Mastering

Autodesk®
3ds Max® Design 2011

Autodesk®
Official Training Guide

Mark Gerhard

Jeffrey M. Harper

WILEY

Wiley Publishing, Inc.

Senior Acquisitions Editor: Willem Knibbe
Development Editor: Kim Wimpsett
Production Editor: Rachel Gigliotti
Editorial Manager: Pete Gaughan
Production Manager: Tim Tate
Vice President and Executive Group Publisher: Richard Swadley
Vice President and Publisher: Neil Edde
Book Designer: Maureen Forys and Judy Fung
Compositor: Chris Gillespie, Happenstance Type-O-Rama
Proofreader: Candace English
Indexer: Ted Laux
Project Coordinator, Cover: Lynsey Stanford
Cover Designer: Ryan Sneed
Cover Image: © John Foxx / Stockbyte / Getty Images

Copyright © 2010 by Wiley Publishing, Inc., Indianapolis, Indiana

Published simultaneously in Canada

ISBN: 978-0-470-88262-7
ISBN: 978-0-470-92557-7 (ebk)
ISBN: 978-0-470-92559-1 (ebk)
ISBN: 978-0-470-92558-4 (ebk)

Dear Reader,

Thank you for choosing *Mastering Autodesk 3ds Max Design 2011*. This book is part of a family of premium-quality Sybex books, all of which are written by outstanding authors who combine practical experience with a gift for teaching.

Sybex was founded in 1976. More than 30 years later, we're still committed to producing consistently exceptional books. With each of our titles, we're working hard to set a new standard for the industry. From the paper we print on, to the authors we work with, our goal is to bring you the best books available.

I hope you see all that reflected in these pages. I'd be very interested to hear your comments and get your feedback on how we're doing. Feel free to let me know what you think about this or any other Sybex book by sending me an email at nedde@wiley.com. If you think you've found a technical error in this book, please visit http://sybex.custhelp.com. Customer feedback is critical to our efforts at Sybex.

Best regards,

Neil Edde
Vice President and Publisher
Sybex, an Imprint of Wiley

This book is dedicated to my wife, Rhonda, who puts up with me; to my four children, Kai, Sakina, David, and Sam, who bring me so much joy; and to my grandsons, Mateo and Zev, may they enjoy the future. And to my mother and father and sister, who gave me the encouragement to do whatever I wanted, no matter how wacky it seemed at the time.

—Mark Gerhard

This book is dedicated to my family and friends, for always encouraging me in my endeavors, for providing their emotional support, and for their understanding when I missed events or disappeared from the face of the earth to finish projects such as completing this book on schedule.

—Jeffrey M. Harper

Acknowledgments

Thanks to everyone at Wiley and Sybex for their continued support over the years. Big thanks to Tom Hudson for pursuing his dream that turned into this software, and to Gary Yost, Dan Silva, Rolf Bertteig, and Jack Powell for creating a program that has turned into my life's work. I'd like to acknowledge Frank Moore, for getting me into this mess by hiring me at Autodesk in 1990. And my gratitude goes to Gary Rackliff for hiring me exactly at the right moment in my life. Thanks to Jeff Harper for incredibly hard work under the gun. Additional thanks to Jennifer O'Connor for the MAXScript information. And double thanks to my wife Rhonda, for keeping me sane when my computer was driving me otherwise.

—*Mark Gerhard*

I would like to acknowledge the support of Mark Gerhard in helping update and write *Mastering Autodesk 3ds Max Design 2011*. I would also like to acknowledge Willem Knibbe, Pete Gaughan, Kim Wimpsett, Connor O'Brien, Jenni Housh, Rachel Gigliotti, and everyone else on the Wiley/Sybex team who helped keep us on schedule, assisted with graphics and figures, and made edits and corrections.

I would also like to thank Scott Onstott for allowing us to use his models as examples for a number of chapters in this book. Thanks also go out to Michael Clamp for the use of his wonderful photograph of Notre Dame de Haut in Chapter 3 and to Brian P. Skripac, former architectural consulting expert at IMAGINiT Technologies, for the Revit model used in Chapter 5.

A great deal of thanks goes to Barbara Vezos and Michael Sehgal at Autodesk for helping us make sure that we cover the right topics for *Mastering Autodesk 3ds Max Design 2011* to be the official training material for those brave enough to tackle the certification examinations for 3ds Max Design 2011.

I have to thank my family and friends again for all their love, support, encouragement, faith, and patience.

—*Jeffrey M. Harper*

About the Authors

Mark Gerhard is a 3ds Max guru. He has devoted the past two decades to this software in all its forms. Mark was one of the first artists hired by Autodesk in 1990 to test the first version of 3D Studio on MS-DOS. In his 14-plus years at Autodesk, he worked as an instructor, product manager, demo artist, application engineer, and technical writer. He wrote many of the tutorials that shipped with 3ds Max, from version 3 to the present. He has been an ATC instructor, teaching 3ds Max to countless individuals at high schools, community colleges, and universities around the world. He has been the technical editor on numerous books on 3ds Max for New Riders, Wiley/Sybex, friends of ED, Apress, 3DATS, and Focal Press. He has been coauthor of several books as well.

Currently Mark teaches 3ds Max to architects and engineers across the United States and Canada. He is also a forum assistant on Area, Autodesk's forum for all things 3D.

Mark has a bachelor's degree in practice of art from University of California, Berkeley, with a focus on painting and sculpture. He is the author of the children's book *The Elf of the Shelf Sees Himself* (Push Press, 1983). He is also a trained musician, proficient in the tradition of North Indian classical music, having studied tabla with Ustad Shankar Ghosh and Pandit Jnan Prakash Ghosh of Calcutta. He has also studied vocal music with Ustad Ali Akbar Khansahib. Additionally, he is a student of Indian folk music, having studied and performed with the Bauls of Bengal (Babukishan Das Goswami Baul).

Jeffrey M. Harper started using Autodesk products (initially AutoCAD 9) in his architectural drafting classes when he was in high school. Jeff was very excited to see AutoCAD add 3D modeling to its toolset and he merged this with his love of photography and started thinking cinematographically, creating renderings of his CAD files with AutoShade. Soon he began using 3D Studio R3 (for DOS) to help visualize his projects while he studied architecture at the University of Colorado at Boulder. He upgraded to 3D Studio Max 1.0 for Windows when it was released, and he has used every version of 3ds Max since; he has also used Lightscape 3.2 and a few versions of Autodesk VIZ.

Jeff has used 3ds Max to create architectural and civil engineering visualizations from a combination of aerial and terrestrial LiDAR, USGS NED data, high-resolution digital orthophotography, stereo-compiled mapping data, and CAD files from different packages and disciplines. He has also used 3ds Max to create models, stills, and animations used in computer-based training programs for aircraft maintenance. Jeff has even used 3ds Max to create an STL file used to build a rapid-prototyped form from which he hand-pressed ceramic tiles used in the backsplash for a kitchen remodeling project. Jeff also uses 3ds Max to create visual effects elements for a variety of media.

As a CADD manager and data manager for a large multistate, multidiscipline engineering firm, Jeff wrote a number of workflow/training documents to assist users with certain CAD and GIS functions and assisted users with AutoCAD, Revit Structure, Civil 3D, MicroStation, InRoads, Adobe Photoshop, ArcGIS, and GeoMedia.

Contents at a Glance

Contents

Introduction

A significant portion of your work as a designer will involve sketching and drawing throughout the design process. Not only will these visual explorations help convey your ideas to others, but they will help you see problems within a design and help you refine your ideas. 3D computer modeling and animation take design visualization beyond hand-drawn sketches and foam-core models by allowing you to create a complete replica of your design and study it from any point of view in any lighting condition.

With 3ds Max Design 2011, you can apply color, texture, lighting, and other effects to see how variations of these elements affect your design. You can get a realistic look at your design to help you make better decisions as you progress through the design process.

Mastering Autodesk 3ds Max Design 2011 is intended to help architects, designers, and visualization artists present their designs through 3D models, rendered still images, and animations. This book focuses on the use of 3ds Max Design 2011 as a modeling and presentation tool. Because *Mastering Autodesk 3ds Max Design 2011* is focused on design issues, you will not find comprehensive information about character animation or advanced special effects. You also will not find descriptions of every single tool or function available in 3ds Max Design 2011.

In this book you will find step-by-step tutorials covering the primary functions of the software that you will use in the process of visualizing design projects. These tutorials are based on years of experience using 3ds Max on real projects with real requirements and deadlines. By completing the tutorials, you will learn how to construct complex geometric forms and how to apply realistic textures and lighting to study a design. You will also learn how to create effects to help emphasize parts of your design for presentations.

Mastering Autodesk 3ds Max Design 2011 is also an Official Training Guide for Autodesk's 3ds Max Design 2011 professional certification exams. See Appendix D for more information about certification.

How to Use This Book

The goal of this book is to give you the appropriate skills to produce professional-level presentations of your ideas, from conceptual designs to finished renderings and animated walkthroughs. Once you have mastered those fundamental skills, you will be equipped to confidently explore 3ds Max Design 2011 and its robust set of tools and options on your own.

To get the most value from this book, you should read the chapters sequentially from front to back, doing all the exercises as you go. Each chapter builds on skills you learned in previous chapters, so you can think of this book as your personal, self-paced course on 3ds Max Design 2011. As you are doing the exercises, don't be afraid to try things not in the tutorials. 3ds Max Design is too robust and complicated a piece of software to completely teach in one volume.

The first two chapters of this book will help you become familiar with how 3ds Max Design 2011 works and how it is organized. If you are already familiar with 3ds Max, 3ds Max Design, or Autodesk VIZ, you may want to skim these chapters to become accustomed to the new user interface and to be introduced to some of the new features of 3ds Max Design 2011. Chapters 3 through 7 will show you how to build fairly complex geometry using a variety of tools. These chapters introduce you to the more common methods of constructing and modifying objects in 3ds Max Design 2011. Chapters 8 through 10 show you how to use lights, materials, and cameras. Chapter 11 covers scene management to help you work with large complex scenes and external files. Chapters 12 and 13 introduce and then expand on animation topics. Chapter 14 discusses advanced rendering techniques with the mental ray renderer. Chapter 15 covers using more mental ray effects, rendering those effects to high dynamic range files, and then compositing elements from your renderings and tweaking those materials in 3ds Max Composite to enhance your visualizations.

At the back of the book there is a set of appendices that offer general reference information on some of the most common tools used in 3ds Max Design 2011. Once you have completed the first few chapters of the book, you can use the appendices as an aid in your own exploration of 3ds Max. You can then refer to the appendices as you continue to work through the rest of the book. If you are interested in taking the certification examinations for 3ds Max Design 2011, Appendix D will help you find the information in this book, the 3ds Max Design Help System, or other resources that will help you prepare to take the tests.

The Tutorial Files on the Website

It's very important that before you start going through the tutorials in this book, you need to go to this book's page on the Sybex website (www.sybex.com/go/mastering3dsmaxdesign2011) and download the compressed files with the content that will be used in the tutorials throughout this book. The website includes archive files of the *.max and support files necessary to complete the exercises in this book. You must extract the chapter archive files to a folder on your computer that you will use to complete the tutorials in the book. You should not try to open the max files directly from the website.

CONNECTING 3DS MAX TO THE CHAPTER FILES

It is important that you configure 3ds Max Design 2011 to recognize the location of the tutorial files from the Sybex website (www.sybex.com/go/mastering3dsmaxdesign2011). Make sure that you perform the instructions given in the section titled "Adding a Map Path to Help 3ds Max Find Bitmaps" in Chapter 9. If you like, you can set up 3ds Max as described in that section right after you have extracted the files.

What You'll Find

To give you a better idea of what you'll find in this book, here is a summary of the chapters and their contents:

Chapter 1: Getting to Know 3ds Max Design 2011 In Chapter 1, you will get an introduction to 3ds Max Design 2011 and the user interface, and you'll get a first look at 3ds Max objects and how they are created and animated. Toward the end of Chapter 1 you will be introduced to the different ways you can view your designs in 3ds Max Design 2011.

Chapter 2: Introducing 3ds Max Objects Chapter 2 delves deeper into the workings of 3ds Max objects. You'll learn about the different types of objects available in 3ds Max Design 2011 and how you can use them to create the shapes you want. You will learn how to manipulate 3ds Max's core set of shapes, called *primitives*, and turn them into more complex shapes. You will also learn about the different methods you can use to duplicate shapes and how these methods can help you quickly complete your design.

Chapter 3: Creating Shapes with Splines In Chapter 3 you will look at how you can create complex forms from simple lines. Here you will learn how to manipulate a basic type of object called a *spline shape* and turn it into a wineglass. You will look at creating walls and 3D text objects as well.

Chapter 4: Editing Meshes and Creating Complex Objects Chapter 4 introduces you to object creation and editing methods that are common to architectural projects. You will start modeling a well-known building, using a hand-drawn sketch as a template. You will also focus on drawing objects that have unusual shapes.

Chapter 5: Working with External Design Data Chapter 5 introduces you to concepts and workflows that will be helpful with importing data from other programs into 3ds Max Design 2011 and using that data to enhance your models and scenes.

Chapter 6: Creating AEC Objects Chapter 6 introduces you to the parametric AEC (architectural, engineering, and construction) objects included with 3ds Max Design 2011, such as walls, windows, doors, stairs and railings, and foliage objects.

Chapter 7: Organizing and Editing Objects In Chapter 7 you will continue working on the main scene from Chapter 5 by exploring ways to organize the components of the design. You will learn how to use object names and layers to help identify parts in the design. You will also continue your exploration of modeling complex forms by creating additional objects and modifying existing objects to add detail and depth to the scene.

Chapter 8: Light and Shadow Chapter 8 continues to use the well-known building started in Chapter 5 to introduce you to the concepts of lighting and rendering your digital models. You will also learn about the different types of lighting and shadows and how to use them together. In addition, you will learn how you can create more realistic renderings by the careful placement of additional lights in strategic locations.

Chapter 9: Enhancing Models with Materials In Chapter 9, you will continue to build on what you learned in Chapter 8 by exploring materials. You will experiment with the many properties of materials and maps in 3ds Max Design, such as diffuse color, bump map textures, and reflections. You will learn how to align a texture to a surface, and you will be introduced to methods for adding 2D entourage, such as trees and people, to scenes.

Chapter 10: Using the 3ds Max Camera Chapter 10 discusses placing cameras in your model and creating environments to surround your models. You will learn how to control the background to affect the mood of your renderings. You will also experiment with rendering only selected portions of your scene to save time.

Chapter 11: Organizing Objects and Scene Management Chapter 11 shows you different ways to use 3ds Max files. You will learn how to combine different files efficiently to allow you to work collaboratively with other members of a design team. You will discover ways to share data between project files. You will also see how you can share your models on the Internet.

Chapter 12: Understanding Animation Chapter 12 offers you an introduction to animation in an architectural context. You will learn to create and control the animation of a camera to create a flyby of one of the buildings you worked on in earlier chapters. You will also learn how to edit an animated object's motion, create previews of your animation, and control lights over time.

Chapter 13: Creating Animations Chapter 13 continues your look at animation by exploring the options for outputting your animations to files, creating shadow studies, adding other animated elements to add to the realism of your visualizations, and creating effective walkthroughs of your designs. You will also learn about other animation topics, such as creating and animating particle systems, as well as animating using rigid body physics in dynamic simulation systems.

Chapter 14: Advanced Rendering Using mental ray In Chapter 14 you will learn how to take advantage of the advanced features of the rendering engine in 3ds Max Design 2011 to optimize rendering your stills and animations with global illumination and caustics.

Chapter 15: Finishing It Off: Atmosphere, Effects, and Compositing Chapter 15 shows you how to take your 3ds Max Design 2011 renderings to the next level, adding depth and mood to your renderings and using effects available with mental ray and adding effects to your final renderings with 3ds Max Composite, adjusting how your final renderings look, and how to composite anaglyph stereo renderings.

In addition to the main chapters in this book, there are four appendices:

Appendix A: The Bottom Line Appendix A has the solutions for the "Master It" exercises found at the end of each chapter.

Appendix B: Modifiers, Maps, and Materials Appendix B is a reference for the modifiers and materials in 3ds Max Design 2011.

Appendix C: Inverse Kinematics and MAXScript Appendix C is a reference for finding information on MAXScript and inverse kinematics (IK).

Appendix D: The Autodesk 3ds Max Design 2011 Certification Exams Appendix D is a reference for finding information that will help you prepare for taking the Autodesk certification exams related to 3ds Max Design 2011.

System Requirements

This book assumes that you already have Autodesk 3ds Max Design 2011 and a computer that can properly run the software. Additionally, you should perform a complete installation of 3ds Max Design 2011, including the optional tutorials and plug-ins. Many of the extra and demonstration plug-ins are not covered in this book; however, you should experiment with them on your own. The following list shows you the minimum system requirements necessary to run 3ds Max Design 2011; you should exceed these values whenever possible for better system performance and stability:

◆ Intel Pentium4 1.4GHz or AMD-based equivalent processor with SSE2 technology

◆ 2GB of RAM (4GB recommended)

◆ 2GB of swap space (4GB recommended)

◆ 3GB of free disk space after 3ds Max Design 2011 software installation

◆ Microsoft Internet Explorer 7.0 or newer

◆ Direct3D 10, Direct3D 9, or OpenGL-capable graphics card supporting 1024 × 768, 32-bit color display; 256MB video memory (1GB or higher recommended)

◆ DVD-ROM drive

◆ A three-button mouse with the appropriate driver software

◆ Microsoft Windows XP Professional (Service Pack 2 or higher); Microsoft Vista Business (SP2 or higher); or Microsoft Windows 7, 32-bits or 64-bits

◆ Internet connection for web downloads and subscription access

Autodesk does not support running 3ds Max Design 2011 on Windows Me, NT 4.0, 98, or prior versions.

You can find the complete system requirements for 3ds Max Design 2011 on the Autodesk website (www.autodesk.com/3dsmaxdesign).

The 3GB of free disk space includes space for the sample files and general workspace for your projects. For later chapters, you may want to install AutoCAD 2007 or newer and Adobe Photoshop CS or newer. You can obtain a trial version of Photoshop from the Adobe website. You can also download a 30-day trial version of AutoCAD 2011 from the Autodesk website. These additional software applications are not crucial, but you may find them to be useful companions to 3ds Max Design 2011.

Chapter 1

Getting to Know 3ds Max Design 2011

Welcome to *Mastering Autodesk 3ds Max Design 2011*. Autodesk 3ds Max Design is the premier software package for design visualization and animation and has many features specifically designed to assist architects, engineers, and designers in many disciplines in the realization of their projects. It is comparable to 3ds Max, the entertainment software, and is essentially the same product without the Software Developer Kit (SDK), which is used to develop plug-ins that give the programs additional functionality. In addition to having all the features that 3ds Max has, 3ds Max Design offers two exclusive tools. The Lighting analysis tool is used to help meet the Leadership in Energy and Environmental Design (LEED) 8.1 certification standards. The Civil Visualization Extension, which will be available as a download for those users on Autodesk 3ds Max Design Subscription, is a customized version of the Dynamite VSP plug-in for importing design data from Civil 3D or the Bentley MX design tools. In this book, we refer to the program as both 3ds Max and 3ds Max Design.

Autodesk 3ds Max Design 2011 provides users with cutting-edge rendering technology, easy-to-use architectural materials, improved interoperability with other related design and CADD software, enhancements to modeling and animation tools, and better viewport interactivity than ever before.

This chapter introduces some of 3ds Max Design 2011's special features and then gets you started working with the 3ds Max interface. In this chapter, you will learn to:

- ◆ Navigate and configure the viewports
- ◆ Dock and float toolbars
- ◆ Copy objects and use the transform tools
- ◆ Create a named selection set

Introducing the New 3ds Max Design 2011 Features

3ds Max Design 2011 is a significant release that extends the comprehensive features and functionality with new exciting capabilities and also updates many existing features. This is an important release with a long list of improvements and additions that will greatly impact your projects whether you have been using 3ds Max for a number of years or are new to design visualization.

Each new version of 3ds Max incorporates fresh and exciting tools to enhance your capabilities and workflow while also increasing the performance of the program on your computer system. Utilizing these new features is key to improving your skills and decreasing the time it takes to complete your projects. To help you find information, 3ds Max Design 2011's Learning

Movies dialog box (see Figure 1.1) includes links to essential skills movies that teach many of the basic skills for using 3ds Max, as well as links to movies that explain the new features and additional 3ds Max–related tutorials. Note that if you don't see this dialog box, you can go to the Help menu and launch the Essential Skills Movies from there.

FIGURE 1.1
The Learning
Movies dialog box

Here, in no particular order, are some of the high points of 3ds Max Design 2011:

Viewport canvas paint system There was a viewport canvas feature in the previous release, but it has been reworked and extended so much that it is like it's completely new in 2011. You can paint directly on the 3D objects in the viewport to create your bitmaps using a layered composite paint system. It has a 2D mode as well as a 3D mode, so you can paint on the flat unwrapped map or paint on the 3D objects in space—take your pick. Paint with bitmap textures, just like the Clone brush in Adobe Photoshop, into any channel you want. Make automatic masks by rendering surface maps of your elements, and then drop them into the mask channel of the layered composite. To learn more about the viewport canvas system, see Chapter 9, "Enhancing Models with Materials."

3ds Max Composite Based on the video compositing package that used to called Autodesk Toxik, 3ds Max Composite now comes *for free* with 3ds Max 2011. 3ds Max Composite features completely node-based compositing, allowing you to work on still images or video sequences, and works seamlessly with new OpenEXR support for render element channels. If you use Combustion, Adobe Premiere, Adobe After Effects, or even Video Post, you will want to explore the features and possibilities provided by 3ds Max Composite. To learn more about 3ds Max Composite, see Chapter 15, "Finishing It Off: Atmosphere, Effects, and Compositing."

Slate Material Editor Slate is a node-based schematic material editor, where you can wire material properties together, and wire the material to the object in the viewport. Multiple views and material groups let you organize your material work more easily than ever. Now you can spot with no trouble at all which maps are instanced and which are copies. The original material editor is still available, now called the Compact Material Editor. The old

Material Map Browser has been removed from 3ds Max Design 2011. To learn more about the Slate Material Editor, see Chapter 9.

Autodesk Materials　Moving files from Inventor or Revit into the latest release of 3ds Max Design now uses a shared library of standardized materials. These materials replace the role ProMaterials played in 3ds Max Design 2010. Based on MetaSL shaders, there are 1,200 new materials that you will find in both Revit and 3ds Max.

Enhanced viewport material display　MetaSL shaders are now used in the viewport if your graphic card meets the minimum requirements. That means you can get real-time reflections in the viewport. Future 3ds Max development is going to continue improving the viewport experience and making it appear closer to the rendered image. Eventually there will be no need to render; saving a screen capture of the viewport will be all you need.

Graphite Modeling Tools　New additions to the Graphite Tools feature an Object Paint system that lets you paint 3D objects onto surfaces. The objects can be animated and the animations and scaling of the objects can be offset. Use this to plant trees blowing in the wind. There have been scripts to do this over the years, but now it's officially part of the base package. Other new Graphite Tools features include the ability to mirror elements and the capability to customize the ribbon. To learn more about Graphite Tools, see Chapter 4, "Editing Meshes and Creating Complex Objects."

Other UI improvements　You can minimize the Command panel, float it, or put it in a mode that automatically appears when you need it. When you need more screen real estate, this is a great new way to work. Also, many of the floating dialog boxes that appeared as part of Edit Poly editing have been replaced with "Caddies," a new UI that floats under your cursor in the viewport. Also, the Make Preview feature has been moved to the Tools menu under Grab Viewport ➢ Create Animated Sequence File.

Snaps and selection　There's a new Snap handle at the center of the Transform gizmo that makes snapping simpler and more straightforward. Autodesk also changed the behavior of selection when using the Ctrl key. In previous versions, 3ds Max had the maddening behavior of using Ctrl to both add to and subtract from a selection set. Now Ctrl *only adds*; it doesn't subtract. Use the Alt key to subtract from a selection set.

FBX linking　3ds Max Design 2011 now supports the FBX file format for file linking. Previous versions did this with only DWG; now you can use the much more intelligent FBX from Revit 2009 and onward to link into your scene. This means that updates made to the Revit file and saved over the linked FBX file can automatically be reflected in the 3ds Max file as well. Note that FBX is still a huge file, so you may have to break up your Revit project into pieces to assemble the whole thing in 3ds Max.

CAT character animation toolset　Previously available only to subscription customers, CAT is a plug-in that was a competitor to Biped and is now part of 3ds Max. CAT complements the Biped system; it's designed to do the things Biped has trouble with. CAT comes with prebuilt rigs designed for all kinds of characters besides humans, whether they walk on 2, 4, or 100 legs. Horse, centipede, and dragon templates are just some of the possible choices. CAT comes with a muscle system and lets you do things like walk along a path, something Biped doesn't provide. A collection of prerigged skinned characters is included in the partners folder of your 3ds Max Design installation.

Save to previous versions 3ds Max Design will now let you save your 3ds Max files backward to the previous version number. In 3ds Max Design 2011 you can save back to the 2010 version to make sharing of your project files easier if you are collaborating with other users who haven't transitioned to the newest version yet. This is a first; 3ds Max has never had this capability in its 20-year history!

File-related improvements You can now import SketchUp (SKP) files directly. You can also import and export solids as SAT files from Inventor and Revit as Body Objects. This means you can actually round-trip a file from Revit to Max and back to Revit without losing all the intelligence in the model.

Inventor support has been improved. You no longer need to have Inventor installed on the same machine as 3ds Max to open an IPT or IAM file.

The OpenEXR file format has been updated, so it now holds all the render element and GBuffer channels in a single file. Just like the old RPF/RLA file type, the new OpenEXR file saver gives you access to all the various channels as separate layers for compositing, masking, and so on. OpenEXR has been exposed to MAXScript as well.

The SGI file format support has been extended to support all formats. This includes an option to turn off Compression as part of a save operation. If you're working with Open Flight, you'll appreciate this improvement.

Quicksilver hardware rendering Another new rendering engine has been added to the 3ds Max toolset. Quicksilver is a lightning fast high-quality renderer that leverages the power of the GPUs and CPUs in your workstation for blazing fast rendering. Competitive with mental ray, once it has completed the file translation, you will find subsequent renders are much faster than anything you have seen before.

Local edits to containers Containers have seen significant work in this release. A new Rules rollout improves the workflow when using containers. Now you can allow others to access and edit the contents of inherited containers locally while still inheriting your changes. The previous version offered only the options of No Access or Only Edit in Place, but the new rules include Only Add New Objects and Anything Unlocked. This lets you lock objects or object attributes so others can change anything except your locked content. A new Containers preference panel lets you define the container behavior.

Containers also now have a proxies feature (such as XRefs) that lets you substitute a proxy container for an existing one in the scene. This is a nice improvement, because previous versions only let you unload the existing container.

Windows 7 support Autodesk 3ds Max Design 2011 is now fully supported on the Microsoft Windows 7 operating system.

Bitmap Pager The Bitmap Pager has been enabled by default to page large texture images and renderings to disk to save memory.

Extras galore The installation DVD for 3ds Max Design 2011 comes with a number of special tools, evaluation plug-ins, and exciting new content. Note that these are available only on the install DVD or via the subscription website. If you download the trial version, you won't have these.

The extras include the following:

- ◆ A Vegetation Library of trees from Marlin Studios
- ◆ Biped and CAT rigged high-resolution characters from aXYZ Design
- ◆ High-quality vehicles from aXYZ Design
- ◆ Low-polygon vehicles from Cacheforce
- ◆ Assorted motion clips from Mixamo
- ◆ Pedestrian motion capture clips (male and female)
- ◆ Craft Animation plug-in for animating cars and moving cameras
- ◆ A special edition of the stand-alone CityScape program from PixelActive that can import some GIS data and formats and then export an FBX file for linking into 3ds Max Design 2011

For more information about new features and improvements in 3ds Max, go to the What's New in Autodesk 3ds Max Design 2011 section of the help system. You can also find information on the Autodesk website or the Autodesk Media and Entertainment forums called The Area.

What Was New in 3ds Max Design 2010

If you are upgrading from several releases back, you may not be familiar with the new features that were added in the previous release of 3ds Max Design. Here is a brief look at the new features added in the release before the latest:

Graphite Modeling tools The Graphite Modeling tools provide more than 100 additional modeling features for organic sculpting, texture painting in the viewports, and advanced polygon modeling. They are available on the Graphite Modeling ribbon. These tools bring a higher level of interactivity to modeling in 3ds Max.

Containers Containers are an enhanced toolset within 3ds Max designed to improve project collaboration and workflows by aggregating multiple objects into containers. Similar objects in a scene can be added to a container so you can interact with them as one unit. Containers can be loaded and unloaded from the viewports as necessary to improve the performance of 3ds Max Design.

Material Explorer The Material Explorer introduced in 2010 is a hierarchical display that allows you to review and manage all materials in a scene. Unlike the Material Editor, the Material Explorer does not suffer from a limitation of how many materials it can display at one time.

Exposure lighting validation When architectural or engineering visualizations are being created, accurate simulation of lighting conditions can be vitally important to a project's success. The Exposure feature, available only in 3ds Max Design, allows you to create more sustainable design projects by analyzing the interaction of artificial lighting, sun, and skylight directly in your models. This information can be studied right in the viewports. Although the Exposure name is trademarked by Autodesk, you won't actually find "Exposure" anywhere in the Help file or 3ds Max interface, but you can access the feature via the Lighting Analysis menu.

xView Mesh Analyzer The xView Mesh Analyzer feature allows you to check your models in the viewport for common mesh errors such as overlapping UV coordinates, isolated vertices, duplicate and flipped faces, and other geometry errors. This feature can help you avoid potentially costly modeling mistakes before projects proceed too far down the production pipeline.

ProSound The ProSound system allows you to work interactively with up to 100 unique audio tracks directly in your scene using the Track View dialog box. ProSound can be used to help when working with lip-syncing or creating preliminary audio tracks for your animated projects.

Review3 Review3 helps artists get a better idea of how their final renderings will turn out by previewing the scenes directly in the viewports with interactive shadows (hard and soft), ambient occlusion, real-time HDR generated lighting, and interactive exposure control, and it takes advantage of the mental mill shader technology.

mental mill/MetaSL support Integral to the improvements in the interactive viewports is the inclusion of support for mental mill (a shader technology from mental images), which allows users to create, test, and distribute hardware-independent shaders that provide real-time feedback and look the same in the viewport as they do in renderings.

Multi-Map shader The Multi-Map shader for use with metal ray allows you to create materials with built-in variations that can be applied randomly to scene objects or applied based on specific object properties. This is a great way to create more natural-looking variations among similar scene objects, such as trees, vehicles, furniture, or any anything else you want.

Render Surface Map The Render Surface Map can create grayscale bitmaps of selected UVW-mapped poly objects based on the unique properties of the objects. The four types of maps that can be rendered are Cavity Map, Density Map, Dust Map, and SubSurface Map.

Viewport Canvas The Viewport Canvas tools allow you to paint your maps directly on your poly objects right in the 3ds Max viewports using familiar paint software concepts. The Viewport Canvas has been expanded significantly in the 3ds Max Design 2011 release.

SteeringWheel and ViewCube objects The SteeringWheel and ViewCube objects are located in the viewports and are used to navigate through a 3D scene and to quickly orient or provide feedback regarding your current viewpoint. The SteeringWheel and ViewCube widgets are common across several Autodesk products.

ProMaterials A library of physically accurate materials, called ProMaterials, is now available from the Material Editor. ProMaterials are for use exclusively with the mental ray rendering system and can add a significant degree of realism to a scene. In the 2011 release, the ProMaterials have been replaced with Autodesk Materials. If you open files saved from 3ds Max Design 2010, the ProMaterials will render without issue.

mental ray The mental ray renderer that shipped with 3ds Max Design 2010 was upgraded to the latest available version of this high-level, production-quality rendering system. An entirely new subdivision surface implementation makes this version faster and more efficient. The mental ray renderer is now the default renderer for 3ds Max Design.

Updated Biped system 3ds Max has had the Biped system, used to create the bone system for animating two-footed characters, for several releases. The 2010 version introduced an ability that allows a biped's hands to act as feet in regard to the plane on which the character is walking. This feature makes it easier to use Biped to animate characters with four feet rather than two.

FBX file format The FBX file format was improved in the 2010 release and can be used to exchange files between 3D programs, including 3ds Max, Autodesk Maya, Autodesk Mudbox, and Softimage. You will want to make sure you download and install the newest update for the FBX software from the Autodesk website.

Updated Recognize Scene-Loading Technology Data from Revit Architecture 2010 files, such as geometry, lighting parameters, camera information, and materials, can accurately be imported into 3ds Max using the new Recognize Scene-Loading Technology. Recognize is also based on the FBX format mentioned earlier.

Getting Started with 3ds Max

Although many of 3ds Max's components are typical for a Windows program, quite a few are unique to 3ds Max; therefore, a solid understanding of them is essential to effectively using the program. To begin exploring the 3ds Max Design 2011 interface, start the program by doing one of the following:

◆ Double-click the 3ds Max Design 2011 icon on the Desktop.

◆ Choose Start ➢ Programs ➢ Autodesk ➢ Autodesk 3ds Max Design 2011 ➢ 3ds Max Design 2011.

You'll see a variety of components in the 3ds Max window (see Figure 1.2)—some that may be familiar and others that may not.

FIGURE 1.2
The standard 3ds Max Design 2010 window

THE LARGE ICONS OPTION

The images in this book use the Large Icons option to better display the toolbar buttons. To activate this option, choose Customize ➤ Preferences to open the Preference Settings dialog box. In the UI Display section of the General tab, select the Use Large Toolbar Buttons option, and then shut down and reopen 3ds Max for the option to take effect.

At the top, you see a typical Windows menu bar and the 3ds Max Main Toolbar. Depending on your default settings, you may also see up to nine more floating or docked toolbars containing additional 3ds Max tools. In the center, you see the viewport area, which currently shows the Perspective, Top, Left, and Front viewports. At the lower-right corner of the screen, you see the viewport navigation tools for adjusting your views in the current viewport. You also see the time controls for creating and playing animations, the prompt line and status bar, and the MAXScript MiniListener (for creating macros). On the right side of the user interface, you see the Command panel, which contains nearly all the tools you'll use to create and edit objects in 3ds Max. Let's take a closer look at each of these components. 3ds Max often provides several methods, including toolbars, Command panels, menus, and shortcuts, for accomplishing the same task.

Touring the Interface

3ds Max offers a wealth of tools, and their sheer number can be overwhelming. To get a basic understanding of the 3ds Max window, we'll present each of the window components individually, starting with the Menu Bar.

The Menu Bar

At the top of the screen is the Menu Bar. Here you find the typical Windows commands for file maintenance, as well as commands specifically for 3ds Max.

Standard to 3ds Max 2011 is the Application button (Figure 1.3), which replaced the traditional File menu in the last release. The Application button is a graphical representation of the tools from the traditional File menu, including opening and saving files, importing, exporting, and referencing files. The Application button is also where you can set a project folder, access the Asset Tracking tool, and check statistics about the current file. If you are more comfortable using the traditional File menu, you can restore it to the 3ds Max interface using the dialog box that appears when you select Customize ➤ Customize User Interface.

FIGURE 1.3
The Application
button

The options in the Menu Bar are organized the same way they are in most Windows applications. Clicking an option issues a command, and you're expected to take some action. An option

that's followed by three periods, called an *ellipsis*, opens a dialog box, usually to allow you to make changes to settings related to the option. An option with a right-pointing arrow displays more options in what is called a *cascading menu*, as shown in Figure 1.4.

FIGURE 1.4

A typical cas-
cading menu

Try out the Menu Bar by taking a look at the Units Setup dialog box:

1. Choose Customize ➢ Units Setup. The Units Setup dialog box displays.

2. Select the US Standard radio button, and make sure that Feet w/Decimal Inches is selected below it and that the Inches radio button is selected for Default Units, as shown in Figure 1.5.

FIGURE 1.5

Defining the units
in the Units Setup
dialog box

3. Click the System Unit Setup button, and you will see the System Unit Setup dialog box shown in Figure 1.6. Make sure 1 Unit is set to 1.0 Inches. Do not change anything else in the System Unit Setup dialog box, and click OK twice to close both dialog boxes.

By setting the Units Setup options, you ensure that you'll be working with the same units that are discussed in this book.

FIGURE 1.6
The System Unit
Setup dialog box

REVERTING TO THE STARTUP LAYOUT

3ds Max Design 2011 is something of a chameleon. It can change its appearance, depending on the focus of your modeling needs. Users of 3ds Max 2011 will see a somewhat different interface, with the tools designed more for the game and entertainment industries featured. If your 3ds Max Design 2011 window doesn't look the way it does in the figures in this book, choose Customize ➤ Revert To Startup Layout. You'll see a warning message telling you that any user interface (UI) changes you have made will be lost. Click Yes to set up your 3ds Max windows to match the interface you see in this book. You can also reload Custom UI schemes to reset the interface or use the Custom UI and Defaults Switcher to accomplish the same thing, plus more. See the "Working with the Custom UI and Defaults Switcher" section later in this chapter for more information on this topic.

The Quick Access Toolbar

Just to the right of the new Application menu is the Quick Access toolbar, another standard feature in 3ds Max 2011. As its name implies, it provides quick access to a number of useful commands, including New Scene, Open File, Save File, and the Select Project Folder Browser.

The Quick Access toolbar is also the home for the enhanced Undo Scene Operation and Redo Scene Operation tools. Click these buttons to undo your last actions, up to 25 by default, or redo any undone actions. Clicking the drop-down button next to either the Undo or Redo button opens a list of actions from which you can select.

You can customize the Quick Access toolbar by clicking the down-arrow icon at the far right of the toolbar.

The Information Center Toolbar

All the way across the screen at the upper-right corner of the interface, near the traditional Windows Minimize, Maximize, and Close buttons, is the Information Center toolbar. The Information Center toolbar provides a search function for 3ds Max topics in the local Help files

and on the Autodesk website; the Subscription Center (if you have Subscription Center access); the Communication Center, where you'll receive notices of program updates and other relevant announcements; a Favorites panel, where you can store links to commonly accessed websites; and pages and elements from the 3ds Max Help menu.

The Main Toolbar

Just below the Menu Bar is the Main Toolbar. The tools on this toolbar offer tooltips, which are exposed when the cursor pauses over them, to help you identify their purpose.

The first set of tools is for linking and selecting objects. The two linking tools, one for linking and the other for unlinking, cause one object to move, rotate, or scale based on commands applied to another object. The third linking tool, the Bind to Space Warp tool, can be used to attach objects and space warps together. The selection tools let you select objects by clicking them or by selecting them by name. The selection filter allows you to limit what can be selected with the cursor. You can also specify the method for selecting objects by using a *selection window*, which lets you indicate a selection by placing a rectangle, circle, or other border around the objects.

To the right of the selection tools are the transform tools. This set of tools lets you move, rotate, and scale objects. You can also choose the reference coordinate system, set the center of the transform using the pivot options, toggle the keyboard shortcut overrides, use different snap options, work with named selection sets, and use tools to mirror and align objects.

The next group of tools to the right includes access to the Layer Manager, the Graphite Modeling tools display toggle, the Track View Curve Editor, the Schematic View tools, and the Materials and Rendering tools. The Layer Manager gives you control over all the settings for layers in your scene and the objects contained in those layers. The Graphite Modeling tools are a complete set of more than 100 tools to improve creating and editing poly objects within 3ds Max. (Note that the Graphite Tools are the first 3ds Max tools available on a customizable ribbon interface. You will explore the Graphite tools interface in Chapter 4.) The Curve Editor tools display your scene information as graphs or wiring diagrams to indicate the functionality or relationships of scene objects. The Schematic View tools provide a visual graph and control how all the elements of your scene are linked. The Materials tools give you control over the appearance of objects by defining and applying their surface properties. With these tools, you can create color, texture, opacity, and other material characteristics and then apply these characteristics to objects in your model. You can also open the Render Setup dialog box, select the render type, and perform a quick render with the buttons on the far right.

The rendering tools give you control over the image output of your 3ds Max scene. Unlike output from most applications, output from 3ds Max Design 2011 is most likely to be image or animation files, or real-time virtual models. The rendering tools let you set the type and size of output, from single, large-format stills to video-ready animations.

WORKING ON A LOWER-RESOLUTION SYSTEM

If you're working with a screen resolution less than 1280 × 1024, you will not be able to see all the tools on the Main Toolbar. Some of the tools are off the screen to the far right. To access these tools, place the cursor on the toolbar so that a Hand icon appears, and then click and drag the toolbar to the left. If you have trouble with this, move your cursor under one of the drop-down lists on the Main Toolbar to access the Pan Hand. The hidden tools will emerge. You can also click the Rendering menu item to access all the rendering tools. The smallest supported screen resolution for the UI in 3ds Max Design 2011 is 1024 × 768, but the recommended resolution is 1280 × 1024 or higher. All the screenshots presented in this book are using the 1280 × 1024 resolution.

Docked and Floating Toolbars

In addition to the Main Toolbar, you may see several "floating" toolbars sitting on top of the viewport. These toolbars may be hidden by default. You can open hidden toolbars by right-clicking a blank part of any open toolbar. A context menu will appear listing the available toolbars. Let's take a quick look at the floating toolbars (see Figure 1.3).

1. Right-click a blank area of the Main Toolbar and click any of the toolbar items that do not have a check mark next to them.

2. Repeat the process until all the floating toolbars are exposed.

All the toolbars float over the viewports and have titles such as Layers, Render Shortcuts, Snaps, Axis Constraints, and Extras. As with most toolbars, you can dock these floating toolbars to the side or hide them altogether to gain better access to objects in the viewports. The toolbars can be resized by clicking and dragging any of their edges.

CONSIDER A DUAL-SCREEN SYSTEM

In 3ds Max and many other graphics programs, screen space is always at a premium. You can use a two-monitor system to help unclutter your screen. Simply move items such as floating toolbars, the Material Editor, Curve Editor, Rendered Frame Window, and so forth to the second monitor, freeing up as much screen real estate as possible.

Layers are like overlays that help you organize the objects in your model. If you are an AutoCAD or Adobe Photoshop user, you should have an idea of how layers work. You'll learn more about layers in Chapter 6, "Creating AEC Objects."

Render shortcuts contain predefined render settings, such as resolution and output file type, that are used to create content from your 3ds Max scenes. The Render Shortcuts toolbar is where you will find the tools for saving and storing your preset values. You'll learn about rendering in Chapters 9 through 13.

Snaps are features that control where the cursor jumps to, adding a degree of precision to your scene, when the cursor is near a characteristic in the scene. Using snaps, you can easily move the corner of one object to the midpoint of another, or nearly any other characteristic combination.

Objects are frequently transformed (moved, rotated, or scaled) along a particular axis, or direction, relative to the object or the scene. This functionality is usually utilized through the Transform gizmo, an onscreen tool used to facilitate the transforms. The Axis Constraints toolbar also contains these tools.

The Extras toolbar contains tools that don't fit cleanly into other categories. With the AutoGrid button, you can turn on a creation grid relative to the surface of any object in the scene. You can also create an *array* (numerous, precisely placed clones) of objects in matrices, along a path or at equal intervals.

Several tools found within 3ds Max utilize a paint brush analogy in their implementation. The location and intensity of the effects are determined by how the *brush* cursor is dragged over an object's surface. The Brush Presets toolbar gives you access to the standard brushes and the Brush Preset Manager so you can modify and save a brush's parameters. This toolbar is grayed out unless a tool that utilizes it is active.

The Animation Layers toolbar lets you access tools that control the layering of objects' animated parameters. *Layering* allows you to designate which animated features are enabled and which are not, allowing for many possible combinations.

Large scenes and projects can become very complicated quickly. Containers help you organize assets by combining them into groups. They can be loaded and unloaded at will to reduce the size of files and how much information is active at one time. By refreshing the link to a container, you can help coordinate data and project changes among project teams. By limiting write access to data files, you can protect project scene files. Use container proxies to reduce the size of the file while still seeing the container contents.

Interactions between objects (for example, collisions, fluid surfaces, and jointed constraints) can be difficult to animate manually. Using reactor, a physics simulation toolset, you can quickly and accurately create simulations that account for properties such as gravity, friction, and wind.

You can dock the floating toolbars or float the docked toolbars. Try the following exercise to see how to change the location of toolbars:

1. Click and drag the title bar of the Layers toolbar so that the toolbar is below the Main Toolbar. The Layers toolbar appears ghosted as a horizontal outline just before you release the mouse button.

2. When the outline is in the position shown in Figure 1.7, release the mouse button. The Layers toolbar is now in a docked position.

FIGURE 1.7
Docking the Layers toolbar under the Main Toolbar

3. Click and drag the Extras toolbar and dock it just to the right of the Layers toolbar (also just under the Main Toolbar), as shown in Figure 1.8.

4. Right-click the two vertical lines (called the *toolbar handle*) on the left side of the Extras toolbar to open the context menu shown in Figure 1.9.

5. Select Float from the context menu. The Extras toolbar returns to its floating position. Another way to do this is to drag the toolbar by its handle down into the viewport.

6. Toolbars can be docked on any side of the viewports. However, you should avoid docking toolbars to the left and right sides of the interface if the toolbars have drop-down lists; otherwise, the lists will not appear. Select the Axis Constraints toolbar and dock it to the left side of the user interface (Figure 1.10).

7. Select the remaining floating toolbars and dock them on the top, right, or left edge of the viewport.

In this brief exercise, you learned how to dock and float toolbars and how to access the context menu where you can toggle the toolbars on and off. Most of the toolbars aren't required in the early chapters of this book, and they occupy a portion of available screen space. You can hide or float the toolbars however you like.

FIGURE 1.8
Docking the
Extras toolbar

FIGURE 1.9
Floating the toolbar

FIGURE 1.10
Toolbar docked left

Toolbar Flyouts

You may have noticed that some of the tools in the Main Toolbar show a small arrow in the lower-right corner of the tool's icon (Figure 1.11).

That arrow indicates that the tool is one of several offered in a *flyout*. A flyout is like a graphical version of options in a menu bar. If you click and hold a tool that's part of a flyout, you see a set of additional, similar tools appear. For example, if you click and hold the Select and Uniform Scale tool, two additional tools appear, as shown in Figure 1.12.

Once you select an option from a flyout, it becomes the default button that you see in the toolbar.

FIGURE 1.11
Flyout arrow

FIGURE 1.12
The Select and
Scale flyout menu

The Viewports

At the center of the window are the *viewports* (see Figure 1.13). You'll be doing most of your modeling work in a viewport. In a blank file, the viewports show a grid that you can use as a reference for orientation and size.

FIGURE 1.13
A typical viewport
configuration

If you look in the lower-left corner of the viewport, you will see the World Axis Tripod that indicates the orientation of the X-, Y-, and Z-axis. The World Axis Tripod helps you get your bearings when you are looking at camera and perspective views.

Currently, there are four viewports named Top, Left, Front, and Perspective, as indicated by the labels in the upper-left corner of each viewport. You can also tell that the Perspective

viewport is different from the others by the way the grid squares get smaller and converge in the distance. As you'll see toward the end of this chapter, you can configure and view your model in a variety of ways, depending on your needs.

Tools for Working with the Viewports

At the bottom of the window are several other options that are grouped into six sections: the status bar, the prompt line, the time controls, the time slider, the track bar, and the viewport navigation tools (see Figure 1.14). Most of these tools affect the viewport, either by modifying the display of the viewport directly or by affecting the way you interact with objects within the viewport.

FIGURE 1.14
The bottom sections of the 3ds Max Design 2011 window

The viewport navigation tools give you control over the main graphic display in the center of the window. With these tools, you can zoom and pan over the display as well as alter the viewpoint of your model. You can also switch between multiple views and a single view. Try the following:

1. Note which viewport is surrounded with a yellow border, and then click the Maximize Viewport Toggle in the far lower-right corner of the window. This is a tool you'll be using often. You can also press Alt+W on the keyboard.

 The graphic display changes to display a single viewport showing only the viewport that had the yellow border, as shown in Figure 1.15.

FIGURE 1.15
The viewport area showing only the Perspective viewport

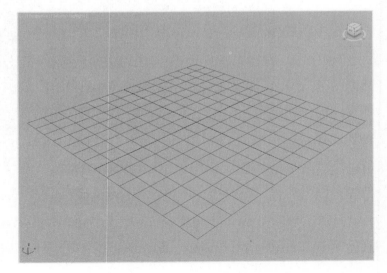

2. Click the Maximize Viewport Toggle to divide the viewport area into four individual viewports again.

3. Click the upper-right viewport, labeled Front. Notice that the border of the Front viewport becomes highlighted in yellow.

4. Click the Maximize Viewport Toggle again. Now the Front viewport fills the graphic area. Notice how you can quickly expand the view of a viewport to see more detail.

5. Click the Maximize Viewport Toggle again to return to a four-viewport layout.

6. Place your cursor at the intersection of the four viewports until it changes to a crossed-arrows cursor. Click and drag to resize all viewports simultaneously, as shown in Figure 1.16. You can also place the cursor between just two viewports to resize the viewports in only one direction.

7. Right-click the border between two viewports and choose Reset Layout from the context menu to return to the default layout, as shown in Figure 1.17.

You've just seen how you can display a single viewport or expand the graphic area into multiple viewports showing the Top, Front, Left, and Perspective viewports. Several other views and viewport arrangements are available, as you'll see later in this chapter.

FIGURE 1.16
Resize the viewports by dragging their intersection.

FIGURE 1.17
Reset Layout option

To the left of the viewport navigation tools are time controls. These tools give you control over the animation functions of 3ds Max. Here you can set your creations in motion by selecting the length of time for your animation, as well as set the precise location of objects within that time frame.

Near the bottom center of the interface is a large button with the symbol of a key on it and two smaller buttons to the right that are used to create animation keyframes, called *keys*.

The long horizontal elements across the bottom of the viewport are the Time slider and track bar, which are used for animation. You can hide the track bar to save space on the screen. Choose Customize ➤ Show UI ➤ Show Track Bar to toggle this part of the interface off until you're ready to make animations.

Just to the left of the animation controls are the transform type-ins. This area displays the location of your cursor in X, Y, and Z coordinates. It also displays other types of data, depending on your current activity. For example, if you're rotating an object, the coordinate readout displays the rotation angle of the object being rotated. If you're scaling the data, these text boxes will show percentages.

In addition to the transform type-ins, there is a Grid panel, which may be hidden to the right if your display is set to low resolution. To find it, if necessary, place the cursor on the vertical bar just to the left of the prompt line until you see a double-pointed arrow.

When you see the arrow, click and drag to the left. The Grid panel will be revealed to the right of the transform type-ins.

The Grid panel displays the default setting for the grid size in the current scene. You can hide or display a grid in the current, active viewport by clicking the G shortcut key. Right-click the Snaps Toggle, Angle Snap Toggle, or Percent Snap Toggle in the Main Toolbar, and then click the Home Grid tab of the Grid and Snap Settings dialog box to set the grid spacing and other grid parameters.

Finally, to the far left at the bottom of the 3ds Max window is the MAXScript MiniListener. MAXScript is a programming language that allows you to create custom applications or *macros* in 3ds Max. A macro is like a prerecorded series of instructions. The MAXScript MiniListener serves two functions: the pink area displays your activity when the MAXScript MacroRecord function is turned on, and the white area provides a space where you can enter commands using the keyboard.

Getting to Know the Command Panel

You'll be using the Command panel for most of your work in 3ds Max. If you're an experienced AutoCAD user, you might think of the Command panel as the equivalent of the AutoCAD command line; it's a single entry point for most of the program's functions. The Command panel offers nearly all the tools for creating and editing in 3ds Max.

Across the top of the Command panel, you'll see a set of six tabs, each displaying an icon.

From left to right, the tabs are Create, Modify, Hierarchy, Motion, Display, and Utilities. If you place the cursor on a tab, you'll see a tooltip displaying the name of the tab. When you click a tab, the functions relating to the tab appear in the rest of the Command panel. Here's a brief rundown of what each tab offers:

Create This tab allows you to create two- and three-dimensional objects. You can also create light sources, cameras, and helper objects that are used to determine distance and relationships between objects. Light sources, cameras, and helpers are objects that don't appear when your view is rendered.

Modify This tab gives you control over the dimension, shape, and parameters of your objects. On it, you'll find tools to extrude, twist, and bend your objects. You can also control methods for applying material definitions to objects (called *mapping coordinates*) on this tab.

Hierarchy This tab offers a set of tools aimed primarily at animation. The options on this tab let you build relationships between objects to simulate joint movement or to constrain motion of one object in relation to another. It also offers a way to control the location of an object's pivot point.

Motion This tab also gives you control over animation. Here, you can control the actual motion or parameter change of objects over time and view the objects' trajectories.

Display This tab lets you turn the visibility of objects on or off in your model. There may be times when you don't want a particular object visible while you render your model or while you're editing a complex model full of objects. Display lets you temporarily hide objects from view or lock them out from being selected. Objects can be hidden individually or by category.

Utilities This is a kind of catchall tab that provides access to special features and plug-ins. Here you find the Camera Match utility that lets you match your model view to a photograph. You can also get access to the MAXScript customization features on this tab.

FLOATING AND HIDING THE COMMAND PANEL

You can move the Command panel just like any other toolbar, or you can close the panel entirely by clicking the Close button (the one with the X, in the upper-right corner of the window) when the panel is floating. To bring the Command panel back, right-click the blank area of any toolbar and then select Command Panel from the context menu. You can also right-click the Command panel's title bar to dock the panel on the left or right side of the screen or minimize the Command panel to autohide it when it's not in use.

Understanding 3ds Max's Tools

There are a few ways of working in 3ds Max that are a bit unusual for a Windows program. In this section, you'll explore the Create tab of the Command panel as a way to understand some of 3ds Max's quirks. There aren't many, but understanding them now will make it easier for you to learn how to use the program.

GETTING TO KNOW SCROLLING PANELS AND ROLLOUTS

3ds Max Design 2011 has a rich set of creation and editing tools—so many, in fact, that 3ds Max's programmers had to come up with a way to get to them easily without making the program too arcane. Two of these tools help you navigate its interface: the *scrolling panel* and the *rollout*. A scrolling panel is an area that can be scrolled up or down using a Hand cursor. A rollout is a set of tools that can be opened or closed, much like a drawer in a dresser. Let's start by looking at how a scrolling panel works:

1. Click the Create tab of the Command panel. Notice the row of icons just below the title of the tab. These icons are buttons, or tools, that offer different categories of objects.

2. Place the cursor over the tool that looks like a movie camera. Notice that a tooltip displays, offering the name of the tool.

3. Click the Cameras tool. You see the options change below the tools.

4. Click the Target button. A set of additional options appears. Although it may not be obvious, these options extend beyond the bottom of the Command panel.

5. Move your cursor down to a blank spot in the Command panel. The cursor changes to a hand.

6. Click and drag up with your mouse. Notice that the options in the Command panel scroll up, following the motion of your mouse. This is an example of a scrolling panel. This scrolling action exposes the rest of the options in the lower portion of the Command panel. Release the mouse button at any time once you've seen how this scrolling action works.

7. Place the cursor on a blank area again so that the Hand cursor displays. Then click and drag down to view the Target and Free buttons under the Object Type bar.

8. You can also scroll the Command panel by rolling the wheel on your mouse or by dragging the dark-gray slender vertical scroll bar on the right side of the Command panel. Try both of these methods.

9. Another way to see more of the Command panel is to increase its width by dragging the vertical border between the Command panel and the viewport. Position your cursor along this edge, drag to the left, and expand the Command panel to two and then three columns.

10. The advantage to having a two- or three-column Command panel is obvious—you can see all the controls within the Command panel at once. The disadvantage is equally apparent—the viewport area becomes much smaller. Drag the Command panel back to one vertical column to give yourself the maximum amount of screen space. In a one-monitor system, it's better to learn how to scroll within the Command panel than to sacrifice valuable viewport space.

11. New to 3ds Max Design 2011, you can minimize the Command panel. Right-click the Command panel's title bar and choose Minimize. The Command panel is reduced to a single narrow border tab. Move your cursor over it to reveal it; move it off it to autohide. This works really well if you have a two- or three-column format.

In this exercise, you learned that you can change the entire set of options by clicking a single tool. You can also see that the set of tools can extend beyond the bottom of the Command panel. You can scroll the options up or down within the panel in several ways. This allows 3ds Max to offer a wide variety of options within the limited space of your display.

The Main Toolbar also acts like a scrolling panel whenever a portion of the toolbar extends beyond the screen area. For example, if your screen resolution is 1024 × 768, a portion of the Rendering toolbar isn't visible to the right of the screen. If you place the cursor on a blank area of the Main Toolbar, it turns into a Hand cursor. You can then click and drag to the left to display the additional tools.

When you clicked the Target button in step 4 of the preceding exercise, a set of options appeared under a bar labeled Parameters. There are three other bars, labeled Depth of Field Parameters, Object Type, and Name and Color. Notice the minus (-) sign to the far left of these bars. These bars display the titles of the *rollouts*. They let you open and close a set of options to get them out of the way or to roll them out for use. Try the following:

1. Click the rollout labeled Parameters. The options below the Parameters rollout disappear. Also notice that the minus (-) sign to the left of the rollout changes to a plus (+) sign. This indicates that the rollout is in its closed state. The plus tells you that there is more information inside, waiting to be rolled out.

2. Click the rollout labeled Name and Color. It also closes and displays a plus (+) sign to the left. Click the rollout to open it again. Right-click a blank part of the interface within any one of the rollouts, and you'll see a context menu. Select Close All.

3. Notice that the Parameters and Depth of Field Parameters rollouts closed but Object Type and Name and Color remained open. This is because all objects on the Create Panel have Object Type and Name and Color rollouts, and these always remain open by default. Any additional rollouts belong to the object you have chosen to create and can be controlled with this context menu. Try dragging the Depth of Field Parameters rollout above the Parameters rollout.

4. You will see a horizontal blue bar appear with an image of the rollout you are dragging ghosted. When you release the mouse, the rollout you are dragging gets docked where the blue bar was. Now the Depth of Field Parameters rollout should appear above the Parameters rollout.

5. Click the Parameters and Depth of Field Parameters rollouts again to display the options.

Now you can see how easy it is to control and customize the Command panel interface. In this and later chapters, you'll explore the rollouts that appear in the Command panel.

CREATING OBJECTS AND SETTING THEIR PARAMETERS

By now, you've seen most of 3ds Max's interface and how it functions. However, you should know about a few more tools and methods before you delve into using 3ds Max. In the following exercises, you'll get a chance to create a simple object, and in the process you'll be introduced to a few new tools.

1. On the Create tab of the Command panel, click the Geometry tool at the top of the panel, as shown in Figure 1.18. Make sure that Standard Primitives appears in the drop-down menu, and you will see the Object Type rollout with a set of object types.

2. Click the Box button. Additional rollouts appear in the Command panel. They include Creation Method, Keyboard Entry, and Parameters. Notice that a message in the prompt line at the bottom of the screen says, "Click and drag to begin creation process." Also, the cursor in the graphic area displays as a cross, telling you that you're in Object Creation mode.

3. In the Perspective viewport, place the cursor at the center of the graphic area at coordinates 0,0, where the two darker grid lines intersect, and click and drag diagonally to the upper-right corner of the screen—don't release the mouse button yet. As you move the mouse, a rectangle follows your cursor. Notice that the values in the Length and Width input boxes in the Parameters rollout change as you move the mouse.

4. Place the cursor so that the rectangle looks similar to the one shown in Figure 1.19, and then release the mouse button. (You don't need to match the rectangle in the figure exactly.) Now, as you move the cursor, the rectangle changes in height. Notice that the Height value in the Parameters rollout also follows the change in height.

FIGURE 1.18
Click the Geometry tool, and the available Standard Primitive object types will appear.

FIGURE 1.19
The box object so far

5. Adjust the height so that the Height parameter shows about 3′0″ and left-click your mouse. The box is now fixed at the height you selected. It should look similar to Figure 1.20.

FIGURE 1.20
The finished box

CREATE A NEW BOX IF NECESSARY

The following steps work as directed only if you have not deselected the box. If you have, click the Undo button in the Main Toolbar until the box disappears, create a new box, and then proceed with the following steps.

You've just created your first object in 3ds Max, and in the process, you've seen how the dimensions of an object are reflected in the Parameters rollout. Once you've created an object, you can continue to modify its parameters, as the following exercise demonstrates.

1. In the Parameters rollout, locate the Width input box and click the up arrow to the right of the box several times. Arrows like this one are called *spinners*, and they allow you to graphically adjust the value of the associated input box. Notice that the box in the Perspective viewport begins to widen as the value in the Width input box increases.

2. Click and hold down the left mouse button while pointing to the up arrow of the Width spinner. Notice that the box continues to grow in width as you hold down the mouse button. When you hold down the mouse button and move the mouse forward or backward, the rate of change on the values is accelerated.

3. Right-click the spinner arrow. The box shrinks in width to 0. Right-clicking any spinner changes the spinner value to its lowest possible non-negative value, which is 0′0.0″ in this case.

4. Click the Width spinner and drag the mouse up. The box grows wider. Click and drag down, and the width decreases.

5. Click and drag the Width spinner up until the cursor reaches the top of the screen. Then continue moving the mouse up the screen, and notice that the cursor reappears at the bottom of the screen and continues moving up the screen. This *circular* action of the spinner lets you scroll continuously without being limited by the screen area.

UNDOING SPINNER CHANGES

While adjusting a spinner, you can immediately undo any changes you make by right-clicking the mouse while still holding the left mouse button. This allows you to quickly experiment with spinner settings while you work.

You've just seen how you can change the parameters of an object by using the spinner. Now let's take a look at the absolute way of entering values into input boxes.

1. Double-click the Length input box in the Parameters rollout and type **60↵**. Notice how the box's length changes and the Length value changes to 5′0.0″, the feet and inches equivalent of 60″.

 Notice that it's not necessary to enter the inch (″) symbol to indicate a measurement in inches. You are, however, required to enter the foot (′) symbol when entering a measurement in feet. This is because you selected the Inches option as the default units in the Units Setup dialog box earlier in the chapter.

2. Press the Tab key. Notice that the Width value is now highlighted.

3. Type **60↵** for the width and press Tab again. The Height value is highlighted.

4. This time enter **5′↵**. The box is now a cube 60″ square.

USING THE CUBE CREATION METHOD

You can also create a cube directly by selecting the Cube radio button in the Creation Method rollout.

USING THE TAB KEY

If there is a series of related input boxes—such as the Length, Width, and Height boxes in the previous exercise—the Tab key lets you advance from one field to the next. You'll find that numeric input boxes and spinners are quite common throughout 3ds Max Design 2011.

SETTING THE SPINNER RATE OF CHANGE

If you hold down the Ctrl key while you move a spinner, the rate of change in the spinner value increases. The Alt key has the opposite effect, decreasing the rate of change. The higher the numeric value in the spinner, the faster the rate of change, and vice versa.

Working with Objects

Now that you've seen the main elements of the 3ds Max interface, we'll cover how you interact with objects in the viewport. You'll start by looking at a way to move the box you've just created. Then you'll learn how you can view your box from different angles.

Selecting and Moving Objects

3ds Max's basic editing tools are simple and straightforward, although it may take a little explaining for you to grasp the finer points. As with most graphics programs, you use a Selection tool to select objects. This tool is typically shown on the toolbar as an up arrow that looks like the standard Windows cursor.

1. Click the Select Object tool in the Main Toolbar.

2. Click a blank area of the viewport. This clears any selections that may currently be active.

3. Move the cursor over the box. Notice that the cursor turns into a plus (+) sign. This tells you that the cursor has found a selectable object.

4. Click the box to select it. A graphic displays, showing the X, Y, and Z orientation of the box in relation to the viewport (see Figure 1.21). Also notice that in the perspective view, marks like 3D *corner marks* appear at the corners of the box. These are called *selection brackets*, and they indicate graphically the objects that are selected.

With the box selected, you can go to the Modify tab of the Command panel and edit its properties, or you can use any number of other editing tools to affect the box.

FIGURE 1.21
The selected box

Let's continue by looking at one of the more basic editing tools you'll use—the Select and Move tool.

1. Click the Select and Move tool in the Main Toolbar. Notice that the graphics indicating the box selection change and new ones appear.

2. Place the cursor on the box. It changes into the Select and Move icon.

3. Click the box if it isn't still selected. A manipulator known as the Move Transform gizmo appears, showing the X, Y, and Z orientation of the box in relation to the viewport. Selection brackets also appear at the corners of the box.

4. Place the cursor on the blue Z-axis handle of the Move Transform gizmo; the blue arrow represents the Z-axis. Notice that the Z-axis and axis label highlight in yellow and the X-axis and axis label turn back to red. When you move the cursor away from the Z-axis, the X-axis is highlighted again and the Z-axis returns to blue.

The yellow highlighting shows you which axis is currently active. The X-axis is the default constraint direction. If the Constraints toolbar is still open, you'll see that the X-axis button is selected. As you've seen in this step, you can select an axis to constrain just by placing your cursor on the axis coordinate arrow.

5. Place the cursor on the XY-plane handle, the square that joins the X and Y handles of the Move gizmo. Notice that the XY-plane handle highlights in yellow (see Figure 1.22). Click and drag the box on the grid. The box now moves in the XY-plane. When you click and drag the X arrow, movement is constrained along the X-axis only.

6. Click and drag the blue Z-coordinate arrow up. Now movement is constrained in the Z-axis, away from and toward the grid. As you may guess, clicking and dragging the green Y-coordinate arrow constrains movement in the Y-axis.

FIGURE 1.22
Moving the box in
the XY-plane

THE LAST AXIS TRANSFORMED IS HIGHLIGHTED IN YELLOW

The axis that is highlighted in yellow is the last axis constraint that was used. For example, if you transform an object in the Y direction, the next time you start to transform an object, the Y-axis will be highlighted.

If you click an object in a location other than the coordinate arrows, you can freely move the object in the current axis or plane restriction. Notice that the coordinate location of the object is displayed in the status line just below the Drafting tools.

CONSTRAINING MOTION

The tools in the Axis Constraints toolbar constrain the motion of an object in the X-, Y-, or Z-axis. For example, to constrain motion in the X-axis, click the Select and Move tool, and then click the X tool in the Constraints toolbar. The selected object's motion is constrained to the X-axis. In early versions of 3ds Max, this was the only method available to constrain motion.

Another important function that the Axis Constraints toolbar offers is the selection of the default *free motion* plane. In step 5 of the preceding exercise, you were able to move the box freely in the XY-plane, but you were constrained to that plane. The Constraints toolbar lets you select the default plane to which you are constrained. The Restrict to XY-Plane tool is a flyout offering three options: XY, YZ, and ZX. You can select the plane in which you want to constrain motion by selecting one of these three options. The XY option is fine for nearly all of your work; every now and then, though, you'll want to use one of the other options, so it's good to be aware of this tool. You can also access these constraint planes simply by dragging the appropriate parts of the Transform gizmo—it's very intuitive.

If you prefer to use shortcut keys instead of a toolbar, the F5, F6, and F7 keys toggle the Y-, Y-, and Z-axis constraints, respectively. Pressing the F8 key repeatedly cycles through the XY-, YZ-, and XZ-plane constraints.

Finally, a tool that is related to the transform tools is the Selection Lock Toggle tool.

Any objects that are selected when this tool is clicked will remain selected as long as the Selection Lock Toggle is toggled to the On position. This tool helps prevent the accidental loss of a selection due to a mouse click. It also allows you to use the transform tools without actually placing the cursor on the selected objects. You can also toggle this tool on and off by clicking it or by pressing the spacebar while in a selection mode.

As you see, moving an object in 3ds Max is fairly straightforward. But what if you want to move an object a specific distance or to a known position? The following exercise demonstrates how this is done:

1. With the box still selected and the Select and Move tool still active, click the Absolute Mode Transform Type-In button at the bottom of the 3ds Max window, as shown in Figure 1.23. The tool changes to show that the Offset mode is active.

 When the Absolute/Offset Mode Transform Type-In button is in the Absolute mode (up), you can enter the specific coordinates of the point where you want to move your object. When it's in the Offset mode (down), you can enter a relative distance from the object's current location.

FIGURE 1.23
Absolute Mode
Transform Type-In
(top); Offset mode
(bottom)

2. Click in the X input box in the coordinate readout and type **10**↵. The box moves 10 inches in the positive X direction.

3. Click and drag the Z-coordinate readout spinner up. The box moves vertically.

4. Click the Absolute/Offset Mode Transform Type-In button to switch to Absolute mode. Then click in the Z-coordinate readout input box and enter **1**↵. The box moves so that its base is exactly at 1′ for the Z-coordinate.

5. Right-click the X-coordinate readout spinner. Remember that right-clicking a spinner converts the value associated with the spinner to its lowest value, which is 0′0.0″ in this case. Notice that the box moves to 0 for the X-coordinate.

6. Right-click the spinners for the Y- and Z-coordinates in the coordinate readout. The box moves to the center of the screen at the origin (coordinates 0,0,0), as shown in Figure 1.24.

FIGURE 1.24
Moving the box to
the origin

Just as with the spinners in the Command panel, the Transform Type-In spinners let you set values by clicking and dragging. You can also return to the default values of zero by right-clicking the spinners. When in Offset mode, the spinners automatically reset to zero because the values represent numerical values away from the current, baseline location. The spinners in the coordinate readout appear when you turn on the Select and Move, Select and Rotate, or Select and Scale tool from the Main Toolbar.

ACCESSING THE TRANSFORM TYPE-IN DIALOG BOXES

If you are accustomed to earlier versions of 3ds Max, you can still use the floating Transform Type-In dialog boxes that appear when you right-click the Select and Move, Select and Rotate, Select and Scale tools. Most recently, this functionality has been added to the quad menu; by clicking the settings box to the right of Move, Rotate, or Scale, you are taken to the Transform Type-In dialog box automatically. You can also access the Transform Type-In dialog box by using the F12 key.

Rotating and Scaling Objects

Besides the Move tool, the transform tools also include the Rotate and Scale tools. Try the following set of exercises to see how these tools work.

1. With the box selected, click the Select and Rotate tool in the Main Toolbar. The Rotate Transform gizmo, a kind of virtual trackball, appears, with rings representing the rotation about the X-, Y-, and Z-axes.

2. Place the cursor on the red ring that circumscribes the X-axis. Notice that the ring is highlighted in yellow. Click and drag the X-axis ring up. The box rotates about the X-axis as shown in Figure 1.25. A tangent indicator arrow will appear, indicating the direction of rotation, and a transparent red slice along with a text tooltip will appear, displaying the amount of rotation. Release the mouse button to set the rotation angle.

 Make sure the Absolute/Offset Mode Transform Type-In button is in the Absolute mode and look at the coordinate readout. Notice that the X value is not zero, because you rotated it in step 2. It now shows a number of degrees.

3. Right-click the X spinner in the coordinate readout to set the X value rotation back to zero. Notice that the box snaps back to its original orientation.

The Select and Rotate tool's methods are the same as the Select and Move Tool's. You can rotate an object graphically by clicking and dragging the object, or, with an object selected, you can enter an exact rotation value in the coordinate readout. When the Absolute/Offset Mode Transform Type-In button is in the Absolute mode, you can control the orientation in relation to the object's original orientation when it was created. In the Offset mode, you can control the orientation relative to the object's current orientation.

FIGURE 1.25
Rotating the box
about the X-axis

Now try the Select and Scale tool:

1. With the box selected, click the Select and Uniform Scale tool in the Main Toolbar. The Scale Transform gizmo appears, showing the X, Y, and Z orientation of the box in relation to the viewport.

2. Click in the center of the Scale gizmo that appears or on the box itself and drag up. The box grows uniformly in size.

3. Click and hold the Select and Uniform Scale tool. Then, from the flyout select the middle tool, which is the Select and Non-uniform Scale tool, as shown in Figure 1.26. This step is not absolutely required; it is presented here to clarify the concept. The axis handles alone can be used to scale an object nonuniformly.

4. Drag the XY-plane handle of the Scale gizmo (highlighted in yellow on-screen) to non-uniformly scale the box in the XY-plane in this case, but not along the Z-axis. Similarly, the axis handles can be dragged individually to constrain the scaling of an object to one axis (Figure 1.27).

FIGURE 1.26
The Scale flyout

FIGURE 1.27
Using the Non-uniform Scale transform on the box

Now take a look at the coordinate readout. The values you see are percentages of scale. When the Absolute/Offset Mode Transform Type-In button is in the Absolute position (up), the values are percentages of the original size of the object. When it's in the Offset position (down), the values are the scale in relation to the current size and are immediately reset to 100 percent when you release the mouse button.

1. With the Absolute/Offset Mode Transform Type-In tool in the Absolute position, click and drag the Z spinner up. Notice that the box grows in the Z-axis.

2. Right-click the Y-axis spinner. The box distorts to a 0 value in the Y-axis.

3. Click in the X-value input box and enter **100**↵. The box's X value is restored to its original size.

HOW 3DS MAX SEES THE SCALE TRANSFORM

Look at the box's Length, Width, and Height values in the Parameters rollout in the Command panel. They all read 5′0.0″ even though the box has been scaled. This is an important indicator as to how 3ds Max handles object data. For example, if you have a box that is 1 unit long on each side and then you scale it to twice its size, 3ds Max does not now see this as a box that is 2 units on each side; it sees it as a 1-unit box with a 200 percent scale factor applied.

4. Press the Tab key to move to the Y-value input box and enter **100**↵.

5. Press Tab again to move to the Z-value box and enter **75**↵. The box is now slightly shorter than it is wide and long.

The Select and Scale tool works in a slightly different way from the other two transform tools. For one thing, a zero value in the coordinate readout doesn't return the selected object to its original shape. This is because the values in the coordinate readout represent percentages, where 100 percent is the object's original size.

The Scale gizmo allows you to both uniformly and nonuniformly scale an object by automatically switching between scale modes. Which operation you perform depends on which part of the Scale gizmo you drag.

1. Try dragging the center of the Scale gizmo. You will see the object get uniformly bigger or smaller when you drag up or down, as shown in Figure 1.28.

2. This time, put your cursor over one of the edges of the Scale gizmo. When you drag over one of the plane handles, you are performing a nonuniform scale in two directions at once. Look closely at the gizmo, and you can see the axes labeled. Try nonuniformly scaling the box in the YZ plane (see Figure 1.29).

FIGURE 1.28
Using the Uniform Scale transform on the box

FIGURE 1.29
Using the Uniform Scale transform, in two axes, on the box

3. The last operation you can perform using the Scale Transform gizmo is a nonuniform scale in one direction. To accomplish this, put your mouse directly over the axis handle at the tip of an axis. For example, put your mouse over the green dot at the end of the Y-axis and drag to scale in that direction only, as shown in Figure 1.30.

FIGURE 1.30
Using the Uniform
Scale transform,
along one axis, on
the box

Once you master the mechanics of the new Transform gizmos, you will find that you have much finer and more intuitive control over your objects as compared to earlier versions of 3ds Max.

Copying an Object

We've covered just about all the ways of moving, rotating, and scaling an object in the Perspective viewport. If you want to copy an object, you use the same methods you would use to move, rotate, or scale objects—with the addition of holding down the Shift key. Try the following steps to see how copying, or *cloning*, as it's called in 3ds Max, works. (Copying is one of the forms of a more general function called *cloning*.)

1. From the File menu, choose Open and click No in the dialog box that opens asking whether you want to save the changes in your current file. The Open File dialog box appears. Navigate to the Chapter 1 files you downloaded from the book's accompanying web page, www.sybex.com/go/mastering3dsmaxdesign2011. Select the Chair.max file and then click the Open button.

2. Click the Select Object button in the Main Toolbar and then select the chair.

3. Click the Select and Move button.

4. While holding down the Shift key, move the cursor over the XY-plane of the Transform gizmo, and then drag the chair to the left. A second chair appears.

5. Release the mouse button. The Clone Options dialog box displays (see Figure 1.31). This dialog box lets you control the quantity and type of copies you're making as well as the name of the new objects.

6. In the Object group of the Clone Options dialog box, select Copy.

7. Click OK. The new chair is added to your model, as shown in Figure 1.32.

FIGURE 1.31
The Clone Options
dialog box

FIGURE 1.32
The original and cloned chairs

CREATE A COPY IN THE SAME LOCATION AS THE ORIGINAL

You may want to make a copy of an object in exactly the same location as the original object. To accomplish this, first select the object you want to copy, and then select Edit ➤ Clone from the Menu Bar or press Ctrl+V on the keyboard. You will see a Clone Options dialog box similar to the one that you saw in the preceding exercise. Set your options and click OK. Note that the new copy doesn't appear at first, because it occupies the same space as the original. (You can accomplish the same thing by Shift+clicking an object with the Select and Move tool or by selecting Clone from the Transform quad menu, which can be accessed by right-clicking the object.)

In step 6, you selected the Copy option in the Clone Options dialog box. This option creates a distinct copy of the original object. The other two options, Instance and Reference, create clones that are related to the original, in such a way that changes in one object affect the other. You'll learn more about these options in Chapter 2, "Introducing 3ds Max Objects."

 Real World Scenario

PARKING CURBS AND BOLLARDS

Jon McFarland, one of the authors of this book's 2010 edition, says that every project has features in it that vary from interesting and cool to mundane and repetitive. Although we all like to work on the exciting projects, we will all do our share of the latter. When those less-than-exciting projects pop up, it's best to crank them out quickly and accurately and then move on to the next portfolio-quality project down the line.

While the main effort of McFarland's company was being applied to the creation of a mall, complete with an entertainment center and several freestanding buildings for restaurants and other shops, someone had to work on the parking lot. He was hired to accurately place several thousand parking curbs and bollards (vertical posts used to restrict vehicular traffic) throughout the parking lot and around the entrances to the structure. Parking curbs are usually identical and placed equidistant from each other (usually 9′0″ apart), so the layout wasn't difficult. After modeling the simple curb, he placed one at the end of each parallel run of parking spaces. He selected the first curb on each run, held the Shift key down, and moved it 9′ in the proper direction. In the Clone Options dialog box, he set Number of Copies to the number of curbs in the longest run and then deleted any superfluous curbs.

This process was repeated several times for the remaining curbs, and then a similar process was used to place the bollards. Upon receiving the completed work, the company assigned McFarland the task of creating the traffic islands and the screen walls around the service areas. He says, "I'm sure one of these days they'll give me a fun job to do."

Selecting Multiple Objects

You've now learned how to select, move, and copy a single object, but what do you do if you want to move or copy several objects at once? You can select multiple objects, or create *selection sets*, as they are called in 3ds Max, using two methods. The first is one that is also employed in other graphics programs.

1. Click the Select Object tool on the Main Toolbar.

2. Click a blank area of the viewport to clear any selections you may already have, or click Ctrl+D on the keyboard.

3. Click and hold your cursor at a point below and to the left of the chair copy. Then drag to the right and up. Notice that a dotted rectangle follows your cursor, as shown in Figure 1.33.

4. Continue to drag the cursor up and to the right until it encloses both chairs. Then release the mouse button. Both chairs are selected.

FIGURE 1.33
Placing the selection rectangle around the chairs

Notice that selection brackets (or bounding boxes) appear at the corners of both chairs, and a gizmo appears between them, indicating that the two objects are selected. You can select objects in a couple of other ways, which you'll learn about in a moment, but first, let's use the current selection to make a few more copies of the box.

1. Click the Select and Move tool in the Main Toolbar.

2. Hold the Shift key down and drag the X-axis arrow of the Move Transform gizmo back so that copies of the two chairs appear in the location shown in Figure 1.34. (You don't need to be exact about the placement of the copies.)

FIGURE 1.34
Place the copies
just beyond your
first two objects.

FIGURE 1.34
Place the copies
just beyond your
first two objects.

3. When the copies are in place, release the mouse button.

4. In the Clone Options dialog box, make sure Copy is selected in the Object group and click OK.

The four chairs help to demonstrate some of the other selection methods available to you. First, let's look at another property of the selection window.

1. Click the Select Object tool, or right-click and choose Select from the quad menu.

2. Click a blank spot in the viewport to clear your selection set.

3. Click and drag the cursor from the point indicated in Figure 1.35.

4. Drag the rectangle up and to the right so that it completely encompasses one chair but just a portion of two other chairs, as shown in Figure 1.35. Then release the mouse button. Three of the four chairs are selected.

Notice that you didn't need to enclose the chairs completely to select them. In the current selection mode, you only need to have the selection window cross over the desired objects. This is known as a *crossing window*. If you're an AutoCAD user, this type of window should be familiar to you.

FIGURE 1.35
Selecting points for
a crossing window

...to here

Click and drag from here...

You can change the way the selection window works by using the Window/Crossing Selection tool. The following exercise demonstrates this:

1. Click a blank area in the drawing in order to clear your selection set.

2. Click the Window/Crossing tool in the Main Toolbar.

 Notice that the icon highlights in blue and changes to one showing a cube that's completely within a dotted rectangle. This tells you that you are now in Window Selection mode.

3. Click a point above and to the left of the front left chair in the foreground, as shown in Figure 1.36.

4. Drag the rectangle down and to the right until it completely encompasses the two chairs in the front, as shown in Figure 1.36. Then release the mouse button. Notice that the only objects selected are the two chairs on the left.

FIGURE 1.36
Placing a Window
Selection window

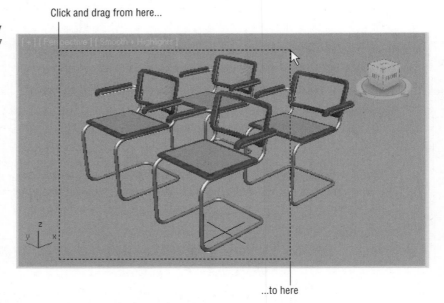

Click and drag from here...

...to here

When you use Window Selection mode, only objects that are completely within the selection window are selected. Unlike with the crossing window, objects that are partially inside the selected window are omitted from the selection.

You can use the Ctrl key in conjunction with any selection method to continue to add more objects to your selection set. You can also remove objects from your selection set by using the Alt key. This is a new behavior in 3ds Max Design 2011. Previously the Ctrl key would both add to and subtract from selection sets. Now the Ctrl key is only for addition, and the Alt key only for subtraction. The following activity demonstrates how adding and subtracting from selections works:

1. Switch back to the Crossing Selection method, and then Ctrl+click and hold a point below and to the right of the chair near the bottom of the viewport. Notice the small plus (+)

sign next to the cursor indicating that selected objects are to be added to the current selection set, as shown in Figure 1.37.

2. Drag the window up and to the left so that it encloses a portion of the two chairs on the right. Then release the mouse button. Now all four chairs are selected.

3. Hold down the Alt key and then click the chair in the upper right of the screen. Now all chairs except the upper-right one are selected, as shown in Figure 1.38.

FIGURE 1.37
Adding objects to your selection set using the Ctrl key

FIGURE 1.38
Removing an object from your selection using the Alt key

You can change the shape of your selection window to help select objects. There are rectangular, circular, polygonal, lasso, and paint Selection Region options. The next exercise explores the lasso selection region that allows freeform sketching for a selection.

1. Drag open the Selection Window flyout and click the Lasso button.

2. Switch back to the Window selection option.

3. Sketch a lasso selection region by dragging the mouse in a freeform manner around two of the chairs to select them, as shown in Figure 1.39. Because the Ctrl button was not held down during the selection process, only the two chairs fully encompassed by the lasso are selected while the rear-left chair, which was previously selected, is now unselected.

Right now, you have only a few objects in your model, but as your model develops, you'll find that selecting objects in a crowded model becomes more of a challenge. Knowing about the different selection modes will go a long way toward making your work easier.

FIGURE 1.39
Selecting objects using a lasso selection region

One more selection method will be an invaluable tool as your model becomes more complex. You can select objects by their names, using the Select from Scene dialog box. The following is a quick exercise that will introduce you to this important tool.

1. Click the Select by Name tool in the Main Toolbar or press H on the keyboard.

 The Select From Scene dialog box displays. It contains a list showing the names of the objects in your drawing on a blue background with the currently selected objects appearing (see Figure 1.40). Groups of objects appear preceded by an icon consisting of an overlapping circle and square contained within brackets. Right now, the list shows the default names given to the objects by 3ds Max. You can always change the name of an object in the Command panel. (You can rename an object on every tab except Utilities.)

2. Click the Select None button on the second row of icons on the dialog box. This clears the selection set.

3. Click MeshChair01 and then Ctrl+click MeshChair03 in the list of object names. This list lets you select multiple names as you would in a typical Windows list box. You can Shift+click to select a group of adjacent names or Ctrl+click to select a group of individual names. Figure 1.41 shows the Select Objects dialog box with the new selection.

4. Click the OK button. The two chairs are selected.

FIGURE 1.40
Selected objects appear on a blue background in the Select From Scene dialog box.

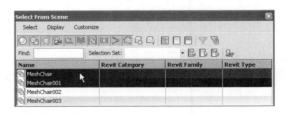

FIGURE 1.41
The Select From Scene dialog box with the new selection set

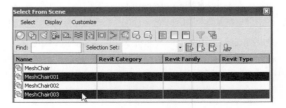

The preceding exercise showed you how to select objects based on their names, but it also indirectly showed you the importance of the names of objects. Giving objects meaningful names helps you locate and select them more easily, especially in a crowded model.

EACH OBJECT HAS ITS OWN NAME AND PARAMETERS

3ds Max is a parametric, object-oriented program, and every object has its own name. Each object has its own parameters that can be accessed from the Modify tab.

Whenever you create an object in 3ds Max Design 2011, you have the opportunity to give the new object a name. If you don't indicate a new name, 3ds Max provides a name for you. If the new object is a copy of an existing one, the new name that 3ds Max provides is the name of the original object, with a number appended to its name. If you don't give an object a meaningful name when you create it, it's easy enough to change the name later. Just select the object, and then enter a new name in the object name input box at the top of the Modify tab or in the Name and Color rollout of the Create tab.

Naming Selection Sets

Suppose you've gone through a lot of effort selecting a set of objects, and you know you will want to select the same set of objects again at a later time. 3ds Max offers the Named Selection Sets tool, which lets you name a selection set for later recall. Here's how it works:

1. Make sure two of the chairs are selected. It doesn't matter which two, because you're just practicing using the Named Selection Sets tool.

2. Click inside the Create Selection Set input box that's just to the left of the Mirror tool in the Main Toolbar.

3. Type the name **Sample**.↵. You've just given the current selection set a name. (You can enter a selection set name up to 15 characters long.)

4. Click in a blank area of the viewport to clear the current selection set.

5. In the Main Toolbar, click the down arrow to the right of the Named Selection Sets input box. Select Sample. The two boxes you selected earlier are now the current selection set.

In these early stages of learning 3ds Max, the concept of named selection sets may seem simple, but you'll likely use named selections quite a bit as you expand your skills.

OTHER METHODS FOR SELECTING OBJECTS

The Edit option in the Menu Bar offers some additional selection commands, such as Select All, Select None, and Select Invert. You can also use the Edit ➤ Select By cascading menu to select objects by color, name, or layer.

Editing Named Selection Sets

Named selection sets are not set in stone. You can add to or subtract from them, or you can delete them entirely through the Named Selection Sets dialog box.

1. Open the Named Selection Sets dialog box by choosing Edit ➤ Manage Selection Sets or by clicking the Edit Named Selection Sets button just to the left of the Named Selection Sets input box you used before. The Named Selection Sets dialog box appears with a list of all of the selection sets that have been created (Figure 1.42).

2. Click the plus (+) symbol next to your Sample named selection set to see which objects are contained within this set, as shown in Figure 1.43.

3. Click Sample in the list. Then click the Select Objects by Name button in the Named Selection Sets toolbar (Figure 1.44).

FIGURE 1.42
Edit Named Selection Sets

FIGURE 1.43
The Named Selection Sets dialog box showing the contents of the Sample selection set

FIGURE 1.44
Select Objects by Name

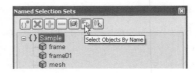

4. The Select Objects dialog box displays—this is identical to the Select From Scene dialog box that you used in the previous exercise. Select one of the names in the list that doesn't already appear in the Named Selection Sets dialog box, as shown in Figure 1.45, and then click the Select button. This selects the listed objects in the scene but doesn't add them to the named selection set.

FIGURE 1.45

Selecting an object with the Select Objects dialog box

SEVERAL OBJECTS ACTING AS ONE

It may appear that objects in the Select Objects or Select From Scene dialog boxes are different from the objects listed in the Named Selection Sets dialog box. This is only partially correct. The chairs used in these exercises are *groups*, collections of objects that react as if they were a single object. The Select Objects and Select From Scene dialog boxes display the names of the groups, but the Named Selection Sets dialog box displays the names of the component objects that make up the groups. Groups are covered in more detail in the "Working with Groups" section in Chapter 2.

5. Click the Add Selected Objects button in the Named Selection Sets dialog box (Figure 1.46).

The names of the objects you selected now appear in the list of objects contained in the selection set, as shown in Figure 1.47.

FIGURE 1.46

Add Selected Objects

FIGURE 1.47

The expanded list of objects in the Named Selection Sets dialog box

6. Close the dialog box and deselect all by clicking off to the side in the viewport.

7. Select Sample from the Named Selection Set drop-down list. Now you see that three of the chairs are selected.

8. Click a blank area of the viewport to clear the selection set again.

There are several other tools in the Named Selection Sets dialog box. These tools let you select objects from a set, highlight selected objects, delete objects from a set, or remove a set altogether. You can also create new named selection sets using the Create New Set tool at the far left of the Named Selection Sets toolbar.

You've now seen most of the selection tools you'll need to get started with 3ds Max. You'll learn about a few other selection tools as you work with 3ds Max, and you'll also get a chance to apply the tools you've already learned as you start to build and edit 3D models in later chapters.

In the next section, you'll learn about the tools that enable you to view your model from different angles, and how these different views can aid you in creating and editing your model.

Named selection sets can also contain selections of sub-objects, such as vertices, edges, or polygons, the components that make up an object. When a sub-object named selection set is created, it is available only when that object is selected and the sub-object level is accessed. You will learn about sub-objects in Chapter 4.

Getting the View You Want

So far in this chapter, you've done all of your work without making any modifications to the *point of view* of your model. Now let's take a look at ways you can control your view. Understanding the viewport controls is essential for manipulating objects in your model, so take some time to become familiar with all the tools discussed in this section.

Understanding the Perspective Viewing Tools

If you look at the viewport navigation controls in the lower-right corner of the 3ds Max window, you'll see some tools that are common among most graphics programs. They include the magnifying glass and the hand. Other tools in this area may be a bit more mysterious. In this section, you'll learn how these tools let you get around in your model.

PANNING AND ZOOMING YOUR VIEW

Let's begin by looking at the tool with the Hand icon, known as the Pan View tool. Like similar tools in other programs, the Pan View tool displaces your view up, down, left, or right. But in 3ds Max's Perspective viewport, you're also changing your point of view. Do the following to see what this means:

1. Click the Pan View tool.

2. Click and drag the viewport to the left and up until the chairs are roughly centered in the viewport.

3. Click and drag the viewport in a circular fashion. Notice that your view of the model appears to change as if you were moving sideways while looking at the boxes.

Next, try the Zoom tool:

1. Click the Zoom tool.

2. Click and drag the Zoom tool up from the center of the viewport. Notice how you appear to get closer to the chairs.

3. Click and drag the cursor down in the viewport. Now you appear to be moving away from the chairs.

4. Continue to click and drag down until your view looks similar to the one shown in Figure 1.48.

FIGURE 1.48
Zooming out to
view a larger area

Depending on your settings, as you moved farther away, the grid may have become denser. Then, at a certain point, the grid changed to a wider interval. 3ds Max does this so that the grid doesn't overwhelm the view when it becomes too dense.

If the grid does not increase in size to fill the viewport, right-click the Snaps Toggle in the Main Toolbar. Click the Home Grid tab in the Grid and Snap Settings dialog box and uncheck the Inhibit Perspective View Grid Resize option.

Again, as with other graphics programs, the Zoom tool enlarges or reduces your view. In addition to the Zoom tool, the wheel of the mouse can be used to zoom in and out within a viewport. In 3ds Max's Perspective viewport, zooming has the effect of moving you closer to or farther away from the objects in your model.

Now, suppose you don't like the last view change you made and you want to go back to the previous view. Try the following steps to return to the previous view:

1. Choose Views ➢ Undo View Change. You return to the previous view. (Alternatively, press Shift+Z.)

2. Choose Views ➢ Undo View Change or press Shift+Z again. Your view returns to the view prior to the last view.

3. Choose Views ➢ Undo View Change a third time. You return to the view you had before you panned your view.

The Views ➢ Undo View Change command lets you step back to a previous view in case the last view change you made is one you don't like. Views ➢ Undo View Change undoes any view change, regardless of which Viewport tool you used last.

UNDO VIEW IS DIFFERENT FROM UNDO

Don't confuse Views ➢ Undo View Change with the Edit ➢ Undo command. Edit ➢ Undo undoes creation and editing operations but not view changes.

SAVING A VIEW YOU LIKE

If you happen to get a view that you know you want to go back to later, you can save the view with the Views ➢ Save Active command from the Menu Bar. Use it in the next exercise to save a view that you'll return to later in this chapter. And, as you'll see in Chapter 8, "Light and Shadow," you can also create a camera object and align it to an existing view.

1. Click the Zoom Extents tool to set up your view for the next exercise. Zoom Extents causes the viewport to display the entire model.

2. Save this view by choosing Views ➢ Save Active Perspective View.

The Zoom Extents tool repositions your view so that the entire model just fits within the viewport, filling the viewport as much as possible. If you're an AutoCAD user, you're familiar with this tool, because its counterpart in AutoCAD performs the same function.

RESETTING THE PERSPECTIVE VIEW

You can also restore the perspective viewport (the one you see when you open a new file) in a blank file by clicking the Zoom Extents tool or by choosing File ➢ Reset to reset the scene.

CHANGING YOUR VIEWING ANGLE

Three other tools are specifically designed for viewing 3D objects: Field-of-View, Orbit Selected, and the ViewCube. The Field-of-View tool changes your field of view, the Orbit Selected tool lets you rotate your view around a selected object, and the ViewCube contains several tools for modifying your viewpoint.

The Field-of-View tool appears to do the same thing as the Zoom tool, but as you'll see in the following exercise, there is a significant difference between the Zoom and Field-of-View tools.

1. Save the current view by choosing Views ➢ Save Active Perspective View. This lets you return to the current view later.

2. Click the Field-of-View tool.

3. Place the cursor in the viewport, and click and drag down until your view looks similar to Figure 1.49.

FIGURE 1.49
The Perspective
viewport after
increasing the field
of view

In one sense, it appears as though you've zoomed out from the chairs, but if you compare this view to the zoomed-out view in the previous exercise, you'll notice a difference. When you use the Zoom tool in the Perspective viewport, your view changes as though you were physically moving closer to or farther away from the chairs. As the name implies, the Field-of-View tool widens or narrows your field of view, much as a zoom lens on a camera does. You're not actually changing the distance from the object; instead, you're changing the area that your viewport displays. The Field-of-View tool has the potential to distort your view, just as a super-wide-angle fish-eye lens or a super-telephoto lens tends to distort a photograph. Until you are in a situation where you really need to change the field of view, you may want to refrain from using the Field-of-View tool.

Now let's take a look at the Arc Rotate Selected tool:

1. Return to the view you had before you used the Field-of-View tool by choosing Views ➢ Restore Active Perspective View.

2. Click the Select Object tool, and then click a blank space in the viewport to clear any selections that may be active. In the next exercise, you'll see why this is significant.

3. Click the Orbit Selected tool (this may be hidden on the Orbit flyout menu).

You see a yellow circle with squares at each of the four cardinal points on the circle. If you place the cursor inside the circle, the cursor looks like two overlapping ellipses.

4. Place the cursor on the square at the far left of the circle. Notice that the cursor changes shape to what looks like a horizontal ellipse.

5. With the cursor on the square, slowly click and drag the cursor to the right. Notice how the view rotates.

6. Place the cursor on the square at the top of the circle. Now the cursor changes to a vertically oriented ellipse.

7. With the cursor on the square, click and drag the cursor down. The view now rotates in that direction.

The squares on the yellow circle are like handles that you can grab and turn to change your view orientation. The left and right squares constrain the rotation to the horizontal plane, and the top and bottom squares constrain the rotation to the vertical plane. If you prefer, you can adjust the view freely without constraint in the vertical or horizontal direction by clicking and dragging the cursor anywhere within the circle. You can also rotate the view by clicking and dragging anywhere outside the circle. The following exercise demonstrates these features. Pay attention to the shape of the cursor in each step.

1. Place the cursor anywhere within the circle. Then slowly click and drag in a small, circular motion. Notice how the view changes as if your point of view were rotating around the group of chairs.

2. Place the cursor anywhere outside the circle. Then slowly click and drag in an up-and-down motion. Now the view rotates around the circle as if you were tilting your head from side to side.

You may have noticed that the cursor changes, depending on whether you're inside or outside the circle. This gives you further cues regarding the way the Orbit Selected tool affects your view.

You've been introduced to nearly all of the viewport tools. However, there's one more feature of the Orbit Selected tool that you'll want to know about before you continue. The Orbit Selected tool uses the center of the viewport as the center about which it rotates when no object is selected. But the Orbit Selected tool works in a slightly different way when objects are selected. Try the following exercise to see how this variation works:

1. Choose Views ➤ Restore Active Perspective View to restore the view you saved earlier.

2. Click the Select Object tool from the Main Toolbar.

3. Click the chair on the left side in the back row, as shown in Figure 1.50.

4. Click the Orbit Selected tool again.

5. Slowly click and drag the cursor within the circle. Notice how the view appears to be fixed at the center of the selected chair.

FIGURE 1.50
Selecting a chair in
the back row

6. Slowly click and drag the cursor in a vertical motion outside the circle. The view appears to rotate around the selected chair.

7. Return to the saved view by choosing Views ➢ Restore Active Perspective View.

If you click and hold the Orbit Selected tool, you'll see two other Orbit tools in the Orbit flyout. The tool at the top, called simply the Orbit tool, rotates the view about the view center, regardless of whether an object is selected. You've already seen how the second tool, the Orbit Selected tool, works. The tool at the bottom of the Orbit flyout is the Orbit SubObject tool. This tool rotates a view about a sub-object-level selection. You'll learn about sub-object-level editing in Chapter 4.

ORBIT ON THE FLY

You can orbit on the fly, without leaving the current command, by holding down the Alt key on the keyboard and holding down the wheel button while you move the mouse. This is a huge time-saver because you'll find that you don't have to spend time clicking the Orbit button when you want to rotate your viewing angle.

USING THE VIEWCUBE

Changing the viewpoint to view your scenes is especially important in a 3D environment because you are more likely to encounter a situation where foreground objects obscure background objects. The ViewCube, the tool in the upper-right corner of the viewport, is used to quickly access common views, return to a saved view, or navigate freely in the drawing area.

The ViewCube consists of a center cube with each face labeled, identifying the standard orthographic view that it represents. Clicking any of these labeled faces changes the viewpoint in the drawing area to display the objects from that point of view. For example, clicking the ViewCube face labeled TOP changes the drawing area to display the scene from the top, with the X-axis pointing to the right and the Y-axis pointing to the top of your screen (see Figure 1.51).

FIGURE 1.51
The functions of
the ViewCube

Click to switch to the Home view.

Click a face to switch to an orthographic view.

Click an edge to switch to a view rotated 45° from the adjacent orthographic view.

Click a corner to switch to an isometric view.

Click and drag to set a nonstandard view.

Click a letter to switch to an elevation view from that direction.

The orthographic views are not the only viewpoints that you can access from the ViewCube. Clicking any corner changes the drawing area to display the objects from an isometric vantage point that is a combination of the three labeled faces. Clicking the corner at the intersection of the TOP, FRONT and LEFT faces (see Figure 1.52) produces a southwest isometric view.

Clicking any of the edges (see Figure 1.53) changes the drawing area to display the objects rotated 45 degrees from one of the adjacent orthographic views. You'll usually perform a Zoom after using the ViewCube.

FIGURE 1.52
Clicking a corner of the ViewCube creates an isometric view.

FIGURE 1.53
Clicking an edge of the ViewCube creates a view adjacent to an orthographic view.

Surrounding the ViewCube is a ring with the compass directions indicated. Clicking any of the letters switches the view in the drawing area to a view from that direction. For example, clicking the letter E on the ring displays the elevation from the east.

Switching to a predesignated view is quick and can often provide the vantage point that you need, but you may have to view your objects from a specific, nonstandard location. Clicking and dragging the ViewCube changes the viewpoint freely without any constraints to the predesignated views.

Another tool, called SteeringWheels, lets you zoom, pan, and orbit in the viewport similarly to these other methods. Because this tool is off by default, we're not going to cover it in this book. The SteeringWheels tool is available in other Autodesk programs; if you are familiar with it and want to use it, you can turn it on by choosing Views ➤ SteeringWheels.

By being able to select an object or set of objects as the center of rotation for your view, you are better able to set up your views for rendering or editing. The combination of the Zoom, Pan, and Orbit tools allows you to obtain just about any view you may need as you work within 3ds

Max's Perspective viewport. But you aren't limited to a perspective view of your model. In fact, there are many situations where the perspective view is not ideal, especially when editing your model. In the next section, you'll look at other viewport types that give you greater flexibility in creating and editing objects in your model.

Using Multiple Viewports

So far, you've done all your work in the Perspective viewport, but this isn't the only view you have available. You currently have four equal viewports, each representing a different view. Let's explore some of 3ds Max's display tools in the other viewports, starting with the way that the Field-of-View tool changes when your active viewport changes.

1. Click the Maximize Viewport Toggle, in the set of viewport navigation controls, if necessary to display a four-viewport configuration.

2. Click anywhere in the viewport labeled Top in the upper-left corner of the display. Notice that the Field-of-View tool changes to a magnifying glass with a rectangle. This is the Zoom Region tool.

 Also notice that the Top viewport now shows a thick yellow border around it, indicating that it is the current, active viewport.

3. Click the Zoom Region tool.

4. Click and drag the cursor on a point below and to the left of the chairs, as shown in Figure 1.54. As you drag the cursor, you see a rectangle appear. Don't release the cursor yet.

5. Position the rectangle above and to the right of the bottom row of chairs, as shown in Figure 1.54, and then release the mouse button. The view enlarges to the region you just indicated with the Zoom Region tool.

The Zoom Region tool acts like the magnifying tools in many other graphics programs. Also, the Zoom and Pan tools perform the same functions in orthogonal views in 3ds Max as they do in other programs, allowing you to zoom in and pan over the view.

FIGURE 1.54
Selecting a view to enlarge with the Zoom Region tool

You may have noticed two other tools in the viewport navigation controls that haven't been discussed yet: the Zoom All and Zoom Extents All tools. Now that you have multiple viewports displayed, you can try these two tools:

1. Click the Zoom All tool.

2. In any viewport, click and drag the cursor up and down. Notice that the view in all of the viewports is enlarged or reduced as the cursor moves.

3. Click and drag the cursor down, and the views expand to show more of the model area.

4. Click the Zoom Extents All tool.

 All of the viewports change to display enlarged views of the chairs, as shown in Figure 1.55.

FIGURE 1.55
The four viewports after using the Zoom Extents All tool

Although not as frequently used as the other viewport navigation tools, the Zoom All tool and the Zoom Extents All tool can be helpful when you need to adjust the overall view of your model in multiple viewports.

You should be aware that the Orbit Selected tool you used in the Perspective viewport also works in the other viewports. Try it out on the Top viewport in this exercise:

1. Click the Orbit Selected tool.

2. Select one chair, and then click and drag the cursor from the center of the Top viewport up and to the right, so it shows a view similar to Figure 1.56.

 The view changes to a type of 3D view known as an *isometric projection.* Also notice that the label in the upper-left corner of the viewport now reads Orthographic. This indicates that the view is a custom view based on your changes.

3. Click the Zoom Extents tool to center the view in the viewport.

The 3D view in the upper-left corner of the display differs in many ways from the perspective view. But, as you'll see in the next section, it's different only because a few of the settings for that viewport are different from those of the Perspective viewport.

FIGURE 1.56
The Top viewport
after using Orbit
Selected

Changing the Viewport Display and Configuration

If you compare the Orthographic viewport with the Perspective viewport, you'll notice one thing that is different. As mentioned in the previous exercise, the Orthographic viewport shows a 3D orthographic projection. Parallel lines do not converge as the distance from the viewpoint increases as they do in the Perspective viewport. You'll notice that the Orthographic viewport is set to the Smooth + Highlights display mode. The chairs appear solid, have color, and texture, and the metal appears shiny. These display characteristics can be modified for each viewport.

Look at the upper-left corner of the viewport, and you will see the Viewport Label menus (Figure 1.57). These three menus provide access to control the characteristics of the selected view.

FIGURE 1.57
The Viewport
Label menus

 General Shading
 Point-of-View (POV)

In the following exercise, you'll see how you can alter viewport settings to obtain specific view characteristics such as shading and perspective:

1. Move the cursor and hover over the Shading Viewport label menu, which is the rightmost set of brackets in the upper-left corner of the viewport. The label inside the brackets turns yellow. Now click the label. A context menu appears, as shown in Figure 1.58.

2. Select Wireframe from the menu. The chairs now appear as wireframes (see Figure 1.59), just as they do in two of the other viewports.

FIGURE 1.58
Shading View-
port label menu

3. Click the Orthographic viewport Shading label again, and then select Hidden Line from the context menu. The Orthographic viewport changes to reflect the contents in the Hidden Line rendering mode.

4. Zoom into the chairs to get a better look at the Hidden Line rendering mode. Your view should be shaded similarly to Figure 1.60.

FIGURE 1.59
The Orthographic viewport in Wireframe mode

FIGURE 1.60
A single chair in Hidden Line rendering mode

Notice that the context menu is the same for both the Orthographic and Perspective viewports. This menu gives you control over the display characteristics of the viewport. Try a few of the other options in the Viewport Label menus:

1. Click the Point-of-View (POV) label, select Perspective, and then click the Zoom Extents button. The Orthographic viewport changes to a Perspective viewport. Notice that the label changes to read Perspective, so that you now have two Perspective viewports, as shown in Figure 1.61.

2. Click the POV label of the upper-left viewport, select Top, and then click Zoom Extents. The view changes back to the original top view. Notice that the chairs are still in shaded mode.

3. Click the Shading label of the Top viewport, and then select Wireframe.

FIGURE 1.61

Two of the four viewports are now Perspective viewports.

Three of the viewports show wireframe views of the chairs. Wireframe views are best for many types of editing operations. Wireframes also redraw faster when your model is very large and full of complex geometry. Another type of view, called a *bounding box*, is even faster than a wireframe view, but bounding-box views reduce the representation of objects to rectangular boxes. The Edged Faces mode, available when the viewport is in any of the available Shaded modes, displays both the Shaded mode and the edges of the visible objects.

Besides changing the way the viewport displays your model, wireframe view also gives you control over the layout of the viewports themselves. The following exercise shows you the variety of layouts you can create in 3ds Max:

1. Choose Views ➢ Viewport Configuration. The Viewport Configuration dialog box appears, as shown in Figure 1.62.

FIGURE 1.62

The Viewport Configuration dialog box

2. Click the Layout tab. You see the current viewport layout at the bottom of the tab. Above it is a set of 14 predefined layouts, as shown in Figure 1.63.

FIGURE 1.63
The Layout tab of the
Viewport Configura-
tion dialog box

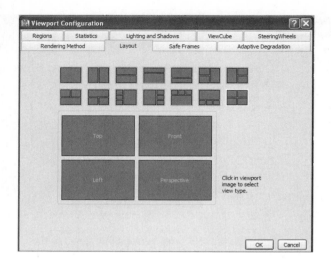

3. Click the layout that looks like three small rectangles stacked on the left side with one large rectangle on the right.

4. Click OK. The viewports change to the selected layout.

5. Click the Zoom Extents All button to zoom all the viewports to show the contents of the scene. Your viewports should look similar to the viewports in Figure 1.64.

FIGURE 1.64
The viewports
after changing the
viewport layout

You aren't limited to the canned layouts either. You may decide that you want the layout to reflect a more traditional mechanical drawing layout, with a top, front, and right side view. Here's how you can set up such a viewport arrangement:

1. Choose Views ➢ Viewport Configuration.

2. With the Layout tab selected, click the layout showing four equal viewports, which is the rightmost layout in the bottom row of layout options (see Figure 1.65).

3. Click the sample viewport labeled Front in the upper-right corner of the large sample layout and select Perspective in the pop-up menu, as shown in Figure 1.66.

FIGURE 1.65
Selecting a four-viewport layout

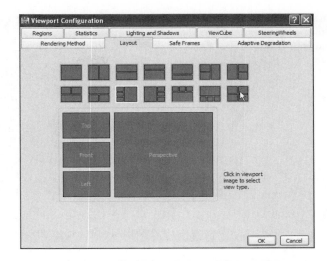

FIGURE 1.66
Changing a specific viewport's view

4. Click the sample Perspective viewport in the lower-right corner and select Right from the pop-up menu.

5. Click the sample Left viewport in the lower-left corner and select Front from the pop-up menu.

6. Click OK. Now you have a layout that shows the top, front, and right views, plus a perspective view, arranged in a more traditional manner. Change the Right viewport to Hidden Line mode. Perform a Zoom Extents All, and your viewports should look like Figure 1.67.

FIGURE 1.67
The four-viewport layout with modifications

As you can see from what you've learned so far, 3ds Max Design 2011 provides a wide array of display options, but most of the time, you'll stick with one viewport layout that is comfortable for you. For the purposes of this book, you'll use the default layout that shows the four equal-size viewports.

Before you conclude your tour of the 3ds Max interface, take a look at how the Move tool acts in the non-Perspective viewports. The following exercise will give you a feel for the ways that you can use multiple viewports:

1. Click the Select and Move tool.

2. In the Top viewport, click and drag the cursor from a point below and to the left of the bottom row of chairs.

3. Drag the selection region above and to the right of the two chairs in the lower row, as shown in Figure 1.68, so that they are enclosed in the rectangle. The two chairs are selected.

4. Right-click in the Right viewport.

FIGURE 1.68
Drag a selection region around the lower chairs.

RIGHT-CLICKING RETAINS THE SELECTION SET

By right-clicking in a viewport, you can make it active without disrupting any selections that may be active at the time.

5. In the Right viewport, click and drag the green Y-arrow up. Notice how the chairs move in the front and perspective views as you do this.

6. Position the chairs so they are higher by about one-half the height of a chair.

7. Click and drag the red X-axis of the chairs to the right of the screen so they merge with the chair to the right, as shown in Figure 1.69.

8. You can save or discard this file. You won't need it anymore.

FIGURE 1.69
Move the selected chairs along the X-axis.

In this exercise, you've seen a number of methods in action. First, you saw how to use the Select and Move tool to select objects as well as move them. This can help you move objects quickly by reducing the number of clicks you need to make. Be careful, though; you might select and move the wrong object when you are in a hurry.

Second, you saw how you can right-click in a viewport to make it active. Had you simply clicked in the Right viewport in step 4, you would have lost the selection set you created in step 3.

Finally, you saw how objects in 3ds Max don't conform to one of the basic rules of physics. In 3ds Max, more than one object *can* occupy the same space at the same time. This characteristic can be useful in a number of ways as you build models in 3ds Max Design 2011.

Working with the Custom UI and Defaults Switcher

The Custom UI and Defaults Switcher provides an easy and unified method for managing all the myriad preference settings within 3ds Max. Let's explore what the Custom UI and Defaults Switcher has to offer.

1. Choose Customize ➤ Custom UI and Defaults Switcher, as shown in Figure 1.70.

2. Click the DesignVIZ initial settings for tool options in the upper-left corner of the dialog box to see the settings listed in Figure 1.71.

FIGURE 1.70

The Customize menu

FIGURE 1.71

Custom UI and
Defaults Switcher
settings

3. Scroll down in the dialog box and read through the changes that the DesignVIZ settings represent in the HTML file that is part of the Custom UI and Defaults Switcher dialog box. There are four possible settings for tool options: Max, Max mentalray, DesignVIZ, and DesignVIZ.mentalray.

The DesignVIZ settings are configured to provide you with good rendering performance in large scenes with many lights; this assumes you'll be using the Radiosity Renderer and photometric lights.

The DesignVIZ.mentalray initial settings are meant to be used in conjunction with the mental ray renderer. Each of these settings automatically configures multiple preferences in layers, the Material Editor, Lights, Daylight System, Rendering, Motion Blur, Cloning, Select by Name, i-drop, Inverse Kinematics, Viewport Shading, and Real-World Texture Coordinates. The Max and Max mentalray initial settings are designed for use when utilizing 3ds Max for game, film, and video production.

On the right side of the Custom UI and Defaults Switcher dialog box, you'll see a default list of UI schemes. Here, you can conveniently select which UI scheme you'd like to use. UI schemes hold in one place all the customizations you can make to the keyboard hotkeys, toolbar, quad menus, standards menus, and color schemes. To make changes to an existing UI scheme, you'll use the Customize User Interface dialog box.

1. Choose Customize ➢ Customize User Interface to display the dialog box shown in Figure 1.72.

2. Click each of the tabs at the top of this dialog box to become familiar with all the ways you can customize your user interface (changes can be made to the keyboard, toolbars, quad menus, pull-down menus, and colors). If you do decide to make any changes, simply click the Save button on the tab in this dialog box to record your specific changes to disk, as shown in Figure 1.73. Each tab saves as a different file type that controls different aspects of the user interface.

FIGURE 1.72
The Customize User Interface dialog box

FIGURE 1.73
Saving the customization

3. Choose Customize ➢ Save Custom UI Scheme. Open the Save As Type drop-down list, shown in Figure 1.74. You will notice five different file formats that can be saved (and loaded) through Save (and Load) Custom UI Scheme from the Customize menu. Each one of the lower four formats—UI File (*.cui), Menu File (*.mnu), Color File (*.clr), and Shortcut File (*.kbd)—corresponds to each of the tabs in the Customize User Interface dialog box—Toolbars and Quads, Menus, Colors, and Keyboard, respectively.

When you choose to save the first format in the Save Custom UI Scheme dialog box (Interface Scheme format), you are saving a composite file that contains all the customizations

present in all the other formats combined. It is this Interface Scheme format (`*.ui`) that is displayed in the UI Schemes portion of the new Custom UI and Defaults Switcher.

FIGURE 1.74
The Save Custom UI
Scheme dialog box

3ds Max Design 2011 Quick-Start

3ds Max Design 2011 is a powerful animation tool. Here is a quick practice exercise that lets you get a little taste of how easy it is to create animation using this software program:

1. Start 3ds Max Design 2011 using either of the methods outlined in the earlier "Getting Started" section.

2. Click the Application menu (the large button at the upper-left corner of the interface), and then click Open.

3. In the Open File dialog box, navigate to the support files for this book, and open the file `Quickstart.max`.

4. On the Main Toolbar, click the Select and Move button.

5. Click the object named Car01 in the viewport. The Transform gizmo appears, with three colorful arrows displayed on the car object.

6. At the bottom of the screen, below the Time slider, click the Auto Key button (next to the icon with the large key). This activates the automatic keyframing mode. The viewport is outlined in red, and the Time slider turns red as well.

7. Drag the Time slider to frame 50. Move the car forward along the X-axis until the car enters the corner where the road turns. Use the Transform gizmo to move only in one constrained direction.

8. Notice that there are now two red dots (keyframes) visible on the track bar, below the Time slider. 3ds Max automatically places a key at frame 0 when you set the initial key at a subsequent frame.

9. Click the Play button in the animation controls. Watch the car move in the viewport between frames 0 and 50.

10. Drag the Time slider to frame 100 and move the car, this time in the Y-axis down the road toward the camera, until it is at the right side of the frame.

11. Play the animation again. The car needs to rotate to follow along the road.

12. To make the car turn the corner, go to frame 35, right-click, and choose Rotate from the Transform quad menu.

13. Rotate the car very slightly around the Z-axis.

14. Go to frame 60 and rotate the car so it turns the corner.

15. At frame 60, also move the car so it's properly situated on the road, not running up on the grass.

16. Go to frame 100 and move the car so it's staying on the road.

17. Turn off Auto Key, and play the animation.

Having fun yet? You can animate almost anything inside 3ds Max Design in this fashion.

The Bottom Line

Navigate and configure the viewports The 3ds Max viewports can be configured in several ways, including setting the quantity and configuration of the viewports.

> **Master It** Configure the viewports so that there are three small viewports stacked on the left side and one larger viewport on the right. From top to bottom, set the three stacked viewports to be Top, Front, and Right, respectively; then set the large viewport to a perspective view.

Dock and float toolbars The 3ds Max user interface has several customizable features, including the ability to hide or expose and dock or float the program's toolbars.

> **Master It** Detach the Command panel from the right side of the 3ds Max window and release it so that it floats in the middle of the 3ds Max window. Select the Command panel again and attach it to the left side. Expose a hidden toolbar and dock it to the left of the Command panel.

Copy objects and use the transform tools The transform tools (Move, Rotate, and Scale) are the most commonly used tools in 3ds Max. With them, you can position, orient, and scale your objects as required in the scene. You can quickly create a copy in 3ds Max, a process called *cloning*, by holding down the Shift key while using any of the transform tools.

> **Master It** Make a box that is 3′ long, 10″ wide, and 8″ high. Make five instance clones of the box and rotate each clone 20 degrees more than the previous clone. Stack the boxes like a spiral staircase, with an increasing amount of swing with each stair and leaving no vertical or horizontal gaps in the stairs.

Create a named selection set Whenever any objects are selected in 3ds Max, the selected objects are referred to as a selection set. Often, you may need to repeatedly select the same objects for different operations. By creating named selection sets, you can quickly select objects by selecting the selections set name from a drop-down list.

> **Master It** Continuing from the previous "Master It" exercise, rename the boxes to Step1, Step2, Step3, and so on, starting with the top step. Make and test two named selection sets, one containing the lower three steps and another containing the even-numbered steps.

Chapter 2

Introducing 3ds Max Objects

If you've never used a 3D modeling program, you may find the behavior of objects in 3ds Max to be rather unusual. Objects in 3ds Max are dynamic and malleable, and they can be basic or extremely complex. In this chapter, you'll be introduced to some of the ways you can create and form objects, and in the process you'll see that you can create just about any shape from just a handful of basic object types and modifiers.

Most 3D modeling programs offer basic building blocks called *primitives*. Primitives are rudimentary shapes on which you can build to form your model. 3ds Max offers three types of primitives that you can use to build forms: standard primitives, extended primitives, and splines. This chapter covers standard primitives and extended primitives. (We'll get to splines in Chapter 3, "Creating Shapes with Splines.")

In this chapter, you will learn to:

◆ Apply a modifier

◆ Make a clone of a 3ds Max object

◆ Manipulate a group

Understanding Standard Primitives

In Chapter 1, "Getting to Know 3ds Max Design 2011," you used the Create tab of the Command panel to create a box. Let's take another look at the Command panel to see what else it has to offer.

1. Start 3ds Max Design 2011.

2. Click the Create tab in the Command panel.

3. Click the Geometry button just below the Create tab label.

You'll see the Object Type rollout that contains the 10 standard primitives. You already created the Box primitive in Chapter 1. The drop-down box provides access to 12 other sets of default objects that you can create in 3ds Max Design 2011. If you install other object plug-ins, additional sets of objects will be listed as well.

CREATING OTHER TYPES OF GEOMETRY

The list box just below the Create tools displays the Standard Primitives option. You can create other types of geometry objects by selecting them from this list box. For now, concentrate on the standard primitives.

Besides the Box primitive, there are nine other object types of standard primitives, as shown in Figure 2.1. To create any of these primitives, you use a method that's similar to the one you used to create the box in Chapter 1.

FIGURE 2.1
A view showing all the standard primitives

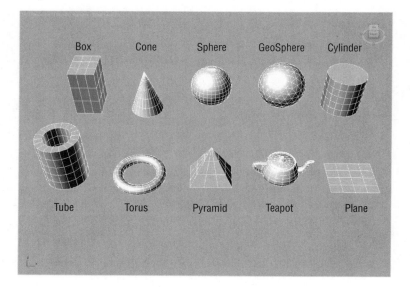

To create a box, click and drag to determine the base dimensions, and then click again to establish the height. To create a sphere, click and hold to set the center point of the sphere and then drag and release to set the radius. Try it out in the following exercise:

1. In the Object Type rollout, click the Sphere button.

2. Click and hold in the Perspective viewport near the origin, where the two darker lines cross.

3. Drag the mouse slowly away from the center point. The sphere grows as you do this. Also notice that the Radius input box in the Parameters rollout displays the radius of the sphere as you move your mouse.

4. Release the mouse to complete the sphere.

 You may recall that you were able to adjust the parameters of the box after you created it. You can do the same with the sphere.

SETTING THE UNITS TO FEET AND INCHES

If the Parameters rollout doesn't display dimensions in feet and inches, choose Customize ➢ Units Setup to open the Units Setup dialog box. Select the US Standard radio button and Feet w/Decimal Inches from the list box.

5. Click the Radius input box in the Parameters rollout.

6. Type **6↵**. The sphere now has a 6-foot radius.

7. Click and drag the Radius spinner, the double arrows to the right of the input field, up. The sphere grows in size.

3DS MAX INPUT IS IN FEET BY DEFAULT

When using Feet w/Decimal Inches as the units, you don't specify feet or inches with the apostrophe (′) or quote (″) characters. 3ds Max uses feet as the default unit. If you prefer to input inches rather than feet, choose Customize ➤ Units Setup to open the Units Setup dialog box and then select the Inches radio button.

By default, 3ds Max places the sphere's center on the plane defined by the grid. The grid shows the World Coordinate System, which is the main coordinate system for your model. As you'll see later, you can also use other coordinate systems.

Adjusting an Object's Parameters

CERT
OBJECTIVE

You can see from the sphere (and from the box example in Chapter 1) that the form of a standard primitive is not fixed. You can change its size and other properties by using the tools in the Command panel. This ability to adjust the parameters of an object is referred to as *parametric modeling*. This means that you don't need to be precise in your initial placement and creation of a primitive object, because you can refine its form later by entering values in the Parameters rollout.

To see the variety of forms you can generate from just one type of object, try modifying the sphere's other parameters:

1. In the Parameters rollout, double-click the Radius input box to highlight the contents and then enter **2↵**. This changes the radius of the sphere to 2′ 0.0″.

Please note that changes to an object's parameters can occur only when the object is selected. If you change the numbers in any of the parameter input boxes and nothing happens, most likely you clicked one extra time in the viewport and deselected your sphere. If that has happened, you have to go to the Modify panel to adjust the object's parameters.

2. Scroll down the rollout until you see the Hemisphere input box, as shown in Figure 2.2.

FIGURE 2.2
The Hemisphere
parameter

3. Click and drag the Hemisphere spinner up and watch the sphere. It starts to collapse into a closed dome from the bottom up. The Chop option deletes any segmentation that existed below the area that the Hemisphere setting eliminated. The Squash option retains all segmentation but condenses it to the area unaffected by the Hemisphere setting. You

can use the F4 key to Toggle on or off the Edged Faces viewport rendering mode, which displays an object's edges as well as its faces.

4. Highlight the entire value in the Hemisphere input box, and then enter **0.5**↵. This gives you an exact hemisphere, as shown in Figure 2.3.

FIGURE 2.3
The sphere is now a hemisphere.

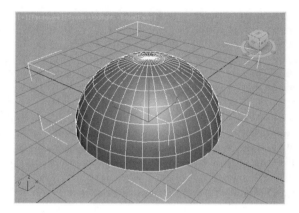

COORDINATES IN 3DS MAX

One feature that stands out in the viewports is the grid. The grid offers some orientation in an otherwise empty space, and it also shows the coordinates of the space. You may remember from high school geometry that the X- and Y-axes form the basis of a standard two-dimensional grid, with the X-axis defining the horizontal (or width) dimension and the Y-axis forming the vertical (or length) dimension. Here, you also have the additional Z-axis, which forms the height dimension.

The grid you see in a new file shows the World Coordinate System, which is the basis of your model's coordinates. In a new file, you can see the *origin* of the World Coordinate System at the center of the grid. The World Coordinate System is also called the home grid in 3ds Max. The origin is where the X-, Y-, and Z-axiz zero coordinates intersect. The origin is frequently used as a reference point for your model. It is also used as a common reference point among separate model files that need to be combined later. If you're an AutoCAD user, you'll know how the World Coordinate System's origin can be used to keep external reference drawings aligned. In 3ds Max, you can use the origin to align different models in a similar way.

The World Coordinate System is fixed and cannot be moved. You can, however, adjust the grid spacing and the type of units you want to use. Later you'll learn about user grids, which allow you to create local coordinate systems that can be placed anywhere.

3ds Max also uses another coordinate system based on what is called *Object Space*. Object Space is the coordinate system of individual objects. When an object is moved or rotated, its Object Space, or Local Coordinate System, is moved or rotated with it. You see evidence of this object space in the form of a graphic showing the X, Y, and Z orientation of an object when it's first created or when it's selected. This graphic, along with the transform gizmos (the Move gizmo, the Scale gizmo, and the Rotate gizmo), represents both the position of the object in World Space and the origin point of the object in its own space—the Object Space. There are two classifications of modifiers—tools to change an object's appearance or features—in 3ds Max: the World-Space Modifiers (WSMs) and the Object-Space Modifiers (OSMs). World-Space Modifiers affect objects relative to the home grid, and Object-Space Modifiers affect objects relative to their local coordinates.

A LEADING ZERO IS NOT REQUIRED FOR INPUT

For the sake of clarity on the printed page, you will see a leading zero before a decimal measurement. However, you don't need to type this zero when you are entering values.

You can further adjust the shape of the sphere by removing a section. The Slice From and Slice To input boxes allow you to do this.

1. Locate the Slice options below the Hemisphere input box. Click the Slice On check box, and then click and drag the Slice From spinner up until it reads 135 (see Figure 2.4). This value is the angle in degrees from the Y-axis to the beginning of the slice.

2. Click and drag the Slice To spinner down until it reads -135 (negative 135). Your hemisphere now looks like a segment was removed, as shown in Figure 2.5.

FIGURE 2.4
Changing the Slice
From option

FIGURE 2.5
The hemisphere
after removing a
segment with the
Slice tool

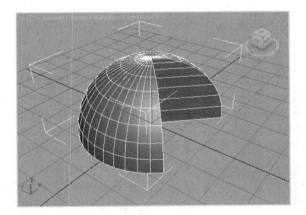

As you can see, you can use a variety of parameters to modify the shape of an object, and each object has a different set of parameters that are appropriate to that object. For example, most of the round primitive objects have the Slice From and Slice To parameters to let you create a segment in a manner similar to the sphere example (see Figure 2.6), while the Cylinder and Tube primitives have Height and Radius parameters to further define their shapes.

In the Parameters rollout for the sphere are a couple of other parameters. The Smooth parameter is a check box that turns smoothing on and off. *Smoothing* is a feature of 3ds Max that's found in most 3D modeling programs. It removes the hard edges between the facets that make up the object. Let's see how smoothing works with the hemisphere you've created.

1. Make sure the sphere is selected.

2. Click the Slice On check box to remove the check mark from this setting. The hemisphere returns to its full shape.

3. Click the Smooth check box to remove the check mark. (The Smooth check box is just below the Segments input box in the Parameters rollout.) Notice in Figure 2.7 that the sphere now looks faceted. (The Edged Faces display was turned off for clarity.) You're seeing the polygons that make up the sphere.

With smoothing turned off, the sphere looks as if it has a rough surface. In fact, all objects are faceted, even if they appear to be smooth; the Smooth parameter merely blends the appearance between adjacent faces to achieve a smooth look. The Smooth parameter is available for all of the curved primitives—the Cone, Sphere, GeoSphere, Cylinder, Tube, Teapot, and Torus types.

FIGURE 2.7
A sphere with
smoothing
turned off

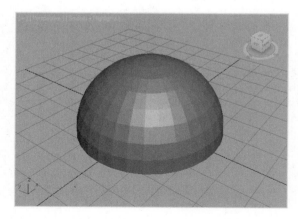

4. To see the construction of the sphere more clearly, click the Smooth + Highlights viewport label in the upper-left corner of the viewport and select Wireframe from the context menu. Only the edges show, as in Figure 2.8.

FIGURE 2.8
A wireframe view
of the sphere

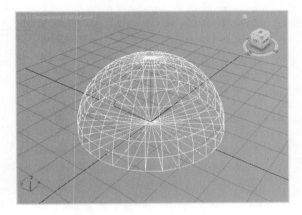

Now let's look at another parameter that is somewhat related to the Smooth parameter. The Segments parameter gives you control over the number of facets that make up an object. Try the following to see how the Segments parameter affects the sphere:

1. Click and drag the Segments spinner down until the Segments value is 12 (see Figure 2.9).

Notice in Figure 2.10 that the sphere appears to have fewer surface segments.

FIGURE 2.9
Adjusting the Seg-
ments parameter

FIGURE 2.10
The sphere with
fewer segments

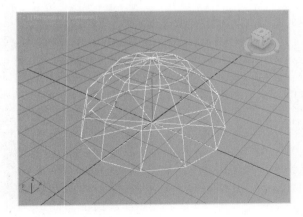

2. Click the [Wireframe] label in the upper-left corner of the viewport and select Smooth + Highlights from the context menu. Figure 2.11 clearly shows the faceting because sphere's Smooth parameter overrides the viewport's Smooth + Highlights rendering mode.

3. Click the Smooth check box to turn on smoothing. In Figure 2.12, the sphere's surface appears smoother, although you can detect the faceting, especially around the perimeter of the object.

4. Click and drag the Segments spinner down so that the Segments value reads 4, the lowest possible value for a sphere. Figure 2.13 shows that the sphere becomes a pyramid shape with the edges smoothed.

FIGURE 2.11
The sphere after changing the viewport rendering mode

FIGURE 2.12
The sphere after smoothing is turned back on

FIGURE 2.13
The smoothed sphere after the number of segments is lowered to four

5. Click the Smooth check box again to turn off smoothing. The sphere now looks like a pyramid with flat surfaces (see Figure 2.14).

FIGURE 2.14
The sphere after
Smoothing is
turned off

Smoothing provides the illusion of a gradual curve, hiding the facets that are required to construct objects. In the extreme case where a sphere is reduced to four sides, smoothing still provides the illusion of a smooth edge, but it does not hide the sharp corners along the profile of the sphere's geometry.

In situations where you need to show a smooth, curved surface, the Smooth parameter is essential. You can apply smoothing to all objects, even if they do not have a Smooth parameter by default. You'll learn more about applying smoothing to objects in later chapters.

Accessing Parameters

Immediately after you create an object, you can set its parameters on the Create tab of the Command panel. However, if you create several objects and then decide you want to modify the parameters of an object you created earlier, you'll need to use the Modify tab of the Command panel.

1. Click the Select Object tool, and then click a blank area of the viewport to clear your selection set. (When you create an object, it is automatically the current selection, so you need to click to clear the previous selection of the sphere, or you can press Ctrl+D on the keyboard to deselect any currently selected objects.)

2. Select the sphere, which at this point looks like a pyramid with flat surfaces. Notice that the sphere's parameters do not appear in the Create tab of the Command panel.

3. Click the Modify tab of the Command panel. You see the parameters for the sphere, as shown in Figure 2.15. You can now make adjustments to the sphere from the Parameters rollout.

The Modify tab displays the parameters of any single object you select. If, however, your selection consists of multiple objects, the individual objects' parameters will not be available. The Modify tab is the doorway to editing all objects in your model, as you'll see a little later in this chapter.

FIGURE 2.15
The sphere's param-
eters shown in the
Modify panel

FIGURE 2.15
The sphere's param-
eters shown in the
Modify panel

Introducing the Standard Primitive Objects

As you've seen, there are 10 standard primitive object types. So far, you've used the Box and Sphere tools to create objects. Now let's take a quick look at how each of the standard primitives works. Although you won't be trying every standard primitive in this chapter, the method of creation for all of these objects is quite similar to the procedure for creating Box and Sphere objects, so you shouldn't have any trouble if you want to experiment with them.

The Plane primitive is perhaps the simplest of all. Click and hold to establish one corner of the plane, and then drag to locate the other corner. Once you are satisfied with the size of the plane, release the mouse. Figure 2.16 illustrates the procedure for creating a plane.

FIGURE 2.16
Drawing a plane

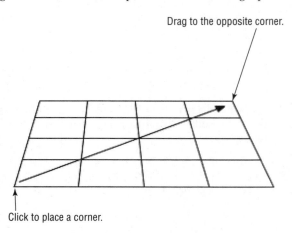

Drag to the opposite corner.

Click to place a corner.

The Box, Cylinder, and Pyramid tools all work in a similar way. First, click and hold to set one corner of the box or pyramid or, for a cylinder, the center point. Drag to locate the other corner of the box or pyramid or the radius of the cylinder. Release the mouse when you are satisfied with the size of the base. Next, move the mouse forward or backward to establish a height. Click when you want to fix the height. Figure 2.17 shows how to create these objects.

The Sphere and GeoSphere primitives are created in the same way. Click and hold to establish the center point, and then drag to locate the radius. When you're satisfied with the radius, release the mouse button. Figure 2.18 illustrates the process.

FIGURE 2.17
Drawing a box, cylinder, and pyramid

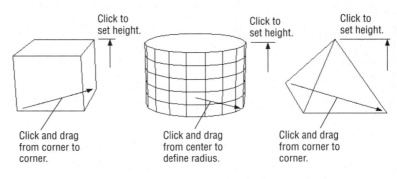

FIGURE 2.18
Drawing a sphere and geosphere

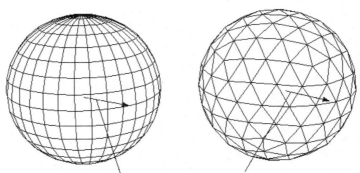

Click and drag from center to radius.

WHAT'S THE DIFFERENCE BETWEEN SPHERE AND GEOSPHERE?

You may notice that both the Sphere and GeoSphere tools create the same thing—a sphere. But if you look at the wireframe view of each of these objects, you'll see that there's a structural difference. The sphere is created with horizontal and vertical segments, much like the longitude and latitude lines on a globe. The geosphere is constructed like a geodesic dome, with triangles.

The sphere's construction lets you convert it into a dome of varying configurations, but the geosphere can only be cut to an exact hemisphere. The advantage of the geosphere is its modeling *plasticity*. Because its shape is derived from a less regular construction, it can be molded more easily into other shapes. Also, it requires fewer facets to simulate a smooth surface, which is important when you're creating a complex model that contains many faces.

The Cone, Torus, and Tube primitives are a bit more complicated to construct, requiring a few more steps than the other types.

Just like the cylinder, the cone starts with a click and drag to establish its center and base. And as with the cylinder, the next step is to establish the height by positioning the mouse and then clicking to set the height. But unlike the cylinder, the cone requires an additional step to establish the radius of the opposite end of the cone, as shown in Figure 2.19.

The Torus object may be the most unusual of the standard primitives in its construction method. First, click and hold to establish the center point of the torus, and then drag to locate the radius of its tubular cross section. Release the mouse button when you're satisfied with the radius. Next, move the mouse forward or backward to establish the radius of the torus body. Click the mouse when you're satisfied with the radius. Figure 2.20 shows how to draw a torus.

FIGURE 2.19

Drawing a cone

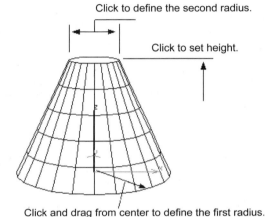

Click to define the second radius.

Click to set height.

Click and drag from center to define the first radius.

FIGURE 2.20

Drawing a torus

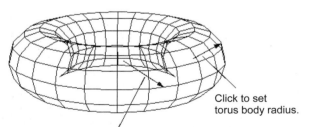

Click to set torus body radius.

Click and drag from center to the radius of the tubular cross section.

UNDERSTANDING THE CONE PRIMITIVE

The Cone primitive is not restricted to a shape with a large base and a smaller top. The second radius defined can just as easily be larger than the first and, with a negative Height value, it can be below the initial radius.

The method for creating a Tube primitive is similar to the method for creating a Cylinder primitive but with a slight twist. Click and hold to select the center of the tube, and then drag to establish the first radius. Release the mouse to fix the first radius. Move it again, and then click the mouse to establish the second radius. The Radius1 and Radius2 parameters reflect the order that the radii are determined and not which radius defines the inside or outside surfaces of the tube. Finally, move and click the mouse to establish the height. Figure 2.21 illustrates this process.

Remember that you can make adjustments to the dimensions of the primitives after their creation. In fact, you may find it easier to just quickly place a primitive in your model, without giving much care to determining its size, and then adjust the dimensions of the primitive in the Parameters rollout to fine-tune its shape.

The method for drawing a teapot (see Figure 2.22) is similar to creating a sphere. Click and hold to select the center of the base of the teapot, and then drag to establish the overall teapot size. There are options in the Parameters rollout to toggle the visibility of the body, handle, spout, and lid elements. As with many of the other primitives, there is a Smooth check box and a Segments parameter to control the density.

FIGURE 2.21
Drawing a tube

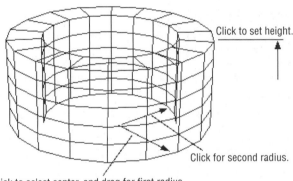

Click to set height.

Click for second radius.

Click to select center, and drag for first radius.

FIGURE 2.22
Drawing a teapot

Click to select center, and drag to set teapot size.

> **THE HISTORY OF THE TEAPOT PRIMITIVE**
>
> The teapot is a sort of mascot of computer graphics. People have been using teapots, with their intersecting and curved surfaces, as test and benchmark objects in renderings ever since Martin Newell modeled the teapot form at the University of Utah in 1975 to test shading algorithms.

Modeling Standard Primitives with Modifiers

You've seen how standard primitives have basic parameters that can be modified any time after the creation of the primitive. Tools called *modifiers* can further act on a primitive to change its form. You might think of modifiers as invisible attachments that add functions to a primitive, in much the same way that a software plug-in adds functions to your Internet browser or other program.

Adding a Modifier

In this section, you'll explore a few of the most commonly used modifiers offered on the Modify tab of the Command panel. Think of this section as a general introduction to modifiers. You'll explore the use of other modifiers in later chapters.

You'll start your exploration of modifiers by creating a box. You'll use the box to try the modifiers.

1. Expand the Application menu, and then choose New ➢ New All to start a new scene while retaining the settings from the previous scene.

2. Click the Zoom Extents All tool to display the default view for a new file if necessary.

3. Click the Create tab in the Command panel, and then click the Box button.

4. Create a box in the Perspective viewport and then, in the Parameters rollout, set the Length and Width to 3′ 0.0″ and the Height to 6′ 0.0″. Your Parameters rollout should look like Figure 2.23.

FIGURE 2.23
Setting the box's
parameters

5. If the box you created is not shaded, click the viewport shading label in the upper-left corner of the viewport and select Smooth + Highlights. Click the label again and select Edged Faces, or press the F4 key on your keyboard, to highlight the edges in your model. You won't see the effect very much on the box now, but the benefits of Edged Faces will be apparent shortly and the effects of changes that you make to the box's parameters will be evident. You should have a view that looks similar to Figure 2.24. Click the Zoom Extents button if you don't.

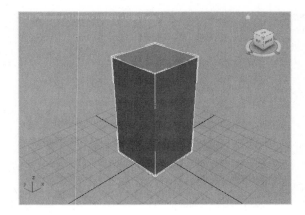

Figure 2.24
The box in the viewport

Now let's add a modifier to change the shape of the box into a curved box:

1. Make sure the Box001 object is selected. Click the Modify tab in the Command panel.

 Notice the list box, shown in Figure 2.25, with only Box listed. This is the *modifier stack*. You'll use it in the following exercises. Also notice the options in the Parameters rollout. You'll see the standard Length, Width, and Height options, as well as the Length Segs, Width Segs, and Height Segs options shown here.

Figure 2.25
Only the Box entry shows in the Modify panel.

In the next section, you'll see what these Segs options do.

2. Click the Modifier List drop-down arrow near the top of the Command panel. This expands to show a scrollable list of modifiers, as shown in Figure 2.26. Notice that the list is divided into three categories.

FIGURE 2.26
The Modifier List
drop-down

3. Click the Bend modifier, which is under Object-Space Modifiers in the list. Notice that Bend now appears in the modifier stack just below the Modifier List drop-down. You'll also see an orange outline appear, superimposed on the box. This orange box is another gizmo, like the Move, Rotate, and Scale gizmos introduced in Chapter 1, and it shows the general effect of the modifier. Figure 2.27 shows that the Parameters rollout changes to show the options for the Bend modifier rather than the parametric options for the box.

4. In the Bend group of the Parameters rollout, click and drag the Angle spinner up, and watch what happens to the box: it cants to the right, but it does not bend, as you can see in Figure 2.28. You can see the orange Bend gizmo showing the optimum result of the modifier, which is achieved only when the object is pliable enough to match it.

FIGURE 2.27
The Bend modi-
fier's parameters

FIGURE 2.28
The canted box
shows the curved
Bend gizmo.

5. Adjust the Angle spinner so that its value reads 60. Alternatively, you can highlight the Angle value, and then enter **60**↵.

The Bend modifier has its own set of parameters that can alter the shape of an object. This is typical for any modifier you might use on an object. However, adding a modifier doesn't mean that you cannot return to the original parameters of the object to make changes there.

Accessing Modifier Parameters

You've just applied the Bend modifier to the box, but the result may not be exactly what you expected. The box now looks like a trapezoid. To get the box to appear curved, you need to adjust the Segs parameters you saw earlier as part of the box's parameters.

Currently, the object's modifier stack contains Bend, the modifier you just added, and Box, which is the current object type (see Figure 2.29).

1. Click Box in the modifier stack (beneath the Modifier List drop-down). Notice that the original box parameters appear in the Parameters rollout.

2. Click the up arrow of the Height Segs spinner repeatedly and notice what happens to the box.

Horizontal lines appear, dividing the box horizontally. The value in the Height Segs input box shows the number of segments. Also notice that the box now appears to be curved, as shown in Figure 2.30.

3. Set the Height Segs value to 8.

FIGURE 2.29
The box's
modifier stack

FIGURE 2.30
The increased
Height Segs
value allows for a
smoother bend.

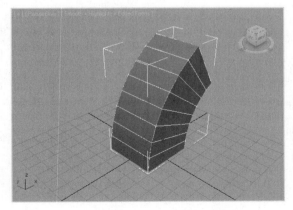

In this exercise, you saw how you can increase the number of segments in the box, allowing the Bend modifier to give the box a curved appearance. You also saw how the modifier stack offers access to the box's original parameters. The modifier stack plays a key role in your ability to edit objects in 3ds Max, as you'll see as you work through the examples in this book.

Now let's try making another adjustment to the Bend modifier's parameters:

1. Click Bend in the modifier stack. The Bend modifier's parameters reappear.

2. Click the Direction spinner in the Parameters rollout and drag it up. Notice how the top of the box rolls around as you change the Bend Direction parameter, while the base remains fixed.

3. Adjust the Direction value to 180. This causes the Bend modifier to point in a direction that is at an angle of 180 degrees from its original direction. You can see the result in Figure 2.31.

Once again, you moved from one set of parameters to another. This time, you switched from the box's basic parameters to the Bend modifier's parameters. When you adjusted the Direction spinner in step 2, you saw how the box appeared to roll around as it changed the direction of the bend.

You may have noticed the plus (+) sign to the left of the Bend item in the modifier stack. If you click the plus sign, the modifier expands to show additional parameters, also called sub-objects, available for the modifier, as shown in Figure 2.32. For the Bend modifier, Gizmo and Center are two additional options.

As noted earlier, the Gizmo option refers to the orange shape superimposed over the box. It lets you see how the modifier is being applied to the object. The Center option refers to the origin of the modifier object, which is usually the first point you click when you create the object. Both the Gizmo and Center options can be edited, as you will learn in later chapters.

FIGURE 2.31
Changing the Direction parameter alters the bend direction.

FIGURE 2.32
The Bend modifier's sub-objects

Now let's try another modifier. The Taper modifier does just what you might guess: it tapers an object.

1. Start by changing the view to one that will show the box from a lower angle. Click and drag the ViewCube slightly up and to the right.

2. Click the Zoom Extents tool in the viewport navigation controls.

3. Click the Modifier List drop-down arrow and select Taper from the list. (It's in alphabetical order under Object-Space Modifiers in the list.) Now the Parameters rollout shows a different set of options (see Figure 2.33) specific to the Taper modifier.

FIGURE 2.33
The Taper modifier's parameters

QUICKLY NAVIGATING THE MODIFIER LIST

The modifier list shows all modifiers that can be applied to the selected objects. This list can be long and extend beyond the display area. To quickly navigate to a modifier, press the key that corresponds with the first letter of the modifier's name to highlight that modifier in the list. When multiple modifiers exist with the same first letter (for example, Taper, Tesselate, TurboSmooth, and so on), press the key repeatedly to continue moving down the modifier list. Press ↵ when the desired modifier is highlighted to add it to the stack.

1. In the Parameters rollout, click and drag the Amount spinner down. The box tapers vertically. You also see the orange gizmo change shape as you adjust the Amount spinner.

2. Click and drag the Curve spinner up and watch how the box bulges, as shown in Figure 2.34.

3. Set the Curve spinner back to zero for now.

FIGURE 2.34
After the Amount and Curve settings have been changed, the box changes shape.

Although this is an interesting form, you may have expected the box to taper along its curved length instead of straight up. You can change the effect of the Taper modifier by changing its position in the modifier stack, as explained in the next section.

Placing Modifiers Where You Want Them

The modifier stack is a collection of modifiers, each one stacked on another one. It is important to understand that each modifier in the stack is applied to the result of the modifier, or the original object, located directly below it. An object that is twisted and then bent yields a much different result than an object that is first bent and then twisted. Currently, Taper is at the top of the modifier stack because it is the last modifier you added to the box. Below Taper is Bend, and below Bend is the Box object itself. You can change the order of the modifiers in the stack to obtain a slightly different effect on the box. Try the following to see how this works:

1. If the Taper entry in the modifier stack is not highlighted in gray, click to select it. If it highlights in yellow, this is an indication that one of the sub-objects in the collapsed list is selected—click it again to return to the modifier itself.

 Take care not to click the plus sign or the lightbulb icon in the list. (Clicking the plus sign shows additional levels of the modifier, as you saw earlier, and clicking the lightbulb toggles the modifier off and on, as you'll learn in the next section.)

2. Right-click and select Cut from the context menu to remove the Taper modifier from the stack and place it temporarily into the computer's memory.

3. Click the Box entry in the stack to select it.

4. Right-click and select Paste from the context menu. The Taper modifier is pasted just above Box in the list, changing the order of the modifiers. Notice the change in the shape of the box. It now tapers along the length of the bend, as shown in Figure 2.35.

This exercise demonstrated a couple of things. First, you saw how to change the order of modifiers in the modifier stack. You also saw how a change in the order affects the way multiple modifiers work on the box. When the Taper modifier is below the Bend modifier, the box is tapered *before* it is bent, giving the modified box a completely different shape. Therefore, you can see how 3ds Max evaluates the stack from the bottom up in sequential order. Remember that the order of the modifiers in the stack affects the way the modifiers work.

FIGURE 2.35
Changing the location
of the Taper modifier in
the stack changes the
appearance of the box.

WHAT CAN YOU DO WITH PRIMITIVES AND MODIFIERS?

Some examples of objects built with the help of modifiers are the binoculars and drawer pulls shown here:

Several objects were used for the binoculars, including cylinders and a few splines. A Taper modifier was used to taper the large end of the binoculars, and a combination of Taper and Skew modifiers was used in the main body. The drawer pulls are just cylinders with a Squeeze modifier applied. The Squeeze modifier gives the cylinder a slight bulge at the top while tapering the sides down.

DRAGGING TO RELOCATE MODIFIERS IN THE STACK

Instead of cutting and pasting to move a modifier in the modifier stack, you can simply click and drag a modifier into a different location in the list. The blue bar previews where you will paste the modifier in the stack before you release the mouse button. You can also highlight the modifier stack entry below where you want a new modifier inserted, before selecting the modifier from the list. New modifiers are inserted above the currently highlighted entry or at the top of the stack if no entry is selected.

You also saw how the context menu lets you manipulate the modifiers. You can cut, paste, and even delete modifiers using the context menu that appears when you right-click a modifier label.

Using the Modifier Stack Tools

You've seen how you can make changes to the modifier stack to fine-tune the shape of an object. Some additional tools offer ways to manage the modifier stack. The following set of exercises will let you see what these tools do:

1. Choose Edit ➢ Hold from the Menu Bar or select Ctrl+H. This command acts as a place marker to which you can return, using Edit ➢ Fetch, if you want to experiment.

SAVING YOUR SCENES USING HOLD AND FETCH

The Edit ➢ Hold command performs the same function as AutoCAD's Mark option under the Undo command. You can save your drawing in its current condition in case you want to return to this condition later. It lets you try various what-if scenarios without the risk of losing your work up to a certain point. Hold writes the maxhold.mx file to the AutoBackup folder specified in the Configure User Paths dialog box, and you do not have to be in the same 3ds Max session to use the Fetch command. Be aware that there is only one maxhold.mx file. Each time Hold is used, it is overwritten and the previous file is saved as maxhold.bak. The Fetch command is not undoable.

2. Roll up the Bend modifier by clicking the minus (-) sign to the left of its entry in the stack.

3. Click the lightbulb icon to the left of the Bend modifier.

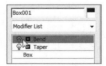

Clicking the lightbulb icon turns off the modifier. Notice that the box changes to a shape with a taper but without the Bend modifier.

4. Click the Bend lightbulb again to turn Bend back on.

5. Click the lightbulb next to the Taper modifier. Notice how the box reverts to the shape it had before Taper was added.

6. Choose Edit ➢ Fetch or select Alt+Ctrl+F. You see a message box asking if it's OK to restore. Click Yes. Your box returns to its original state (as it was before step 1), but the object is no longer selected.

The lightbulb icon lets you turn on or off a modifier so you can quickly view the effects of removing a modifier from the stack without actually deleting it. A somewhat similar means is to use the Show End Result tool. When it is turned off, the Show End Result tool simply shows

you the shape of the object at the currently selected modifier stack level. The following example demonstrates this:

1. Select the object in the viewport, and then select Taper in the modifier stack.

2. Click the Show End Result tool in the toolbar just below the modifier stack.

The viewport shows the box in its form before the Bend modifier is applied. Also notice that the Show End Result icon changes into a half gray and half white bar. This helps you remember whether the Show End Result tool is on or off.

3. Click the Select Object tool in the Main Toolbar, and then click a blank area of the model to clear the selection. The box returns to its original form, with all of the modifiers active.

4. Click the box to select it again, and then choose Taper from the modifier stack. The box again returns to the form it had before the Bend modifier was applied. This shows that the Show End Result tool doesn't actually affect the end result of the box's modifiers, just how the box is displayed in the viewport when it is selected.

5. Click the Show End Result tool to turn it on again. The viewport displays the box in its final form.

Now suppose you want to simply delete a modifier from the stack. This is easy to do with the context menu.

1. Right-click the Taper modifier in the stack and select Delete from the context menu. Now the Taper modifier is removed from the modifier stack. The box reverts to the form it had before you added the Taper modifier.

2. Choose Edit ➢ Fetch to restore the box with the Taper modifier intact.

REMOVING MODIFIERS FROM THE STACK

Another way to remove a modifier from the modifier stack is to select it and then click the garbage can icon in the toolbar below the modifier stack. This is the Remove Modifier from the Stack tool. Do not press the Delete key on the keyboard; this deletes the selected object rather than the modifier.

The Delete context-menu option is a quick way to remove a modifier. You can accomplish the same thing by selecting the Cut option from the context menu. Another modifier stack tool (available on the toolbar beneath the modifier stack) is Make Unique. This tool works with special types of clones, which you'll learn about in the "Making Clones That Share Properties" section, coming up shortly.

How 3ds Max Sees Objects

Let's take a break from the tutorial for a moment to understand how 3ds Max Design 2011 sees objects. When you create and edit an object in 3ds Max, you are creating data that 3ds Max evaluates to display your model. The order in which that data is evaluated is known as the *object data flow*. 3ds Max sees objects as a stream, or flow, of data in a particular order. The order in which this data is evaluated affects the outcome of the data; in other words, the order affects the behavior and appearance of the object in your model.

When you rearranged the modifiers in the modifier stack, you saw an example of object data flow. You saw that the order in which modifiers appear in the stack affects the shape of a box. 3ds Max also applies this data flow to the overall object by evaluating all modifications made to an object in a specific order.

The first piece of data 3ds Max looks at is the *master object*. This is the object as you first create it, including a set of parameters, its position, and its orientation.

The next item is the modifier or set of modifiers you apply to an object. Modifiers are evaluated in their order in the modifier stack, as you've already seen. Of course, if there are no modifiers, 3ds Max skips to the next piece of data.

The third item in the data flow consists of the *transformations* applied to the object. Transformations refer to the movement, cloning, scaling, or rotation of an object. For example, even though you may have moved the object *before* you applied modifiers, 3ds Max will evaluate the object's Move transformation after it evaluates its modifiers. The one exception to this occurs when you use the XForm (transform) modifier, which places transform operations within the bounds of the modifier stack.

3ds Max evaluates the properties of an object last. Properties include the object's name, color, layer assignment, display, rendering, shadow casting and receiving, motion blur, and so on. For example, even though an object acquires a default color and name as soon as it's created, 3ds Max evaluates the name and color last.

To summarize object data flow, 3ds Max looks at object data in the following order:

1. Master object

2. Modifiers

3. Transforms

4. Properties

The ramifications of object data flow are not obvious at first, but keep the concept in the back of your mind as you work with 3ds Max. It will help you understand the behavior of the program and ultimately give you better control over your models.

Making Clones That Share Properties

The modifier stack plays a major role in allowing you to mold objects to a desired form, but you can go a step further and have modifiers act across several objects instead of just one. In Chapter 1, when you learned about copying objects, you may have noticed three clone options in the Clone Options dialog box: Copy, Instance, and Reference.

Instances and references are more than just clones of objects; they share modifiers, so the changes you make to one clone affect all the other clones. This can be a great editing aid when you have multiple copies of the same object, such as columns in a building, or lighting fixtures. By making instance clones, for example, you can place the objects in your model before you've finalized the particular parameters of the objects. Instances and references also reduce file size by defining a single object or modifier that is repeated in multiple locations, rather than defining the parameters of each identical object.

Creating an Instance Clone

The instance and reference clones are quite similar but with a subtle yet powerful difference. You'll start by examining the simpler of the two types of clones—the instance clone.

1. Open the Clone Window.max file, which you'll find in the Chapter 2 archive at this book's accompanying web page, `www.sybex.com/go/mastering3dsmaxdesign2011`. This file consists of a Fixed Window object with a Taper modifier applied.

 If you see a File Load: Units Mismatch dialog box when you open the file, this indicates that the file's System Units setting is different than the current scene's System Units setting. Select the Adopt the File's Unit Scale option and then click OK.

2. In the Perspective viewport, select the Window object, and then click the Select and Move tool.

3. Hold the Shift key down and drag the red X-coordinate arrow to the right. Then move the copy of the window along the X-axis toward the upper-right corner of the viewport until it is beyond the extents of the original window.

4. Release the mouse button. The Clone Options dialog box displays, as shown in Figure 2.36.

5. If it is not already selected, click the Instance radio button in the Object group, increase Number of Copies to 2, and then click OK. You now have two instance clones of the original window arranged similarly to the windows in Figure 2.37.

 Pan and zoom as required to get a better view of the scene. You now have three identical windows. The similarities of the three boxes go beyond appearances, as the following steps demonstrate.

FIGURE 2.36
The Clone Options
dialog box

6. With the Window object to the far right selected, click the Modify tab in the Command panel.

7. Make sure the Taper modifier is selected in the modifier stack.

8. In the Parameters rollout, click and drag the Amount spinner down until its value reads -0.9 and the windows have a more tapered appearance.

9. Click the FixedWindow entry in the modifier stack. In the Rails and Panels section of the window's Parameters rollout, change # Panels Horiz to 3 and # Panels Vert to 2.

10. Notice that all three windows change their shapes and parameters simultaneously, as shown in Figure 2.38.

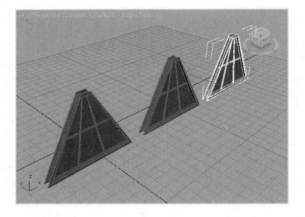

Any parameter change you make to any of the windows will be reflected in all of the instanced clones. Furthermore, if you add additional modifiers to any of the clones, each will have the modifier applied to the same position in its modifier stack. This is true because instance clones share modifiers in their respective modifier stacks. This sharing of its modifiers is what distinguishes an instance clone from an ordinary copy. 3ds Max identifies clones by displaying their entries in the modifier stack in a bold font.

Creating a Reference Clone

Like an instance clone, a reference clone shares modifiers in its modifier stack, but in addition it allows you to include modifiers that are not shared. The following example shows how this works:

1. Select the middle window.

2. With the Select and Move tool, Shift+click and drag the Move gizmo's XY-plane to the foreground. Relocate the window to a location similar to the one shown in Figure 2.39.

3. In the Clone Options dialog box, click the Reference radio button, and then click OK.

4. Click the clone farthest to the right (FixedWindow003) to select it.

5. Change the Taper modifier's Amount parameter to -0.5. Now all four of the clones change shape.

6. Click the newest clone to select it. Look carefully at the modifier stack, and you'll see a gray bar at the very top of the stack (see Figure 2.40). This line divides the shared modifiers from potentially unshared modifiers.

FIGURE 2.39
The location of the reference clone

FIGURE 2.40
The reference
clone's modifier
stack

The shared modifiers of all the clones are still accessible through the reference clone.

1. With the reference clone selected, select Taper from the modifier stack.

2. In the Parameters rollout, adjust the Amount spinner down to read -0.8. All of the clones change shape, as shown in Figure 2.41.

3. With the reference clone selected, click the blank, gray line at the top of the modifier stack.

4. Open the Modifier List drop-down list and select Skew. (It's in alphabetical order under Object-Space Modifiers in the list.) The Skew modifier is now added to the top of the modifier stack of the selected window.

5. In the Parameters rollout, set the Skew Axis to Y and then set the Amount value to approximately -2′ 7″ until the left edge of the window is vertical. Notice that the reference window changes shape independently of the other windows, as shown in Figure 2.42.

FIGURE 2.41
Changing the reference clone's Taper Amount spinner affects all four windows.

FIGURE 2.42
Changing the reference clone's Skew Amount spinner affects only the reference clone.

Here, you see that the blank line in the modifier stack delineates the modifiers that are shared between the clones from those that are specific to the selected object. Try testing this by moving the Skew modifier below the line.

1. In the modifier stack, select Skew and then drag it below the gray line (see Figure 2.43).

 Now all four windows share the Skew modifier, as shown in Figure 2.44.

2. Select the Skew modifier, right-click, and select Delete to remove it.

FIGURE 2.43
Moving the Skew
modifier

FIGURE 2.44
After the Skew
modifier is relo-
cated in the modi-
fier stack, all clones
become affected.

As you see, you can manipulate the reference clone's modifier stack in quite a number of ways to achieve an effect across multiple objects. Next, you'll see another way that the stack can be used in conjunction with a modifier to apply the transform tools to multiple objects.

> **3DS MAX INSTANCES ARE SIMILAR TO AUTOCAD BLOCKS**
>
> If you're an AutoCAD user, you might think of instance and reference clones as being similar to blocks in AutoCAD. But as you can see from these exercises, they are far more flexible in 3ds Max. Reference clones can share some parameters and also include parameters that are independent of other instances.

Scaling and Rotating Objects with Transform Tools

Now that you have a set of objects in your scene, let's take a break from our look at modifiers to examine the transform tools. In Chapter 1, you learned how you can scale and rotate a single object using the transform tools in the Main Toolbar. You can also scale and rotate a collection of objects by selecting the set of objects and applying the Scale or Rotate tools. When you do this, by default 3ds Max affects all the selected objects uniformly. For example, if you rotate a collection of objects, they all rotate about a common axis, as illustrated in the top of Figure 2.45. If you

scale a collection of objects, they all change their scale, including the distance between objects in the collection, as illustrated at the bottom of Figure 2.45.

3ds Max offers a few options that alter the way objects are affected by the transform tools. In this section, you'll learn how the Transform Center options give you a higher degree of control over the transform tools.

FIGURE 2.45
Rotating objects in a selection set (top) and scaling objects in a selection set (bottom)

First, try rotating one of the clones by itself:

1. Click the Select and Rotate tool on the Main Toolbar.

2. Select the window in the middle of the viewport.

3. Click and drag the red X-coordinate axis up. The window rotates independently of the clones.

4. Click the Undo button in the Quick Access toolbar to return the window to its original orientation.

CLONES AND THE TRANSFORM TOOLS

Although this exercise involves a set of cloned objects, the transform tools in the Main Toolbar do not consider whether the selected objects are clones of one another or a set of dissimilar objects.

Here, you see that the Rotate tool affects only the currently selected clone. You also see that you can use the Rotate gizmo's rings to control the orientation of the rotation.

Now, let's take a look at how the Rotate tool affects a group of objects:

1. Click the Select Object tool, and then select all four objects. You can either click and drag a region enclosing all of the objects or Ctrl+click each object.

2. Click the Select and Rotate tool in the Main Toolbar.

3. Click the Use Pivot Point Center tool on the Main Toolbar. If you don't see it, click and hold the tool just to the right of the View drop-down list in the middle of the Main Toolbar (see Figure 2.46), and then select the Use Pivot Point Center tool from the flyout.

4. Click and drag the red X-axis ring. Now all of the cloned windows rotate in unison with the original box, each on its own axis, as shown in Figure 2.47.

FIGURE 2.46
Selecting the Use Pivot Point Center option

FIGURE 2.47
All the selected windows rotate in unison.

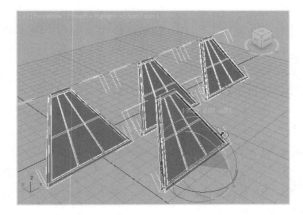

THE TRANSFORM COORDINATE CENTERS ARE TRANSFORM SPECIFIC

It is important to understand that the Transform Center options are specific to the current transform and are not global across all the transforms. For example, if the Use Pivot Point Center option is current for all transforms and then, with the Rotate Transform active, you make the Use Selection Center option active, it is active for only the Rotate Transform. For this reason, the transform must be selected before the Transform Center option is changed. You can change this default parameter by clicking Customize ➤ Preferences... on the Application menu and then checking the Constant option in the Ref. Coord. System area under the General tab of the Preference Settings dialog box.

Next, try the Select and Uniform Scale tool:

1. Click the Undo button to return the windows to their original orientation.

2. Click the Select and Uniform Scale tool from the flyout on the Main Toolbar.

3. Click the Use Pivot Point Center tool on the Main Toolbar, and then click and drag the center of the Scale gizmo. Each of the windows now scales in unison with the others, each about its own pivot point, as shown in Figure 2.48.

4. Click the Undo button to return the windows to their original size.

FIGURE 2.48
The windows scale about their own pivot points.

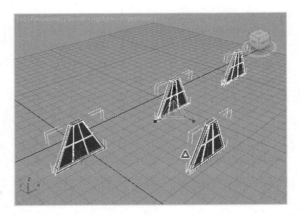

You've seen how the Use Pivot Point Center tool affects the Rotate and Scale transform tools. Next, try the Use Transform Coordinate Center tool to see its effect on the Scale tool:

1. Click and hold the Use Pivot Point Center tool, and then select the Use Transform Coordinate Center tool from the flyout.

 Notice that the Transform gizmo now appears at the origin of the World Coordinate System on the home grid, as shown in Figure 2.49.

FIGURE 2.49
With the Use Transform Coordinate Center option, the Transform gizmo relocates to the origin.

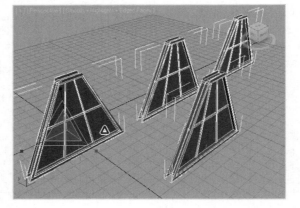

2. Click and drag the Scale gizmo or any of the windows. Notice that they all change in scale about the origin of the scene.

3. Click the Undo button to return all the clones to their original scale.

SETTING THE NUMBER OF UNDO LEVELS

You can use the Undo tool to undo as many as 20 steps back by default. You can also set the number of steps 3ds Max will allow for Undo. To set the number of steps, click the Options button on the Application menu, choose the General tab of the Preference Settings dialog box, and then set the Scene Undo Levels option to the value you want. Holding more undo steps consumes more memory.

As you can see from the previous exercise, the Transform Center options allow you to select the center location of the currently active grid. They are a simple set of options that enhance your ability to control the transform tools. You haven't had a chance to try all the options with all the transform tools, so here's a summary of the Transform Center tool functions:

Use Pivot Point Center This tool places the center of the transformation at the pivot point of the selected object. If multiple objects are selected, each object is transformed about its own Object Space.

Use Selection Center This tool places the center of the transformation at the center of the set of selected objects. This differs from Use Pivot Point Center in that all objects move, scale, or rotate about a common, single point, rather than about their individual pivot points.

Use Transform Coordinate Center This tool places the center of transformation at the origin of the World Coordinate System. Or, if you're using a user grid, the center of transformation will be at the origin of the user grid. This option, in conjunction with a user grid, is useful for moving, scaling, or rotating an object or set of objects in relation to a specific point in a model.

ADDING TRANSFORMS TO THE MODIFIER STACK

The XForm modifier lets you scale and rotate objects from the modifier stack. This has the advantage of allowing you to apply transform tools to cloned objects without needing to individually select the objects. It also has the effect of applying the transform tools to a specific position in the object data flow. Normally, transforms are evaluated after the modifiers, but you can insert transforms within the modifier stack using the XForm modifier.

Making a Clone Unique

At some point, you may decide that you want to turn a clone into a unique object so that it no longer reacts in unison with other clones. You can do this easily with the Make Unique button in the modifier stack toolbar.

1. Click the Select Object tool, and then select the instanced clone to the far left.

2. Make sure the Modify tab is selected in the Command panel and that the Taper modifier is highlighted in the modifier stack.

3. Click the Make Unique button on the toolbar below the modifier stack. The selected window is now an independent object that is no longer connected to the other two clones.

Notice that the entries in the modifier stack are no longer bold, indicating that the object is independent of all others and no longer an instance.

Cloning a Modifier

You've learned the many ways in which you can clone an object and edit those clones together. You've also seen most of the major methods used to create objects from primitives. However, there is one more feature related to clones and modifiers that you'll want to understand. At times, you may want to clone just one modifier instead of an entire object. This allows you to have an object maintain a degree of uniqueness and still have at least one modifier cloned so that it acts on a set of objects. The following exercise will demonstrate the principle.

First, make a copy of one of the clones:

1. Click the Select and Move tool, and then Shift+click and drag the green Transform gizmo handle for the instanced window clone in the center of the scene.

2. Drag the copy to a location behind the initial row of clones, so the set of windows forms a rough X shape.

3. In the Clone Options dialog box, click the Copy radio button, and then click OK.

4. Using the Modifier List drop-down, add a Lattice modifier to the window copy. The struts and joints unique to that modifier appear on the selected window only, as shown in Figure 2.50.

FIGURE 2.50
The Lattice modifier affects the copy clone only.

Now let's add a cloned Lattice modifier to the instanced clones. You can do this by copying the modifier to the Clipboard and then pasting it back into the modifier stack.

1. With the newest window selected, click the Lattice modifier in the modifier stack, right-click, and select Copy.

2. Select the window at the center of the scene.

3. In the modifier stack, right-click Taper, and then select Paste Instanced from the context menu to place the new Lattice modifier above the Taper modifier. Notice that the new instanced Lattice modifier is italicized to indicate that it is an instanced modifier.

You've just created an instance clone of the Lattice modifier that affects all the windows in the scene except the window that was made unique in a previous exercise. Now let's see the results:

1. Click the instanced window nearest to the top-right corner of the viewport.

2. Click Taper in the modifier stack.

3. Try adjusting the Amount spinner in the Parameters rollout. The instance and reference clones change in unison, but the newest copy and the unique window do not, as shown in Figure 2.51.

4. Click the instanced Lattice modifier in the stack.

5. Change the Radius value in the Joints area to 0´ 9.5˝. Four of the objects change their shape, as shown in Figure 2.52.

FIGURE 2.51
The cloned Lattice modifier affects three of the five windows.

FIGURE 2.52
Adjustments to the Joints Radius value affect four of the windows.

By placing an instance copy of a modifier in an object's modifier stack, you can apply a cloned modifier to an object, so a unique object can share a few characteristics with other similar objects. An example of this might be a set of windows across the facade of a building, as shown in Figure 2.53.

FIGURE 2.53
A facade of a building using cloned references for windows

Most of the windows are identical. The window design can be modified for one window, and all the windows will be affected. Some of the windows may need to share only a few (but not all) of the parameters of the rest of the windows. It saves memory to make instances of objects that are identical.

Introducing Extended Primitives

Before moving on to the next chapter, you may want to be aware of the *extended primitives*. They are a set of primitives that offer a few more parameters than the standard primitives. In most cases, the extended primitives offer shapes with adjustable smoothing along their edges. Some of the other extended primitives are complex shapes, such as the Hedra and Gengon objects. Figure 2.54 shows the extended primitives in their default configurations.

You can get to the extended primitives by clicking the Geometry tool on the Create tab of the Command panel and then selecting Extended Primitives from the drop-down list that appears just below the Create tools.

For several of the extended primitives, you'll see a Fillet parameter. This controls the radius of the edges. For example, the Chamfer Cylinder (ChamferCyl) primitive has a Fillet parameter that works in conjunction with a Fillet Segments parameter to control the rounding of its top and bottom edges. The Oil Tank and Spindle primitives use a Blend parameter to round their corners.

FIGURE 2.54
Examples
of extended
primitives

Modeling a Couch

Up until now, you've been creating random forms using the primitives. In this section's exercises, you'll get a chance to create a small couch by trying some of the tools you've learned about so far.

Start by setting up a new file:

1. Save your scene as MySample.max if you like.

2. Open the Application menu and then choose New ➢ New All.

3. Set the units to Feet w/Fractional Inches.

You'll start your model by creating the base. For this, you'll use one of the extended primitives:

1. Click the Create tab of the Command panel.

2. Click the Geometry tool and select Extended Primitives from the drop-down list, as shown in Figure 2.55.

FIGURE 2.55
Selecting Extended
Primitives from
the drop-down list

3. Click the ChamferBox tool, and then expand the Keyboard Entry rollout, as shown in Figure 2.56.

4. Double-click the Length input box in the Keyboard Entry rollout and enter **20˝↵**. Press Tab to accept the value and advance to the Width input box, where you will enter **44˝↵**.

5. Press Tab again to advance to the Height input box and enter **9˝↵**.

6. Press Tab and enter **1˝↵** for the Fillet value.

7. Click Create. Figure 2.57 shows the new base that is created.

8. Display all four viewports if necessary then click Zoom Extents All to get an enlarged view of the base in all the viewports.

FIGURE 2.56
Expand the Keyboard Entry rollout.

FIGURE 2.57
The base of the couch

In this exercise, you created the base strictly by using the Keyboard Entry rollout. Now create the back of the couch:

1. Double-click the Length input box of the Keyboard Entry rollout to select the entire value, and then enter **8˝↵**.

2. Press Tab twice to go to the Height input box, leaving the Width input box unchanged. Then enter **26˝↵**.

3. Press Tab again, and then enter **2˝↵**.

4. Click the Create button. The seat back is created in the middle of the base.

5. Click the Select and Move tool in the Main Toolbar, and then right-click the Top viewport to make it active.

6. Click and drag the green Y-axis arrow of the seat back up to move the seat back to the back side of the base, as shown in Figure 2.58. Click the Zoom Extents All tool to get a better view.

FIGURE 2.58
Move the seat back into position. The Smooth + Highlights rendering mode is used for clarity.

Let's also rotate the seat back so it is angled slightly backward:

1. Click the Select and Rotate tool in the Main Toolbar. Then right-click in the Perspective viewport to make it active.

2. Click and drag the red X-axis ring up, and watch the coordinate readout on the Transform gizmo. When the readout shows approximately -8 (negative 8) degrees, as shown in Figure 2.59, release the mouse button.

FIGURE 2.59
Rotating the back of the couch

USE THE TAB KEY TO HIGHLIGHT INPUT FIELDS

Rather than pressing ↵ and then highlighting the next input field with your cursor, consider using the Tab key. Tab accepts the value in the current field and then highlights the next available field. Pressing Tab repeatedly highlights the subsequent fields in an object's Create or Modify panel.

To add an arch to its shape, apply a Squeeze modifier to the back:

1. Click the Select Object button to exit the Rotate transform, and then click the Modify tab in the Command panel.

2. Open the Modifier List drop-down and select Squeeze.

3. Go to the Axial Bulge group in the Parameters rollout, and click and drag the Amount spinner up until its value reads 0.14.

4. Press Tab and set the Curve value to 3. Notice that the seat back shows a gizmo bending up, but the back itself does not bend (see Figure 2.60). This is because the back is made up of only a single segment in the horizontal direction.

 To allow the Squeeze option to take effect, you need to increase the number of horizontal segments in the seat back.

5. Select ChamferBox in the modifier stack and locate the Width Segs input box in the Parameters rollout.

6. Click the Width Segs input box and enter **20**↵. The back divides into 20 segments, and a curve appears at the top of the back, as shown in Figure 2.61.

FIGURE 2.60
The back of the couch with the Squeeze modifier applied

FIGURE 2.61
The back of the couch with additional Width segments

Now let's add the arms. Once again, you'll use the ChamferBox extended primitive, but this time you'll use a different modifier to adjust its shape:

1. Click the Create tab in the Command panel, and then click ChamferBox again.

2. Click the Keyboard Entry rollout to open it. Enter 28˝↵ for the length, 7˝↵ for the width, 22˝↵ for the height, and 2˝↵ for the Fillet value.

3. Click the Create button. The arm appears in the center of the base, as shown in Figure 2.62.

4. Click the Select and Move tool. Right-click the Top viewport to make it active, and then click and drag the arm into the position shown in Figure 2.63.

FIGURE 2.62
The first side object created

FIGURE 2.63
Moving the arm into position

Move the arm to this position.

USING THE TRANSFORM PLANE HANDLES RATHER THAN THE AXIS HANDLES

If you place the Select and Move cursor on the rectangular plane handle at the intersection of the Move Transform gizmo, you can move the arm freely in the XY-plane.

5. Shift+click and drag the red X-axis arrow of the arm to the right until you see a copy of the arm in the position shown in Figure 2.64.

FIGURE 2.64
Creating a copy
of the arm

6. In the Clone Options dialog box, click the Instance radio button and then click OK. (You made an instance clone because you want to modify both arms simultaneously.)

7. Click the Modify tab of the Command panel.

8. Open the Modifier List drop-down and select Taper.

9. In the Parameters rollout, click and drag the Amount spinner until its value reads 0.2. Both arms taper, widening at their tops.

10. Click the ChamferBox object in the Modifier Stack and change the Width Segs value back to 1.

You've nearly finished with the couch. The final part consists of the seat cushions. For that, you'll use a copy of the base:

1. Click the Select and Move tool in the Main Toolbar.

2. Right-click in the Left viewport to make it active. This viewport offers the clearest view of the seat base.

3. Click the seat base to select it, and then Shift+click and drag the green Y-axis arrow up until you have a copy of the seat base, as shown in Figure 2.65.

FIGURE 2.65
The copy of the
seat base

4. In the Clone Options dialog box, click the Copy radio button, and then click OK. You don't want this clone to be instanced to the base.

You need to change a few parameters for the cushion. It's a bit too thick, and you want two cushions to fit in the seat, so you need to reduce the width of the cushion.

5. In the Parameters rollout, change the Length and Width values in the Parameters rollout to **22**″, and change the Height value to **7**″.

6. With the Select and Move tool selected, right-click the Top viewport. Then click and drag the red X-axis arrow of the cushion to the left to place the cushion, as shown in Figure 2.66.

7. Shift+click and drag the red X-axis arrow to the right to make a copy of the cushion on the right side of the couch.

8. In the Clone Options dialog box, click Instance and then click OK.

FIGURE 2.66
The new position of the cushion

The couch is complete. Let's get a better view of it:

1. Right-click in the Perspective viewport to make it active.

2. Click and drag the ViewCube to get a view that better shows the couch.

3. Click the Zoom Extents All tool.

You will notice that the fillets on the couch have only one segment and look very sharp. You will now select the primitives of the couch and increase the number of fillet segments on each object to round the edges of the couch.

4. Select one of the armrests of the couch and then in the modifier stack, click the ChamferBox entry and change the Fillet Segs value to 3. Both ends of the couch are now much rounder than before.

5. Starting with the back of the couch, select the remaining objects of the couch and, one by one, increase the number of fillet segments to three. Because you made the second seat cushion of the couch as an instance, you will only have to modify one of the seat cushions.

6. Right-click the viewport rendering label and turn off Edged Faces.

7. Click the Maximize Viewport Toggle. Your view should look like Figure 2.67.

8. Save the file as MyCouch.max.

FIGURE 2.67
The completed couch

Working with Groups

Now that you modeled a couch in the previous section with extended primitives, it is important to organize the primitive objects that compose this piece of furniture into a group. That way, you'll be able to easily select and transform this piece of furniture within your architectural spaces as a single object.

Grouping the Components of the Couch

The couch consists of six ChamferBox extended primitive objects. For convenience, you'll want this set of objects to act like one object when it is selected. To do this, you can use 3ds Max's Group feature. You'll create a group containing only a few objects; then you'll add other objects to that group.

1. Select the seat cushions and base of the couch.

2. Choose Group ➢ Group from the Menu Bar. The Group dialog box displays, as shown in Figure 2.68.

3. Replace the default Group001 name with **Couch001** and then click OK.

4. Click a blank area of the viewport to clear the selection set, and then select and move any of the objects that you just added to the group. All the objects react as if they are a single object.

FIGURE 2.68
The Group dialog box

5. Click Undo to return the group to its original location.

6. Select the couch back and both arms, and then choose Group ➤ Attach.

7. Place the cursor over a couch cushion and notice that a selection cursor displays, as shown in Figure 2.69. This selection cursor, showing the name of the group and the individual object, will display whenever the cursor passes over a group. Click the seat cushion, which is now part of the Couch001 group. Now all the components of this piece of furniture are contained in the Couch001 group.

8. Click the Select by Name tool on the Main Toolbar to open the Select from Scene dialog box. You'll see the name Couch001 preceded by a circle overlapping a box icon in square brackets, indicating that Couch001 is a group. Click Cancel when you're done looking at the list.

Even though you could have created the Couch001 group all at once by selecting all the components of the couch in step 1, this exercise gave you the opportunity to see how you can add objects to a group that has already been created.

The couch will now act as a single object for selection and transform operations. It will be much easier to locate this piece of furniture in a complex scene because it shows up in the Select by Name dialog box as Couch001, rather than six rather anonymous-sounding chamfer boxes.

FIGURE 2.69
The selection cursor appears as you pass the cursor over the couch back.

Working within Groups

After you've contained objects within a group, you can always open the group up to work on the objects inside. When you're done making changes, remember to close the group to stay organized.

1. Select the Couch001 group you made previously.

2. Choose Group ➢ Open. All of the open groups will display pink selection brackets, as shown in Figure 2.70.

3. In the Left viewport, select the couch back.

4. Click the Angle Snap Toggle icon on the Main Toolbar to turn on the Angle Snap feature.

5. Right-click the Angle Snap Toggle icon to open the Options tab of the Grid and Snaps Settings dialog box, as shown in Figure 2.71.

 Notice that the Angle snap option is set to 5 degrees; you'll keep this option to restrict the rotation of the back of the couch to 5 degree increments. After you have reviewed the settings on the Options tab, you can dismiss the dialog box by clicking the red X icon.

FIGURE 2.70
The open groups display pink selection brackets.

Pink bounding box indicates an open group.

FIGURE 2.71
The Grid and Snaps Settings dialog box

6. With the back of the couch still selected, click the Select and Rotate button, and in the left viewport rotate it back 5 degrees more to have a more relaxed seating position, as shown in Figure 2.72.

7. Move the couch back forward to eliminate any gap that may have opened up between the back and seat, as shown in Figure 2.73.

FIGURE 2.72
Rotate the couch-back cushion counterclockwise.

FIGURE 2.73
Move the couch-back cushion to eliminate any gaps.

8. Open the Select From Scene dialog box by pressing H on the keyboard, and observe how the objects within the group are displayed while the group is open. Notice how the objects belonging to the group are indented to let you know they belong to the Couch001 group, as shown in Figure 2.74. If the group members are not indented, choose Display ➢ Display Children in the Select From Scene dialog box.

9. Click Cancel to close the Select From Scene dialog box.

10. Now that you have finished editing the objects contained within the group, it is time to close the group. Make sure that at least one group member is selected, and then choose Group ➢ Close.

FIGURE 2.74

The Select From Scene dialog box showing the open group

11. Open the Select From Scene dialog box again. Note that the edited-and-then-closed group looks just like the group did right after you created it (see Figure 2.75).

12. Save your file.

FIGURE 2.75

The Select From Scene dialog box showing the closed group

Disassembling Groups

Groups are convenient for making multiple components react as a single object, but the relationship does not have to be permanent. As easily as groups are created, they can be disbanded.

1. Select the Couch001 group you made previously.

2. Choose Group ➢ Open.

3. Select the two arms of the couch.

4. Choose Group ➢ Detach.

5. Open the Select From Scene dialog box. As you can see in Figure 2.76, the two chamfer boxes that represented the arms are no longer part of the group and are no longer listed under Couch001. Close the dialog box when you have finished.

6. Select a remaining member of the Couch001 group and then choose Group ➤ Close.

7. Choose Group ➤ Ungroup to permanently disband the Couch001 group and remove any relationship between the objects.

8. Close your file without saving it.

FIGURE 2.76
The Select From Scene dialog box after the arms are detached

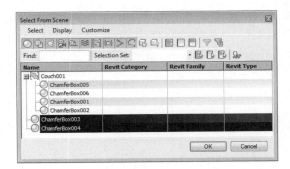

You have seen how easy it is to work with groups. If you're familiar with blocks in AutoCAD, you will recognize the similarity to groups in 3ds Max. They are both structures that contain objects and yield higher levels of organization for your data. They differ in that 3ds Max does not automatically instance the objects contained within groups, whereas in AutoCAD, blocks are always made as instances. Grouping in 3ds Max is independent of cloning; the choice of whether to instance, reference, or copy is yours to make separately from any organizational structures of convenience you choose to make with groups.

Groups can contain not only individual objects but other groups as well. This is called *nesting* groups. To manipulate members of a nested group, open the parent group, select the nested group, and then open that as well. Similar to the Ungroup option, Group ➤ Explode disbands all selected groups as well as any nested groups contained within them.

Similar to groups are the new containers. Containers are like groups in that they take a number of objects and put them into one single unit that can be transformed easily and can be used to condense long lists of objects in a list view, such as the Select by Name dialog. Containers have the added attraction that they can be "unloaded" from the scene to relieve memory problems and unclutter the viewport.

The Bottom Line

Apply a modifier Modifiers provide many ways to manipulate an object that may not be possible by manually transforming the object's sub-objects. The order in which the modifiers appear in the modifiers stack determines the final result.

Master It Create a Teapot primitive and apply the Slice modifier to it. Raise the Slice plane sub-object until it passes through the middle of the object. Choose the Remove Top option from the Slice Parameters rollout to delete everything above the Slice Plane. Add a Cap Holes modifier to the top of the stack.

Make a clone of a 3ds Max object The type of clones you make determines whether modifiers and parameter changes affect the clones as well as the original. Copies are distinct objects, instances maintain the changes between all clones, and references maintain all changes below the reference bar.

Master It Select the teapot from the previous exercise and make two clones: one instance and one reference. Turn off the Slice modifier for the instance, and then apply a Twist modifier and increase the amount of twist reflected in the objects. Select the reference clone, and apply a Spherify modifier to the top of the stack.

Manipulate a group Groups provide a method for associating separate objects so they act as if they are a single object. Groups can be opened, allowing individual member objects to be selected or exploded, or the members associated with it to be changed.

Master It Make one clone each of the teapots from the previous exercise. Select the three original objects and make them into a group. Remove the spherified teapot from the group, and then add the remaining two non-spherified teapots to the group.

Chapter 3

Creating Shapes with Splines

In the previous chapter, you learned about 3ds Max's geometry primitives and how they can be shaped by parameters and modifiers into an infinite variety of forms. In this chapter, you'll continue your introduction to primitives with an exploration of *splines*. Splines are a type of primitive, and they are classified as shapes in 3ds Max. In a way, shapes are even more primitive than the geometry primitives you looked at in Chapter 2, "Introducing 3ds Max Objects." You can create more varied forms with splines than you can with the geometry primitives, but they require a bit more work to use.

In general, you can think of splines as objects composed of straight-line or curved-line segments. Splines can be two- or three-dimensional; however, unlike solid geometry, splines do not define surface areas or volumes. Splines are defined only along their edge segments. Strictly speaking, a spline is a line or curve whose shape is controlled by its *vertices*, which are the points along the spline. *Bezier* splines are a type of spline that includes features, called handles, for controlling the curvature of the spline as it enters or exits each vertex. Splines are initially created as two-dimensional objects (with the exception of the Helix spline primitive, which is a line that curves in 3D space like a spring or a DNA strand). Like the standard primitives in 3ds Max, most splines are parametric; that is, they can be modified using parameters such as the Width and Length parameters of the Box standard primitive. All the splines can be made three-dimensional by editing their vertices and handles.

A benefit of splines is that you can use them to create an outline of virtually any two-dimensional shape and then *extrude* (project into the third dimension to define a volume) the outline into the third dimension. You can use splines as paths for a variety of purposes, such as camera motion for animated sequences or the path for a *loft*, which is a type of extruded form along a path. Splines can be *lathed* (revolved around an axis), making a surface or volume. You can also create a complex 3D armature with splines over which a surface can be draped.

A *shell* defines a volume that can be extruded out of a three-dimensional surface, which itself may be generated from splines. Suffice it to say that splines are used almost everywhere in 3ds Max and are definitely worth learning to use well.

In this chapter, you'll learn how to use splines to create complex extruded and lathed forms. You'll see how you can apply modifiers to enhance splines, just as you did with geometry primitives. You'll also begin to explore methods for editing objects on what are called *levels*, similar to the modifiers that we discussed in Chapter 2. These are levels of editing at which you can manipulate the components that make up an object.

In this chapter, you will learn to:

◆ Draw shapes with splines

◆ Outline and extrude splines

◆ Modify closed splines with Boolean tools

Drawing with Splines

As you'll see in this and later chapters, the ability to edit the location and characteristics of an object's vertices is an essential part of creating and editing objects in 3ds Max. In this chapter, you'll begin working with splines and their associated vertices to gain a better understanding of how you can manipulate objects in general. You'll start with the most primitive of the shape objects: the line. With the Line tool, you can draw line segments, curves, squares, circles, or just about any shape you want. Such shapes can then be extruded, in a manner similar to the way the box and cylinder standard primitives are created, as you saw in the previous chapter.

THE NONPARAMETRIC SHAPES

We mentioned that most 3ds Max shapes are *parametric*, which means they offer a set of parameters that let you modify the shape at will. The Line spline is an exception. Once you've created a Line spline, you cannot use parameters to modify its shape. Lines behave more like the common splines used in other computer design and drafting programs. The Section shape, which is created by following the intersection of a 3D object's edges and a slice plane, is another nonparametric shape. All shapes that are converted to editable splines lose their parametric capabilities.

Let's get started by drawing a simple rectangle using a Line spline:

1. Start 3ds Max Design 2011, or choose Reset from the Application menu.

2. Click the Maximize Viewport Toggle, if necessary, to display all four viewports, and then right-click in the Top viewport.

3. If required, choose Customize ➤ Units Setup and set the units to Feet w/Decimal Inches, set Inches as the default units, and then click OK.

4. If it isn't selected already, click the Create tab in the Command panel.

5. Click the Shapes tool. Notice that the drop-down list shows Splines; if it doesn't, expand the drop-down list and select it as shown in Figure 3.1.

6. Click the Line button in the Object Type rollout.

Notice that a set of new rollouts appears in the bottom half of the Command panel. The Line options that appear offer a variety of ways to construct a spline from line segments.

FIGURE 3.1
Selecting Splines as the shapes to create

Drawing Straight-Line Segments

Now you're ready to draw a spline made of line segments. Use the finished rectangle in Figure 3.5 as a guide to help you select points as you draw the spline in this exercise. You don't need to be too exact, because you're just practicing.

1. Maximize the Top viewport, and then click a point near coordinate 0′0.0″,10′0.0″,0′0.0″ just above the 0,0 origin in the viewport. You can use the coordinate readout at the bottom of the 3ds Max window to locate the point. Now, as you move the cursor, a rubber-banding line follows from the point you just clicked, as shown in Figure 3.2.

2. Place the cursor near the 15′ X-coordinate, directly to the right of the first point, and click. You may need to pan or zoom to avoid clicking on the ViewCube.

FIGURE 3.2
Drawing a line
with the Line tool

3. You can use the coordinate readout again to locate a relative coordinate near 15′0.0″, 0′0.0″, 0′0.0″. Click to create the second line segment fixed between the last two points you selected, as shown in Figure 3.3. (Don't worry if your line segment is not exactly straight.)

4. Place the cursor over a point near the origin of the grid, and then click again.

5. Click the beginning of the line segment near where you started drawing the line. You'll see a dialog box asking you whether you want to close the spline (see Figure 3.4).

6. Click Yes. The rectangle is complete, and 3ds Max awaits your next point selection to draw another spline. Figure 3.5 shows the entire rectangle procedure.

FIGURE 3.4
Closing the spline

FIGURE 3.5
Drawing a rectangle with the Line tool

You've just drawn a rectangle. It's not necessarily straight, but now you know that you can draw a rectangle by clicking points in the drawing area. You also saw that you can close the set of line segments by clicking the beginning point. The Spline dialog box appears, offering you the option of either closing the set of line segments or leaving it open. When you select Yes, the beginning and ending points of the spline are connected exactly end to end.

Constraining Lines Vertically and Horizontally

Some of the lines you drew in the previous exercise may not be perfectly horizontal or vertical. 3ds Max offers some tools that constrain your lines to perfectly horizontal and vertical lines, much as a T-square and triangle constrain your lines when you draft on a drafting board.

One way to constrain lines vertically or horizontally is to use the Shift key. Let's try drawing another rectangle using this technique:

1. Make sure the Line button in the Object Type rollout is still active; it should be pale green and appear to be in a down position.

2. Click a point about 10″ directly below the 0,0 coordinate. Once again, you see a rubber-banding line as you move your cursor around the screen.

3. Hold down the Shift key as you move the cursor. The rubber-banding line is constrained in a vertical or horizontal direction.

4. Point the cursor down and click a point 5′ below the last point. A vertical line is drawn.

5. Right-click to exit the Line tool, and then press the Delete key to delete the line you just drew.

6. Select and delete the original rectangle as well.

Drawing Curves

The Spline tool also allows you to draw curves, as the following exercise demonstrates:

1. With the Line button selected, change the Drag Type to Bezier in the Creation Method rollout.

2. Click and drag the mouse while still holding down the left mouse button from a point near the origin to the right, as shown in Figure 3.6.

FIGURE 3.6
Placing the first
point of a curved-
line segment

3. Continue to drag the mouse approximately 10′ to the right, and then release the left mouse button. You can use the coordinate readout to estimate your distance. Now, as you move the mouse, the line becomes a curve emerging from the starting point in the general direction indicated by the first two points you selected or indicated (see Figure 3.7).

FIGURE 3.7
Placing the second
point of a curved-
line segment

4. Click a point about 10′ to the right and 10′ down, as shown in Figure 3.8. The spline's curved shape is now fixed, and a straight rubber-banding line appears from the last point you picked.

FIGURE 3.8
Drawing a
curved spline

Click and drag the line
from here to the right.

And lastly here. Next Click here...

5. Click another point below and to the left of the origin of the drawing at coordinate -3′,-6′. A straight-line segment is added.

6. Right-click to end your line input. (See Figure 3.8.)

7. Press the Delete key to erase the lines. You won't need them anymore.

CREATING CURVED OR STRAIGHT SPLINE SEGMENTS

It is fairly easy, especially when you're in a hurry, to accidentally click and drag a point, in which case you'll get a curve in your line segment. If you just want a straight-line segment, take care not to accidentally drag your mouse while clicking. You can also set the Drag Type option to Corner in the Creation Method rollout of the Line object to ensure that you'll get a straight line even if you drag. This is the default behavior in 3ds Max Design 2011.

You have seen that by clicking and dragging a point, you can add a curve to the spline. A single click gives you a straight *corner* point. Once you've drawn a spline, you can later edit a curve in the spline, add more vertices, remove existing ones, or even convert a corner vertex into a curved one for rounded corners.

You can add accurate lines to a 3ds Max scene in several ways. Two other common methods are setting up an appropriately sized grid and snapping to the grid points, or importing 2D linework from Autodesk's AutoCAD family of products or Adobe Illustrator. Snaps are covered later in this chapter, and utilizing AutoCAD files is covered in Chapter 5, "Working with External Design Data."

Lathing a Spline

Next, you'll create a wineglass using a spline. This will give you a chance to see how you can edit a spline to achieve a desired effect. A wineglass provides a fine example of the versatility of the Line tool, and you can use the Lathe modifier to create any type of revolved object, from a bowling pin to a banister post, using a spline. You will create a model of the wineglass shown in Figure 3.9.

FIGURE 3.9
The wineglass
you will model

When creating objects for visualization, it is important that the models you build are at the correct real-world size. This is important for many reasons, including how 3ds Max Design and mental ray treat light and material properties, which you will learn about later in this book. Another crucial reason for modeling to real-world dimensions is that when you bring many models together to create a more complex and compelling scene, if the models you use are not built to real-world dimensions, an object like this wine glass could be significantly larger than the table it needs to be placed on, and then you will have to spend time scaling all the objects in the scene to fit together appropriately.

1. To view all the viewports if necessary, click the Maximize Viewport Toggle in the viewport navigation controls. Then right-click in the Front viewport to activate it.

2. Click the Rectangle button in the Object Type rollout of the Create tab.

3. Expand the Keyboard Entry rollout, and enter **7.125″** for the Length value and **3.125″** for the Width, and click the Create button.

4. Click the Zoom Extents button to make the rectangle fill the Front viewport.

5. Click the Line button in the Object Type rollout of the Command panel's Create tab.

6. Draw the initial profile of the wineglass, starting at the lip and working down to the base. You can use the grid and Figure 3.10 to locate the points indicated in the figure. If the grid doesn't already appear, press the G key to turn it on.

 Don't click and drag any of the points, and don't worry if your placement isn't exact. You just need to create the general outline. Later, you'll learn how to apply a curve to a spline. It is easier to start with straight-line segments and later curve them to your liking than it is to start directly with imperfect curved segments.

7. Right-click to terminate the command when you have finished.

FIGURE 3.10
Drawing the initial wineglass profile

DELETING A VERTEX WITHOUT TERMINATING THE LINE TOOL

Don't try to click the Undo button when you're using the Line tool; this will place a vertex in the scene at a location behind the button. If you click a point accidentally, you can go back to the previous vertex by pressing the Backspace key.

The next step is to turn the profile into a 3D wineglass.

8. With the spline profile selected, click the Modify tab in the Command panel.

9. Open the Modifier List drop-down. Then click the Lathe modifier.

A somewhat cylindrical shape is created by revolving the profile of the spline, as you can see in Figure 3.11.

The shape isn't quite what you would expect. The Lathe tool wrapped the spline profile about the profile's center, which is not necessarily where you want the action to occur. You can make some simple adjustments to a spline on a sub-object level to get the exact shape you want, as described in the next section.

FIGURE 3.11
The result of applying the Lathe modifier to the spline

USING THE LATHE MODIFIER'S MIN OPTION

You could also click the Min button in the Align section of the Lathe modifier's Parameters rollout without resorting to entering a sub-object level, but you would still need to make some fine adjustments to make sure the stem had some volume.

Modifying a Shape Using Sub-object Levels

Objects in 3ds Max are fairly complex entities that offer built-in parameters for controlling their shape. As you saw in Chapter 2, you can add even more control by using modifiers. However, parameters and modifiers are limiting when it comes to some of the more minute and detailed changes you might want to make to objects. For example, parameters allow you to adjust the overall height and width of a box, and modifiers allow you to taper the overall shape—but what do you do when you want to add a bulge to one surface or remove one side of a box? To make these types of changes, you need to access objects on a more fundamental level than parameters and modifiers provide. 3ds Max offers that access through sub-object modeling.

There are four basic methods for gaining access to an object's sub-object levels:

◆ One method, not available to all objects or modifiers, is to use the red buttons in the Selection rollout on the Modify tab of the Command panel.

◆ Another method is to click the plus (+) sign next to the name of an object in the modifier stack, and then select the sub-object level from the expanded list.

◆ You can also use the 1 through 6 key, at the top of the keyboard (but not in the numeric keypad) to act as shortcut keys. The 1 through 5 keys access the different sub-object levels when available, and the 6 key returns 3ds Max to the object or modifier top level. The 6 key does not work with editable splines.

◆ Still another way to access an object's sub-levels is to use the quad menus that appear when you right-click in a viewport. The tools 1 quad menu contains a listing of each of the available sub-object levels as well as the top level.

Sub-objects in a spline are the lines or curve segments of the spline and the vertices at each line-segment intersection. When you enter the sub-object level of an object, you gain access to these sub-objects. You can alter the characteristics of each sub-object to fine-tune the overall object's shape.

There are three sub-object levels in a spline: Vertex, Segment, and Spline. Vertices are points in space that define both the endpoints of each segment and the curvature of the segments as they enter or exit the vertex. Segments are the visible portions of the spline that display in the viewports. Segments consist of one or more straight steps that further define the curvature of the segment. The number of steps between each vertex is set in the spline's Interpolation rollout. Every segment is terminated at each end by one vertex, but a single vertex can terminate many segments. This may be a bit confusing, but splines can also consist of several noncontiguous spline sub-objects. A *spline sub-object* consists of all contiguous segments that were created at the same time. A Donut spline primitive and text objects consist of more than one spline sub-object that can be selected and edited independently of the others.

You can also edit modifiers on a sub-object level, although you are usually more limited in the number of levels to choose from within modifiers. Still, using these levels, you can make adjustments to the way modifiers affect the object. You'll start your exploration of sub-object editing by adjusting the Lathe modifier's axis level.

Adjusting the Lathe Axis

The wineglass profile you created in the previous exercise isn't quite where it should be in relation to the center of the Lathe axis. You can move the center axis of the Lathe modifier to the location you want by moving the modifier's axis of rotation. Let's try that now:

1. Click the plus sign to the left of the Lathe listing in the modifier stack. Axis appears as an option under the Lathe modifier.

2. Click the Axis option, and it will be highlighted in yellow to indicate that you can now edit on this level. Also notice that the Select and Move tool in the Main Toolbar is automatically selected and that the Move gizmo appears at the center of the lathe object.

3. In the Front viewport, click and drag in the X-axis handle of the Transform gizmo to the left until it looks like Figure 3.12. Now the lathed spline looks more like a wineglass.

4. Click the Zoom Extents All tool to get a better view. Your Perspective viewport should look similar to Figure 3.13.

FIGURE 3.12
Moving the
Lathe axis

Click the red arrow at the end of
the X-axis handle, and drag it left.

LOOK OUT FOR YELLOW

Yellow is a warning color in 3ds Max and is meant to grab your attention. Whenever a sub-object is selected, you can select and manipulate only sub-objects of the currently selected object, and you are prohibited from selecting anything else in your scene.

The sub-object button turns yellow whenever a sub-object level is accessed.

The Selection Lock Toggle, the icon that looks like a padlock to the left of the transform type-ins at the bottom of the user interface, also displays in yellow to indicate that the user has locked the current selection to ensure that the selection set remains selected even if a blank area of a viewport is clicked. The shortcut key for the Selection Lock Toggle is the spacebar. If you find that you cannot select an object, ensure that a sub-object level is not accessed and that the Selection Lock Toggle is not active.

FIGURE 3.13
The wineglass
so far

Transforming the Axis Gizmo

As a shortcut to steps 1 and 2 of this exercise, you can click the plus sign next to Lathe in the modifier stack so that it is expanded. You can first use the Min button in the Align group of the Parameters rollout to get a shape closer to the one you want, and then fine-tune the shape by entering the Axis level and transforming the gizmo.

Here, you see how the Transform gizmo can be moved to alter the way the Lathe axis affects the resulting three-dimensional object. The Lathe axis offers control over the way modifiers act on an object.

Flipping Surface Normals

At this point, you might notice that your perspective view of the wineglass looks a bit odd. Some of the parts seem to be missing. As you model other objects in 3ds Max Design 2011, you may find that sometimes surfaces seem to disappear. This can also be a problem when files are imported from some CAD programs. You know the surfaces are there, because you can see them in wireframe view. Where do these surfaces go? This problem happens less as video card hardware and drivers increase in quality and speed, so it may not occur on your system. If the wineglass appears correct on your system, as shown in the earlier Figure 3.13, you can skip to the "Smoothing Spline Corners" section.

To understand why surfaces disappear, you need to know one basic fact about 3D computer models: A surface has only one visible side. The other side of a surface is invisible. Like a one-way mirror, an object appears solid from one direction and transparent from the other.

CERT OBJECTIVE

Surfaces are visible or invisible, depending on the direction of their normals. A *normal* is a mathematical concept indicating a vector pointing perpendicularly away from a plane (as defined by at least three points); the direction of the normal is determined by the order and direction in which these points are created. Figure 3.14 shows an example of a typical object face and its normal.

FIGURE 3.14
A typical 3D surface and its components and normal

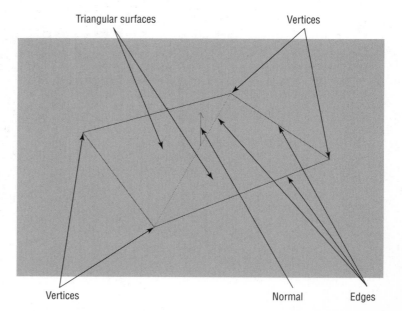

Triangular surfaces Vertices

Vertices Normal Edges

You will now flip the normals of the wineglass so that the surface faces the opposite direction:

1. Select the top level of the Lathe modifier by clicking Lathe in the modifier stack.

2. Check the Flip Normals option in the Parameters rollout.

Observe how the surface appeared to flip to the other side (see Figure 3.15). Now you can see the exterior of the wineglass while the interior becomes hidden.

FIGURE 3.15
Flipped normals on the wineglass

In most situations, you'll create objects in 3ds Max that have volume rather than objects with flat, two-dimensional faces. When you create a volume such as a box or the lathed outline of a wineglass, 3ds Max will automatically align the normals of the surfaces so that they all point outward, away from the interior of the volume. You'll see this happen later, when you use the Outline option on the spline for the wineglass, effectively creating a double-walled surface to represent the glass. Instead of creating a surface using a single layer of surfaces, the Outline option creates a closed volume with a distinct interior and exterior. If you look between the lathed outline splines, you will see that from the inside out, the wineglass is invisible!

In most situations, 3ds Max takes care of the normals in objects, but if you import objects from some CAD packages, sometimes surfaces disappear. You can use a number of methods to fix these disappearing surfaces. One method to fix the normals on a mesh is to use the Shell modifier with values of zero. The Shell modifier works similarly to the Outline option on a spline, by offsetting new faces on the geometry. You'll learn about the other methods as you begin to work with materials later in this book.

Smoothing Spline Corners

You now have a wineglass that looks a bit crude. Next, you'll smooth some of the rough spots by returning to the Spline primitive and editing it.

1. Select Line from the modifier stack. Your view of the wineglass returns to the flat spline you drew earlier. Notice that the options below the modifier stack change to a set of options related to the spline.

2. Click the Vertex option in the Selection rollout so that it is highlighted.

3. Click the second vertex of the spline to select it.

4. Right-click in the viewport to open the quad menu, and then click the Bezier option as shown in Figure 3.16.

FIGURE 3.16

Converting the second vertex to a Bezier vertex

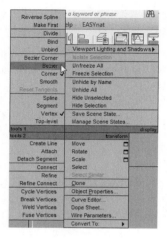

The line changes to a curve and two handles appear, emerging from the vertex as shown in Figure 3.17.

FIGURE 3.17

The second vertex converted to a Bezier vertex

The Bezier option turns a vertex into a control point for a Bezier curve passing through that vertex. You can manipulate the Bezier curves by adjusting the tangent handles that appear:

1. With the Select and Move tool active, click and drag the upper Bezier tangent handle, the green end of the yellow lines protruding from the vertex, to deform the spline to the shape shown in Figure 3.18. If the Move tool is restricted to an axis, press the F8 key repeatedly until the Transform gizmo's XY-plane handle highlights, indicating that it is free to move in both axes. You may also want to drag the vertex itself to a new position by clicking and dragging the axis and plane handles of the Transform gizmo.

2. Click the next vertex toward the stem of the wineglass, as shown in Figure 3.19. Right-click in the viewport after you select the vertex, and then select Bezier Corner from the quad menu. Now you see two handles from this vertex, but this time the handles are not opposite each other. Instead, they point in different directions.

FIGURE 3.18
Click and drag the
vertex and its tan-
gent handles.

Use the Move tool to drag the
selected vertices to a new position.
Also drag the green handles to
adjust the curvature of the spline.

FIGURE 3.19
Convert the next
vertex to a Bezier
Corner vertex.

Select this vertex.

3. Click and drag each of the Bezier handles into position, as shown in Figure 3.20. Notice
that the Bezier Corner option lets you control the curve from the vertex in both directions.

FIGURE 3.20
The new location
for the Bezier
Corner handles

Move the handles as shown to
adjust the curvature at the stem.

4. Click Line to exit the Vertex sub-object level, and then click Lathe in the modifier stack. You now see how your changes to the spline translate to the form of the wineglass, as shown in Figure 3.21.

FIGURE 3.21
The view of the wineglass so far

In this exercise, you have begun to see that splines are really made up of components, or sub-objects. You used the Transform gizmo to reposition the axis used by the Lathe modifier. You also changed the characteristics of a vertex by editing at the Vertex level. For example, the quad menu options allow you to change the shape of a spline just by changing the type of vertex being used. Four of the options on the Vertex shortcut menu relate to the way the vertex affects corners:

Smooth This option turns a sharp corner into a rounded one. This has an effect similar to that of the Bezier option without offering the Bezier handles.

Corner This option turns a Bezier or smooth corner into a sharp corner with no curve entering or exiting the vertex.

Bezier This option converts a corner into a Bezier curve with symmetrical handles that allow you to adjust the pull and direction of the curve.

Bezier Corner This option converts a corner to a Bezier curve with handles that allow you to adjust the pull and direction of the curve. Unlike the regular Bezier option, Bezier Corner allows you to control the handles independently in both directions from the vertex.

Remember that to use these corner options, you need to be editing on the Vertex sub-object level.

USING QUAD SHORTCUT MENUS

In the wineglass exercise, you used a context menu that appeared when you right-clicked the vertex of a selected spline. You may have been a bit surprised by the appearance of this particular shortcut menu—it's really several menus arranged in a quad fashion. In fact, 3ds Max calls this a *quad menu*. The options on the quads vary depending on the context.

Many of the options in the quad menu are actually duplicates of options in the Modify tab of the Command panel and on the Main Toolbar. These options provide a quick way to get to options that relate specifically to the object you're editing. By using the quad menu, you don't need to sort through a set of buttons in the Command panel, many of which may be grayed out.

Be aware that the options in the quad menu are often abbreviated versions of those found in the Command panel, and they frequently don't offer keyboard input. If you want to edit an object visually, the context menu options work just fine. However, if you need to enter exact dimensions, you'll want to go to the Modify tab of the Command panel and use the tools and options there.

Adjusting Tangent Handles

3ds Max has several controls for the way you can work with spline vertices and their tangent handles. Let's explore these features.

1. Above your wineglass, draw a spline in the Top viewport alternating straight and curved segments similar to Figure 3.22. Do this by alternately clicking and clicking/dragging the mouse while using the Line tool. Right-click to finish drawing the spline.

2. Switch to the Modify panel and right-click in the viewport to bring up the quad menu. Select Vertex from the tools 1 quad to enter the vertex sub-object level for editing.

3. Select a few vertices of your choosing either by dragging a selection window or by Ctrl+clicking individual vertices. Figure 3.23 shows three vertices selected.

4. Right-click and change the tangent type for the entire selection to Bezier Corner from the tools 1 quad.

FIGURE 3.22
Draw a curved spline in the viewport.

FIGURE 3.23
Select a few of the spline's vertices.

Being able to change the tangent type of multiple vertices in a selection set is an excellent feature in 3ds Max. This is much better than it was in early versions, where you had to change each vertex one at a time by right-clicking directly on top of the vertex on which you wanted to work. Another valuable feature is the way you can copy and paste tangent handle orientations between handles.

1. While you are still in the Vertex sub-object level for editing, in the Modify panel scroll down in the Geometry rollout and locate the Tangent group. Click the Copy button.

2. When the Copy button is active, you are in a mode where you can select a tangent handle to copy its orientation to the Clipboard. Click one of the handles of either a Bezier or Bezier Corner vertex, as shown in Figure 3.24. You will automatically exit Copy mode when you click.

3. Click the Paste button in the Tangent group.

4. Click the handle of another Bezier vertex. This matches the tangent handle orientation stored on the Clipboard to the vertex where you choose to paste it. Notice that your cursor changes to a Clipboard Paste icon while over a green tangent handle, as shown in Figure 3.25.

FIGURE 3.24
Copying the tangent handle's orientation to the Clipboard

FIGURE 3.25
Pasting one tangent handle's orientation to another

As you copy and paste handle orientations between vertices, you are making these handles parallel to each other (see Figure 3.26). This can be convenient when you're shaping splines in your 3ds Max scene.

FIGURE 3.26
Once you paste the orientation, the handles from different vertices are parallel.

Another feature useful when editing splines is the Reset Tangents option in the tools 1 quad menu. Use this option when you want the orientations of the tangent handles you already copied and pasted to revert to their original orientations. You can think of it as a specialized undo tool for tangent handles. Exit the Vertex sub-object level, and then delete the selected line.

Creating Thickness with a Spline

The wineglass is currently an object with surfaces but no thickness. To make this glass appear more realistic, you can give it some thickness. Here's how it's done:

1. Select the wineglass, and then click Line in the modifier stack.

2. Select the Spline level in the Selection rollout.

3. Click the spline. Notice that now the entire spline turns red, indicating that it's selected.

4. Scroll down the Modify panel until you see the Outline button in the Geometry rollout.

5. Click the input box to the right of the Outline button, and then change its text value from 0′0.0″ to 0′0.125″, and press ↵. The spline is outlined and now represented by a double wall.

6. Go back up to the modifier stack and select Lathe. You now see the entire glass, including those portions of the glass that may not have appeared previously because of the orientation of the normals (see Figure 3.27).

7. Zoom in close; you will see that the wineglass appears chunky, or faceted, as shown in Figure 3.28.

8. Try increasing the number of segments in the Lathe modifier to 36 or so to make it appear more rounded.

FIGURE 3.27
The wineglass
after outlining the
spline

FIGURE 3.28
The rim of the
wineglass

9. Your wineglass appears smoother and less faceted in the Perspective viewport, as shown in Figure 3.29.

10. Choose File ➢ Save and then name and save your wineglass model in you Chapter 3 directory as My_Wineglass.max.

FIGURE 3.29
The smooth
wineglass

In step 5, when you entered a value for the outline, 3ds Max changed the single-line spline into an outline using the spline, thereby creating a double-lined spline. In this context, entering an Outline value has the effect of creating a cross section with thickness.

The Outline option generates an outline using the existing spline as one side of the outline. To determine the side on which the outline appears, check the direction in which the original spline was created. For example, if a spline is drawn from left to right, the outline will appear on the top side, as shown in Figure 3.30.

FIGURE 3.30
Determining the side of the outline

Direction of point selection

Direction of outline

THE OUTLINE TOOL'S CENTER OPTION

The Center check box just below the Outline input box causes the outline to be centered on the original spline instead of creating the outline on either side of the spline.

If you're not sure of the order in which a spline was drawn, select the Line object, select Vertex, and then click the Show Vertex Numbers check box in the Selection rollout of the Modify tab (see Figure 3.31).

With the Show Vertex Numbers check box selected, you'll see each vertex labeled with a small black number, indicating the order in which the vertices were created (Figure 3.32).

FIGURE 3.31
Turning on Show Vertex Numbers

FIGURE 3.32
The vertex numbers shown in
the viewport

If you want the outline to appear on the opposite side, you can either enter a negative value for the offset distance, or you can reverse the order of the vertices using the Reverse button in the Geometry rollout of the Modify tab. The Reverse button is active only when you select Spline from the Selection rollout or the modifier stack. You must also have a spline sub-object selected.

So far, you've used the sub-object options and parameters to adjust the spline curve to a shape that gives the impression of a wineglass. The steps you took while editing the spline are similar to those you would take for other types of objects. As you've seen in some of the rollouts, there is a bewildering array of options you can apply to a sub-object, but you've covered the main points regarding sub-object editing. Throughout this book, you'll continue to work on a sub-object level to edit items such as segments and vertices.

Detailing the Wineglass Base

The wineglass doesn't yet look exactly like the picture you saw at the beginning of these exercises, so let's finish it up quickly so you have an object you can use again later in this book for applying materials and then rendering with some advanced features of mental ray.

1. Click the Line entry in the modifier stack and then select the Segment sub-object level.

2. Select the spline segment that would represent the inside of the stem of the glass, as shown in Figure 3.33, and delete it.

FIGURE 3.33
Select the inner
segment of the
wineglass stem.

3. Switch to the Vertex sub-object of the spline and select the top vertex of the open spline, as shown in Figure 3.34.

4. Right-click in the viewport to bring up the quad menu and click the Transform Type-In button next to Move from the transform panel, as shown in Figure 3.35.

FIGURE 3.34
Select the top vertex of the open spline.

FIGURE 3.35
Activate the Move Transform Type-In dialog box.

5. On the Move Transform Type-In dialog box, enter **0** for the Absolute:World X coordinate.

6. Select the lower vertex of the open spline and, using the Move Transform Type-In dialog box, set its X-coordinate to **0** and its Y-coordinate to **-0′3.4″**.

7. Zoom in on the outer vertices of the base of the wineglass, select the two vertices, and move them in about a .25″ and down so the lower vertex rests at the bottom of rectangle drawn at the very beginning of the wineglass project.

8. Deselect the top vertex by Alt+clicking it, move the lower vertex directly under the top vertex of the base, and then, using the Bezier Corner handle, make the bottom of the glass somewhat flat near the outer edge of the base, as shown in Figure 3.36.

FIGURE 3.36
Fixing the base of the wineglass

Now you need to add some more detail to the top of the base of the wineglass.

9. Select the top segment of the wineglass's base, and click the Divide button in the Geometry rollout (see Figure 3.37).

10. Select the vertex where the base and stem of the wineglass meet and click the Fillet button in the Geometry rollout, as shown in Figure 3.38.

FIGURE 3.37
Click the Divide button to split the selected segment

FIGURE 3.38
Click the Fillet button.

11. Click the selected vertex, notice the mouse pointer changes, and drag the mouse. You will see the vertex interactively fillet; continue dragging the mouse until you set the radius to about 0.35˝, as shown in Figure 3.39.

FIGURE 3.39
Interactively fillet the vertex.

12. Select the middle vertex on the top of the wineglass base, and move it as shown in Figure 3.40.

13. Select the vertex on the top corner of the base and, using the Bezier handle, add some curvature to the segment, as shown in Figure 3.41.

FIGURE 3.40
Move the selected
vertex.

FIGURE 3.41
Adding some defi-
nition to the top of
the base

You have now finished the base of the wineglass, giving it a good surface to rest on a table-top and adding some fine detail to the model. Now you will fix the inside and upper lip of the glass.

1. Using the Select and Move tool, select the vertex on the bottom of the inside of the glass and move it up slightly, as shown in Figure 3.42.

FIGURE 3.42
Moving the inside
of the glass up

2. Select the Bezier handle and move it down to flatten the inside curve of the glass, as shown in Figure 3.43.

3. Select the vertices that make up the top of the glass and move them so they are inside the rectangle, as shown in Figure 3.44.

4. Using the Select and Move tool, select the vertex on the inner lip of the glass and move it close to the outer vertex to make the upper lip of the glass very thin (like the glass in Figure 3.9), as shown in Figure 3.45.

FIGURE 3.43
Flatten the inside of the glass.

FIGURE 3.44
Make the glass spline fit the real-world dimensions of the glass.

FIGURE 3.45
Move the vertex at the lip of the glass.

You are almost done detailing the wineglass so that it is like the one in Figure 3.9. There is one detail left to add: the curves at the top of the stem. You'll add those now:

1. Pan the view so that you can see the top of the glass's stem.

2. Click the Refine button in the Geometry rollout, as shown in Figure 3.46.

3. Move the mouse pointer over the spline in the Front viewport; notice that it changes to show two black line segments, one with a white vertex in the middle. Using the Refine tool will allow you to add new vertices to the spline without changing its shape. Click and add a vertex about half an inch down from where the stem joins the top of the glass, as shown in Figure 3.47.

4. Click the Refine button again to turn off the Refine tool.

5. Click the Insert button in the Geometry rollout and then set the New Vertex Type option to Bezier, as shown in Figure 3.48.

FIGURE 3.46
Click the Refine button.

FIGURE 3.47
Add and a new vertex to the spline.

FIGURE 3.48
Set the New Vertex Type to Bezier.

6. Move the mouse pointer over middle of the short line segment at the top of the glass stem, and notice the pointer changes to show a black line segment and a white line segment that has additional curves. Click once to put a new vertex on the segment, move the mouse to the right, and click and drag to place the new vertex with a Bezier curve, as shown in Figure 3.49. Right-click to stop adding new points to the line segment.

FIGURE 3.49
Add and shape the
new curve on the
spline.

7. Click the Insert button again to turn it off.

8. Select the vertices around the bulge you just created and move them by adjusting the Bezier handles to make the spline look like Figure 3.50, or you can make the spline look any way you want, also known as "season to taste."

FIGURE 3.50
Adjust the Bezier
handles to create
the curves you
desire.

Finishing the Wineglass

You are almost finished making the wineglass; only a few steps remain to make it an object that you can reuse many times in your visualization career.

1. Deactivate the sub-object mode and click the Lathe modifier.

2. Click the Axis sub-object of the Lathe modifier. Earlier you placed the Axis sub-object by hand to create the revolved shape of the wineglass.

3. Press the F12 button on your keyboard to open the Move Transform Type-In dialog box, enter **0** for the Absolute: World: X coordinate, and press Enter on your keyboard to commit that value.

4. Click the Lathe modifier again to turn off the Sub-object mode and then click the Weld Core box on the Parameters rollout. This will make the wineglass a water-tight model.

 You have now finished modeling your wineglass (see Figure 3.51).

5. Save your model as My_Wineglass.max, overwriting the previous file.

FIGURE 3.51
Your finished
wineglass

Outlining and Extruding Splines

You've just seen how you can create a complex wineglass using a spline and the Lathe modifier and sub-object editing. Now, let's look at drawing a type of object that is simpler in many ways but that requires quite a different approach to using splines. Walls are usually drawn with straight-line segments, and they require a fairly high degree of accuracy. In the following exercise, you'll learn how to draw a spline using exact coordinates.

OTHER METHODS FOR CREATING WALLS IN 3DS MAX

This example is intended primarily to demonstrate a technique of working with splines, not necessarily a method you'll use in the real world to draw walls. 3ds Max provides a set of architecture, engineering, and construction (AEC) tools, which includes a Wall tool. The AEC tools offer specialized functions geared toward the creation of building components such as walls and stairs. 3ds Max's AEC Wall tool works in a way that is slightly different from the splines described here, and it offers some time-saving features for inserting doors and windows. You'll learn about the AEC tools in Chapter 6, "Creating AEC Objects." You can also link AutoCAD and AutoCAD Architecture drawings to your scene and manipulate the walls created in AutoCAD using 3ds Max's toolset.

Drawing Accurate Splines

You'll start by setting up a top view in a new file that will include the area in which you'll draw the walls. The walls will cover a 20′-square area, so you'll want to include an area that covers about 20′ square.

1. Expand the Application menu and choose New.

2. Choose Customize ➤ Units Setup. In the Units Setup dialog box, make sure that US Standard and Feet w/Decimal Inches are selected, and click the Inches radio button for the Default Units setting, as shown in Figure 3.52. Then click OK.

FIGURE 3.52
Setting the units
in the Units Setup
dialog box

3. Click the Maximize Viewport Toggle to display all four viewports.

4. Click the Zoom Extents All tool to restore the views to their default zoom factors.

5. Click in the Top viewport, and then click the Maximize Viewport Toggle to enlarge it to fit the entire viewport area.

6. Click the Zoom tool and zoom out until you can see both -12′0″ and 12′0″ in the X direction by alternately zooming and placing the cursor along the edges of the viewport, causing the coordinates to display at the bottom of the user interface.

7. Click the Pan View tool, or hold down the mouse's scroll wheel, and pan the view down and to the left so that the 0,0 origin of the grid is in the lower-left corner of the viewport, as shown in Figure 3.53.

FIGURE 3.53
Pan until the origin
is near the corner
of the viewport.

Now you're ready to start drawing. You'll draw an L-shaped room that is 20′ by 20′ overall, with each leg 10′ long.

1. If it isn't already selected, click the Create tab of the Command panel.

2. Make sure the Shapes tool and Splines are selected. Then click the Line button.

3. Locate the Keyboard Entry rollout at the bottom of the panel, and then click to expand it if necessary.

You see three coordinate input boxes and three buttons labeled Add Point, Close, and Finish. These are the tools you'll use to accurately place the walls.

1. Click the Add Point button. This starts the wall by inserting the start point at the coordinates shown in the coordinate-input boxes. Because the input boxes show the coordinates 0′0.0″, 0′0.0″, 0′0.0″ for the X-, Y-, and Z-coordinates, the line starts at 0′0.0″, 0′0.0″, 0′0.0″.

2. Click the X-coordinate input box and enter **20′**↵.

3. Click the Add Point button again. It may not be obvious, but you've just added a line segment from coordinate 0′0.0″, 0′0.0″, 0′0.0″ to 20′0.0″, 0′0.0″, 0′0.0″.

4. Double-click the Y-coordinate input box, enter **10′**↵, and click the Add Point button. Another line segment is added.

5. Double-click the X-coordinate input box, enter **10′**↵, and click the Add Point button.

6. Double-click the Y-coordinate input box, enter **20′**↵, and click Add Point.

7. Double-click the X-coordinate input box, enter **0′0.0″**, and click Add Point.

8. Click the Close button to create the final segment.

 You've just drawn the basis for the walls.

9. Click the Zoom Extents tool to get an overall view of your walls. You scene should look like Figure 3.54.

As you can see from this exercise, you can enter coordinate values to place the corners of the walls accurately. Because you started at the World Coordinate System origin 0,0,0, it's fairly easy to determine the coordinate location of your walls.

FIGURE 3.54
The walls drawn using the Keyboard Entry rollout

Giving Walls Thickness

Right now, you have only a single-line representation. To give the walls thickness, you can use the Outline tool, which you used earlier in the wineglass exercise.

1. Click the Modify tab of the Command panel. Because you just created the wall outline, that shape is still selected, and you can see the options for the spline in the Modify tab.

2. Click the Spline button in the Selection rollout, and then select the spline.

3. Scroll down the Modify panel to the Geometry rollout so you can see the Outline button.

4. Double-click the input box next to the Outline button and enter 5˝↵. Notice that a new spline outline appears inside the original outline. This is the inside face of the wall.

5. Exit the Spline sub-object level by clicking Line in the modifier stack.

When you used the Outline option in the wineglass example, 3ds Max turned the single, open line into a single, continuous outline of the wineglass section. In this wall example, you actually have two splines, with one closed spline inside the other. Even though there are two splines, 3ds Max considers this to be one object. This is so because the new spline was created while you were in the sub-object spline level of the line. As you'll see in the next exercise, concentric closed splines behave in an unusual manner.

1. Click the Maximize Viewport Toggle to view the other viewports.

2. Click the Zoom Extents All tool to see the entire outline in all the viewports.

3. Expand the Modifier List drop-down and click Extrude, which is in the Object-Space Modifier category.

4. In the Parameters rollout, click the Amount input box and enter 8´↵.

5. Make sure the Segments input box shows a value of 1. Walls are usually vertical planes, so you don't need the extra segments in the wall's vertical plane. You now have a wall that is 8´ tall, as shown in Figure 3.55.

FIGURE 3.55
The walls after extruding them 8´

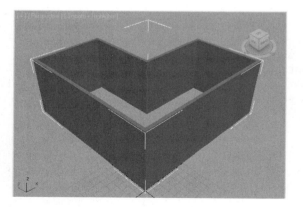

IMPORTING AUTOCAD FILES

AutoCAD users will find it easier to import 2D floor plans into 3ds Max and then extrude the walls of the floor plan in 3ds Max. You'll learn how to import 2D plans in Chapter 5.

If you're an AutoCAD user, you may find drawing walls with accurate dimensions a bit more difficult in 3ds Max. It can be done, but as you've just seen, you need to translate the wall dimensions into coordinates. You can use a tool called the *user grid* as an aid to drawing accurately.

Using Grids and Snaps to Align Objects Accurately

You've seen how you can enter coordinate data for splines using the Keyboard Entry rollout in a simple example. As you can imagine, entering coordinates can become quite cumbersome and tedious for any wall configuration that is even slightly more complex than the simple example you are modeling here. There are a couple of tools that can help make drawing walls easier: user grids and snaps.

User grids These are nonrenderable reference objects that you can align to any orientation or object geometry you want. You can use them to set up a *local* coordinate system in which to add other objects.

Snaps This is a set of options that lets you accurately select specific geometry on existing objects, such as endpoints of line segments, midpoints of lines, and intersections. Snaps also let you select grid points.

In the next exercise, you'll use grid objects and snaps to add some walls to the existing set of walls. Start by setting up a view that will allow you to see your work:

1. Make the Top viewport active and then maximize it.

2. Click and drag the ViewCube to the left and up to view the model from the other side. The view should be somewhat opposite of the Perspective viewport that you have been working in.

3. If it is not already selected, choose the Smooth + Highlights viewport display by clicking the [Wireframe] viewport label and selecting Smooth + Highlights from the context menu.

4. Click the [Orthographic] viewport label and select Perspective from the context menu.

5. Click the Zoom Extents tool or use the Zoom tool to fit the model in the view. Your viewport should look similar to Figure 3.56.

FIGURE 3.56
Changing the view
of the building

Now you're ready to add a user grid. First you'll place it somewhere in the drawing; then you'll move it into a position that makes it easier to add a new wall.

1. Click the Create tab of the Command panel.

2. Click the Helpers button.

3. Click the Grid button in the Object Type rollout.

4. Click and drag down from a point near the upper center of the view, as shown in Figure 3.57. Just approximate the location—it doesn't need to be exact.

FIGURE 3.57
Adding a user grid

First click here to start the grid placement.

Then click here.

You don't need to be too accurate about the shape and size of the grid. As with all other 3ds Max objects, you can fine-tune its parameters in the Command panel after it is created. You can set the width and length, as well as the grid spacing. In this set of exercises, you're just using the grid to create a local coordinate system, from which you can draw additional walls.

Next, you'll move your user grid into a position that will allow you to enter coordinates relative to an existing feature of the walls you've drawn so far. To accurately place the grid, you'll use snaps. First, set up the snaps to connect to the geometry with which you plan to work. In this case, you'll want to snap to grid points and endpoints of objects.

1. Right-click the Snaps Toggle in the Main Toolbar at the top of the 3ds Max window.

 The Grid and Snap Settings dialog box displays as shown in Figure 3.58.

2. Click the Grid Points and Endpoint check boxes. Clear any other check boxes and then close the Grid and Snap Settings dialog box.

3. Click the Snaps Toggle to make it active or press S on the keyboard. (You'll know it's active if the button is highlighted with a yellow background.)

4. Right-click and choose Activate Grid from the tools 1 quad menu. Grids must be activated for 3ds Max to assume their coordinate system as the active coordinate system.

FIGURE 3.58
The Grid and Snap
Settings dialog box

Now you're ready to move the grid using the snap settings to guide your movements:

5. Click the Select and Move tool in the Main Toolbar. Now as you move the cursor over the viewport, you'll see a cyan snap marker appear on the grid.

 The cursor jumps to grid points on the user grid. You may also notice that it jumps to the endpoints of the walls you've drawn so far.

6. Place the cursor so that it is on the 0,0 origin of the user grid, and click (see Figure 3.59). You can spot the origin by the new origin target on the Transform gizmo, which appears as a circle and will highlight when you are snapped to the origin.

7. Click and hold the origin, and then drag the grid to the corner of the wall, as shown in Figure 3.60.

FIGURE 3.59
Start the Move
command at the
origin of the
user grid.

FIGURE 3.60
Dragging the grid
to the corner of
the wall

8. Make sure that the cursor shows the endpoint marker graphic before you release the mouse button.

Now you're ready to start drawing the wall addition:

1. Click the Shapes tool in the Create tab of the Command panel.

2. Click the Line button in the Object Type rollout.

3. Open the Keyboard Entry rollout.

4. Set the X, Y, and Z values to 0 in the Keyboard Entry rollout, and click the Add Point button. This starts the new line at the 0,0 coordinate of the user grid (on the corner of the existing wall).

5. Double-click the X value, enter **12'↵**, and click the Add Point button.

6. Double-click the Y value, enter **10'↵**, and click the Add Point button.

7. Double-click the X value again, enter **-10'↵**, and click the Add Point button.

8. Click the Finish button to exit the Line tool.

MOVING AND ROTATING GRIDS

Grids are helper objects and can be moved or rotated as the need arises. For example, the grid's Z value can be increased to create the walls at an upper floor's height.

By using the user grid, you were able to draw the additional wall lines using coordinates relative to the corner of the existing wall. This is far easier than trying to translate world coordinates into the coordinates relative to the existing walls. You can place as many user grids as you need in a model, and they can be oriented in any direction you choose. You can also align them to the surfaces of objects if you so choose. You'll learn how to do this in later chapters.

3DS MAX GRIDS ARE SIMILAR TO AUTOCAD UCSS

If you're an AutoCAD user, you can think of the user grid as a kind of User Coordinate System (UCS), as it is known in AutoCAD. The methods for using the user grid may differ from those for using the UCS, but its purpose is the same. In addition, 3ds Max offers an autogrid, which is like a quick, temporary grid that works on the fly.

Now let's finish the additional wall by giving it some thickness and height:

1. With the new wall selected, click the Modify tab. (Because the wall has just been created, it's already selected.)

2. Click the Spline level in the stack.

3. Select the spline. Scroll down the Command panel until you see the Outline button, and enter **5″⏎** in the input box next to the Outline button. Once you press ⏎, the wall will be given a thickness of 5″, as shown in Figure 3.61. Exit the Spline level.

4. Apply an Extrude modifier to the new wall shape. Make sure that the Amount value in the Parameters rollout is set to 8′. Your additional wall now appears in place.

5. Click the Zoom Extents tool to get an overall view of your model so far. Your scene should look like Figure 3.62.

FIGURE 3.61
Offsetting the new walls

FIGURE 3.62
The new walls after extruding them 8′

Once again, you used the Outline option to convert a single-line spline into an outline, giving the wall a thickness. Unlike other parameters, an outline cannot be changed by simply changing a parameter once it's in place. This is true for most Spline functions. You can make changes at sub-object levels, such as changes to the vertices or line segments.

While you were working to add the new wall, you got a glimpse of the Grid and Snap Settings dialog box. That dialog box contains quite a few snap options (on the Snaps tab), of which you only used two. Table 3.1 describes the Standard snap options. (You won't use all of these options in this book.)

TABLE 3.1: Grid and Snap Settings Options

SETTING	DESCRIPTION
Standard/Body Snaps/NURBS	Drop-down list revealing different sets of snaps for Standard Max objects, SAT Body Objects, and NURBS objects. (Body Snaps and NURBS aren't listed in this table.)
Grid Points	Snap to intersection of grid lines.
Pivot	Snap to an object's pivot point as represented by the Transform gizmo.
Perpendicular	Snap to perpendicular line segments and edges.
Vertex	Snap to vertices.
Edge/Segment	Snap to the cursor location over an edge or segment.
Face	Snap to the cursor location over a face.
Grid Lines	Snap to any point on the grid lines.
Bounding Box	Snap to bounding box corner.
Tangent	Snap to tangent of curves and circles.
Endpoint	Snap to endpoints.
Midpoint	Snap to midpoints of line segments and edges.
Center Face	Snap to center of face.
Clear All	Clear all snap settings.

SNAP TO GRID POINTS TO CREATE STRAIGHT LINE SEGMENTS

Another way to draw line segments is to set the snap setting to Grid Points (on the Snaps tab of the Grid and Snap Settings dialog box) and then set the grid spacing to the smallest value you need to work with (on the Home Grid tab). Then, as you select points for the line, you can check the coordinates readout at the bottom of the 3ds Max window. You'll see that the coordinates show your current position relative to the last point you selected in the X-, Y-, and Z-coordinate format.

You may have noticed a graphic next to each of the options on the Snaps tab of the Grid and Snap Settings dialog box. When a snap setting is selected, the cursor will display the graphic associated with the snap setting whenever the cursor approaches a geometry that matches the snap setting. For example, if you select the Endpoint Snap setting, when Snap is turned on and the cursor approaches and touches an endpoint, the cursor will display the graphic associated with the endpoint snap.

SNAP OPTIONS ARE ON THE SNAPS TOOLBAR

Most of the common snap options are available on the Snaps toolbar, which is closed by default in most scenes. If the Snaps toolbar isn't visible, open it by right-clicking an open area of any toolbar and choosing Snaps from the pop-up menu. Like other toolbars, the Snaps toolbar can remain floating or you can dock it to the edge of the user interface.

Adjusting a Wall Location

The wall you just added isn't quite aligned properly with the first set of walls. If you look at a top view of the walls, you'll see that one of the 10′ sections of the new wall is offset by the width of the wall where the new wall meets one of the corners of the old wall.

To move the new wall section into place, you need to work with the vertices of the wall. Once again, this means working with the wall on a sub-object level. The following exercise will give you some hands-on experience with some simple vertex transformations. Start by returning to the top view of the walls.

1. Press T to switch to a Top viewport. If it is not already selected, choose Wireframe from the Viewport Label context menu.

2. Click the Select Object tool, click the user grid, and then press the Delete key. You don't need the user grid anymore.

3. Click the Zoom Extents tool to get an overall view of the model and press the G key to turn off the grid. Your view will look similar to Figure 3.63.

FIGURE 3.63
Top view showing
the new wall offset

The wall is offset at this corner.

Now you can see the offset more clearly. Let's go on to the work of moving the wall into alignment with the existing wall. First, set up the snap for endpoints. You don't want to accidentally snap to a grid point.

1. Right-click the Snaps Toggle at the top of the 3ds Max window.

2. In the Grid and Snap Settings dialog box, uncheck Grid Points, make sure that Endpoint is still checked, and then close the dialog box.

 Next, you'll move the wall section.

3. Click the Select Object tool, and then click the new wall.

4. Click the Modify tab of the Command panel and select Line in the modifier stack.

5. Expand Line in the stack and click the Vertex sub-object level.

6. With the Select Object tool active, place a window around the four vertices on the 10' section that you want to move. Do this by clicking and dragging a window. You'll see the selected vertices turn red, as shown in Figure 3.64.

7. Click the Select and Move tool in the Main Toolbar.

8. Place the cursor on the wall vertex, as shown in Figure 3.65. Only one vertex needs to be explicitly moved; all of the selected vertices will move relative to it.

FIGURE 3.64
The four vertices
are selected.

FIGURE 3.65
The four vertices
selected to move

With the endpoint marker on
this point, click and drag down.

9. Use the ViewCube tool until you can see the walls in three dimensions. This changes the current viewport into an Orthographic viewport.

10. When you see the Endpoint Snap marker, click and drag the vertex down to the location of the vertex just below it, as shown in Figure 3.66.

FIGURE 3.66

Selecting the new location of the vertex

When the cursor snaps to the endpoint, release the mouse button.

You've moved the selected vertices into place. Now let's take a look at the results:

1. Click the Maximize Viewport Toggle to view all the viewports.

2. Click the Zoom Extents All tool to show the entire model in the viewport. Notice that the new walls no longer appear as walls. Because you are editing at the Line level in the modifier stack, 3ds Max displays the wall as a spline.

3. In the modifier stack, select Extrude. The wall reappears at its full height.

You've just moved a set of vertices, thereby stretching a wall into a new location. As you can see, you need to enter the sub-object level of editing before you can make changes to vertices, but once you do, you have a good deal of freedom to edit parts of an object. As you've seen through these exercises, you can easily get to the sub-object level by selecting the level, such as Vertex, from the Selection rollout or from the modifier stack.

If you're working with architectural models, you'll use this operation frequently to fine-tune parts of a model. You'll get a chance to edit the vertices of objects in a number of ways as you work through the exercises in this book.

EXTRUDE DOES NOT FOLLOW THE STANDARD MODIFIER CONVENTION

Normally, when you're editing at the sub-object level and a sub-object is active below a modifier in the stack, only those selected sub-objects are passed up to the modifier. The Extrude modifier is one of the few exceptions to this rule. Regardless of the sub-object level active below the Extrude modifier, the entire spline is passed up to it.

Combining and Extruding Primitive Splines

You've learned how you can create walls with simple lines. Lines are perhaps the most basic type of object you can draw with, and you'll use them often when creating your models. However, for walls of a floor plan, you can use another object type that can simplify your work.

3ds Max offers a number of 2D shapes that can help make quick work of your modeling efforts, as long as you know how to apply them. In this section, you'll use the Rectangle spline to add a room to your current plan.

1. Change the Orthographic viewport into a Top viewport, and then click the Maximize Viewport Toggle to enlarge it if necessary.

2. Click the Zoom tool, and then click and drag down on the Top viewport so that you get a view of a larger area.

3. Click the Create tab of the Command panel and click the Rectangle button in the Object Type rollout.

4. Right-click the Snaps Toggle to open the Grid and Snap Settings dialog box, and then click the Grid Points option. You'll use the Grid Points snap to help you create the next set of walls. Make sure Endpoint is turned off as well.

5. Click the Home Grid tab of the Grid and Snap Settings dialog box, set the Grid Spacing to **0´6.0˝**, and then press ↵.

6. Close the dialog box and turn the grid back on.

7. Make sure the Snaps Toggle is turned on. Then click and drag from coordinate 26´,14´,0 to coordinate 41´,-1´,0 to draw a rectangle that is 15´ wide by 15´ deep. You can use the coordinate readout at the bottom of the screen to read the dimensions of your rectangle as you move the mouse. Use the scroll wheel on your mouse to zoom out if necessary. The Snap functions do not work if the points are not displayed in the viewport.

In the exercise in the previous section, you started out with a single-line representation of the wall. In this case, it's a rectangle that is 15´ × 15´. You were able to use the grid and snap together in this exercise to place the rectangle and determine its size.

The next step in adding the wall is to combine it with the existing walls. The rectangle needs to have a portion of its upper-left corner removed. To make the plan a little more interesting, you'll also add a curve to the lower-right corner.

 Real World Scenario

USING EDITABLE SPLINES FOR MODELING

A while back, one of the original authors of this book was given a project that entailed creating a model of a large, complex sign that was to be placed at a major downtown intersection. Most of the sign's components were structural steel members consisting of tubular, channel, and I-shaped posts and beams. The purpose of the model was to investigate the visual appeal of the sign from angles that were not provided with the designer's two-dimensional renderings and construction drawings.

Using the information provided by the designer, we found it easy to use the objects under the Shapes panel's Extended Primitives category that matched the sign's components. When we could not make the available extended primitives match the members' profiles by adjusting their parameters, we converted the shapes to editable splines and then edited them manually by adjusting their vertices and using the Spline Boolean tools.

Once we created the shapes, we moved them to their proper locations and oriented them accordingly. We took care to use instance clones whenever possible to maintain consistency when duplicate parts were used in the sign's design. Then we extruded each shape to the proper length and examined it for accuracy. We then modeled the remaining parts of the model, including light fixtures and informational panels, and added them to the project. The total project time was less than a day, and the model that resulted helped gain approval for the sign's design and placement.

Combining Splines

You've learned that Spline objects can be composed of multiple splines, accessible on the Spline sub-object level. In this section, you'll see how to combine two Spline objects into one and edit the new object to form new shapes.

1. Turn the grid off if you like, and then click the Select Object tool in the Main Toolbar, and click the 10′ × 20′ wall that intersects the rectangle you just drew, as shown in Figure 3.67.

2. Click the Modify tab in the Command panel and select Line in the modifier stack.

3. Scroll down the Command panel to the Geometry rollout and click the Attach button.

FIGURE 3.67
Select the wall you created in a prior exercise.

Select the previously created walls.

 4. Move the cursor on top of the rectangle you added in the previous exercise. You'll see the Attach cursor appear (see Figure 3.68) when the cursor finds an available object to attach.

 5. Click the rectangle. Notice that it turns white as it becomes part of the selected object.

 6. Click the Attach button again to deactivate it.

FIGURE 3.68
Attach the new rectangle to the existing wall.

You've just attached the rectangle to the wall you selected at the beginning of this exercise. Earlier, you saw how the Outline option created two concentric rectangles to form a rectangular wall. That was a clue that objects can contain multiple splines. The outer and inner walls of that rectangular wall are separate splines contained within the same object. In this exercise, you added the rectangle you just created to the wall of the previous exercise.

 Next, you'll see how you can trim the parts of the rectangle that you don't need:

 1. Click the Zoom Region tool.

 2. Place a Zoom window around the intersection of the walls and the intersecting rectangle. Your drawing area should look like Figure 3.69.

 3. With the wall selected, click the Spline button in the Selection rollout.

FIGURE 3.69
Zoom into this area.

4. Locate the Trim button in the Geometry rollout (you may need to scroll down the rollout) and click it.

5. After you click the Trim button, place the cursor on the upper-left corner of the rectangle. Notice how the cursor changes to a graphic that indicates the Trim operation.

6. Click the rectangle in the location shown in Figure 3.70. The corner of the rectangle is trimmed back to the wall.

7. Click the Trim button to deactivate it.

8. Click the Zoom Extents tool to get an overall view of the walls.

The Trim tool will trim a spline to the nearest spline that is a part of the same object. Trim ignores any splines that are not included in the current object. This is why you needed to attach the rectangle before you used the Trim tool.

You can continue to trim a spline by clicking the side you want to trim. The spline will then trim back to the nearest spline that is part of the currently selected object. Figure 3.71 shows an example of what the rectangle would look like if you continued to click the remaining endpoints of the rectangle with Trim activated.

FIGURE 3.70
Select the portion of the rectangle to be trimmed.

FIGURE 3.71
Click the endpoints of the rectangle to trim it back to the outside of the wall.

You won't be trimming the rectangle any farther than you have in step 6. Instead, in a later exercise in this chapter, you'll use the rectangle in its current configuration to learn how you can merge two sets of lines using the Boolean tools.

Now let's see how you go about adding a rounded corner to a spline using the Fillet tool:

1. Scroll to the Selection rollout and click the Vertex option.

2. Click the Select Object tool and click the lower-right corner of the rectangle. You'll see the axis tripod appear at the corner along with the Bezier handles, as shown in Figure 3.72.

3. Scroll down the Command panel until you see the Fillet button in the Geometry rollout.

4. Click/drag the Fillet input box spinner up. Notice what happens to the corner: as you move the spinner, the corner turns into a radius. Don't release the mouse button just yet.

5. Adjust the spinner until the Fillet value reads 5′0.0″ and then release the mouse button. (If you release the mouse button before you get to 5′0″, click the Undo button and try again.) You could also just type **5**↵ in the Fillet text box. Your completed fillet should look like Figure 3.73.

FIGURE 3.72
Select the lower-right vertex of the trimmed rectangle.

FIGURE 3.73
Filleting the corner

The Fillet tool is an option of the Vertex sub-object level, so you need to be in the Vertex sub-object editing mode before you can use it.

Now, to finish off the new wall, use the Outline tool once again:

1. Access the Spline sub-object level.

2. If it isn't already selected, click the Select Object tool, and then click the filleted rectangle. It turns red when it's selected.

3. Scroll down the Command panel to get to the Outline tool on the Geometry rollout.

4. Enter 5″↵ in the Outline tool's input box. The rectangle is outlined.

5. Click the Maximize Viewport Toggle to view all of the viewports.

6. Scroll up the Command panel, and then click Extrude in the modifier stack.

7. Save the walls you've drawn as a file named My_Walls.max.

Because the rectangle is attached to the Wall spline you created earlier, it's also affected by the Extrude modifier. Look at your model from the Perspective viewport to see this effect. Figure 3.74 shows your model up to this point, from an angle that shows all the components.

As you work with splines, you'll see that the type of tool options you can use to edit a spline depend on the sub-object type you select in the Selection rollout or the modifier stack. Fillets and Bezier curves can be edited when the Vertex sub-object level is selected. Trim is available when you select the Spline sub-object level. The Attach option is available in object mode as well as in all sub-object levels.

FIGURE 3.74
The perspective
view of the walls

Joining Closed Splines with Boolean Tools

In the previous exercise, you combined the rectangle with a wall to form a wall object that is made up of two splines. The added rectangle protrudes into the wall that it is joined with, as shown in an enlarged view of the walls in Figure 3.75.

FIGURE 3.75
The walls joined
at a corner

These wall intersections are
actually overlapping splines.

Although these wall intersections do not adversely affect your ability to work with the model in many situations, you may eventually want to merge the wall intersections into a clean joint. This is important, however, when working with several of the advanced lighting tools. You can clean up these intersections by using spline Boolean operations. Boolean operations combine two spline sub-objects using one of three distinct operations. The Union Boolean operation combines two overlapping splines to form a single spline by creating vertices where the segments cross and by deleting any segments that are within the shared area of the new shape. The Subtract operation deletes one spline and any area shared by the two splines. Finally, the Intersection operation deletes all areas that are not shared by both splines. Spline Boolean operations work only when both splines are closed.

1. Make sure the Top viewport is active, and then click the Maximize Viewport Toggle to display only the Top viewport.

2. Select Line from the modifier stack.

3. Access the Spline sub-object level, select the filleted wall, and then scroll down the Command panel to the Geometry rollout until you see the Boolean button.

4. Next to the Boolean button, click the Union button and then click the Boolean button. In the Top viewport, move your cursor to the other wall that is connected with the currently selected wall, as shown in Figure 3.76.

Notice that the cursor shows a graphic indicating that it has found a candidate for the Boolean operation.

FIGURE 3.76
Selecting the wall
for the Boolean
operation

5. Click the wall. The wall intersections form a neat connection.

6. Scroll up the Command panel and click Line in the modifier stack to exit the sub-object level. You can now see the corners more clearly, as shown in Figure 3.77.

7. Select Extrude from the modifier stack to restore the wall height.

You can use the Boolean tool to join any closed splines, such as those that form the two walls from the previous exercise. Figure 3.78 shows some examples of other splines that are joined using this tool. Besides joining spline outlines, you can subtract outlines or obtain the intersection of two outlines.

FIGURE 3.77
The wall intersections after using the Boolean tool

FIGURE 3.78
Examples of Boolean operations on closed splines

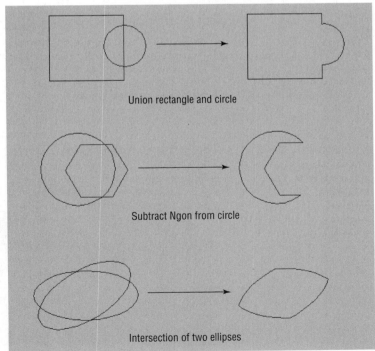

Union rectangle and circle

Subtract Ngon from circle

Intersection of two ellipses

SPLINE BOOLEANS DIFFER FROM BOOLEAN COMPOUND OBJECTS

In Chapter 4, "Editing Meshes and Creating Complex Objects," you'll learn about the ProBoolean compound objects, which create new objects by combining existing ones through Boolean operations. Boolean operations with compound objects are different from those created through the Boolean options in the object's Spline sub-object level.

To perform these other types of Boolean operations, follow the same steps you used to join the wall intersections in the previous exercise; however, before you select the object to be joined, click the appropriate Boolean option (the buttons to the right of the Boolean tool button).

Creating a Solid Form with Splines

You've been using splines to create outline shapes such as the profile of the wineglass and the walls of a floor plan. You can also create solid forms like those of the primitive objects you saw in the previous chapter. Splines let you go beyond the primitive forms of circles, rectangles, and squares to make just about any shape you need.

In the following exercise, you'll use a spline to create a ceiling for the walls that you've created so far. This involves creating an outline of the walls and then using the Extrude modifier to give the outline some thickness.

Start by setting up a view that will make it easier to add the ceiling:

1. Adjust the view of the Perspective viewport so that you can see the entire top edge of the walls, as shown in Figure 3.79.

2. Next, set up the snaps to accurately place the spline at the perimeter of the walls. Right-click the Snaps Toggle.

3. In the Grid and Snap Settings dialog box, click Clear All, and then click the Endpoint check box.

4. Close the Grid and Snap Settings dialog box.

5. Make sure the Snaps Toggle option is on.

FIGURE 3.79
The completed
structure so far

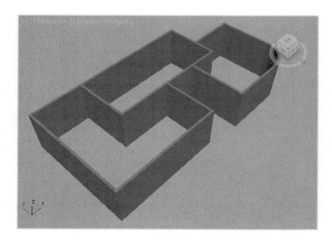

Now you're ready to add the spline that will become the ceiling:

1. Click the Create tab of the Command panel, and then click the Shapes tool if it isn't already selected.

2. Click the Line tool.

3. Click the outside corners of the walls, as shown in Figure 3.80. When you get to the rounded corner, click the point indicated in the figure. You'll move and reshape that corner later.

4. When you return to the starting corner, click it. In the Spline dialog box, click Yes to close the spline.

FIGURE 3.80
Drawing the
Roof spline

Select the new endpoint at the top outside
of the wall for the rounded corner.

Start the line
at this corner.

Continue to select the
top outside endpoints.

Now you have the Roof plane outlined with a spline. Next, you need to make an adjustment to the corner where the walls are rounded:

1. With the Ceiling spline selected, click the Modify tab in the Command panel.

2. Turn off the Snaps Toggle and access the Vertex level; then click the Select and Move tool in the Main Toolbar.

3. Click the vertex at the corner where the wall is rounded, as shown in Figure 3.81.

FIGURE 3.81
Moving the vertex

FIGURE 3.81
Moving the vertex

4. Click the Absolute Mode Transform Type-In button at the bottom of the 3ds Max window to switch to Offset mode. While in Offset mode, you don't enter the actual coordinates, just the distance from the current location.

5. Enter -5′ in the Y input field as shown in Figure 3.82, and then press ↵. The lines are aligned with the original wall.

6. Scroll down to the Geometry rollout in the Modify tab of the Command panel until you see the Fillet tool.

7. Click the Fillet input box so that the entire value is highlighted, and then enter 5′↵. The corner is filleted to match the wall, as shown in Figure 3.83.

8. Click the Offset Mode Transform Type-In button to switch back to Absolute mode.

FIGURE 3.82
Moving the vertex using the Transform Type-In spinner arrows

FIGURE 3.83
The spline after filleting

For the final operation, you need to give the new spline an area with thickness. Typically, you would make a ceiling around 10″ to 12″ thick between floors of a building. Use the Extrude modifier to extrude the spline to a thickness of 12″.

1. Click the Line level in the modifier stack so you're not on any sub-object level. Scroll up to the top of the Command panel and click the Modifier List drop-down arrow.

2. Click the Extrude modifier.

3. Go to the Parameters rollout, click the Amount input box, and enter **12″**↵. The spline extrudes into a thick, slablike object in the shape of the wall outline, as shown in Figure 3.84.

4. Click the Maximize Viewport Toggle to see the walls in all the viewports.

5. If any of the ceiling's corners appear rounded instead of sharp, select Line in the modifier stack and then access the Vertex sub-object level.

6. Select any offending vertices, right-click, and choose Corner from the quad menu.

7. Save your scene, overwriting the file named My_Walls.max.

You extruded the ceiling outline only 12″, but it could easily have been extruded several feet. You can also copy the spline vertically and use the Outline tool to form the exterior walls of a second floor.

You've seen a few examples of using splines to create walls and a ceiling. There are many ways to create walls, as you'll learn in later chapters. For now, let's move on to the other spline types.

FIGURE 3.84
The finished ceiling on top of the walls

Introducing the Other Spline Types

You've already used the Line spline and the Rectangle spline, and you've gotten some practice in editing them. Before you continue, you'll want to know a little about the other spline types. Table 3.2 shows the various spline options, how they are created, and some of the editing characteristics of each object.

TABLE 3.2: Creation Methods for Splines

SPLINE NAME AND FUNCTION	CREATION METHOD	CREATION OPTIONS*	PARAMETERS*
Line—Draws splines	Click points to place line segments. Click and drag adds smoothing when Smooth is selected for Initial or Drag Type group.	*Initial Type:* Corner/Smooth *Drag Type:* Corner/Smooth/ Bezier	Lines are not parametric objects.
Circle—Draws circles	Click center and drag radius [Center]. Or click two points to locate points on circumference edge [Edge].	Edge/Center	Radius.
Arc—Draws arcs	Click to place first endpoint and drag to place second endpoint, and then adjust and click for radius [End-End-Middle]. Or click center, drag to radius and first end, and click second end [Center-End-End].	End-End-Middle/ Center-End-End	Radius, From, To, Pie Slice (creates pie-slice shape with line segments from the center to each endpoint), Reverse.
NGon—Draws regular polygons	Click center, and then drag to place radius [Center]. Or click to place one edge, and then drag for other edge [Edge].	Edge/Center	Radius, Inscribed/ Circumscribed, [number of] Sides, Corner Radius, Circular.
Text—Draws text	Click to place text.	Input box for entering text	Font, Size, Kerning, Justification, Italic, Underline Leading, Text, Manual Update.
Section—Draws a section plane and creates a 2D spline along the location where an intersecting object crosses the plane	Click to place section center point, and drag to place corner. Create Shape button creates the spline outline.	*Update:* When section moves/ When section selected/ Manually *Selection Extents:* Infinite/Section Boundary/Off	Length, Width.
Rectangle—Draws rectangles with or without curved corners	Click first corner and drag for other corner [Edge]. Or click center and drag for corner [Center].	Edge/Center	Length, Width, Corner Radius.

TABLE 3.2: Creation Methods for Splines (*CONTINUED*)

SPLINE NAME AND FUNCTION	CREATION METHOD	CREATION OPTIONS*	PARAMETERS*
Ellipse—Draws ellipses	Click first tangent edge and drag for other edge [Edge]. Or click center and drag for edge [Center].	Edge/Center	Length, Width.
Donut—Draws a donut shape: two concentric circles	Click first point on circumference and drag for second point on circumference; click for second radius [Edge]. Or click center and drag for first radius; click for second radius [Center].	Edge/Center	Radius 1, Radius 2.
Star—Draws star shape	Click center and drag for first radius; click again for second radius.		Radius 1, Radius 2, [number of] Points [of star], Distortion [twist], Fillet Radius 1, Fillet Radius 2.
Helix—Draws a 3D helix (spiral)	Click first circumference point, drag second circumference point, click height, click second radius [Edge]. Or click center, drag first radius, click height, and click second radius [Center].	Edge/Center	Radius 1, Radius 2, Height, Turns, Bias, CW [clockwise]/CCW [counterclockwise].

Items separated by a slash (/) denote radio button options. Italics denote button group names.

You may want to experiment by creating some different splines in a separate file. Remember that you can extrude most of them into the third dimension by using the Extrude or Bevel modifiers and the Loft compound object, which extrudes a shape along a spline path (you'll learn about lofting in Chapter 7, "Organizing and Editing Objects").

Common parameters among all of the shape primitives are found in the Rendering and Interpolation rollouts. In the Rendering rollout, you can force 3ds Max to render a two-dimensional spline as if it were a three-dimensional object complete with surfaces. The Interpolation rollout contains controls for adjusting the number of steps, or straight segments, between each vertex. The more steps a shape has, the smoother the curves are, but this results in a more complex object when the shape is lofted or extruded.

In addition to the Splines group of objects that are created from the Shapes tool, there are also NURBS curves and a small library of newer shapes called Extended Splines consisting of common structural steel cross sections. The NURBS Curves and Extended Splines options are accessed from the drop-down list above the Object Type rollout when the Shapes button is active. Table 3.3 discusses the Extended Spline types and options.

TABLE 3.3: Creation Methods for Extended Splines

SPLINE NAME AND FUNCTION	CREATION METHOD	CREATION OPTIONS*	PARAMETERS*
WRectangle—Draws offset rectangular splines with or without corner radii	Click first corner and drag for other corner; then click for inner offset [Edge]. Or click center and drag for corner, and then click for inner offset [Center]	Edge/Center	Length, Width, Thickness, Sync Corner Fillets, Corner Radius 1, Corner Radius 2.
Angle—Draws an "L" shape	Click first corner and drag for other corner; then click for inner offset [Edge]. Or click center and drag for corner, and then click for inner offset [Center]	Edge/Center	Length, Width, Thickness, Sync Corner Fillets, Corner Radius 1, Corner Radius 2, Edge Radii.
Wide Flange—Draws an "I" shape	Click first corner and drag for other corner; then click for inner offset [Edge]. Or click center and drag for corner; then click for inner offset [Center]	Edge/Center	Length, Width, Thickness, Corner Radius.
Channel—Draws a "C" shape	Click first corner and drag for other corner; then click for inner offset [Edge]. Or click center and drag for corner, and then click for inner offset [Center]	Edge/Center	Length, Width, Thickness, Sync Corner Fillets, Corner Radius 1, Corner Radius 2.
Tee—Draws a "T" shape	Click first corner and drag for other corner; then click for inner offset [Edge]. Or click center and drag for corner; then click for inner offset [Center]	Edge/Center	Length, Width, Thickness, Corner Radius.

*Items separated by a slash (/) denote radio button options.

Editing Splines

You've seen how you can edit the rectangle and line through the Modify tab of the Command panel. In most cases, you need to select the Edit Spline modifier from the Modifier List dropdown to gain access to the sub-object levels of a spline where parametric controls are usually shown.

The exception to this is the Line spline, which will display its sub-object level options as soon as you select the Modify tab.

Once you've selected Edit Spline, you can make changes to the vertices, segments, or splines by entering the corresponding sub-object level of the Edit Spline modifier. You can even attach or detach components of a spline to create new forms, as you'll see in the next chapter.

Another way to access a spline's sub-object level is to convert it into an editable spline. This is accomplished by right-clicking the object name in the modifier stack and selecting Convert To: Editable Spline from the context menu.

You can also right-click the object in the viewport and choose Convert to ➤ Convert to Editable Spline from the quad menu.

This exposes the sub-object level of the selected spline in a way similar to the Edit Spline modifier, but it does so by permanently converting the spline to an editable spline. The spline then loses its parametric functions.

After modifying a spline's sub-objects using the Edit Spline modifier, especially if vertices are added or removed, editing the spline at its top level may yield unpredictable results. For this reason, converting a parametric shape into an editable spline is often preferred over using the Edit Spline modifier. If you want to experiment with the spline's sub-objects but are not sure if the end result will be adequate, use the Edit Spline modifier first. If the desired shape is created, convert the object into an editable spline. If not, simply delete the modifier to return the shape to its unaltered configuration.

In this chapter, you have learned how to draw splines with the traditional tools in 3ds Max Design 2011. The Graphite Modeling Tools provide some alternate ways to sketch splines that can be used for many purposes. For example, you can use the Polydraw panel to sketch splines on grids or on the topology of other Edit Poly objects that can automatically create polygons when you create quadrilaterals with the splines you draw.

COLLAPSING TO AN EDITABLE SPLINE REDUCES MEMORY USAGE

Collapsing a spline with modifiers to an editable spline helps reduce the memory usage for your scene. 3ds Max must use additional memory from your system in order to maintain the parameters of objects as well as the modifiers in the stack. If you convert a spline to an editable spline, 3ds Max no longer needs to draw on that additional memory for the spline. As your scene becomes larger, these memory issues become more important. On the other hand, using the Edit Spline modifier consumes more memory than converting a primitive spline shape to an editable spline, but you have the best of both worlds—parametric and explicit control.

Placing and Beveling Text

3ds Max treats text as a parametric spline with parameters that control many features found in word processing software. Text can be justified, bold, and italicized; the space between letters can be adjusted (kerned); the space between lines can be adjusted (leaded); and the 3ds Max text object can use any Windows fonts. 3ds Max is far from a robust text editor, but you will find most of the tools necessary to add text-based geometry to your scenes, including cutting and pasting text from TXT files into the Text tool's Text field.

You've noticed that, when you create objects, they are created on and oriented to either the home grid or a user grid. 3ds Max also has the ability to create grids on the fly using the surfaces of scene geometry as the basis for the grid's location and orientation. This feature is accessed by checking the AutoGrid check box in the Object Type rollout. AutoGrid is available whenever you create any type of geometry or shape primitive and remains active until the box is unchecked.

The following exercises explain the use of Text, AutoGrid, and the Bevel modifier:

1. Choose File ➢ Open and open the `Signage.max` file from the book's companion web page. The file consists of a rectangular sign with a curved border, as shown in Figure 3.85. The sign has been rotated off the home grid.

2. Click Create ➢ Shapes ➢ Splines in the Command panel.

FIGURE 3.85
The rectangular sign from the Signage.max file

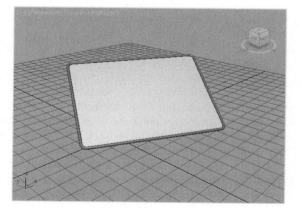

3. Click the Text button in the Object Type rollout and then select the AutoGrid check box.

4. Drag your cursor over the sign in the viewport and notice that the axis tripod orients its axes to whichever face the cursor is over at any given time, as shown in Figure 3.86.

5. With the cursor over the central part of the sign, click the mouse to place the default "MAX Text" text in the scene and on top of the sign. The text is created, but it is too large for the sign (see Figure 3.87). Uncheck AutoGrid.

FIGURE 3.86
With the AutoGrid feature active, the axis tripod orients itself to the face over which the cursor is placed.

FIGURE 3.87
Placing new text on the board with AutoGrid turned on

THE START NEW SHAPE OPTION

You may have noticed the Start New Shape option near the top of the Splines Object Type rollout. When this option is unchecked, each shape created becomes a spline sub-object of a greater spline object, rather than individual, parametric spline objects. This option is checked by default.

6. In the Parameters rollout, select a font from the drop-down list and then adjust the Size value to change the text to a more appropriate size. Select the text in the Text field and replace it with the words that you want to appear on your sign.

Different fonts can yield different results when modifiers are applied to them. This is usually the result of using a font with tight corners or thin areas, and then beveling the text in such a manner that it is forced to cross over itself. In other cases the fonts are designed poorly and don't work well when extruded or beveled. This exercise uses the Book Antiqua Bold font with a Size parameter set to 2´3˝.

CYCLING THROUGH THE FONT OPTIONS

With the font highlighted in the Parameters rollout, use the up and down arrow keys to cycle through the fonts and observe how each looks in the viewports. If you use the arrows in the numeric keypad, make sure Num Lock is not turned on.

The text assumes the characteristics that you assigned, but its location on the sign is too low. To move it properly, you must use the Local Reference Coordinate System, which uses the X-, Y-, and Z-orientation of the selected object rather than using the World Coordinate System.

1. Click the Select and Move button on the Main Toolbar.

2. To the right of the transform tools, expand the Reference Coordinate System drop-down list and select Local as shown in Figure 3.88.

3. Select the text and notice that the Move Transform gizmo is oriented to the text. Place the cursor over the XY-plane handle and move the text into place, as shown in Figure 3.89.

FIGURE 3.88
Choose the Local coordinate system

FIGURE 3.89
Moving the text into place

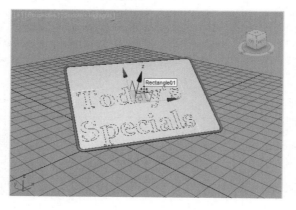

Most real-world objects that you will find outside of a machine shop do not have perpendicular faces that join at sharp angles. They usually have a curved (filleted) or straight (chamfered) transition between the surfaces. Although it may not be obvious visually, this transition in your scene will appear more realistic to the viewers by creating a condition that they are used to seeing. With proper lighting, the transition surfaces can generate a specular highlight, subtly

calling attention to the condition. The Extrude modifier does not provide for a fillet or chamfer, but these features can be found in the Bevel modifier's option, as explained in the following steps. Although this example uses text, the Bevel modifier can be used with any spline.

The Bevel modifier's Bevel Values group has controls for setting the height and outline amount at three different locations perpendicular to the spline's current location. The Outline value is an offset size that the shape assumes, at the specified Height value, relative to its original size.

Add the Bevel modifier to your text using the following steps:

1. Select the text, click the Modify tab, and then choose Bevel from the Modifier List drop-down.

2. In the Bevel Values rollout, set the Level 1 Height parameter to 3″ and leave Outline set to 0.0″. This will generate an initial straight segment for the letters.

3. Check the Level 2 check box. Set the Level 2 Height to 0.25″ and the Outline to -0.25″.

4. Zoom into the letters to see the chamfered effect of the Bevel modifier, as shown in Figure 3.90.

5. In the Parameters rollout, select Curved Sides in the Surface group, set Segments to 4, and select the Smooth Across Levels check box. These settings will generally soften the transition between levels and, when a small Outline value is present, can create a ridge around the perimeter of the splines, as shown in Figure 3.91.

FIGURE 3.90
The chamfered effect of the Bevel modifier

FIGURE 3.91
Smoothing the transition between surfaces

The Bottom Line

Draw shapes with splines Two-dimensional splines can be used as the building blocks for more complex, three-dimensional objects. You can draw splines from scratch using the Line tool or start with a parametric shape and then collapse it to an editable spline.

Master It Create a rainbow-shaped set of splines—in other words, a series of concentric arcs.

Outline and extrude splines Outlining splines provides a way to create a new spline subobject that parallels the original. This is faster and more accurate than creating the second spline manually and then attaching it to the original. Extruding splines is the most common method for creating 3D objects from 2D splines.

Master It A column surround is a shell that covers a structural column to give it a more appealing appearance. Create a 16′-tall, 2″-thick, semicircular column surround with a 16′ outside radius.

Modify closed splines with Boolean tools Nearly any shape can be formed using the standard Editable Spline two or more simple shapes and combine them for a more complex shape.

Master It Using the spline Boolean tools, create the cross-sectional shape of a fluted column, similar to the shape shown here.

Chapter 4

Editing Meshes and Creating Complex Objects

In the three previous chapters, you spent some time becoming familiar with 3ds Max. In this chapter, you'll continue exploring 3ds Max's features while exercising your newfound skills. You'll start by learning how to add openings to the walls you created in Chapter 3, "Creating Shapes with Splines." Then you'll learn how you can import scanned images that you can use to trace. In the process of tracing a floor plan, you'll further explore methods for creating and editing forms using splines. You'll also be introduced to ways you can edit the extruded shapes that you have created, as well as edit any other mesh object. In this chapter, you'll learn to:

- Create openings with ProBoolean operations
- Designate a modeling template image
- Create and modify objects using box modeling
- Attach objects to a mesh
- Create clones with Array and Snapshot

Creating Openings in a Wall with Boolean Operations

In Chapter 3, you created a set of walls that completely enclosed a space. Now you need to add wall openings between the enclosed spaces of your model. To do this, you'll use *Boolean* operations to remove portions of a wall.

A BRIEF HISTORY OF BOOLEANS

Boolean operations are named after George Boole, who developed a mathematical branch of symbolic logic. Boolean logic includes AND, OR, and NOT operators, which correspond to geometric union, intersection, and subtraction.

Boolean operations are methods you can use to join two objects, subtract the shape of one object from another, or obtain a shape that is the intersection of two objects. Figure 4.1 illustrates the effect of Boolean operations on some sample shapes.

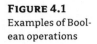

FIGURE 4.1
Examples of Boolean operations

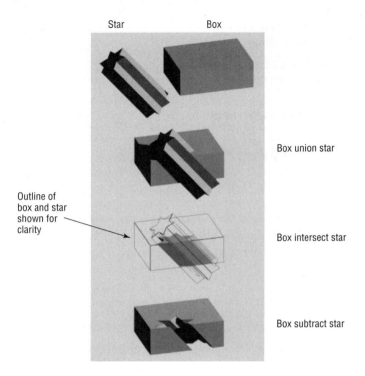

Star Box

Box union star

Outline of box and star shown for clarity

Box intersect star

Box subtract star

3ds Max allows you to use two existing objects to form one new object using Boolean operations. The original objects are referred to as the *operands* of the Boolean operations, and they are not deleted when the operation is performed; they become sub-objects of the resultant Boolean object. In the following exercise, you'll use a simple box to define the opening in your walls. The existing wall is one operand, and the box that forms the opening is the other operand.

3ds Max now has the ProBoolean and ProCutter compound objects. The ProBoolean compound object has the classic three Boolean operations and adds Merge, Attach, and Insert. You can also use the Imprint and Cookie Cutter options to further enhance your operations. The ProBoolean tools keep the history of operations; you can modify the operators or change the ordering of operators anytime you want. You can even change an operation's type (for example, change a subtracted operand to a union operand). The ProBoolean operations create better geometry than the original Boolean tools in 3ds Max. They provide you enormous flexibility in creating objects for your visualizations.

Hiding Shapes That Get in the Way

Start by setting up your wall model and creating an object you'll use to subtract from the walls.

1. Open the My_Walls.max model you created in the previous chapter, or open MyWalls04 .max that you downloaded from www.sybex.com/go/mastering3dsmaxdesign2011.

2. If your 3ds Max window shows only a single viewport, click the Maximize Viewport Toggle to view the four viewports.

 You'll need to hide the ceiling of your model in order to more easily work on the model. Here's a quick way to temporarily hide objects if they're in your way.

3. Right-click in the viewport, choose Select from the quad menu, and then click to select the ceiling.

4. Click in the Name input box in the Name and Color rollout in the Command panel and change the name to **Ceiling**, as shown in Figure 4.2. This will help you find the ceiling later.

5. Right-click in the viewport and choose Hide Selection from the quad menu (see Figure 4.3). The ceiling disappears.

6. The ceiling hasn't really gone anywhere—you've just hidden it. Just so you know where to look when you do need to turn it back on, right-click again and choose Unhide by Name from the quad menu, as shown in Figure 4.4.

The Unhide Objects dialog box appears, as shown in Figure 4.5.

7. You can see that Ceiling is listed in the dialog box. To turn it back on, you would click the name in the list and then click Unhide. You want to keep it off for now, so click Cancel.

The display functions shown in this section are also available from the Display tab of the Command panel and by selecting Tools ➢ Display Floater.

FIGURE 4.2
Rename an object in the Command panel.

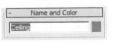

FIGURE 4.3
Using the quad menu, hide the selected object.

FIGURE 4.4
Unhide the selected object.

FIGURE 4.5
The Unhide Objects dialog box

Creating the Shape of the Opening

Now you're ready to get to work on the walls. Your first step is to create the shape of the opening. You can think of this shape as the negative space of the opening or as the shape that is to be removed from the wall.

1. Click in the Top viewport to make it active.

2. Click the Zoom Extents tool so that you can see the entire plan in the viewport.

3. Click the Geometry tool in the Create tab of the Command panel and make sure Standard Primitives is selected in the drop-down list.

4. Click the Box button in the Object Type rollout. Then, in the Top viewport, click and drag a rectangle that is roughly 3′ × 3′ square to the location shown in Figure 4.6. You don't need to draw the box precisely, because you'll enter the exact dimensions in the Parameters rollout.

5. Make the height of the box roughly 7′.

6. Go to the Parameters rollout of the Create tab and set the Length and Width values to 3′ and Height to 6′8″.

 You now have a box that will be used to create an opening. The next steps are to place the box in the locations for the openings.

7. Click the Select and Move tool in the Main Toolbar and move the box to the location on the left, as shown in Figure 4.7. Remember that you need to place the cursor on the selected object. Then, when you see the Move cursor, click and drag the object into position.

8. Shift+click and drag the box to make a copy of the box in the location to the right, as shown in Figure 4.7.

9. In the Clone Options dialog box, click Copy and then click OK.

FIGURE 4.6
Placing the box
in the plan

FIGURE 4.7
Positioning the boxes in the doorway locations

Move the box here. Make a copy here.

Subtracting the Opening from the Wall

Now that you have the object ready, you can use the ProBoolean tool to subtract it from the wall. First, you'll select the object from which you want to subtract the opening—this is referred to as *Operand 0*. Afterward, you'll select the object to subtract, called *Operand 1*.

1. Click the Select Object tool and click the first wall you created, as shown in Figure 4.8.

2. Click the drop-down list under the row of tools near the top of the Command panel, and then select Compound Objects as shown in Figure 4.9.

3. Click the ProBoolean button in the Object Type rollout. The ProBoolean options appear in the Command panel.

FIGURE 4.8
Selecting the wall for the Boolean operation

Operand 0; select Operand 1; select
this object first. this object second.

FIGURE 4.9
Starting the creation process for compound objects

4. Scroll down the Command panel to the Parameters rollout and make sure that the Subtraction radio button is selected (Figure 4.10).

5. Click the Start Picking button in the Pick Boolean rollout.

6. Click the box that intersects the wall, as shown in Figure 4.8.

If you look in the Perspective viewport, you'll see that an opening appears in the wall where you located the box, as shown in Figure 4.11.

FIGURE 4.10
Choose the Boolean operation to be performed.

FIGURE 4.11
The opening in the wall

PROBOOLEANS ARE MORE POWERFUL THAN BOOLEANS

You may have noticed the Boolean option under the Object Type rollout. This is the older Boolean tool developed with 3ds Max. This tool is at least 15 years old; it was part of the first release of 3ds Max in 1995. ProBoolean was a more powerful plug-in available for 3ds Max that has been incorporated into the program.

Now repeat the operation for the other wall:

1. Click the Select Object button to exit the ProBoolean tool and then click the second wall, as shown in Figure 4.12.

 This becomes the first operand for the next Boolean operation.

2. Click the ProBoolean button in the Object Type rollout of the Command panel.

3. Click the Start Picking button, and then select the box, as shown in Figure 4.12. The second opening appears, as shown in Figure 4.13. You may need to Orbit your viewport a little to get a better view of the new opening.

FIGURE 4.12
Selecting the wall and box for the second opening

Select the wall object first. Select the box second.

FIGURE 4.13
The Perspective viewport showing the second opening

In this example, you created a simple rectangular opening in the wall. The shape of the opening can be anything you want it to be. You just need to create the geometry, using primitives or extruded splines. In addition, the object that you're subtracting from doesn't need to be thin like the wall in this example. It can be any geometry you want, and the subtracted shape will leave its impression. Figure 4.14 shows some examples of other Boolean subtractions to give you an idea of other possibilities.

FIGURE 4.14
Some samples of Boolean subtractions

Creating Multiple Openings in a Single Wall

You can perform multiple ProBoolean operations on any 3D object, such as creating several openings in one wall. To do this, you only need to continue selecting objects while the Start Picking button is selected. All of the objects selected become operands of the Boolean operation.

If you've deselected a ProBoolean object, simply reselect it, click the Modify tab, click the Start Picking button, and then continue picking operands. If you have a number of objects to subtract from another, after you have clicked the Start Picking button, you can press the H key on the keyboard to bring up the Select from Scene dialog box and select all of the objects for your operation. All of the objects will appear in the Operands display; they can still be reordered and modified as if you had selected them individually.

If you collapse a ProBoolean object to an Editable Mesh or Editable Poly you lose the operands history. This means you cannot edit the openings by going back and changing the size of the boxes. You can, however, edit openings in the object at sub-object levels.

Making Changes to the Opening

Suppose that you decide to increase the size of one of the openings. You can go back and modify the box used as the Boolean operand so that it's wider. This, in turn, will increase the opening size.

1. Click the Select Object tool in the Main Toolbar and click the first wall, as shown in Figure 4.15.

2. Click the Modify tab in the Command panel. Scroll down to the Display section of the Parameters rollout and click the Operands radio button. The box reappears in the viewports.

3. Scroll down to the bottom of the Parameters rollout, and then click the 1: Subtr – Box001 item in the selection field. See Figure 4.16.

FIGURE 4.15
Moving the operand to change the location of the wall opening

Select this wall.

Resize operand and move to this location.

FIGURE 4.16
Selecting the subtraction operation

4. Notice that Box is now listed in the modifier stack at the top of the Command panel. Click the Box item. See Figure 4.17.

The Command panel options change to show the parameters for the box.

5. In the Parameters rollout, change the Width value to 6′. Notice how the box changes in the viewports as you edit the Width parameter.

6. Go back to the top of the modifier stack and select ProBoolean.

7. Scroll down to the Parameters rollout and click the Result radio button, shown in Figure 4.18.

FIGURE 4.17
Selecting the Box
in the stack

FIGURE 4.18
Display the result.

Now you can see the result of your edit in the Perspective viewport. The opening is now 6′ wide instead of 3′ wide.

Besides altering the shape of the box, you can also reposition it to change the location of the opening in the wall. Here's how it's done:

1. Click the Operands radio button in the Parameters rollout again to view the box.

2. Scroll up the Command panel to the modifier stack and click the plus (+) sign next to the ProBoolean option, and then click the Operands entry. It highlights to indicate that it is selected. See Figure 4.19.

3. Click the Select and Move tool in the Main Toolbar. Then click and drag the box to the left, in the -X direction, so that it passes through the corner of the wall, as shown earlier in Figure 4.15.

4. Click Operands again in the modifier stack, or click the top ProBoolean entry to exit the sub-object level (the yellow color disappears).

FIGURE 4.19
Selecting the Oper-
ands sub-object

5. Scroll down the Parameters rollout and click the Result radio button. The new wall opening configuration appears in the Perspective viewport, as shown in Figure 4.20.

6. Save the `Mywalls04.max` file incrementally by choosing File ➢ Save As and clicking the plus (+) button in the Save File As dialog box. The file will be named `My_Walls01.max` if you continued from the previous chapter or `Mywalls05.max` if you used the file provided.

FIGURE 4.20
The result of moving the box operand

The tricky part of moving the opening in this exercise is making sure that the sub-object level is active and that the proper operand is selected at the bottom of the Parameters rollout.

These exercises demonstrate that you can alter the shape of the opening by modifying the parameters of the object you used to create the opening. The trick here is to know how to get to the box operand in order to edit its parameters. It's a good idea to first make the subtracted operand visible. It's not absolutely necessary, but it helps to see the operand as you make changes. Use the modifier stack to gain access to the operand. Once there, you can access the operand's parameters and make changes to its geometry or change its location. To change the location of either of the operands within a compound object, go to the Operands sub-object level and select the operand. The operands are considered sub-objects of the ProBoolean compound object. Like almost everything else in 3ds Max, this can be animated. You can use ProBoolean animations to make quick animations of objects appearing or disappearing.

Tracing a Sketch

You cannot always predict when or where you'll have a brilliant design idea. Frequently, ideas arise when you're sitting at a table during a brainstorming session or perhaps even while you are out eating lunch. The basic tools of pencil and paper offer the spontaneity needed to express your ideas freely.

Once you've created an inspired sketch, 3ds Max offers a way to quickly transfer your inspiration into a 3D model. Among its view options, 3ds Max supplies a tool that displays a bitmap image in the viewports for a variety of purposes, including the tracing of scanned design sketches.

In this section, you'll continue your exploration of splines by importing a sketch and tracing it. You'll use a sketch that roughly approximates the floor plan of Notre Dame du Haut, more commonly known as the Chapel at Ronchamp, which was designed by Le Corbusier in 1950.

Figure 4.21 shows a photograph of one view of the famous building. If you use Google to search for images of the Ronchamp Chapel you'll find hundreds of photos that give views of all sides of this masterpiece of modern architecture.

By modeling this building, you will have the opportunity to examine how you might use splines to create shapes other than simple straight walls like those you created in the previous chapter. You'll also be introduced to other methods for modeling forms by combining splines and primitives.

FIGURE 4.21
Notre Dame du
Haut in Ronchamp

ENSURING YOUR BITMAPS APPEAR CORRECTLY

Depending on your installation, bitmaps used as template images may appear pixelated and be unusable. To ensure they look their best, before you start the next exercise, save your file and then choose Customize ➢ Preferences ➢ Viewports ➢ Configure Driver. In the Appearance Preferences Group, under Download Texture Size, select the highest resolution size listed and check the Match Bitmap Size as Closely as Possible option. Next, click OK, exit and restart 3ds Max, and then continue with the next exercise.

Using a Bitmap Image

Using a bitmap image as a modeling template is fairly simple, but you need to watch out for a few settings. In the following exercise, you'll import an image that is a sketch of the Ronchamp Chapel floor plan. The sketch shows a grid that is spaced at approximately 4.5 meters, as shown in Figure 4.22.

FIGURE 4.22
The bitmap image
of the Notre Dame
du Haut floor plan

You will apply this image onto a plane object, so first set up 3ds Max so that you can see only the maximized Top viewport.

ACCESSING THE BACKGROUND IMAGE

To access the background image, you'll need a file from this book's website (www.sybex.com/go/mastering3dsmaxdesign2011), so make sure you've installed the sample files before you start.

1. Choose File ➢ Reset, and click Yes at the reset query message.

2. Click the Create tab of the Command panel, and click the Plane button.

3. Press Alt+W to display four viewports, and then activate the Top viewport. Press Alt+W again to display the Top viewport as a single view. Now draw a plane that is about 20´ × 20´, and deselect the Real-World Map Size check box at the bottom of the rollout, as shown in Figure 4.23.

FIGURE 4.23
Creating the
image plane

4. With the Plane001 object selected, right-click the Select and Move icon on the Main Toolbar to open the Move Transform Type-In box.

5. Enter **0** for both the X and Y locations, and press Enter to center the plane on the world origin, as shown in Figure 4.24.

 Now you're ready to set up your scanned floor plan.

6. Click the Material Editor icon on the Main Toolbar to open the Material Editor, shown in Figure 4.25. Note there are now two different Material Editors in 3ds Max; here we're using the Compact Material Editor. The icon on the Main Toolbar is a flyout now, so make sure you've chosen the correct one. The icon should look like the one in the margin here.

 The Material Editor uses the renderer to display the sample spheres. If the sample spheres display as black holes, you'll need to change the renderer to the mental ray renderer. Choose Rendering ➤ Render Setup, close the Common Parameters rollout, and open the Assign Renderer rollout. Locate the Production Renderer field, and click the Choose Renderer button, marked with three dots. Choose the mental ray renderer and click OK. The Material Editor should now display the sample spheres correctly.

FIGURE 4.24
Centering the plane on the world origin

FIGURE 4.25
The Material Editor

You will be using the Material Editor here to set up your sketch to use as a modeling template. The Material Editor will be covered in more detail in Chapter 9, "Enhancing Models with Materials."

7. Pick the second sphere in the upper-left corner of the material samples. The thick, white border around the sample will indicate that it is selected.

8. Click in the Material Name box and rename 02 – Default to **RonchampPlan** so that you will know where you will use the material. Click the button to the right of the material name currently labeled Arch & Design to change the material type. In the Material/Map Browser's Materials rollout, click Architectural in the Standard materials and then click OK. This should change the material type to Architectural for the new material you are making. Note that changing the material type changes the available parameters and rollouts for the new material.

9. In the Physical Qualities rollout, click the button currently labeled None to the right of the Diffuse Map item. This will again bring up the Material/Map Browser.

10. To open the Select Bitmap Image File dialog, open Standard in the Maps rollout, and double-click the Bitmap entry at the top of the listing of available maps.

11. Navigate to where you downloaded the ronchampscan.gif file, select the file, and click the Open button.

12. In the Coordinates rollout, which is now visible in the Material Editor, deselect the Use Real-World Scale option. This causes the Width and Height fields to change to U and V.

13. Change the Tiling value for both U and V mapping coordinates to 1, and deselect the Tiling option for both. Click the Go To Parent button to go to the top level of the material you just created. Leave the Material Editor open.

14. Select the Plane001 object you created at the beginning of these exercises, and in the Name and Color field, rename the Plane to **RonchampPlanTemplate** so that you will be able to identify the object in the scene in the future.

15. With the RonchampPlanTemplate object selected, click the Assign Material to Selection button.

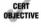

16. Click the Show Standard Map in Viewport button. The scanned image appears on the plane object in the Perspective viewport, as shown in Figure 4.26.

FIGURE 4.26
The Ronchamp image plane in the Perspective viewport

> ### How Resetting 3ds Max Differs from Starting a New File
>
> The difference between choosing File ➢ Reset and choosing File ➢ New is subtle, but there is an important distinction. When you reset the scene, you are starting completely over and everything defaults to the way it was when you first launched 3ds Max. When you create a new scene, it merely erases all the objects, leaving your scene seemingly empty; however, the new scene still has all the materials, units, and other settings as they were set before you chose File ➢ New.

Scaling the Image Plane to the Model's Size

The image appears stretched across the 20′ × 20′ plane that you created at the beginning of the exercise. You'll want to size the image plane so that it's to scale—that is, so that the distances represented by the image are the same as those in the 3ds Max model. You can approximate the correct scale, although you won't be able to get it exactly the same. Here's how it's done:

Start by setting up the units with which you'll be working.

1. Choose Customize ➢ Units Setup. The Units Setup dialog box displays (see Figure 4.27).

2. Click the Metric radio button and make sure Meters is displayed in the Metric drop-down list. Then click OK.

 You'll use meters in this example because this is a European building project. Now let's scale the image plane to the proper size.

3. Type **G** to toggle off the grid display.

 If you look at the scanned image carefully, you'll see a grid whose spacing is about 4.5 meters.

You see 10 reference grid spaces in the horizontal direction. By inspecting the image in an application such as Photoshop, you can determine that the grid lines are about 63 pixels apart and that the image is 640 × 470 pixels. You can use these numbers and the grid spacing interval estimate of 4.5 meters to determine that the entire image is 45.85 meters × 33.57 meters.

Figure 4.27
The Units Setup
dialog box

Now you will adjust the size of the image plane to accommodate the measurements of the sketch.

1. Select the RonchampPlanTemplate object and then click the Modify tab of the Command panel (see Figure 4.28).

 The Length and Width values are now shown in meters.

2. Set the Length value to 33.57 and the Width value to 45.85, based on the image scaling calculations. Change the image plane's Length and Width Segments to 4, as shown in Figure 4.29.

3. Press the **G** key to turn on the grid.

4. Click the Zoom Extents All button.

5. Press Alt+W to display four viewports if you're still in a single viewport.

6. Save your scene as **MyRonchamp01.max**

You will see your modeling template displayed in the Top and Perspective viewports, as shown in Figure 4.30.

FIGURE 4.28
The Parameters rollout for the Ronchamp PlanTemplate object

FIGURE 4.29
Sizing the Image Plane object

FIGURE 4.30
The ronchamp-scan.gif image applied to your plane object in the Top viewport

The RonchampPlanTemplate image plane that you have created may not be exactly the same size as the real chapel, but based on the estimate of the grid size of the hand-drawn sketch, it is probably as close as you can make it. If you had accurate dimensions from the actual structure that related to parts of the sketch, and if you knew the sketch was very accurate, you could get a much closer approximation of the size of the structure.

When creating 3D objects for visualization, it is crucial that you build all your objects at their real-world size. Doing so will help you significantly as you build a collection of objects and buildings that you can merge together to create more visually interesting scenes. If your objects are not built to real-world size, the objects will not relate to each other, and you will have to manually scale and guess at the sizes of objects to make them fit together correctly.

There are other reasons for building your objects at their real-world size. The mental ray materials that you will learn about in Chapter 9 are designed to work in real-world units. If you use those materials on objects that are not real-world size, the results can be unpredictable. The photometric lights are also intended to be used in models that are real-world size, and you will get the best results if your models are built to the correct real-world size.

> ### Avoid Distortion by Using BitMap Fit
>
> There is another way to make sure that the image you apply the plane doesn't get distorted. Applying a UVW Map modifier to the plane and choosing Bitmap Fit will lock the proportions of the UVW coordinates to the original bitmap, avoiding distortion.

Now that you have set the image plane to a size that makes some sense scale-wise, you are ready to get on with the real work of building the model.

Tracing the Image

To trace the bitmap, you'll use the Line tool that you were introduced to in the previous chapter. You won't trace all of the walls at first.

Start by tracing the small, U-shaped wall on the exterior of the chapel:

1. Continue with the previous exercise or open `Ronchamp01.max`. If you use the provided file, you may need to retarget the `ronchampscan.gif` image in the Material Editor.

2. In the Top viewport, use the Zoom Region tool to zoom into the U-shaped wall area so that your view looks similar to Figure 4.31. Don't select too small an area.

FIGURE 4.31
Tracing the wall

Continue creating points in
a counterclockwise fashion.

3. Click the Create tab of the Command panel, and then click Shapes.

4. Click the Line button in the Object Type rollout of the Command panel.

5. Open the Creation rollout and set the Initial type to Corner, and Drag type to Bezier, if these are not already checked.

6. Trace the outside of the wall, using single clicks in a counterclockwise fashion to select the points shown in Figure 4.31.

USE THE COLORCORRECTION MAP TO CHANGE BRIGHTNESS

You may have trouble seeing the line against the texture map. You can change the brightness of the sketch easily by going to the Material Editor and navigating to the Coordinates rollout. Click the button marked Bitmap just above the Coordinates rollout to launch the Material/Map Browser. In the Maps > Standard rollout, choose ColorCorrection and click OK. In the Replace Map dialog, choose Keep Old Map as Sub-Map. The map will disappear in the viewport. To see the map again, click the Show Standard Map in Viewport button. Scroll down till you see the Lightness rollout, where you can adjust the brightness of the sketch.

Another alternative is to change the color of the line you are drawing by using the color swatch in the Name and Color rollout.

7. For the last point, click the beginning of the spline. In the Spline dialog box, click Yes to close the spline.

 If the line disappears and is not visible when you finish drawing it, try selecting and moving the plane slightly in the Z dimension to assure that it is just below the home grid. You can do this by right-clicking the plane and then choosing the Move settings button on the right side of the quad menu. Use the Transform Type-In spinners to move the plane down in the negative Z direction.

The line needs to be curved, so use the Bezier Vertex option to adjust the curvature of the wall:

1. Click the Modify tab of the Command panel and then right-click in the viewport to open the quad menu.

2. Click the Vertex option in the tools 1 quad menu (see Figure 4.32) to access the Vertex sub-object level for the spline. You can also click the plus (+) sign next to Line in the modifier and then click Vertex in the expanded list or click the Vertex button in the Selection rollout of the Modify tab.

3. With the Select Object tool, click the middle vertex of the wall, as shown in Figure 4.33.

FIGURE 4.32
Accessing the Vertex sub-object level

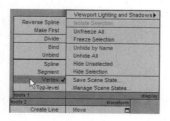

FIGURE 4.33
Editing the
middle vertex

4. Right-click to open the quad menu and select Bezier from the list of Vertex options.

5. Click the Select and Move tool in the Main Toolbar, and the Transform gizmo appears. Drag the XY gizmo (the yellow box) and then drag the tangent handles to a position similar to the one shown in Figure 4.33. Note that the tangent handles honor the last used Transform gizmo setting, so if you have it set to X only, you'll be able to move only the handles in X. This is not obvious, but once you understand this, you'll be a happy spline camper.

You'll want to smooth the bottom curve to match the bitmap image.

6. Right-click the vertex to the left of the one you just edited and select Bezier from the shortcut menu. Adjust the tangent handles until the curve of the line matches the sketch, as shown in Figure 4.34.

7. Right-click the vertex to the right of the first vertex that you edited, select Bezier from the shortcut menu, and adjust the Bezier handles so that the wall looks symmetrical, as shown in Figure 4.35.

FIGURE 4.34
Editing the sec-
ond vertex, to the
left of the middle
vertex

FIGURE 4.35
Editing the third
vertex, to the right
of the middle vertex

SETTING THE AXIS LOCKS

If the handles still will not move in the direction that you want, the axis locks may be active. Use the F5 through F8 keys to set the proper lock axis. These cycle through the Axis Constraints. F5 locks the X axis, F6 locks the Y axis, an d F7 locks the Z axis. F8 cycles through the XY, XZ, and YZ planes.

Now you have the basic outline of the wall. You could extrude the spline now to get the general shape of the wall, but the design calls for a bit more elaboration.

Building Objects from Traced Lines

The shape of the wall starts at its base as a solid form, and as you move up the height of the wall, it becomes partially open. In the transition area, you have a sloped roof that covers the enclosed portion of this piece of the chapel, as you can see in Figure 4.36.

FIGURE 4.36
Looking at the form of the U-shaped wall

Sloped roof

To obtain this shape, you'll make a copy of the wall outline you've just drawn and then form it to create an object matching the void of the upper part of the piece. Once you have the void object, you can subtract it from the main outer part of the wall using the Boolean operation you learned about earlier in this chapter.

CREATING THE VOID OUTLINE

While you're creating the void object, you'll get a chance to explore some spline-editing tools. First, you'll make a copy of the existing wall outline, and then you'll edit the copy to get the outline of the void object.

1. Click Line in the modifier stack to deactivate the Vertex sub-object level.

2. With the Select and Move tool selected, Shift+click and drag the wall you just created to the right so that you have a copy, as shown in Figure 4.37.

3. In the Clone Options dialog box, click Copy and then click OK. You don't need an instance or reference copy for this part because the new object is destined to be different from the original.

FIGURE 4.37
Copy the wall as shown here.

Next, you'll work on the copy to form the void outline:

1. With the copy of the line selected, right-click in the viewport and choose Spline from the quad menu. (You can also click the Spline tool in the Selection rollout or the modifier stack.)

2. Click the Spline to select the shape at the Spline level, scroll down the Command panel to the Outline input box in the Geometry rollout, double-click the input box, and enter **0.4**↵. This creates an outline that is 0.4 meter thick.

3. Right-click and choose Segment in the quad menu to access the Segment sub-object level of the spline (see Figure 4.38).

4. Click the straight-line segment at the top of the interior wall outline, as shown in Figure 4.39, and then press the Delete key to delete the segment.

FIGURE 4.38
Accessing the Segment sub-object level

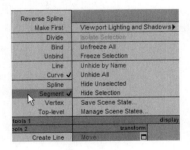

FIGURE 4.39
Delete the straight-line segment.

With the straight-line segment deleted, you can extend the remaining portion of the line to the outside edge of the wall.

1. Enter the Spline sub-object level again, and then click the remaining portion of the interior wall outline so that it turns red.

2. Scroll down the Command panel and click the Extend button in the Geometry rollout.

3. Place the cursor on the left endpoint of the inside wall so that the Extend cursor displays, as shown in Figure 4.40, and click the line. It extends to the outside line.

4. Click the other end of the inside wall so that it too extends to the straight-line segment of the outside line, and then click the Extend button in the Command panel to deactivate the tool.

5. Click the inner spline to select it and then click the Close button in the Command panel. This generates a new straight-line segment across the top.

6. Click the Select Object tool, click the outside spline, as shown in Figure 4.41, and then press the Delete key to delete it.

7. Right-click and choose Top-Level from the quad menu to exit the sub-object level.

FIGURE 4.40
Extending the inside wall to the straight-line segment of the outside wall outline

FIGURE 4.41
Select the outside wall and then press the Delete key.

You have the outline of the shape you want to subtract from the wall. Now move it into position.

1. Right-click the Snaps toggle in the Main Toolbar.

2. In the Grid and Snap Settings dialog box, click the Clear All button and then click Midpoint. Close the Grid and Snap Settings dialog box.

3. If it isn't already active, click the Snaps toggle to make it active.

4. With the Select and Move tool selected, place the cursor on the midpoint of the straight-line segment of the wall copy.

5. When you see the Midpoint cursor appear on the line, click and drag the wall outline to the straight segment of the original wall, as shown in Figure 4.42.

6. Save the file as **MyRonchamp02.max**.

FIGURE 4.42
Selecting and moving the wall copy using the Midpoint snap

FORMING THE WALL VOID

Now you're ready to extrude both the wall and the wall void. First, move the void object to the elevation where the void begins.

1. Click the Maximize Viewport Toggle to see all four viewports, if necessary.

2. Right-click the Perspective viewport and then click the Zoom Extents tool.

3. With the inside wall line selected, right-click to open the quad menu and click the Move Settings button, the small square symbol next to Move (see Figure 4.43), to open the Move Transform Type-In dialog box.

FIGURE 4.43
Click the Settings button next to the Move option in the quad menu.

Vertex	Save Scene State...
Top-level	Manage Scene States...
tools 1	
ools 2	transform
Create Line	Move
Attach	Rotate

USING THE TRANSFORM TYPE-IN FIELDS IN THE UI

You can also use the transform type-ins that are integrated into the bottom of the user interface. Opening the Transform Type-In dialog box from the quad menu is just a way of focusing your attention on entering coordinate values. The dialog box has the advantage that you can see both absolute and offset (relative) values simultaneously.

4. Double-click the Z input box of the Absolute: World group to highlight the current value, and then enter **3.0↵**, for 3 meters. Close the Move Transform Type-In dialog box.

5. Click Zoom Extents again to see both wall outlines. The inside wall outline now appears above the outside wall outline.

Now it's time to extrude the two outlines. This piece of the chapel is about 7.5 meters high, so you can extrude both pieces to this height. The height of the void is somewhat arbitrary, because it's to be subtracted from the main, outside form of the wall.

1. Click the Snaps toggle or press S on the keyboard to turn it off. It may be a distraction during the next few operations.

2. Click the inside wall line to select it.

3. In the Modify tab, select Extrude from the Modifier List drop-down.

4. In the Parameters rollout, click the Amount input box and enter **7.5↵**, for 7.5 meters. The inside wall appears at its full height.

Now extrude the exterior shape.

5. In the Top viewport, click the outer wall line, as shown in Figure 4.44.

6. Select Extrude from the Modifier List drop-down again. The object extrudes to the same height as the other wall. 3ds Max applies to the current extrusion the last value you entered for the first extrusion.

7. Right-click in the Perspective viewport, and then click the Zoom Extents tool to get a better look at the two extrusions. Because one extrusion is inside the other, you won't really see both extrusions completely.

FIGURE 4.44
Select the form of the exterior wall line.

Select the larger outer line.

Adding a Skew to the Void Object

You're almost ready to subtract the interior void object from the outer wall object. You need to apply the Skew modifier to the void object to get the sloping roof (shown earlier in Figure 4.36).

1. With the Perspective viewport selected, click the Maximize Viewport Toggle to enlarge the view.

2. Click the Orbit Selected tool, the middle tool in the Orbit flyout menu, in the viewport navigation controls. The yellow Orbit circle appears in the viewport.

3. Click and drag the left square on the circle's perimeter to the right so that you get a view similar to Figure 4.45.

4. With the interior void object selected, right-click and select Isolate Selection from the displayed quad menu. The viewport changes to show only the interior wall object, and the Isolated Selection dialog box displays.

FIGURE 4.45
Using the Orbit Selected tool, match this view.

By using the Isolate Selection tool, you can more easily view and edit an object that may be partially obscured by other objects in your scene. Now you can apply the Taper modifier to the selected object and see its effects more clearly.

1. Select Skew from the Modifier List drop-down.

2. In the Parameters rollout, click the Y radio button in the Skew Axis group. This causes the taper to occur in the Y-axis.

3. In the Parameters rollout, set the Amount input box to **-0.76m** to specify the amount of the skew, and change the Direction to 90.0. The top of the extrusion now slopes down toward the flat surface, as shown in Figure 4.46.

FIGURE 4.46
The result of using the Skew modifier

4. Click the Exit Isolation Mode button in the Warning: Isolated Selection dialog box to restore the view of the other wall object.

You're just about ready to subtract the inside wall shape from the outside shape, but there are a couple of little details you'll want to handle. You now need to align the skew to the extrusion.

ALIGNING THE SKEW MODIFIER TO THE OBJECT

The Skew modifier acts on the shape in a direction that is aligned with the World Coordinate System. You really want the Skew modifier to be aligned with the void object, which is slightly rotated in relation to the World Coordinate System. You may recall from earlier chapters that you can adjust the orientation of a modifier by adjusting its gizmo. In the next exercise, you'll rotate the Skew gizmo to align it with the inside wall shape.

1. With the Skew modifier still active, click the plus (+) sign next to Taper in the modifier stack. You should see Gizmo and Center in the expanded list.

2. Click Gizmo, and then click the Select and Rotate tool in the Main Toolbar.

3. Carefully click and drag the blue Z-axis ring of the Transform gizmo down until the rectangular Skew gizmo is aligned with the top edge of the wall, as shown in Figure 4.47.

4. Click the Skew level in the stack again to return to modifier-level editing.

The skew is now aligned with the extrusion.

FIGURE 4.47
Click and drag the Z-axis to rotate the Skew gizmo.

Align the Taper gizmo's edge with top edge of the object.

Drag the blue Z-axis ring down to align the Taper gizmo with the object.

FIRST SELECT THE OPERAND TO REMAIN

The rule of thumb with Boolean subtractions is to always select the object that is to remain before you select any other objects.

You're now ready to subtract the void object from the outer wall object.

1. Click the Select Object tool in the Main Toolbar. In the Top viewport, select the outer wall object, as shown in Figure 4.48.

2. Click the Create tab in the Command panel, and then click the Geometry icon.

3. Click the drop-down list just below the Create buttons and select Compound Objects.

4. Click the ProBoolean button, and then click the Start Picking button in the Pick Boolean rollout. Make sure Subtraction is still selected in the Operation group in the Parameters rollout.

5. Click the void shape. It is subtracted from the outer wall object to form the final shape of the wall. You can see the result in the Perspective viewport, as shown in Figure 4.49.

You've just created part of the Chapel at Ronchamp building. The method shown here is just one of a number of ways you could have created the wall. By using this method, you were able to try some spline-editing tools, and you also got a chance to practice using some other modeling methods you learned in previous chapters.

FIGURE 4.48
Selecting the outside wall shape

Select the larger outer object.

FIGURE 4.49
The newly created void

LOCKING OBJECT TRANSFORMS

When you are modeling using an image applied to a plane, it can be troublesome if you accidentally click the plane object and move it, misaligning it with from the rest of your objects. To prevent this, you can turn off the ability to move, rotate, or scale the plane.

1. Save your work from the previous section as **MyRonchamp03.max**.

2. Select the RonchampPlanTemplate object.

3. Click the Hierarchy tab of the Command panel and click the Link Info button.

4. In the Locks rollout, click in all nine check boxes to prevent accidentally changing one of the transforms.

Now even if you accidentally select the RonchampPlanTemplate, you will not be able to move, rotate, or scale it.

A good trick to accomplish the same thing is to freeze the selection, which can be done through the Object Properties dialog box, which you can access from the quad menu. If you deselect Show Frozen in Gray in the Object Properties dialog box, you can freeze objects and still see their textures in the viewport.

USING SEE-THROUGH MODE

Another technique that can help you when you are modeling with image planes is to set your objects to See-Through mode.

1. Select the object you just created in the previous exercise.

2. Right-click to bring up the quad menu and select Object Properties.

3. On the General Tab of the Object Properties dialog box, go to the Display Properties group and click the ByLayer button. This changes the mode for this object to ByObject.

4. Now click the See-Through check box.

Now you can see through the object to the sketch applied to the image plane. This technique can help you when you are building objects such as buildings, cars, or packaging designs from sketches.

Now let's move on to another part of the building to examine another way of editing objects.

Editing Meshes

You've been introduced to 3ds Max objects in the form of the standard primitives, splines, and compound objects. It also helps to think about 3ds Max objects in terms of parametric and non-parametric objects. This can be a bit confusing, because virtually all objects in 3ds Max start out as parametric objects. But, as you'll see, a lot of your work with objects will depart from the parametric level of editing as soon as you begin editing objects in earnest. In fact, you've already seen this with the spline examples in this and the previous chapter.

The term *mesh* is somewhat generic and refers to a nonparametric geometry object composed of vertices, edges, and surfaces. 3ds Max can convert geometry into two types of meshes: Editable Mesh and Editable Poly. Both object types consist of comprehensive toolsets, located

in the rollouts under the Modify tab, for editing geometry. The Editable Poly is newer and has a more robust toolset, including the new Graphite Modeling toolbar. Many of the Graphite Modeling tools have both dialog and visual input methods, and will be the tools used in these exercises. The tools available for the Editable Mesh and Editable Poly objects are also available with the Edit Mesh and Edit Poly modifiers.

In your introduction to 3ds Max objects, you created simple forms and adjusted them using the object's parameters. Parameters are great for establishing the initial dimensions and characteristics of an object. They can also serve as a convenient way to make adjustments to objects as you progress through the design process. But eventually, you'll begin to make changes on a deeper level, bypassing the parameters altogether. At this point, you'll be editing 3D objects as *editable polys*. Editing 3D objects as editable polys is similar to the sub-object level editing you've already performed on splines. The main difference is that you have some additional sub-object levels to work with, in the form of edges, borders, and polygons.

In this section, you'll begin to explore editable polys by creating the south wall of the chapel. You'll learn how you can convert an extruded spline into an editable poly, and then you'll proceed to modify the mesh on a sub-object level.

Creating a Tapered Wall

The part of the chapel you just created was unusual because it was a curved wall. Ronchamp contains many curved walls, but they shouldn't pose a problem to you because you've had some experience drawing such shapes and extruding them. One wall of the chapel is quite unusual, however. The south wall tapers in two directions, plus it has a curve in it. In the following set of exercises, you'll look at a way to create such a wall in 3ds Max—and in the process, you'll be introduced to some additional methods for editing sub-objects.

You'll start, as usual, by outlining the plan of the wall. Once again, you'll trace the imported bitmap sketch using a line. First, set up your view to prepare for tracing:

1. Click the Top viewport to make it active, and then click the Maximize Viewport Toggle to enlarge the view.

2. Click the Pan tool and pan the view so the south wall is centered in the view. Then use the Zoom Region tool to enlarge the south wall to fill as much of the viewport as possible, similar to Figure 4.50.

FIGURE 4.50
Zoom to the outside wall shape

Now you're ready to trace the wall:

1. If it isn't already selected, click the Create tab of the Command panel and click the Shapes tool.

2. Click Line, and draw the line, as shown in Figure 4.51. Pay special attention to the vertices at the curved portion of the wall. You'll want to place three vertices around the curve so that you can change them into Bezier vertices later.

3. At the last point, click the beginning of the line and close the spline.

4. Click the Modify tab of the Command panel, and then enter the Vertex sub-object level of the spline.

5. Click the Select and Move tool in the Main Toolbar, right-click the vertex shown in Figure 4.52, and select Bezier from the quad menu.

FIGURE 4.51

Trace the south wall as shown here. The vertices are shown for clarity.

Trace the line starting here. Then select points in a clockwise direction.

FIGURE 4.52

Selecting and editing the vertex on the top of the wall

Right-click this vertex and select Bezier. Then adjust the handles to achieve the curve shown here.

6. Using the tangent handles, adjust the curve of the wall so that it looks similar to Figure 4.52. You'll want the curve of the wall to join the straight portions of the wall in a tangent.

7. Right-click the vertex across the wall from the one you just edited and select Bezier.

8. Adjust the curve of this vertex so it looks similar to Figure 4.53. Exit the Vertex sub-object mode when you're finished.

FIGURE 4.53
Selecting and editing the vertex on the bottom of the wall

Right-click this vertex and select Bezier.
Then adjust the curve to match the one shown here.

Now it's time to extrude the wall. The wall forms a peak at its easternmost end, and that peak is approximately 14 meters high. You'll want the wall to be at least 14 meters high so that you have enough material with which to work.

1. You're already in the Modify tab of the Command panel, so open the Modifier List dropdown and select Extrude. If you're continuing from the previous section, the wall will extrude to the last height you entered.

2. In the Parameter rollout, change the value in the Amount input box to **14**. Also, make sure that the Segments value is set to 1.

3. Click the Maximize Viewport Toggle, right-click the Perspective viewport, and then click the Zoom Extents Selected tool on the Zoom Extents flyout to get a better look at the south wall so far.

4. Click the Orbit Selected tool, and then click and drag the rightmost square of the navigation circle to the left until your view looks similar to Figure 4.54. Alternatively, you can drag the ViewCube ring to the left to achieve the same result.

5. Click the Maximize Viewport Toggle to enlarge the Perspective viewport.

You now have the basic form of the wall, but the actual wall tapers vertically. Not only that, but the taper is not uniform across the entire wall. It tapers more at its west end, and it doesn't taper at all at its east end. You won't be able to use the Taper modifier to accomplish this nonuniform taper. Instead, you'll edit the mesh directly by rotating some of the edges.

FIGURE 4.54
The Perspective viewport after rotating with the Orbit Selected tool or the ViewCube

Converting the Spline to a Mesh

To edit the south wall, you need to convert the extruded spline to an editable poly to take advantage of the special features of the editable poly tools. You can then make the appropriate changes at the sub-object level of the mesh to get the volume you want. Start by setting up the view to aid in your editing:

1. Right-click the Perspective label in the upper-left corner of the Perspective viewport and select Wireframe.

2. Use the Orbit Selected tool or ViewCube to adjust your view until it looks similar to Figure 4.55. You want to get a good view of the top of the wall.

3. Click the Zoom tool, and then click and drag up in the viewport to enlarge the view of the wall.

FIGURE 4.55
Rotate the view to see the top of the wall.

EDITING THE EDGE OF A MESH

Now you're ready to start editing the wall. You'll convert the object to an editable poly to access the sub-object tools, and then you'll learn how to use the Lasso Selection Region tool to select an edge of the wall for editing.

1. Make sure that the south wall is selected.

2. Right-click in the viewport and choose Convert To ➢ Convert to Editable Poly from the quad menu, as shown in Figure 4.56.

FIGURE 4.56
Converting the
selected object to
an editable poly

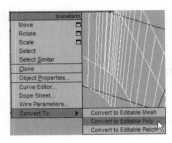

You've just converted your extruded spline into an editable poly; the editable poly tools appear in the Modify panel.

The quad menu options you will see when you right-click an item in the modifier stack depend on the item that is currently selected. Usually, this menu will include the Editable Mesh and Editable Poly options. Now let's proceed with editing the wall:

1. Expand the Polygon Modeling item on the Graphite Modeling toolbar and click Edge, as shown in Figure 4.57.

FIGURE 4.57
Selecting the Edge
sub-object mode

THE GRAPHITE MODELING TOOLBAR

The Graphite Modeling toolbar is an expanded feature in 3ds Max 2011. It provides more than 100 modeling tools for working on Editable Poly objects. If you do not see the Graphite Modeling toolbar, you can click the Graphite icon on the Main Toolbar.

When it is docked to the top of your 3ds Max interface, the Graphite Modeling toolbar has three modes. You can access these modes with the drop-down icon to the right of the Selection tab of the Graphite Modeling tools. They include showing the full ribbon interface using tabs, and minimizing to show just panel titles or panel buttons. This functionality provides you with a great number of options for working with the Graphite Modeling tools and conserving screen real estate.

The Graphite Modeling toolbar, like many user-interface (UI) features, can be turned into a floating toolbar or docked to another side of the 3ds Max UI. New to 3ds Max Design 2011, you can also customize the ribbon, making your own collection of tools. You can assign a shortcut to the floating ribbon to make it appear and disappear at your command.

2. In the Main Toolbar, click and hold the Rectangular Selection Region tool until its flyout displays, and then drag the mouse down to the near-bottom option, the Lasso Selection Region tool (see Figure 4.58).

 You're going to select the top edge of the wall that is closest to you, so you'll need a selection tool that lets you select a freeform area.

3. Click the Crossing Selection tool in the Main Toolbar so that it changes to the Window Selection tool (the icon changes to a dotted square enclosing a sphere). This causes 3ds Max to select only objects that fall completely within the selection window.

4. Click the Select Object tool, and then start dragging a selection lasso around the wall, as shown in Figure 4.59.

5. Continue to drag the lasso so that the front, top edge of the wall is completely enclosed by the selection. Release the mouse button, and your selection should turn red and appear as shown in Figure 4.60.

FIGURE 4.58
Selecting the
Lasso Selection
Region tool

FIGURE 4.59
Drawing the
lasso selection

Drag a lasso around the top edge
to make a freehand selection.

FIGURE 4.60
The top edge
selected

Now that you have the edge selected, you want to rotate it. The best view for this operation is the top view, so the first thing to do is to go to the Top viewport.

1. Press T to switch the maximized Perspective viewport into the maximized Top viewport. If the geometry disappears, do a Zoom Extents by pressing Shift + Z.

2. Click the Select and Rotate tool in the Main Toolbar.

3. Place the cursor on the ring of the Rotate gizmo, and then click and drag clockwise until the selected edge is rotated in such a way that it appears to be parallel to the opposite edge of the wall. You can look at the coordinate readout and set the angle to approximately -7 (negative seven) degrees or, better yet, just type **-7** in the Z field of the transform type-ins at the bottom of the user interface.

4. Click the Select and Move tool, and then click and drag the edge up so that the top edges are closer together, as shown in Figure 4.61.

5. Exit the Edge sub-object level and return to the top level.

FIGURE 4.61
Move the selected edge so it's closer to the top edge of the wall and parallel to it.

Moving a Single Mesh Vertex

You've managed to taper the south wall. The right end of the wall is a vertical surface that does not taper, so you need to realign the upper corner to its original location. You can do this by moving the vertex and using the endpoint snaps.

1. Enter the Vertex sub-object level.

2. Click the vertex at the corner of the top of the wall to select it, as shown in Figure 4.62.

FIGURE 4.62
Select the corner of the top of the wall.

Select the vertex.

Before you move the vertex, activate the endpoint snaps so you can get a perfect alignment.

3. Right-click the Snaps toggle button in the Main Toolbar.

4. In the Grid and Snap Settings dialog box, click the Midpoint check box to deactivate it (no snaps should be active now), and then click Endpoint. Close the Grid and Snap Settings dialog box.

5. Click and hold the Snaps toggle to expose its flyout. Select the 2.5D Snaps Toggle tool. The 2.5D Snaps Toggle tool snaps to a point projected from the location selected to the active grid beyond or in front of it. This allows you to visually snap from one vertex to another located away from and below it, but to only move the selected vertex in the XY-plane.

Snaps have been reworked in this release. If you are an experienced user upgrading to 2011, you'll notice that snapping behavior has changed somewhat from the previous versions of the software. There's now a snap handle at the center of the Move Transform gizmo.

6. Click the Select and Move tool. Then place the cursor on the selected vertex so that the Endpoint Snap cursor displays as shown in Figure 4.63.

7. Click and drag the cursor to the vertex shown in Figure 4.64. When the Endpoint Snap cursor displays, release the mouse button.

8. Click the Maximize Viewport Toggle to view the results in the Perspective viewport, and then exit the sub-object level.

Now that you have the east end of the wall back to its original configuration, you can move on to editing the interior side of the wall.

FIGURE 4.63
Select the corner of the top of the wall.

FIGURE 4.64
Moving the vertex

FLATTENING A SURFACE

The interior side of the wall also tapers in toward the top, but that taper occurs only along the straight portion of the wall, starting from the curve and progressing to the left. In this situation, you need to move only the vertex at the end of the wall corner.

1. Change back to four views. In the Left viewport, click the Zoom Extents tool. You'll use this view to help adjust the taper of the wall.

2. Right-click in the Perspective viewport, and then use the Select Object tool to select the wall, if it's not still selected. Go to the Vertex sub-object level, and then select the two vertices on the top-left corner of the wall. You can use the Rectangular Selection Region setting from the Main Toolbar to select the vertices with a rectangular window, as shown in Figure 4.65.

FIGURE 4.65
Selecting the corner vertices

Select these two vertices with a rectangular region.

Verify that only two vertices are selected by reading the display at the bottom of the Selection rollout, as shown in Figure 4.66.

3. Right-click the Left viewport and then turn off the Snaps Toggle if it is still on.

4. With the Select and Move tool selected, click and drag the red X-axis to the right. Adjust the wall so that it looks similar to Figure 4.67.

FIGURE 4.66
The Selection rollout shows the number of vertices selected.

FIGURE 4.67
In the Left viewport, move the vertices so the wall looks like this.

Now you have both sides of the wall tapering in. But there's one problem with the wall: the west end to the left of the wall is twisted and not flat because of all of the changes you've made to the vertices. You can quickly flatten that end of the wall using the View Align tool.

1. Click the Select Object tool. In the Top viewport, click and drag a selection region so that all of the vertices of the left end of the wall are selected, as shown in Figure 4.68.

2. Right-click in the Left viewport to make it active.

FIGURE 4.68
Selecting the vertices of the left side of the wall

Select all of the vertices at this end of the wall.

3. Scroll down the Command panel until you see the View Align button toward the bottom of the Edit Geometry rollout, and then click it.

The selected vertices are aligned to the Left viewport, forming a flat plane (see Figure 4.69). The View Align tool flattened the left side of the wall so that it became a plane parallel to the active viewport (the Left viewport in this case).

4. If your Top viewport is still in wireframe mode, change to Smooth + Highlight so you can see the sketch plane. With the four points at the left end of the wall selected, click the Select and Rotate tool from the Main Toolbar and rotate the points so they are inline with the sketch, as shown in Figure 4.70.

5. Using the Select and Move tool, finish moving the points so they line up with the sketch.

FIGURE 4.69
Aligning the vertices of the left side of the wall

FIGURE 4.70
Rotating the vertices of the left side of the wall

OTHER ALIGNMENT TOOLS

You might have noticed a few other buttons in the group with the View Align button. Grid Align aligns the points to the current active user grid or to the nearest grid line in the home grid. Make Planar causes all of the selected points to be coplanar, taking the average location of all of the points to determine the plane. Collapse, near the top of the Edit Geometry rollout, causes all of the selected points to converge into a single point.

Tapering the Top of the Wall

To finish the wall, you need to slope the top of the wall down from right to left. This will be a uniform slope, so you can use the Taper modifier for the operation.

1. Right-click the Front viewport, and then click the Zoom Extents tool to get a better view of the wall.

2. Exit the sub-object level.

3. Open the Modifier List drop-down and select Taper. (You may need to scroll to the bottom of the list to find it.)

4. In the Parameters rollout, set the value in the Amount input box to 0.35.

5. In the Taper Axis group of the Parameters rollout, click the X Primary and Z Effect radio buttons. This causes the taper to occur only on the X-axis.

The Taper occurs from roughly the midpoint of the wall, which causes the left side to drop and the right side to rise, as with a balance scale. However, you want to maintain the height of the wall at its highest point instead of having it rise. You can adjust the taper by moving the Center sub-object with the Transform gizmo.

1. Expand Taper in the modifier stack and select the Center option.

2. Make sure the Select and Move tool is selected. Then, in the Front viewport, click and drag the red X-axis arrow to the right until the Y-axis arrow is aligned with the right edge of the wall as shown in Figure 4.71.

3. Exit the Center sub-object level.

FIGURE 4.71
Moving the Center sub-object of the Taper modifier (Smooth + Highlight shading used for clarity)

Notice that the wall drops in height. If you adjust the Amount parameter spinner, you'll see that the top of the wall now changes its taper angle in relation to the right end of the wall. Make sure that you set the Amount value back to 0.35 when you've finished experimenting.

The wall is also tapered to the north, so you want to apply the Taper modifier again.

1. Select Taper from the Modifier List drop-down.

2. In the Parameters rollout, set the Taper Amount input box value to -0.1. This is equivalent to roughly 10 degrees.

3. In the Taper Axis group of the Parameters rollout, click the Y Primary and Z Effect radio buttons. This causes the taper to occur only on the Y-axis.

4. Save your work as **MyRonchamp_TaperedWalls.max**.

USING THE EDIT POLY MODIFIER

In the beginning of this section, you converted an extruded spline into an editable poly. You could have used the Edit Poly modifier to gain access to the same mesh sub-object level you used to edit the south wall. The advantage to using the modifier is that you can return to the Spline level in the modifier stack to make changes at that level. The disadvantage is that your model uses more memory to store the Edit Poly modifier's parameters. The Edit Poly modifier also inserts more complexity into the object data flow, which can cause unpredictable results if you make changes to the geometry or modifiers below it in the modifier stack.

The Edit Poly modifier is a great option while you're in the process of creating an object and you aren't quite sure you want to commit to a particular set of changes. It allows you to return to other levels of the modifier stack and experiment. It also helps to maintain the parametric characteristics of objects so that you have more flexibility in shaping an object, and you can always delete the modifier if the edits don't work out as expected. But once you've created an object you're satisfied with, it's a good idea to convert objects to editable polys for the sake of data, flow simplicity and efficient memory use.

You now have an editable poly to which you've applied two Taper modifiers. You could convert the wall to an editable poly again, thereby combining the effects of the Taper modifiers into a single editable poly object. But later you'll need to make further adjustments to the taper of the wall to fit the roof, so for now keep the modifiers in place.

Now you've completed the main shape of the south wall. Next to the roof, the south wall is the most complex part of the building, so it took quite a bit of effort to construct. In the next set of exercises, you'll create the towers of the chapel. These towers are somewhat easier to build, but they're also a bit tricky.

CREATING SPLINES FROM MESHES

It is possible to create a flat 2D spline from a 3D mesh object. You can create a spline where a section plane intersects the 3D form. This can be useful when you are trying to create section drawings of complex forms, as in the following example.

1. Continue from the previous exercises, or open MyRonchamp_TaperedWalls.max that you downloaded from the book's web page.

2. Select Isolate Selection from the quad menu to isolate the curved wall you have been working on or press ALT+Q.

CONTINUES

CREATING SPLINES FROM MESHES *(CONTINUED)*

3. Click the Create tab and click the Shapes button. Make sure Splines is shown in the drop-down list and then click the Section button.

4. Drag out a section plane on the home grid at the base of the curved wall. It doesn't matter how large you make this plane, because it is only a placeholder representing the section cut you are making through the curved wall. The actual cutting plane extends infinitely in two directions.

5. Turn off the Snaps toggle and then move the section plane up in the Z direction.

As you move the section plane, a yellow highlight shows where the section plane cuts through the mesh. Observe how the yellow highlighting changes shape as the section plane moves because the curved wall's cross section changes height.

6. Try rotating the section plane. See how the highlighting always represents the intersection of the section plane with the mesh object.

7. With the selection plane still selected, switch to the Modify tab of the Command panel. Click the Create Shape button.

8. Assign a name to the new spline you are creating in the Name Section Shape dialog box and then click OK.

9. Delete the section object. Notice that something is still intersecting the mesh—this is the new spline you created from the mesh.

10. Select the object that is intersecting the mesh. It is an editable spline, as shown in the Modify panel. Finally, delete this spline and exit Isolation mode.

You have seen how you can use the Section tool to highlight the relationship between your 3D mesh object and a plane. After positioning and orienting the section plane, you created a spline crystallizing this intersecting relationship. This procedure can be useful when you go to generate any number of splines from a mesh.

Using Instanced Clones to Create Symmetrical Forms

The towers of Ronchamp enclose smaller mini-altars apart from the main altar at the east end of the building. The towers' forms reflect the shape of a nun's hat. To create the towers, you'll create half of the tower plan, and then mirror that half to complete the rest of the plan. This will ensure that the walls are symmetrical, and it will also give you the parts you need to construct the top of the tower.

Adding a User Grid to Aid Tracing

First, set up the Top viewport to trace the plan of the tower. The tower is slightly skewed from the axis of the main floor, so adding a user grid will help you create it.

1. Click the Top viewport to make the viewport active, and then click the Maximize Viewport Toggle to enlarge the view of the Top viewport.

2. Click the Pan tool and pan the view so that the large tower plan is centered in the viewport, as shown in Figure 4.72.

3. Click the Zoom Region tool and place the zoom region around the tower plan, as shown in Figure 4.72.

4. Click the Create tab in the Command panel, and then click the Helpers button.

5. Click Grid, and then click and drag a grid across the viewport, starting in the lower-left corner of the viewport, as shown in Figure 4.73. As you're aligning the grid, place its vertical centerline at the center of the plan, as indicated in the figure.

FIGURE 4.72
Centering the tower plan and selecting the zoom region

Select this area with the Zoom Region tool.

RonchampPlanTemplate

FIGURE 4.73
Adding a grid to the viewport

Place the grid so it is centered on this point.

Drag the grid helper starting from here.

ACTIVATING A USER GRID

As soon as a user grid is created, it can become the currently active grid. If your system does not react this way, choose Tools ➤ Grid and Snap Settings ➤ User Grids and check the Activate Grids When Created check box. When multiple user grids exist in a scene, to activate the selected a grid, right-click and then choose Activate Grid from the quad menu.

6. The grid is a bit too dense. To adjust its spacing, go to the Spacing group in the Parameters rollout and change the Grid value to 2, for 2 meters.

7. To align the grid with the tower, click the Select and Rotate tool in the Main Toolbar, and then carefully click and drag the Z-axis ring clockwise so that it is aligned with the lines indicating the top edge of the tower, as shown in Figure 4.74. The angle is very small, around -1.5, so you need to rotate the grid only slightly.

FIGURE 4.74
Aligning the grid
with the tower plan

Rotate the grid so that it is aligned
with this line from the sketch.

Building the Tower Walls

Now you're ready to lay out the tower. Start by tracing the left side of the tower plan.

1. Click the Shapes button in the Create tab of the Command panel, and then click the Line tool in the Object Type rollout.

2. Draw the lines shown in Figure 4.75, starting from the upper-left corner of the plan. Finish the lines at the centerline of the grid. Right-click when you've finished drawing the lines.

FIGURE 4.75
Drawing the left half
of the tower plan

3. Click the Modify tab in the Command panel and then click the Vertex tool in the Selection rollout (or select Vertex from the quad menu).

4. Right-click the last vertex in the lower half of the viewport and select Bezier from the quad menu.

5. Click the Select and Move tool and adjust the Bezier handle of the selected vertex to shape the spline as shown in Figure 4.76.

6. Right-click the middle vertex, choose Bezier from the shortcut menu, and adjust the handles so that the line looks similar to Figure 4.77.

7. To add thickness to the wall, enter the Spline sub-object level, select the spline, and then scroll down the Command panel to find the Outline option.

8. Click the Outline input box and enter **0.5**↵. The line becomes a wall with a thickness of 0.5 meter.

FIGURE 4.76
Moving the vertex handle of the end of the line

FIGURE 4.77
Adjusting the middle vertex

The next step is to mirror the wall you just created. You want to use the X-axis of the user grid you set up earlier as the mirror axis.

1. Click Line in the modifier stack to exit the sub-object level.

2. In the Main Toolbar, click the Reference Coordinate System drop-down list (see Figure 4.78) to view its options.

3. Select Grid. Notice that the Transform gizmo rotates slightly to match the user-grid orientation, and the reference coordinate system is displayed as Grid001 on the Main Toolbar.

FIGURE 4.78
The Reference
Coordinate System
drop-down

4. Click the Mirror tool in the Main Toolbar.

5. In the Mirror: Grid Coordinates dialog box, make sure that the X radio button in the Mirror Axis group is selected, as shown in Figure 4.79.

6. Click the Reference radio button in the Clone Selection group. You see a mirrored copy of the wall you just drew. Adjust the Offset using the spinners so the corners of the mirror segments are close to touching each other. Click and drag up and down on the spinner to see the effect, and then gently move the copy into the correct location.

7. Zoom into where the two clones are close. Click the Select and Move tool and click the Snaps toggle button to turn on Snaps. Right-click the snaps toggle, choose Clear All, and then check Vertex.

8. Using the vertex snaps, click and drag the bottom vertex of the wall spline half you just created to the bottom vertex of the original wall so that they meet end to end, as shown in Figure 4.80.

FIGURE 4.79
The Mirror: Grid Coor-
dinates dialog box

FIGURE 4.80
Offset the clone so
there is only a narrow
gap between the orig-
inal and the clone.

Offset the clone from here…

…to here.

The plan of the tower is a bit too wide at the opening. You can adjust one side of the plan, and because the two halves are references, adjustments you make to one side will affect the other side.

1. Turn off the Snaps toggle. Then select the left half of the tower plan.

2. Go to the Vertex sub-object level and then use the Rectangular Selection Region setting to select the two wall corner vertices at the top of the wall, as shown in Figure 4.81.

3. Click the Select and Move tool. Make sure Grid is selected from the Reference Coordinate System drop-down list.

4. Click and drag the red X-axis handle of the Transform gizmo to the right a slight amount so that the walls look similar to Figure 4.82.

 Because they are reference clones, both ends of the wall move in unison toward the centerline of the tower plan.

5. Save your work as **MyRonchamp_MirroredWalls.max**.

FIGURE 4.81
Select these
two vertices.

FIGURE 4.82
Moving the ends
of the tower wall to
the right, centered
over the wall in the
sketch

Adding the Vaulted Ceiling

You need another copy of the wall half to use later to cap the tower. This copy will be extruded using the Lathe modifier to form the vaulted ceiling of the tower.

1. Exit the Vertex sub-object level and then, using the Select and Move tool, Shift+click and drag the right half of the tower plan to the left.

2. In the Clone Options dialog box, click Copy. Then enter the name **Vault** in the Name input box and click OK.

Now you're ready to extrude the plan into a tower. The overall height of the tower is 22 meters. Subtract 2 meters for the vaulted ceiling, for a height of 20 meters for the straight portion of the tower.

1. Click the Maximize Viewport Toggle.

2. Click the Select Object tool and click the left half of the tower plan.

3. In the Command panel, select Extrude from the Modifier List drop-down.

4. In the Parameters rollout, change the value in the Amount input box to **20m**.

5. Right-click the Perspective viewport and click the Zoom Extents tool to get a better view of your model.

To finish the basic shape of the tower, you need the vaulted ceiling.

1. In the Top viewport, select the rightmost copy of the tower plan outline.

2. In the Command panel, select Lathe from the Modifier List drop-down.

3. In the Parameters rollout, change the Degrees value to 180. The ceiling won't look quite right, but in the next step, you'll fix things.

4. Click the plus (+) sign next to Lathe in the modifier stack and select Axis.

5. Use the Select and Move tool to click and drag the red X-axis arrow to the left until the shape of the vault appears to be about the same width as the extruded tower plan, as shown in Figure 4.83. Zoom in on the apex of the lathed roof to ensure that the axis is moved accurately.

FIGURE 4.83
Using the Lathe modifier to form the ceiling

Drag the Lathe axis to the left.

You need to prepare the tower and ceiling to be combined into a single object, but first save a copy of them to use in case you want to use a different approach to create the towers in a later exercise.

1. Select both the extruded tower wall and vaulted ceiling objects.

2. Click the Select and Move tool, hold down the Shift key, and move the objects off to the left, as shown in Figure 4.84.

FIGURE 4.84
Move the selected
objects to the left

3. In the Clone Options dialog box, choose Copy and then click OK.

4. Right-click and choose Hide Selection from the quad menu to remove these objects from the display.

To join the walls and ceiling, you start by attaching the two wall objects and then you complete the task by bridging the gap between the objects.

1. Right-click the Perspective viewport Shading label and choose Smooth + Highlights from the shortcut menu.

2. Right-click the label again and select the Edged Faces option. This will display both the surfaces as well as the edges in the viewport.

3. Select the left wall object.

4. Right-click and choose Convert To ➢ Convert to Editable Poly to convert it to an editable poly object.

5. Click the Modify tab, scroll down to the Edit Geometry rollout and click the Attach button, and then click the right wall object. The two walls are now part of one object.

6. Zoom into the area where the two walls touch.

7. Go to the Polygon Modeling panel of the Graphite Modeling tools and turn on the Polygon sub-object mode. Polygons are contiguous, coplanar surfaces bound by visible edges.

8. Click the Select tool from the Main Toolbar and then change the selection mode to Window.

9. Make a selection window just around the edge between the two halves of the wall, as shown in Figure 4.85. You can confirm that only two faces are selected on the Selection rollout.

FIGURE 4.85
Make a selection
around the edge
of the two wall
halves.

10. Press the Delete key on the keyboard to delete the two interior faces.

11. Switch the sub-object mode to vertex and make a selection the same size as the one you made in step 9.

12. You should have eight vertices selected. Click the Zoom Extents Selected button to get a close up view of the selection, as in Figure 4.86.

13. Click the Settings box next to the Weld button on the Edit Vertices rollout.

14. The Weld Vertices caddy appears. Move it to the right so you can see the vertices. Adjust the Weld Threshold value until it reads about .048 meters. This should cause the Number of Vertices feedback to display 120 vertices before the weld and 116 after the weld, as shown in Figure 4.87. Click the green check mark to approve this change.

FIGURE 4.86
The selected vertices

FIGURE 4.87
The Weld Vertices settings

This closes the mesh so there will be no more modeling issues with this section of the building—or any more problems if you render the scene with radiosity or mental ray.

Now we need to remove the faces at the top of the wall to prepare to move the vault and attach the faces to the tower object.

1. Right-click in the Front viewport to make it active.

2. Change the sub-object mode to Polygon and make a selection around the top of the joined walls. You should have two polygons selected.

3. Press the Delete key on the keyboard to delete the selection.

The polygons are deleted (Figure 4.88). Portions of the vertical side walls may appear to be missing; however, this is just a function of the direction of the face normals. When the normal of a face is directed toward you, the face is visible. If the normal is pointed away from you, it will not display in the viewport.

FIGURE 4.88
The top polygons
have been deleted.

A similar procedure must be completed for the bottom of the vaulted ceiling object. Here's how:

1. Select the vaulted ceiling object and then isolate the selection.

2. Use Orbit Selected or the ViewCube to adjust the view so that you can see the bottom surfaces of the ceiling, as shown in Figure 4.89.

3. Right-click and choose Convert To ➤ Convert to Editable Poly to convert the lathed spline to an editable poly object.

4. Enter the Polygon sub-object level.

5. In the Front viewport, use a rectangular selection region to select all the polygons on the bottom surface of the ceiling, as shown in Figure 4.90. Be careful not to select any polygons above the bottom surface.

FIGURE 4.89
Rotate the Perspective viewport as shown.

FIGURE 4.90
Select the bottom surface using a selection region.

6. Press Delete to remove the selected polygons. Your model should look similar to Figure 4.91.

7. Exit the Polygon sub-object level.

8. Exit isolation mode.

FIGURE 4.91
The vault model with the bottom polygons deleted

Next, you'll move the vaulted ceiling into position and adjust its width to fit exactly over the vertical walls of the tower. You don't want the next operation to operate on a sub-object level, so begin by turning off this option.

1. Click the Select and Move tool.

2. In the transform type-ins at the bottom of the user interface, change the Z input box to 20.5 to raise the vault to 20.5 meters.

The vaulted ceiling is near its proper Z-axis location. Now you need to place the ceiling exactly over the vertical wall.

1. Right-click the Perspective viewport, and click the Maximize Viewport Toggle to enlarge the viewport. This will help you move the ceiling more accurately.

2. Click the Snaps toggle to activate the 3D Snap mode, and then place the cursor on the upper-left corner of the vaulted ceiling, as shown in Figure 4.92.

FIGURE 4.92
Moving the vaulted ceiling into place above the vertical wall

Move the vault from this corner…

…to this corner of the extruded walls.

3. When you see the Snap cursor, click and drag the mouse to the upper-left corner of the wall, as shown in Figure 4.92.

4. Turn off the Snaps toggle.

5. If the width of the vault is different from the walls, you'll need to do the following steps. First center the vault over the walls by pressing Alt+A and then clicking the extruded wall object. Choose Center for both the current and target objects, and align only the X and Y positions. Click OK. Next, go to the Hierarchy panel, click Affect Pivot Only, and then click Center to Object. Turn off Affect Pivot Only. This forces the pivot point into the center of the object. Now adjust the width of the object by right-clicking and selecting Scale on the quad menu. Drag the red handle to scale in the X direction only.

6. Click the Attach button in the Edit Geometry rollout, and then click the corresponding wall object to join the two objects as one editable poly. Click the Attach button again to turn it off; you don't need to attach any additional objects.

7. Click the Maximize Viewport Toggle to view the other viewports.

8. Select the Vertex sub-object level from the quad menu.

9. In the front view, drag a selection box around the vertices where the vault and the walls meet, as shown in Figure 4.93.

10. Click the Settings button next to the Weld button in the Edit Vertices rollout.

11. Scroll the Weld Threshold until it looks like all areas with multiple vertices have been welded together; a value such as 0.2 meters should work, but depending on your modeling, the values may be different. Orbit around the model and adjust the Weld Threshold, watching the result. See where it is too much, back away from that value a little, and then orbit more to confirm the setting is what you need. Click the green check mark to approve this change.

12. Exit the sub-object level and then delete the user grid you created earlier. You won't need it anymore.

13. Save your work as **MyRonchamp_AttachedVault.max**.

FIGURE 4.93
Select the vertices
where the objects meet.

Creating the Smaller Towers

You have completed one tower. There are two smaller towers of a similar configuration. You can make a copy of the large tower you just created, and then edit the copy to create the smaller tower. First, copy the tower and move the copy into its new location at the north side of the building.

1. Continue from the previous exercise, or load MyRonchamp_AttachedVault.max. Click the Top viewport and click the Maximize Viewport Toggle to enlarge the viewport.

2. Click the Zoom Extents tool to get an overall view of the plan so far.

3. Click the Select Object tool and select the existing tower.

4. Click the Select and Move tool, and then Shift+click and drag the tower to the location of the smaller tower, as shown in Figure 4.94.

5. In the Clone Options dialog box, click Copy and click OK.

FIGURE 4.94
Moving the tower copy to a new location

The copy is a bit too large, and it's oriented in the wrong direction. You need to rotate the tower copy and then scale it down.

1. Pan the view so that the tower copy is centered in the viewport, and use the Zoom Region tool to enlarge the view of the tower, as shown in Figure 4.95.

FIGURE 4.95
Centering the tower copy in the viewport and selecting a region to enlarge

Use the Zoom Region tool to enlarge this area.

2. Click the Select and Rotate tool, and then click and drag the blue Z-axis ring clockwise until the tower is aligned with the image of the smaller tower in the imported bitmap sketch. You can use the centerline in the sketch to help you align the tower. Tip: Alt+X is the shortcut for SeeThrough mode, which will help to check the size against the sketch when you're in the Top Viewport.

3. Use the Select and Move tool to center the tower over the sketch.

4. Click the Select and Uniform Scale tool and click and drag the Scale Transform gizmo's triangular handle down until the tower is about the same width as the sketch of the smaller tower, as shown in Figure 4.96.

5. Recenter the tower using the Select and Move tool. Use the Select and Scale tool to refine the size of the tower until you are happy with its position relative to the sketch. If necessary, set the Transform Coordinate System to Local prior to using the Scale transform.

FIGURE 4.96
Fine-tune the size and location of the tower over the sketch so that it looks similar to this figure.

You may also need to experiment with the rotation of the tower to get it in the correct orientation. You don't need to be too fussy about the tower, however. Just use this as an opportunity to get accustomed to 3ds Max's Move, Scale, and Rotate tools.

When you scaled the copy of the tower, 3ds Max scaled it down in all directions. This caused the tower copy to appear to be floating in space because its pivot point was not at the base of the object. It now needs to be brought back down to the ground level.

1. Click the Maximize Viewport Toggle, and then right-click in the Front viewport.

2. On the Hierarchy panel's Pivot tab, under the Adjust Pivot rollout, click Affect Pivot Only, and then in the Alignment group select Center to Object.

3. In the Front viewport, move the pivot down in the Z-axis until it is at the base of the tower, as shown in Figure 4.97. Zoom in to get it accurate.

FIGURE 4.97
Moving the pivot to the base of the small tower

4. Turn off Affect Pivot Only.

5. Lower the small tower to the ground, as shown in Figure 4.98, by right-clicking the Z Transform Type-In spinner at the bottom of the interface.

FIGURE 4.98
The smaller tower
on the ground

You have the tower in the location and orientation you like. Now you need to copy and rotate it to represent the other small tower.

1. Use the Select Object tool to select the tower you just created.

2. In the Main Toolbar, expand the Reference Coordinate System and choose View as the new coordinate system.

3. Click the Mirror tool in the Main Toolbar.

4. In the Mirror: Screen Coordinates dialog box, make sure the X radio button is selected in the Mirror Axis group and the Instance option is selected in the Clone Selection group. Then click OK.

5. Click the Select and Move tool, and then move the tower instance left to the location of the first smaller tower, as shown in Figure 4.99.

6. Use the Select and Rotate tool to rotate the new tower so that it is oriented in a way similar to that shown in Figure 4.100.

Move it again, if necessary, to center it on the sketch.

7. To see your results so far, click the Maximize Viewport Toggle.

The smaller towers could use a little more work to refine their forms, but for now you have the general form of the towers in place.

FIGURE 4.99
Moving the second
smaller tower into
place

FIGURE 4.100
The final location
and orientation of
the second smaller
tower

Drawing the Remaining Walls

A few other walls, as well as the roof, still need to be added to the model. As a review of some of the earlier skills you've learned, go ahead and add the other walls, starting with the west wall on the left side of the floor plan.

1. Click the Maximize Viewport Toggle to enlarge the Top viewport again. Then click the Zoom Extents tool to view the entire top view.

2. Use the Zoom Region tool to zoom into the area shown in Figure 4.101.

3. In the Create tab of the Command panel, click the Shapes button if it isn't already selected, and then draw a line on the left side of the wall, shown in Figure 4.101.

4. Click the Modify tab of the Command panel, and then click the Vertex button in the Selection rollout.

5. Select all the vertices and then right-click to open the quad menu. Convert all of the points on the line to Bezier curves. Adjust the tangent handles to match as closely as possible the curve shown in Figure 4.102.

FIGURE 4.101
Draw the west wall
as shown here.
The vertices are
marked for clarity.

FIGURE 4.102
Match the curve
shown here.

6. In the Modify tab, click the Spline tool in the Selection rollout. Then scroll down the panel to the Outline input box and enter **0.5**↵. The west wall will convert to a thick wall.

7. Scroll up to the top of the Command panel and select Extrude from the Modifier List drop-down.

EXTRUDE ACTS ON THE ENTIRE OBJECT

When a sub-object selection is active, most modifiers only pass that selection to the modifiers in the stack. The Extrude modifier is one exception where the entire shape is extruded, not just the selected vertices, edges, or splines. In the case where a sub-object selection has been passed to a modifier and you want to start passing the entire object up the stack again, apply a Poly Select modifier to the top of the stack. Without a sub-object selection at the Mesh Select modifier, all subsequent modifiers are applied to the entire object.

8. In the Amount input box of the Parameters rollout, enter **9.5**↵.

The west wall will need some editing later. For now, continue with the addition of the north wall.

1. Choose Views ➢ Undo View Change, and then zoom into the area shown in Figure 4.103.

2. Draw the line shown in Figure 4.103 and convert the vertex indicated in the figure to a Bezier curve. Adjust the Bezier handles so the line follows the curve of the sketch. By now, this should be a familiar process.

3. Access the Spline sub-object level and then, in the Modify panel, scroll down to the Outline input box to set the wall outline to 0.5 meter. If your wall outline appears on the wrong side of the line, click the Undo tool and reenter the Outline value as **-0.5** (or you can click the Reverse button and reenter the **0.5** Outline value).

4. Scroll up to the top of the Command panel and select Extrude from the modifier stack list. 3ds Max uses the last value you entered for the Extrude amount, so the wall automatically extrudes to 9.5 meters.

5. Save your work.

FIGURE 4.103
Drawing the
north wall

Convert the middle vertex to a Bezier curve.

OBJECT DATA FLOW, SCALED PARAMETRIC OBJECTS, AND EDITABLE POLYS

When you scale an object, the object's apparent size is affected, but the parameters of the object are not. For example, if you create two spheres, the first with a radius of 2 and the second with a radius of 1, the first appears twice as large as the second, just as it should. When you then scale the first sphere to 50 percent of its size, it appears equal in dimensions to the second sphere. Select each sphere in turn and verify its Radius value in the Modify panel. Although they appear to be the same size, the Radius of the first sphere is 2 and the second is 1. This can cause a good deal of confusion.

The reason for this seemingly odd behavior becomes clearer when you consider the object data flow in 3ds Max. You may recall that 3ds Max evaluates the data associated with an object in a particular order before the object is displayed. The order of that data evaluation is master object, modifiers, transforms, and then properties. The object's parameters fall under master object, which is the first item in the object data flow. Transforms are third in the evaluation order. Transforms affect the way the master object is displayed, but they have no effect on the master object's internal parameters or other data at its sub-object level. The net result of this is that when parametric objects are scaled up or down in size, their parameters remain at their original values before being scaled, even though the object itself appears larger or smaller than its original size.

Another way of saying all this is that the object really exists in its own space, called Object Space (*Object Space* means a 3D Cartesian coordinate system with an origin and a grid). Objects are defined, sculpted, and modified in Object Space. Objects can be transformed in Object Space using the XForm modifier. Moving, rotating, and scaling (in other words, transforming) an object actually occurs in World Space and is applied later in the object data flow. (Objects can be transformed in World Space to align with Object Space by using the Local Reference Coordinate System.)

An alternative way to look at it is to consider the master object as having internal data, which includes its own unit of measure and coordinate system, called Object Space. These internal data are unaffected by modifiers, transforms, and properties. The modifiers, transforms, and properties you apply to an object only affect the object's appearance in the 3ds Max viewport.

This all changes when you convert an object to an editable poly. In terms of 3ds Max data, an editable poly is a more fundamental way of representing the object on a mathematical level, even though its appearance is identical to that of the original object from which it was derived. Once you convert an object to an editable poly, the editable poly becomes the master object in the data flow. This new master object then inherits the properties and structure of the original object, while the modifiers are collapsed into the original master object. You can then apply more modifiers and transforms to this new master object, and the process goes on.

Finally, add the east wall to the model.

1. Choose View ➢ Undo View Change, or press Shift+Z to return to the overall view of the plan. Then zoom into the area shown in Figure 4.104.

2. Draw the line shown in Figure 4.104.

3. Convert the vertices shown in Figure 4.105 to Bezier curves and adjust the tangent handles to match the curve of the sketch.

ADDING VERTICES TO A SPLINE

To add a vertex to an existing spline, click the Refine button in the Geometry rollout at either the Vertex or Segment sub-object level. To delete an unnecessary vertex, simply select it and press the Delete key. 3ds Max spans the gap created with a segment to maintain the spline's integrity.

FIGURE 4.104
Drawing the
east wall

FIGURE 4.105
Convert these
vertices to curves.

Convert these two vertices to Bezier curves.

4. Use the Outline option to create an outline that is 0.5 meter wide.

5. Extrude the east wall to a height of 11 meters.

6. Click the Maximize Viewport Toggle to view all of the viewports.

7. Save your work as **MyRonchamp04.max**.

You've created most of the major structure of the chapel. If you're familiar with the Chapel at Ronchamp, you'll see that there are a few areas where the model doesn't quite match the real building, but in general, you do get the overall flavor of the design. Refining the details will come later. For a view of the chapel so far, see Figure 4.106.

FIGURE 4.106
A view of the
chapel so far

Attaching Objects to a Mesh

As you have been modeling the Chapel at Ronchamp, you have been creating a series of objects. Sometimes, and particularly in more complicated projects where you anticipate creating hundreds of objects, it can be helpful to attach multiple objects to a mesh. By aggregating objects by attachment, you reduce the total number of objects in the scene. It often makes sense to attach the objects that logically belong together to a mesh object for simplified organization of your scene, but it is not strictly necessary. You will learn how to attach objects to a mesh next.

1. Select the north wall (Figure 4.107), which is the second-to-last object you made.

2. In order to attach other objects to this one, you'll have to first either convert this object to an editable poly or use the Edit Poly modifier. Apply the Edit Poly modifier to this wall.

3. Click the Attach button in the Edit Geometry rollout.

4. Click the adjacent tower to attach it to the north wall, as shown in Figure 4.108. You could also click the small Attach List button to the right of the Attach button to select the objects to attach from a list.

5. Click the Attach button again to turn it off.

6. Press H on the keyboard to open the Select Objects dialog box. Notice that the object you attached no longer appears in the list because it has become part of the east wall (currently named Line04).

7. Now that you have seen how attachment works, try the opposite—detaching. Enter the Element sub-object level of the north wall's Edit Poly modifier.

FIGURE 4.107
The scene with the north wall selected

FIGURE 4.108
Attaching the adjacent tower to the north wall

Attach the adjacent tower to the north wall.

8. Select the element that was formerly the independent tower within the east wall object, as shown in Figure 4.109.

9. Click the Settings button next to the Detach button in the Edit Geometry rollout, as shown in Figure 4.110.

FIGURE 4.109
Selecting elements within a mesh

FIGURE 4.110
Selecting the Settings button for the Detach option

DETACHING AN OBJECT CREATES AN EDITABLE POLY

Once you detach an object from a poly, it too becomes an editable poly. The modifiers you may have used before the attachment occurred are lost. Because of this, it is important not to attach objects to a poly until you are done editing their modifier stacks.

10. The Detach dialog box appears to prompt you for the name of this new object. Type **Vault02** in the Detach As field and then click OK.

11. Exit the Element sub-object level. Observe how the tower is no longer part of the bounding box of the east wall object, as shown in Figure 4.111. It has become its own "object" once again.

FIGURE 4.111
The scene after you've detached an element from the mesh

You have seen how you can organize a complex scene by attaching multiple objects to a single poly object. You have also learned how to detach elements from a poly, returning them to their former object status. Utilizing the two opposites of attaching to and detaching from meshes is an optional way to organize your scenes.

CHOOSING MESHES OVER GROUPS

You may choose to organize your scene using Attach as an alternative to using groups. Objects that are attached to a mesh lose the modifiers in their stacks and often require the use of more complicated Multi/Sub-Object materials. However, mesh elements require much less memory than grouped objects.

Smoothing Meshes

You learned in Chapter 2, "Introducing 3ds Max Objects," that many of the 3ds Max primitive objects have a Smooth parameter. *Smoothing* is an inherent quality of mesh objects.

All meshes are composed of vertices that are themselves connected by straight lines called edges. Sets of edges define surfaces called faces or polygons (depending on whether they are three-sided or multisided). Multiple polygons form elements, as you previously learned.

The relatively simple surfaces set up by the sub-objects literally define a faceted overall surface. Smoothing is an illusion, created by blending the appearance of adjacent surfaces to give the appearance of a continuously curved surface over a discrete set of vertices, edges, faces, and so on. The left image in Figure 4.112 shows the actual surfaces or a sphere while the right image shows the same sphere with smoothing turned on.

Each mesh object stores smoothing information that can be edited. You will learn two different ways to adjust smoothing—both within a mesh and by using the Smooth modifier.

FIGURE 4.112
Compare a faceted sphere and a smooth sphere.

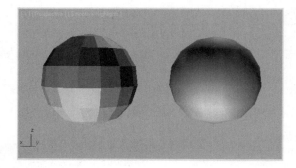

Smoothing within a Mesh

You can adjust smoothing at the sub-object level within a mesh object. The smoothing data is part of the mesh itself. Next you will learn how to convert an object to an editable mesh and adjust its smoothing.

1. Select the tapered wall of the Ronchamp model, as shown in Figure 4.113, that you modeled earlier in this chapter.

FIGURE 4.113
Select the tapered wall.

2. Right-click in the viewport and choose Convert To ➤ Convert to Editable Poly, and the object becomes an editable poly.

3. Zoom into the area indicated in Figure 4.114.

FIGURE 4.114
Zoom into the curved area on the back side of the tapered wall.

ZOOM REGION WITH PERSPECTIVE VIEWPORTS

The Field-of-View navigation tool in a Perspective viewport is actually the top button in a flyout. Hold down the button to extend the flyout and expose the Zoom Region tool underneath.

1. Observe that there is a smoothing discontinuity, or *seam*, that shows up along the back side of the tapered wall, as shown in Figure 4.115. This is typical of many modified mesh forms. Turn off Edged Faces in the viewport's label shortcut menu to see this seam.

FIGURE 4.115
Smoothing discontinuity, or "seam"

Observe the seam here.

2. Add another Edit Poly modifier to the top of the stack, and then go to the Polygon sub-object level.

3. Select all polygons within this object by pressing Ctrl+A on the keyboard.

4. Scroll way down in the Modify panel and locate the Polygon Properties rollout. Click the Clear All button in the Smoothing Groups area (see Figure 4.116).

5. Deselect all polygons by clicking off to the side in the viewport. Notice that all the smoothing information that was previously stored in the editable poly has been cleared out, as shown in Figure 4.117. Each surface appears faceted and is easily discernable from the adjacent surfaces.

6. Select all polygon sub-objects again by pressing Ctrl+A.

7. Click the Auto Smooth button near the Clear All button.

8. Deselect all polygon sub-objects and exit Polygon mode. The seam that was present in Figure 4.115 has been smoothed out now that you've smoothed the mesh—see Figure 4.118. Look carefully, as the effect is subtle.

FIGURE 4.116
Clearing the smoothing groups

FIGURE 4.117
The editable poly has been cleared of all smoothing.

FIGURE 4.118
The resmoothed mesh

> **UNDERSTANDING SMOOTHING GROUPS**
>
> Smoothing groups are the numbers in the 8 × 4 grid in the Surface Properties rollout. Each polygon sub-object can have a smoothing group number assigned. Just select a polygon and click the number button to assign a smoothing group. When adjacent polygons have the same smoothing group number, their surface appearance is smoothed together. When the angle between adjacent faces exceeds the threshold value in the input box next to the Auto Smooth button, the faces are not smoothed together. You can manually edit the smoothing groups for maximum control over the illusion.

The Smooth Modifier

Another way of applying smoothing to any object—whether it is a mesh or a parametric object—is to use the Smooth modifier.

1. Select the tapered wall again.

2. Apply the Smooth modifier.

3. Check Auto Smooth in the Parameters rollout.

4. Adjust the Threshold value to 0.0 degrees. This effectively removes smoothing from the object.

5. Drag the threshold spinner up. As you do, observe how more and more of the object gets smoothed. Set the threshold to 30 degrees. Figure 4.119 shows the object properly smoothed.

6. Set the threshold at 90 degrees and observe how the illusion of smoothing extends now across the top edge. This is an example of incorrect smoothing. Figure 4.120 shows a case where the threshold value was set too high so that the crisp edges that you want to remain are smoothed.

FIGURE 4.119
Smoothing threshold
set at 30 degrees

FIGURE 4.120
Smoothing threshold
too high

7. Delete the Smooth modifier after you are done experimenting by clicking the Remove Modifier from the Stack tool below the modifier stack.

8. Save your file as **MyRonchamp_Smoothed.max**.

Creating and Modifying Objects Using Box Modeling

The toolsets included with 3ds Max's editable poly and editable mesh objects are extensive, giving you an immense amount of control over the objects in your scene. Using either mesh type, you can manipulate, delete from, or add to the sub-objects to create nearly any object imaginable. This modeling technique, often called box modeling because the initial mesh begins as a box primitive, is very powerful and often used to create objects in 3ds Max scenes where primitives, extrusions, and modifiers are not flexible enough to complete a project or feature.

Preparing a Box for Box Modeling

Figure 4.121 shows a 3D model of the type of pew found in the Ronchamp chapel. This is an example where you could use box modeling. The pews consist of poured concrete supports and carved wooden planks that can be quickly modeled using a combination of polygon editing tools.

FIGURE 4.121
An example where box modeling could be used

In the next exercise, you'll model a pew similar to those shown in Figure 4.121:

1. Click the Application Button and select Reset to prepare for working on a new scene.

2. Set the units to Feet w/Decimal Inches and set the default units to Inches.

3. In the Perspective viewport, make a box primitive near the origin and set its Length to 0´ 2˝ and Width to 0´ 7˝, and set its Height to 0´10˝. Your Parameters rollout should look like Figure 4.122.

FIGURE 4.122
The Parameters rollout after creating the box primitive

Parameters	
Length:	0'2.0"
Width:	0'7.0"
Height:	0'10.0"
Length Segs:	1
Width Segs:	1
Height Segs:	1

4. Right-click the viewport label and choose Edged Faces to display the objects edges. Orbit the viewport so you can see the back side of the box. Your Perspective viewport should look similar to Figure 4.123.

5. Right-click in the viewport and convert the box into an editable poly.

CONNECTING THE EDGES

Starting on the back side, the next step is to connect the edges to divide the one polygon into three polys, which you can then extrude.

1. Click the Polygon Modeling tab of the Graphite Modeling toolbar and then access the Edge sub-object level.

2. Click to select the two vertical edges on the right side of the box.

3. Right-click to access the quad menu. In the lower-left quad (tools 2), click the Connect Settings button, as shown in Figure 4.124.

4. The Connect Edges caddy appears, as shown in Figure 4.125. Move it to the side, and then change the number of segments to 2, the Pinch setting to 24, and the Slide setting to 10. Notice that the caddy label changes as you move your cursor over each field. Also notice the new edge positions on the box as you adjust the values.

5. Click the green check mark to approve the changes. Next you'll start extruding polygons to build the pew support.

FIGURE 4.124
Accessing the connect settings

FIGURE 4.125
The Connect Edges settings

EXTRUDING POLYS

The Extrude modifier projects a 2D object into 3D space by building vertical faces and capping the top and bottom surfaces. The Extrude tool in the editable poly toolset projects a selected set of faces away from their existing locations by building new perpendicular faces. Here, you'll extrude the faces at the top and bottom of the box to model the supports for the kneepad and the prayerbook rest.

1. In the Main Toolbar, set the Crossing/Window option to Crossing.

2. Click the Polygon Modeling Tab on the ribbon, and select the Polygon sub-object model, or press 4 on the keyboard to go to that mode.

3. Ctrl+click the polys to get the top and bottom vertical polygons, as shown in Figure 4.126.

4. In the Perspective viewport, zoom into the base of the support. In the Polygons tab of the Graphite Modeling toolbar, click the drop-down arrow and then click the Extrude Settings button to open the Extrude Polygons dialog box.

5. Set the Extrusion Type to Local Normal so that each polygon extrudes perpendicular to the angle of its surface and so that the intersection between adjacent selected polys is maintained. Set the Extrusion Height to 5˝, as shown in Figure 4.127.

6. Click the green check mark to approve the changes. The extrusions are executed and the dialog box closes.

7. Select the polygon on the top right of the model, then choose the Extrude settings from the quad menu. Using the quad menu is the fastest method to get to the basic tools; more advanced tools require you use the ribbon.

FIGURE 4.126
Selecting the top and bottom polygons

FIGURE 4.127
Extruding the polys

8. Set the extrusion to 6″ and click OK. Your model should look like Figure 4.128.

Repeat the process now on the two front vertical edges of the newly extruded polygon. Select the two edges, and use Connect Edges to divide them into two polys, as shown in Figure 4.129.

9. Select the polys and extrude them 4″. Repeat the process once more, selecting the new top poly and extruding it about 7″. Your model should resemble Figure 4.130.

FIGURE 4.128
The box model
so far

FIGURE 4.129
The base after scaling the top corner vertices

FIGURE 4.130
The pew support

10. You can add a slant to the back support by selecting two vertices and moving them to angle the vertical faces on the back side of the support. Select two vertices and move them to the right in the Y-axis only. You can do this on each set of vertices, as shown in Figure 4.131. For the seat, select the pair of vertices and move them downward slightly.

FIGURE 4.131
Slanting the pew's
back support

Next you'll add the horizontal pieces for the prayerbook rest, kneepads and the bench for seating. You'll use the Bevel tool and the Chamfer Edge function to shape and round the cross pieces.

BEVELING POLYS

So far you've used Connect to create new polygons and Extrude to build additional geometry. You can use the Bevel tool and the Chamfer Edge function to make rounded sections of your model.

1. In the perspective viewport, zoom out so that you can see the entire editable poly, and then click the top of the stack so you're out of the sub-object level.

2. On the Edit menu, choose Clone. Create an instance of the support by clicking OK.

3. Move the clone 5″ away from the original object by using the Move tool and watching the transform type-in.

4. Create a box for the bench by going to the Create panel, turning on Box and AutoGrid, and then dragging out a box starting on the slanting surface on the support, as shown in Figure 4.132. Since the surface is angled and AutoGrid is on, the box should lay flat on the angled surface. Name the object **Bench**.

FIGURE 4.132
Creating the bench
with AutoGrid

CREATING USER GRIDS WITH AUTOGRID

If AutoGrid is on and you hold down the Alt key, the newly created grid will be displayed and remain active in the viewport. The grid object will remain in the file unless you delete it, so you can always activate it and reuse it to create additional objects.

5. Adjust the height, width, and length to taste. You can use Length = 2″, Width = 6″, and Height = 1″.

6. Add an Edit Poly modifier to the bench.

7. Select the front polygon and choose the Bevel settings button. Set the bevel height to around 1.6″ and the outline to -0.3″, as shown in Figure 4.133. Click OK to commit the changes.

8. Repeat the process to create the rest of the bench. Bevel as before, then add a second bevel where you make the outline larger. Move the last polygon up so it fits in the cutout area, as shown in Figure 4.134.

9. You can round individual edges by using the Chamfer tool. In the Edit Edges rollout, choose Chamfer settings and then select the edge, adjust the chamfer size and segment number, and click the green check mark to approve and commit. See Figure 4.135.

FIGURE 4.133
Beveling the
bench polygons

FIGURE 4.134
Completing the
bench polygons

FIGURE 4.135
Chamfering
the edges

10. For practice, create the kneepad and the prayerbook rest to finish the pew assembly. The finished pew should look something like Figure 4.136.

11. Save your work as **MyPew_boxmodel.max**.

Now that you've been introduced to box modeling techniques, let's use soft selection methods to adjust the Ronchamp chapel model.

FIGURE 4.136
The finished pew

SHAPING THE WALLS WITH SOFT SELECTION

Soft selection allows you to select sub-objects in a graduated set. When a soft selection is applied to a sub-object selection, transforms and modifiers affect the selection with a falloff. This allows you to build gentle, graceful curves with ease.

1. Open **Ronchamp_shapeWall.max**, or continue from your own model if you prefer.

2. Select and navigate to the West Wall object (Line006 West Wall in the supplied file), the wall between the tallest tower and the shorter two towers.

3. Add an Edit Poly modifier to the object if needed.

4. Select a pair of vertices in the top center of the wall.

5. In the Soft Selection rollout turn on Use Soft Selection. Adjust the value for the falloff, and watch as a rainbow display appears over the vertices (see Figure 4.137; you can download the color file at **www.sybex.com/go/mastering3dsmaxdesign2011**).

FIGURE 4.137
Soft selection of
the wall vertices

6. Make sure Pinch and Bubble are set to zero, then use the Select and Move tool to move the selected vertices down in the Z-axis. The move transform is applied in a graduated effect over the soft selection, and the wall is given a gentle, graceful undulation, as shown in Figure 4.138.

7. Try the same thing on the opposite wall for practice. Select the vertices at the end of the wall, near the outdoor altar, rather than adding a curve in the middle. Your wall should look something like Figure 4.139. If the bottom of the wall is affected, move those vertices back into place by turning *off* the soft selection, and use the Transform gizmo on vertices one at a time or in small groups. You can right-click the Z transform type-in to zero out (flatten) the vertices.

8. Save your work as **MyRonchamp_curvedWalls.max**.

FIGURE 4.138
Curved wall created with soft selection

FIGURE 4.139
Curving the east wall

Using the Transform Toolbox

Another tool that can be helpful in your daily use of Editable Poly objects in 3ds Max Design 2011 is the Transform Toolbox. Choose Edit ➢ Transform Toolbox to display the floating toolbox, as shown in Figure 4.140. The toolbox allows you to easily rotate, scale, adjust the pivot points, and move/clone objects in your scene. The toolbox is divided into four sections: the Rotate tools, Size tools, Align Pivot tools, and the Object tools. The Transform Toolbox is dockable to any side of the 3ds Max user interface.

FIGURE 4.140
The floating Trans-
form Toolbox

The Rotate group of tools will rotate a selected object or sub-object clockwise or counter-clockwise based on the current view. You can select the amount of rotation in degrees by using the presets in the provided drop-down, or by entering a value in the Degrees field. You can type in a value or use the spinners.

1. Continue from your previous file, or open Ronchamp_pew.max.

 If you haven't already opened the Transform Toolbox, choose Edit ➤ Transform Toolbox to display the dialog box.

2. Select the Pew Support object you created in the previous series of exercises. Isolate this object by pressing Alt+Q.

3. Click the drop-down in the Rotate group of the toolbox and select the 30 Degrees preset.

4. In the Top viewport, click the clockwise-curving arrow. See how your pew support has changed its rotation, as shown in Figure 4.141.

5. Press Ctrl+Z or the Undo Scene Operation button on the Quick Access toolbar to return the pew support to its original rotation.

When using this tool with Perspective, User, or Camera viewports, you have to watch for which axis the object is rotated around.

FIGURE 4.141
The rotated
pew support

The Size group of the toolbar does not directly resize the object as if you were adjusting parameters in the Modify tab; it acts like the Scale command that you were introduced to in Chapter 1, "Getting to Know 3ds Max Design 2011." The tool can calculate the current size of an object in a given dimension and, based on the new measurement you enter, the tool will figure out the correct scaling factor to apply to the object to make it the desired size. If you look at the parameters of a primitive object that you have resized, you will see the sizes are the original values. This can be a very helpful tool in adjusting your models, but you need to be aware of the impact of using this tool on your objects.

1. Select the pew support again and click the Get button in the Size group of the Transform Toolbox.

 The Get button queries the selected object and returns the bounding box dimensions of the object in a new Size dialog box, shown in Figure 4.142.

2. The pew is 23 inches tall, which seems too short. In the Transform Toolbox's Size field, enter **26** and make sure the Z radio button is selected.

3. Click the Set Size button. This will scale your pew to be 26˝ in height. See Figure 4.143.

FIGURE 4.142
The Size dialog box is returned when you click the Get button.

FIGURE 4.143
The pew support scaled to 26 inches tall

The Align Pivot tools allow you to easily modify an object's pivot point to help with modeling and scene building operations, applying modifiers to shapes or objects, or animating the objects in you scenes. You can quickly move the object's pivot point to the Minimum, Maximum, or center of the object in any given dimension, or you can set the pivot point right on the scene's World Origin regardless of the object's current position, which can be helpful for creating radial

arrays. You will learn to use radial arrays later in this chapter. Changes to the object's pivot take effect immediately; there is no Apply button, so be careful.

The Object tools section has two buttons: Center and QClone.

The Center tool This moves the currently selected object so that its pivot point is on the scene origin (0,0,0). This can be helpful for when you need to reset an object that isn't near the origin, or if you want to use the Save Selected option to extract an object from a scene.

The QClone (Quick Clone) button This creates a copy of an object directly to the right (offset by the object's width) in the current viewport. Three keyboard modifiers enhance the way the QClone tool works. If you hold down the Shift key and press QClone, you will make an instanced copy of the selected object. If you hold down the Alt key, QClone will make two copies of the object. If you hold down Shift+Alt, you will create two instances of the original object.

Creating Clones with Array and Snapshot

As you saw earlier, clones, particularly instanced clones, are great time-savers in 3ds Max. Using the Shift key in conjunction with any of the transform tools (Move, Rotate, or Scale), you can quickly create multiple copies by entering a value in the Number of Copies input box. Each subsequent clone will be created at the same interval as the initial from the original object clone. This is adequate when only one transform is required for a clone operation.

The Array and Snapshot tools both create organized patterns of clones with much more creative control than the Shift+Transform clone methods. The Array tool creates patterns in three magnitudes of complexity: 1D, 2D, and 3D. A 1D array moves, rotates, and scales an object's clones in an axis or combination of axes to create a row of cloned objects. The 2D and 3D array options are used to create fields (2D) of the first array or stacks (3D) of the 2D array.

The Snapshot tool creates clones of animated objects at any time interval you choose. An instanced clone retains a parameter link to all other instances while the Copy option creates an object that holds the animated object's shape only at the time that it was cloned.

Creating a Pew Grid with Array

The pews must be repeated over a grid pattern to lay out the seating for the congregation inside the main space. This makes the pew layout a fine example for explaining the Array tool.

1. Open the file `Array_Pew.max`. This consists of a single column created from an Extended Spline primitive and the Extrude modifier. Select the Pew_LeftSupport object, and then right-click in the Top viewport to activate it.

2. Right-click a blank area of any toolbar and select Extras from the shortcut menu (see Figure 4.144) to open the Extras toolbar if it isn't already open.

3. In the Extras toolbar, click the Array tool.

FIGURE 4.144
Opening the
Extras toolbar

The Array dialog box that opens (see Figure 4.145) may appear formidable at first, but it is broken down into a few logical groups. At the top of the dialog box is the Array Transformation section. Input information into the left (Incremental) side to specify the distance, degrees, or percentage difference between each clone, and 3ds Max will transform each clone per the input values. Input information into the right side (Totals) of the Array Transformation section to specify the distance, degrees, or percentage difference between the original object and the last clone created. 3ds Max divides the total value by the number of clones to determine the incremental value. Both halves are arranged in columns and rows, with the columns determining the axes in which each transform is affected. Enter data in the top row to set the distance between clones, the middle row to set the angular displacement, and the bottom row to set the percentage change between each clone.

FIGURE 4.145
The Array dialog box contains controls for creating arrays of clones.

INCREMENTAL VALUES

When working with incremental values, it's important to understand that each increment is applied to the clones in relation to the state of the previous clone. For example, a 15-degree Z-rotation increment rotates each clone 15 degrees more than the previous clone's rotation. This is especially important when working with the Scale transform in the Array dialog. If a tubular column is 10′0″ tall and the Incremental X Scale value in the Array dialog box is set to 10′ and the Z Scale value is set to 90 percent, how many columns are created before the Z height becomes zero? The answer is that the height will never be zero because each 90-percent Z-scale reduction is applied to the total height of the current column. The first clone will be 9′0″ tall, the next will be 8′1″ (90 percent of 9′0″), then 7′3″, and so on.

The Type of Object section at the bottom of the Array dialog box contains controls for specifying the type of clones to create. The Array Dimensions section contains controls for the type of array and the offset distance between 2D and 3D arrays. The Preview button generates a preview in the viewports for your review before the array operation is committed. In the following exercise, you create a 3D array of pews using the Array dialog box:

1. Turn on the Preview button. Enter **-2′ 9″** in the X Incremental input box, make sure the Instance radio button is checked in the Type of Object section, and enter **7** in the 1D Count input box (see Figure 4.146), and then click the OK button.

2. The viewport displays a series of seven columns at 2′ 9″ increments, as shown in Figure 4.147. The last object created is the currently selected object.

FIGURE 4.146
The settings in the
Array dialog box

FIGURE 4.147
The seven supports
created using the
Array dialog box

NO VIEWPORT CHANGES ARE AVAILABLE IN PREVIEW MODE

The Array Preview tool can be useful when you're creating a complex array. One drawback is that, when in Preview mode, you cannot zoom or pan in a viewport to inspect a sprawling array.

3. Click the Undo button in the Main Toolbar or press the Ctrl+Z to undo the array.

4. Click the Array tool again and notice that the previous settings remain in the Array dialog box.

5. In the Array Dimensions area, click the 2D radio button and enter **2** in the 2D Count input box. Click the Preview button. It appears as if nothing happened because the six copies of the array are collocated over the original array. There was no offset specified in the Array dialog box.

6. Click the Preview button again to exit the Preview mode. In the Array Dimensions area, enter **4′ 5″** in the Y Incremental Row input box for the 2D array to create clones of the pew supports to fill the trapezoidal base evenly. The dialog box should look like Figure 4.148.

7. Click the Preview button again. This time all the supports appear in the viewport, as shown in Figure 4.149.

8. There's an extra pew support object you can delete, and then select the bench object and array it. Repeat the process for the kneepad and prayerbook-rest objects. Your finished array should look like Figure 4.150. Save your file as **MyRonchamp_PewArray.max**.

FIGURE 4.148
The Array Dimensions section of the Array dialog box should now look like this.

FIGURE 4.149
The pew supports created using the 2D Array Dimensions option

FIGURE 4.150
The finished pew array

As you can see, the Array tool can quickly and accurately construct many clones in a structured pattern. The tool can also be used to form clones with multiple transforms applied simultaneously, as you will see in the next exercise.

Creating a Multitransform Polar Array

A polar array is an array with an angular displacement controlling the spacing between objects, rather than a lateral increment. In 3ds Max, when you rotate an object, it is rotated about its pivot. To effectively create a polar array, you need to first move the pivot point away from the geometry of the object.

1. Open the Array Polar.max file. This consists of a single, short tubular column. Select the column.

2. Click the Hierarchy button in the Command panel to access the hierarchy and Pivot tools.

3. Ensure that the Pivot option is selected at the top of the Hierarchy panel and then click the Affect Pivot Only button in the Adjust Pivot rollout. The button (see Figure 4.151) turns blue and the axis tripod changes shape in the viewports.

4. Click the Select and Move tool and then, in the Top viewport, move the pivot point to the left, near the origin. Be sure to click and drag on the red X-axis to restrict the movement to a single direction. Only the pivot point moves while the geometry stays in a fixed location, as shown in Figure 4.152.

5. Click the Affect Pivot Only button to turn it off.

6. Open the Array dialog box and then click the Reset All Parameters button at the bottom of the dialog box to clear any settings from the previous exercise.

7. In the Incremental Z Rotate input box, enter **30** to create a 30-degree rotation in the Z-axis between each column.

8. Click the right-facing arrow next to the Scale label to activate the Scale Totals input boxes.

9. Enter **600** in the Totals Z Scale input box. This will cause the last column in the array to be 600 percent larger than the first.

10. In the 1D Count input box, enter **7**. This is a setup to create a semicircular array of columns with ascending heights. Your Array dialog box should look like Figure 4.153.

FIGURE 4.151
Changing the
Pivot option

FIGURE 4.152
Moving the pivot
point

FIGURE 4.153
The Array dialog
box prepared for a
polar array

11. Click the Preview button. The array is displayed properly in the viewport, as shown in Figure 4.154.

12. Click the Preview button again to turn off Preview mode. Make any adjustments that you want to in the Array dialog box, and then click OK to create the array.

FIGURE 4.154
The polar array

The Array tool's capability to create a vast number of clones is significant and deserves additional experimentation. Consider using Array to generate all of the windows in a high-rise or fields of cars or light posts.

USING THE ARRAY TOOL TO CREATE WINDOWS

Modern office buildings are often designed with large, redundant surfaces covered with windows or glass panes. The windows are usually of the same size and design and equally distributed throughout large portions of a building's vertical surfaces. A common practice is to use the Array command to reproduce the windows in an accurate and orderly fashion. As long as the on-center distance between windows is known both vertically and horizontally, the Array tool can be a great timesaver.

Creating Multiple Clones Using Snapshot

When an object is animated, it may have a change in its transforms (Move, Rotate, and Scale), parameters, modifier settings, and so on. The Snapshot tool, located on the Array flyout, captures the state of the selected object at the specified time interval. You can create copy, instance, or reference clones as well as mesh clones (that is, clones collapsed to editable meshes). The Snapshot tool requires an animated object; animation is covered thoroughly in Chapter 12, "Understanding Animation," and Chapter 13, "Creating Animations, Particles, and Dynamics."

1. Open the Snapshot.max file. This scene consists of a single wrought-iron fence post and three rails forming a 50′ × 50′ square (see Figure 4.155). The post's vertical scale reciprocates between approximately 7′0″ and 6′0″ every 20 frames and travels along the 200′0″ perimeter over 400 frames.

FIGURE 4.155
A fence with rails
and a single post

FIGURE 4.155
A fence with rails
and a single post

A FRAME IS A POINT IN TIME

A *frame* is a point on a timeline that corresponds to one displayed image and is measured in frames per second (fps). This scene is set up to create and play back animation at 30 fps.

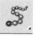

2. In the Perspective viewport, select the fence post.

3. In the Extras toolbar, click and hold the Array tool and select the Snapshot tool.

4. The Snapshot dialog box opens as shown in Figure 4.156. Click the Range radio button to instruct 3ds Max to create copies over a specified period of time.

5. In the Snapshot area, set the From input box to 0, the To input box to 400, and the Copies input box to 200. The 200 clones will be generated during the entire 400-frame animation, or one clone every 1/15th of a second.

6. In the Clone Method section, choose Instance and then click the OK button.

7. The posts, reciprocating heights and all, are created as shown in Figure 4.157.

FIGURE 4.156
The Snapshot
dialog box

FIGURE 4.157
The Snapshot tool
created 200 evenly
spaced instanced
post clones.

The only slight problem in the scene is that there are three posts in the corner where the original post started. These are the original post and the posts created at frames 0 and 400 with the Snapshot tool. Only one is necessary, so we will re-create all of the posts with slightly different parameters:

1. Click the Undo button, or press Ctrl+Z to undo the Snapshot tool.

2. Click the Snapshot tool again to open the Snapshot dialog box.

3. Set the From value to 2 and the To value to 398. Reduce the number of copies to 198, and then click the OK button.

The posts are created again, this time without the additional objects at the starting point. Because all of the posts are instances, changes to any single object will be instantly reflected in all of the others. When the posts are required to be closer together, set the number of copies higher to increase the clone count generated in the same amount of time. A similar tool on the same flyout as the Array and Snapshot tools is the Spacing tool. Use Spacing instead of Snapshot when there is no animation involved or when the precise distance between objects is pertinent, rather than the count.

The Bottom Line

Create openings with ProBoolean operations Using the ProBoolean operations, you can join meshes (union), delete one object and any volume it shares with another object (subtraction), or delete two objects while retaining the volume of the share (intersection).

> **Master It** Using the ProBoolean tools, cut an archway into a box primitive representing a wall. The archway is to be 3´ wide and 8´ high at the top of the arch.

Designate a modeling template image Using a template image applied to geometry, such as a plane or a box, can be very helpful in the modeling process. These image planes can be used to display reference information, such as plans, sections, or elevations, needed to aid the modeling process.

> **Master It** So you can use it to model the building's elevation, add an image plane that uses the House.jpg file provided with 3ds Max to your Front viewport.

Create and modify objects with box modeling Virtually any real-world object can be created using box modeling methodology. Instead of combining primitive objects, you can take a plane or a box and extrude/bevel, inset, and otherwise build up new polys to model anything you wish.

> **Master It** Create any object you want using box modeling techniques.

Attach objects to a mesh The Attach option of an Editable Poly object causes objects to become Element sub-objects of an existing Editable Poly. This creates a single object from multiple objects and reduces the memory requirements of the object.

> **Master It** Create a short tube primitive to act as a simple, round picture frame. Taper the tube. Create a short cylinder to represent the picture backing. Use the Attach option to attach the backing to the frame.

Create clones with Array and Snapshot The Array and Snapshot tools both provide a method of creating many clones of scene objects. The Array tool creates them in patterns of rows and columns, and the Snapshot tool creates clones by capturing their appearance at any point in time.

Master It Create a window that's 4′ wide by 6′ tall. In the Front viewport, create an array of windows that are spread out 8′ on-center horizontally and 12′ on-center vertically.

Chapter 5

Working with External Design Data

3ds Max Design is a complete and powerful product. 3ds Max Design 2011 is so robust that it can take advantage of the other design and drafting programs produced by Autodesk. Other products that are useful with 3ds Max Design are AutoCAD-based applications, including AutoCAD, AutoCAD LT, AutoCAD Mechanical, AutoCAD Architecture, AutoCAD Civil 3D, and the Revit family of products. In this chapter, you'll look at ways that you can use AutoCAD-based applications more directly with 3ds Max in your design and visualization workflow. You'll explore the common practices of importing 2D AutoCAD line drawings as a starting point in the creation of 3ds Max geometry and the direct linking of the AutoCAD drawings. The latter procedure incorporates the entire DWG file into the 3ds Max scene with a one-way pipeline; any changes to the AutoCAD file are reflected in the 3ds Max scene. Finally, you'll look at the procedure for incorporating Revit files into 3ds Max.

In this chapter, you'll learn to:

◆ Create topography with splines

◆ Import AutoCAD plans into 3ds Max

◆ Use the Substitute modifier

◆ Import Revit files into 3ds Max

Creating Topography with Splines

In 3ds Max there are many ways to add detail to an object created with splines, as you saw with the wineglass in Chapter 3, "Creating Shapes with Splines," and modeling the Ronchamp cathedral in Chapter 4, "Editing Meshes and Creating Complex Objects." In Chapter 9, "Enhancing Models with Materials," you will learn to create geometry by using a displacement map. A *displacement map*, which is similar to a bump map, creates a deformed surface based on the light and dark areas of a bitmap image. A *bump map*, on the other hand, simply applies shadows to your rendered objects, giving the illusion of texture. You can create terrain in a 3ds Max scene by painting light and dark areas in an image and then importing that image and using it as a displacement map, as shown in Figure 5.1.

FIGURE 5.1
A bitmap image (left) and the terrain created by using the image as a displacement map (right)

INTEGRATING AUTODESK PRODUCTS INTO YOUR WORKFLOW

The tight integration between all of Autodesk's AutoCAD-based products and 3ds Max Design 2011 allows you to maximize the strengths of each program in your workflow. By using CAD and 3ds Max together, you can maintain a single design database that carries through your entire workflow. 3ds Max will never overwrite an AutoCAD DWG or DXF file that you import or link into your scene, so you can be sure of the integrity of your design database.

Depending on your particular needs and skill level with each program, you will need to consider several strategies for planning the tasks to perform in each software package.

Although it is possible to create your entire project in 3ds Max alone, if you have access to and proficiency with AutoCAD, we don't recommend you do so. 3ds Max's real strengths are in modeling complex forms, assigning materials, lighting, composing scenes, rendering, and animating. 3ds Max is not as proficient at managing the complex 2D linework needed in drafting—this is AutoCAD and AutoCAD LT's traditional strength. Therefore, if you have both programs, it is more efficient to utilize AutoCAD for what it is best at and use 3ds Max for its strengths.

AutoCAD and AutoCAD LT are excellent tools for creating 2D geometry. Much of your work as a designer will require accurate renditions of your designs in the traditional plan and elevation views. Frequently, designs begin as 2D plans anyway, so having the ability to import or link to a DWG or DXF file is a natural extension of 3ds Max. In the most common strategy, the 2D linework is handled by CAD, and the rest of the workflow is handled by 3ds Max.

Another strategy to consider is to bring a well-developed 3D model into 3ds Max from AutoCAD, AutoCAD Architecture, or AutoCAD Mechanical. Some veteran AutoCAD users (or those very new to 3ds Max) may prefer to do basic 3D modeling in AutoCAD and use 3ds Max later in their workflow to add materials and create animation.

Although the 3D aspects of AutoCAD have been addressed in the most recent releases, AutoCAD's 3D modeling tools can seem quite primitive in comparison with 3ds Max's modeling tools. 3ds Max is much better for modeling curving, organic forms such as those found in furniture, ornamentation, and luminaries.

AutoCAD Architecture is designed to build a 3D model as you work, so it makes sense to link an AutoCAD Architecture model into 3ds Max and use 3ds Max for the visualization aspects of the workflow.

There is a strong push in the architectural industry to incorporate the Revit family of building information modeling (BIM) products into the construction pipeline. Using Revit, for example, wall objects are more than simple lines or flat structures. They are data-rich elements that define every aspect of the wall, such as construction type, coatings, surface properties, or surface area. Changing a wall type from stud with a brick façade to 8″ block not only changes the appearance of the structure but also cascades data throughout the file. Incorporating Revit files into a 3ds Max scene is discussed near the end of this chapter.

AutoCAD Architecture and Revit 2011 include mental ray as their core renderer—the same mental ray that is incorporated into 3ds Max. Using the lights, cameras, and materials included with the program, you can render your scenes in AutoCAD Architecture or Revit, but the 3ds Max rendering toolset is more complete.

IMPORTING AUTOCAD FILES THE OLD WAY

You can still access the legacy DWG importer if you want importing files to work the way it did in Autodesk VIZ 2008. Click the Application menu and select Import. Then click the Files of Type drop-down list and select Legacy AutoCAD (*.DWG) to access the old importer.

This type of terrain modeling is fine for creating freeform shapes. Displacement maps for terrain can also be created from Geographic Information System (GIS) and mapping programs so that you will have a good approximation of a project site to quickly create large areas of land for visualization projects. If you want to have a very accurate model of terrain based on survey data, you need to use other tools to create your terrain model, such as AutoCAD Map 3D or AutoCAD Civil 3D, or contour lines created in AutoCAD. In this section, you'll learn how you can quickly create a terrain model from contour lines generated in AutoCAD. You'll also get a look at ways of linking files from AutoCAD to allow you to maintain one data source for both AutoCAD and 3ds Max. The importer for DWG and DXF files has been refined in 3ds Max 2011 to support files from the latest versions of the software. Both DWG and DXF files are imported through the same dialog box.

1. Start 3ds Max; click the Application menu and choose References ➢ File Link Manager.

ACCESSING THE FILE LINK MANAGER FROM THE COMMAND PANEL

You can also use the File Link Manager as a utility. From the Utilities tab of the Command panel, choose More ➢ File Link Manager.

2. In the File Link Manager dialog box, make sure the Attach tab is selected; then click the File button.

3. In the Open dialog box, locate and open the contour.dwg file as shown in Figure 5.2. The contour lines are AutoCAD splines.

FIGURE 5.2
The contour.dwg file

4. Back in the File Link Manager dialog box, click the Attach This File button. The contours appear in the 3ds Max Perspective viewport, as shown in Figure 5.3.

5. Close the File Link Manager.

FIGURE 5.3
The imported
contour lines in
the Perspective
viewport

TURN OFF THE GRID IF NECESSARY

You may want to toggle the grid off if it makes the scene appear too cluttered.

By linking an AutoCAD file, you keep the imported geometry associated with the original AutoCAD file. As you'll see a bit later, this link will enable you to update the 3ds Max scene whenever changes occur to the AutoCAD file.

Now let's see how the contours can be turned into a surface model:

1. Click the Select by Name button to open the Select from Scene dialog box. Select both objects in the list; then click OK.

2. Make sure that the Geometry button is selected in the Create tab of the Command panel; then choose Compound Objects on the Create drop-down list.

3. Click Terrain on the Object Type rollout.

Figure 5.4 shows the surface that appears over the contour lines.

FIGURE 5.4
The surfaces created
using the Terrain
compound object

3ds Max creates a Terrain object based on the contour lines. You can improve the visibility of the terrain's shape by using the Color by Elevation option:

1. In the Command panel, scroll down to the Color by Elevation rollout and open it.

2. Click the Create Defaults button in the Zones by Base Elevation group.

The Terrain object changes to show a series of colored bands, as shown in Figure 5.5.

FIGURE 5.5
The contour line surfaces shown as a series of colored bands

The values in the Zones by Base Elevation list box tell you the base elevation for each of the colors. You can change the color and the base elevation:

1. Select the first elevation value in the list box of the Zones by Base Elevation group.

2. In the Color Zone group, click the Base Color swatch.

3. In the Color Selector dialog box, click a cyan color in the Hue/Blackness field and then click OK.

4. Click the Modify Zone button in the Color Zone group. The base of the Terrain object changes to the cyan color you selected.

You can also change the vertical location for a color by changing the Base Elev value in the Color Zone group. This doesn't have any effect on the shape of the Terrain object; it only changes the location of the color.

Updating Changes from an AutoCAD File

You imported the AutoCAD contour map by clicking the Application menu and choosing the References ➤ File Link Manager option. By using this option, you link your 3ds Max scene to the `contour.dwg` file in a way that's similar to XRef files in both 3ds Max and AutoCAD. The conceptual difference between file linking and external references is that with XRefs, you are bringing in native files, whereas with file linking, you are bringing in files that were made in another application. Just as with changes made to an XRef, changes in the `contour.dwg` file will affect any 3ds Max file to which it's linked.

Let's suppose that you have some corrections to make to the AutoCAD contour drawing that will affect the Terrain object you've just created. You can change the AutoCAD drawing file and then update the 3ds Max scene to reflect those changes:

1. If you have AutoCAD 2004 or later, open the `contour.dwg` file in AutoCAD and make the changes shown in Figure 5.6. Save the file when you are done, overwriting the original.

FIGURE 5.6
Stretch these points outward.

Stretch these points.

2. If you don't have AutoCAD, use Windows Explorer to delete the `contour.dwg` file; then make a copy of the `modified contour.dwg` file and rename it `contour.dwg` to replace the file you deleted. The `modified contour.dwg` file contains the changes shown in Figure 5.6.

3. In 3ds Max, click the Application menu and choose References ➤ File Link Manager.

4. In the File Link Manager dialog box, select the Files tab; then click the `contour.dwg` listing in the Linked Files list box at the top of the dialog box.

5. Click the Reload button. The File Link Settings: DWG Files dialog box displays.

6. In the File Link Settings: DWG Files dialog box, click OK. The file is reloaded, and the changes are applied in the current 3ds Max scene.

THE SCENE MAY LOSE THE TERRAIN COMPOUND OBJECT PARAMETERS

Some installs of 3ds Max Design have a problem updating changes from AutoCAD regarding the Terrain compound object. This is a known issue and is being looked into by Autodesk. If your file doesn't update properly (in other words, the Terrain compound object gets deleted), reselect the two contour objects and re-create the Terrain compound object.

7. Close the File Link Manager dialog box. The changes to the drawing are reflected in the 3ds Max scene. See Figure 5.7.

8. Save your terrain as `Mycontours.max`.

Like XRef files, 3ds Max scenes that are linked to AutoCAD files can be updated to reflect changes that are made to the source AutoCAD file. You'll get a chance to take a closer look at this feature later in this chapter.

FIGURE 5.7
The modified DWG file after reloading it into the 3ds Max scene

Exploring Terrain Options

The Terrain object has quite a few parameters that allow you to make adjustments to the terrain. For example, if you prefer, you can have the terrain appear as a terraced form instead of a smooth one, as shown in Figure 5.8.

FIGURE 5.8
The Terrain object with the Layered Solid option. The scene is shown rendered for clarity.

THE LAYERED SOLID OPTION IS SIMILAR TO A TRADITIONAL MODEL

The Layered Solid option of the Terrain object creates a surface that resembles a traditional site-plan physical model made of plywood, foamcore, or similar a material.

You've already seen how a few of the Color by Elevation rollout options work. Here's a rundown of the rest of the Terrain object parameters. These options allow you to add additional splines to, or delete splines from, an existing Terrain object.

THE PICK OPERAND ROLLOUT

The Pick Operand rollout, shown in Figure 5.9, allows you to add other splines to an existing Terrain object. The splines used for the Terrain object are referred to as the operands of the Terrain object. When a Terrain object is created, a Reference clone of the selected splines is added as part of the Terrain object. This is the default option in the Pick Operand rollout. When adding additional splines, you can choose the type of clone you want to use instead of the Reference clone. The Override option lets you replace one operand with another.

FIGURE 5.9
The Pick Operand
rollout

THE PARAMETERS ROLLOUT

The Parameters Rollout, shown in Figure 5.10, offers settings that control the overall form of the Terrain object. The Operands group lets you selectively delete operands from the terrain.

The Form group gives you control over the way the contour data is shaped into the terrain. Graded Surface creates the type of terrain you've seen in previous exercises. Graded Solid creates a solid form that encloses the entire terrain, including the underside. Layered Solid creates a terraced form. The Stitch Border option improves the formation of terrain where open splines are used in the contour. Retriangulate helps to generate a terrain that follows the contours more closely, especially when they are close together.

The Display group allows you to view the terrain as a surface terrain only, as contour lines only, or as both. The default is to show only the terrain.

FIGURE 5.10
The Parameters
rollout

At the bottom of the rollout, the Update group lets you control the way that the Terrain object is revised when the operands are edited. The Always option updates the Terrain object as soon as a contour is modified. The When Rendering option updates when you render the scene. You can also use the Update button with the Manually option to selectively update the terrain.

THE SIMPLIFICATION ROLLOUT

3ds Max uses the vertices of the original contour polylines to generate the Terrain object. The Simplification rollout (see Figure 5.11) options give you control over the number of vertices used to generate the terrain.

FIGURE 5.11
The Simplification rollout

In the Horizontal group, both the Use 1/2 of Points option and the Use 1/4 of Points option reduce the number of points used from the contour line. These procedures reduce the accuracy of the terrain, but they also reduce the complexity of the geometry, thereby making the terrain's memory requirements smaller and rendering time shorter. The Interpolate Points options increase the number of points used. Interpolate Points * 2, for example, doubles the number of vertices used by interpolating new points between the existing points in the contour.

The Vertical group determines whether all of the selected contour lines are used. You can reduce the terrain's complexity by using either the Use 1/2 of Lines option or the Use 1/4 of Lines option.

THE COLOR BY ELEVATION ROLLOUT

3ds Max lets you color the Terrain object by elevation, using the rollout shown in Figure 5.12. This enables you to visualize the terrain more clearly and helps you identify elevations by color-coding them.

FIGURE 5.12
The Color by Elevation rollout

The Maximum Elev. and Minimum Elev. options display the maximum and minimum extents of the terrain, based on the contour data. The Reference Elev. option lets you establish a reference elevation that is used for assigning colors to the terrain. If this value is equal to or less than the lowest contour, 3ds Max generates five color zones for the terrain, as you saw in an earlier exercise. If the Reference Elev. is greater than the lowest contour, 3ds Max treats the lower elevations as water, using the Reference Elev. value as the water level. Water is given a blue color by default.

The Zones by Base Elevation group gives you control over the individual colors for each color zone. As you've seen from the exercise, the Create Defaults button applies the colors to the Terrain object based on the current settings of the rollout. You can also change the color of each zone by selecting the zone elevation from the list box and using the Base Color swatch to select a color.

The Blend to Color Above and Solid to Top of Zone options let you choose to blend colors between zones or to have each zone one solid color. By default, colors are blended. You can change from blended to solid by selecting the zone elevation from the Zones by Base Elevation list, selecting Solid to Top of Zone, and then clicking the Modify Zones button. The Add Zone and Delete Zone options add and delete zones.

Setting Up an AutoCAD Plan for 3ds Max

If you're an experienced AutoCAD, Revit, AutoCAD Architecture, or AutoCAD Mechanical user, you may find it easier to create at least part of your 3D model in your CAD program and then import the model into 3ds Max to refine it. If this is the case, simply import or link the CAD model into 3ds Max and then resume your design visualization workflow at the point of assigning material, or adding lights and cameras. Then you can animate and render the scene.

On the other hand, you can also import 2D plans and elevations and build your 3D model entirely in 3ds Max. In this section, you'll explore the ways you can set up an AutoCAD or AutoCAD LT 2D drawing to take advantage of 3ds Max's superior modeling tools.

One of the drawbacks of importing fully developed 3D models from AutoCAD is that frequently, the surface normals of the AutoCAD model are not all oriented in the proper direction. You can use 3ds Max to adjust the normals to point in the correct direction, but that takes time. In this situation, it's sometimes more efficient to apply two-sided materials to the offending objects and leave it at that. Using two-sided materials increases rendering time; however, this disadvantage is often offset by the amount of time it would have taken to identify and adjust misaligned normals. You can also use the Normal modifier or apply the Edit Poly modifier to selected objects and adjust individual sub-objects in order to correct problems with surface normals.

This is less of a problem when the 3D geometry is created in Revit and then linked into 3ds Max Design using the Filmbox (FBX) file format. The geometry almost always comes in correctly using this method. Be sure to update to the latest FBX version by using the Web Update button in the FBX import dialog. The FBX importer has been updated since the release of 3ds Max 2011. FBX also imports materials and lights from Revit; its only real drawback is that it has a huge file size, so you often have to import pieces of your Revit project and assemble them inside 3ds Max Design 2011.

You can avoid the normals problem altogether by importing a specially prepared 2D drawing from AutoCAD into 3ds Max.

In the next set of exercises, you'll use AutoCAD to prepare a plan for export to 3ds Max. If you don't have AutoCAD, you can skip to the section "Importing AutoCAD Plans into 3ds Max Design."

1. Open AutoCAD 2004 or later; then open the `savoye-ground.dwg` file, which you'll find in the Chapter 5 archive at this book's accompanying web page, `www.sybex.com/go/mastering 3dsmaxdesign2011`. This is the ground floor plan of the Villa Savoye. This is an early twentieth-century residential design built at Poissy, outside of Paris, France, by the world-famous architect Le Corbusier (see Figure 5.13).

FIGURE 5.13
The Villa Savoye
drawing

USING A LEGACY VERSION OF AUTOCAD

All the files provided with this book are saved in the AutoCAD 2004 file format. If you have a version of AutoCAD previous to 2004, you will not be able to open the provided files. You can download the Autodesk DWG TrueView application from `www.autodesk.com` and install it on your system to open and save the files to a previous version of AutoCAD's file format so you can open the files and work along with these exercises.

2. Select WALL-3ds-EXT from the Layer drop-down list on the Layer Properties toolbar, as shown in Figure 5.14. You may need to unhide the toolbar if it is hidden in your AutoCAD UI layout.

FIGURE 5.14
Select the appropri-
ate layer in the Layer
drop-down list.

3. Use the Zoom Window tool to enlarge your view so that it looks similar to Figure 5.15.

4. Choose Draw ➢ Boundary. The Boundary Creation dialog box displays.

5. In the Boundary Creation dialog box, click Pick Points. The dialog box temporarily disappears to allow you to select points.

 At times, you might encounter an error message while selecting areas with the Boundary Creation dialog box. This is usually caused by one of two reasons: either the area you select isn't completely closed or a single line intrudes into the space you're trying to outline. In these cases, you will have to manually trim away intruding lines or join lines that do not meet.

6. Click the points shown in Figure 5.15. Press Enter when you're finished. A magenta outline of the wall appears, outlining the areas you selected.

FIGURE 5.15
Selecting points inside the exterior walls

Click the interior of these objects.

The magenta outline is a continuous closed polyline, which will become a closed spline in 3ds Max. Closed splines are preferable entities because they extrude without any problems with surface normals in 3ds Max. Because the WALL-3ds-EXT layer is current, the outline is placed on this layer. The layer's color is magenta, so the wall acquires the layer's color.

MAKE SURE YOU CAN SEE THE ENTIRE BOUNDARY

Depending on your version of AutoCAD, you may be required to see the entire boundary on the screen before picking a point to create a boundary object. The Boundary Creation tool may fail unless the boundary is visible because the older algorithm analyzes what is visible on the screen only. Try zooming out a bit and choosing Draw ➢ Boundary again if you get the message "Boundary Definition Error: Valid hatch boundary not found." Boundary creation will also fail if you click outside the lines, or if the point you click is directly on an object.

Next, continue to add the outlines of the exterior walls using the Boundary Creation dialog box:

1. Use the Pan tool to adjust your view to look similar to Figure 5.16.

2. Open the Boundary Creation dialog box again and then click the Pick Points button.

3. Select the points indicated in Figure 5.16.

4. Press Enter when you've selected all the points.

5. Adjust your view so it looks like Figure 5.17.

6. Use the Boundary Creation dialog box again to select the areas indicated in Figure 5.17. Press Enter when you're done.

7. Select WALL-3ds-INT from the Layer drop-down list on the Layer Properties toolbar.

8. Use the Boundary Creation dialog box to create outlines of the interior walls. When you're done, the interior walls should all appear in the cyan color, which is the color for the WALL-3ds-INT layer.

FIGURE 5.16
Selecting other points for the exterior wall

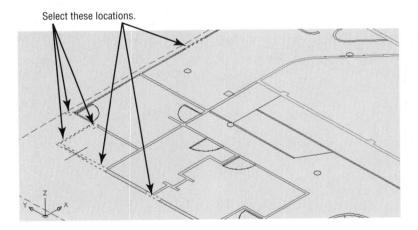

Select these locations.

FIGURE 5.17
Select points in the walls near the curved glass.

Select these locations.

You want the interior walls to be on a different layer from the exterior walls so that when the drawing is imported into 3ds Max, you can apply separate materials to the interior and exterior wall objects. By default, 3ds Max converts AutoCAD objects into 3ds Max objects based on their layers, although you can have 3ds Max use other criteria for converting objects if you choose.

Go ahead and use the Boundary Creation dialog box to outline the other portions of the drawing:

1. Choose the WALL-3ds-EXT-HDR layer; then use the Boundary Creation dialog box to outline the door headers over the exterior doors.

2. Turn off the Glass layer; then make the WALL-3ds-SILL layer current.

3. Use the Boundary Creation dialog box to outline the areas where the windows are indicated in the plan, as shown in Figure 5.18.

4. Finally, turn off the MULLION-VERT layer, set the current layer to MULLION-3ds-HORIZ, and outline the areas indicated in Figure 5.19.

FIGURE 5.18
Outline the window areas.

Select the window sill areas.

FIGURE 5.19
Outline the areas that are the horizontal mullions.

Select the outline of the curved windows.

5. Make sure all the layers are turned back on; then choose File (the Application menu in AutoCAD 2009 and newer), choose Save As, and save the file as MySavoye-ground-max.dwg.

The main point of these exercises is that you want to segregate the different parts of the drawing so that later, in 3ds Max, you can control the extruded heights of the separate layers individually. You ensure that you can do this by using layers in AutoCAD to organize the closed polylines that are to be extruded in 3ds Max.

You used the Boundary Creation dialog box to ensure that the polyline outlines are continuous and closed. Alternatively, you can just use the Polyline tool on the Draw toolbar to trace over the wall outlines if you prefer. The Boundary Creation dialog box makes the work a lot easier because it relieves you from having to click every point in each boundary.

Importing AutoCAD Plans into 3ds Max Design

Now that you've got the plan set up, you can import it into 3ds Max and make fairly quick work of the conversion to 3D. You've done all of the organizing in AutoCAD, so all that is left is to extrude the building parts to their appropriate heights:

1. Open 3ds Max, or click the Application menu and choose Reset if it is already open. You don't have to save your changes from the terrain exercise, so click No at the "Do you want to save your changes?" warning and click Yes at the "Do you really want to reset?" warning.

2. Click the Application menu and choose Import. The Select File to Import dialog box displays.

3. In the Select File to Import dialog box, select AutoCAD Drawing (*.DWG, *.DXF) from the Files of Type drop-down list; then locate and open the MySavoye-ground-max.dwg file. If you haven't done the preceding AutoCAD exercises, you can open the savoye-ground-max.dwg file.

4. In the AutoCAD DWG/DXF Import Options dialog box, make sure the settings are the same as those shown in Figure 5.20.

FIGURE 5.20
The AutoCAD DWG/DXF Import Options dialog box showing the settings needed for this exercise

5. Make sure that the Orient Normals of Adjacent Faces Consistently check box is selected. This is an important setting because it tells 3ds Max to align all the normals so that they are pointing outward.

WHEN TO TURN OFF ORIENT NORMALS OF ADJACENT FACES CONSISTENTLY

This option should be turned off when you are working with 3D objects created in AutoCAD Architecture or Revit.

6. Click OK to import the AutoCAD file. The plan appears in the viewport.

The next step is to set up a comfortable view of the model so that you can easily maneuver within it:

1. Right-click the POV label in the upper-left corner of the viewport, and then select Views ➤ Orthographic or press U. Your view changes to an orthographic projection instead of a perspective view.

TURN ON THE MATERIAL COLOR OPTION

When AutoCAD files are imported, they often appear uniformly as a dull gray color; in rendered viewports, that may be similar to the viewport background color. A common solution to this situation is to open the Display tab in the Command panel and select the Material Color radio button in the Shaded area of the Display Color rollout. If the objects' material colors don't have a good contrast with the background color, try the Object Color option instead.

2. Orbit so your point of view is above and at a 45-degree angle to the plan. Alternatively, you can click the corner of the ViewCube where the Front, Left, and Top faces intersect.

3. Press the G key to hide the grid for a clearer view.

4. Click the Zoom Extents tool to view the plan so that it looks similar to Figure 5.21.

FIGURE 5.21
The view so far

Extruding the Walls

The next step is to start extruding the walls. The polyline outlines that you created in AutoCAD are converted to closed splines in 3ds Max, so you need only to select the splines and apply the Extrude modifier:

1. Right-click in the viewport and choose Unhide All from the quad menu to unhide the Layer:MULLION-VERT and Layer:GLASS objects. Layers that are turned off in AutoCAD are imported as objects that are hidden in 3ds Max.

2. In the Unhide All dialog box that opens, click Yes to unhide the layers these objects are on.

3. Click the Select by Name tool on the Main Toolbar to open the Select from Scene dialog box. Click the Name column title to sort the object names alphabetically.

4. Select Layer:Wall-3ds-INT, Layer:Wall-3ds-EXT, and Layer:MULLION-VERT from the list, and then click OK. Remember that you can select multiple, nonconsecutive items from a list by holding down the Ctrl key while you click.

> **COMBINING OBJECTS BY LAYER**
>
> Objects that were combined by layer in the conversion from AutoCAD to 3ds Max have "Layer:" preceding their AutoCAD layer name.

5. Select the Modify tab in the Command panel, and then select Extrude from the Modifier List drop-down.

6. In the Parameters rollout, set the Amount input box to **9´6˝**. The walls and mullions display in the viewport as shown in Figure 5.22.

In this exercise, you applied the same modifier to three objects: Layer:Wall-3ds-INT, Layer: Wall-3ds-EXT, and Layer:MULLION-VERT. Whenever you change the Extrude Amount parameter for one object, it changes for the others because the Extrude modifier is instanced across the objects you selected in Step 4, applied to in Step 5. The two sets of walls and the vertical mullions were segregated in AutoCAD so that you could apply a different material to each of them in 3ds Max; but because all of these items are the same height, you applied a single modifier to all three of them.

FIGURE 5.22
The building after extruding the selected objects

If you decide that you need to give each set of walls its own Extrude modifier, you can do so by clicking one of the walls, selecting the italicized Extrude modifier in the stack, and then clicking the Make Unique button in the modifier stack, as shown in Figure 5.23.

FIGURE 5.23
Make the instanced modifier unique.

ITALIC AND BOLD MODIFIERS

Modifiers that appear in italics in the stack are instanced. Modifiers that appear in bold in the stack are modifiers applied to instanced objects.

Extruding Exterior Wall Headers

Now let's continue with the exterior door headers and the walls around the windows:

1. Open the Select from Scene dialog box again. Then select Layer:WALL-3ds-EXT-HDR and Layer:Wall-3ds-SILL.

2. Select Extrude again from the modifier list; then change the Amount value in the Parameters rollout to 1′6″.

3. Click the Select and Move tool; then click the Absolute/Offset Mode Transform Type-In tool next to the coordinate readout so that you are in the Offset mode. You'll see values appear in the coordinate readout.

4. In the coordinate readout, change the Z value to 8′0″. Figure 5.24 shows the door headers all moved to their positions above the doors.

FIGURE 5.24
The headers moved to an elevation of 8′0″

You may have noticed that in step 3, the coordinate readout showed values only when you selected the Offset mode from the Absolute/Offset Mode Transform Type-In tool. This is because you have more than one object selected. The Absolute mode has no significance for multiple selections because several objects can have different locations in the scene.

Also, just as with the walls, you used a single instanced Extrude modifier to effect changes to multiple objects.

Now, take a closer look at the windows. You have the window headers in place, but you also need a portion of wall to fill in below the windows. You'll need to copy the window headers and change their Extrude amount:

1. Select the Layer:WALL-3ds-SILL object. You can use the Select from Scene dialog box to do this, or you can simply click one of the window headers toward the back of the building.

2. With the Select and Move tool selected, Shift+click the blue Z-axis arrow of the Transform gizmo and drag the selected header down to make a clone of the window header object, roughly placing the copy at ground level.

3. In the Clone Options dialog box, click the Copy radio button to enable it. You can keep the Layer:WALL-3ds-SILL001 name. Click OK to accept the clone settings.

4. Click the Absolute/Offset Mode Transform Type-In tool to change to the Absolute mode; then right-click the Z spinner arrows to change the Z value in the coordinate readout to 0.

5. Change the Amount value in the Parameters rollout of the Modify tab to 2´8˝.

Extruding the Mullions

You now have the walls in place. Because you did some prep work in AutoCAD, the work in 3ds Max went fairly quickly. Even so, you still need to take care of a few items. The horizontal mullions for the curved window need to be created:

1. Use the Zoom Region tool to enlarge your view of the plan near the entrance to the right, as shown in Figure 5.25.

2. Select the horizontal mullion outline named Layer:MULLION-HORIZ.

3. Select the Extrude modifier in the Modifier List drop-down; then change the Amount parameter to 2˝.

FIGURE 5.25
A close-up view of the entrance and curved window

4. Choose Edit ➤ Clone; then, in the Clone Options dialog box, click Instance, and then click OK. The clone is now the selected object.

5. Click the Select and Move tool; then change the absolute Z value in the coordinate readout to 32″ or 2′8″.

6. Choose Edit ➤ Clone again; then click OK in the Clone Options dialog box.

7. With the Select and Move tool still selected, change the Z value in the coordinate readout to 9′4″. The horizontal mullions for the curved window are now in place.

Creating Interior Wall Headers

You used the Extrude modifier to create the headers for the exterior walls of the Villa. You are going to use a different method to create the headers for the interior walls.

1. Select Layer:WALL-3ds-INT object.

2. On the Modify tab, select the Extrude modifier and then select the Make Unique button that was mentioned earlier in the chapter.

3. In the Parameters group of the Extrude modifier, change the number of segments to 2.

4. Right-click the Shading viewport label and select Edged Faces. You should see the extra segment on your interior walls, as shown in Figure 5.26.

FIGURE 5.26
Extra segments on
the interior walls

5. With the Layer:WALL-3ds-INT object selected, add an Edit Poly modifier to the stack.

6. Expand the Edit Poly modifier and select the Vertex sub-object mode.

7. Right-click to make the Left viewport active and make a selection window through the middle of the first floor, as show in Figure 5.27, to select the newly added vertices.

8. In the Mini-Transform Type-In field, change the Z value to 8′.

9. Deselect the vertices you just moved.

10. Change the sub-object mode to Polygon and select the polygon, as shown in Figure 5.28.

FIGURE 5.27
Select the center vertices with a crossing window.

FIGURE 5.28
Select the polygon at the top of the wall.

11. Using View-Rotate-Sub-Object, arrange the view so you can see the opposite side of the closet.

12. Ctrl+click and select the polygon opposite the currently selected polygon.

13. On the Graphite Modeling toolbar, go the Polygons tab and select the Bridge command, as shown in Figure 5.29.

FIGURE 5.29
Select the Bridge command to close the gap between the selected polygons.

The Bridge tool connects the selected polygons, removing any interior polygons and welding the polygons of those faces. See Figure 5.30 to view the bridged polygons.

FIGURE 5.30
The bridged poly-
gons form the
header over the
closet opening.

Using this technique, you need to create the headers over the remaining four interior door openings on the ground floor of the villa. Once you are done creating the remaining interior headers, deselect all the polygons and close the sub-object mode of the Edit Poly modifier.

Using the Edit Poly modifier and the Bridge tool allows you to create a model that is well suited for radiosity or mental ray rendering, or even for sending out for rapid prototyping.

Adding Glass

Let's continue to model the ground floor of the villa. Next you need to add the glass:

1. Open the Select from Scene dialog box and select Layer:GLASS.

2. Select Extrude from the modifier list; then change the Amount parameter to 9´6˝ and make sure that the Segments value is set to 1.

The glass appears in only one or two areas. This is because the Glass object is a single spline and not an outline. You may recall from Chapter 3 that the normals of a surface will render the surface visible in only one direction. To compensate for this limitation, you can turn the Layer:GLASS spline into an outline:

1. In the Command panel, select Editable Spline from the modifier stack. The glass disappears in the viewport because you are below the Extrude level in the stack.

2. Right-click in the viewport, and then click the Spline option in the quad menu to enter that sub-object level for editing.

 3. Click the Zoom Extents Selected tool to view the entire Layer:GLASS object.

4. Select Ctrl+A to select all the spline sub-objects of the Layer:GLASS object.

5. Scroll down to the Outline button and input field in the Geometry rollout. Enter **0.2˝**⏎ for the Outline value. You won't see any changes at this viewing distance, but the glass is now a closed outline instead of a single line. Deselect the spline by clicking Ctrl+D.

6. Select Editable Spline in the modifier stack to exit the sub-object level.

7. Click Extrude in the modifier stack. The glass appears in all of the appropriate places (see Figure 5.31) because it now has two surfaces that both have normals that face outward.

8. Save this file as **Mysavoye-ground-max.max**.

FIGURE 5.31
The Ville Savoye model after outlining the glass splines

You could have left the glass as a single line. That would make the glass difficult to see in a shaded viewport, but you could apply a two-sided material to the glass so that it would appear in a finished rendering. Although a two-sided glass material takes a bit longer to render, the single-line glass material is a less-complex geometry. This makes the file a bit smaller. For this reason, if your model contains lots of curved glass, it may make sense to leave the glass as a single line. Otherwise, you may want to convert all of the glass in your model to outlines. As you've seen here, that's fairly easy to do in 3ds Max. It takes a bit more work to accomplish the same results in AutoCAD by using the Boundary tool.

Also, in the previous exercise, you may have noticed that you gave the glass a full height of 9´6˝, even though, in many cases, the glass only filled a height of 64˝ or less. You can do this because 3ds Max takes care of the small details of object intersections. In those places where the glass occurs within a wall, 3ds Max hides most of the glass, and it is displayed only where it appears in an opening, as shown in Figure 5.32. 3ds Max also takes care of the intersection of the vertical and horizontal mullions.

FIGURE 5.32
The window showing the glass

RADIOSITY REQUIRES BETTER MODELING

The creation methods used in these exercises are fine when using the 3ds Max Standard lights and Scan Line Renderer. If you intend to render your project using radiosity, the modeling must be cleaner, with no overlapping of faces, for the renderer to create an accurate radiosity solution. Good clean geometry and models are said to be water-tight, meaning the geometry is completely enclosed. If you're using mental ray, it's also a good idea for the geometry to be non-overlapping.

Creating a Floor with Openings

You've seen how the ground floor of the villa can be set up in AutoCAD to make quick work of the extrusions in 3ds Max. The second floor and rooftop can be done in the same way, but the floors between the different levels require a slightly different approach.

Both the second floor and the roof surface have openings that need some special attention when you are setting up to export to 3ds Max:

1. Go back to AutoCAD and open the savoye-second.dwg file. If you don't have AutoCAD, skip ahead to the "Importing the Second Floor" section later in this chapter.

2. Click the Layer Properties icon, and in the Layer Properties Manager dialog box, click the New Layer button. Create a layer named **FLOOR-2ND-3ds**. Right-click the new layer and select Set Current from the context menu to make it the current layer.

3. Use the Rectangle or Polyline tool to outline the second floor, as shown in Figure 5.33.

4. Turn off all the layers except **FLOOR-2ND-3ds**, STAIR, and RAMP; then zoom into the stair, as shown in Figure 5.34.

FIGURE 5.33
Outline the second floor.

Place a rectangle or closed polyline around the perimeter of the second floor plan.

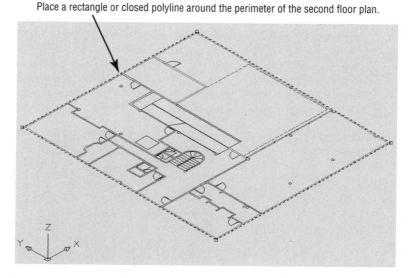

FIGURE 5.34
Outline the stair.

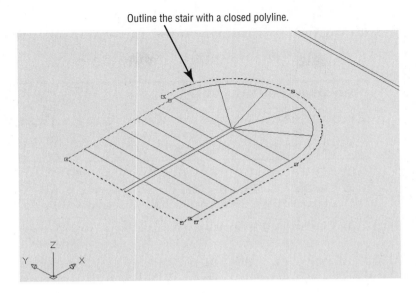

Outline the stair with a closed polyline.

FIGURE 5.34
Outline the stair.

5. Outline the stair with a closed polyline, as shown in Figure 5.34. (In this operation, you're drawing the outline of the stair opening in the floor. You will have to toggle between Arc and Line modes while drawing with the Polyline tool in AutoCAD to complete the outline shown in the figure.)

6. Pan over to the ramp. Then draw an outline of the ramp with a closed polyline (you can use the Rectangle tool), as shown in Figure 5.35.

FIGURE 5.35
The outline of the ramp floor opening

Outline the ramp with a closed polyline or rectangle.

You've got all of the additional linework you need to export the floor of the second story to 3ds Max, but you still need to take a few more steps to complete the setup for 3ds Max:

1. Freeze all the layers except the FLOOR-2ND-3ds layer.

IMPORTING FROZEN LAYERS

Frozen layers are automatically excluded from importing into 3ds Max. However, it is possible to manually select which layers will be included upon import, regardless of their layer state in AutoCAD (but the workflow is less efficient).

2. Use the Zoom Extents tool to view your work so far (see Figure 5.36). You now have the outline of the second floor and the two openings through the floor.

3. Choose File (the Application menu in AutoCAD 2009 and newer), and choose Save As to save your changes to a file named **Mysavoye-second-max.dwg**.

Basically, you've outlined the second floor and its openings with closed polylines. In addition, you've frozen all the layers except the floor outline and openings. This last step lets you automatically limit the objects that 3ds Max imports to only those items you added to the AutoCAD file.

FIGURE 5.36
The outline of the second floor

IMPORTING THE SECOND FLOOR

The next step is to import your work into 3ds Max:

1. Go back to 3ds Max, click the Application menu, and choose Reset. You can go ahead and reset the scene because you've already saved your work.

2. Click the Application menu and choose Import. Then, in the Select File to Import dialog box, locate and open the `Mysavoye-second-max.dwg` file you just saved from AutoCAD. If you don't have AutoCAD, open the `savoye-second-max.dwg` file.

3. In the AutoCAD DWG/DXF Import Options dialog box, adjust the settings to match those shown in Figure 5.37.

4. Click the Layers tab in the AutoCAD DWG/DXF Import Options dialog box. Note that the Skip All Frozen Layers radio button is selected by default. This setting lets you automatically skip importing the layers you froze in AutoCAD.

FIGURE 5.37
The AutoCAD
DWG/DXF Import
Options dialog box

FIGURE 5.37
The AutoCAD
DWG/DXF Import
Options dialog box

When you click the Select from List radio button on the Layers tab of the AutoCAD DWG/DXF Import Options dialog box, you are able to manually check which layers are imported by toggling the large check mark along the left edge of the list. The layer states shown in the list (on/off, freeze/thaw, lock/unlock) represent the current state of the DWG or DXF file and are not functional; they are for your information only.

5. Click OK to import the drawing and close the AutoCAD DWG/DXF Import Options dialog box.

You now see the outline of the second floor that you created in AutoCAD.

The final step is fairly easy. You only need to extrude the spline, and the openings will appear automatically:

1. Click the Select Object tool; then click the floor outline.

2. Select the Modify tab in the Command panel; then select Extrude from the Modifier List drop-down.

3. Set the Amount parameter to 18˝. You now have the floor of the second story, complete with openings as shown in Figure 5.38.

4. If you'd like, save this file as **mysavoye-secondfloor.max** for future reference.

When creating an extrusion, 3ds Max automatically subtracts the nested splines, closed subsplines that are enclosed by other subsplines, of the same spline object. On the second floor, ramp and stair openings are automatically subtracted from the second floor perimeter.

FIGURE 5.38
The extruded
second floor

You were asked to freeze all the layers in AutoCAD except the Max-floor layer. This allowed you to automatically limit the objects that were imported from AutoCAD into 3ds Max. You can go back to the AutoCAD file; thaw the wall, header, and other layers; and then freeze the Max-floor layer. Once you've done that, you can import the other second-story elements into a 3ds Max file and then merge the floor and the walls. On the other hand, you can choose exactly which layers will be imported on the Layers tab of the updated AutoCAD DWG/DXF Import Options dialog box. Of course, you can also thaw all the layers and import the entire AutoCAD drawing at once. But importing parts of an AutoCAD file can help simplify your work and keep it manageable.

USING BUILDING ELEVATIONS AND WALL PROFILES FROM AUTOCAD

In the preceding section, you learned how to convert outlines of a building plan into a floor with openings. You can employ the same procedures for converting building elevations from AutoCAD to 3ds Max scenes. For example, in AutoCAD you can outline an elevation of the villa using concentric rectangles for the second floor outline and the windows. You can then import the outlines to 3ds Max and extrude them, just as you did with the floor. That will give you the exterior walls of the building that you can rotate into a vertical position. This 3ds Max technique is similar to real-world tilt-up wall framing construction.

Using this method, you can even include other details such as the window mullions. Once you've done this for all four exterior walls, you can join the walls to form the second floor exterior walls, complete with window openings and even window detail.

Another great tool for forming building exteriors and interiors is the Loft tool. Sometimes a simple vertical extrusion won't be enough for walls. You may be working with a design that uses strong horizontal elements, such as a wide cornice or exaggerated rustication. You can make quick work of such detail by using 3ds Max's Loft tool. Draw the profile of the wall and the building footprint in AutoCAD. Be sure each of these items is on a separate layer and is made of polylines. You can then import the AutoCAD file into 3ds Max and use the Loft compound object or the Sweep modifier to loft the wall profile along the building footprint in a way similar to the exercises in Chapter 7, "Organizing and Editing Objects." This is especially helpful if the building footprint contains lots of curves and corners that would otherwise be difficult to model.

As an alternative, in AutoCAD, you can convert the closed splines of the stair, ramp, and floor into regions, and then subtract the stair and ramp regions from the floor outline. AutoCAD regions are converted into 3ds Max mesh surfaces. You then have to extrude the floor with the tools within the polygon level of the Editable Poly, rather than with the Extrude modifier.

Exploring the File Link Manager

Earlier in this chapter, you were introduced to the File Link Manager when you imported topographic contour lines from AutoCAD. In that example, the File Link Manager allowed you to update the 3ds Max terrain model when a change was made to the AutoCAD DWG file. You can also use the File Link Manager with floor plans to help maintain design continuity between AutoCAD and 3ds Max.

Try using the File Link Manager with the second floor of the villa in the following exercises:

1. To reset 3ds Max, click the Application menu and choose Reset.

2. Click the Application menu and choose References ➤ File Link Manager.

3. In the File Link Manager dialog box, select the Attach tab and then click the File button.

4. Locate and open **savoye-second-link.dwg**.

Now let's take a closer look at some of the options in the File Link Manager:

1. In the File Link Manager dialog box, click the Presets tab (see Figure 5.39).

FIGURE 5.39
The Presets tab of the File Link Manager dialog box

The Autodesk FBX (Revit) presets contain the settings most commonly used when linking to FBX files saved from Autodesk's Revit family of BIM programs. The AutoCAD drawing presets provide defaults for linking DWG files from various Autodesk applications. We will create a new preset based on one of the AutoCAD profiles.

2. Select the DWG File Saved from AutoCAD preset and notice that the New button (visible when no presets are selected) changes to Copy. Click the Copy button to bring up the New Settings Preset dialog box.

3. In the New Name field enter **My_DWG_fromAutoCAD** and click OK to close the dialog box.

4. Select the preset you just created and click the Modify button. The File Link Settings: DWG Files dialog box appears and defaults to the Advanced tab, as shown in Figure 5.40.

5. In the Derive AutoCAD Primitives By drop-down list, notice that the Layer, Blocks as Node Hierarchy, Split by Material option is selected and the Create Helper at Drawing Origin option is checked.

FIGURE 5.40
The Advanced tab of the File Link Settings: DWG Files dialog box

6. Click the Basic tab and check Orient Normals of Adjacent Faces Consistently.

7. Click Save. Then, in the File Link Manager dialog box, select the Attach tab and select My_DWG_from_AutoCAD from the Preset drop-down menu.

8. Click the Attach this File button. The plan displays in the viewports.

 A good tip to know is that by double-clicking the Helper object, you will select all the objects linked from the source file.

9. Close the File Link Manager dialog box.

10. Click the Manage Layers tool in the Main Toolbar. The AutoCAD layers are re-created in 3ds Max in the Layer dialog box.

With the file link settings, you can control layers as you would in AutoCAD, using the AutoCAD layer names preserved in 3ds Max. You can also create your own settings for special conditions by using the File Link Manager's Presets tab and adjusting your custom presets as you need them.

To confirm that you have full control over the linked drawing, try the following steps:

1. Open the Select from Scene dialog box; then select the Layer:WALL-3ds-INT and Layer:WALL-3ds-EXT objects.

2. Click the Modify tab in the Command panel; then choose Extrude from the Modifier List drop-down.

3. Set the Amount parameter to 9′6″ or 114″. The interior and exterior walls are extruded in the scene.

As you can see, the method for extruding the walls in the linked file is exactly the same for the imported AutoCAD file. You can now select and extrude objects as you did for the savoye-ground.dwg file that you imported earlier. The difference with the linked file is that changes made in the AutoCAD file can be reloaded in 3ds Max, much like the way XRefs work in both AutoCAD and 3ds Max.

Editing Linked AutoCAD Files

Now let's take a look at one of the key advantages of using the File Link Manager instead of the simpler DWG file import.

1. In AutoCAD, open the `savoye-second-link.dwg` file.

2. Turn on and thaw all the layers, and use the Stretch command to stretch the walls as shown in Figure 5.41.

3. Choose File ➢ Save to save the changes.

4. In 3ds Max, click the Application menu and choose References ➢ File Link Manager.

5. In the File Link Manager dialog box, click the Files tab and then select `savoye-second-link.dwg` in the Linked Files list box.

6. Click the Reload button. The File Link Settings dialog box displays.

7. In the File Link Settings dialog box, click OK. Then close the File Link Manager dialog box.

The 3ds Max scene is updated according to the changes made in the AutoCAD file.

FIGURE 5.41
Stretch these walls
as shown here.

Stretch these walls outward.

CONTINUING THE EXERCISE WITHOUT AUTOCAD

If you don't have AutoCAD, rename the existing `savoye-second-link.dwg` file to **savoye-second-link-bak.dwg** and then use Windows Explorer to save a copy of the `savoye-second-link-mod.dwg` file as **savoye-second-link.dwg** to replace the existing file. The savoye-second-max-mod.dwg file contains the modifications described in the preceding steps; however, linking to a different drawing will cause the Extrude modifiers to be deleted from the scene.

You've seen how you can update 3ds Max scenes when changes occur in a linked AutoCAD object. If you add objects in AutoCAD, those objects are also added to the 3ds Max scene. If the new object is added to a layer that already exists, and the objects associated with that layer are attached to a modifier, the new object is also controlled by the modifier. For example, if you add a rectangle to the AutoCAD drawing on the WALL-3ds-EXT layer, the new rectangle will be extruded to the 114″ height, just like all the other objects on the WALL-3ds-EXT layer. New objects on that layer that have a thickness or that are extruded within AutoCAD will be ignored by 3ds Max unless they are placed on a newly created layer.

Understanding the Block Node Hierarchy

Previous to 3ds Max 6, AutoCAD blocks translated into *Maxblocks*, which were collections of entities treated as a single object (which worked like a compound object).

ENCOUNTERING MAXBLOCKS

You can still encounter Maxblocks in 3ds Max 2011 if you choose to derive AutoCAD primitives by Layer, Entity, Color, or One Object only.

Beginning with 3ds Max 8, blocks are linked in a *node hierarchy* when you choose to derive AutoCAD primitives by Layer, Blocks as Node Hierarchy or Entity, or Blocks as Node Hierarchy. To understand how this works, let's do a short exercise:

1. Click the Application menu, choose Reset, and do not save the changes you made to the scene earlier.

2. Click the Application menu, choose References ➢ File Link Manager, and click the Attach tab.

3. Click the File button and select the `Blocks.dwg` file; then click Open.

4. Click the Presets tab and without selecting any Named Preset, click New. Give the new preset the name **Entity Blocks**, select AutoCAD Drawings from the Format drop-down, and click OK.

5. Select Entity Blocks in the Named Presets list and click Modify.

6. Click the Advanced tab in the File Link Settings: DWG Files dialog box. Click the Derive AutoCAD Primitive By drop-down list and select Entity, Blocks as Node Hierarchy. In this example, it makes sense to also combine by entity (rather than layer) because there are only a few simple objects.

7. Click Save to close the File Link Settings: DWG Files dialog box.

8. Click the Attach tab of the File Link Manager dialog box and select Entity Blocks from the Preset drop-down list if it is not already selected. Finally, click Attach This File and close the dialog box. The drawing appears in the viewport as shown in Figure 5.42.

 The `Blocks.dwg` file contains two simple blocks called BlockA and BlockB. BlockA contains a circle and a rectangular polyline. There are three instances of BlockA in the scene. BlockB has only one instance and contains a triangular polyline and BlockA nested within it.

9. Select the circle of BlockA, as shown in Figure 5.43.

10. Click the Select and Move tool and move the circle you selected a short distance in the XY-plane.

 Notice that all the child circle nodes move relative to their block headers (like the insertion point of AutoCAD blocks). In AutoCAD lingo, entities in the block definition are moving relative to the insertion points in their block instances.

FIGURE 5.42
The block node hierarchy

Click here to select a child node of this instance of BlockA

FIGURE 5.43
Moving one portion of the BlockA object

11. Select Ctrl+Z to undo the transform you did in step 10.

12. Open the Select from Scene dialog box and notice which node is selected—the circle in the third instance of Block:BlockA (see Figure 5.44). Select Block:BlockA, which is the block header node. The block header node contains all the nested objects but doesn't represent an object itself.

13. Using the Select and Move tool, drag the selected block header a short distance in the XY-plane. Notice that this time the entire block moves, and only the third instance of BlockA moves.

FIGURE 5.44
Selecting an object
with the Select from
Scene dialog box

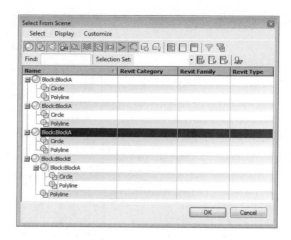

14. Click the Modify tab of the Command panel. Notice that the block header shows up as Block/Style Parent in the stack. Click the Reset Position button in the Linked Geometry rollout to return the block instance to the original position it had in the linked DWG file.

15. Save your work as **MyBlocks.max**.

As you can see from this exercise, selecting a block node on the screen selects a child in the block hierarchy. Transforming a child node actually transforms all instances of that child relative to their block headers.

On the other hand, when you select the top node in the hierarchy, called the block header, moving the block header allows you to transform a unique block instance independently of all other block instances. When you transform a parent node, the relative positions of its children do not change. AutoCAD blocks are now handled essentially as kinematic chains in 3ds Max.

BLOCKS IN 3DS MAX DIFFER FROM BLOCKS IN AUTOCAD

The block node hierarchy works much as it does in AutoCAD, with the exception that you do not have to explicitly redefine a block each time you make a change to the constituent geometry of the block definition. In 3ds Max it is easy to change the relationship between what is inside a block definition (by moving the child nodes) and the block instance (by moving the block header). No block redefinition is required in 3ds Max because it all happens automatically, depending on which node you select in the block hierarchy. The entire block node hierarchy brings block behavior much more in line with how AutoCAD handles blocks as compared with the more limited functionality of Maxblocks.

Understanding the File Link Manager Options

In the preceding exercises, you were able to try out a few of the File Link Manager options. The File Link Manager, like so many other 3ds Max features, offers numerous options to tailor your workflow to the particular needs of your project. Given the limited space of this book, an

example of every option available won't be shown, but you can get started with this feature after reviewing the exercises. Here's a summary of the File Link Manager's options, organized by tabs.

THE ATTACH TAB

As you've already seen, this tab lets you locate a file using the File button. The File drop-down list shows a history of previously attached files from which you can select. The Preset drop-down list lets you select from a collection of presets that you've saved earlier.

The Select Layers to Include button opens the Select Layers dialog box, which allows you to select or deselect specific layers that you may want to include or exclude from the link.

The Attach This File button lets you attach an AutoCAD DWG, DXF, or Revit FBX file to the current 3ds Max scene. Files can be attached from versions 12 through 2011 of AutoCAD, AutoCAD Architecture, AutoCAD Mechanical, and the Revit family of products. If you're using a CAD program other than AutoCAD, you can use the DXF file format instead of the DWG format, although many CAD programs today support the DWG file format directly.

USING OBJECT ENABLERS

Many Autodesk products, including AutoCAD Architecture, AutoCAD Mechanical, and AutoCAD Civil 3D, require that Object Enablers be installed to properly import certain objects. To find the proper Object Enabler to install, go to www.autodesk.com and search for "Object Enabler." An absent Object Enabler results in the appearance of a Proxy Object Detected dialog box when you attempt to import or link to the offending DWG files. You can still use the drawings without the enablers present; however, the associated geometry may not properly come into 3ds Max.

THE FILES TAB

The Files tab allows you to control how a file is linked to the current 3ds Max file.

As you've seen in previous exercises, the Reload option lets you manually reload a linked file. The File Link Settings dialog box displays when you click this button if you have the Show Reload Options check box selected.

Detach removes a linked file from the current 3ds Max scene. Use this option with caution, as it deletes all of the linked objects in the scene even if they have been modified in 3ds Max.

The Bind option removes any links to the source AutoCAD file while maintaining the objects in the current 3ds Max scene. The 3ds Max scene then becomes an independent scene file and can no longer be affected by the source AutoCAD file.

BINDING LINKED FILES ELIMINATES INTEROPERABILITY

Binding a former link will increase your file size as the data is migrated from CAD into 3ds Max when the link between them is broken. Do this with caution as changes made in the CAD file will no longer affect the 3ds Max scene.

Finally, the Files tab displays a list of DWG, DXF, or FBX files that are currently linked to the 3ds Max scene file. An icon next to the filename indicates the status of the linked file:

◆ A paper clip indicates that the source file has not changed and that there are no errors in the link.

◆ A question mark indicates that the file cannot be found.

◆ A red flag indicates that the file has changed since import and that it must be reloaded using the Reload button.

◆ A grayed-out page indicates that a different file has been selected through another path.

◆ A curved arrow indicates that the Dynamic Reload option has been turned on for the file.

THE PRESETS TAB

You saw in an earlier exercise how you can create a preset, which determines the settings when files are linked. The Presets tab also lets you modify an existing preset through the Modify button or rename or delete an existing preset. When you create a preset, it appears as an option in the Attach tab's Preset drop-down list. You'll learn more about the actual preset settings in the next section.

Understanding File Link Settings

When you import a linked AutoCAD file, you have the option of controlling the way that file is imported through the File Link Settings dialog box. This dialog box appears by default when you've selected a file for linking, but you can set 3ds Max to avoid this dialog box by deselecting the Show Reload Options check box in the Files tab of the File Link Manager dialog box.

As you saw in previous exercises, the options selected in the File Link Settings dialog box can make a huge difference in the way the resulting 3ds Max file is organized. Because AutoCAD and 3ds Max use entirely different ways of organizing data, this dialog box is necessary to make some sense of the way AutoCAD DWG files are converted to 3ds Max files. To help in the translation process, 3ds Max uses a type of node called Linked Geometry. All linked AutoCAD objects are converted to Linked Geometry or 3ds Max blocks, which occurs only when you choose to derive AutoCAD primitives by Layer, Entity, Color, or One Object.

For example, objects in an AutoCAD file that reside on layer 0 are collected into a single 3ds Max block. The name of the 3ds Max block will depend on the settings you choose in the File Link Settings dialog box. In an earlier exercise, you chose the Layer option in the File Link Settings dialog box's Derive AutoCAD Primitives By drop-down list. You can further refine the way 3ds Max combines objects through a combination of layer, thickness, and color, or you can have 3ds Max import each AutoCAD object as a single object in 3ds Max.

Most of the time, you will probably choose to derive your AutoCAD primitives using one of the Blocks as Node Hierarchy options in the File Link Settings dialog box, due to the improved way that you can work with blocks using these options. Therefore, the objects that appear in 3ds Max will most often be Linked Geometry nodes.

Linked Geometry nodes have only one parameter on the Modify tab of the Command panel: the Reset Position button. Click Reset Position when you want to restore the node to the location it has in the linked DWG or DXF file. Any transforms you apply to Linked Geometry nodes are stored in 3ds Max alone and there is no chance that 3ds Max will ever overwrite your AutoCAD files.

> **AVOIDING SYSTEM INSTABILITY**
>
> You'll want to avoid several things when working with Linked Geometry due to its connection to a foreign file format. System instability may occur if you include Linked Geometry in groups or assemblies, attach them to an Editable Mesh or Editable Poly, change animation controllers, create hierarchical links, or make instance clones of Linked Geometry. However, you can confidently make copy clones and apply transforms, modifiers, and materials to Linked Geometry without any problems.

THE BASIC TAB

The options in the Basic tab, shown in Figure 5.45, give you control over the way imported objects are converted into 3ds Max objects. These options are similar to those found in the Geometry Options group of the AutoCAD DWG/DXF Import Options dialog box that you see when you import a DWG or DXF file using the Application menu's Import option.

FIGURE 5.45

The Basic tab of the File Link Settings dialog box

Weld Nearby Vertices This option determines whether coincident vertices of imported objects are joined, or *welded*, together to form a contiguous object. When Weld is turned on, the Weld Threshold setting is used to determine how close together objects need to be before they are welded.

Auto-Smooth Adjacent Faces This option determines whether to apply smoothing to contiguous surfaces in imported objects. When Auto-Smooth is turned on, the Smooth-angle setting is used to determine the minimum angle to which smoothing should be applied.

Orient Normals of Adjacent Faces Consistently This option attempts to align all the normals of an object so that they point outward from the center of the object.

Cap Closed Splines This option causes 3ds Max to apply an Extrude modifier to closed objects such as closed polylines or rectangles.

Texture Mapping The options in this drop-down list determine whether 3ds Max generates mapping coordinates for imported mesh objects. The Generate Coordinates for All Objects option creates mapping coordinates for all mesh objects, which may take a while with a complex 3D AutoCAD file. This option should always be used when importing AutoCAD Architecture files that already have mapping coordinates assigned to their objects. The Generate Coordinates On-Demand option causes 3ds Max to automatically assign mapping coordinates to Linked Geometry when a mapped material is assigned to it.

Curve Steps This option gives you control over the way curves are converted. A low Curve Steps value causes curves to appear as straight segments, and higher values generate a more accurate curve.

Maximum Surface Deviation for 3D Solids This option controls tessellation in 3ds Max on objects that are converted from AutoCAD 3DSOLID entities. Small numbers produce accurate surfaces with a greater number of faces, whereas larger numbers use less memory but produce less accurate surfaces with fewer faces.

Include group This group of options has a number of check boxes that can be toggled to indicate which categories of objects you want to link into 3ds Max. The choices include External References (these are XRefs from AutoCAD, not 3ds Max), Hatches, Points, Lights from AutoCAD, Sun and Sky objects, Views and Cameras, and UCSs (Grids) (UCS stands for User Coordinate System).

LINKED HATCHES INCREASE FILE SIZE

It is generally not a good idea to include Hatch patterns in a file link. 3ds Max cannot store the entities making up the pattern in as efficient a way as AutoCAD, and the result usually consumes far too much memory, results in too large a file size, and requires too much translation time.

THE ADVANCED TAB

The options on the Advanced tab, shown in Figure 5.46, give you control over the way AutoCAD primitives are derived, as well as several important settings and the possibility of selectively reloading only a portion of the linked file.

FIGURE 5.46
The Advanced tab of the File Link Settings dialog box

Derive AutoCAD Primitives By This option lets you determine how entities from AutoCAD are treated in 3ds Max. Perhaps the simplest choice from this drop-down list is Layer, Blocks as Node Hierarchy, which converts AutoCAD layers to Linked Geometry and blocks into a node hierarchy. The similar Layer, Blocks as Node Hierarchy, Split by Material option converts AutoCAD layers to Linked Geometry and then further subdivides the AutoCAD objects on each layer by the materials assigned to them. Blocks using this option are assigned a node hierarchy. The next option is Entity, Blocks as Node Hierarchy, which converts AutoCAD entities to Linked Geometry and blocks into a node hierarchy.

You may also choose Layer, Entity, or Color, which groups AutoCAD objects by their layer, entities, or color and then converts them to Maxblocks. The Entity option creates an object for each entity in the AutoCAD file. The One Object option turns the entire AutoCAD drawing into a single Maxblock.

The Derive AutoCAD Primitives By drop-down option is available only when modifying a preset.

Select Layers To Include Click this button to open the Select Layers dialog box (see Figure 5.47), where you can choose the option Skip All Frozen Layers (default) or Select from List. The Select Layers to Include button is grayed out unless you are reloading a linked file. Layers that are checked are linked, regardless of their layer state in AutoCAD. Note that the layer state data shown in the dialog box is for your information only—it is not functional and does not update in AutoCAD. This button is also available on the Attach tab.

Figure 5.47
The Select Layers
dialog box

Create Helper at Drawing Origin This option will include an Origin Point helper object with the linked file. This helper is placed at the origin of the linked file to help identify its origin and to facilitate alignment of other files.

Use Extrude Modifier To Represent Thickness When checked, this setting will apply an Extrude modifier, matching the height of any entities that have a thickness value. Note that thickness is a very old concept (prior to AutoCAD release 12) from the early days of 3D modeling in AutoCAD and is not in wide use today. Most contemporary 3D modeling is done with surfaces or solids in AutoCAD.

Create One Scene Object for Each AutoCAD Architecture One When this option is checked, AutoCAD Architecture-specific objects, such as doors and windows, are imported as single objects rather than each component being imported separately.

Use Scene Material Definitions This option matches material names coming from an AutoCAD file with material names in 3ds Max. When there is a match, the material names in 3ds Max are used when checked. When unchecked, the material names are always taken from the DWG file. Note that DXF files do not support materials.

Use Scene Material Assignments on Reload This important option allows you to maintain the materials you have assigned in 3ds Max after you reload a DWG file. When unchecked, the materials from AutoCAD will overwrite materials made in 3ds Max when the linked file is reloaded.

Selective Reload Check Selective Reload when you want to reload only a subset of all the objects in the linked file. You may want to do this if you do not want subsequent changes made in the CAD file to be linked into 3ds Max. Selective Reload can also be used in complex scenes to minimize the time spent loading the entire linked database.

When Selective Reload is on, either you can select the objects to reload in the scene manually, or you can select them from the Select Linked Objects dialog box (see Figure 5.48) by clicking the Linked Objects button. This option is available only when reloading a linked file.

FIGURE 5.48
The Select Linked
Objects dialog box

Real World Scenario

AUTODESK PRODUCTS THROUGHOUT THE PRODUCTION PIPELINE

A major jewelry store chain was redesigning its free-standing stores complete with a customer lounge, jewelry design rooms, and a child care area. A Cleveland-based architectural firm was tasked with defining the store design and creating the construction documents (CDs) for the new store template. Part of the design process included creating renderings for approval by the client. The firm's pipeline for larger projects used Autodesk products at each phase.

Revit (see "Importing Revit Files into 3ds Max" later in this chapter) was first used to design the building and create the construction documents. Walls, doors, windows, partitions, and so on were all modeled in Revit. AutoCAD or AutoCAD Architecture was then used to model the interior components such as the display cases, point-of-sale features, fixtures, and signage. The AutoCAD drawings were imported into Revit, and then elevations, sections, views, and notes were all defined and assembled into a complete set of drawing sheets.

To create the renderings, the structural components from Revit and the interior components from AutoCAD were then linked to a 3ds Max scene. Materials, lighting, and animation were completed in 3ds Max and sent electronically to the client for review. Required changes were made in Revit or AutoCAD, and were reflected in the 3ds Max scene or in 3ds Max itself, and then revised renderings or animations were made.

Through the interoperability of several Autodesk products, the architectural firm was able to increase productivity and quickly address the client's needs.

The Spline Rendering Tab

The options in the Spline Rendering tab, shown in Figure 5.49, give you control over the way AutoCAD splines and polylines are imported into 3ds Max. Renderability, appearance, smoothing, and mapping coordinates are controlled through this tab.

Figure 5.49

The Spline Rendering tab of the File Link Settings dialog box

Enable in Renderer When this option is checked, imported shapes are rendered as 3D geometry using the settings in the Viewport/Renderer section. See the Viewport/Renderer description later in this list for a description of these settings.

Enable in Viewport This option determines whether the shape is displayed in the viewports using the Viewport/Renderer settings. When Enable in Viewport is on, the Use Viewport Settings option becomes available. Use Viewport Settings toggles on the Viewport option in the Viewport/Rendering group.

Generate Mapping Coords. When checked, mapping coordinates are applied to the shapes, thereby allowing control over the appearance of mapped materials. The default U mapping direction consists of a single loop around the shape, and the V mapping direction follows the length of the shape.

Real-World Map Size This option determines whether a map's scaling is controlled by the material's Use Real-World Scale settings.

Auto-smooth This option controls the smoothing of the splines based on the Threshold parameter. When this option is checked, adjacent segments are smoothed when their angular difference is less than the Threshold value.

Viewport/Renderer Turn on these options to set the rendering appearance of splines in the viewports and in rendered scenes. The Radial option creates a rounded cross section while the Rectangular option consists of straight sides. It is common to have different Viewport and Renderer settings with less dense geometry created in the viewports and more dense geometry in rendered views. The Viewport option is available only when Enable in Viewport is checked.

Linking files into 3ds Max allows you to maintain a single design database that begins in AutoCAD and continues seamlessly into 3ds Max. File linking makes a good alternative to simply importing an AutoCAD file directly by clicking the Application menu and choosing the Import

option because of the connection that carries into the future between the AutoCAD and 3ds Max databases. You can always use the Bind option to sever the link and make the imported data a stand-alone 3ds Max file, but be aware that you lose the benefits that accrue to those who use both AutoCAD and 3ds Max together in a continuing relationship throughout the design workflow.

Using the Substitute Modifier with Linked Geometry

You can substitute a complex piece of furniture modeled in 3ds Max for a simple outline drawn in AutoCAD. Designers often do space planning in AutoCAD with simple 2D blocks that are drawn to scale. You can link a space planning drawing into 3ds Max and then proceed to substitute a complex 3D version of a piece of furniture for a simple 2D block. After seeing the more realistic depiction of the scene in 3ds Max, a designer may want to revise the space plan in AutoCAD. The AutoCAD DWG file can then be reloaded in 3ds Max, and the changes automatically affect the complex 3D models in the scene. Let's try out this idea:

1. Open the MyBlocks.max file you saved earlier, or open Blocks.max.

2. Select the rectangular polyline in the foreground. Note that it appears as Linked Geometry in the modifier stack.

3. Apply the Substitute modifier to the object.

4. Click the Select XRef Object button in the Parameters rollout, as shown in Figure 5.50. Note that you also have the option to pick an object that is already in the scene for the substitution.

FIGURE 5.50
The Substitute modifier's Parameters rollout

5. Select the Worktop.max file and click Open. This is a free 3D model of a desk worktop from ScottOnstott.com.

6. The XRef Merge dialog box appears, listing the objects that are in Worktop.max. Select Worktop01 and click OK.

7. Answer Yes to the Substitution Question dialog box that asks, "Do you want to assign the substitute object's material to this object?" The 3D model appears in the viewport, now substituting for the rectangular polylines that were there before (see Figure 5.51).

8. Select the circle in the foreground and apply the Substitute modifier to this Linked Geometry.

9. Click the Select XRef Object button again and select the Chair.max file (this is part of the collection of free designer furniture models at the same website). Click Open.

FIGURE 5.51
The substituted geometry in the viewport

10. Select the object Chair01 from the XRef Merge dialog box and click OK.

11. Answer Yes again at the Substitution Question dialog box that appears.

12. Rotate the chair and observe that it behaves exactly as the circle did within the linked block node hierarchy. All the block instances of the chair rotate accordingly, as shown in Figure 5.52.

13. Save your file as **MyBlocks_Sub.max**.

FIGURE 5.52
The substituted geometry behaves like the linked geometry.

RENDERING LINKED SPLINES

You can make linked splines render by applying the Renderable Spline modifier.

You have now seen how easy it is to link a 2D space plan drawn in AutoCAD into 3ds Max, and then substitute more complex geometry in 3ds Max for the simple blocks from CAD. The benefits of such an approach are that you are using each application for what it does best: AutoCAD for drafting and 3ds Max for visualizing 3D models. Not only are you focusing on

the strengths of the applications you use in your workflow, but there is a dynamic link between the programs so that there can be a design dialogue, and changes can be incorporated using the best tools for the job.

Importing a Truss

Frequently, you may be called on to include a truss in your design. If it's a flat truss, you can draw a side view of the truss in AutoCAD using closed polylines, and then import the drawing to 3ds Max and extrude it in a way similar to the floor of the earlier savoye-second.dwg example. If you import the truss line drawing as a single object, 3ds Max will automatically subtract the truss web from the outline of the truss, as shown in Figure 5.53.

Tubular trusses can be created easily from engineering 3D line diagrams. Figure 5.54 shows an AutoCAD diagram of a truss whose components are to be made of tubular steel. The different diameters are represented by different layers in this model.

FIGURE 5.53
An AutoCAD drawing of a truss at the top and the extruded 3ds Max object

FIGURE 5.54
A 3D line diagram of a truss in AutoCAD

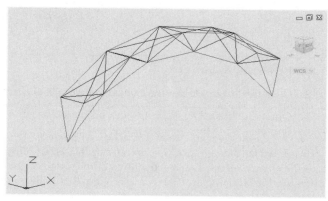

The following exercise will show you how the model can be turned into a renderable truss in 3ds Max:

1. Click the Application menu and choose Reset to reset 3ds Max.

2. Click the Application menu, choose Import, and then select and open the `truss.dwg` file.

3. The AutoCAD DWG/DXF Import Options dialog box displays.

4. Make sure that the settings in the AutoCAD DWG/DXF Import Options dialog box are the same as those shown in Figure 5.55. Click OK.

FIGURE 5.55
The AutoCAD DWG/DXF Import Options settings

The truss displays in the 3ds Max viewport.

With the truss imported into 3ds Max, you only need to change a parameter to alter the way the lines are rendered:

1. Select one of the truss's struts. Layer:brace appears in the name field at the top of the Command panel. You can also use the Select from Scene dialog box to select the Layer:brace object.

2. Click the Modify tab of the Command panel.

3. Open the Rendering rollout, check both the Enable in Renderer and Enable in Viewport options and change the Thickness to 4″.

4. Select the Layer:main object, the main frame around the truss.

5. In the Command panel, check both the Enable in Renderer and Enable in Viewport check boxes and change the Thickness value to 6″.

6. The viewports now display the linework as tubes, as shown in Figure 5.56.

7. Save your scene as **My_Truss.max**.

FIGURE 5.56
The tubular truss

METHODS FOR RENDERING SPLINES

You can use the File Link Manager to import linked AutoCAD drawings and still use the Spline Rendering tab parameters to create the truss shown in the preceding exercise. You can also use the Renderable Spline modifier if you prefer. To create actual geometry around the splines, consider using the Sweep modifier.

You saw this earlier in Chapter 4, where you were quickly introduced to the Rendering rollout of the Editable Spline object. Here you see a practical use for this set of options. Without much effort in 3ds Max, you can create a reasonable-looking truss. You just need to remember to place the different-diameter truss members on different layers in AutoCAD before you import the file to 3ds Max.

You can also make quick work of window mullions using this method. Typically, mullions are square, but if they are to be viewed from a distance, you can use single lines for mullions and set up the Rendering rollout to have them render as rectangular section tubes.

Importing Revit Files into 3ds Max

The Revit family of software products appears to be the next step in BIM. Using AutoCAD Architecture or a similar CAD program, you can draw a 3D Wall object that has the form and volume of a wall but is still a simple 3D mesh. These objects tend to be flat sided, and there is little or no true information associated with the object. Anybody viewing the drawing, as either a hard copy or within the CAD package, can deduce the composition of the wall only by reading a note or associated attribute.

Even the parametric wall objects in 3ds Max are little more than mesh objects with a few parameters to control and adjust their appearance.

Revit handles walls and most other aspects of drawing a building differently. Walls, for example, are first created in families that define their construction. A 16″ on-center 2 × 4 stud wall with ⅝″ drywall and a 2-hour fire rating is different than an 8″ CMU (concrete masonry unit) wall with a brick fascia on one side and furring strips and drywall on the other. When either wall family is used in Revit, each component of the wall is created in the file. An estimator can query the file to determine the amount of each component necessary for the structure's construction. It's a snap to select one wall type and switch its family to determine how the project is affected.

Revit had a small but loyal following through its acquisition by Autodesk in 2002. Since then, its capabilities, stability, and integration with the other Autodesk products have led to a significant increase in the size of the Revit user base. As its integration into the workflow of many companies increases, the chances that you may work with a Revit file increase as well.

Export the Revit File

In Revit 2009 and newer you can directly export to 3ds Max via the Filmbox (FBX) file format. This works really well, and carries lights and materials across platforms without hassle. The only drawback to FBX is that the file size is gigantic when compared to the alternatives. A 10MB Revit file can become a 70MB FBX file. For this reason, you often have to import your model in pieces to work with manageable file sizes.

There is no direct import of Revit files into 3ds Max; you can export the scene from Revit to AutoCAD and then link the AutoCAD file to the 3ds Max scene or use the FBX file format as an interim format that can be linked or imported into 3ds Max.

CERT OBJECTIVE

One of the benefits of using Revit 2011 with 3ds Max 2011 (and AutoCAD 2011) is the inclusion of the new Autodesk Materials and the Autodesk Common Material Library, a set of more than 1,200 preset textures and materials that are common across all of Autodesk's 2011 products that use the mental ray renderer. We will discuss materials in Chapter 9, but you will be introduced to the Autodesk Common Materials here as we link an FBX file from Revit 2011 into 3ds Max Design 2011. If you don't have Revit 2011, you can skip to the "Link the Exported FBX File in 3ds Max" section.

1. Open Revit Architecture 2011.

2. Open Shop_r2011.rvt, a Revit file of a small retail store (see Figure 5.57).

FIGURE 5.57
The Show_r2011
.rvt file

REVIT FILES ARE FORWARD COMPATIBLE ONLY

Revit files are not backward compatible, and there is no method for saving a file to be compatible with a previous version of Revit. When a file from an older version of Revit is opened in a newer version of the software, the file is automatically upgraded to the newer version's file format. Included in the upgrade process with Revit 2011 is the immediate conversion of all materials in the older Revit file to the new Autodesk Common Materials. If you have older Revit projects with materials that you are very happy with, you may not want to open those projects in Revit 2011, because you will lose those materials. You can still export them to the FBX format from the prior release of Revit; make sure to update to the most current version of the FBX software for that version of Revit. Once you have the FBX file, you can link to or import the file in 3ds Max Design 2011, keeping your original materials.

Revit can output 3D views as well as 2D sheets suitable as construction documents. When 2D views are exported, the model is flattened, resulting in a 2D representation of the file. A 3D view must be active when you export to AutoCAD for eventual linking to 3ds Max.

1. There are three views specific to this project, as well as the standard {3D} view, listed in the 3D Views section of the Project Browser, as shown in Figure 5.58. Make sure one of these views is active by double-clicking it. You could also create a new camera and make that camera view active.

2. From the Revit application menu, choose Export ➢ FBX.

3. In the Export 3ds Max (FBX) dialog box that opens, navigate to an appropriate folder to place the new file and accept the default filename.

4. Click Save to export the Revit file to the FBX format.

FIGURE 5.58
The Revit Project
Browser

Link the Exported FBX File in 3ds Max

Now that the FBX file has been created, you can link it to a 3ds Max scene. It is important that you have your System Units be configured to feet for elements such as lights and cameras to come in properly. Let's link in the FBX file you created in the previous exercise.

1. Open or Reset 3ds Max.

2. Choose Customize ➤ Units Setup and then click the System Unit Setup Button.

3. On the System Unit Setup dialog box, use the drop down menu to select Feet as the unit.

4. Click OK to close the System Unit Setup dialog box and OK again to close the Units Setup dialog box.

5. Click the Application menu and choose References ➤ File Link Manager.

6. On the Attach tab, click the File button, navigate to the location where you saved the exported FBX file, and select it. If you did not complete the previous exercise, select the `Shop-r2011-3DView-{3D}.fbx` file.

7. Back in the File Link Manager, select Autodesk Revit FBX – Do Not Combine Entities from the Preset drop-down list.

8. Click the Presets tab, again pick the Autodesk Revit FBX – Do Not Combine Entities preset, and then click the Modify button.

9. In the File Link Settings dialog box that opens, make sure that the Use Scene Material Definitions and Use Scene Material Assignments on Reload options are selected; then click Save.

10. Click the Attach This File button on the Attach tab of the File Link Manager. The system processes the file briefly; then the shop appears in the viewport.

11. Close the File Link Manager.

12. Zoom into the scene, as shown in Figure 5.59.

Next you will see how the materials assigned in Revit are imported into 3ds Max.

13. To see the materials assigned to the shop building, on the Menu Bar choose Rendering ➤ Material/Map Browser.

The use of the Material/Map browser will be covered in greater detail in Chapter 9.

FIGURE 5.59
The imported building

14. In the Material/Map Browser, use the scroll bar next to the right edge of the dialog box to find the Scene Materials group and open the group, if it is closed by clicking the group heading. It might help to close the Autodesk Material Library group. The Scene Materials group expands to display the Autodesk Materials that are applied to the shop building (see Figure 5.60). If the Scene Materials group appears short, you can increase the size of its window by clicking and dragging the lower divider bar of the group to extend it.

15. Save your scene as **My_Shop.max**.

FIGURE 5.60
The Material/Map Browser showing the imported Revit materials

Using the Scene Explorer

Now that you have linked the shop file into 3ds Max Design as an FBX file exported from Revit and seen how the Autodesk Common Materials transport, let's look at some of the geometry of the model using the Scene Explorer. The Scene Explorer is a modeless dialog box that you can use to accomplish many logistical tasks in 3ds Max, including viewing, sorting, selecting, renaming, hiding, and freezing objects in the scene; creating or modifying object hierarchy trees; and editing groups of objects at the same time. You can also use the Scene Explorer to see how many faces are on a particular object.

1. On the Menu Bar choose Tools ➢ New Scene Explorer to create the first Scene Explorer in the scene (see Figure 5.61).

2. The Scene Explorer dialog box opens up and the title bar of the dialog box says Scene Explorer – Scene Explorer 1, as shown in Figure 5.62. You can create and save as many uniquely configured Scene Explorers as you need to maximize your workflows.

FIGURE 5.61
Accessing the
Scene Explorer

FIGURE 5.62
The Scene Explorer

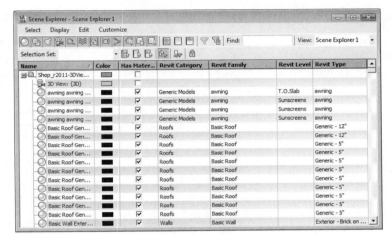

The Scene Explorer is showing you the contents of the Revit file that was linked using the Do Not Combine Entities preset, so every item in Revit is a unique item in 3ds Max. If you used the Combine by Revit Material preset, you would see the just the Revit Material names, but because of the way the items are combined, you would lose access to additional information about the individual objects that can be displayed in the Scene Explorer.

Looking a Figure 5.62, you can see the specific Revit properties of each object in the file, such as Category, Family, Level, and Type. To see how many faces are on each object, you need to customize the Scene Explorer.

3. On the Scene Explorer dialog box, choose Customize ➢ Configure Columns to open the Configure Columns floater, as shown in Figure 5.63.

FIGURE 5.63
Some of the additional columns available on the Configure Columns floater

Configure Columns
Display Vertex Channel
Viewport Lighting
Viewport Locked Lighting
Viewport Shadows
Light Color
Light Intensity
Shadow Map Size
Light On
Shadow On
Shadow Type
Light Map Bias
Shadow Sample Range
Application Origin

The Configure Columns floater is a dynamic list of columns that are available to add to the Scene Explorer dialog box, or you can move columns currently in the Scene Explorer back to the Configure Columns floater if you don't want them to display.

4. In the Configure Columns floater, drag the Faces button to the Screen Explorer dialog box and drop it between the Has Material and Revit Category columns.

Now you can see how many faces each object in the scene has, as shown in Figure 5.64.

FIGURE 5.64
The Scene Explorer now showing how many faces each object consists of

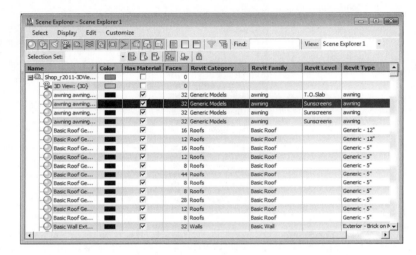

Looking at the details of what is displayed in the columns currently in the Scene Explorer, the Revit Level column isn't providing you with a lot of detail. Because it is an empty field for the majority of the items in the file, you can move that column back to the Configure Columns floater.

5. Drag the Revit Level column header to the Configure Columns floater.

Now that you have the faces column in the Scene Explorer, you can sort the objects in the scene to see which objects have the most faces.

6. Click the Faces column header in the Scene Explorer dialog box and notice the up pointing triangle after the heading Faces, and that the objects in the scene are sorted in ascending order of number of faces per object.

7. Click the Faces column header again to see the list sorted in descending order of number of faces, as shown in Figure 5.65.

8. Close the Scene Explorer dialog box: closing the Scene Explorer dialog will close the Configure Columns dialog box at the same time.

9. Now that you have linked in your FBX file, you can use the Units Setup dialog box to reset your system unit to inches.

As you've seen in these exercises, Revit files are incorporated in 3ds Max scenes by exporting them as FBX files and then linking or importing those files into 3ds Max. You have also seen how the new Autodesk Common Materials help improve workflow across the Autodesk 2011

product line. To maintain an effective workflow, changes to the Revit files should be exported as a new FBX file, overwriting the existing, linked file. This way, any changes in the Revit file will be reflected in 3ds Max when the linked file is reloaded. If you reload an FBX file, you should reset your System Units setting to Feet to avoid scaling issues with Lights and Camera objects.

FIGURE 5.65
The Scene Explorer sorted to display object face count in descending order

The Bottom Line

Create topography with splines Using the Terrain compound object, you can create flowing or layered surfaces defined by the height, shape, and location of the included splines.

> **Master It** Create a Terrain object in a shape that represents a valley that extends between two peaks. The summit of the peaks should be approximately 1,000′ above the ground plane and the valley should extend approximately 200′ below it. Contour lines should be present for every 100′ of elevation change.

Import AutoCAD plans into 3ds Max The File Link Manager is a utility that incorporates an AutoCAD drawing into a 3ds Max scene while maintaining a link between the two files. Changes made to the DWG file are reflected in the 3ds Max scene whenever the drawing is reloaded.

> **Master It** Create a File-Link Preset so you can repetitively use the same settings when you file-link a drawing file into the 3ds max scene.

Use the Substitute modifier It is best to use your CAD application and 3ds Max Design to each of their strengths: drafting 2D plans with blocks for laying out space arrangements and then linking that plan into 3ds Max, extruding walls, and then using the Substitute modifier to replace 2D CAD blocks with the appropriate 3D models for rendering your views and presenting to the designers or clients.

> **Master It** Using the File Link Manager, attach Classroom01.dwg into a new 3ds Max scene. Using the Substitute modifier, replace the circles of the StudentDesk blocks with the Chair.max file and the rectangles with the Worktop.max file.

Import Revit files into 3ds Max Revit is Autodesk's premier building information modeling (BIM) software. Using Revit, every element of a building's construction is modeled as a 3D component. Revit's lights, materials, and views can all be incorporated into a 3ds Max scene.

Master It What is one method of bringing the components of a Revit file into 3ds Max?

A. Use the File Link Manager to link the Revit file to the 3ds Max scene.

B. Save the Revit file in Revit 2009 or earlier, and then use the File Link Manager to link the Revit file to the 3ds Max scene.

C. Save the Revit file in Revit 2009 or earlier, and then click the Application menu and choose References ➢ Import to import the Revit file to the 3ds Max scene.

D. Export the Revit file as an FBX file, and then use the File Link Manager to link the exported Revit file to the 3ds Max scene.

E. Use the Layer Manager to define the Revit layers to import, and then drag the file from Windows Explorer to a 3ds Max viewport.

Chapter 6

Creating AEC Objects

In the previous four chapters, you spent time getting familiar with 3ds Max Design and exploring the available modeling tools. You can use these tools for a variety of modeling purposes. The primary intent of 3ds Max Design is to generate visualizations of existing or proposed architectural facilities. These may consist of external images and animations of a building's outward appearance, a multi-building development, internal layouts of rooms and offices, or a combination of both. In this chapter, you'll focus on the tools contained in the 3ds Max toolset designed specifically to create parametric architectural objects (walls, windows, railings, and so on) in your scenes. If you don't have a parametric building program like Autodesk Revit, you can use AEC (architectural, engineering, construction) objects to construct models of buildings.

Items added to a scene for purely aesthetic purposes (for example, people, cars, plants, and things that are not part of the architectural structure) are referred to as *entourage*.

Buildings exist in many forms, from homes, condominiums, and office buildings to shopping malls, prisons, and airports. The AEC items common to all modern buildings are walls, doors, and windows, and 3ds Max contains a parametric library of these objects as well as stairs, railings, and foliage. Design and visualization time can be reduced significantly by using 3ds Max's AEC objects to help construct your scenes. This includes both the initial scene-building period as well as time spent making modifications.

In this chapter, you will learn to:

◆ Create a wall with a linked door or window

◆ Build a staircase

◆ Create a railing

◆ Add parametric plants

Creating a Parametric Wall

3ds Max allows you to create parametric walls easily and quickly. If you are working with AutoCAD drawings that are only 2D, it's simple to add 3D walls by using the Parametric Walls feature. These walls have an added benefit—if you add windows or doors to Parametric Wall objects, 3ds Max will automatically create an opening for the door or window once the door or window object is linked to the wall. If you move the door or window the opening will move with it!

Throughout this and the following sections, you will add and modify the AEC objects required to complete the modeling portion of an architectural scene.

Creating and Adjusting a Parametric Wall

You create parametric wall objects by clicking in the viewport to place the wall's corner points and then right-clicking to terminate the process. This scene contains a line object that is used to define the significant point of the wall.

1. Open the Condo AEC.max file, which you'll find at this book's accompanying web page, www.sybex.com/go/mastering3dsmaxdesign2011. This is a partially completed model of a high-end condominium suite complete with a mezzanine level and three balconies.

2. In the Top viewport, use the Zoom Region tool to zoom into the area shown in Figure 6.1.

3. In the Command panel, choose Create ➢ Geometry and then choose AEC Extended from the drop-down menu. The Object Type rollout changes to display buttons to create three types of AEC objects. Click the Wall button in the Object Type rollout.

4. In the Parameters rollout, make sure Width is set to 0′5″ and Height to 8′0″. In the Justification area, select the Right option (see Figure 6.2).

5. Ensure that the Snaps Toggle is set to 2D, right-click the button, and make sure the Endpoint and Vertex snap options are active. Then click the Snaps Toggle to turn it on. This will ensure that the corners of the wall are placed precisely on the vertices of the existing line that you'll use as a guide.

Walls are either created on the centerline of the selected points or offset to one side by one half the thickness of the wall. For example, a 5″-wide wall, set to be created on the right side of the selection point, is shifted 2 ½″ to the left so that the right side of the wall falls along the selection points.

FIGURE 6.1
Zoom into this area to begin constructing the wall.

FIGURE 6.2
The Parameters rollout for the new wall

6. Click the far-left endpoint of the black line object when the cursor is over it, and the Endpoint or Vertex snap marker appears. Move the mouse and notice that the new wall segment follows the cursor and rubber bands from the initial point, as shown in Figure 6.3.

7. Click three more times, once on each of the remaining vertices of the line, until the new wall object butts against the existing, far-right wall (see Figure 6.4).

8. Right-click to terminate the Wall tool.

FIGURE 6.3
Start creating the first wall.

FIGURE 6.4
The first three wall segments

Adjusting the Wall's Parameters

The wall fits cleanly in the space provided, but it is much shorter than it needs to be considering the high ceilings in the condo. As with most objects in 3ds Max, you can adjust a wall's parameters and sub-objects to achieve the result that you want.

1. With the wall selected, click the Modify tab of the Command panel.

2. Expand the Wall listing in the modifier stack by clicking the plus sign next to it, and then highlight the Segment sub-object level.

3. In the viewport, select all three wall segments. Feel free to use a selection region to quickly select all of the segments; you cannot select any additional objects while in sub-object mode.

4. In the Edit Segment section, increase the Height parameter to 19′8″. The selected wall segments extend up and now match the height of the other walls in the suite, as you can see in the CamWall viewport.

5. Click Wall in the modifier stack to exit the sub-object level.

6. Right-click the [CamWall] label in the viewport and choose Perspective from the context menu to change the camera viewport into a Perspective viewport. If you would like more information about cameras, see Chapter 10, "Using the 3ds Max Camera."

7. Pan the view down, and drag the ViewCube up in the Perspective viewport to look at the wall. You may want to change the Field-of-View setting so you can see more of the room. Right-click the Field-of-View icon in the viewport navigation controls and then change it to a higher value, if you like. Now you can visually confirm the new wall height. To return the view to its previous appearance, press C on the keyboard, and select the CamWall camera view. The C key is the shortcut for the camera view. If a scene has multiple camera views, you'll get a list to choose from. To convert to a Perspective view, press P on the keyboard. Leave it as a Perspective viewport for the time being.

UNDERSTANDING THE WALL OBJECT'S HEIGHT AND BOTTOM OFFSET PARAMETERS

The Bottom Offset parameter, in the Edit Segment rollout, controls the location of the bottom of the wall relative to the initial elevation at which it was created. The Height value is the distance from the base of the wall to the top. For example, a positive value raises the wall above the floor level and also raises the top of the wall the same amount.

Adding Doors and Windows to Walls

Doors and windows not only need to be located and oriented properly in a wall, they also need an opening within which to exist. Without an opening, only the door or window frame, which can protrude through the wall, is visible and not the door leaf or window panes. If a wall is a simple box primitive or a mesh object, openings can be formed using the Boolean techniques discussed in Chapter 4, "Editing Meshes and Creating Complex Objects." When a wall is a parametric 3ds Max wall object, the door and window objects can be created and their openings generated at the same time. Using the latter method results in openings that move whenever the door or window is moved, and the openings automatically adjust in size to match changes in the door or window size.

1. Click the top of the stack so you're no longer in segment sub-object mode. Press Alt+Q to isolate the selection and hide all other objects in the scene.

2. Right-click the Perspective viewport's rendering mode label and change the rendering mode to Wireframe, or press F3. It's easier to see the door's creation in Wireframe mode when the wall does not obstruct your view.

3. Pan, zoom, and orbit to adjust the Perspective viewport until you can see the top of the wall, similar to Figure 6.5.

4. Right-click the Snaps Toggle in the Main Toolbar to open the Grid and Snap Settings dialog box. Clear all snap options and then activate the Edge/Segment option only. The Edge/Segment option will snap the door or window to the proper location and orientation in relation to the wall. Close the Grid and Snap Settings dialog box.

5. Hold down the Snaps Toggle and then choose the bottom option, 3D Snap, from the flyout.

FIGURE 6.5
Pan, zoom, and use the ViewCube tool in the Perspective viewport to see the top of the walls.

6. In the Command panel, choose Create ➢ Geometry and then choose Doors from the drop-down menu. Click the Pivot button in the Object Type rollout. For convenience, you may want to hide the grid by pressing the G key.

7. Place your cursor over the left edge of the short, middle wall, and when the Edge/Segment snap marker appears, click and hold to set the left edge of the door.

8. Move the cursor near the opposite end of the same edge and release the mouse button to set the width of the door, as shown in Figure 6.6.

9. Place the cursor over the opposite edge of the same wall and then click to set the depth or thickness of the door (see Figure 6.7). This is determined by the thickness of the wall.

FIGURE 6.6
Setting the width of the door

FIGURE 6.7
Setting the thickness of the door

10. Move the cursor down and click to set the height of the door, as shown in Figure 6.8. You don't need to set the height to anything realistic; it can be a very short door for the moment, because you will be moving and modifying the door shortly.

FIGURE 6.8
Setting the height
of the door

FIGURE 6.8
Setting the height
of the door

11. In the Parameters rollout, set the Height value to 7´6˝, the Width value to 2´6˝, and Depth to 5˝.

12. Click the Select and Move tool in the Main Toolbar; then, in the Top viewport, move the door so that it is centered in the wall.

13. In the transform type-in boxes at the bottom of the user interface, right-click the spinner to set the Z value to 0´0˝. This moves the pivot point of the door, located at the bottom center, to the 0 (zero) Z-coordinate in the World Coordinate System. The bottom of the door is now at the same elevation as the bottom of the wall.

14. Pan and zoom in the Perspective viewport to get a better view of the new door, and change the viewport render mode back to Smooth + Highlights with Edged Faces. If necessary, change the color of the door to help differentiate it from the wall.

Changing the Door's Parameters

You can change many of the door's parameters, including the frame and leaf size and complexity, to meet the requirements of the design. Here's how:

1. With the door selected, click the Modify tab and, in the Parameters rollout, increase the Open value to see which direction the door swings, as shown in Figure 6.9.

2. Check the Flip Swing and Flip Hinge options to reverse the swing direction and move the hinge to the opposite side of the frame (see Figure 6.10).

FIGURE 6.9
The Open param-
eter determines
how many degrees
of swing the door
follows.

FIGURE 6.10

Flipping the door's Swing and Hinge options

Although most people consider a door to be the large, rectangular object that swings when you push it, this is not the case in 3ds Max. In 3ds Max, this is called a *leaf* and a door object consists of both the frame and the leaf. The leaf has its own set of parameters that control its appearance and complexity.

3. In the Leaf Parameters rollout, change the # Panels Horiz value to 2 and # Panels Vert to 5. The door immediately reflects the changes.

TOGGLE THE EDGED FACES MODE

You can press the F4 key, or choose Edged Faces from the rendering mode label's right-click menu, to enter and exit Edged Faces mode and to better see the results of changing the door's parameters. This way you can see the underlying geometry structure or hide it to just view the form in Smooth + Highlight shading.

4. In the Panels area of the Leaf Parameters rollout, select the Beveled radio button. As you can see, you can make the door become very detailed just by adjusting its parameters.

5. Click the Exit Isolation Mode button to reveal all the objects that were hidden when the wall was isolated.

6. Adjust your Perspective viewport to clearly see the large opening to the right of the new wall.

Adding Doors to Existing Openings

Parametric doors are not limited to being components of parametric walls. Doors can also be incorporated into walls drawn using other methods, such as boxes, extrusions, or walls imported from other programs. In these cases, an opening should exist before the wall is created. In the following exercise, you'll place a sliding glass door into the openings provided.

1. In the Perspective viewport, switch back to the Wireframe rendering mode.

2. Select the Wall06 object and then isolate it to temporarily clean up the scene. Adjust your view, if necessary, to see the opening.

3. Click the Create button, and then click the Sliding button.

4. Open the Grid and Snap Settings dialog box, deselect Edge/Segment, check Vertex and Endpoint, and close the dialog box.

5. Click the bottom-left inside corner of the opening to set the start point for the door; then drag and release the cursor over the right inside corner to set the door's width, as shown in Figure 6.11.

6. Click the bottom-right outside corner to set the thickness of the door to match the thickness of the wall (see Figure 6.12).

7. Lastly, click the top-right outside corner of the opening to set the height of the door to match the height of the existing opening, as shown in Figure 6.13.

FIGURE 6.11
Set the width for the new sliding door.

FIGURE 6.12
Set the thickness for the sliding door.

FIGURE 6.13
Set the height for the sliding door.

When doors and windows are created using the method described in the previous exercise, the frame is placed outside the locations picked rather than inside. You'll often have to edit the objects' parameters to properly fit the opening:

1. Zoom into the bottom of the sliding door. If you have trouble zooming, change from Perspective to Orthographic view; the shortcut to do this is the U key. Changing back and forth from Perspective to Orthographic seems to restart the zoom.

2. As you can see in the Frame area of the Parameters rollout, the width of the door frame is 0´2˝. This means that the width of the door object must be reduced by 4˝.

3. At the top of the Parameters rollout, change the Width parameter from 5´4˝ to 5´0˝. The door shrinks toward its initial creation point of 4˝.

4. Click the Select and Move tool.

5. In the transform type-ins, turn on Offset mode and enter **minus 2**↵ in the Y field. The door shifts 2˝ to center itself in the opening, as shown in Figure 6.14.

6. Set the door's Height value to 7´10˝ to match the door's height to the opening's height.

FIGURE 6.14
The sliding door after shifting it into place

The door looks a bit industrial for the condo setting, so you'll adjust a few parameters to make it look more appealing.

1. Set the door's Depth parameter to **0´2˝** so the frame doesn't fill the depth of the opening.

2. Use the transform type-in to move the door -3˝ in the X direction to relocate it near the middle of the opening as shown in Figure 6.15.

FIGURE 6.15
The sliding door after reducing its depth and centering it in the opening

3. In the Leaf Parameters rollout, set both the Stile/Top Rail and Bottom Rail parameters to 0´1″ to provide only a thin border around the perimeter of the glass door.

4. Increase the Open value to see how the door opens (see Figure 6.16).

5. Create two more sliding doors in the other large openings, noting that the far-right opening is 4″ wider than the others.

6. Click Exit Isolation Mode to view the rest of the scene when you're finished.

FIGURE 6.16
The sliding door after adjusting the location and parameters

Creating a Parametric Window

Perhaps your wall needs a window to allow light into the room. Follow these steps to add one:

1. To create the window, you'll use a similar process as door creation, only using the window object instead. You'll create a window on the new wall and in the existing openings above the sliding doors. Choose Create ➤ Geometry, and then choose Windows from the drop-down menu.

2. To create the window in the new wall, click the Sliding button in the Object Type rollout, and using the Edge/Segment snap, place the window in the long segment of the new wall. In the Wireframe rendered viewport, the window should look similar to Figure 6.17.

3. Move the window lower on the wall, and then adjust its parameters to your liking. Open the window using the Open field in the Open Window area. Your window should look similar to Figure 6.18.

4. Click the Select and Move tool; then, using the X- and Y-axis handles, relocate the window on the wall. Notice that when you move the window, the hole in the wall moves as well. Your window should look similar to the one shown in Figure 6.19.

FIGURE 6.17
Adding a sliding window to the parametric wall

FIGURE 6.18
Move the window lower on the wall.

FIGURE 6.19
Move the window into position on the wall.

5. Switch to Wireframe mode; then, using the Vertex snap, place a Fixed window type into the opening above the first sliding door that you made. The procedure is identical to the one you used to create the sliding door.

6. Change the Depth value to 4″ and switch to Smooth + Highlights mode. Notice how the window's frame does not extend beyond the opening, as shown in Figure 6.20.

7. Create another Fixed window, or a window type of your choice, in each of the two remaining large openings.

FIGURE 6.20
The new fixed window above the sliding door

Changing Elevations with Stairs

Elevation changes in buildings can be controlled and facilitated through the use of ramps, stairs, escalators, or elevators. Parametric ramps, escalators, and elevators are not part of the base package of 3ds Max 2010, but constructing either is not beyond the capabilities of the program. However, 3ds Max does come with a set of four parametric stair types that you can use to quickly add access to the upper levels of a scene. Stairs can be straight, with a single turn (LTypeStair), with a double turn (UTypeStair), or a standard spiral staircase. To create a stair, you simply define the base and height and then adjust the stair's parameters. In this next exercise, you will add an AEC Stair object that goes from the lower level of the condominium to the mezzanine level.

1. Continue with the current project or open the Condo AEC2.max file from the book's accompanying web page.

2. Make the Top viewport active, click the Zoom Extents button, and then perform a Zoom Region and zoom into the area shown in Figure 6.21.

3. In the Command panel, choose Create ➤ Geometry, and then choose Stairs from the drop-down menu. Click the Straight Stair button in the Object Type rollout.

4. In the Top viewport, click and drag to define the length of the stairs. Start to the right of the first window you created and end near the edge of the mezzanine, as shown in Figure 6.22.

5. Move the cursor down and click to set the width of the stairs (see Figure 6.23).

6. Move the cursor up and click to set the overall height of the stairs, as shown in Figure 6.24. Watch in the Perspective, Front, or Left view while setting the height.

FIGURE 6.21
Before creating the stair, zoom into the area shown.

FIGURE 6.22
Click and drag to set the length of the stairway.

FIGURE 6.23
Set the width of
the stairway.

FIGURE 6.24
Set the overall
height of the stair
object.

RESTRICTING THE ORIENTATION OF THE STAIRS

Unlike with many other tools in 3ds Max, holding down the Shift key does not restrict the orientation of the stair objects to 90-degree increments.

7. With the staircase selected, click the Select and Rotate tool. In the transform type-ins at the bottom of the 3ds Max window, enter **90** in the Z input box. (Make sure Absolute Mode is on, not Offset Mode.) This rotates the stair slightly so that it is parallel with the wall nearest to it.

8. In the Layout section of the Parameters rollout, set Length to 9′0″ and Width to 3′0″.

CREATING HANDRAILS

The options to create handrails and rail paths on the sides of the stairs are in the Generate Geometry section of the stair's Parameters rollout. The Handrail option simply creates the handrail as if it were to be affixed to a wall, without the option to also create handrail posts. Posts can be made using at least two different methods. First, you can manually create a single post and then clone that post at each location as necessary. The Array tool (discussed in Chapter 4, "Editing Meshes and Creating Complex Objects") may be appropriate for generating the clones for straight or spiral staircases. A second option is to use the 3ds Max rail object, which is discussed in the next exercise. Rails can be created by clicking the vertex points for the base or by designating a path for the rail to follow. Using the Rail Path option for the staircase creates a line object that the rail can be instructed to follow. The stair's rail path is at the same standard elevation that the rail should be, relative to the size of the staircase; the rail object, when following a path, is created with its base on the path. Therefore, when using a stair's rail path with a rail object, you will have to move the rail down into position after it is created.

Three parameters define the height of a staircase: the overall height, the height of each riser, and the total number of risers. You need to define one of these values in the Rise area of the Parameters rollout and then click the Pin button to the left of the parameter label. When one parameter is pinned, its value is fixed and the other two parameters define the height and riser parameters for the stair.

9. In the Rise area of the Parameters rollout, set the Overall value to 11´6″. This is the elevation change from the first floor to the second, minus the height of one riser. You want the last step that a person takes up the staircase to be onto the floor of the next level.

10. After you set the overall height, click the Pin Overall Height button to hold that value.

> **PINNING THE OVERALL VALUE**
>
> The overall height is always determined by multiplying the riser height by the riser count. Pinning the Overall value keeps the value close, but does not always keep it exact as it does when you pin either of the other two values. To determine the riser height, divide the overall height by the riser count.

11. Set Riser Height to 0´9 ⅛″ and Riser Count to 15.

12. Move the staircase until it butts against the mezzanine as shown in Figure 6.25.

The stairs are currently supported by a single stringer centered on the steps, but a double-stringer situation would be more stable.

FIGURE 6.25
Move the stairs against the mezzanine.

13. Expand the Carriage rollout, and then click the Carriage Spacing button.

14. Choose Start Offset from the drop-down list in the Carriage Spacing dialog box, and then set the Count value to 2, Spacing to 2´0″, and Start Offset to 4″, checking the check boxes as necessary (see Figure 6.26). Close the Carriage Spacing dialog box.

15. Move the stairs away from the wall if necessary.

16. Move the window if it interferes with the stairs. The stairs are complete (see Figure 6.27), and the residents have access to the upper level. Continue experimenting with the stairs' parameters—many values can be set in the Carriage, Railings, and Stringers rollouts that change the appearance of the staircase and customize it to the owner's preference. You can also convert it to an editable poly and continue editing at the sub-object level.

FIGURE 6.26
The Carriage Spacing dialog box

FIGURE 6.27
The staircase after setting the proper parameters

Setting Boundaries with Railings

Another AEC object available in the 3ds Max toolbox is the rail object. Rails consist of straight, horizontal rail elements with vertical posts at each vertex and pickets spread between them. Rails can be customized in many ways, including the shape and count of the rails, pickets, and posts, and whether the fencing area is a solid fill. In the following exercise, you will add a railing along the perimeter of the mezzanine opening.

1. Continue with the current project or open the Condo AEC3.max file.

2. Zoom in the Top viewport to get a good view of the mezzanine area (see Figure 6.28) and also adjust the Perspective viewport to observe the mezzanine's edge.

FIGURE 6.28
Zoom into the mezzanine area.

3. In the Command panel, choose Create ➤ Shapes, click the Line button, and then click the AutoGrid check box at the top of the Object Type rollout. The AutoGrid option causes the line to be drawn on top of the highest object that the cursor is over when the mouse is clicked. In this case, it will be the top surface of the mezzanine.

4. Turn off the Snaps Toggle option. If it is on, that will complicate the vertex-creation process.

5. Click to place the vertices at the points shown in Figure 6.29 and draw the line that the rail will follow. Be sure to click, rather than click and drag, to create Corner type vertices, and then right-click to terminate the Line tool.

6. In the Command panel, choose Create ➤ Geometry, and then choose AEC Extended from the drop-down menu. Click the Railing button in the Object Type rollout.

7. In the Railing rollout, click the Pick Railing Path button, and then click the line that you created in step 5. The cursor changes to a cross with an oval and a line near it to indicate when it is over an acceptable path object, as shown in Figure 6.30.

FIGURE 6.29
Click to draw
the line for the
rail path.

Click here to place the vertices for the line.

FIGURE 6.30
Selecting the
railing path

The railing is created (see Figure 6.31), but it spans from the first vertex to the last in a single segment, while the four posts are located on the line. Increasing the Segments value in the Railing rollout causes the railing to more closely follow the railing path. This can be useful when the spline path is curved. Selecting the Respect Corners check box, however, causes the railing to turn at each vertex, regardless of the Segments setting.

8. In the Railing rollout, click the Respect Corners check box. The railing now follows the path cleanly, as shown in Figure 6.32.

FIGURE 6.31
The straight railing path

FIGURE 6.32
Click Respect Corners to force the railing to follow the straight-line segments.

9. In the Top Rail area, set the following parameters:

Profile = Round

Depth = 2″

Width = 3″

Height = 4′0″

In the Lower Rail(s) area, set the following:

Profile = Round

Depth = 2″

Width = 1″

Figure 6.33 shows the Railing updates.

FIGURE 6.33
The railing after
updating the
parameters. Edged
Faces is off for
clarity.

10. Expand the Posts rollout, and then set the Profile parameter to Square.

11. In the Fencing rollout, set the Profile parameter to Round, and then click the Picket Spacing button to open the Picket Spacing dialog box.

12. The Picket Spacing dialog box contains controls for defining the number of pickets, how they are spaced, and what types of clones are created. Set Count to 40, click the Instance radio button in the Type of Object area, and then choose Divide Evenly, No Objects at Ends from the drop-down list, as shown in Figure 6.34.

13. Close the Picket Spacing dialog box. Figure 6.35 shows the railing with the new picket spacing.

FIGURE 6.34
The Picket Spacing
dialog box

FIGURE 6.35
The railing with
the new picket
spacing

The pickets are created and placed properly in the rail system. As you can see, railings can be created and customized quickly to fit the desired appearance or local building requirements. The Solid Fill option in the Picket's Type drop-down list replaces the pickets with a solid form that can represent glass, canvas, or any other substance defined by 3ds Max's Material Editor. Materials are covered in Chapter 9, "Enhancing Models with Materials."

Adding Foliage to a Scene

Plants and trees can add life and color to a scene in addition to adding a visual clue as to the structure's size and the scene's geographic location. 3ds Max ships with a small collection of plants and trees: the AEC foliage objects. These plants and trees are fully parametric and feature controls for determining the height, spread, density, and so on.

Trees and plants can consist of thousands of distinct elements, including trunks, branches, twigs, and leaves. Creating these manually would consume an enormous amount of time for each plant required and is beyond the expectation of any project. In earlier years, trees in computer graphics were made by photographing a real tree and then applying that image to the surfaces of two crossing planes placed in your scene. This approach may be acceptable for distant objects, but it often fails to provide enough realism when these objects are in the foreground. Several parametric tree objects that can quickly populate a barren scene are included in 3ds Max's base program. Here's how to use them:

1. Continue with the current project or open the Condo AEC4.max file from this book's accompanying web page.

2. Make the Top viewport active, click the Zoom Extents button, and then perform a Zoom Region and zoom into the area shown in Figure 6.36. Adjust the Perspective viewport to look at the northernmost balcony door.

FIGURE 6.36
Zoom into the area shown before creating the AEC foliage object.

3. In the Command panel, choose Create ➤ Geometry, and choose AEC Extended from the drop-down menu. Click the Foliage button in the Object Type rollout.

4. Select a tree in the Favorite Plants rollout; the example shown in Figure 6.37 uses the yucca tree.

5. Drag the tree into the Top viewport and drop it in the planter between the left and middle balcony doors (see Figure 6.38). The tree appears in the viewports.

6. Switch to the Perspective viewport and adjust the view to see the tree. Move the tree into the pot if necessary.

FIGURE 6.37
Select a tree from
the Favorite Plants
rollout.

FIGURE 6.38
Drag the tree into
the Top viewport.

7. Expand the Parameters rollout in the Command panel.

8. Reduce the Height value to lower the top of the tree to a more realistic elevation.

9. The Seed parameter is the random number that 3ds Max uses to determine the minute details that affect the plant's appearance, including bend amounts, directions, and branch location. Click the New button several times to see various versions of the tree that use the same general parameters but with different appearances.

CREATE SIMILAR PLANTS USING THE SEED PARAMETER

To create several similar, but not identical, trees in your scene, create Copy clones of one tree and then change the Seed value in the Parameters rollout for each clone. The Seed value is a reference number used in the algorithm that builds the foliage. Changing the Seed value changes the appearance of the trees while maintaining the other parameter values.

10. In the Viewport Canopy Mode area, make sure the When Not Selected radio button is selected. This replaces the leaves on the tree with a green "bubble" in the viewports when the tree is not selected to reduce the load on your system's video card.

11. Rotate the tree and move the tree and planter, if necessary, to prevent any part of the tree from protruding into the wall. With the foliage objects, as well as most other objects in 3ds Max, there is no collision detection utility to prevent objects from intersecting each other.

12. Deselect the tree and notice that the leaf area is replaced with low-density, substitute geometry, as shown in Figure 6.39.

13. Save your scene as Condo AEC5.max.

FIGURE 6.39
The Canopy mode geometry displays much faster in the viewports.

FIGURE 6.39
The Canopy mode geometry displays much faster in the viewports.

The Bottom Line

Create a wall with a linked door or window Many walls in actual structures contain doors and windows, and the tools for creating them in your 3ds Max scenes can significantly reduce the amount of time required to complete a project.

> **Master It** Draw a spline to represent the floor area of a rectangular room 20′ × 40′ in size. Create walls around the perimeter that are 15′ tall and do not encroach inside the perimeter line that you drew. Fill one of the tall walls with floor-to-ceiling fixed windows and place a door in the opposite wall.

Build a staircase Staircases can be complex assemblies that must meet a fixed set of parameters, including transitional height and stair count. 3ds Max comes with a library of parametric stairs that can meet most of your needs.

> **Master It** Delete the stair that you made for the condo scenes in this chapter. Replace it with a spiral staircase that transitions from the lower floor to the mezzanine.

> Using a procedure similar to the one described in the "Changing Elevations with Stairs" section, replace the straight staircase with a spiral staircase using Create ➤ Geometry ➤ Stairs ➤ Spiral Stair. Use the same count, riser height, and other parameters from the straight stair object. Your scene should look similar to the following image.

Create a railing Railings partition spaces and guide or restrict foot traffic through a facility or room. The Railing parametric object included in the 3ds Max toolset provides many parameters, such as ones for setting the number and style for the railings and posts.

> **Master It** Select the railing on the mezzanine level of the condo scene in this chapter. Modify it so that the lower railing, which currently passes through the middle of the railing system, is moved to the bottom. Replace the pickets with solid fill.

Add parametric plants The AEC foliage objects included in 3ds Max can quickly populate a scene with any number of trees found in the library. Each tree can be unique or an instance of others.

> **Master It** Replace the yucca tree in the condo scene with a small weeping willow from the plant library. Make sure it doesn't encroach into the nearby walls. Adjust the tree to your liking, and then copy it and the planter to two more locations. Change the Seed value to make the two new trees different from the original and from each other.

Chapter 7

Organizing and Editing Objects

In this chapter, you'll continue to work on the condo model. You'll be introduced to the Loft compound object and the Sweep modifier, which allow you to extrude a shape along a path to create more complex forms. To be able to see your work clearly and continue working on the building, you'll need to employ some organizational tools. You'll learn more ways to create and edit extruded spline shapes. Along the way, you'll learn how to organize your work using object names and layers and aligning one object's location based on the location of another.

In this chapter, you will learn to:

- ◆ Loft a shape
- ◆ Organize objects with layers
- ◆ Deform an object with the Noise modifier
- ◆ Model with the Symmetry modifier
- ◆ Extrude with the Sweep modifier
- ◆ Align objects
- ◆ Rename objects

Naming Objects

Perhaps one of the simplest and most important things you can do to help keep your model organized is to give the objects in your model meaningful names. You were introduced to this concept in Chapter 2, "Introducing 3ds Max Objects." Let's go ahead and name some of the parts of the condo project that you worked on in Chapter 6, "Creating AEC Objects," to prepare for creating more objects:

1. Open the ch07a.max file. This is similar to the condo project you worked on in Chapter 6 but with additional objects displayed and named.

2. If the file opens with a single viewport displayed, press Alt+W, or click the Maximize Viewport Toggle.

3. Click the Zoom Extents All tool to get a view of all the parts of your model.

4. In the Top viewport, zoom in and use the Select Object tool to select the wall you created in Chapter 6, as shown in Figure 7.1.

FIGURE 7.1
Selecting the
wall in the Top
viewport

5. In the Name and Color rollout of the Create tab of the Command panel, change the existing name to **Wall_Den**. If you're in the Modify tab, change the name that appears just below the Modify label at the top of the tab. (In fact, you can change the name of an object in any tab except the Utilities tab.)

6. Select the pivot door that you created, change its name to **Door_Den,** and then rename the sliding window to **Window_Den**.

7. Repeat this process for the three sliding doors, renaming them, from top to bottom in the Top viewport, to **Door_Patio_East**, **Door_Patio_Middle**, and **Door_Patio_South**, as shown in Figure 7.2.

8. Next rename the fixed windows over the sliding doors to **Window_Patio_East, Window_Patio_Middle**, and **Window_Patio_South**, as shown in Figure 7.2.

FIGURE 7.2
Renaming the
sliding doors and
fixed windows

Now that you've renamed the new wall, windows, and doors, the next step is to rename the deck for each patio. Right now, it's difficult to access the decks because the railings are in the way in the plan view, and their arrangement in the other views is overlapping. The easiest way to get to the decks is to temporarily turn off the visibility of the rails. Let's do that in the next exercise:

1. Click the Select by Name tool on the Main Toolbar or type **H** on the keyboard.

 The Select from Scene dialog box appears (see Figure 7.3.)

2. Click the Name column label to organize the objects alphabetically by name, and then Ctrl+click all of the objects with names that start with "Railing." Alternatively, you can select the first Railing object in the list and then Shift+click the last one to highlight all of them.

3. Click OK. The dialog box closes and the objects are selected in the viewports.

4. Right-click in the viewport and choose Hide Selection from the quad menu.

 The Railing objects disappear, as shown in Figure 7.4.

FIGURE 7.3
The Select from
Scene dialog box

5. Using Figure 7.4 as your guide, rename the patio deck objects as you did the wall, window, and door objects. Use the Select Object tool to select a deck, and then use the Name and Color rollout to enter the new name.

 Although you can use the Modify tab to change the name of an object, using the Create tab is faster for changing the names of multiple objects, because you don't need to wait for the object's parameters to load each time you make a selection.

6. To finish the process, redisplay the hidden railings. Right-click in the viewport and choose Unhide by Name in the quad menu.

 The Unhide Objects dialog box displays, as shown in Figure 7.5.

 This is basically the same dialog box as the Select from Scene dialog box, but instead of listing all objects that are on, it shows only the objects that have been hidden.

7. Click the Select All button on the toolbar on the right side of the dialog box, and then click Unhide. The railings reappear.

FIGURE 7.4
Renaming the
patio decks

Patio_East

Patio_Middle

Patio_South

FIGURE 7.5
The Unhide
Objects dialog box

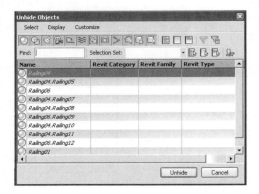

If you simply want to unhide all the objects that were hidden, you can click the Unhide All option in the quad menu. In this exercise, you used the Unhide Objects dialog box just so you'll know how to selectively unhide objects by name if necessary. This demonstrates the usefulness of meaningful names for objects. If the object names are not descriptive, you'll have a difficult time determining which object in the list is the one you want to turn on.

Another point to consider when naming objects is their alphabetical listing. In the Sort group of the Select from Scene and Unhide Objects dialog boxes, you have the option to sort the objects in a variety of ways. By default, names are sorted alphabetically. To help you keep track of an object, you might consider how its name will appear in the alphabetical listing. For example, you named the patio door and window objects in a way that keeps them grouped together in the listing. The name Door or Window appears first, then the location (patio), and then the direction that the object faces, such as east or south. This hierarchical naming scheme helps keep objects grouped together in a listing. When you have several objects to sort through in the list, this is a handy practice to maintain.

USING THE RENAME OBJECTS TOOL

Renaming a large number of objects can be a tedious and time-consuming procedure. When several objects need to be renamed, try to use the Rename Objects tool (Tools ➢ Rename Objects) whenever possible. The Rename Objects tool completely changes the names of all selected objects, or you can use it to add or remove a prefix or suffix from the objects' names.

In a recent project, several objects had names such as 3DRCab223, 3DRCab224, 3DRCab225, and so on. These names made sense to the consultant who designed the kitchen, but the objects needed more descriptive names that adhered to the company's standard naming convention. We quickly renamed these objects to Cabinet Kitchen 3 Drawer01, Cabinet Kitchen 3 Drawer02, Cabinet Kitchen 3 Drawer03, and so on, using the Rename Objects tool. Rename Objects can also rename objects when they currently have identical names, a condition that 3ds Max allows.

To use this feature, select the objects to be renamed.

1. In the Base Name input box, enter a new name for the objects, such as **Cabinet** or **Chair** or an even more descriptive name.

2. If you leave this input box blank and deselect the corresponding check box, it will retain the existing name while modifying it using the following options.

3. Add a prefix or suffix by selecting those options' check boxes and entering the text in the matching input box. Start or end the line with a space if you want to have a gap between the existing or base name and the new prefix or suffix.

4. You can use the Remove First or Remove Last Digits option to delete the leading or trailing letters of the current names, or you can set the numbering procedure using the Numbered options.

5. Click the Rename button at the bottom of the dialog box to execute the process.

The objects will be renamed and the Rename Objects dialog box will remain on the screen. It will not indicate that the objects were successfully renamed, but you can verify it in the Select from Scene dialog box. Alternatively, you can choose the Pick option at the top of the Rename Objects dialog box, rather than the Selected option. Pick opens the Pick Objects to Rename dialog box, which works similarly to the Select from Scene dialog box, where you selected the objects to be renamed.

Renaming the Ceiling Fixtures

Several pairs of objects that represent the glass cover and support ring for the recessed ceiling lamps are spread across the ceilings of the condo. They all have nondescriptive names such as 3Ring20 and D3Glass22. In this exercise, you'll use the Rename Objects tool to quickly rename all of these objects in the scene.

1. Continue with your existing scene, or open the ch07b.max file from the Sybex website.

2. Click the Select by Name button, select all the objects with names that start with "3Ring" (see Figure 7.6), and then click OK.

3. Choose Tools ➢ Rename Objects to open the Rename Objects dialog box.

4. Make sure the Selected radio button and Base Name check box are selected, and then type **Fixture_Ceiling_Ring** in the Base Name field.

5. Select the Numbered option, and then make sure Base Number is set to 0 and Step is set to 1, as shown in Figure 7.7. With these settings, all the fixture rings will be renamed to Fixture_Ceiling_Ring00, Fixture_Ceiling_Ring01, Fixture_Ceiling_Ring02, and so on.

6. Click Rename, and then verify the success of the operation in the Select from Scene dialog box (see Figure 7.8).

FIGURE 7.6
Selecting the "3Ring" objects

FIGURE 7.7
Renaming the selected "3Ring" objects

FIGURE 7.8
The objects
are renamed.

7. Repeat the process and rename the fixtures' glass objects as follows:

 A. Select all of the D3Glass objects.

 B. Open the Rename Objects dialog box if necessary.

 The Selected, Base Name, and Numbered options should still be active.

 C. Type **Fixture_Ceiling_Glass** in the Base Name field. Again, select the Numbered box.

 D. Click Rename.

 E. Verify the success of the operation.

 F. Close the Rename Objects dialog box.

As you can see, you can use the Rename Objects dialog box to quickly rename objects in a scene. In the previous exercise, you renamed 46 objects in a matter of minutes.

Organizing Objects by Layers

Another way to keep your model organized is through layers. The idea of layers comes from drafting, where different disciplines literally drew their parts of a design on different layers of media. For example, in an architectural drawing, the mechanical engineer would draw duct-work and piping on a separate sheet, which was overlaid on the floor plan of the drawing. The different overlays were eventually combined into one sheet through reprographic techniques.

In computer-aided drafting (CAD), layers are used to help keep drawings organized and easy to manage. This concept is taken a step further by organizing types of graphics into walls, doors, reflected ceiling information, and so on. In addition, notes and dimensions are usually separated into their own layers.

In 3ds Max, you can use layers in a similar way by organizing parts of your model by the type of material you'll be applying to each object. For example, the walls that will be stucco might be placed in a layer called Walls_Stucco. In the condo scene, if the bulkhead for the mezzanine is to be given the same appearance as the walls, you might combine it into the Walls_Stucco layer as well. Roof and floor components will be given their own layers, too. You might even go further and create layers for window glass, mullions, wood detail, and so on, if these components are not parts of a single-piece object. As you've learned in Chapter 5, "Working with External Design Data," another way of working with layers is to link or import your CAD data into 3ds Max.

In this section, you'll begin to explore layers by using them to organize objects in the condo model by their material assignments. You'll use these different layer/material assignments in later chapters to apply materials to objects.

Setting Up Layers

Start by setting up a few layers that you'll use for objects in your condo scene:

1. Click an empty area in the viewport to clear the selection set, and then click the Layer Manager button on the Main Toolbar. This button is also available in the Layers toolbar, which you can access by right-clicking a blank area of any toolbar and choosing Layers from the shortcut menu.

 The Layer dialog box displays (see Figure 7.9).

FIGURE 7.9
The Layer
dialog box

2. Click the Create New Layer (Containing Selected Objects) button. Layer01 appears in the list box. If any objects were selected at this time, they would be assigned to the new layer. In this case, the layer is empty.

3. Click Layer01 to highlight the name for editing and type the name **Windows**↵. It appears in place of the Layer01 name.

4. Click the Create New Layer (Containing Selected Objects) button again, select the layer, and type **Doors**↵.

5. Click the Create New Layer (Containing Selected Objects) button again and name the new layer **Walls**↵.

6. Click the Create New Layer (Containing Selected Objects) button again and name this final layer **Patios**↵.

 If you're an AutoCAD user, you'll notice that most of the 3ds Max methods for creating and using layers are identical to those for AutoCAD.

You might have noticed that one layer already exists. Layer 0 is always present and is the default layer on which all objects in a new file are created. All of the objects that already existed when you started the project and all the objects you've created in the condo scene reside on layer 0. You may even notice that the Color column in the Layer dialog box shows a particular color for layer 0. This is the same color that you see on objects when you look at the shaded view in the Perspective viewport, unless the objects color is manually changed.

The color that you see on newly created objects is the color of layer 0 by default. This is because the new nodes that are created default to a setting of By Layer, meaning an object's color is controlled by the layer that it is on, rather than having a different color assigned By Object.

In 3ds Max, layer 0's color is randomly chosen when you start a new scene. If you don't like the particular color that was chosen, you can easily change the color in the Layer Manager. See the section "Assigning Color to Layers" later in this chapter for information about changing layer colors.

Assigning Objects to Layers

Now that you have some new layers, go ahead and assign some of the objects to the proper layers. This is fairly easy to do: you select the object and then use the Layer drop-down list on the Layers toolbar to select a layer for the object:

1. Click the Select by Name tool on the Main Toolbar. The Select from Scene dialog box appears with a list of all of the objects in the file.

2. Highlight the three Window_Patio objects and the Window_Den object. Click OK.

3. If necessary, open the Layers dialog box.

4. Select the Windows layer in the Layer dialog box to highlight it, and then click the Add Selected Objects to Highlighted Layer button, as shown in Figure 7.10.

5. The selected objects are now on the Window layer. Click the plus (+) sign next to the Windows entry in the Layer dialog box, as shown in Figure 7.11, and you'll see a listing of all the objects on that layer.

6. Select the four Door objects that you created, and add them to the Doors layer. The Door_Den object is found indented under the Wall_Den object.

FIGURE 7.10
Add the objects selected in the viewport to the layer.

FIGURE 7.11
Objects on the Window layer

7. Use the Ctrl key and a crossing selection window to select the patio decks and railings, as shown in Figure 7.12, and add them to the Patios layer.

8. Finally, select the three Wall objects and move them to the Walls layer.

FIGURE 7.12
Selecting the patio components

Another way to add objects to a layer is to create the layer with the objects preselected:

1. Select all the objects with names that start with the word "Lamp." These are the objects that combine to represent the six suspended lights in the kitchen and dining area.

2. Click the Create New Layer (Containing Selected Objects) button on the Layer dialog box's toolbar.

3. The objects are moved to the new layer automatically as the layer is made. Give the new layer the name **Lamp Suspended** (see Figure 7.13).

FIGURE 7.13
The Lamp Suspended layer

Now try a little experiment to see how you can control the visibility of objects based on their assigned layers.

1. Click the Hide column next to the Patios entry in the Layers dialog box. A lightbulb icon appears in place of the horizontal line, and all the objects on the Patios layer disappear, as shown in Figure 7.14.

HIDDEN OBJECTS AND HIDDEN LAYERS

In 3ds Max, you cannot show an object that is on a hidden layer. However, you can hide an object that is on a visible layer.

FIGURE 7.14
Hiding the objects
assigned to the
Patios layer

2. Click the Freeze column next to the Windows entry. The windows turn gray, and a snowflake icon appears in the Freeze column (see Figure 7.15). You can freeze selections of objects in your scene by right-clicking in a viewport and then choosing Freeze Selection from the quad menu.

 Try to select one of the windows, and you'll find it to be impossible. When an object or object's layer is frozen, those objects are visible in the viewports but cannot be selected and, therefore, cannot be changed.

3. Click the Patios lightbulb symbol to unhide the Patios layer. The patio components reappear in the viewports.

4. Click the snowflake icon next to Windows to unfreeze the Windows layer.

 Earlier, you used the quad menu to hide individual objects. You can see from this exercise that you can also hide an object through its layer assignment by hiding a layer. In this exercise, you used the Hide and Freeze columns in the Layer dialog list to hide and unhide the Patios layer and to freeze and unfreeze the Windows layer.

 When a layer is frozen, choosing Unfreeze All from the quad menu opens a dialog box that asks whether you want layers unfrozen as well as the objects that were frozen using the Freeze Selection quad menu option.

FIGURE 7.15
Freezing the
objects on the
Windows layer

Assigning Color to Layers

Another way to help you keep track of objects and their layers is to assign a unique color to layers. This helps you visually keep track of layer assignments and can help in your everyday editing tasks by toning down the appearance of objects that you are not currently editing. Layer colors also give you a visual reference for object organization.

1. In the Layer dialog box, click the color swatch associated with the Windows layer to display the Layer Color dialog box.

 You can toggle to the AutoCAD Color Index (ACI) palette in the Object Color dialog box if you are more familiar with the arrangement of palette colors in AutoCAD.

2. Click the medium-green color swatch in the bottom row, as shown in Figure 7.16.

3. Click OK. The objects assigned to the Windows layer now appear in this color.

4. Set the colors for the rest of the new layers. Use Figure 7.17 as a guide.

FIGURE 7.16
Selecting the color for the Windows layer

FIGURE 7.17
Use this view of the Layer Color dialog box to set the colors for the rest of the layers.

WHAT IF AN OBJECT DOESN'T CHANGE TO ITS LAYER COLOR?

Color can be confusing if you don't understand the distinction between setting color By Layer or By Object, especially when you open up a legacy scene made in an older version of 3ds Max. You may find that some older scenes don't use layers at all, although you still have the option of taking them or leaving them in 3ds Max 2011. It's important to note that layers are best used to organize complex scenes and are especially appropriate to use if you import data from any CAD-based application into 3ds Max.

If each object that you create has a different color, then your scene is set to assign color By Object, meaning that each object created is assigned a random color. If the scene is set to By Layer, the objects will assume the color of the layer on which they reside.

A preference setting in 3ds Max lets you change the default creation method for new nodes to either By Layer or By Object. Choose Customize ➤ Preferences. Then select the General tab and in the Layer Defaults group, select the Default to By Layer for New Nodes check box. If you plan on using layers, it is best to leave this setting selected.

No matter which way you decide to set the preferences, each individual object can have its color assigned By Layer or By Object. One quick way to tell whether an object's color is assigned By Object or By Layer is to look at the color swatch next to the object's name in the Modify panel.

If the color swatch shows stacked black and white swatches, its color assignment is By Layer. If it shows a single color, its color assignment is By Object.

You can change an object's property setting from By Object to By Layer. This change will cause the object to inherit its display properties from its assigned layer. To make this change, use the Select Object tool to select an object, and then right-click the object and select Object Properties from the quad menu. The Object Properties dialog box displays.

CONTINUES

WHAT IF AN OBJECT DOESN'T CHANGE TO ITS LAYER COLOR? *(CONTINUED)*

Click the By Layer button in the Display Properties group. This will cause the Display Properties check boxes to be enabled. The check boxes are properties that are available for each object if you enable the By Object mode.

You'll also see that the By Layer button is available for the Rendering Control and Motion Blur groups of the Object Properties dialog box. Just as with Display Properties, the By Layer button lets you determine whether the Rendering Control and Motion Blur properties are controlled by the individual object or by the layer to which the object is assigned. You'll learn more about Rendering properties in Chapter 13, "Creating Animations, Particles, and Dynamics."

Notice that there are also tabs in the Object Properties dialog box for Advanced Lighting (Radiosity Renderer) and mental ray. These tabs control specific properties for these renderers that you will be learning about in Chapter 14, "Advanced Rendering with mental ray."

Clicking the color swatch at the top of the dialog box (also available next to the object name in the Command panel) opens the Object Color dialog box, where the object color can be changed from By Object to By Layer.

Not all of the objects, including the original walls and the patio components, respect the assigned layer color. This is because the colors of these objects are assigned on a per-object basis rather than per layer color. This problem can be fixed globally using the Object Color dialog box.

1. Choose Edit ➤ Select All or press the Ctrl+A shortcut key combination. All the nonhidden and nonfrozen objects in the scene turn white to indicate that they are selected.

2. Click the color swatch in the Command panel to open the Object Color dialog box.

3. Click the Mixed button once or twice until it changes to read By Layer and the Current Color field changes to stacked black and white swatches. Mixed indicates that the objects selected include objects with colors assigned By Layer and By Color.

4. Choose Edit ➢ Select None or press the Ctrl+D shortcut key combination to clear the selection set.

5. All the objects in the scene now respect the color designated to their assigned layers.

6. Save your scene as ch07c.max.

Once your layers are set up, you can use a layer as a selection criterion.

1. In the Layer dialog box, make the Doors layer current by double-clicking the layer name and then clicking the square icon to the right of the layer's name. It changes to a check mark to indicate that Doors is the current layer.

2. Click the Select Highlighted Objects and Layers button on the Layer dialog box's toolbar. The objects on that layer are selected.

You can also set the current layer by first selecting an object. This technique can be useful if you want to model additional objects on the same layer as something you see on the screen.

1. Select a window object.

2. Click the Highlight Selected Objects' Layers button in the Layer dialog box. The Windows layer is highlighted.

3. Click the Select Highlighted Objects and Layers button. The objects on the Windows layer are selected.

One nice thing about this method is that you don't even have to know the name of the layer you are changing to, because you are getting that information by picking the object.

The layer color or object color property you've been working with so far defines the color of the objects only as you work with them in wireframe views. These colors also appear in shaded

views until you assign materials to the objects. At that point, the shaded views of objects will show a facsimile of the materials assigned to objects rather than the object's Color property. The Color property is only there to help you differentiate between objects and is not meant to represent the surface qualities of the material. You will learn more about materials in Chapter 9, "Enhancing Models with Materials."

Understanding the Icons in the Layer Dialog Box

In a previous exercise, you used the Layer dialog box to hide and unhide and freeze and unfreeze objects. The Layer dialog box provides layer-based controls for several 3ds Max features. Here is an overview of some of the control options:

1. Open the Layer dialog box, if it isn't already open.

2. Click the plus (+) sign next to the Doors layer. The list expands to show the objects that are assigned to the Doors layer.

Dots appear next to the object names in the Render, Color, and Radiosity columns. This indicates that those properties are controlled by the layer to which the objects are assigned. Dashes in the Hide and Freeze columns indicate that nothing object-specific has been set.

RENDERING AND RADIOSITY

Rendering is the process that 3ds Max uses when the effect of lighting on materials and geometry is calculated and output to an image file. *Radiosity* is a lighting system that calculates indirect illumination—that is, bounced lighting—to determine the coloration of the pixels in a rendering. Radiosity is a Global Illumination system; other systems that work similarly include mental ray and V-Ray.

3. Next to the Door_Patio_South entry, click the dot in the Render column repeatedly. The icon cycles through a dot, a teapot, and a dash sequence.

 The icons define whether the object's rendering capabilities are defined by the layer's settings (dot) or if the object is not rendered, regardless of the layer's rendering setting (dash). The teapot icon indicates that the object will render, even when the layer is set not to render.

Similarly, you can control whether an object or layer is considered when calculating a radiosity solution. Omitting objects from the radiosity calculations can speed up the rendering process but will also lower the accuracy of the rendered image.

You can also control the color of individual objects by clicking the icon in the Color column. In fact, if you click the Color option for an object in the Layer dialog box, you'll see the Object Color dialog box you saw earlier.

The By Layer/By Object option allows you to toggle the method of assigning color to the object. If you select an object that currently has its color assigned By Layer, as soon as you select a color for the individual object, the By Layer button changes to By Object to indicate the new state. If the object doesn't change to the color of its layer, you can choose By Layer to force the object to observe the layer's color. You can also choose a color from the color palette to give the object a different color from its layer color to make it easier to identify on screen.

Lofting an Object

Now that your model is a bit more organized, you're ready to model a few new components. In this section, you'll look at how you can use splines to create unique forms—in this case, a pedestal for showcasing a statuette or plant.

Lofting is a process whereby a cross-sectional shape is extruded along a path. The result of this lofting is called a loft object. Loft objects are a bit like Boolean objects in that they are the compound result of the combination of multiple objects, namely cross-sectional shapes and the path. The term *lofting* comes from shipbuilding, and it refers to the method of laying out the contours of a ship's hull. Like a ship's hull, the cross-sectional shape of a loft can vary along the path. As you'll see later, you can adjust the shape of the loft along the path by adjusting the profile at various points along the path.

Setting Up the Shapes to Form the Pedestal

The pedestal that you'll create has a fairly common shape: a square base and cap with a round, fluted body. The goal is to make a form similar to the one shown in Figure 7.18. This shape may pose a challenge to most modeling programs, but 3ds Max can easily create this unique shape.

To begin the process, you'll draw two splines. One spline will represent the cross-sectional shape of the base, and the other spline will define the length and direction the form follows. The cross-sectional shape is projected, similar to the behavior of the Extrude modifier, along the path shape, to form the new 3D loft object.

FIGURE 7.18
A pedestal created using the Loft tools

Let's start the lofting process by hiding most of the model so you can see your work more clearly. You'll leave the den wall and floor visible.

1. Make a new, empty layer named Pedestal, and make it the current layer.

2. Use the Select Object tool to select the Wall_Den and Floor407 objects. If you prefer, you can practice using the Select from Scene dialog box to do this.

3. Right-click in the viewport, and then click Hide Unselected in the quad menu.

All of the objects disappear except for the den wall and the lower level floor. Now, draw the cross section for the pedestal base:

1. Use the Zoom Region tool to zoom into the portion of the Top viewport near the den window, as shown in Figure 7.19.

FIGURE 7.19
Use the Zoom Region tool to enlarge this portion of the Top viewport.

2. Click the Create tab of the Command panel. Then click the Shapes button and click Rectangle.

3. Select the AutoGrid option, and then in the Top viewport, click and drag a rectangle just below the den wall. You don't need to be exact about the placement or size of the rectangle. The AutoGrid option ensures that the rectangle is drawn at the same elevation as the top of the floor.

4. In the Parameters rollout of the Command panel, change the Length and Width values to **12″** and the Corner Radius value to ⅛″.

You now have the profile ready, so it's time to create the path over which the profile will be lofted. This time, you'll create a shape in the Front viewport.

1. Right-click in the Front viewport and zoom into the area near the rectangle.

2. In the Transform Type-In area at the bottom of the user interface, turn on Offset mode.

3. Click the Create tab in the Command panel. Click the Shapes button, if it isn't already active. Click the Line button, and then deselect AutoGrid.

4. Draw the line shown in Figure 7.20. Starting from the top of the floor and while holding the Shift key down to force a straight line, draw a line.

FIGURE 7.20
Draw this line, starting at the square shown at the bottom of the line.

5. When the Z Transform type-in field shows approximately 2´10˝, right-click to terminate the Line tool.

6. Click the Modify tab. Then click the Vertex button in the Selection rollout (or open the quad menu and select Vertex).

7. Select both vertices and, if necessary, convert them to Corner vertices.

You now have the path you need to create the loft object.

OBJECT CREATION AND THE CURRENT VIEWPORT

If you zoom out in the Top viewport and turn on the grid, you'll notice that 3ds Max placed the path line on the X-axis as you see it in the Top viewport. By default, 3ds Max places objects on the planes defined by the X-, Y-, and Z-axes of World Space. When you draw objects in the Top or Perspective viewport, they are placed on the plane defined by the X- and Y-axes of the World Coordinate System. For the Front and Back viewports, objects are placed on the plane defined by the X- and Z-axes, and for the Left and Right viewports, objects are placed on the plane defined by the Y- and Z-axes.

For this exercise, it's not imperative that the path be near the cross-section shape, but you can move it closer if you prefer.

Lofting a Shape Along a Path

Now you're ready to loft the shape you created earlier. You'll use the Loft compound object in the Create tab to perform this maneuver.

1. Click the profile rectangle shape you created earlier to select it.

2. Click the Create tab in the Command panel. Then click the Geometry button.

3. In the Create drop-down list, select Compound Objects.

4. Click the Loft button in the Object Type rollout. Note that the Loft button will be grayed out if you do not first select a spline to act as either the loft path or shape.

5. Click the Get Path button in the Creation Method rollout, and make sure the Instance radio button is selected, as shown in Figure 7.21.

6. Move the cursor over the line you created in the previous exercise. The cursor shows an ellipse marker, indicating that the cursor has found an object that can be used as a path for the loft. Click the line. The profile extrudes along the shape of the path, as shown in Figure 7.22.

FIGURE 7.21
The Creation Method options for Loft compound objects

FIGURE 7.22
The lofted shape

UNDERSTANDING WHAT A LOFT DOES

A loft is constructed by creating a cross section (the shape object) at each vertex of the path object, starting at the path object's first vertex. If the resultant loft appears backward, select the path object, access the Spline sub-object level, and then click the Reverse button in the Geometry rollout. With an open spline, the vertex at the opposite end of the spline will become the designated first vertex. With a closed spline, the same vertex will remain the first vertex; however, the direction to the subsequent vertices will be reversed.

When you create a loft, you are given the option of having the loft make an instance or reference copy of the shape to place at the beginning of the path. The default is to create an instance copy. This allows you to modify the original profile object, which will modify the cross-sectional shape of the loft. When you create the loft, a clone of the original shape is placed at the starting point of the path. The clone is placed in the same location as the original shape, so it isn't obvious that a clone has been created. Also, the clone of the original shape becomes a sub-object of the loft (as you'll see in a later exercise).

When you select a spline, initiate the Loft tool, and then choose the Get Shape option; the current object becomes the path object and the shape object, or a clone of it, is moved to the first vertex of the path. When you choose the Get Path option, the current object becomes the shape object, and the path object, or a clone of it, is moved to the shape. The loft emerges from the shape object as if the path were perpendicular to the face of the profile shape. You can later adjust the location of the loft using the transform tools. Any shape object can be the shape component of a loft object, but only shapes with a single, contiguous spline can be the path object. For example, text can be a shape but it cannot be a path. When you need to extrude a shape along a complex, noncontiguous spline, consider using the Sweep modifier discussed later in this chapter.

Using Different Shapes Along the Loft Path

The loft object you just created is basically a uniform shape along its length. But suppose you want the form of the loft to change along the path. You can do this by introducing additional shapes along the path. Here, you'll begin to see some of the powerful capabilities of 3ds Max's Loft tool.

The goal here is to have a 2″-thick square base and cap with each of these transitioning to an 11″-diameter circular cross section and then a 9″ cross section. Try the following exercise to see how to switch the shape object in a loft:

1. Choose Create ➢ Shapes, activate the AutoGrid option, and then click the Circle button.

2. In the Top viewport, create one circle with a radius of 5.5″ and one with a radius of 4.5″.

3. Click the Select Object tool to exit the Circle tool, and then select the Loft compound object.

4. Click the Modify tab. You should see the name Loft001 at the top of the Command panel.

5. Scroll down the Command panel to the Path Parameters rollout and click to open it. Path Parameters lets you select a location along the path where you can place a new shape (see Figure 7.23).

FIGURE 7.23
The Path Parameters rollout

6. Click/drag the Path spinner up to about 40 percent. As you do this, you see a small, yellow X, called the *path marker*, move along the loft path, as shown in Figure 7.24.

 Often, the loft object obscures your view of its component objects. You can toggle off the visibility of the loft object in the Display section of the Skin Parameters rollout, as shown in Figure 7.25. The Skin option sets the display of the loft in Wireframe viewports, and the Skin in Shaded option affects Shaded viewports. The loft objects appear in renderings regardless of the Display settings.

7. Click the Distance radio button and then enter **2″⏎** in the Path field. This places the yellow X marker at a point that is 2″ from the first vertex of the path object. The Distance option causes the Path value to reflect an actual measurement, rather than a percentage of the path length.

8. Scroll up the Command panel to the Creation Method rollout and click Get Shape.

9. Place the cursor on the larger of the two circles and click it. The loft object changes to include a transition of the cross section from the original shape to the new shape, as shown in Figure 7.26.

FIGURE 7.24
The path marker appears as an X.

FIGURE 7.25
The Skin Parameters rollout

FIGURE 7.26
The new loft shape with the modified profile in place

Holding One Cross Section

The result of the new loft isn't quite right. You want the square base to be maintained for the first two inches and then instantly switch to a circular cross section. In this case, the transition begins immediately. A multi-cross-sectional loft object will always transition from one shape to the next without holding a shape for any length of the path. To maintain the rectangular shape for any portion of the path, you must bracket both ends of that portion with the same shape.

1. In the Path Parameter rollout, highlight the Path value and enter **1.99**↵.

2. Make sure the Get Shape button is still active and then place the cursor over the rectangle shape at the base of the pedestal.

 It's important to understand what you accomplished here. The rectangle shape isn't actually maintained from the beginning of the path; for a length of 1.99″, the loft transitions from one rectangle to another, identical rectangle over that distance. The cross section quickly transitions to a circle over the next 0.01″ (see Figure 7.27).

FIGURE 7.27
Transition from one shape to another.

Completing the Loft Cross Sections

The last steps required to finish the basic shape of the pedestal are to place the remaining cross sections at the proper distances from the first vertex in the path.

1. To place the first smaller circular shape, change the Distance value to 4″, click the Get Shape button, and then select the smaller circle. The base of the pedestal's circular area shrinks, as shown in Figure 7.28.

FIGURE 7.28
The base of the loft after placing the small circular shape

The top of the pedestal is a reciprocal of the base. You'll need to add the same shapes, but in the reverse order.

2. Change the Path value to 2´6˝, make sure Get Shape is still active, and then click the small circle. This causes the 4½˝ radius to be held for most of the pedestal's height.

3. Set the Path value to 2´8˝ and then select the large circle as the shape.

4. Finally, enter **2´8.125˝** in the Path field and then select the rectangle at the base of the pedestal, as you did in step 2 of the prior exercise. You don't need to place the rectangular cross section at the top of the pedestal; when there is no shape at the end of the path, the last shape given is continued to the end. Your pedestal should look like the one shown in Figure 7.29.

5. Save your file as **mych07d.max**.

The basic form of the pedestal is complete. In the next section, you'll learn some techniques for fine-tuning the loft.

FIGURE 7.29
The pedestal with multiple cross sections

Fine-Tuning a Loft Object

You now have a pretty good piece of furniture for your condo, but let's suppose you want to refine the shape. For example, you might want to make some slight adjustment in the diameter of the main shaft so that it bows outward slightly. Although you could accomplish this with additional path shapes, this technique might cause a noticeable change between shapes and would require calculating and creating additional shapes. Instead, you'll use Loft Deformations to change the overall shape of the loft object.

USING LOFT DEFORMATIONS

Loft Deformations are a set of tools that alter the shape of the loft object as a whole, rather than changing the shape of path sub-objects. Deformations use a graph to adjust the parameters of each deformation type: Scale, Twist, Teeter, Bevel, and Fit. The deformations are available only from the Modify tab of the Command panel.

1. Continue with the previous exercise or open ch07d.max, which you downloaded from this book's website.

2. With the pedestal selected, click the Modify tab in the Command panel.

3. Expand the Deformations rollout and then click Scale, as shown in Figure 7.30. Scale changes the size, in the X or Y direction, of the loft object. The Z direction always points along the path; the X- and Y-axes are always perpendicular to the path.

 This opens the Scale Deformation (X) dialog box shown in Figure 7.31. The red line, currently at a value of 100, indicates that the scale of the loft is consistently at 100 percent of its designed size. In other words, all the cross sections appear at the same size as their instanced counterparts. The black boxes at the end of the red line represent the corner points where the scale is defined. To change the scale, you would move a corner point upward to increase it or downward to decrease it.

FIGURE 7.30

The Scale Deformation button

FIGURE 7.31

The Scale Deformation (X) dialog box for the pedestal loft object

4. Make sure the Make Symmetrical button in the Scale Deformation box's toolbar is active. In this exercise, only the scale of the X-axis is changed, but the Make Symmetrical button forces the Y-axis to match the X-axis.

5. You want to change the scale at the middle of the object, but not at the ends, so you'll need to add a new corner point at the midpoint of the path. Click the Insert Corner Point button.

6. Click on the red line, about halfway along its length. A white box appears showing the location of the new corner point. Like most objects in 3ds Max, selected corner points are white. Unselected corner points are black.

 There are two fields at the bottom of the dialog box. The left field is the location, as a percentage of the path, of the selected corner point. The right field is the value, as a percentage of scale, of the loft at that corner point.

7. In the left field, enter **50**↵. In the right field, enter **125**↵ (see Figure 7.32).

 The pedestal shaft bows outward at 50 percent along the path (see Figure 7.33).

FIGURE 7.32
Moving the
midpoint vertex

FIGURE 7.33
The pedestal after
increasing the
scale to 125 percent
at the midpoint

The main, tubular shaft isn't the only part of the pedestal with an increased scale. The entire length is in a constant state of increased or decreased scale. Here, you'll restrict the scale deformation to the shaft section only.

The vertical dashed lines indicate the points along the path where shapes are placed. The solid line indicates the location specified in the Path field of the Path Parameters rollout.

1. Select Insert Corner Point and then click on the red line at approximately 12 percent, where the 4½″ radius circular cross sections begins, and then click again, at about 88 percent, where it ends (see Figure 7.34).

2. To find the exact percentage value for the smaller circular cross sections, click the Percentage radio button in the Path Parameters rollout and then use the Previous Shape and Next Shape buttons to jump to those shapes in the loft object, as shown in Figure 7.35.

FIGURE 7.34
The Scale Deformation
points are inserted.

FIGURE 7.35
The Previous Shape
and Next Shape
buttons

3. Select a corner point in the Scale Deformation dialog box that corresponds to the current cross section in the Path parameters rollout, and then enter the Path value into the left input field and **100**↵ in the right. Your path scale should begin and end with flat sections, indicating no change in scale, and have a peak in the middle when the increase in scale occurs (see Figure 7.36).

FIGURE 7.36
Flat sections
and peaks

The last item to adjust is the sharpness of the corner point at the middle of the loft. Like the vertices of a spline, the corner points can be either sharp or smooth.

1. Select the corner point at the middle of the path, and right-click and choose Bezier-Corner from the pop-up menu, as shown in Figure 7.37.

2. Two handles appear, projecting from the selected corner point, as shown in Figure 7.38. Move each handle upward to soften the transition into the corner point. Be sure not to move the handles higher than the corner point, or the shaft diameter will become larger on one side of the corner point and then recede back to 125 percent at the corner point.

When you're done, the pedestal should look like Figure 7.39.

FIGURE 7.37
Choose the Bezier
Corner option.

FIGURE 7.38
The Bezier handles

FIGURE 7.39
The pedestal after adjusting the middle corner point

3. Close the Scale Deformation (X) dialog box.

4. Save your file.

TURNING DEFORMATIONS ON AND OFF

Each of the deformation types has a lightbulb icon next to it in the Deformations rollout. Turning any of these off preserves the settings while preventing the deformation from affecting the loft object. This is similar to clicking the lightbulb icon in the modifier list to turn off a modifier.

Feel free to experiment with the other deformation options. Each has a unique function, as listed here:

Twist Like the Twist modifier, the Twist deformation turns a loft object around the path. Using the deformation, you can change the twist direction and vary the rate of change over the length.

Teeter By default, the cross-section shape is perpendicular to the path. Using the Teeter deformation, you can adjust the shape's pivot along the path.

Bevel Usually used at the ends of a loft, Bevel reduces the size of a cross section to give a tapered appearance.

Fit Fit doesn't work like the other deformation curves; it doesn't affect the loft along the path. Rather, you define the shapes in the X- and Y-axes, and the lofted shape is conformed to those shapes, along their related axes, as it is lofted.

ADJUSTING THE DENSITY OF THE LOFT

Look in a Wireframe viewport or activate the Edged Faces option, which is accessed from the Viewport Shading Label right-click menu, and you'll see the pedestal is broken into several vertical segments along the path and several along the perimeter of each shape. Each series of segments adds to the total number of faces in the object and, in turn, the file size and rendering time. Just as with many other objects in 3ds Max, you can set the number of segments used to create a loft.

The Shape Steps setting determines how many subdivisions occur between each vertex of the loft object's cross section. The Path Steps setting determines the number of segments between

each cross-section shape, or between each deformation corner point, when they exist. Neither of these values affects the original shape and path objects used to create the loft. To get a less-dense loft, decrease the number of segments along the path and shape. Here's how it's done:

1. Select the loft object.

2. In the Modify panel, scroll down to the Skin Parameters rollout label and expand it (see Figure 7.40).

3. Change the Shape Steps value to 4 and the Path Steps value to 3. This reduces the number of faces in the loft from about 4,000 to approximately 2,000. Your pedestal should look like Figure 7.41.

FIGURE 7.40
The Skin Parameters rollout

FIGURE 7.41
The pedestal after reducing the number of path and shape steps

Using the Instance Clones to Edit the Loft

In an earlier exercise, you drew the original loft path so that it was close to the rectangle shape. You did this so you could have a clear view of the path in order to select it. In the next exercise, you'll make changes to the loft by editing the original line you used to define its path and the cross-section shapes.

Start by adjusting the line that defines the loft path of the pedestal:

1. To temporarily save the model in its current state, choose Edit ➤ Hold.

2. In the Front viewport, select the line you created to define the path of the loft, as shown in Figure 7.42, and then click Vertex in the modifier stack.

3. In the Geometry rollout, click the Refine button (see Figure 7.43). Refine is one tool that can be used to add segments to a spline.

4. Click in two locations along the path to add two new vertices, as shown in Figure 7.44. The segmentation of the loft object increases to accommodate the new vertices.

FIGURE 7.42
The path selected with the Vertex sub-object mode active

FIGURE 7.43
The Refine button on the Geometry rollout

FIGURE 7.44
Adding new vertices to the path

5. Use the Select and Move tool to move the new vertices. Observe how the loft reacts to the changes, as shown in Figure 7.45.

6. Undo the changes made in step 5.

The transforms (Move, Rotate, and Scale) placed on a shape are disregarded when they are considered to be components of a loft object. For example, a shape object's position or rotation does not matter when the loft is created. Understanding this is very important when the Scale transform has been used on a shape. A 4″-diameter circle scaled to 50 percent so that it appears to be 2″ in diameter will still loft with a 4″ diameter. This is due to the method that 3ds Max uses to evaluate data. If a shape to be used in a loft has been scaled, use the Reset XForm Utility (Utilities Command Panel ➤ More ➤ Reset XForm) to set the current transforms to be the object's default.

FIGURE 7.45
Moving the vertices in the path

Here's an example where the transforms do not affect a loft:

1. Exit the Vertex sub-object level, and then select the smaller circular shape near the loft object.

2. Click the Select and Uniform Scale button, then click and drag upward on the scale gizmo. As you can see in Figure 7.46, the scaling of the shape instance has no effect on the loft.

3. Undo the Scale operation.

4. In the Parameters rollout, change the Radius parameter to 6″. Figure 7.47 illustrates how changing the Radius value is reflected in the loft.

5. Choose Edit ➢ Fetch and then click Yes in the "About to Fetch. OK?" dialog box. Your scene is restored to the state it was in when you chose Edit ➢ Hold at the beginning of the prior exercise.

6. Save your scene as **mych07e.max**.

FIGURE 7.46
Using the Scale transform has no effect on the loft object.

FIGURE 7.47
Changing the radius of the instanced shape is reflected in the loft.

EXPLORING THE DIFFERENT MODELING TECHNIQUES

You should experiment on your own with the many different modeling techniques available in 3ds Max. There are usually several ways to achieve the same three-dimensional form.

Using the Noise Modifier

Straight lines, flush surfaces, and perfect spheres, are easy to accomplish in computer-generated (CG) graphics but they are often the downfall of CG images. Randomness and imperfections, although sometimes subtle, are normal in the real world and their absence is very noticeable. Noise, in CG, is the addition of apparent randomness as a feature to an object and, when properly used, can add a sense of realism in a scene. In this exercise you'll add the Noise modifier to a primitive to move the object's vertices, adding some randomness.

1. Continue from the previous exercise, or open ch07e.max, which you downloaded from the book's website.

2. Right-click in a viewport and choose Unhide All from the quad menu.

3. If necessary, move the pedestal so that it is located under the stairs.

4. In the Top viewport, zoom in on the large planter.

5. Make sure AutoGrid is off, and then create a Cylinder primitive with a Radius value of approximately 13″ and a height of 2″. The perimeter of the cylinder should overlap the inside edges of the planter.

6. Move the cylinder in the Z-axis so that its top is below the upper rim of the planter, as shown in Figure 7.48.

FIGURE 7.48
The cylinder primitive inside the planter

7. Expand the Modifier List drop-down and click the Noise modifier.

8. In the Strength area, increase the Z value to 3″. In this case, we want the noise to affect only the cylinder in the Z-axis and not the X- or Y-axis. A small amount of change has occurred on the surface of the cylinder, but not enough to be easily noticeable.

The Scale parameter sets the size of the noise effect, but not the strength in a particular direction. Smaller Scale values produce rougher noise patterns.

9. Reduce the Scale value to 5. The noise becomes more apparent, as shown in Figure 7.49.

The Noise modifier accomplishes its task of moving vertices as well as it can given the assets is has. By default, a cylinder has only a single cap segment at each end. This isn't enough segmentation to create a rough surface.

FIGURE 7.49
The Noise parameters for the planter object

10. To increase the amount of segmentation and provide the Noise modifier with additional vertices to work with, click the Cylinder entry in the modifier stack to access the cylinder's parameters, as shown in Figure 7.50.

11. Set the Cap Segments to 5. The surface change is now smoother, as shown in Figure 7.51.

12. Select Noise in the modifier stack.

As you can see, the Noise modifier can add randomness that would be difficult and time consuming to achieve by moving the vertices manually.

13. Save your file as **mych07f.max**.

FIGURE 7.50
Choose Cylinder in the modifier stack.

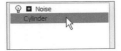

FIGURE 7.51
Smoothing the surface

Modeling with Soft Selection

Soft selection gives you a way to gently deform an object by transforming the vertices. When soft selection is used, unselected sub-objects have the same transforms or modifiers applied to them as the sub-objects that are explicitly selected—but to a lesser degree. You can partially select multiple vertices and apply your transform gently across the entire selection set. You'll use soft selection here to pull out the sides of the planter to form spout type ends. You've already experimented with soft selection in Chapter 4, when you curved the far wall on the Ronchamp Chapel.

1. Select the planter, right-click and then choose Isolate Selection so that only the planter remains in the viewports.

2. Expand the Modifier List drop-down list and click the Edit Poly modifier, as shown in Figure 7.52.

3. Go to the Polygon Modeling tab on the Graphite toolbar and activate the Vertex sub-object level, as demonstrated in Figure 7.53.

4. Drag a window selection region in the Front viewport, similar to the one shown in Figure 7.54. As expected, the selected vertices turn red while the unselected vertices remain blue.

5. Use the Select and Move tool to move the vertices in the X direction. The vertices move and the edges between the selected vertices and the unselected vertices remain straight, as shown in Figure 7.55.

6. Undo step 4.

FIGURE 7.52
The Edit Poly
modifier

FIGURE 7.53
The Vertex sub-
object level on the
Graphite ribbon

FIGURE 7.54
Drag a selection set in
the Front viewport.

FIGURE 7.55
Moving the vertices
in the X direction

7. Expand the Soft Selection rollout and then select the Use Soft Selection option.

As you can see in Figure 7.56, the vertices now change colors from red to orange, yellow, green, and then blue. The red vertices are still fully affected by the transform, and the blue vertices are still unaffected; however, the remaining colored vertices are affected based on their distances from the selection set.

8. Too much of the planter is affected by the soft selection. Adjust the falloff to about 7″ to affect a smaller region around the selected vertices (see Figure 7.57).

FIGURE 7.56

The colors of the soft-selected vertices indicate the amount they will be affected by a transform.

FIGURE 7.57

Soft Selection rollout's Falloff setting

DEFINING THE SOFT SELECTION METHOD

You can adjust the way the Soft Selection options affect the vertices by making changes to the Pinch and Bubble settings just below the Falloff setting. Pinch causes the selection to create a spiked form when a selection of vertices is transformed. Bubble causes the selection to create a wavelike form. The graphic below these settings displays a visual sample of their effects.

9. Move the selected vertices along the X-axis. Watch as the softly selected vertices get pulled along according to the degree to which they were selected (Figure 7.58).

FIGURE 7.58

Moving the planter vertices with soft selection

10. Right-click in the Top viewport, and then click the Select and Uniform Scale button. Click and drag downward on the Y-axis handle to narrow the spout a bit, as shown in Figure 7.59.

As you can see, the Soft Selection tool can effectively create objects with soft, flowing curves.

11. Exit the Vertex sub-object level.

FIGURE 7.59
Forming a
gradual spout

EDITING BELOW THE EDIT POLY MODIFIER

It's important to understand how 3ds Max manipulates objects, and the restrictions that are in place. When you moved the selected vertices, you moved a set of distinct, numbered vertices. Making changes to an object or modifier below the Edit Poly modifier might renumber the vertices—an act that is lost on the Transform modifier that remembers the vertex numbers, but not their specific locations. As an example, if you were to click the Lathe modifier in the stack, you would see a Warning dialog box noting that the Edit Poly modifier is dependent on the selected modifier. It's highly recommended that you select No to cancel the attempt to access the lower modifier or Hold/Yes to save the file in its current state if you need to fetch it later.

When you access the Lathe level in the modifier and make changes that affect the vertex count, such as increasing the number of segments, there can be unexpected results.

If you work beyond the number of available Undos, you can use the Fetch command to return to the previous state only if you selected Hold/Yes in the Warning dialog box.

COMPLETING THE PLANTER WITH THE SYMMETRY MODIFIER

To complete the planter, you need to make the right side look like the left side. One option is to perform the same steps that you did in the prior section on the opposite side of the object. This would be the ideal procedure when the goal is to make both sides similar, but not identical. In this exercise, you'll use the Symmetry modifier to make the left side of the planter a reciprocal of the right side.

1. Make sure the planter is selected, expand the Modifier List drop-down and then select the Symmetry modifier, as shown in Figure 7.60.

 Figure 7.61 shows that the initial result is not the intended result. The Symmetry modifier is acting along the wrong axis.

2. In the Mirror Axis area of the Parameters rollout, click the Y radio button and then the Z radio button, as shown in Figure 7.62. Neither option results in the proper symmetry of the planter's geometry.

FIGURE 7.60
The Symmetry modifier

FIGURE 7.61
The initial result after applying the Symmetry modifier

FIGURE 7.62
The results after changing the mirror axis

3. The problem is that, when using Z as the mirror axis, the left side of the planter is mirrored over to the right side of planter. In the Mirror Axis area, select the Flip option. This results in the right side mirroring over to the left, as shown in Figure 7.63.

FIGURE 7.63
The planter after you've chosen the Z-axis and flipped the result

4. Select Exit Isolation Mode to bring the other scene objects back into view.

5. Select the cylinder object, apply the Edit Poly modifier, and use soft selection and the Symmetry modifier to fit it to the newly shaped planter.

6. If necessary, rotate the planter and dirt so that they do not intersect the wall.

7. Now it is time to do a little scene housekeeping. Select the cylinder and rename it **Planter_Dirt** and assign a brown color to it. Select and rename the planter to **Planter** and the tree to **Planter_Yucca**. Leave their colors set to By Layer.

8. Finally, select the planter, dirt, and tree and place them on a new layer named Planter.

9. Set the current layer to layer 0.

10. Save your file as **mych07g.max**.

ACTIVATING USER GRIDS

A user grid is still active even when hidden. If a user grid does not become the active grid immediately after you create it, select the Activate Grids When Created box in the User Grids tab of the Grid and Snap Settings dialog box. When you have multiple user grids in a scene and need to change the active grid, select it, right-click, and choose Activate Grid from the quad menu. Choose Activate Home Grid from the quad menu to switch back to the home grid.

Extruding with the Sweep Modifier

The Loft compound object is an excellent tool for creating complex extruded shapes with multiple cross sections and smooth transitions between them. For quick and simple extrusions of shapes along a path, nothing beats the Sweep modifier. Sweep projects a cross-sectional shape along a path regardless of the number of noncontiguous spline sub-objects that it contains. The Sweep modifier comes with a library of premade shapes to use as the cross section, or you can use a shape that you make yourself. The following exercise demonstrates the application of the Sweep modifier:

1. Click the Application menu and select Reset to reset 3ds Max and start a new scene from scratch.

2. Create a text object in the Top viewport using the default Size of 100. Alternatively, you can open the `Sweep.max` file from the Sybex website.

3. Select the text object and apply the Sweep modifier. The default Angle cross section is applied to all splines in the shape, as shown in Figure 7.64.

4. Expand the drop-down list in the Built-In Section area of the Section Type rollout and choose Pipe (see Figure 7.65).

The cross section changes to a tube shape throughout the object, as shown in Figure 7.66.

FIGURE 7.64
The text shape with the default Angle cross-section shape

FIGURE 7.65
The Pipe Built-In Section shape

FIGURE 7.66
The text with the Pipe cross section selected

THE SWEEP MODIFIER AND STRUCTURAL STEEL COMPONENTS

Using the Sweep modifier, you can quickly create the structural steel used in a construction project. Many of the shapes found in the Built-In Section drop-down list correspond with common structural steel components.

5. In the Parameters rollout, reduce the Radius value to 2.0, as shown in Figure 7.67. The Thickness parameter will not apply unless a transparent material is used or the ends of an open spline are visible.

6. Create a small 2D shape object in the scene. This example uses a five-pointed star with radii of 2.5 and 1 (see Figure 7.68).

7. Select the text object and then click the Modify tab.

8. In the Section Type rollout, select the Use Custom Section radio button and then click the Pick button, as shown in Figure 7.69, in the Custom Section Types area. Make sure the Instance option is selected near the bottom of the rollout. In a complex scene, you can click the Pick button in the same section to select the cross-section shape from a list.

9. Click the shape that you created in step 2. The text object's cross section assumes the same configuration as the shape object, as shown in Figure 7.68. Because the Instance option was selected, any changes made to the shape are instantly transferred to the text object.

FIGURE 7.67
The Pipe
Radius value

FIGURE 7.68
The text with the custom cross section selected

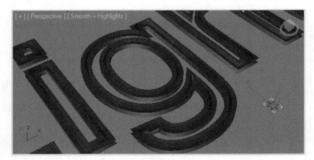

FIGURE 7.69
Select the Pick button on the Section Type rollout.

THE SWEEP PARAMETERS ROLLOUT

The Sweep modifier contains several controls, located in the Sweep Parameters rollout, for adjusting the cross section's shapes as well as its alignment with the paths that it follows. By default, the pivot point of a shape is located at its geometric center, and this point is used as the center of the cross section for the Sweep modifier. This may not be the optimum location for a project, but this can be fixed within the Sweep modifier's Sweep Parameters rollout. For example, if you draw a line that follows the intersection of the walls and ceiling in a room to use as the path that the crown molding will follow, then the default location of the pivot, at the center of the crown molding's shape, will force half of the molding behind the wall or above the ceiling. By choosing the Pivot Alignment button (out of a grid of nine buttons) that corresponds with the molding cross section's corner, the molding will be properly aligned with the path.

The cross section's location can be further refined using the X Offset and Y Offset fields, and the Angle input box and spinners adjust the cross section's rotation around the spline path.

Aligning Objects

To look professional and accurate, objects in your 3ds Max scenes must be aligned with one another so that their intersecting surfaces are touching rather than overlapping or in a condition where one object inexplicably hovers over another. The Align tool, found on the Main Toolbar, is used to align one object's bounding box with the bounding box of another. A *bounding box* is an implicit box defined by the boundaries of an object or the smallest possible box that completely surrounds it. To begin this exercise, open the Align.max file. In this exercise, you will align an end plate and an angle beam to an I-beam. Align can just as easily be used to place objects on a shelf or table or to locate windows on a wall.

1. Select the Plate object, the box near the end of the beam. The object selected when the Align command is initiated becomes the *current* object and is the object that is moved. The second object selected becomes the *target* object; the current object is moved in relation to it.

2. In the Main Toolbar, click the Align button. The cursor changes to the Align cursor, similar in appearance to the Align button, with the addition of a cross whenever the cursor is over an applicable target object. Instructions to pick the target object appear in the status bar, as shown in Figure 7.70.

FIGURE 7.70
Pick Align
Target Object

3. Click the Wide Flange object to designate it as the target. The Align Selection dialog box opens, as shown in Figure 7.71, and the plate relocates to the default location, aligning the pivot points of both objects.

The X, Y, and Z Position check boxes refer to the current viewport's coordinate system. Aligning an object's Y position in the Front viewport is the same as aligning its Z position in the Top or Perspective viewport.

The plate must be moved to the end of the beam and centered. The Align Position section contains four options for each object: Minimum, Center, Pivot Point, and Maximum. The Minimum and Maximum options refer to the extreme locations of the objects' bounding boxes in the directions identified with the Position check boxes at the top of the dialog box. The Center option refers to the center of the bounding box, again only in the directions identified by the Position check boxes. The Pivot Point applies to each object's pivot point.

4. Deselect the X and Z Position check boxes if they are selected. Align allows you to address the concerns for each axis independently. Select the Y Position check box if necessary, as shown in Figure 7.72.

5. The positive Y-axis points to the far end of the beam, as indicated by the axis tripod in the lower-left corner of the Perspective viewport. Therefore, the near end of the beam's bounding box would be its lowest, or minimum, Y value. In the Target Object area, select the Minimum radio button.

6. Similarly, the highest Y value for the plate is the surface facing away from the viewport and the lowest Y value is facing the viewport. Because you want the back of the plate to touch the front of the beam, click the Maximum radio button in the Current Object section. With each option selected, the current object changes location.

FIGURE 7.71
The Align Selection dialog box

FIGURE 7.72
Align Position (World)

7. Your Align Selection dialog box should look like Figure 7.73. Click the Apply button on the right side of the dialog box. Apply executes the Align command, moving the current object into position, and then clears the Position check boxes and awaits further position modifications.

8. The plate must be centered on the beam to complete the repositioning shown in Figure 7.74. In the Align Selection dialog box, select both the X and Z Position check boxes and click both Center radio buttons. Then click OK to execute the Align command and close the dialog box.

FIGURE 7.73
Apply the alignment parameters to the flange.

FIGURE 7.74
The plate is aligned with the I-beam.

9. Complete the exercise by aligning the angle object to the bottom-right edge of the wide flange object. Each position must be aligned independently. Here is a summary of the steps:

10. Select the Angle beam, click the Align button, and then click the beam.

11. Click the X Position option, choose Maximum for both objects, and then click Apply.

12. Click the Y Position check box, choose Minimum for both objects, and then click Apply.

13. Click the Z Position check box, choose Maximum for the current object, choose Minimum for the target object, and then click OK. Figure 7.75 shows the completed exercise.

FIGURE 7.75
The angle is
aligned with
the I-beam.

USING THE QUICK ALIGN TOOL

To quickly align the pivot points of two objects, use the Quick Align tool. With one object selected, choose Tool ➤ Align ➤ Quick Align or press Shift+A and then select another object. The first object is moved so that its pivot point is also located at the second object's pivot point.

Using the Align tool, you can quickly and accurately position objects in your scene. You are not restricted to using a single current object. To place several objects on a table, you can select all of the objects, click the Align button, and then select the table. Choosing Minimum for the object's Z Position and Maximum for the table's Z Position will align the base of all the objects simultaneously with the table's top. The objects can then be moved manually on the X- and Y-axes.

The Bottom Line

Loft a shape Lofting is the practice of extruding a two-dimensional shape along the length of another two-dimensional shape. There are few restrictions on the shape component of the loft object, but the path component must consist of a single spline.

Master It Use the Loft tool to create a table leg that is 32″ tall. The table leg is to start as a 1″-diameter circle and end as a square that is 1½″ on a side.

Organize objects with layers By assigning the objects in your scenes to layers, you can define which layers are hidden, frozen, rendered, and subject to a radiosity calculation. New objects are always created in the current layer using the current layer's color.

Master It Make three instance clones of the table leg from the previous Master It exercise. Also make two teapot primitives and a 32″-long, 32″-wide, and 2″-tall box. Place the two-dimensional shapes in one layer and hide the layer. Place the legs in one layer, the square in one layer, and the two teapots in one layer. Assign each layer a unique name and layer color.

Deform an object with the Noise modifier Applying the Noise modifier to any object adds apparent randomness to the object's surfaces. This can often add a sense of realism to a scene by eliminating the perfect roundness and flatness of many objects created in 3ds Max.

Master It Select the potted tree in the last condo scene you saved, add the Noise modifier to it, and then adjust the Noise parameters so that the trunk of the tree is slightly more jagged than it currently is.

Model with the Symmetry modifier In many cases, objects are symmetrical across one or more axes. Rather than attempting to model both sides of an object, you can model one side and then, using the Symmetry modifier, adjust the other side automatically to appear as its reciprocal.

Master It Being able to quickly modify objects you have already built to create new objects is an important skill. Open the last condo scene in which you modified the pedestal. Create a clone of the first pedestal you built, modify one side of the pedestal, and then make the new pedestal model symmetrical.

Extrude with the Sweep modifier Similar to the Loft compound object, the Sweep modifier extrudes one 2D object along the length of another. While the Loft tool is more powerful, with more controls and features, the Sweep modifier is faster, can be applied to multiple objects, and comes with a library of 2D shapes.

Master It The goal of this exercise is to make a round bumper to fit around the box that you made in the previous exercise. The large, flat surfaces of the box should transition seamlessly into the bumper. Use the Sweep modifier to extrude a half-round shape that fits precisely around the box.

Align objects Visualization Specialists frequently must move one object so that it sits directly on, or butts precisely against, another object with no gaps or overlaps. The Align tool is often the best choice when you need to align the minimum or maximum axis values of different objects.

Master It Continuing from the previous exercise, you need to align the table legs with the box so that the top of each leg is aligned to the bottom of the table and two of the rectangular edges at the top of each leg are aligned with the outside edges of the box. Move the teapots so they lie within the perimeter of the box, and then align the bottom of the teapots with the top of the box. Align the bumper so that it is centered around the box.

Rename objects A good naming convention is invaluable when a scene becomes complicated, with many objects to control and select. The Rename Objects tool is invaluable for quickly renaming several objects to a standard naming convention.

Master It Again continuing from the previous exercise, use the Rename Objects tool to rename the four table leg clones to objects named Table_Leg_01, Table_Leg_02, Table_Leg_03, and Table_Leg_04.

Chapter 8

Light and Shadow

Up until now, you've been concentrating on methods of constructing models and scenes in 3ds Max. In this chapter, you'll learn some of the ways you can control the appearance of the objects you build by manipulating light and shadow.

After your model is built, three main elements affect the look of your models: materials, cameras, and lighting. This chapter will introduce you to the influence of lighting.

Lighting is one of the most interesting subjects in 3ds Max. You can use lighting to create effects, emphasize parts of your model, or simply set up a daytime scene. Through lighting, you can control shadows, manipulate reflective color, calculate the bending of light passing through a transparent material, and simulate lighting fixtures, based on specifications from a lighting manufacturer. It's best to think of lighting in 3ds Max as a kind of paint tool to add emphasis, color, or a sense of realism to your model.

In this chapter, you'll learn to:

◆ Create and adjust the different light types

◆ Render a scene

◆ Define shadow effects

◆ Save and restore scene states

Lighting Your Model

When you are creating 3D graphics, lighting is one of the most important tools at your disposal. Whether you are able to render your model successfully depends largely on your ability to control and manipulate the lighting in your model. A poor lighting setup can ruin an outstanding modeling effort, while proper lighting can emphasize the best parts of a scene. There's a lot to cover in this topic, so let's start with an overview of the different types of lights available in 3ds Max.

Understanding the Types of Lights

So far, you've been depending on the default lighting in 3ds Max Design. Until you add a light to a scene, in a Perspective viewport with Smooth + Highlights turned on, one light source is above the origin and shifted in the negative X direction, while the other is below the origin and shifted in the positive X direction. In a Camera viewport, the default light source is in the same location as the camera, behaving as if you had a light mounted on a video camera.

3ds Max Design 2011 offers a bewildering array of light types. There are five standard light types, two mental ray lights, the Skylight, two lighting systems (Daylight and Sunlight), and three photometric lights. The reason there are so many light types in 3ds Max Design 2011 is historical and has to do with the various ways that you can render your model, using the standard scanline rendering system, the Radiosity advanced renderer, or mental ray.

ADDING THE DEFAULT LIGHTING TO A SCENE

3ds Max has the ability to display the effects of lighting interactively in your viewport. If you have the "classic" version of 3ds Max, you will see the following behavior. When you place your first light in the scene, the hidden default lights that were illuminating the scene previously are automatically disabled when the scene is rendered but remain as the only lighting visible in the viewports. If you have the 3ds Max Design version, the default lights are not automatically disabled when lights are added in the viewport, and you won't see the lighting in the viewport right away.

To disable the default lighting in the viewports and display the effect of the lights you add, click the General viewport label to open the Viewport Configuration dialog box. Select the Lighting and Shadows tab, and locate the Illuminate Scene With group. In this section, deselect the Default Lighting option by selecting the Scene Lights option. The light that you see in the shaded viewports now comes completely from the sources you have placed.

You can convert the default lights into actual, editable scene light objects by choosing Create ➢ Lights ➢ Standard ➢ Add Default Lights to Scene. This command is available only when Default Lighting is enabled and the 2 Lights option is selected in the Rendering Method tab of the Viewport Configuration dialog box (Views ➢ Viewport Configuration).

Once the viewport displays the effect of the lighting, you can also enable the display of shadows directly in the viewport. The ability to display soft shadows in the viewport was new to the 2010 release. On the Viewport shading menu, choose Lights and Shadows, Enable Hardware Shading, and then Illuminate with Scene Lights and Enable Shadows. You will need to verify that your video card and driver are supported by 3ds Max Design 2011 to get the most out of these features.

As mentioned, there are three photometric lights; however, with the settings available in those lights, they can act as many more different types of lights.

This book focuses on using the default configuration of 3ds Max Design 2011 and uses the mental ray renderer and photometric lighting systems. If you are using 3ds Max 2011 with this book, you will need to change your 3ds Max 2011 defaults using the Custom IU and Defaults switcher, as discussed in the "Working with the Custom UI and Defaults Switcher" section of Chapter 1, "Getting to Know 3ds Max Design 2011." You'll also need to make sure to set your system to the DesignVIZ.mentalray preferences. Also, if you are using 3ds Max 2011, you will not have access to the Light Analysis features that will be used in Chapter 14, "Advanced Rendering with mental ray."

With the improvements with hardware and software available to designers and visualization artists, there has been a convergence in the styles and techniques used to create compelling visualizations. More and more visualizations are created in the same way that Hollywood blockbuster feature films or television series are, and they use many of the same lighting, camera, compositing, and special-effects techniques, as you will learn in Chapters 10, 14, and 15.

The standard lights are Target Spot, Target Direct, Free Spot, Free Direct, and Omni. As you might guess from their names, the spot and directed lights come in two versions.

The lights that have *Target* in their name use a target point helper that is linked to the light source but can be moved independently from it. A light source always points at its own target, so you change the light's orientation by moving the target.

Lights that have *Free* in their name are light sources that don't require the placement of a target point. You can freely rotate and move Free lights without having to transform a target location. The drawback to Free lights is that they're a bit more difficult to aim because you must rotate the sources to orient these lights. The advantage is that they're a bit easier to move in animated scenes because you do not have to move their targets too.

For better control over the rotation, always use the Local Reference Coordinate System when you are rotating Free lights.

Here's a brief rundown of these various types of standard lights:

Target Spot Like a spotlight in a theater or headlights on a car, a Target Spot projects a focused beam of light from a single point source that can be aimed in a specific direction. The light rays emitted from a spotlight diverge as they get farther from the source. The Target Spot is perhaps one of the most versatile light sources offered in 3ds Max.

Target Direct Otherwise known as directional lighting, a Target Direct is a source whose light rays remain parallel, rather than diverging with distance from the source. A Target Direct is like a single, very distant light source, such as our sun, with rays that are nearly parallel when they reach Earth.

Free Spot The Free Spot is similar to the Target Spot, except that it has no target point helper. With a Target Spot, you must move the target location to rotate the light. A Free Spot can be freely rotated in any direction using the Transform tools.

Free Direct A Free Direct light is the same as the Target Direct light, except that it doesn't use a target point helper. Like the Free Spot, the Free Direct can be rotated freely without involving a target point.

Omni The Omni light acts similarly to an incandescent lightbulb, radiating light in all directions. Like the Target Spot, Omni is a versatile light source that you'll use frequently. Because an Omni light has no particular direction, it doesn't have a target version.

DON'T MIX 3DS MAX LIGHT TYPES

If you are using the mental ray renderer, it is not recommended to mix using standard and photometric lights. You will get the best results using only Photometric lights with mental ray.

CERT
OBJECTIVE

A feature that is extremely helpful in using lights in 3ds Max is the ability to take a targeted light and toggle off and back on the target helper so that you can have complete freedom for positioning and rotating the lights in your scene. You cannot toggle the targets on and off on the Create tab, but you can do so on the Modify tab.

When working with the lights in 3ds Max Design, an important piece of information to be aware of is the *angle of incidence*. The angle of incidence is calculated using a vector from the light object and the face normal of the geometry that the light is affecting. If the angle of incidence is zero degrees, indicating that the light rays are perpendicular to the geometric surface, the geometry will be lit by the full intensity of the light. When the value of the angle of incidence raises above 0 degrees, the surface will be affected less and less by the light.

Another lighting feature you'll grow to understand and use is *ambient lighting* (also called *global lighting*). Ambient lighting can best be described as the secondary, indirect light that doesn't come directly from a particular source. You can think of ambient light as the light you get on an overcast day, when the light seems to be coming from all directions. You can use ambient lighting to bring out hidden detail or, conversely, to suppress detail. Proper usage of ambient light contributes a great deal toward photorealism. In Chapter 14, you will use the advanced features of the mental ray renderer, a Daylight system, and photometric lights to calculate global illumination as a way to accurately calculate indirect (ambient) lighting in a scene.

It is best to increase the ambient light in a scene with great care. In actuality, no additional illumination is included in a scene, but the surface colors of the scene's objects are brightened, which may cause a loss of surface texture or appearance. In this chapter, you will begin your ambient-light journey by learning how to make quick approximations of indirect light. But first, let's learn about the obvious light in the scene—the light that comes directly from illumination sources.

In traditional photography or filmmaking, setting up your lighting to create the desired impact of a scene is an important aspect of making your images (or *shots*, as they are commonly called) engaging for the viewer or to set a specific tone or mood for the image or sequence.

One of the simplest and most overused lighting setups is the *three-point* lighting method. The benefit of the three-point setup is that the photographer/cinematographer can control the amount and direction of illumination on the subject, including the appearance of shadows.

Figure 8.1 shows what you might commonly see arranged on a tabletop in a beginning drawing, painting, or photography class; recognizable objects set about to allow the students to see how light falls across the shapes as the directionality of the lighting changes.

It is good lighting practice to set up your initial lighting with all objects using a neutral diffuse gray material. This is because the human eye is more perceptive to changes in brightness than it is to changes in color. Therefore, it is easier and more informative to make decisions about lighting and layout in gray tones. Your eye can get fooled if you add color and complex materials too early in the process of setting up your scenes.

FIGURE 8.1
A collection of objects on a tabletop

The three-point lighting setup has a key light, a fill light, and a back light. Figure 8.2 presents a top view of the mock tabletop scene and indicates the three-point lighting that is used in the scene.

The primary key light provides the majority of the light on the subjects and casts the most discernible shadows. Figure 8.3 shows the scene illuminated by just the key light.

FIGURE 8.2
Three-point lights identified in the scene

Back light

Fill light

Key light

FIGURE 8.3
The scene using just the key light

Typically fill lights are placed with a lower angle to the subject to add light in shadow areas and are typically set at about 50 percent the intensity of the key light, as shown in Figure 8.4.

FIGURE 8.4
The scene using
just the fill light

The back light, shown in Figure 8.5, is used to help separate the subject from the background and give a little kick of light around the perimeter of the objects in the scene. It is often seen as the highlight or halo in the top/back of an actress's hair in photographs or recorded interviews.

FIGURE 8.5
The scene using
just the back light

Figure 8.6 shows a render of the scene with all the lights on.

In the last few images, you have seen how lighting in the 3D scene accumulates to form the three-point lighting technique. The three-point lighting technique is one of many basic techniques used to light objects or actors for photography or film recording; however, it is not used very much in architectural renderings.

FIGURE 8.6
A rendering of the scene with all lights on

SUGGESTED ADDITIONAL READING

Mastering Autodesk 3ds Max Design 2011 is designed to give you a fundamental understanding of how to use 3ds Max Design 2011 to create your visualizations, from modeling through final rendering, quickly and efficiently; therefore, it cannot cover all the fundamentals of basic photographic, studio, or stage/set/location lighting. Some information about traditional lighting techniques is discussed in this book, but for a much greater appreciation of the history of set and production lighting, you should consider reading these books:

◆ *Painting with Light* (fourth edition) by John Alton (ISBN-13: 978-05-20-08949-5)

◆ *The Art of 3D Computer Animation and Effects* (fourth edition) by Isaac Kerlow (ISBN-13: 978-0-47-00849-08)

◆ *[digital] Lighting & Rendering* (second edition) by Jeremy Birn (ISBN-13: 978-0-321-31631-8)

Adding a Spotlight to Simulate the Sun

3ds Max offers a way to accurately simulate the sun, including the correct sun angle, depending on the time of day and the location of the illuminated object on the earth. You'll see how you can accurately place the sun in your scene in the sidebar "Creating an Accurate Daylight Environment with the Daylight and Sunlight Systems." (You can find a complete tutorial on placing the sun in your scene in Chapter 14.) First, to get a feel for how lighting works in general, you'll use a spotlight to simulate the sun.

UNDERSTANDING SPOTLIGHTS

Although a spotlight may not be the best type of light to simulate the sun, it's a type of light that you'll use often, so it makes a good introduction to lighting.

3ds Max lets you control the intensity as well as the *spread* of the spotlight. You can focus the light down to a narrow beam like the headlights of a car, or you can spread the light out in a wide angle like the light from a desk lamp. To simulate the sun with a spotlight, you can place a standard Target Spot in your scene at a relatively large distance from the objects. Like the Target Spot camera you created earlier, this Target Spot requires the placement of both the light source and the target of the light. In the following steps, you will add a Target Spot to the scene.

ADDING OMNI OR FREE LIGHTS

The process for creating all lights is the same. The steps to add an Omni or Free light are nearly identical to those for adding a spotlight. The main difference is that an Omni or Free light doesn't require a target point.

1. Open the Savoye08.max file which you'll find at this book's accompanying web page, www.sybex.com/go/mastering3dsmaxdesign2011. This file displays a residential building, the Villa Savoye, that you modeled parts of in Chapter 5. If the File Load: Units Mismatch dialog box opens, make sure the Adopt the File's Unit Scale radio button is selected, as shown in Figure 8.7, and then click the OK button.

2. Right-click the Top viewport; then use the Zoom tool to zoom out (make your top view look similar to the one shown later in Figure 8.9).

3. Click the Create tab of the Command panel; then click the Lights category button.

4. Change the Light Type drop-down list to Standard, and click the Target Spot button in the Object Type rollout to activate it, as shown in Figure 8.8.

FIGURE 8.7
The File Load:
Units Mismatch
dialog box

FIGURE 8.8
Activating the
Target Spot tool

5. Click and hold at a point in the lower-left corner of the viewport, as shown in Figure 8.9.

As you move the cursor, the light appears at the point where you clicked and the spotlight target follows your cursor.

6. Move the cursor to a point in the center of the model plan (shown in Figure 8.9). Then release the mouse button.

Once the Target Spot is placed, it takes over as the light source in the model. To get the Perspective viewport to change to show the light you placed in the scene, right-click the Smooth + Highlights + Edged Faces viewport label, and then choose Lighting and Shadows ➤ Illuminate with Scene Lights.

7. Type **SUN001** in the Name and Color rollout's input box so that you can identify this new light source.

As you can see from the options in the Command panel, quite a few alternatives are available for controlling the characteristics of a spotlight. You can always go back and make changes to a spotlight. For now, accept the default settings created with the spotlight.

FIGURE 8.9
Placing the
Target Spot

Moving a Light

Notice that in the Front viewport, the spotlight is oriented horizontally. 3ds Max places the light and target objects flat along the XY-plane when the light is created in the Top viewport. You must then move the light into position to simulate the sun high in the sky. Let's move the light to a point higher in the Z direction.

1. Right-click the Front viewport to make it active.

2. Use the Zoom and Pan tools to adjust the Front viewport so that it looks similar to Figure 8.10.

3. Click the Select and Move tool on the Main Toolbar. Then click and drag the Y-axis handle of the Transform gizmo of the SUN001 spotlight into the position shown in Figure 8.10. Once you've moved the light source, you'll see a change in the lighting of the Perspective viewport.

FIGURE 8.10
Moving the spot-
light and spotlight
target

Move the spotlight to this location.

Move the target up to this point.

4. Click the Select by Name tool on the Main Toolbar. Then click SUN001.Target in the list, and click Select. Alternatively, with a light selected, you can right-click and choose Select Light Target from the tools 1 quad menu to select the target.

5. With the Select and Move tool active, click and drag the spotlight target's location up, as shown in Figure 8.10. You can use the SUN001 light cone in the Perspective viewport to help match the target position.

The light source and its target move independently, yet they are linked to each other. If you need to move both objects simultaneously, you can select and move the light-blue line that connects them. You also see that viewports using the Smooth + Highlights rendering mode give you immediate feedback regarding the light's effect on your model.

CREATING AN ACCURATE DAYLIGHT ENVIRONMENT WITH THE DAYLIGHT AND SUNLIGHT SYSTEMS

The Daylight system can be useful for shadow studies and for creating an accurate daylight representation of your design. It simulates the color, intensity, and surface reflections of a scene, and it takes into account the "sky glow" or general diffuse lighting from the sky. When the DesignVIZ settings are chosen in 3ds Max 2011, the Daylight system places a special light source called an Illuminating Engineering Society (IES) Sun that more accurately simulates the position and intensity of sunlight according to geographic location, time of year, and time of day. The Daylight system is intended for use in conjunction with Radiosity. Another lighting system, called Sunlight, works very much like the Daylight system. The Sunlight system is meant to be used with the Default Scanline Renderer because it uses a direct light source instead of an IES Sun.

To get the most from the Daylight and Sunlight systems, you need to set a North Direction parameter to accurately orient your model in the north-south direction. You also need to know the location of your building or site and the date and time you want to use for the sun's position. Once you've established these criteria, you can set up your system of choice fairly easily. You'll learn more about this feature in Chapter 14.

When 3ds Max is set to use the DesignViz.mentalray (mr) settings, the Daylight system defaults to creating an mr Physical Sun and Sky for producing accurate shadow studies and sunlight simulation. It is designed to work with mental ray as the renderer and is also required when doing lighting analysis using the new Light Meter objects. The process of creating a daylight system is similar whether you are creating one for the Scanline Renderer, Radiosity, or mental ray.

Editing a Spotlight

Many settings are available for your new spotlight. You can set the intensity, the color, and even the shape of the light, just to mention a few. But the two settings you'll be using the most adjust the light intensity and the light cone. The light intensity is set in the Intensity/Color/Attenuation rollout, and the light cone is set in the Spotlight Parameters rollout.

Let's start by looking at the Hotspot and Falloff settings:

1. Use the Select Object tool to select the SUN001 Spotlight object (not its target).

2. Click the Modify tab in the Command panel; then scroll down and click to open the Spotlight Parameters rollout.

3. Click and drag the Falloff/Field spinner down until its value reaches 12 degrees (Figure 8.11). Notice that the light is reduced in size, shining on only a small part of the scene. Also notice that when you reduce the Falloff/Field value, the Hotspot/Beam value also drops. The Hotspot/Beam will always be at least two degrees smaller than the Falloff/Field value.

FIGURE 8.11
Reduce the Falloff/
Field value.

4. Click and drag the Hotspot/Beam spinner up until it reaches a value of about 50. The light spreads out to cover a larger area. Notice that the Falloff/Field value also increases, staying slightly larger in value.

5. Now, click and drag the Hotspot/Beam spinner down to about 20. This time the Falloff/Field value remained where it was last set while the hotspot got smaller.

6. Set the Hotspot/Beam value to about 34 and the Falloff/Field value to about 36.

The Hotspot/Beam and Falloff/Field spinners control the *spread* of the Target Spot. The Hotspot/Beam value controls the area covered by the most intense portion of the light; everything within the Hotspot cone will receive the full intensity of the light. The Falloff/Field value controls where the light intensity is reduced to zero; nothing beyond the Falloff cone receives any illumination from the light. There is a continuous gradient between the maximum intensity of the light within the hotspot and the zero intensity at the edge of the Falloff cone. The greater the difference between the Hotspot and Falloff is, the smoother the transition will be from bright to dark at the edge of the light pool. This is difficult to see in the Perspective viewport, but it will be more obvious in a rendered view; you'll see this better when you learn to make a quick rendering later in this chapter. Directional lights have identical Hotspot and Falloff controls; however, their cones are cylindrical or box shaped.

Now, try setting the light intensity. This is done through the Multiplier input box.

1. On the Modify tab of the Command panel, expand the Intensity/Color/Attenuation rollout; then click and drag the Multiplier spinner down.

As you reduce the Multiplier value, the view in the Perspective viewport dims. Remember, this is because the SUN001 Target Spot is now the only light illuminating the scene. If you set this light's multiplier to zero, there will be no light at all.

2. Click the Undo tool on the Main Toolbar to return the Multiplier value to 1.0.

CREATING NEW LIGHTS AFTER ADJUSTING EXISTING LIGHTS

When you create a new light after adjusting an existing light's Multiplier value, the new light's default Multiplier will match the previous light's modified value.

The Multiplier spinner controls the overall intensity of the light source. Technically, this parameter is multiplied by the color value to result in the total output intensity. You can change the color of the light source using RGB (Red, Green, and Blue) or HSV (Hue, Saturation, and Value) values. You select a color using the Color Selector shown in Figure 8.12.

To open the Color Selector dialog box, click the color swatch next to the Multiplier spinner in the Intensity/Color/Attenuation rollout.

The Color Selector dialog box lets you see your chosen color as a sample in the lower-right corner of the dialog box. Adjacent to this on the left is the original color that was in the swatch when you opened the Color Selector. This feature can be helpful when you want to compare the new with the old. If the light color that you chose is not appropriate and you have not exited the Color Selector, use the Reset button to return the light to its color prior to making any modifications.

Finally, if you decide that the light you selected originally isn't appropriate for the task at hand, you can use the Light Type drop-down list in the General Parameters rollout to change the type of light used, as shown in Figure 8.13. You can switch the light type only within the same category of lights (Standard, Photometric, or mental ray), but not between the different categories.

This tool, along with the Targeted option in the same group, offers a convenient way to change a light type without having to erase the light and create a new one.

FIGURE 8.12
The Color Selector
dialog box

FIGURE 8.13
Changing the
type of light

Changing the Light Type

As mentioned in the preceding section, once you've placed a light in your model, you aren't stuck with your choice of light type. You can change it in the Modify tab of the Command panel.

You were asked to create a sunlight source using a Target Spot. There is nothing wrong with using such a light for the sun, but the Target Direct is a more appropriate standard light source for the sun.

TREAT THE SUN AS A DIRECT LIGHT

The light rays from a 3ds Max Target Direct or Free Direct light are parallel, just as the rays from our sun are basically parallel in relation to the earth. The rays from the sun are almost parallel because of the relative sizes of the sun and the earth and the vast distance between them. Even though the sun is effectively an Omni light source, it is about 93 million miles from Earth; so from our perspective, the rays of light from the sun striking Earth are essentially parallel.

Here's how you can change a light from Target Spot to Target Direct:

1. Click the Light Type drop-down list in the General Parameters rollout and select Directional (see Figure 8.14). Also make sure that the Targeted option is checked. The light pool produced by a directional light that has been created from a spotlight can be very small compared to the original expanse of the spotlight.

 Notice that the light changes its icon in the viewports to indicate a Target Direct light object. You might also notice that, instead of showing a cone, the light shows a narrow cylinder to indicate the direction and parallel spread of the light rays. You can see this cylinder more clearly in the Left viewport after you click the Zoom Extents button.

2. Scroll down the Modify panel and open the Directional Parameters rollout (Figure 8.15).

FIGURE 8.14
Choosing directional light

FIGURE 8.15
The Directional Parameters rollout

3. Click and drag the Hotspot/Beam spinner up until its value reads around 800m. Click and drag the Falloff/Field spinner until its value reads 850m. You see the light enlarge to form a large cylinder, as shown in Figure 8.16.

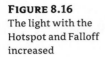

FIGURE 8.16
The light with the Hotspot and Falloff increased

As described earlier, the Target Direct light source produces a light whose rays are parallel, so the light appears as a cylinder. The light rays from a Target Spot diverge, so the light forms a cone. Both light sources offer a Falloff option to soften the edge of the light.

Many other parameters are associated with the light objects, and you'll get to use a few more in later chapters. For now, let's see how lighting and camera locations affect your rendering.

Rendering a View

One of the main reasons for using 3ds Max Design is to get an idea of how your project will look before it is built. Although you can get a fairly decent idea of how it looks in the Perspective viewport, you need to render your model to get a finished image.

The rendering facilities that 3ds Max offers let you create a wide range of images, from quick-study renderings to photorealistic images. You can also generate animated walkthroughs or virtual-reality environments.

All of these types of output are produced through the Render Setup dialog box. Clicking the Render Setup button on the Main Toolbar opens this dialog box, and the Render Production button executes the rendering, using the Render Setup parameters without opening the dialog box. In this section, you'll get a look at some of the ways you can control your rendered output through Render Production. The Render Setup dialog box will be covered in Chapter 10, "Using the 3ds Max Camera," and Chapter 14. This chapter was written, and its accompanying files were created, with the Scanline Renderer in mind.

Try the following exercise to get a good look at the rendering options you have available:

1. Make sure the Perspective viewport is active, use Orbit to get a better view of the Villa Savoye model if desired, and then click Render Production on the Main Toolbar (see Figure 8.17).

 The Rendered Frame Window appears, as shown in Figure 8.18, and the view is rendered with the Scanline Renderer.

FIGURE 8.17
The Render Production button

FIGURE 8.18
The Rendered Frame Window

Rendering is the process of calculating image pixels from mathematical vectors or, in other words, generating a picture based on the objects, lights, and materials in a scene. A *frame* is a single still image on the timeline (animations are composed of numerous frames). Notice that the lighting looks a bit more realistic in the Rendered Frame Window when compared with the viewport, and it includes shadows.

2. In the upper-left corner of the Rendered Frame Window, click the Save Image button.

3. The Save Image dialog box appears, as shown in Figure 8.19. Click the Save As Type drop-down list. A wide variety of output formats is available. Scroll through the drop-down list to get an idea of the choices.

4. Select PNG Image File (*.png) from the drop-down menu. Type in the filename **FirstRendering** and click the Save button. The .png file extension is automatically appended to the output file. The default location for the file is the same folder as the current project.

5. The PNG Configuration dialog box appears, as shown in Figure 8.20. Click OK to accept the defaults, and the file is saved to your hard drive. Each one of the output formats will have its own configuration dialog box with information that must be selected that is specific to each format. You will learn more about image and video formats in later chapters.

FIGURE 8.19
The Save Image
dialog box

FIGURE 8.20
The PNG Configu-
ration dialog

6. Close the Rendered Frame Window.

7. Click the Rendered Frame Window button from the Main Toolbar to view the last rendering you made in your scene. The next time you make a rendering, the contents of the Rendered Frame Window will be overwritten.

Because you haven't added materials to the model yet, the rendering displays with the default colors assigned to all surfaces. Your rendering has the appearance of a cardboard model painted gray. Although it definitely is not the greatest rendering, it does offer a fairly accurate representation of the design. This is really just a start. The process of creating a finished rendering or animation involves a repeated cycle of rendering, adjusting (lights, materials, and camera settings), and rendering again (and again) until you've reached a look that pleases you or, more importantly, your client or employer. Rendering is representative of the magic of computer graphics—seeing your beautiful renderings appear can be quite fulfilling to you as a designer and to your clients. As you progress through the chapters in this part of the book, you'll learn these processes firsthand. In the next chapter, you'll learn the method for adding materials and for further enhancing the rendered image. But for now, let's continue with more on light and shadow.

WHEN OBJECTS APPEAR TO BE MISSING

If you're familiar with the Villa Savoye design, you may notice that some parts of the building are missing or suffer from overlapping surfaces called display *artifacts*. All of the parts are there, but because their normals aren't aligned properly—a common occurrence when using CAD-generated models—they disappear when the model is rendered. You can use the 2-Sided option in the Shader Basic Parameters rollout of the Standard Material or on the Physical Qualities rollout of the Architectural Material to force 3ds Max to render both sides of a surface, regardless of the direction of the normals.

Ambient Light

The rendering shows a picture with lots of contrast. The lighted areas are bright enough that you can clearly see the building features; however, you cannot see any detail in the shadows. This is because there is no ambient light in the model. In the real world, there is usually some ambient light that bounces off the surrounding objects. Indoor ambient light comes from light that is bounced off walls, floors, and ceilings; outdoor ambient light comes from clouds and the general glow from the sky overhead.

If you add ambient light to your scene, you'll begin to see more of the objects in the shadows, and you'll give your rendering a little friendlier appearance. As mentioned earlier, ambient light can be calculated in many ways. The most realistic methods for calculating ambient light (Radiosity or Light Tracer with the Scanline Renderer and using Global Illumination and Final Gather in mental ray) generally take much longer to process. Although it is often better to fake bounced light (see the "Faking Radiosity" section), here's how you can quickly increase the ambient light while using the Scanline Renderer:

1. Close the Rendered Frame Window to make more room on the screen.

2. Choose Rendering ➢ Environment from the menu bar or press 8 on the keyboard. The Environment and Effects dialog box displays, open to the Environment tab (Figure 8.21).

3. For now, you will just be dealing with the Common Parameters rollout on the Environment tab. Click the Ambient color swatch in the Global Lighting group.

 The Color Selector displays (Figure 8.22).

FIGURE 8.21
The Environment tab

4. Click and drag the triangular slider in the Whiteness column downward, as shown in Figure 8.22. This adjusts the general brightness of the ambient light.

FIGURE 8.22
Adjusting the Whiteness value

Drag the Whiteness slider downward.

5. As you move the triangular slider, notice that the Value spinner changes. Adjust the Value setting to approximately 80; then click OK.

6. Click the Color swatch in the Background group. In the Color Selector, adjust the Whiteness slider so that the Value setting shows 150. This will make the background lighter.

7. Click OK in the Color Selector; then close the Environment and Effects dialog box.

 You've increased the ambient light so that objects in shadow will be more visible. To see the results, you'll have to render the model.

8. Make sure the Perspective viewport is selected, and then click the Render Production button in the Main Toolbar. The Default Scanline Renderer quickly calculates the new rendering, as shown in Figure 8.23.

FIGURE 8.23
The model with ambient lighting and background color increased

In this exercise, you only increased the amount of ambient light in your model and changed the brightness of the background. This is clearly the simplest approach to ambient lighting—that of approximating all the indirect light with a single color. As you can see in the Color Selector dialog box, you can also tint the ambient light with hue and saturation if you so choose. This can be useful for interior views of rooms that have a predominant color or for sunset exterior views.

Because artificial lighting usually has a slight orange cast, as a general rule adding an orange cast to interior scenes helps give them a more natural appearance. Likewise, outdoor scenes can be improved by adding a bit of blue to the light source to simulate the ambient light in the sky. Keep the color saturation levels very low to avoid strange results. You can imagine that if you increased the ambient color value to 255, or pure white, all the darker areas in the rendering would disappear as the contrast was eliminated. Using a particularly bright ambient color washes out the rendering and makes lighting irrelevant, because all surfaces seem to emit their own brightness. Therefore, avoid using an overly bright ambient color, or there will be no point to making a rendering at all.

Faking Radiosity

As you will learn in Chapter 14, Global Illumination is a much more sophisticated way of calculating ambient light than the method you have seen so far. Using Radiosity can help you generate photorealistic renderings. The downside to using Radiosity is the greatly increased render time.

To save time, you might find it useful to learn to fake the look of Radiosity ("fakiosity") using standard lights and the Default Scanline Renderer. The downside of using this method is that it isn't nearly as realistic or convincing as Radiosity or Global Illumination in mental ray for simulating ambient light. Even though mental ray is the default renderer for 3ds Max Design, there are many situations where it is faster and easier to switch to using standard materials and the Scanline Renderer.

> **SIMULATING AMBIENT LIGHTING**
>
> It is relatively easy to simulate "direct light"—that is, light striking surfaces on a beeline from the light source. What is somewhat more difficult in computer graphics is efficiently simulating ambient light, all the light striking the surfaces in a space. Ambient light is influenced by light bouncing everywhere in a space from every angle and represents a huge number of calculations.

1. Open Savoye08C.max, another version of the Villa Savoye model you have been working with. Choose Adopt the File's Unit Scale, and then click OK if you see the File Load: Units Mismatch dialog box.

2. Right-click in the Perspective viewport. Click Render Production. A view of the interior courtyard appears in the Rendered Frame Window, as shown in Figure 8.24.

Because the entire scene is lit only with the SUN001 direct light, the courtyard looks flat and cartoon-like. In real life, the light reflected from the floor would bounce up and illuminate the courtyard walls. Although the Default Scanline Renderer doesn't simulate light this way, you can add some lighting of your own to help simulate ambient light.

Although it is fast, the Scanline Renderer is historically the oldest and least realistic rendering algorithm. In chapters 14 and 15, you will learn how to use the mental ray renderer for increased realism.

FIGURE 8.24
The courtyard
rendering

In the next exercise, you'll add some Omni lights and adjust their color settings to fake your own "bounced light" from the courtyard floor:

1. Close or minimize the Rendered Frame Window.

2. Right-click the Top viewport to make it active, and then zoom out until your viewport looks like Figure 8.25.

3. Click the Maximize Viewport Toggle to enlarge the Top viewport.

4. Click the Create tab in the Command panel; then click the Lights category button.

5. Choose the Standard option, click the Omni button, and then click the location shown in Figure 8.25 to place an Omni light in the courtyard.

6. Give this new Omni light the name **Omni-court** in the Name and Color rollout input box.

FIGURE 8.25
Placing an Omni light
in the courtyard

Place the Omni light here.

The Omni light is at 0 elevation. You'll want to raise it to a location that's just above the second-floor surface in order to simulate the light bouncing off that surface:

1. With the Omni courtyard light selected, click the Select and Move tool on the Main Toolbar.

2. In the Transform type-in area at the bottom of the user interface, make sure the Absolute/Offset Mode Transform type-in tool is set to Absolute; then change the Z value to 3.81 meters. This will raise the Omni light from the ground level to a level just above the floor of the courtyard.

Because the light bouncing off the courtyard floor represents a broad area, it would throw off a very diffuse light in the real world. The Omni light, on the other hand, is a point source. You'll want to spread the bounced light source around a bit to create a more diffuse appearance. To do this, make a few clones of the Omni light:

1. With the Select and Move tool still active, Shift-drag the X-axis of the Omni light's Transform gizmo and make a clone just to the right of the current Omni light's position (see Figure 8.26).

2. In the Clone Options dialog box, click Instance. You'll see the importance of making the clone an instance in the next few exercises.

3. Click OK to close the Clone Options dialog box.

4. Make two more Instance clones, as shown in Figure 8.27.

FIGURE 8.26
Cloning the
Omni light

Drag an instance to the right.

FIGURE 8.27
Adding more Omni
light instances

Make two more Omni light instances.

With the lights in place, you can make a few adjustments to them to simulate the bounced light from the floor. First, you'll want to reduce the intensity of the light. Right now, the Omni lights are at full intensity. You can adjust the intensity of all four of the lights simultaneously by adjusting any one of the clones. This is because you created Instance clones rather than Copy clones. Just as with primitive objects, lights can be instanced so that the edits made to one clone are propagated to all the other clones:

1. With the last clone created still selected, click the Modify tab in the Command panel.

2. Set the Shadows parameter to Shadow Map on the General Parameters rollout.

3. Go to the Intensity/Color/Attenuation rollout; then set the Multiplier spinner to 0.14.

4. Click the color swatch next to the Multiplier spinner to open the Color Selector: Light Color dialog box.

5. Set Hue to 20 and Saturation to 60; then click Close. This will give the light a slight orange cast, as if it were picking up the color of the floor.

 Do not use highly saturated lights or you will overly influence the materials used. For example, if you shine a saturated red light on a blue surface, it will appear red (drowning out the blue material) because of the strong influence of the light.

6. Click the Maximize Viewport Toggle; then right-click the Perspective viewport to make it active.

7. Click the Render Production tool to get a view of your model so far. Your view will be similar to Figure 8.28.

FIGURE 8.28
A rendered view of the courtyard after adding the simulated bounced light

Now you begin to see more detail in the courtyard. The area around the ramps is better defined, and the alcove to the right shows more depth. You see the ceiling of the room in the foreground beginning to appear. Using colored lights can be an effective way to simulate color bleeding off large surfaces, such as the courtyard or the ceiling. It is a little like color painting with light.

When faking ambient light, don't be afraid to place lights in physically impossible places, like under the floor, behind a solid wall, or above the ceiling. As you'll learn later in this chapter, lights that do not cast shadows penetrate through surfaces and illuminate what lies beyond. The best "fakiosity" results come from using multiple strategically placed low-intensity lights to simulate the light bounced off large surfaces.

Adding a Highlight with an Omni Light

Next, you'll learn how to add a highlight to the glass. By adding a highlight, you will be able to see that there is indeed glass in the windows, and doing so adds a bit of interest to the rendering. You'll also get a chance to see some of the advanced features of an Omni light.

1. Select the Create tab in the Command panel, and click the Lights button. Then click the Omni button in the Object Type rollout.

2. In the Perspective viewport, click to place an Omni light anywhere. You don't need to be exact about the location, because the Highlight tool you'll use later will place the light accurately for you. You might notice that the shaded Perspective viewport lightens thanks to the addition of a new light source.

3. With the Omni light selected, choose Tools ➤ Align ➤ Place Highlight, press Ctrl+H, or hold down the Align tool and release the mouse over the Place Highlight button. The cursor changes to the Place Highlight icon.

4. Go to the Perspective viewport, and click and hold the location shown in Figure 8.29.

 A blue normal arrow will appear at your cursor position. Release the mouse button when you see the normal arrow pointing near the middle of the column.

FIGURE 8.29
Click here to place the highlight on the column.

The blue normal arrow represents a direction vector that is perpendicular to the surface over which the Place Highlight tool is positioned. The Place Highlight tool's job is to relocate the selected light somewhere along the normal vector. In other words, you will find the new Omni light some distance in a straight line away from the normal vector. This is helpful because it provides you with a quick way of orienting a light source in relation to a surface.

You may notice that the Omni light was moved but now it lies outside of the room. As long as the Omni is set to cast a shadow, it will be blocked from entering this room.

5. With the new Omni still selected, click the Modify panel and deselect On in the Shadows group of the General Parameters rollout, as shown in Figure 8.30. Now the light will illuminate but will not cast shadows (which is not possible in the real world).

6. Set the light's Multiplier to 0.8.

7. Click the Render Production button on the Main Toolbar and observe the highlight that appears on the glass, as shown in Figure 8.31.

FIGURE 8.30
Turning off the shadows

FIGURE 8.31
A rendered highlight on glass

The Place Highlight tool places the currently selected light in a location that produces a highlight reflection at the location you selected in step 4 of the previous exercise. But the Omni light also shines on the rest of the building, washing out some detail. Fortunately, you can set 3ds Max's lights to affect only selected objects instead of the entire model:

1. With the Omni light selected, click the Modify tab of the Command panel.

2. In the General Parameters rollout, click the Exclude button.

3. In the Exclude/Include dialog box, click the Include radio button in the upper-right corner.

4. In the Scene Objects list, click [Glass.03] to select it; then click the Transfer button that points right, as shown in Figure 8.32. Glass.03 moves from the list on the left to the list on the right.

FIGURE 8.32

The Exclude/Include dialog box set to include only the glass in the Omni light's list of objects

Select the Glass.03 group and then click the right arrow transfer button.

You could have excluded all the objects except Glass.03 to create the same effect; however, that would mean all objects subsequently added to the scene would have to be added to the Exclude list for this light.

5. Click OK to close the Exclude/Include dialog box; then click the Render Production button. Now the highlight is limited to the glass, as shown in Figure 8.33.

At times, you may need to stretch reality a bit when you produce renderings. The highlighted glass adds some interest to the rendering, even though it isn't necessarily a realistic portrayal of the lighting in the model. The highlight effect is not exclusive to the Omni light. The same effect can be achieved using virtually any type of light you choose.

The ability to select the objects that individual lights affect, although not possible in the real world, gives you some freedom to play with a scene, adding emphasis to some areas while downplaying others.

FIGURE 8.33
The villa rendered
with a highlight on
the glass

Looking at Omni Light Options

Because you're working with Omni lights, let's take a look at some of the other Omni light parameters. You've seen how you can choose which objects are affected by Omni lights. The Exclude/Include dialog box is a feature common to all lights. Just as with all other lights, you can include or exclude shadows in the manner described in the previous exercise. You can also control the Attenuation settings of the Omni light. These settings let you control the distance of the light's reach.

CONTROLLING LIGHTS WITH ATTENUATION

Attenuation adds another bit of control over 3ds Max lighting that you do not have over real-world lights. Think of it as the ability to control how much illumination a light contributes to a scene as a function of how far the light travels from its source.

By default, Attenuation is turned off. Try the following exercise to see how you can control the attenuation of an Omni light:

1. Save the file as **MyVilla01.max**.

2. Open the Omni.max file from this book's companion web page. This is the file shown in Figure 8.34.

FIGURE 8.34
An Omni light used
to light a simple
scene

The `Omni.max` model is a simple scene of a light pole, a ground plane, and a wall. The light pole has an Omni light at the center of its globe. The globe itself has been excluded from the effects of the Omni light so that the light is obstructed beyond the globe, with the exception of the pole beneath it. The Omni light in this rendering has been inserted into the scene with its default settings unchanged.

You can adjust the attenuation, however, to limit the range of the light. Try the following exercise to get a feel for the Attenuation settings:

1. Click the Select by Name button. In the Select from Scene dialog box, choose Omni001 from the list, and click OK.

2. Click the Modify tab of the Command panel, scroll down the panel to the Intensity/Color/Attenuation rollout, and open the rollout if it is closed.

3. Click the Use check box in the Far Attenuation group, as shown in Figure 8.35.

FIGURE 8.35
Click the Use
check box

A pair of Sphere gizmos appears around the Omni light, as shown in Figure 8.36.

4. Click and drag the Far Attenuation End spinner up so that its value reads 37′.

5. Click and drag the Far Attenuation Start spinner up so that its value reads 10′.

FIGURE 8.36
The Perspective viewport showing the Far Attenuation gizmos

THE FAR ATTENUATION'S SHOW PARAMETER

The Show check box causes 3ds Max to display the Attenuation gizmos even when the light is not selected. The gizmos will always show when the light is selected, regardless of the Show setting. This is similar to the Show Cone option for spot and direct lights.

6. Click the Render Production button. The Render Production button is on the Main Toolbar, it has been located previously in the chapter. You now see the light limited to a distance of 37´. It casts a dim light against the wall (see Figure 8.37).

FIGURE 8.37
The rendering with Attenuation turned on and the Far Attenuation End distance set to 37´

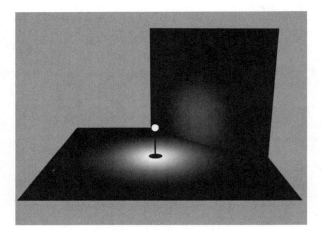

The End distance setting controls the farthest reach of the light. You can also set the distance of maximum brightness using Far Attenuation's Start setting:

1. Click and drag the Far Attenuation Start spinner up so that its value reads 28´. At this distance, the lighter center gizmo just touches the wall and passes through the floor.

2. Click the Render Production button. Now the light on the wall is much brighter (see Figure 8.38).

FIGURE 8.38
The rendering with the Far Attenuation Start setting at 28´

The Start and Far Attenuation settings act a bit like the Hotspot and Falloff settings in direct lights and spotlights, except that they act according to the distance away from the source rather than the angular spread of the light. All areas from the light source to the Far Attenuation Start gizmo receive the full intensity of the light, and all areas beyond the Far Attenuation End gizmo receive no illumination from the light.

You've probably noticed that Attenuation parameters also offer a Near Attenuation group. The settings in this group give you control of where the Omni light begins to take effect, as demonstrated in the following exercise:

1. Click the Use check box in the Near Attenuation group. Blue Attenuation gizmos display in the viewport.

2. Set the Near Attenuation Start value to 15´ and the Near Attenuation End value to 17´.

3. Click the Render Production button. Notice that the shadow of the pole appears to expand and soften, as shown in Figure 8.39.

FIGURE 8.39
The scene rendered using the Near Attenuation parameters

This time, the Near Attenuation settings are limiting the near distance that the light begins to affect. In this scene, we created the effect of a larger, softer shadow being cast by the pole, even though the dark area is actually the result of the Near Attenuation setting limiting the near range of the light cast by the Omni light.

Adding Shadow Effects

You've seen how a single direct light can be used to simulate the sun. You can also use lighting to add emphasis or to provide a sense of drama. Shadows can be controlled to provide a seemingly sharp, strong light source or a softer, more diffuse interior light. In this section, you'll look at some of the more commonly used lighting options, starting with shadows.

By default, the Shadow option for lights is turned on so that when you render your model, you see shadows cast.

1. Open the file Savoye08e.max.

2. Right-click in the Perspective viewport and then click Render Production on the Main Toolbar. The front of the Villa Savoye is rendered with shadows, as shown in Figure 8.40.

FIGURE 8.40
With the current shadow settings, the shadows are not completely correct.

Light is "leaking" through in some places.

Shadows don't touch columns.

SETTING THE DEFAULTS

The default shadow settings are controlled by the Custom UI and Defaults Switcher. See Chapter 1 for more information on this feature.

If you look carefully at your last rendering, you'll see that there are indeed shadows from the columns and the rest of the building. The shadows are not exactly right, however. Parts of the model show light *leaking* through the shadows, as shown in Figure 8.40. You might also notice that the shadows from the columns don't quite start at the column bases.

There are a few options you can use to correct these problems. Let's start with the Shadow Map parameters of the Target Direct light object you're using to simulate the sun:

1. Select the Target Direct light object named SUN001. This is the light in the lower-left corner of the building in the Top viewport.

2. Click the Modify tab in the Command panel to view the parameters for SUN001.

3. Scroll down the panel to the Shadow Map Params rollout and click it to open, as shown in Figure 8.41. You see the Bias, Size, and Sample Range settings.

4. Click the Bias setting and enter **0.2**↵ to change its value from 1 to 0.2. By reducing this number, you bring the shadow closer to the object that is casting the shadow.

5. Open the Rendered Frame window, and then click the Render button in the upper-right corner to render the scene. This time the shadows are rendered more accurately, filling in those portions missed in the previous rendering (see Figure 8.42).

FIGURE 8.41
The Shadow Map
Params rollout

FIGURE 8.42
The new rendering
with the filled-in
shadows

Softening Shadow Edges

Another option that lets you control the softness of the shadow edge is Sample Range. In some situations, you may want the edge of the shadow softer for partially cloudy outdoor scenes or for interior views with combined diffuse and direct lighting. The following exercise shows the effect of Sample Range:

1. Set Sample Range for the SUN001 direct light to 10.

2. Click the Render Production button to see the effects of the new Sample Range setting, as shown in Figure 8.43.

Softened shadow edges

You can see the subtle effects of a softer shadow by looking at the shadows of the columns. Also notice that the shadows of the columns disappear on the ground below the building. The Sample Range setting is high enough to obliterate the thin column shadows.

A soft shadow edge lends realism to objects in indoor settings and in close-up views of outdoor objects; however, in some situations, a sharp, crisp shadow edge is more desirable. There are two ways to achieve a sharp shadow edge. You can manipulate shadow settings in 3ds Max to obtain a high degree of accuracy in the shadow representation, or you can go with an entirely different shadow rendering method offered by 3ds Max, called *ray tracing*. This method models the actual path of light to generate shadows. Ray-traced shadows are more accurate, but they can add a lot of time to the rendering process. They also produce a sharp shadow edge, so in situations where a soft shadow is desired, you will have to use the default shadow-mapped type of shadow or some combination of both ray-traced and shadow map shadows.

In the next section, you'll look at how you can set up a shadow map to create a sharper shadow edge.

Understanding Shadow Maps

So far, you've been using the default *shadow mapping* method for casting shadows. A shadow map is a temporary *bitmap* image (made of pixels) of the shadows cast by objects in the model. You never actually see this bitmap. 3ds Max determines the shape and location of the shadow by determining where the light is obscured and placing the shadow map on all surfaces beyond that point. Because the shadow map is really a bitmap image, a shadow's sharpness depends on the resolution of the shadow map. If the shadow map has a small Size setting, it creates a shadow that is rough around the edges, like a low-resolution rendering. Figure 8.44 shows a sample model with a very low-resolution shadow map that clearly displays the shadow map pixels around the shadow edge. The chair used in these examples is the Reaction Work Chair model from Herman Miller, which is available as a free 3ds DOS file from their website along with a good selection of seating and office furniture models.

You can increase the Shadow Map Size setting to reduce the stairstepping effect of the shadow edge. This stairstepping comes directly from the pixels that make up the shadow map. Figure 8.45 shows the sample image again with the Size setting doubled from the previous figure.

FIGURE 8.44
This image shows a shadow with a low Shadow Map Size setting coupled with a low Sample Range setting of 0.1.

FIGURE 8.45
Increase the Shadow Map Size setting to reduce the stairstep effect.

A larger shadow map makes for a more even shadow edge. If the shadow map size is too great, however, it will consume greater amounts of memory and increase rendering time.

Another setting that is directly related to shadow map size is the spread of the light source. The shadow map is directly related to the area that is lit by the light source casting the shadow. If the area or spread of the light is decreased, the shadow map must also include a smaller area. If the shadow map size is reduced relative to the object casting the shadow, more of the shadow map area can be devoted to the shadow outline. This has the effect of reducing the jagged edge of the shadow. Figure 8.46 shows the same model and light source as shown in Figure 8.45, but the hotspot and falloff have been reduced in size so the light is focused on a smaller area. Notice that the edges of the shadow appear less jagged because the shadow map isn't as stretched as it was in Figure 8.45.

You can control the jagged edge of the shadow to some degree by using the Sample Range setting. In the previous exercise, you saw how the Map Sample Range setting controls the softness of the edge of the shadow. A smaller Map Sample value makes for a sharper shadow but also reveals more of the shadow map's bitmap edge. If the Sample Range setting is too low, you begin to see the stairstep edges of the pixels of the shadow map, as shown in Figure 8.44.

FIGURE 8.46
The chair and light
with a decreased
hotspot and
falloff area

The Sample Range value is actually the number of pixels in the rendered image that are blended to soften the edge of the shadow. This has the effect of hiding the pixelated shadow edges, as shown in Figure 8.47. Here you see the same image as in Figure 8.46 but with an increased Sample Range value.

FIGURE 8.47
The same image
as in Figure 8.46,
but with a Sample
Range of 6

If you look carefully at the shadow that runs vertically up the right edge of the image, you can still detect the stairstep edge of the pixelated shadow map (it appears as a slightly wavy edge). If you aren't looking for it, you may not notice it. You can also further increase the softness of the shadow edge by increasing the difference between the Hotspot and Falloff settings. As the Sample Range setting decreases, however, the hotspot/falloff difference has less effect.

Taking all of this into account, you need to increase the shadow map size and reduce the Sample Range setting to sharpen the shadow edge. You also need to keep the lighted area as narrow as possible while still keeping all of the objects in your scene lighted. Therefore, to get the sharpest shadow with a shadow map, you need to find a balance between the map size, sample range, light spread, and, to some degree, the hotspot/falloff difference. Figure 8.48 shows

the sample scene and light with a Sample Range value of 1, a Shadow Map Size setting of 2048, and a Falloff setting as close to the hotspot setting as possible.

FIGURE 8.48

A fairly sharp shadow achieved with a high Size setting and a low Sample Range

To see firsthand the effects of these settings, try sharpening the shadows on the villa model:

1. In the Shadow Map Params rollout for the SUN001 light source, change the Size value to 2048.

2. Change Sample Range to 1.

3. Make sure that the Perspective viewport is selected and then click the Render Production button. Notice how the shadow appears to be sharper. You may also notice that the shadow is more jagged around the edges in some locations (see Figure 8.49).

4. Save the villa model as `MyVilla2.max`.

FIGURE 8.49

The villa rendered with a sharper shadow map

Using Ray-Traced Shadows

You may feel that using the shadow map settings in the previous exercise requires too many compromises to achieve the sharpest shadows. If you want the sharpest, most accurate shadows possible, you'll want to use ray tracing.

Ray-traced shadows derive the shadow boundary by modeling the path of light from the light source to the shadow surface. The benefit is a very accurate shadow with no stairstep edges, because ray tracing is not based on a projected bitmap. You do pay a penalty in increased rendering time, but in many cases, the time is well worth it. Figure 8.50 shows two images of a fairly complex model that contains transparent elements as well as some detailed structural elements. The top image is the model rendered with a shadow map, whereas the second is rendered using ray-traced shadows. The ray-traced shadows show much more detail.

FIGURE 8.50
An image using shadow map shadows (top), and the same image using ray-traced shadows (bottom)

RAY-TRACED SHADOWS AND TRANSPARENCY

Only shadows created using the Ray Traced Shadows (and Advanced Ray Traced) options consider the transparency of the objects they encounter. Shadow map shadows are consistent regardless of an object's transparency.

With ray-traced shadows, you don't have to be concerned with map sizes and sample ranges. Try the following exercise to see how ray-traced shadows affect the villa model:

1. In the Modify tab of the Command panel, scroll up to the General Parameters rollout.

2. Click the Shadow Map drop-down menu in the Shadows group and select Ray Traced Shadows (see Figure 8.51).

3. Click the Render Production button on the Main Toolbar. The villa is rendered with smoother-looking shadows, as shown in Figure 8.52.

Although the differences are not as dramatic as those shown in Figure 8.50, the ray-traced shadows rendering of the villa does show smoother shadows, particularly on the lower-right side of the image. You can also see more detail in the shadow behind the window at the right side of the image. You can increase the spread of the light source now without affecting the sharpness of the shadows.

FIGURE 8.51
Select Ray Traced
Shadows.

FIGURE 8.52
The villa rendered
using the Ray
Traced Shadows
option

Using Advanced Ray Traced and Area Shadows

Both the Advanced Ray Traced and Area Shadows options create ray-traced shadows, but they offer a few additional properties that the standard ray-traced shadows do not have.

BLURRING SHADOW EDGES

The Advanced Ray Traced option allows you to add a softer edge, or *penumbra*, to shadows (see Figure 8.53), which is a feature absent in the standard ray-traced shadow.

The area shadow consists of two primary parts, the *umbra* and the *penumbra*. The umbra is the darkest part of the shadow, represented by the dark triangular area behind the monolith in Figure 8.53. The penumbra is area that blends between the darkest parts of the shadow and the unshadowed ground around the monolith.

FIGURE 8.53
The components of an area shadow

To use the Advanced Ray Traced option, you can select Adv. Ray Traced from the Shadows group of the General Parameters rollout of any light.

This selection displays the Adv. Ray Traced Params rollout, where you can control the quality with the Basic Options drop-down list. Select 2-Pass Antialias for maximum quality.

The Shadow Bias option works like the Bias option for map shadows. If the shadow appears to "bleed" around the edge of the object casting the shadow, forming a dark edge, you can increase the Shadow Bias setting to remove the dark edge. If the shadow appears to begin too far from the object, you can decrease the Shadow Bias setting.

The Jitter Amount setting smoothes out the effect of the blurred shadow edge. If you look carefully at a blurred shadow, you will see that it is made up of several gradations of values, each with its own distinct edge. The Jitter Amount setting will blend the gradations together to further soften the shadow edge.

CONTROLLING SHADOW SHARPNESS OVER DISTANCE

If you look at the shadow of a tree on a bright, sunlit day, you'll notice that parts of the tree closer to the ground cast sharper shadows than those farther away. This is caused by the combined effect of direct sunlight and the general ambient glow given off by the sky. You can simulate this effect using the Area Shadows shadow type. Area shadows will vary the width of shadow edge blurring or penumbra, depending on the distance between the object casting the shadow and the surface on which the shadow falls. Figure 8.54 shows this effect.

FIGURE 8.54
The shadows from the top of the post are softer than those from the bottom.

To use the Area Shadows shadow type, select it from the Shadows group of the General Parameters rollout of any light. Once you've selected it, you can add the shadow penumbra effect to the shadow edge by increasing the Shadow Quality value under the Area Shadows rollout in the Antialiasing Options group (Figure 8.55).

As with the Adv. Ray Traced settings, Shadow Bias controls how close or far away the shadow starts from its object, and Jitter Amount smoothes the effect of the blurred shadow edge.

FIGURE 8.55
The Area Shadows rollout

A couple of other options in the Area Shadows rollout are important in controlling shadows. The first is the Basic Options drop-down list (Figure 8.56).

FIGURE 8.56
The Basic Options
drop-down list

These options—Simple, Rectangle Light, Disc Light, Box Light, and Sphere Light—affect the shape and quality of the shadow being cast. For example, a Rectangle light casts a shadow in the manner of a flat ceiling light fixture. A Sphere light casts a shadow like a globe. The light itself does not take on any of these shapes, but you can think of these Area Shadow modes as the "virtual" shape of the light fixture.

In conjunction with the Basic Options settings are the Area Light Dimensions settings at the bottom of the Area Shadows rollout. These options control the size of the "virtual" shape of the light as set by the Mode setting. A larger Area Light Dimension tends to increase the spread of the shadow edge blur, just as a larger light fixture would tend to spread shadow edges in the real world.

You won't use these shadow options in any of the exercises of this book, so you should experiment with them on your own by creating a simple scene with a box, a plane for a ground surface, and a single standard light source.

The mental ray shadow map type will be covered in Chapter 14.

Playing in the Shadows

You've seen how you can bring out the depth of a space by adding lights to simulate reflected light. In the villa example you looked at earlier, you had a combination of direct light simulating the sun and a set of Omni lights to simulate ambient light. In this section, you'll learn how to play with shadows by using a combination of lights and objects.

In the previous section, you learned that if you use a bitmap shadow, you can soften the edge of your shadows, and you were shown that ray-traced shadows can bring out detail in your model. Obtaining both effects in the same rendering can be a little tricky, but you may find that you need to do just that in some situations. The following series of exercises will show you how you can mix these two types of shadows to control the composition and appearance of a rendering.

Using Two Suns

You'll use a model that was created for the Avery Aquatic Center on the Stanford campus in Palo Alto, California. You'll be working on a view of the entrance to the center. The entrance consists of a tree-lined, paved walkway with a sign and a set of monuments. Let's take a look at the file and a first rendering:

1. Open the Aquatic.max file from this book's companion web page.

2. Make sure that the Perspective viewport is selected; then click the Render Production button. The rendering appears as shown in Figure 8.57.

FIGURE 8.57
The Avery Aquatic
Center rendered

Notice the large, square shadow in the foreground. This is a shadow of the tree in the foreground. You can see a small part of this tree in the upper-left corner of the rendering. All the trees in this scene project rectangular shadows, although this is less obvious in the trees toward the back. Also notice the odd shadows of the Avery Aquatic Center sign. The saw-tooth pattern on the shadow is the result of the low resolution of the shadow map used by the direct light that simulates the sun. To give you a better idea of what the sign is supposed to look like, Figure 8.58 shows a better view of the sign's design.

This sign poses an unusual problem in lighting because it contains a wavy, perforated screen. At a distance, this screen looks like a translucent material, so it is given a material that is partially transparent. Even so, a shadow map shadow doesn't work with this design, nor does it work well with the trees.

FIGURE 8.58
The design of the
Avery Aquatic
Center sign

You can improve the look of the sign by using a ray-traced shadow for the sun, but the complexity of the model combined with a ray-traced shadow will substantially increase the rendering time. You want to minimize the rendering time if you can, especially if you are working under a deadline. Figure 8.59 shows the same rendering with the sun's shadow type changed to a ray-traced shadow. Compared to the rendering with shadow maps, which took 2 seconds to render on a quad-core system with 8GB of RAM, the ray-traced shadows took 10 seconds to render. That might not sound like a lot, but on a complex project, an increase is significant in rendering time of 500 percent.

FIGURE 8.59
A second rendering, with the Ray Traced Shadow setting and with the sun's shadow type changed

With a ray-traced shadow, the sign looks fine, but the tree shadow looks a bit odd because the trees in the scene are really just flat, vertical planes with materials applied. In reality, the tree would cast a larger shadow. The tree shadow in the foreground would also have a softer edge.

To obtain a fast rendering speed and still maintain a crisp shadow on the sign, you can use two different light sources for the sun. One light will project a ray-traced shadow specifically for the sign and trees, while the other will project a shadow map shadow for the rest of the model.

Adding a Second Sun

You saw in previous examples that you can select objects for illumination and shadow casting for each light in your model. In the following exercise, you'll remove the sign and trees from the effects of the current sunlight; then you'll create a second sun that will affect only the trees and the sign. This second sun will be set to create ray-traced shadows.

1. Close the Rendered Frame Window; then select the target directional light in the Orthographic viewport. This is the light used to simulate the sun.

2. In the Modify tab of the Command panel, click the Exclude button in the General Parameters rollout. The Exclude/Include dialog box is displayed.

3. Scroll down the Scene Objects list box to the left and select each object with a name that begins with *SIGN:* SIGNbody, SIGNmetal, SIGNmetal2, SIGNscreen, SIGNtext01, and SIGNtower.

SELECTING AND MOVING SIMILARLY NAMED OBJECTS

You can select similarly named objects in the Exclude/Include dialog box by typing the first few letters of their names in the input box in the upper-left corner. For example, typing **SI⏎** selects all objects that begin with the letters *SI*. Pressing ⏎ again moves the selected objects from the left window to the right window only when the items were selected using the input box.

4. Click the right-pointing double arrow button to move the selected items to the list box to the right.

5. Scroll further down the list on the left and select each item whose name begins with *Tree* except Treeshadow. These are Tree01 through Tree04 and the three Treecamphor items.

6. Click the right-pointing arrow button again to include these trees in the list box on the right.

7. Make sure the Exclude and Both radio buttons are selected at the upper-right corner of the dialog box. This has the effect of excluding these objects from both illumination and shadow casting.

8. Click OK to exit the dialog box.

9. Right-click the Perspective viewport to activate it and click the Render Production button. Now you see the rendering with the trees and sign appearing rather dark and failing to cast shadows, as shown in Figure 8.60.

FIGURE 8.60
The rendering with the trees and sign excluded from the sunlight object

You need to illuminate the sign and trees with a light. To do this, make a copy of the existing sun and change its shadow type to Ray Traced Shadows:

1. If it isn't selected already, select the SUN direct light in the Orthographic viewport.

2. Choose Edit ➢ Clone.

3. In the Clone Options dialog box, choose the Copy radio button and enter **SUNraytraced** for the name. Click OK to close the dialog box. The new light remains selected.

4. In the Modify tab, click the Exclude button in the General Parameters rollout. The Exclude/Include dialog box displays. Notice that the list on the right includes the same items that you excluded from the original SUN light object.

5. Click the Include radio button in the top right of the dialog box. This causes the new light to include only the items listed in the list box to the right, instead of excluding those items.

6. Click OK to close the dialog box.

You've created a second sun that illuminates only the sign and the trees. The original SUN directed light illuminates everything else. Now you've got one more important step to take: you need to set the new sun to cast ray-traced shadows.

LIGHTS AND THE VIEWPORTS

You may notice that the Perspective viewport has become very bright. The Smooth + Highlights viewport rendering mode does not consider the inclusion or exclusion of any object's illumination while displaying the scene. The viewport is bright because of the two direct lights illuminating the scene.

1. Scroll in the Command panel to the General Parameters rollout and open it if it isn't already open.

2. Click the Shadows drop-down list and select Ray Traced Shadows.

3. Make sure the Perspective viewport is selected; then click the Render Production button. The rendering will take a bit more time when it gets to the sign. Once it's done, you'll see a view similar to Figure 8.61.

FIGURE 8.61
The design rendered with the Shadow Map and Ray Traced Shadow light sources

Although the view took longer to render, it still rendered considerably faster than if you had used a ray-traced shadow for the entire scene. But there is something missing: the sign and trees don't cast shadows. This is because the ground plane isn't included in the set of objects affected by the SUNraytraced sun object. You could include the ground in the SUNraytraced light, but you'd greatly increase the rendering time, and you'd have the same effect as you would if you had simply changed the original sun to project a ray-traced shadow.

To get around this problem, you can add some additional props that will cast shadows from the original SUN directed light that is casting a shadow map shadow.

Using Unseen Objects to Cast Shadows

The trees in this model produce a good deal of shade—considerably more than even the shadows created by the Ray Traced Shadow version of the rendered Perspective viewport you saw earlier. To simulate the shade from the trees, you can employ 2D shapes in the form of a tree shadow. These shapes can be used to cast shadows from the SUN directed light that uses a shadow map shadow. This combination will produce a softer shadow, which offers a somewhat more pleasing effect, especially for shadows in the foreground.

To save some time, these shadow shapes have already been added to the Avery Aquatic model. In the next exercise, you'll turn these shadow objects on and render the view to see how they work:

1. Right-click in a viewport to open the quad menu.

2. Click Unhide All in the display quad. The 2D shadow objects will appear in the model, as shown in Figure 8.62. They may be difficult to see in the Perspective viewport.

FIGURE 8.62
The 2D shadow objects appear in the model.

The 2D tree shadow objects

3. Click the Render Production tool. The view is rendered with the additional shadows being cast by the 2D shadow objects, as shown in Figure 8.63.

FIGURE 8.63
The scene rendered with tree shadows

The character of the rendering changes dramatically with the addition of shadows. The walkway has a more inviting appearance instead of the somewhat harsh, sunlit open space. Also, the shadow in the foreground helps soften the composition by introducing a change in the ground plane.

Because you were spared the work of actually building and placing the shadow objects, you'll want to know some of the details of their construction. The shadow objects, named Treeshadow in the model, are 2D surfaces formed into the shape of a tree shadow. If you look in the Perspective viewport, in Wireframe mode, you'll see that they are placed at about the height of the bottom of the tree canopy (see Figure 8.64). This location offers a more accurate placement for the shadow on the ground plane.

FIGURE 8.64
The Perspective viewport with the Treeshadow objects at the level of the bottom of the tree canopy

2D Treeshadow objects Tree objects

If you look carefully at the Top viewport, you'll see that the Treeshadow objects aren't centered on the trees for which they cast shadows. Instead, they are offset to the left and downward in the direction away from the light source. This simulates the way a tree shadow might be cast, given the relationship it has to the sun angle in the design.

Something else is quite unusual about the Treeshadow objects. Although they cast shadows in the rendering and are plainly visible in the Perspective viewport, they don't appear in the rendered view. You may recall that when you created a wineglass in Chapter 3, "Creating Shapes with Splines," parts of the glass disappeared when it was rendered. This was due to the alignment of the normals on a single surface. Remember that a surface has only one visible side. The Treeshadow object takes advantage of this fact by orienting its normals toward the sky and away from our point of view. The end result is that 3ds Max doesn't render the Treeshadow object, but the trees still cast shadows.

You can create a Treeshadow object by starting with a plane or a star spline shape, editing its vertices to form a shape like the shadow of a tree. You can also form one random shape, and then make multiple copies and join the copies into one object.

Another technique for creating shadows is to use a *gobo light*. In this technique, you assign a projector map (a bitmap usually) to a light, and the light will cast a shadow in the shape of the bitmap. A projector map can be added to a light through the Projector Map group of its Advanced Effects rollout. Projector maps can also be animated to simulate the shadows of trees being blown by the wind or a movie being projected on the big screen.

Using a Clone to Cast Shadows

The Avery Aquatic Center rendering is just about finished. Unfortunately, the sign itself looks as if it were floating in the rendering—as though it were pasted in. It appears to be dislocated because it doesn't cast a shadow.

You want the sign to cast a shadow using the original SUN direct light that uses a shadow map shadow. To do this, you'll make a copy of the main sign components that cast shadows. Those copies will be included in the set of objects that cast shadows from the original SUN direct light.

1. Click the Select by Name tool on the Main Toolbar.

2. In the Select from Scene dialog box, select the SIGNbody and SIGNtower objects from the list; then click Select. These are the two main components of the sign.

3. Choose Edit ➤ Clone; then in the Clone Options dialog box, make sure that Copy is selected and click OK. 3ds Max creates copies of the objects you've selected, appending the number 001 to the name of each object.

You don't want these new objects to affect the rendered scene in any way other than to cast a shadow from the SUN directed light. To avoid any interference with other objects, you can reduce the size of these new objects so that they are smaller than the objects from which they were cloned.

1. Click the Select by Name tool again; then in the Select from Scene dialog box, select SIGNbody001.

2. Click the Select and Uniform Scale tool on the Main Toolbar.

3. In the Transform Pivot Point flyout, next to the Reference Coordinate System drop-down in the Main Toolbar, select Use Pivot Point Center. This will cause the SIGNbody001 object to remain centered within the original SIGNbody object as it is scaled down, thereby keeping the SIGNbody001 object completely nested within the SIGNbody object (see Figure 8.65).

4. In the Transform type-ins at the bottom of the user interface, change the X spinner value to 98.

FIGURE 8.65
The SIGNbody001 object is nested within the SIGN-body object.

The white outline shows the SIGNbody001 clone.

You've made the SIGNbody001 object slightly smaller than the original object from which it was cloned. Repeat the process for the SIGNtower001 object:

1. Click the Select by Name tool again; then in the Select from Scene dialog box, select SIGNtower001.

2. In the Transform type-in, change the coordinate readout's X spinner value to 98. 3ds Max maintains the Use Pivot Point Transform option.

3. Click the Select by Name tool once again and select SIGNbody001 and SIGNtower001.

4. Choose Group ➢ Group.

5. In the Group dialog box, enter **Signshadow** and then click OK. By grouping the newly created objects, you can keep them together and manage them more easily. From now on, you'll see the pair of objects listed as a single entity called Signshadow in the Select from Scene dialog box and it will have an icon that looks like an overlapping circle and square surrounded by square brackets.

The new objects are automatically included to cast shadows from the original light source, and because you haven't explicitly included them with the objects lit by the SUNraytraced directed light, they aren't affected by that light.

It is possible to use lights that have negative multipliers. This has the amazing effect of removing light from the scene—something that is clearly not possible in the real world. Try using negative lights to soak up light from washed-out areas in scenes that use the Default Scanline Renderer. Negative lights will not be effective in physically based lighting simulations with Radiosity or the mental ray renderer.

Using the Light Lister

In more complex scenes, you will find that you need to have dozens or perhaps even hundreds of lights. Managing these lights can become a huge problem if you have to edit the parameters for each light source—one at a time.

As you do test renderings, you will undoubtedly see problems in the levels of illumination, light color, shadow casting, and so on that require you to edit many light parameters. Fortunately, there is a special tool called the Light Lister that is designed to help you with light management.

Be sure to instance lights that are meant to be wired together in the real world. For example, you'll save quite a bit of time by making instance clones of downlights in the same room. That way, changes that you make to one instance are immediately updated in all of its siblings.

1. Create two Omni lights located as shown in Figure 8.66. Create the right one first.

2. In the Front or Top viewport, move the new lights to a height of approximately 60′.

3. Choose Tools ➢ Light Lister.

 The Light Lister is shown in Figure 8.67. It lists each of the light sources in your scene and allows you to change almost all of the relevant parameters in one convenient dialog box.

FIGURE 8.66
Add two Omni lights to the scene.

New Omni lights

FIGURE 8.67
The Light Lister

This vertical bar indicates the selected lights.

Using the columns shown from left to right in Figure 8.67, you can select a light object, turn each light on or off; change the name, the multiplier, or the color; toggle shadows on or off; change the shadow type; and alter many of the relevant shadow parameters. This is obviously much faster than individually selecting each light and changing its parameters in the Modify panel. Furthermore, any object selected when you open the Light Lister remains selected throughout any modifications that you make to the lights in your scene.

4. By using the General Settings feature, you can make changes to selections of lights all at the same time. Click the General Settings radio button in the Configuration rollout (Figure 8.68).

FIGURE 8.68
The General Settings rollout in the Light Lister

5. In the General Settings rollout, click the All Lights radio button. Any changes you make here will now affect all the lights in the scene.

6. Select the All Lights radio button in the Configuration rollout to display the options for all the lights in the scene.

 You can make changes to a series of lights (but not to all the lights in the scene) by first selecting those light objects you want to change and then using the Selected Lights radio button in the General Settings rollout. The Selected Lights radio button in the Configuration rollout displays only the lights selected in the scene in the Lights rollout, rather than all the lights that are displayed when All Lights is selected.

7. Turn off the shadows for the first Omni light, and then change the shadow type to Shadow Map for the second Omni light.

8. Turn off both the Omni lights, as shown in Figure 8.69.

FIGURE 8.69
Adjusting lights in the Light Lister

As you can see, the Light Lister provides quick access to the most common properties of all the lights in a scene. In the next exercise, you will learn how to save and retrieve the status of your lights to instantly re-create a lighting scheme.

Using Scene States

Throughout the course of a project, you will experiment with lighting setups, materials, and layer schemes, trying to make your scenes as appealing, accurate, and streamlined as possible. In the event that the lighting does not work out or a material's appearance needs to be re-created, there are several methods to retrieve your work. You can undo the most recent steps, use the Edit ➤ Hold and Edit ➤ Fetch tools, or simply reopen your scene without saving any changes. The problem with all of these methods is that they are destructive and all steps, even those that you want to retain, are lost. The Scene States tool solves this issue by saving only certain features to be restored by you.

1. Continue with the current project or open `Scene State.max` from this book's web page.

2. Choose Tools ➤ Manage Scene States from the Main Menu. The Manage Scene States dialog box opens.

3. Click the Save button.

4. In the Save Scene State dialog box (Figure 8.70), hold down the Ctrl key; highlight the Light Properties, Light Transforms, and Environment items; and then deselect any others. Enter **Aquatic Day** in the Enter a Scene State Name input box, and then click the Save button. The current parameters and transforms for the lights and all the environment information are saved as a scene state.

FIGURE 8.70
The Save Scene
State dialog box

5. Choose Rendering ➤ Environment to open the Environment tab of the Environment and Effects dialog box.

6. Click the Ambient color swatch and then choose a very dark gray in the Color Selector dialog box that opens. Close the Environment and Effects dialog box when you are done.

7. Open the Light Lister.

8. Turn off the SUN and SUNraytraced lights. Turn on the Omni001 and Omni002 lights.

9. Set the Omni001 light's Multiplier to 1.0 and Omni002 to 0.5.

 Real World Scenario

SCENE STATES

Clients can often be demanding regarding the amount of information they require. This can be especially true when renderings are produced on a computer and the clients believe that a few mouse clicks can generate a large amount of changes to the output.

A recent residential project that one of the authors of *Mastering Autodesk VIZ 2008* (Sybex, 2007) book worked on quickly blossomed into a time-killer when the owner started requesting images of the home under various lighting conditions. The owner wanted to see what the home looked like during the day in each season, at night with the interior lights on but the exterior lights off, at night with the interior lights off but the exterior lights on, and under a few more conditions. With dozens of lights in the project, each situation required many parameter (intensity, attenuation, position, orientation, color, and so on) changes.

By saving the lighting schemes as scene states, the author was able to quickly return to any state that was saved to make client-requested changes and to return to the feature images that he was originally commissioned to produce.

10. Click the color swatch of one of the Omni lights and assign it a pale orange color. Drag the color swatch that you just modified over the other Omni's color swatch to clone the colors. In the Copy or Swap Colors dialog box, choose Copy.

The left half of the Light Lister should look like Figure 8.71.

11. Make sure the Perspective viewport is active, and then click the Render Production button. The scene renders with a darker appearance, indicating that evening is quickly approaching, as shown in Figure 8.72.

FIGURE 8.71
The Light Lister after modifying the lights

FIGURE 8.72
The darker scene after adjusting the lights

12. Open the Manage Scene States dialog box if it isn't already open and click the Save button.

13. Highlight the Light Properties, Light Transforms, and Environment options again. Enter **Aquatic Evening** as the state name, and then click the Save button. The new scene state is saved, as shown in Figure 8.73.

FIGURE 8.73
Save the new
scene state.

THE LIGHT LISTER AND SCENE STATES

If the Light Lister is open when a scene state is restored, it does not refresh to indicate the restored light parameter values. The Light Lister must be closed and then reopened to display the updated values.

14. Select Aquatic Day in the Manage Scene States dialog box and then click Restore, as shown below in Figure 8.74. In the Restore Scene State dialog box, highlight all three options and then click Restore.

15. Save your scene as **MyScene State.max**.

 The light and environment parameters are returned to their settings from the beginning of the exercise. You can repeat the process, selecting Aquatic Evening to restore the evening lighting scene state.

FIGURE 8.74
The Restore Scene
State dialog box

The Bottom Line

Create and adjust the different light types Lighting is an important component of any 3ds Max scene, and proper lighting schemes add to its quality. The various types project light into the scene in different ways.

Master It What is the difference between a spotlight's falloff and its far attenuation?

Render a scene 3ds Max scenes are generally output to image files or animated files for viewing. Choosing the proper output file type is important to manage the file size and quality.

Master It Render a camera view, and save the file as a JPEG file with a Quality value of 100. Render it three more times with Quality values of 90, 50, and 30. Compare the four files for both quality and file size.

Define shadow effects Shadows are an important feature of any 3ds Max scene. They convey information regarding the intensity and type of illumination. Shadows also define where in the scene an object resides by tying it to the surrounding objects.

Master It What is the procedure for causing an object to not cast shadows from a specific light?

Save and restore scene states Scene states let you save and restore the parameters of the lights in a scene. They can save a great amount of time by eliminating the need to note each light's parameters and on/off status, and other parameters, to accommodate different lighting conditions.

Master It Open the file you saved in the "Using Scene States" section in this chapter. Save the light parameters as a lighting scheme, change the parameters, and then restore the new scheme.

Chapter 9

Enhancing Models with Materials

The material and mapping features of 3ds Max Design 2011 let you simulate surface qualities such as color, texture, transparency, and even reflectance, roughness, and bumpiness. The Material Editor in 3ds Max lets you create and modify materials that you can then apply to objects to achieve realistic effects.

This chapter will introduce you to both forms of the Material Editor (the Compact Material Editor and the new Slate Material Editor) and how to design, edit, and use materials. You'll see how you can use materials to add color, texture, and realism to your models. In this chapter, you'll learn to:

◆ Create and edit materials

◆ Select shaders

◆ Use bump maps

◆ Create a material with sub-materials

◆ Add entourage

◆ Use the Autodesk Materials

◆ Use the Displacement modifier

Understanding Bitmap Texture Maps

To simulate a surface material, 3ds Max offers a number of preset material libraries. These are libraries of simulated materials that you can assign to objects. Each material contains properties such as color, reflectance, transparency, and roughness. Many materials also use images, or *bitmaps*, to simulate the look of complex surfaces such as marble, wood, or brick. Other materials use *procedural* maps, which are mathematical simulations of actual materials.

A bitmap is an image file composed of an array of pixels that represent a graphic sample of the material. One common bitmap image is marble; another is brick. You might think of a material that uses bitmaps as a kind of decal or sticker that is placed on a surface. You can use bitmaps in the properties of a material in several ways: texture maps, bump maps, opacity maps, specular maps, shininess maps, self-illumination maps, and reflection maps, to name a few. Diffuse color maps are the most common use of bitmaps and are the easiest to understand.

Procedural maps use mathematical formulas instead of bitmap images to simulate a texture. Unlike bitmaps, procedural maps often have parameters that can be set to control their visual appearance; they also have a more uniform appearance when applied to objects that have unusual shapes or that are sliced or cut open in some way. For example, you can apply

the Wood procedural map to create the look of an elaborately carved wood sculpture. The wood grain is mathematically defined three-dimensionally, so you can see the grain running throughout the carved regions. Phenomena such as smoke, which might normally be difficult to simulate, can also be simulated effectively using a procedural map.

3ds Max Design 2011 has many types of materials available, including the following:

- Standard material
- Architectural material
- Arch & Design (mi)
- Car Paint Material (mi)
- Autodesk Materials (mi)

Arch & Design (mi), Car Paint Material (mi), and the Autodesk Materials (mi) are used with the mental ray renderer, which will be covered in Chapter 14, "Advanced Rendering with mental ray." Many of the principles regarding the construction of materials span most material types. Not all bitmap channels are available with all materials, and the following sections do not include every possible bitmap option. In this introduction to materials, you'll focus on bitmap texture maps.

Diffuse Color Maps

The diffuse slot of the material represents the color the material reflects in direct light. The diffuse component is the most basic element used in creating the appearance of a real-world material. Some of the many predefined materials that 3ds Max offers are brick materials. Brick is an example of the use of bitmaps to define the appearance of a material. Whenever you assign the Brick material to an object, 3ds Max *pastes* a bitmap image of a brick wall onto the object when it is rendered so that the object looks like a brick surface. Figure 9.1 uses a modified version of the `Brick_Uniform_12Inch_Running_Burgundy.png` image that ships with 3ds Max Design 2011.

FIGURE 9.1
A bitmap image (left) used as a texture map to simulate a brick wall (right)

DIFFUSE MAPS

3ds Max calls texture maps, such as the brick example in Figure 9.1, *diffuse* color maps because the bitmap is reflected in diffused light. To get a better idea of the different types of light an object reflects, look at Figure 9.2. It shows a sphere that indicates the different ways light is reflected off an object.

FIGURE 9.2
A sample sphere showing different types of reflected light

Specular Diffuse Ambient

When the ambient light in a scene is increased, you begin to see the dim portions of an object or those parts that are in shadows. The ambient map appears in these areas where indirect light strikes the surface. The diffuse color map appears in the brighter portions of a model, which are lit by light directly emanating from light sources in the scene. The ambient and diffuse color maps blend together so that, as the ambient light increases, the ambient maps seamlessly merge with the diffuse maps.

SPECULAR COLOR MAPS

Specular color maps that are full-color image bitmaps appear only in specular highlights of a surface. On a shiny object, the specular portion of the object would normally appear white, as shown in Figure 9.2. You can have the specular region of an object display a surface feature by using specular color maps, as shown in Figure 9.3.

FIGURE 9.3
A sphere with a specular color map displaying a shiny pattern

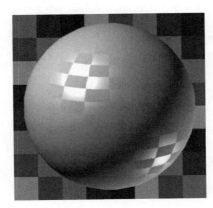

> ### SHADERS DEFINE THE APPEARANCE OF A MATERIAL'S COMPONENTS
>
> *Shaders* control how the ambient, diffuse, and specular components of a material blend together. You will learn more about shaders later in this chapter.

SPECULAR LEVEL MAPS

The Specular Level setting of a material determines how intense the specular highlight, also called the *specular bloom*, of a material is. The specular level maps determine where on the object the specular highlight appears.

GLOSSINESS/SHININESS MAPS

Glossiness maps also affect the specular region of a shiny object, but instead of displaying a colored texture, a glossiness map controls the level of glossiness on a surface. You would use a glossiness map on an object whose surface is not uniformly glossy but instead is alternately rough and shiny, like a troweled stucco wall where the flat areas appear to be glossy and the depressions matte. The glossiness map is usually identical to the specular level map.

SELF-ILLUMINATION/LUMINANCE MAPS

Using the self-illumination feature, you can create materials that appear to glow or emit their own light. A self-illumination map is a grayscale bitmap or procedural map that determines the *brightness* of a surface based on the map's grayscale intensity. White is the brightest part of the texture, whereas black areas have no self-illumination at all. The self-illuminated areas of a material do not actually emit light or add illumination to a scene; they are merely areas with brighter colors and less surface definition to give the appearance of illuminated objects such as fluorescent bulbs or lampshades.

You will learn other more advanced ways to make objects emit light when using the mental ray renderer in Chapter 14.

FILTER COLOR MAPS

Filter color maps control the color of light as it passes through transparent or translucent materials. For example, a filter color map of a stained-glass window would cause the light passing through that window to pick up the window's color and cast it on the floor. Lights must use ray-traced shadows to pick up the colors from a filter color map.

OPACITY/TRANSPARENCY MAPS

Opacity maps use grayscale bitmap images to control opacity and transparency. For example, you can turn a solid surface into an intricate filigree using an opacity map, as shown in Figure 9.4.

FIGURE 9.4
A single, blank surface can be made to appear quite intricate by using opacity/transparency maps. The bitmap image on the left was used to turn a simple rectangular object into the intricate screen on the right.

BUMP MAPS

You can also simulate a bumpy surface texture using grayscale bitmap images. Figure 9.5 shows a 2D bitmap image and objects rendered with a material that uses the bitmap to simulate a bumpy surface. 3ds Max converts the different intensities of light and dark tones of the grayscale bitmap into high and low points on the bumpy surface. The bump effect is an illusion created when 3ds Max applies a bitmap to the surface of the objects. The bitmap defines the shadows that would appear on the surface of the objects, based on the locations of the lights in the scene if there were actual surface deviations. Bump maps are often variations of the same image map used as the diffuse color map.

Maps accept both grayscale and color images as input. However, most maps only use the grayscale information to affect a material. The exceptions where color information is actually used by the maps are the diffuse color, ambient, filter color, and reflection maps.

FIGURE 9.5
A bumpy surface can be simulated using a grayscale bitmap (left). The light portions of the bitmap translate to high points in the bumpy surface, while the darker portions of the bitmap translate to low points (right).

REFLECTION MAPS

A reflection map is a special type of bitmap assignment. It is used where you want a material that appears to be reflective, such as the glass in an office building or a lake or pond. In an animated scene, the reflection map you use can move (if you select an animated image format), just as reflections move when you pass by a reflective surface. Use caution with reflection maps because reflections that appear to be too intense can ruin the illusion, as shown in Figure 9.6.

FIGURE 9.6
Reflection maps give the impression of a reflective surface, such as the glass and tile floor in this rendering of the Villa Savoye.

REFRACTION MAPS

A refraction map is similar to a reflection map; however, instead of giving the appearance of a reflection, such as a chrome ball, it gives the appearance of a refracted image, such as a crystal ball. A refraction map simulates the properties of glass, water, or other transparent material that bends light.

DISPLACEMENT MAPS

A bump map simulates a bumpy surface, but it doesn't actually change the geometry of the model. Displacement maps are similar to bump maps in that they seem to alter the shape of a surface, but displacement maps go one step further and actually modify the geometry of the object to which they are applied. You can, for example, turn a flat surface into a dome by using a displacement map. You need to be cautious when you use a displacement map, because it can generate a large number of faces on an object, thereby increasing the file size and rendering time. You can think of displacement maps as a modeling technique based on materials.

Surface Properties

There are some materials that rely solely on the properties of color, specularity, and opacity and don't use maps of any kind. Instead, they use color and specular levels to simulate the appearance of a substance (see Figure 9.7).

Most materials are mixtures of diffuse color, bump, and opacity maps as well as color, specularity, and transparency. Maps and material properties are combined to simulate detail you would otherwise find impossible to re-create through surface or solid modeling alone (see Figure 9.8).

FIGURE 9.7
Surface materials that don't require bitmaps

FIGURE 9.8
A simple sphere object with a single material that uses many of the different types of maps and properties available in 3ds Max

The Physical Qualities Rollout

The Architectural material's Physical Qualities rollout contains the most important and most obvious aspects of the Architectural material. You will use the Physical Qualities rollout to accurately simulate the character of the material with the following controls:

Diffuse Color Use this swatch to open the Color Selector so you can assign the diffuse color, often the most important aspect of a material. The ambient color is managed automatically, so you don't have to think about it.

Diffuse Map Click the None button in this channel to open the Material/Map Browser to assign a map. There is an Amount spinner that varies as a percentage from 0 to 100. The Amount spinner controls what percentage of the map is used in the Diffuse channel. Whatever percentage remains (out of 100) is blended with the diffuse color.

Next to the Amount spinner there is a check box that allows you to quickly toggle the map on and off. This helps when you are doing test renders and want to accelerate a rendering by temporarily leaving out certain maps (especially the time-consuming ray-trace map).

The Arrow button to the right of the diffuse color swatch and directly above the Diffuse Map slot becomes enabled whenever you assign a diffuse map. Clicking this arrow calculates the average pixel color of the diffuse map and copies it into the diffuse color swatch. This is especially helpful in radiosity renderings, as the diffuse color controls what color surfaces will emit in the form of bounced light.

Shininess This parameter controls both the specular level and glossiness parameters that you may have used before in the Standard material. You may also notice that you do not have to select any shaders with the Architectural material. The shaders used are automatically

handled based on the template that you choose from the drop-down menu in the Templates rollout.

The percentage used in the Shininess amount is entered automatically by the template, so you don't have to alter it unless you want to further customize your material.

Instance the diffuse map in the Shininess channel when you want the bright areas of the map to represent the shiny areas as well.

Transparency Transparency is the opposite of Opacity (from the Standard material). Transparency is the amount of light that passes through the material without illuminating it (as with most kinds of architectural glass).

You won't be able to see any diffuse color on objects that are 100 percent transparent, but you will still be able to see the shiny areas.

Translucency Use this channel when you are simulating objects that allow some light through, but scatter it within the object. Art glass or frosted privacy glass are some examples of translucent materials.

Index of Refraction The Index of Refraction (IOR) is the measurement of a physical property that all objects naturally have, but it is most apparent in translucent and transparent materials. Light reflects and/or refracts at the interface between two materials with different IOR. The template will set this value for you. There are no units with this spinner, but be aware that it is not a percentage. Table 9.1 lists the IOR values for some basic materials. You can find more complete IOR tables online so you can apply the proper values to the materials you are creating to help you with your photometric renderings.

TABLE 9.1: IOR Values for Some Basic Materials

MATERIAL	IOR
Vacuum	1.0000
Air	1.0003
Water	1.3330
Glass	1.50 to 1.70
Diamond	2.41
Gold	0.47
Vodka	1.363

Luminance cd/m² Set this value if you want the material to glow with its own light. The units are in candelas per square meter. You can think of one candela as roughly the light emitted from one wax candle.

Set Luminance from Light If you are using the Radiosity Renderer, chances are you are using photometric lights that simulate real-world intensities. Click the spotlight icon near the bottom of the Physical Qualities rollout and then click a photometric light to copy its

intensity into the Luminance Amount spinner. This is a quick way to make your material emit the light intensity of a known luminaire without having to remember the numerical intensity values.

Check boxes The 2-Sided check box is useful when you are rendering imported surfaces that have their normals facing in the wrong direction. Be aware that your rendering will take longer (especially if you are ray tracing).

The Raw Diffuse Texture check box is used only in radiosity rendering. It excludes the surface from illumination and exposure control, so your whites stay pure white. This is helpful when you are simulating the surface of a luminaire and want it to read as pure white but don't want the surface itself to emit light.

The Special Effects Rollout

The Special Effects rollout for Architectural materials contains four channels that simulate advanced features. Earlier in this chapter you saw how to use a bump map, and this channel is the same as the Bump channel found in the Maps rollout of the Standard material.

Bump Bump simulates low relief by manipulating surface normals (similar to how smoothing works). Any type of map will work in this channel. Noise is often used to make a rough, uneven surface. On the other hand, you can instance the diffuse map into this channel, and only the grayscale equivalent of a color image will be used to lift, or bump, the surface upward.

Displacement Displacement differs from Bump in that this channel actually alters the geometry that it is applied to at render time. Displacement can be used to simulate surfaces that are difficult to model with other techniques. Typically bitmaps are used in this channel, although most map types are supported.

Intensity This channel simulates the brightness or *intensity* of a material. It can be used for positive effect to simulate roughness, which you can think of as variable brightness across a surface.

Try using a noise map in the Intensity channel to make your material more realistic and to avoid that flat look that is so common in computer graphics.

Cutout This is similar to the Opacity channel in the Standard material but better. When you place a bitmap in the Cutout channel, not only are the black areas of the bitmap transparent, but the *cutout* area will not have any reflections, refractions, or shininess. In other words, the black areas of a map in this channel are completely and utterly cut out. This is perfect for creating entourage, covered later in this chapter.

Other rollouts The Advanced Lighting Override rollout is used only for tweaking radiosity solutions and works the same as the Advanced Lighting Override material from earlier versions of 3ds Max.

The SuperSampling rollout allows you to apply antialiasing at the material level. You can opt to control supersampling at the global or local levels. In other words, you can enable supersampling within one material if you want its settings to differ from the global supersampling options.

The mental ray Connection rollout is to be used only with the mental ray renderer (see Chapter 14).

Adding Materials to Objects

For our tutorial, you'll start by selecting a few materials from a list and applying them to the model. Then, after checking the appearance of the materials with a test rendering, you'll look at ways to adjust the materials to better suit your model.

Before you dive in, it is important to let 3ds Max know where the dependent files are that you plan to use in your project.

Adding a Map Path to Help 3ds Max Find Bitmaps

Maps and other support files are not contained within the 3ds Max files; this would make the files enormous and hinder the ability to update and share those files. Instead, the filenames and paths are referenced in 3ds Max and accessed whenever the files are opened or rendered. 3ds Max needs to know where different types of files are located for its use. 3ds Max stores its standard bitmap images in subfolders under the \map folder within the main 3ds Max 2011 application folder. When you start to create your own materials, it may be a good idea to keep your own bitmap files in folders that are separate from the standard 3ds Max \map folder. For example, you might create a folder under the 3ds Max 2011 folder called Custom Maps to store your own bitmap files, or you might make a series of subfolders on your server so that the same set of maps can be shared within your office. Keeping your personal bitmaps separate from the maps that ship with 3ds Max will also make it easier when you upgrade 3ds Max or migrate to a new PC. The program first searches the folder where the current file is located and then searches through a list of paths specified by the user.

You can also define a folder to be the project folder; this provides a common root location to store a scene's assets, including nonstandard map and rendering output. 3ds Max places the project folder, and the subfolders that are automatically created, in the same location where 3ds Max was initially installed. You can set a new project folder by clicking the Application menu, choosing Manage ➢ Set Project Folder (or using the Project Folder button on the Quick Access toolbar), and then navigating to the preferred location with the Browse for Folder dialog box. When you are working on a team project, a consistent project folder location is crucial; not using one can significantly impact the collaboration process.

In the exercises in this chapter, you'll use bitmap files from the website. You first need to let 3ds Max know where to look for the files:

1. Choose Customize ➢ Configure User Paths. The Configure User Paths dialog box appears.

2. Click the External Files tab. You see a list showing the current path where 3ds Max searches for bitmap files and photometric files, among others (see Figure 9.9).

YOUR PATHS MAY BE DIFFERENT

The paths shown will likely differ from those on your system.

3. Click the Add button to the far right. The Choose New External Files Path dialog box appears. This is a typical file dialog box that lets you search for and select a folder.

FIGURE 9.9

The External Files tab of the Configure User Paths dialog box

4. Locate and select the folder that contains the downloaded and unzipped files; select Add Subpaths to add all the folders under the selected path, and then click Use Path to add the new folders to the search path, and close the Choose New External Files Path dialog box.

5. Click OK to close the Configure User Paths dialog box.

RELATIVE USER PATHS

Sharing a project between team members, especially those in different physical locations, has always been difficult, especially when support files are used in a project. In early versions of Autodesk VIZ and 3ds Max, the paths to support files and maps were absolute, meaning the programs would look in a specific drive and folder for the files. For example, if your 3ds Max scene file is located in the `C:/Projects/Restaurant` folder and search paths for the maps used in the scene are in the `C:/Projects/Restaurant/Maps` folder, then 3ds Max, as expected, would search in that folder for the referenced files. Problems would start to occur when you gave the Restaurant folder and its subfolders to a colleague, client, or contractor and they placed it in a different drive or folder. 3ds Max would still search the `C:/Projects/Restaurant/Maps` path for the required files, but the path would be invalid.

3ds Max 2010 and newer have the ability to set the paths for a scene's support files and maps to be relative to the project location, rather than in an absolute folder location. By selecting a path in the Configure User Paths dialog box and then clicking the Make Relative button, the path becomes relative to the current project and is no longer an absolute location. Now when you send the files to someone else, 3ds Max is more likely to locate the referenced files. You can switch paths back to absolute paths by clicking the Make Absolute button.

Now you're ready to start using the bitmap files from the book's website (`www.sybex.com/go/mastering3dsmaxdesign2011`). You may have noticed other tabs in the Configure User Paths dialog box. As you might guess, these other tabs let you indicate additional places to search: File I/O and XRefs, as the names of the tabs indicate. The File I/O tab lets you determine where 3ds Max should look for various components of the program. The XRefs tab lets you indicate where 3ds Max should look when searching for XRef files. XRefs are scenes or objects that have been externally referenced into a file. XRefs do not become part of the file into which they are

imported but remain separate files that are merely referenced when needed. In Chapter 11, "Organizing Objects and Scene Management," you'll get a chance to learn more about XRefs.

You have the ability to save, load, and merge user paths. These options, located at the bottom of the Configure User Paths dialog box, allow the easy transfer of the paths, saved as MXP files, from computer to computer or between project team members.

HOW 3DS MAX SEARCHES FOR FILES

After searching in the folder where the current project (*.max file) is located, 3ds Max searches the search path starting at the top of the Configure User Paths dialog box and working down. Once 3ds Max locates the referenced filename, the search is terminated and the file is used. If multiple files in the search path have the same name, 3ds Max will use the first one that it finds, which may not be the one you want.

There are several utility programs that help you work with paths, and you'll learn more about them later in this chapter. Now that 3ds Max knows where to find the dependent files, you are ready to begin the tutorial.

In this exercise, you'll render a model of the condo project and see that the materials that are assigned to the objects in the scene generally consist of a light beige color and very few other characteristics. There is no difference between the countertop and the cabinet materials. The glass in the model appears transparent but doesn't have any other glass-like qualities. 3ds Max offers a glass material that's both transparent and shiny, and it includes accurate reflections. In the exercise, you'll add this glass material to the model. The rendering process in this exercise might appear different to you because it is using the mental ray rendering system with Final Gather. You will learn more about mental ray in Chapter 14.

1. Open the ch09_A.max file from the sample files on the website.

2. Click the Compact Material Editor button on the Main Toolbar or press M on the keyboard.

The Compact Material Editor appears, as shown in Figure 9.10.

FIGURE 9.10
The Compact
Material Editor

At the top you see a set of sample slots, which are preview images of materials. Right now, there are no custom-designed materials in the Material Editor. The top two rows are the default materials when mental ray is the assigned renderer: some are Arch & Design materials, and others are Autodesk Materials. All the remaining slots show the same blank sphere representing an unaltered Arch & Design material. Also notice that the first material slot in the third row is outlined with a thick, white border. This tells you that it is currently the active slot. Any changes made to the material's parameters affect the material in this slot.

3. Click the Get Material button on the toolbar just below the sample images of spheres. The Material/Map Browser (see Figure 9.11) appears.

FIGURE 9.11
The Material/
Map Browser

4. Near the top-left corner of the Material/Map Browser, click the Material/Map Browser Option button, and then click the Open Material Library button. This lets you load a material library into the Material/Map Browser.

The Import Material Library dialog box displays, listing the material library files that are available, as shown in Figure 9.12.

FIGURE 9.12
The available material library files

WHERE ARE THE LIBRARIES?

The Open Material Library dialog box may open to the C:/My Documents/3dsmax/material libraries folder or the folder the current Max file was loaded from, but this is not the location where 3ds Max installs the libraries. Navigate to the C:\Program Files\Autodesk\3ds Max Design 2011\materiallibraries folders for the default 3ds Max libraries. If you installed 3ds Max Design 2011 from the commercial or educational DVDs, you should have also installed the Samples content. The 2011 samples content installs the extra material libraries to C:\Autodesk\ Autodesk_3ds_Max_2011_&_Autodesk_3ds_Max_Design_2011_English_Win_Samples_ Files\Samples\Maps and Materials\MatLibs folder. If you are using the 3ds Max Design 2011 Trial download, you will not have those additional material libraries; instead, we've provided a Mastering3dsMaxD2011.mat file with the Chapter 9 files that you downloaded from the book's website. Load that material library for these exercises.

You can create your own library files as you become more familiar with 3ds Max. For now, you'll use a predefined material from the material library you will load in the next exercises and make a few simple adjustments:

1. Select Design.Architectural.Materials.Woods&Plastics.mat from the list, and then click Open.

 The newly loaded library will appear in the Material/Map Browser as a group listed by its filename, and it will have a gray LIB indicator at the right edge of the group header, as shown in Figure 9.13. You can see the materials in the library by clicking the + sign on the group's header and expanding the library if it isn't already expanded.

 When you have loaded a material library, you can add materials to it, save it with a new name, or remove materials from the library. Be careful removing materials from a library; once you do, if the material isn't saved in any scene file where you can find it to reload it, that material is lost forever.

FIGURE 9.13
The loaded material library

2. Scroll down the list and click Woods & Plastics.Finish Carpentry.Wood.Teak (Architectural).

3. Double-click the name of the material, and it appears in the Material Editor in the currently selected sample slot. Also notice that the name Woods & Plastics.Finish Carpentry .Wood.Teak (Architectural) appears in the drop-down list just below the horizontal toolbar.

4. Click the Select by Name button. In the Select from Scene dialog box, select all objects with *Draw*, *Cab* (drawers and cabinets), *Crown Moul*, *Microw*, and *Fridge* in the name, but do not select objects that also have *handle* in the object name. Also select the object named Base Moder, and then click Select.

5. In the Material Editor toolbar, click the Assign Material to Selection button. The current material is assigned to the selected objects.

6. In the Main Toolbar, click the Render Production button. The scene is rendered and the material is displayed, as shown in Figure 9.14. The wood grain appears on all the surfaces, including those behind the cabinet doors in the foreground. The material for those doors will be addressed in a later exercise.

As you can see, assigning library materials to scene objects is a fairly quick and easy procedure.

FIGURE 9.14
The rendered scene
with the wood
applied to the cabi-
nets and drawers

Understanding Material Libraries

**CERT
OBJECTIVE**

You imported the Woods & Plastics.Finish Carpentry.Wood.Teak (Architectural) material from
the Design.Architectural.Materials.Woods&Plastics.mat material library. You can find
this and other material library files in the materiallibraries subfolder of the 3ds Max 2011 folder
or with the samples content. You aren't limited to this one material library, however. You can use
all the files with the .mat extension in this folder, you can create your own library from materi-
als you create in the Material Editor, or you can even use libraries from third-party producers.

To open a different library, you need to be in the Material/Map Browser. Click the Options
button, and then select the Open Material Library item to access the Import Material Library
dialog box. You can have as many open libraries as you want in the Material/Map Browser.

To create a new library, click the Material/Map Browser Options button, and then click New
Material Library. You will see the Create New Material Library dialog box. You can then enter
a name for your library and click OK. This creates a new empty library that you can populate
with the materials you want. The new library is saved in your User folder deep down in the
3dsMaxDesign folder. To save the library to a new location, such as your 3ds Max Design 2011\
materiallibraries folder, right-click the Library group header, choose Path/Name ➤ Save As, and
in the Export Material Library browser, navigate to where you want to save the library. Then
click Save.

To remove a material from a library, in the Material/Map Browser, right-click the material
and select Remove from Lib. You can also use the right-click menu on a material to rename it or
copy it to a temporary library or any other library files that are currently open. If you delete a
library, you will have to reinstall 3ds Max Design 2011 to get it back. You should consider mak-
ing backup copies of all your material libraries prior to making any changes to them.

You can close the Material/Map Browser now if you still have it open. Using the Material
Editor and Material/Map Browser at the same time will take up a lot of screen real estate,
and you will quickly realize that working on a system with two monitors will greatly help your
work process.

Editing Materials

Many 3ds Max materials are ready to use out of the box, but often you'll need to edit the materials to achieve the specific look you want. In this exercise, you'll select materials for the walls and floor and change the parameters to achieve a more pleasant appearance.

1. In the Material Editor, click the unused sample slot next to the Teak material you added in the previous exercises. This is where the next material will be designed.

2. Click the Material Type button, which currently says Arch & Design, as shown in Figure 9.15.

FIGURE 9.15

Click the Material Type button, which says Arch & Design.

3. In the Material/Map Browser, expand the Materials group, expand the Standard group, and double-click the Architectural material to load it into the selected sample slot in the Compact Material Editor.

4. In the Templates rollout, expand the drop-down list, and choose Paint Semi-Gloss, as shown in Figure 9.16.

FIGURE 9.16

Choose Paint Semi-Gloss.

Material templates define many of a material's properties, including Transparency, Shininess, and Index of Refraction, common to several types of real-world surfaces. Templates also define how bounced light is reflected from or transmitted through the objects. The Reflectance and Transmittance numbers are shown just above the toolbar in the Material Editor, as shown in Figure 9.17. Transmittance values are above 0 (zero) only when the material is not 100 percent opaque.

FIGURE 9.17

The Reflectance and Transmittance values

5. In the Physical Qualities rollout, click the Diffuse Color sample swatch to open the Color Selector dialog box.

6. Select a pale green color similar to R = 210, G = 249, B = 213, and then click OK. This assigns a pastel green color to the walls.

7. Assigning descriptive names to your materials is important so that when you access them later or put them in a library, you can quickly understand how they are used in your scene. Click in the Material (Map) Name Field to the left of the Material Type button, and enter **Wall Paint Green Light** as the current material's name, as shown in Figure 9.18.

8. Click the Select By Name tool or press **H** on the keyboard. Using the Select from Scene dialog box, select the three Wall objects, but not the sub-objects of Wall_Den.

9. Click the Assign Material to Selection button to assign the material to the scene's Wall objects.

10. Render the CamWall viewport to see the result of adding the paint to the walls.

11. Save your file as **Mychap09_b.max**.

FIGURE 9.18
Rename the material.

Using Bump Maps

Earlier in this chapter, you saw a bump map sample (Figure 9.5). It showed how a grayscale image creates the impression of a bumpy surface. Bump maps can also generate other types of surface textures. The paint in the condo, for example, is too flat and could use some texture. To add that texture, you'll add a map to the Bump Map channel of the current paint material, as shown in these steps:

1. Open the file you saved earlier as Mych09_b.max, or open the ch09_b.max file from this book's download files.

2. Click the Material Editor button on the Main Toolbar to open the Compact Material Editor.

3. In the Compact Material Editor, double-click the Wall Paint Green Light sample slot, with the triangles in the corner. Double-clicking a material slot opens the Magnify Window dialog box (also accessible under the Material menu) that contains just the selected material. This dialog box can be resized to provide a better view of the material as you develop it.

 The triangles in the corners of the sample window indicate the status of the material in the scene. White triangles denote a material that is in the scene and applied to the currently selected objects; gray triangles are materials that are applied to objects in the scene that are not currently selected. No triangles around a sample sphere indicates a material that resides in the Material Editor but not in the scene.

4. Scroll down to the Special Effects rollout and open it.

5. Click the Bump Map button that is currently labeled None.

6. In the Material/Map Browser, expand the Maps group, and then expand the Standard group.

7. Double-click Noise from the list, as shown in Figure 9.19, to add it to the Bump channel of the Wall Paint Green Light material.

FIGURE 9.19
Select the noise map.

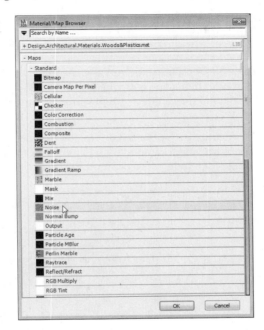

8. With the noise map added to the material, the parameters for the noise map appear in the Material Editor, and the effect of the bump map appears in the sample slots, as shown in Figure 9.20.

FIGURE 9.20
The Material Editor showing the effect of the bump map and the Noise parameters

You may recall that a bump map uses varying shades of gray, or the grayscale equivalent when using a color bitmap, to determine the highs and lows of the bumps on a surface. In computer graphics (CG), noise is added to inject randomness into a scene or image, and the noise map is a procedural map that generates a random pattern of gray tones. As a bump map, the noise map will produce a random bumpy surface.

With the noise map added to the material, let's take a look at the walls as they are rendered:

1. Right-click the CamWall viewport, and then click the Render Production button. You see the walls rendered in the Rendered Frame Window, as shown in Figure 9.21.

 The walls render in a bumpy texture that looks more like a water-damaged, buckling structure than a newly painted wall. This is particularly noticeable on the back wall to the right of the cabinets. You'll want the bumps to be much smaller.

2. In the Noise Parameters rollout, change the Size value from 25.0 to 1.0. This reduces the distance between each bump. Render the scene again. As shown in Figure 9.22, the bumps are much smaller but still too large; the paint looks more like the surface of an orange than the surface of an interior wall.

FIGURE 9.21
The scene after adding the noise map to the material

FIGURE 9.22
The walls after reducing the noise map's Size parameter to 1.0

3. In the Noise Parameters rollout, reduce the Size value from 1.0 to 0.1 and then render the scene again. This time, the surface texture is barely noticeable from the current distance to the walls. The size of the bumps is acceptable, but they appear to protrude from the wall too far. You'll fix this by adjusting the intensity of the bump map.

4. In the Material Editor toolbar, click the Go to Parent button.

 Think of a material as being constructed of components that are organized into a hierarchy. The bump map is considered a "child" of the material. When you added the bitmap file to the Wall Paint Green Light material, you entered a type of sublevel for the material. The Go to Parent tool brings you back up one level—in this case, to the "main" level of the material's parameters.

5. In the Special Effects rollout, change the value in the Bump input box to 25 and then rerender the scene. This time the noise pattern appearing on the surface of the walls is slightly more subtle.

Creating a New Material

You've added a wood and a paint material to your model, and you've made a few modifications. In this section, you'll apply a material to the floor of the condo, but instead of using a preexisting material, you'll create an entirely new one and add a bitmap to define its appearance. The material you create will be fairly simple, but the exercises here will give you a chance to play with some of the settings you haven't tried yet.

1. Open the Material Editor if it is not already open; then click an unused sample slot. You'll use this slot for your new floor material.

2. If necessary, click the Material Type button to the right of the material name, choose Architectural from the Material/Map Browser, and then click OK.

USING THE ARCHITECTURAL MATERIAL

You can use the Architectural material with all types of renderers: Scanline, Ray Tracing, Radiosity, and mental ray. Reflection, Refraction, Radiosity, and Global Illumination parameters are automatically set with this material type.

3. In the Material Name drop-down list, change the name to **Floor_Condo_Wood**.

4. In the Physical Qualities rollout, change Shininess to 75 and Index of Refraction to 1.2. This causes the material to be shiny and to slightly bend the light that bounces off of it.

 Notice how the Floor_Condo_Wood sample slot changes. It looks like a sphere with a shiny surface because of the small, tight specular bloom.

5. At the bottom of the Physical Qualities rollout, select the 2-Sided check box to force this material to render on both sides of each face. If some of the surface materials seem to disappear, this will force them to appear correctly in the rendering.

SELECTING TWO-SIDED MATERIALS

The 2-Sided option is sometimes needed to correct improper normal orientation in models that have been imported from other 3D programs, particularly CAD programs. This option isn't usually as critical for models built entirely within 3ds Max because the surfaces are usually facing in the correct direction and single-sided materials generally are sufficient.

6. Click the None button next to the Diffuse Map label, and in the Material/Map Browser open the Maps group and then the Standard group. Then double-click Bitmap.

7. In the Select Bitmap Image File browser that opens, navigate to the `C:\Program Files\Autodesk\3ds Max Design 2011\maps\ArchMat` folder. Your actual folder path may vary.

8. Double-click the `Woods&Plastics.FinishCarpentry.Urethane.jpg` file to add it to the Diffuse Map channel of the current material and return to the Material Editor.

9. This time, rather than selecting the destination and clicking the Assign Material to Selection button, simply click in the material slot and drag it to the floor as shown in Figure 9.23. A tooltip appears, identifying the object to which the material will be assigned.

10. Render the scene with the floor material added. It's difficult to see any change because the tile pattern isn't evident.

Try changing the lighting in the scene to see how it affects the materials. Remember that a surface's rendered appearance is the result of the combination of its geometry, lighting, and materials.

FIGURE 9.23
Assigning a material by dragging it into the scene

Adding Material Mapping Coordinates

If you just want to manipulate the color, transparency, and shininess of an object, you can usually create or use a material that doesn't use bitmaps to simulate a texture. Once you start to add a texture using bitmaps, you'll need to specify how that texture is applied to the object. You'll want to tell 3ds Max the size of the texture in relation to the object, as well as its orientation on

the object. For example, you wouldn't want the brick pattern to appear with its courses running vertically, as in the example shown in Figure 9.24, nor would you want the brick pattern to be quite so large.

FIGURE 9.24
A brick wall with the brick courses running vertically and at a large scale

To control how materials are applied to objects, you'll want to know how to use the UVW Map modifier. This modifier lets you precisely control the way a material is placed on an object. In the next exercise, you'll add the modifier to the condo floor to establish the orientation and size of the Floor_Condo_Wood material in relation to the object.

WHAT DOES UVW MEAN?

The *UVW* in the name *UVW map* refers to the coordinates of a material map. They indicate the direction of a map in a way similar to the XYZ Cartesian coordinates with which you're already familiar. The letters *UVW* differentiate map coordinates from the standard XYZ-coordinate designation and were chosen simply because they precede XYZ in the alphabet.

UVW map coordinates need to be differentiated from XYZ-coordinates because, although they indicate direction similar to XYZ-coordinates, they are in relation to the length and width of the image map regardless of the object's orientation in space. UVW-coordinates also don't treat measured distances in the same way. In a Cartesian coordinate system, distances are measured at specific intervals of feet, meters, or whatever measurement system you're using. UVW map coordinates, on the other hand, are measured as a percentage of width and height of a surface. Instead of feet or meters, UVW maps use real values from 0 to 1. The value used represents a percentage of the overall width of the surface being mapped, with 1 being equal to 100 percent of the surface width.

Because the coordinate values in a UVW map are based on a percentage, a U value of 0.5 can represent a measured distance that's different from a V value of 0.5. For example, imagine a rectangular surface with a UVW-coordinate system whose origin is the lower-left corner of the rectangle. The upper-right corner of the rectangle would then be the coordinate 1,1, even though the length and width of the rectangle are not equal to each other. This may seem a bit odd at first, but if you consider that material maps are used to match an image to a surface, you begin to see the rationale behind the UVW map system. The relationship between a map and a surface is more important than their actual dimensions. You can think in terms of "What percentage of the surface does the map cover?" rather than "How many square inches does the map cover?"

A UI DISCREPANCY

Oddly, the modifier in the Modifier List drop-down is named UVW Map although UVW Mapping appears in the modifier stack.

1. Right-click the Top viewport; then use the Zoom Extents tool to zoom out so that your view looks similar to Figure 9.25.

FIGURE 9.25
The condo in the
Top viewport

2. Click the Select by Name tool and use the Select from Scene dialog box to select the Floor407 object.

3. Click the Modify tab of the Command panel, expand the Modifier List drop-down, and then assign the UVW Map modifier to the Floor407 object.

4. In the Parameters rollout, make sure Planar is selected as the mapping type and then deselect the Use Real-World Map size option at the bottom of the Mapping group. Turning this option off allows you to manually control the number of times the map repeats itself.

5. In the Alignment section, click the Fit button to adjust the gizmo size to match the size of the floor.

 Let's take a moment to study the UVW Map gizmo. It has one green edge and a small line sticking out on one side. You will have to expand the UVW Mapping modifier and select the gizmo to see the colors. Figure 9.26 gives you a clear picture of what the gizmo looks like. If the map is oriented incorrectly, use the Select and Rotate tool to rotate it properly.

 The colored edge and the small line help you orient the UVW Mapping gizmo on an object by showing you which way is up and which directions are left and right: the short line extending from the frame indicates the top of the image and the green edge denotes the right side. You'll get a more detailed look at the UVW Mapping gizmo after the current exercise. You can increase the amount of tiling two ways: decrease the size of the gizmo or increase the Tile values in the Parameters rollout. Let's continue by adjusting the Tile values to reduce the size of the material on the Floor407 object.

FIGURE 9.26

The UVW Mapping
gizmo assigned to
the Floor407 object

FIGURE 9.26

The UVW Mapping
gizmo assigned to
the Floor407 object

If you were to render the scene now, the woods&plastics.finishcarpentry.urethane .jpg image would be stretched across the floor a single time and appear pixelated. You'll want to scale the Floor_Condo_Wood material to a size that's more in line with the size of the floor object by instructing 3ds Max to repeat, or tile, the material several times. Continuing from the previous steps, you will use the UVW Map modifier to improve the appearance of the floor's texture map.

6. In the Mapping section, enter **20** in both the U Tile and V Tile input fields. This causes any material assigned to the floor object to repeat itself 20 times within the boundary of the UVW Mapping gizmo.

7. Render the scene. The linear pattern of the image map becomes apparent, as shown in Figure 9.27.

There is one final step that you are going to do to make the floor material pop just a little more. The Architectural materials' Intensity parameter controls the brightness of the material. In the Intensity channel you'll use the same map that you used in the Diffuse color channel.

FIGURE 9.27

Changing the U
and V Tile settings
causes the diffuse
color map to repeat
over the surface of
the object.

REMOVING BITMAPS FROM MATERIALS

There are several methods for removing a map from a material. While the map's parameters are visible (the Coordinates and Bitmap Parameters rollouts), you can click the Reset Map/Mtl to Default Settings button in the Material Editor toolbar and then click Yes in the warning dialog that opens. Finally, you can click and drag any button labeled None in the Maps rollout and drop it over a button containing a map name to clear the map slot.

8. Click the Diffuse Map button and drag the map to the Intensity button in the Special Effects rollout, as shown in Figure 9.28.

FIGURE 9.28
Dragging a map
from one channel
to another

9. In the Instance (Copy) Map dialog box that appears, choose Instance, and then click OK. Using the instance option, changes made to one map are immediately made to the other.

10. Render the scene once more, and you'll see that the wood strips are more defined.

EXPOSING ALL AVAILABLE SAMPLE SLOTS

If your Material Editor displays only 6 or 15 samples, don't worry. You can access the remaining slots by using the vertical and horizontal scroll bars around the slots, or you can expose all of the slots at one time. To expose all of the slots, click the Options button on the Material Editor's vertical toolbar to open the Material Editor Options dialog box.

In the Slots area at the bottom of the dialog box, select the 6 × 4 radio button. Click OK to accept the changes; the Material Editor updates to show all 24 sample slots. There is no practical limit to the number of materials in a scene—the number of materials is limited only in the Material Editor.

Understanding Mapping Coordinates

The UVW Map modifier you added in the previous exercise told 3ds Max the size, location, and orientation of the material on the object to which it is assigned. At render time, the image is usually applied to the object in a repeated, or *tiled*, fashion. You can also set a material to apply the bitmap just once. In this section, you'll take a closer look at the UVW Map modifier.

What Happens When You Add the Mapping Coordinates

The UVW Mapping gizmo you saw in the previous exercise is a visual representation of the mapping coordinates. Its shape and color are aids in helping you see the bitmap's orientation more clearly. As mentioned earlier, the small line at the top of the icon represents the top of the bitmap, while the green shows the right side. These indicators can tell you at a glance whether the bitmap image of the material you are using is upside down or backward in relation to the object to which the coordinates are being applied, as shown in Figure 9.29.

FIGURE 9.29
The UVW Mapping gizmo in relation to a material bitmap

Point

Green edge

The UVW Mapping gizmo

The orientation of the bitmap in the preceding exercise is really not that important, but it can be important for texture maps that do have a specific orientation, such as a brick pattern, or for a single image, such as a wine label or a road sign. The UVW Mapping gizmo shows the approximate size of the bitmap in relation to the object to which it is being applied. When the model is rendered, multiple copies of the image are applied over the entire surface of the object, like tiles on a kitchen counter.

Figure 9.30 shows another way that the gizmo affects the appearance of a material. You see a brick wall with the gizmo rotated. The bricks are angled and aligned with the UVW Mapping gizmo.

FIGURE 9.30
A sample brick wall with the UVW Mapping gizmo rotated 30 degrees

The UVW Mapping gizmo rotated

Adjusting the UVW Mapping Gizmo

You have a number of options for controlling the size, shape, and orientation of the UVW Mapping gizmo. These will be crucial to your ability to place materials accurately on an object or an individual face. Here are descriptions of the Alignment group options as they appear in the Command panel:

Manipulate Activates the Select and Manipulate tool. You can also access this tool by clicking the Select and Manipulate icon on the Main Toolbar. The Manipulate option causes the gizmo to turn green and a cursor to appear like the Select cursor when it is over the edges of the UVW Mapping gizmo. Using the Select and Manipulate transform, you can click and drag the edges of the UVW Mapping gizmo to define the exact size and location for the bitmap.

Region Fit Lets you fit the UVW Mapping gizmo to a specific rectangular area. This is useful for situations where you want a texture map to fit exactly over a specific region of an object. When you choose this option, you can select two points to define the two diagonal corners of the UVW Map gizmo. The process is similar to selecting a zoom region or creating a rectangle. Because this option lets you select any two points, it will stretch and distort the UVW Map gizmo in either the X- or Y-axis. To orient the UVW Map gizmo rightside up, pick two points over the region starting with the lower-left corner (see Figure 9.31).

FIGURE 9.31

A Region Fit UVW Map gizmo is placed on a wall in the Front viewport (left). A rendered view is shown with the UVW Map gizmo superimposed on the view (right).

Click here first. Then click here.

Drag to form a region.

The location of the UVW Mapping gizmo in relation to the final rendered surface

Bitmap Fit Adjusts the UVW Map gizmo's proportion to fit the shape of a particular bitmap image. This option uses the current UVW map size and alters the proportions to fit the bitmap proportions. The option is helpful if you want the bitmap to be displayed accurately in its original form. It also helps if you want a better idea of the bitmap's shape as you assign the mapping coordinates to objects.

View Align Aligns the UVW Map gizmo to a viewport. This option can help you locate a UVW map or quickly align it to a viewport.

Fit Stretches the UVW Map gizmo over the surface of an object to make it fit exactly.

Center Centers the UVW Map gizmo on an object's surface.

Acquire Sets the UVW Map gizmo to match the mapping coordinates of an object that already has mapping coordinates assigned to it.

Reset Resets the UVW Map gizmo to the 3ds Max default size and orientation.

Normal Align Aligns the UVW Map gizmo to the normal of a surface of the object to which the mapping is attached.

Controlling the Tiling Effect

When you added the Floor_Condo_Wood material to the floor object and increased the number for the U and V Tile parameters, the wood striping pattern appeared at a smaller scale and was repeated over the entire surface of the floor in a rectangular array. This repetition of the map is called tiling. If you've ever experimented with the Windows desktop wallpaper, you may already be familiar with the idea of tiling.

Tiling is on by default, but you can turn it off for situations when you want only a single image to appear over the surface. Figure 9.32 portrays the same brick wall shown in Figure 9.31, but this time the Tile option is turned off. The brick pattern appears only in the region defined by the UVW Map gizmo. The rest of the wall surface is rendered based on the Basic Parameters rollout settings of ambient, diffuse, and specular color.

FIGURE 9.32
The brick wall rendered with the Tile option turned off

The tile settings are located in the Material Editor and can be controlled or turned on/off there as well. Here's how to locate the tiling parameters:

1. Open the Material Editor.

2. With the Floor_Condo_Wood material selected, scroll down the list of rollouts and open the Physical Qualities rollout if it isn't already open.

3. Locate the map you want to adjust; then click its button. For example, for the Floor_Condo_Wood material, click the Diffuse Map button labeled `woods&plastics.finishcarpentry.urethane.jpg` (the button displays as much of the name as it can). The parameters for that particular map display in the Material Editor.

4. Open the Coordinates rollout and locate the Tile check boxes, as shown in Figure 9.33. You can click the U and V Tile check boxes to turn off tiling. Don't change this setting for your condo model, however—you want to keep the tile setting turned on.

FIGURE 9.33
The Tile options for
a selected bitmap

UNDERSTANDING THE DIFFERENT TYPES OF MAPPING

When you first apply the UVW Map modifier to an object, 3ds Max uses its default *planar* map type. As you might guess from its name, this map type maps the bitmap image to a plane, or flat surface, as shown in Figure 9.32. This option projects a flat image onto a surface. The orientation of the UVW Map gizmo in relation to the object affects the appearance of the material. Figure 9.34 shows how the same texture map can be projected onto a box with different effects.

As you can see from Figure 9.34, you aren't limited to using a planar map that's parallel to the surface you are mapping. You can create some interesting effects by reorienting the UVW Map gizmo. The streaking that you see on the boxes is the color of the edge pixels projected across the faces that run perpendicular to the gizmo.

FIGURE 9.34
A box with mapping coordinates oriented in different ways. The texture map is identical in each example.

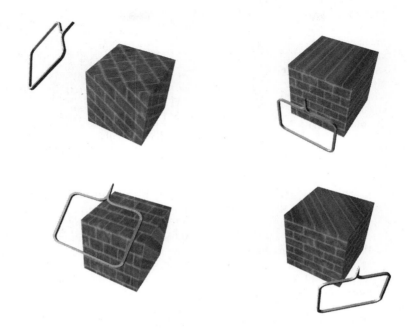

But what do you do if you want to map an image to a cylindrical or spherical object? 3ds Max offers several other mapping types to facilitate mapping to nonplanar surfaces.

If you look at the Parameters rollout for the UVW Mapping modifier, you see the radio button options shown in Figure 9.35.

FIGURE 9.35
Mapping options

The *cylindrical* map curves the bitmap into a cylindrical shape and then projects the map outward from the center of the cylinder. Naturally, you would use this type of mapping on cylindrical objects. You will want to place such a map in the center of the object. The Cap option places the map on the end caps of the gizmo, similar to the Planar option.

When you choose this map, the UVW Mapping gizmo changes to a cylindrical one, as shown in Figure 9.36. You would then place this map in the center of a cylindrical object and assign it to the object. You can also distort the map by moving the UVW Mapping gizmo closer to one side or the other or rotating the map so it isn't aligned with the object.

FIGURE 9.36
A view of the UVW Mapping gizmo when using the Cylindrical mapping type, along with a sample of an object that uses this mapping type

Bitmap Cylindrical UVW Map gizmo Rendering

Spherical mapping curves the bitmap into a spherical shape. To understand how it works, imagine taking the rectangular bitmap image and curling it around a spherical shape; then squeeze the top and bottom ends of the bitmap like a candy wrapper (see Figure 9.37). One use of this mapping type is to portray the surface of a planet. You could use the spherical mapping type to place a flat map of the earth on a sphere.

As with the cylindrical mapping type, the UVW Mapping gizmo changes to a different shape when the spherical mapping type is chosen, as shown in Figure 9.37. You would align this gizmo to the center of the spherical shape that requires mapping.

Shrink wrap is similar to spherical, but instead of wrapping the image around a sphere, as shown in Figure 9.37, imagine wrapping a sphere in plastic wrap with the bitmap image tied at one end. Figure 9.38 shows a rendering using the same sphere and bitmap texture as in Figure 9.37. The only difference is that the sphere in Figure 9.38 uses shrink wrap mapping instead of the spherical mapping of Figure 9.37.

FIGURE 9.37
The Spherical mapping type wraps the bitmap around a sphere.

Bitmap Spherical UVW Mapping gizmo Rendering

FIGURE 9.38
A sample of shrink wrap mapping

Box mapping is similar to planar mapping, but it projects the image onto six sides, as shown in Figure 9.39, instead of a single plane. You may find that you use box mapping the most, especially if your work involves buildings.

Face mapping is similar to box mapping, but instead of projecting the image from a box-shaped gizmo, face mapping projects the image onto each individual face of an object. This is easiest to see in a faceted object, such as the 12-sided sphere shown in Figure 9.40.

FIGURE 9.39
Box mapping

Box UVW Mapping gizmo Rendering with a grid bitmap

FIGURE 9.40
Using face mapping on a sphere

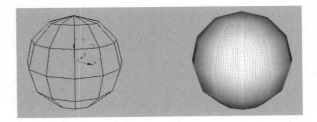

Even if smoothing is used to smooth out the surface of an object, face mapping will project the image onto the individual faces of the object.

XYZ to UVW mapping is mainly used for *procedural maps.* A procedural map is a map that relies on a mathematical formula rather than a bitmap image. The XYZ to UVW map aligns a procedural map to the local coordinates of the object to which it is assigned. This has the effect of *sticking* the map to the object so that if the object is stretched nonuniformly, the map will stretch with the object as if the map were a rubber sheet stretched over the object.

Although we've suggested that you use each map type with its corresponding object shape, you can achieve some unusual effects by mixing map types with different surfaces. For example, if you use a planar map on a cylinder, the image is stretched as it is projected toward the edge of the cylinder, as shown in Figure 9.41.

FIGURE 9.41
A sample of planar mapping used on a cylindrical surface

Planar UVW Mapping gizmo Rendering

Just below the Mapping radio buttons in the Parameters rollout are the Length, Width, and Height input boxes. As you might guess, these options let you enter numeric values for the length, width, and height of the UVW Map gizmo. Their spinners also let you graphically adjust the size of the gizmo.

Finally, if you want to modify the tiling of the bitmap image within the area defined by the UVW Map gizmo, you can do so using the U Tile, V Tile, and W Tile input boxes at the bottom of the Parameters rollout.

These options are set by default to 1.0, causing a single image to appear within the area of the UVW Map gizmo. You can produce multiple images within the gizmo area by increasing the values in these input boxes. This offers a quick way of increasing the density of the tiled image without having to enter the Material Editor window. Figure 9.42 shows the same brick wall displayed in Figure 9.31, but this time the U and V Tile settings have been changed to 2.

FIGURE 9.42
The brick wall sample shown with the U and V tile parameters set to 2

You can also increase the tiling within the Coordinates rollout of the bitmap in the Material Editor. Changes made there affect all objects with the material assigned. In contrast, changes made in the Parameters rollout of the UVW Map modifier affect only the selected object.

The Real-World Map Size option is designed to facilitate the implementation of materials where the map relates to a physical scale in the scene. In the Material Editor, when the Use Real-World Scale option in the Coordinates rollout is used, you can specify in scene units how large the map is. For example, a map showing two courses of concrete block may be given the real-world measurement of 16″ × 32″. After assigning the material to an object with the UVW Map modifier applied, use the Real-World Map Size option to scale the gizmo to the map's assigned size.

These mapping coordinate tools give you a high degree of control over the way your material assignments affect your model. As is the case with many 3ds Max tools, your skill in using them will develop over time. As with any craft, practice makes perfect.

THE GENERATE MAPPING COORDINATES OPTION

Many of the 3ds Max objects you encounter will have a Generate Map Coords check box active as one of their default parameters. This offers another method for applying mapping coordinates.

The Generate Mapping Coords option applies a sort of custom mapping coordinate to standard primitives. For example, if you create a Box standard primitive and select Generate Mapping Coords in the box's Parameters rollout, materials mapped to the box will behave as if the Box Mapping option of the UVW Map modifier were applied to the box. A Sphere primitive with the Generate Mapping Coords option selected will behave as if spherical mapping were applied. As an added benefit, the mapping will conform to any changes applied to the shape of the object. If a box's width is increased, the mapping coordinates will automatically follow the width change (although this may actually be undesirable for some types of material, such as brick or tile).

You have less control over the mapping coordinates with the Generate Mapping Coords option, because objects that use it don't have an adjustable UVW Map gizmo. However, you can still control the UVW tiling to adjust the density of the map over the object. You can do this in the Material Editor's Coordinates rollout for the map with which you are working.

In the case of a lofted object, the Generate Mapping Coords option is the only way to apply a material that will conform to a loft's unusual shape. If you apply a UVW Map modifier, the modifier will take control over the mapping coordinates.

Note that imported objects, such as those found in AutoCAD models, don't have a Generate Mapping Coords option. They require a UVW Map modifier whenever bitmap materials are applied.

Using the Standard Material

Much of this chapter has centered around the Architectural material, the default material in 3ds Max Design 2011 if you are using the DesignVIZ initial settings in the Custom UI and Defaults switcher. Each Architectural material can represent one of many real-world materials often found in a residential, office, or retail setting. The Standard material provides many opportunities to create new and exciting materials by setting many different parameters and accessing several different material-specific map channels that can each hold a unique map to help define a material's appearance. The overall appearance of a Standard material is determined by the shader it uses.

Shaders are a set of methods 3ds Max uses to render materials. When you create a new material, one of the main features you need to determine is which shader to use. Walls are usually matte surfaces, so the wall material should use a shader that's best suited to such a surface. Baseboard and trim might have a semigloss paint, in which case you should select a different shader to simulate the shiny surface.

As you work with the Material Editor, you'll notice that you have a set of options under the Shader Basic Parameters rollout. You can think of shaders as different rendering methods applied to objects when they are rendered. Each shader provides a different way that the primary components of a material (the ambient, diffuse, and specular colors, for example) are blended together, as shown in Figure 9.43.

FIGURE 9.43
The basic areas defined by the Ambient, Diffuse, and Specular settings

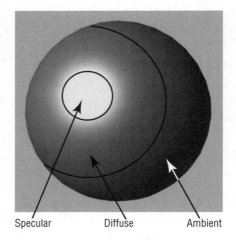

Specular Diffuse Ambient

When the material type is set to Standard, the primary shader options are found in the Shader Basic Parameters drop-down list. This list offers eight shaders: Anisotropic, Blinn, Metal, Multi-Layer, Oren-Nayar-Blinn, Phong, Strauss, and Translucent Shader (see Figure 9.44).

FIGURE 9.44
The eight shaders available in the Standard material

Don't let these strange-sounding names scare you off. They are just different methods that 3ds Max uses to render specular highlights and diffuse and ambient lighting on objects. You choose a shader depending on the type of material to which you are assigning the highlights or lighting. Here's a rundown of the shaders and their specialties:

Anisotropic Measures the difference of shininess from different angles and renders highlights accordingly. The highlight can be oblong rather than round, and you have control over the highlight's shape and orientation. This shader is best used for shiny objects.

Blinn Offers a softer highlight than Phong, particularly for objects with which you want to show highlights from lights bouncing off at low angles.

Metal A shader designed for metallic objects. It is specifically designed to simulate the characteristics of light bouncing off a metallic surface. There is no specular swatch to modify; materials using the Metal shader use the same color for specular highlights that they use as the diffuse color.

Multi-Layer Similar to Anisotropic, but it offers more control, including a second specular highlight. It's especially useful in controlling highlight effects, which makes it highly appropriate for shiny objects.

Oren-Nayar-Blinn Offers a high degree of control over the effects of Diffuse lighting on an object. It's especially useful for matte, soft, or rough objects.

Phong Offers a general shader for smooth, uniform surfaces and can be used as an all-purpose shader.

Strauss Similar to the Metal shader but with fewer, simpler controls.

Translucent Shader Similar to the Blinn shader but with the additional option of translucency. You can use this shader to simulate frosted glass or any situation where a projected light should pass through a material.

When you select one of these shaders from the Shader Basic Parameters drop-down list, the Basic Parameters rollout will change to offer options specifically geared toward that shader. You may want to stick with one or two of these shaders to start out and then experiment with others as you become more familiar with 3ds Max. By offering these shaders, 3ds Max gives you more control over the way objects look and also makes its own rendering faster.

There are four more options in the Shader Basic Parameters rollout that you can add to your material to control its final appearance, as shown in Figure 9.45.

FIGURE 9.45
The Shader Basic
Parameters rollout

The following list explains what these four options do:

Wire Renders an object as a wireframe with the object's edges appearing as lines. You can control the thickness of the wires in the Extended Parameters rollout.

2-Sided Forces a material to render on both sides of each face so that the appearance of a surface is not dependent on its normal.

Face Map Causes the assigned bitmap to appear on each face of an object in a way similar to the Face Map parameter found in the UVW Mapping Modifier's Parameters rollout.

Faceted Discards any smoothing between adjacent faces, which causes objects to be rendered as faceted.

Map Scalar Modifiers

You have seen how you can map materials to objects by generating mapping coordinates (in the case of primitives, this is built in) and by applying the UVW Map modifier. You have also seen how to fine-tune the tiling of a bitmap in the Coordinates rollout in the Material Editor. However, there is another way to approach the issue of mapping materials—using one of the Map Scalar modifiers.

In most cases, map scalars can be used to simplify the issue of mapping. Use the other options if you want greater control, but try Map Scalar first, because it usually works great.

The Map Scalar Object Space modifier (OSM) provides a simplified way to map materials that will scale with the object. The older Map Scalar World-Space Modifier (WSM) is also available for those occasions when you want the map size to be bound to absolute world scale.

1. Open the sample file `Mapping.max` (see Figure 9.46).

 The sample file contains three 5′ cubes that all share the same material. The applied material is using a Checker map in the Diffuse Map slot that is set to tile once in each texture direction, U and V. The pattern that is mapped consists of four squares, alternating white and black, that make a larger square, as shown in Figure 9.47.

FIGURE 9.46
Mapping sample cubes

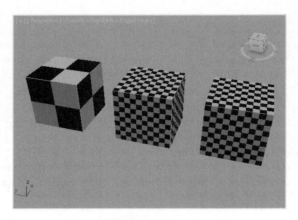

FIGURE 9.47
The mapped pattern

2. Select the first cube on the left and switch to the Modify panel. Note that the modifier stack shows that this Box object has a UVW Map modifier applied with the Box mapping type selected.

3. The pattern shown in Figure 9.47 appears on each of the six faces of the cube because Box mapping was selected in the UVW Map modifier. In the Parameters rollout, change the V Tile parameter to 3. The checker pattern now repeats three times in one direction on each face of the cube.

4. Select the middle cube. Observe how its modifier stack shows a Box object with the Map Scalar Binding (WSM) modifier applied. In this case, WSM stands for World-Space Modifier, meaning that the effects of the map scalar are bound to the absolute size of the home grid. Both Map Scalar modifiers apply box mapping automatically, so you see the pattern tiling on each of the six faces of the cubes.

5. Change the Scale parameter of the Map Scalar Binding (WSM) to 2´6˝.

 Observe how the pattern from Figure 9.47 is tiled exactly twice on each surface of the middle cube, as shown in Figure 9.48. This occurs because the cube's edges measure 5´ and the pattern is bound to precisely half that size in World Space of 2´6˝.

 Use one of the Map Scalar modifiers when you want to bind your mapping to a specific size.

6. Select the cube on the right. Observe how its stack shows a box with the Map Scalar (OSM) modifier applied. OSM is an object-space modifier, meaning its scale is based on the object's transform scale.

FIGURE 9.48
Map Scalar tiles
the map to a spe-
cific size.

7. Change the Scale parameter of the Map Scalar OSM to 2′6″. The pattern tiles twice, just as the WSM version did earlier.

8. Select all three cubes and scale them down to 50 percent of their current size.

Figure 9.49 shows the result. The left cube's pattern gets smaller with the object, but it maintains the same nonuniform tiling. The middle cube's pattern remains the same size as the object gets smaller because its Map Scalar is bound to World Space. The right cube's pattern gets smaller as the object is scaled because its Map Scalar works in Object Space and is subject to the same transforms as the object itself.

FIGURE 9.49
Scaling the objects
reveals the dif-
ference between
WSM and OSM
modifiers.

UVW Mapping maintains non-uniform tiling when it is scaled.

Map Scalar (OSM)'s pattern scales with the object.

Map Scalar (WSM) maintains the size of the pattern when it is scaled.

Spline Mapping

CERT OBJECTIVE

The Spline Mapping tool is used for applying UVW mapping coordinates to irregularly shaped spline-like objects—such as piping or wiring and flat surfaces that have curvature, like paths or architectural archways.

In the next exercise, you will use the Spline Mapping tool to apply a brick paving material to a walkway around the Notre Dame du Haut Ronchamp Chapel you built in Chapters 4 and 7.

1. Open the SplineMapping.max file that you downloaded from the book's website.

2. Activate the Top viewport, if it isn't already active.

3. Press F3 to change the viewport to Wireframe display mode.

4. Hold down the Ctrl key, and click the Path object and the PathSpline.

5. Press Alt+Q to isolate the two objects you have selected. You can move the Warning: Isolate Selection floater out of the way so you can work more easily.

6. In Isolation mode, press F3 again so you can see the texture. Notice that the brick texture is not following the contours of the path, as shown in Figure 9.50.

To make it easier to understand what is happening, you'll switch the brick to a checker pattern while applying the spline mapping.

7. On the Rendering menu, choose Material Editor ➤ Compact Material Editor.

8. In the Material Editor, choose the Checker Test material; it's the second material from the left on the top row. Don't worry if you don't see the checker on the sample sphere.

9. In the viewport, select only the Path object, and then apply the checker test to the Path object. Press F9 to render. Because there are no UVW coordinates, the checker doesn't show up, as shown in Figure 9.51.

10. On the Modify panel, add an Unwrap UVW modifier to the Path object. Expand the Unwrap UVW modifier, and choose the Face level.

FIGURE 9.50
The brick texture not flowing with the curved pathway

FIGURE 9.51
The Checker Test material not flowing with the curved pathway

11. Press Ctrl+A to select all the faces in the path, as shown in Figure 9.52.

FIGURE 9.52
Select all the faces of the Path object in the Unwrap UWV modifier.

12. In the Map Parameters rollout, choose Spline.

13. In the Spline Map Parameters floater, choose Pick Spline, and then select the Path Spline object, which is sticking out of the end of the Path object. Change the Mapping type to Planar in the Spline group, as shown in Figure 9.53.

FIGURE 9.53
Set the Spline Map Parameters option.

The checker pattern on the spline should dramatically change.

14. Press F2 to toggle the red selected faces display off. Also in the stack, click Unwrap UVW to move out of sub-object level (Figure 9.54).

FIGURE 9.54
The Checker Test material spline mapped on the Path object

15. Navigate to the Coordinates rollout of the checker texture. Turn off Real-World Scale, and adjust the U and V tiling while observing the effect. Changing the V tiling to 12 clearly shows the checker following the path contours now, as in Figure 9.55.

16. To exchange the checker pattern with a bitmap, click the Material Type button to open the Material/Map Browser, and then double-click Bitmap. In the Select Bitmap Image dialog box, navigate to `C:\Program Files\Autodesk\3ds Max Design 2011\maps\ArchMat`, and choose `Masonry.Unit Masonry.Brick.Modular.Herringbone.jpg`. Turn off Real-World Scaling again; RWS is automatically activated when you apply a bitmap.

17. Turn on Show Standard Map in Viewport.

18. Adjust the U and V tiling to your taste. Zoom in if necessary so you can see a better view of the mapping, as shown in Figure 9.56.

19. Save your file as `MySplineMapping_Completed.max`. Click the Exit Isolation button, change the view to Perspective view, or add a camera to the scene and render it to see the results.

As you have seen in the previous exercise, the Spline Mapping feature of the Unwrap UWV map modifier makes mapping paved paths, striped roadways, or other splinelike objects easier to map.

FIGURE 9.55
The result of adjusting the V tiling on the Checker Test material

FIGURE 9.56
Adjust the U and V parameters of the brick material.

Adding Entourage

Entourage is a term taken from traditional architectural rendering. It refers to photographic "extras" that are added to a rendering to make it appear more realistic. You can think of entourage as cutouts or props that are added to the scene to make it more lifelike and help define the scale of the scene. Examples of entourage are people, trees and plants, cars, street furniture, and signs. Entourage is not composed necessarily of 3D models, however. As 2D photographic elements, they can be handled mainly through materials.

The key to designing an entourage material is to use an Opacity map to hide unwanted portions of the surface to which the texture is mapped. Generally, entourage materials are applied to Plane or Box primitives that act like flat billboards, displaying their contents for the world to see. Once you apply an opacity-mapped material to an object, it is also important to adjust the object to fit the bitmap's aspect ratio or undesirable stretching will occur.

The AEC Foliage objects, covered in Chapter 6, "Creating AEC Objects," also create entourage objects with varying degrees of complexity.

Hiding Unwanted Surfaces with Opacity Maps

An opacity map is a grayscale bitmap image that tells 3ds Max which part of the surface is opaque and which part is transparent. The black portions of an opacity map become completely transparent, whereas white is completely opaque. Shades of gray create varying degrees of opacity.

To see how this works, look at Figure 9.57. To the left you see an opacity map. The middle figure shows a simple box in 3ds Max without a material assigned to it. The figure to the far right shows the same box that is assigned a material using the opacity map (or a cutout map) at the left. Notice that the portions of the opacity map that are black appear invisible in the box.

FIGURE 9.57
An opacity (cutout) map and an object to which it is assigned

Opacity map Object Object with Opacity
 map material applied

You can also use shades of gray to simulate a semitransparent material or to gradually change the transparency of a surface. Color images can be used for opacity maps as well, although the color information is not used—only the pixel grayscale value is considered.

Now that you understand what opacity maps are, let's design a tree material you can apply to plane objects to use as entourage. While doing this, you'll also have a chance to explore the workflow for using the new Slate Material Editor.

1. Reset 3ds Max. To open the Slate Material Editor, go to the Rendering menu and choose Material Editor ➤ Slate Material Editor. Alternatively, on the Main Toolbar there's a flyout

that lets you choose between Compact and Slate Material Editors if you'd rather use an icon.

2. Right-click in the View1 window of the Slate Material Editor, and choose Materials ➢ metal ray ➢ Arch & Design, as shown in Figure 9.58.

3. Right-click the top bar of the material, as shown in Figure 9.59, and rename this material **Magnolia**. Then click OK.

FIGURE 9.58
Creating a new
Arch & Design
material in the
Slate Material
Editor

FIGURE 9.59
Rename the new
material Magnolia.

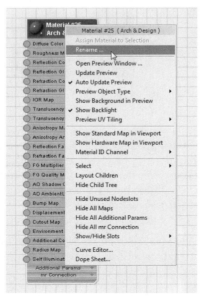

4. Right-click in an empty area of the View1 window of the Slate Material Editor, and choose Maps ➢ Standard ➢ Bitmap, as shown in Figure 9.60, to open the Select Bitmap Image dialog box.

5. In the Select Bitmap Image File dialog box that opens, navigate to and select the `magnoliaIM.jpg` file that you downloaded from the book's website as your diffuse color image, and click Open.

6. Click and drag from the gray circle on the edge of the Bitmap node, called the Output Socket, in the View1 window to the gray circle next to Diffuse Color Map, called an Input Socket, on the Magnolia material, as shown in Figure 9.61.

FIGURE 9.60
Create a new Bitmap node.

FIGURE 9.61
Connect the Bitmap node to the Diffuse Color Map channel.

You have just wired the `MagnoliaIM.jpg` bitmap to the Diffuse Color Map channel of the entourage material.

7. Double-click the Bitmap node to display its properties in the Parameter Editor section of the Slate Material Editor.

8. Deselect the Use Real-World Scale option in the Coordinates rollout, change both the U and V Tiling values to 1, and deselect the U and V Tile boxes.

9. Dial the Blur value down to as low as it will go, 0.01. This will make the texture look as sharp and detailed as possible in your renderings.

10. Change the Preview Object Type to a box by right-clicking the Magnolia material node and choose Preview Object Type ➢ Box, as shown in Figure 9.62.

FIGURE 9.62
Changing the material Preview Object Type

11. Right-click the material node, and click Open Preview Window to see a larger version of a material sample. This opens a small dialog box, which is similar to the Magnify window of the Compact Material Editor, which can be resized and which updates with any parameter changes made to the material, as shown in Figure 9.63.

What is new about the Slate Material Editor Preview Window is that you have one preview window that can show the currently selected material/map, a specific material in the Active View Window, or any maps in the active view using the drop-down at the bottom of the dialog box, as opposed to the Magnify window of the Compact Material Editor, which displays only the material you selected.

12. Right-click in the Active View Window, choose Maps ➢ Standard ➢ Bitmap to open the Select Bitmap Image dialog box, and select the magnoliaOP.jpg file, as shown in Figure 9.64. You see the sample image of the magnoliaOP.jpg file in the lower-right corner of the dialog box.

This file is similar to the `magnoliaIM.jpg` file, but it has been reduced to black and white and shows only the silhouette of the tree. The tree is white, and everything else is black. You can also use the alpha channel of some image formats to store the grayscale opacity data.

13. Click Open, and the new bitmap node is added to the Active View Window.

14. Click and drag from the gray circle on the new Bitmap node's output socket, and wire it to the input socket next to Cutout Map, as shown in Figure 9.65.

FIGURE 9.65
Wire the cutout map.

15. Double-click the Bitmap node wired to the cutout map to open it in the Parameter Editor section of the Slate Material Editor.

16. Go to the Coordinates rollout, deselect Use Real-World Scale, set the U and V tiling to 1, and deselect the Tile boxes for U and V. Notice what happens to the preview window. Now you see the tree without the black background. The change in the sample can sometimes be subtle.

17. Right-click the Magnolia material node, and select Show Background. This will make the cutout material easier to see in the preview window.

18. On the Slate Material Editor toolbar, click the Hide Unused Nodeslots icon, as shown in Figure 9.66. This will reduce the size of the material tree in the Active View Window (see Figure 9.67).

FIGURE 9.66
Hide the unused nodeslots.

FIGURE 9.67
The finished Magnolia entourage node tree

Now let's add geometry for the tree to the empty scene. First, you'll need to create an object to which to apply the Magnolia material. This will essentially be a simple, flat, vertical plane.

1. Minimize the Material Editor to get a clear view of your viewports.

2. Click the Maximize Viewport Toggle to display all four viewports.

3. Click the Create tab in the Command panel; then click the Geometry button if it isn't already highlighted.

4. Click Plane, and then, in the Perspective viewport, create the plane. Use the Length and Width parameter options to set the length to 24′ and the width to 24′.

5. Give the plane the name **Tree001**. You can also use Box primitives (with 0 depth) for entourage elements, but be aware that boxes are visible from both sides and that can have an unwanted impact on your entourage material. Keep the Tree001 object selected.

Don't worry about the placement of the Tree001 object for now. You will first apply the material that you designed earlier to the plane, and then you will rotate the plane into a vertical position.

1. Restore the Slate Material Editor.

2. With the Magnolia material selected, click the Assign Material to Selection button. The Magnolia material is now assigned to the plane you just created. If you don't have the Magnolia node selected, the Assign Material to Selection button will be grayed out.

3. Click the Show Standard Map in Viewport button on the Slate Material Editor toolbar.

4. Deselect the Real-World Map Size option in the plane's Parameters rollout. It's important to do this, or you won't see your bitmap correctly.

5. Use the Select and Rotate tool to rotate the plane so that it is vertical. You may want to turn on the Angle Snap Toggle so it is easier to make the tree perpendicular to the XY-plane.

6. Zoom and pan in the Perspective viewport until the tree fills the view, and then click the Render Production button. The model is rendered with the tree entourage map, as shown in Figure 9.68.

The scene still looks quite bare, but you can easily make several copies of the tree and add some environment to give the impression that the scene is filled with a grove of trees, with very little impact to your scene's size or rendering time.

FIGURE 9.68
The rendered plane with the tree material added

You've just created a material that, when applied to an object, will appear as a tree. Now let's look at a few of the tools that can help you work with and understand all types of materials.

Click the Material/Map Browser button on the Slate Material Editor's top toolbar. This toggles the display of the Material/Map Browser on the left side of the Slate Material Editor. Click the Material/Map Browser button again to open the Material/Map Browser, as shown in Figure 9.69.

FIGURE 9.69
The Material/ Map Browser in the Slate Material Editor

1. On the Slate Material Editor, click the Modes menu, and select Compact Material Editor.

2. Select an unused material sample slot, pick the Pick Material from Object eyedropper, and click the Tree001 object to access the Magnolia material. The materials in the Slate Material Editor are not automatically displayed in the Compact Material Editor.

3. On the Compact Material Editor, click the Material/Map Navigator button. This opens the Material/Map Navigator dialog box shown in Figure 9.70.

 This dialog box gives you a clear picture of the way your material is organized. You see the name at the top with two branches under it. Each branch is a child map that you've added to your material.

FIGURE 9.70
The Material/ Map Navigator

4. Click the Diffuse Color Map listing in the Material/Map Navigator. The parameters in the Material Editor change to those of the selected map.

5. Click the View List + Icons button in the Material/Map Navigator.

 Now you see the actual images used for the maps, plus the resulting material at the top of the list, as shown in Figure 9.71. The arrangement of images shows you the material hierarchy. You can click and drag the edges of the Material/Map Navigator to resize it.

6. Click the Go Forward to Sibling button in the Material Editor. This moves you to the next material or map at the same level in the material hierarchy.

FIGURE 9.71
The Material/Map Navigator showing samples of the maps used

UNDERSTANDING THE MATERIAL STRUCTURE

The family analogy of parent/child/sibling helps you to visualize the material hierarchy.

The parameters in the Compact Material Editor dialog box change to the Cutout Map parameters, and the Cutout Map listing in the Material/Map Navigator is highlighted. The Go Forward to Sibling button lets you advance through the different child levels.

1. Click the Show End Result toggle on the Material Editor toolbar to turn it off.

 The Cutout map appears in the sample slot for the Magnolia material, as shown in Figure 9.72. This tool lets you see the result of any change you make to the child parameters.

2. Close the Material/Map Navigator, and click the Go to Parent button on the Compact Material Editor toolbar to move to the main parameter level.

FIGURE 9.72
The result of turning off the Show End Result toggle

RAY-TRACED SHADOWS RESPECT A MATERIAL'S OPACITY

Objects with opacity maps, such as the tree you just created, will cast a shadow that matches the opacity map when you use ray-traced shadows. If you use a shadow-mapped shadow, objects with opacity maps will cast a shadow in the shape of the object to which the material is mapped. In the case of the trees, using shadow maps would give you a rectangular shadow instead of a shadow in the shape of the tree. Therefore, ray-traced shadows are preferable for entourage.

The method we've shown you here for creating and adding opacity-mapped trees also works for adding people to you scenes. You can also use this method to quickly add text or signage to a model for which the proper fonts are not available in Windows. Adobe Photoshop or another similar program can aid you in creating the texture and opacity maps for people. If you don't want to create your own, you can use one of the many third-party sources for texture maps and models. Here is a short list of companies that provide texture maps and models for 3ds Max:

Marlin Studios www.marlinstudios.com

ScottOnstott.com www.scottonstott.com

TurboSquid www.turbosquid.com

In addition to texture maps, some of these companies offer prebuilt 3D objects such as furniture, cars, appliances, cabinetry, and animals. If you are in a hurry to build scenes quickly, check out the library of objects offered by these and other companies.

3D AND 2D FOLIAGE HAVE THEIR PLACES

Be aware that 3D foliage can consume large amounts of memory and dramatically increase render times because each leaf is modeled as geometry. Opacity-mapped entourage is much more efficient but remains flat. In animations where the camera is moving, 3D foliage can be more convincing, or you can use multiple 2D trees created in star-shaped patterns to add some depth to the simple entourage.

Adjusting an Object to a Bitmap Shape

Sometimes you may find it necessary to match the object's shape to a bitmap's shape. For example, you may create a material that uses bitmap images of people standing. To avoid distorting the shape of the people, you would want to match the object as closely as possible to the aspect ratio of the bitmap image (see Figure 9.73).

FIGURE 9.73
Two renderings with people used as bitmaps. The image to the left has distorted the people.

To do this, choose the Bitmap Fit alignment option under the Parameters rollout of the UVW Map modifier, as shown in Figure 9.74.

FIGURE 9.74
Use the Bitmap Fit option to adjust the aspect ratio of the image.

Locate the bitmap file associated with the material that uses the bitmap. Once the file has been selected, return to the 3ds Max scene, and the Map gizmo will be adjusted to fit the aspect ratio of the selected bitmap.

Once you have the new Map gizmo, you can adjust your object to fit as closely as possible to the Map gizmo proportions. You may not be able to get an absolutely accurate match, but you can get close. Then, once you've gotten the object to the right proportions, use the UVW Map option described earlier in this chapter to align the map exactly to the object.

In the beginning of this chapter, you worked with the condo scene. Let's go back and explore the option of placing more than one material on an object.

Assigning Materials to Parts of an Object

As you work with imported AutoCAD files or complex models in 3ds Max, you'll almost certainly find yourself faced with the situation where you want to add a material to only a single surface, or group of polygons, of an object. This is the situation with the front kitchen cabinet doors in the condo scene where you could enter the sub-object level of those objects and then detach them into separate objects for the purpose of assigning materials

To maintain the connection of the cabinet door surfaces with the rest of the cabinet structure and to add a separate material to their surfaces, you'll need to use another method of applying materials. In this section, we'll discuss a type of material called a *Multi/Sub-Object material*, which allows you to apply multiple materials to a single object. In the condo example, you can use a multi/sub-object material to apply the wood material to the front, sides, and mullions of the cabinet and a glass material to the panes.

Creating a Multi/Sub-Object Material

A multi/sub-object material is like a group of materials collected under one material definition. Each material in this group is assigned a number to identify it within the collection of materials. It's easiest to understand when you've worked with it firsthand, so let's get started:

1. Open the last condo scene that you worked on or ch09c.max from this book's accompanying web page.

2. Click the Material Editor button on the Main Toolbar to open the Compact Material Editor.

3. Click the slot containing the Woods & Plastics.Finish Carpentry.Wood.Teak material and then drag it to another, unused slot to copy the material.

4. With the new material active in the Material Editor, click the Material Type button, currently labeled Architectural, to open the Material/Map Browser.

5. Expand the Materials group and then the Standard group, select the Multi/Sub-Object material, then click OK. In the Replace Material dialog box that opens, choose Keep Old Material as Sub-Material, and then click OK. This option retains the `Woods & Plastics` `.Finish Carpentry.Wood.Teak` material as a sub-material of the current material.

The new material's parameters now appear in the Material Editor. This is the material you assigned to the cabinets and drawers of the condo earlier in the book as a sub-material of the new multi/sub-material. There are nine additional, undefined sub-material slots available in this material.

The next step is to define the rest of the sub-material slots and then assign the material to the cabinet doors:

1. Enter the name `Cabinet_Wood_Glass_Multi` in the Material Name input box. This assigns a new name to the material in the active slot.

 As you can see from the Material Editor, the Multi/Sub-Object Material offers several listings for additional materials. Each material is a sub-material of the main, parent material. In this exercise, you need only six sub-materials, so go ahead and reduce the number of available listings to six:

2. Click the Set Number button in the Multi/Sub-Object Basic Parameters rollout.

3. In the Set Number Of Materials dialog box, enter **6**, and then click OK. Your Material Editor should look like Figure 9.75.

FIGURE 9.75
The Cabinet_
Wood_Glass_Multi
material in the
Compact Material
Editor

Notice how, at the top level of the Multi/Sub-Object Material, the object in the sample slot has the sub-materials applied to different portions of its surface. Now let's copy the current sub-material to additional slots and add the material that will become the glass panes:

1. Click the material button that's in the number 1 position in the Multi/Sub-Object Basic Parameters rollout, and drag it to the Sub-Material buttons for sub-material numbers 2, 3, 4, and 6 to copy the sub-material to those slots.

2. Each time the Instance (Copy) Material dialog box opens, choose the Instance option, and then click OK.

3. Click the Sub-Material button for sub-material number 5. The Material Editor window changes to show the parameters for the material. It may be difficult to tell that you're working with a multi/sub-object material from the looks of the window, but one clue is the Go to Parent button that's not grayed out in the toolbar.

 You'll use a glass material for the glass panes, so you'll want to open the appropriate material from the editor.

4. Change the material type to an Architectural material if it isn't already and expand the drop-down list in the Templates rollout, and then choose Glass-Clear.

VIEWING TRANSPARENT MATERIALS IN THE MATERIAL EDITOR

Glass is never completely transparent. It must have some opacity, or you wouldn't be able to see it. You can use the Background button, the checkerboard button in the Material Editor's vertical toolbar, to change the current sample slot's background color from black to a multicolor checker pattern. This helps discern the actual transparency of non-opaque objects.

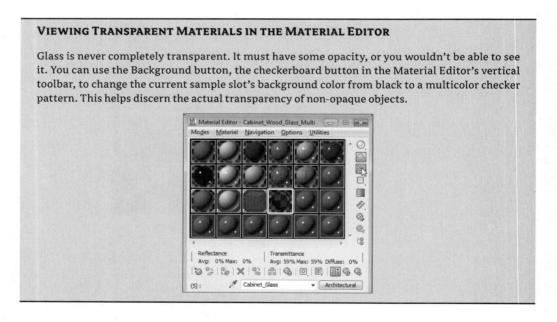

5. Click the Background button in the Material editor's vertical toolbar to better see the new glass material.

6. Rename the sub-material **Cabinet_Glass** then click the Go to Parent button on the toolbar.

Applying a Sub-material to an Object's Surface

The cabinet doors of the condo, named Fixed Wind*x*, were created as AEC Fixed Window objects in 3ds Max and then converted to Editable Meshes. Most AEC objects are created with different material ID numbers assigned to different parts of the object. In the case of Window objects, material ID number 1 is assigned to the front rail surfaces; number 2 to the back rail surfaces; number 3 to the glazing; and numbers 4 and 5 to the front and back frame surfaces, respectively. The cabinet objects have been edited to have material ID numbers 1 through 4 assigned to the frames and railings and number 5 to the glass panes. To apply a sub-material to the polygons of an editable mesh, you'll need to identify the Material ID numbers of the polygons to which the sub-materials are to be applied, as shown in these steps:

1. Select one of the cabinet doors, and then click the Modify tab on the Command panel.

2. Expand Editable Mesh in the stack, and then click the Polygon sub-object level.

3. Scroll down the Modify tab to the Surface Properties rollout.

4. In the Material group, change the Select ID value to 2, and then press ↲, as shown in Figure 9.76. Alternatively, you can use the drop-down box to pick from the material IDs assigned to the selected object.

The front surfaces of the cabinet door turn red (see Figure 9.77) to show that they are selected. Remember that the Woods & Plastics.Finish Carpentry.Wood.Teak sub-material is the number 2 material in the Multi/Sub-Object Basic Parameters rollout. The selected surfaces are assigned the material ID number 2 and, therefore, receive the multi/sub-object material number 2. If you were to change the material ID number of the selected surfaces, they would receive the sub-material assigned to that number.

5. Cycle the Select ID value through the numbers 1–6 to see which surfaces bear which material ID numbers. You'll notice that no surfaces currently are assigned to material ID number 6.

FIGURE 9.76
The front perimeter surfaces are selected when material ID number 2 is selected.

FIGURE 9.77
The selected front panels of the cabinet doors

These polygons are selected, as are the ones tucked under the overhang

ASSIGNING A SUB-MATERIAL WITH A MODIFIER

An alternative method for assigning a sub-material to an object is to use the Material modifier. This modifier offers a single parameter—the Material ID number.

The material is ready, so next you need to assign it to the cabinet door objects:

1. Scroll up to the top of the Command panel; then click the yellow Polygon level to return to the Object level. Alternatively, you can right-click and choose Top-level from the tools 1 quad menu.

2. Select all six cabinet doors.

3. Open the Material Editor, if necessary, and then drag the Cabinet_Wood_Glass_Multi sample slot onto one of the selected doors.

4. In the Assign Material dialog box that opens, choose Assign to Selection, and then click OK. This option assigns the selected material to all selected objects and not just to the object to which it was dragged.

5. Make sure the CamWall viewport is active, and click the Render Production button in the Main Toolbar. The scene renders, with the new Cabinet_Wood_Glass_Multi material assigned to each of the doors, as shown in Figure 9.78.

6. Save your work as **My_chap09c.max**.

FIGURE 9.78
The rendered scene with the new multi/sub-object material assigned to the cabinet doors

USING MULTIPLE UVW MAPS ON A SINGLE OBJECT

If you're able to apply multiple materials to a single object, you may be wondering whether you can apply multiple UVW maps to an object as well. After all, different surfaces may require different UVW Mapping settings. You can indeed apply multiple UVW Map modifiers to a single object. You can then correlate the different UVW Map modifiers to individual sub-materials through *map channels*. You can think of a map channel as a number that links a sub-material to a UVW Map modifier. The concept is simple, but the execution is a bit obscure. Here are the steps that you take to link a sub-material to a UVW map. (These steps aren't part of the main exercise of this book; they are provided only to explain the process for linking multiple UVW maps to multiple material maps.)

1. Open the `Multi_UVW.max` file from the book's website.

2. Open the Material Editor, and then select the multi/sub-object material on which you want to work. In this case, select the Patio_Wood_Bench material.

3. Click the Hardwood Flooring American Cherry material.

4. Click the `american_cherry.png` map, and change the Map Channel to **2**.

5. Select the Patio_Benches object, and add another UVW Map modifier.

6. Change the Mapping setting to Box, and set Map Channel to **2**.

7. Render the scene and see how the cherry paneling is now box mapped on the seating areas of the benches.

8. Save your scene as `My_Multi_UVW.max`.

Exploring the Autodesk Materials

So far you've seen convincing surfaces in your renderings using the Architectural materials. This is because the materials you have made account for light reflecting off surfaces or passing through translucent surfaces (refraction). New to 3ds Max Design 2011 is the inclusion of the Autodesk Materials, a set of approximately 1,200 materials shared with all Autodesk 2011 products that incorporate the mental ray rendering engine. The Autodesk Materials are high-quality 3ds Max materials designed for use with the mental ray renderer and are based on both manufacturer-supplied data and professional high-quality images. To accurately simulate phenomena such as reflectivity and refraction, using a technique called *ray tracing* you will use these materials in your current condo scene. You cannot see ray-traced effects in the viewports—they must be rendered.

USING RAY TRACING AT THE MAP LEVEL ONLY

Alternatively, you can use the Raytrace Standard material instead of a mental ray material if you are using the Default Scanline Renderer.

In the current condo model, there are no objects that would normally be manufactured from a reflective or refractive material. We'll start by building a couple of quick models on the countertop.

1. Continue with the previous exercise, or open the ch09d.max file from this book's companion web page.

2. Maximize the CamWall viewport if necessary; then right-click the POV viewport label and choose Perspective to change the viewport to a perspective view.

3. Zoom in until you can see about half of the front countertop.

4. Choose Create ➤ Geometry, select Standard Primitives or Extended Primitives, and then click one of the primitive object buttons.

5. Click the AutoGrid option and then create an object on the countertop.

6. Repeat steps 4 and 5 and create another object on the countertop. Figure 9.79 shows a teapot and a spindle on the countertop.

FIGURE 9.79
The viewport after creating two primitive objects

7. Open the Material Editor and then click in an unused sample slot.

8. Click the Get Material button. In the Material/Map Browser that opens, expand the Autodesk Material Library group.

9. Scroll down in the Autodesk Material Library group, and open the Metal group.

10. In the Metal group, scroll down and double-click the Copper - Polished material to copy it to the Material Editor; then drag it from the sample slot to one of the primitives that you created.

11. Repeat steps 8 through 10, but choose the Clear material from the Glazing group of the Autodesk Material Library, and drag it to the other object you created.

12. Add the Gray Speckled material, from the Stone ➤ Granite group of the Autodesk Material Library, and drag it to the countertop.

13. Render your scene, and it should look similar to Figure 9.80. This rendering may take some time to complete.

FIGURE 9.80
The rendered scene after adding the Autodesk Materials to the new objects

Adjust the Autodesk Material Parameters

The cabinets, doors, and even the teapot (in this example) look good, but the glass and granite materials need some work. To improve the appearance of these materials, you should follow these steps:

1. In the Material Editor, select the Stone Granite Gray Speckled material slot, and then click the Map button next to Image in the Stone group. This takes you one level lower in the material to the Autodesk Bitmap options.

2. In the Scale group, make the width and height both 1'0".

3. Click the Show Standard Map in Viewport button, in the Material Editor's horizontal toolbar, so that you can see the tiling of the map in the viewport.

4. Click the Go to Parent button to return to the top level of the material.

5. Add a UVW Map modifier to the countertop, set the mapping type to Box, and leave the Real-World Map Size option selected.

6. In the Material Editor, select the Glass Clear material; then in the Solid Glass Materials Parameters rollout, click the Custom Color swatch.

7. Set the colors to a mild blue by setting the RGB values to 0.4, 0.4, 0.8, and then click OK to close the Custom Color dialog box.

8. Scroll back to the top of the Stone Granite Gray Speckled Material Parameters section and change the finish to Matte. Then click the Image button again, set Brightness to 25, and click the Go to Parent button to get to the top of the material.

9. Render your scene and, with the improved materials, it should look similar to Figure 9.81. The shiny copper material reflects the countertop, the spindle, and the rest of the scene while the spindle refracts the light passing through it, distorting the geometry behind it.

10. Save your file as **My_ch09d.max**.

In the next section, you'll take a look at some of the utilities available for working with material and maps in 3ds Max.

FIGURE 9.81
The rendered scene after adjusting the Autodesk Materials

Using the Material Explorer

When you start working on scenes with numerous objects and materials, keeping track of which materials are applied to which objects can become quite a headache. This is where the Material Explorer can be helpful by allowing you to organize all the materials currently applied to objects in your scene. The Material Explorer can be launched by choosing Rendering ➤ Material Explorer. The Material Explorer consists of two main windows, as shown in Figure 9.82.

FIGURE 9.82
The Material Explorer opened in the last condo scene

The upper Scene panel displays all the materials in the scene in a tabular fashion. You can navigate through all the materials in the scene, see the material's type, see whether the material is set to display in the Viewport, and see the material's ID. You can also click any of the column

headings to sort the list of materials by that column and also display the list by the materials or by the objects. The lower Material panel displays properties of a single selected material.

You can drag materials from the Material Explorer onto objects in the viewports the same way you can from the Material Editor. You can also use the Material Explorer to rename materials and maps and change some of the materials properties.

You still need to apply the Stone Granite Gray Speckled material you applied to the Modern Kit object to the Modern Counter object in the back corner of the kitchen, which you will do in the following exercise:

1. In the Scene panel, find the Stone Granite Gray Speckled material, and click the plus sign in front of the material sample to expand it, as shown in Figure 9.83.

FIGURE 9.83
The Material Explorer with the Stone Granite Gray Speckled material selected

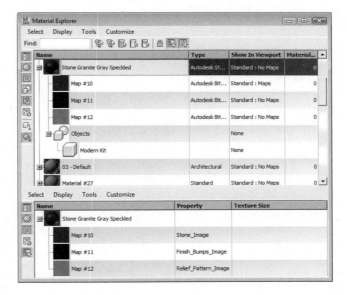

In the Scene panel, you can see that three maps are applied to the material, that one of them is set to display in the viewport, and that the material is applied to the Modern Kit object. The Material panel details the name of the map in the material and the property of the material that the map is applied to, and it is supposed to display the resolution of the bitmap texture.

From Figure 9.83, you can tell that the map for which you adjusted the output value is darker than the other map sample.

2. Select the Map #12 sample, and then click in the Show in Viewport column, which provides a drop-down. Choose the Standard: Maps option. This allows you to see the map on the front counter in the Perspective viewport.

3. Move the Material Explorer window so you can see it and the back countertop in the Perspective viewport.

4. Click the Stone Granite Gray Speckled material, and drag it onto the back counter.

 In the Scene panel, you will see the Modern Counter object listed with the Modern Kit object under the material. The material has been applied to the object in the viewport.

5. In the Material panel, select the Map #10 that is applied to the Stone image property of the Stone Granite Gray Speckled material.

6. Now click Map #10; you can rename this map by adding *Diffuse* at the end of the name. If you go back to the Granite Gray Speckled material in the Material Editor and click the Image button, you will see that the name of that map has been updated. This functionality is a great way to update material/map names so that they are more descriptive and easier to find in your scenes.

The Material Utilities

Utilities are like separate programs that run inside 3ds Max, and there are many utilities that help with materials. Each of the utilities was designed to do a specific job, and they extend the functionality of 3ds Max. Here is how you can access the relevant utilities that help when you are designing, editing, and managing materials:

1. Click the Utilities tab of the Command panel.

 A list of utilities is shown as buttons in the Utilities rollout. You can run each of these utility programs by clicking the appropriate button. There are many more utilities that are not shown as buttons by default.

2. Click the More button in the Utilities rollout. The Utilities dialog box (see Figure 9.84) appears, showing any utilities that are not already shown as buttons in the Command panel.

FIGURE 9.84
The Utilities
dialog box

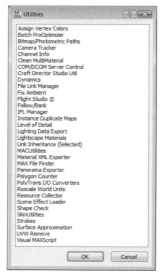

Each of the utilities was designed to do a specific job and to extend the functionality of 3ds Max. The relevant utilities that help when you are designing, editing, and managing materials are as follows:

Bitmap/Photometric Paths Use this utility, shown in Figure 9.85, to change the hard-coded paths that are referenced by your bitmaps. Often incredibly helpful when you open a 3ds Max file made by a person in a different organization or department, this utility lets you repath all the missing bitmaps in one interface. This can be a timesaver when compared to searching each material in the scene for its missing bitmaps.

FIGURE 9.85

The Bitmap/ Photometric Path Editor

Clean MultiMaterial This utility fixes a common problem ("extra" sub-materials that aren't referenced anywhere in the scene) with the multi/sub-object material. Use the utility to remove unused sub-materials without affecting material IDs or sub-materials that are in use.

Color Clipboard Use the Color Clipboard to hold color information in four convenient swatches. Drag a color swatch from anywhere in the Material Editor onto any one of the four swatches in the Color Clipboard rollout, and the color will be stored there during your session.

You can also click the New Floater button to open a separate floating dialog box that has additional color swatches. Click one of the Save buttons to store your 12 favorite colors in a CCB file for later reuse.

Fix Ambient Use this simple program to change any materials that have different colors in the Ambient and Diffuse color channels. The utility copies the settings for the diffuse color to the ambient color for all materials that you select.

Instance Duplicate Maps Figure 9.86 shows the Instance Duplicate Maps dialog box. Use this utility in your projects when you want to convert into instanced maps multiple loaded copies of an identical image used as maps in various materials. This is more efficient than loading each occurrence of the map separately and may save some memory, in addition to giving you more coordinated control over the shared parameters in the instanced maps.

Lightscape Materials Use this utility only if you are importing radiosity solutions from legacy Autodesk Lightscape into 3ds Max. Lightscape is a classic program that brought radiosity rendering to the masses and is still in use in some quarters.

FIGURE 9.86
The Instance
Duplicate Maps
utility

Material XML Exporter The Material XML utility can be used to export the materials in your scene to an XML file that can be used in Autodesk Architectural Desktop 2004 and newer.

You can drag and drop these XML files from a web page into 3ds Max or AutoCAD Architecture. Use this as an alternative to material libraries within 3ds Max and as a new way to communicate with Architectural Desktop (ADT) users.

Resource Collector Use the Resource Collector to copy and optionally compress all your scene's bitmaps (and photometric files) into a single folder. This makes it much easier to send scenes to other organizations because all the associated bitmaps and other support files will be included. The Compress Files option saves all the files into a single, compressed ZIP file.

UVW Remove The UVW Remove utility deletes the UVW mapping information, the assigned material, or both from the selected objects. The Set Gray option changes the objects' color to a neutral gray.

AUTOCAD'S SIMILAR TOOL

The Resource Collector is very similar to AutoCAD's Pack 'n Go or eTransmit tools, depending on which version of the software you are using.

Modeling with Displacement Maps

You've seen how you can use a bump map to simulate a textured surface such as the cabinets in the previous exercises. Another map option, called a *displacement map*, performs a function similar to that of bump maps, but instead of applying a texture, it actually deforms geometry into new shapes. The effect is akin to a vacuum mold in which a flat surface is stretched over a form to create an object. In this case, the form is a bitmap where dark areas represent lower levels of a surface, and light areas represent higher levels, in a way similar to bump maps. Figure 9.87 shows how a displacement map alters the geometry to which it is applied.

FIGURE 9.87
A sample displacement map and resulting mesh.

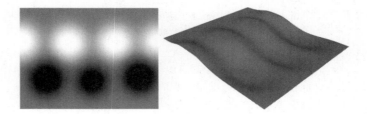

The image on the left, named `disp_dot.jpg`, was created in Photoshop by using the Airbrush tool to create the dots. The background was first filled in with a gray tone; then the black and white dots were sprayed in. As you compare the image with the mesh, you can see that the black dots correspond to the dips in the mesh, and the white dots correspond to the bumps. Because the dots are airbrushed with soft edges, they create a smooth transition from high to low in the resulting mesh.

There are two ways that you can create mesh forms with displacement maps.

◆ You can go through the Material Editor and create a material containing a displacement map.

◆ You can use the Displace modifier to apply a bitmap directly to an object to deform it into a new shape.

Effectively displacing objects using either method requires a dense mesh pattern to accommodate the displacement smoothly.

Using the Displace Modifier

Using the Displace modifier is probably the easiest way to utilize a bitmap to deform a surface. In the following exercise, you'll use the modifier to get a feel for how the process works. These exercises use the Default Scanline Renderer, so make sure you have 3ds Max set properly. You'll create the object in Figure 9.87 by using the `disp_dot.jpg` image file:

1. Choose File ➢ Reset. At the warning message, click Yes if you need to save the changes to the condo scene or No if you don't. Then, at the second warning, click Yes to continue with the reset.

2. In the Create tab of the Command panel, click Plane; then click and drag a plane that is roughly 12′ × 10′. Then use the Orbit, ViewCube, and Pan tools to get a perspective view from the front, as shown in Figure 9.88.

FIGURE 9.88
Draw the plane shown here.

3. Adjust the Length parameter to **12′** and the Width parameter to **10′**. For now, leave the Length Segs and Width Segs at the default 4 value. You'll adjust these settings later.

4. Open the Material Editor, and assign the default (Arch & Design) material in an unused slot to the plane object. This allows you to see the surface features of the plane a bit more clearly.

The plane is perhaps the best type of geometry to use to demonstrate the effects of the Displace modifier, although you can use the Displace modifier on any NURBS surface, patch, Editable Poly, or editable mesh.

ADDITIONAL NURBS INFORMATION

NURBS stands for Non-Uniform Rational Basis Spline. It is a type of object that is especially suited to creating smooth curves.

Now let's apply the bitmap:

1. Click the Modify tab; then select Displace from the Modifier List drop-down. You'll find it under the Object-Space Modifiers heading. Do not apply the Displace Mesh modifier under the World-Space Modifiers heading.

2. In the Image group of the Parameters rollout, click the Bitmap button labeled None.

3. Locate and open the file named `disp_dot.jpg`.

4. Go to the Displacement group and change the Strength setting to **1′**. You'll notice that the plane starts to distort, although it doesn't look anything like the one in Figure 9.87.

You've applied the `disp_dot.jpg` bitmap but haven't gotten the results you might have expected. The reason is that the mesh contains only a 4 × 4 array of segments. You'll need to increase the number of segments in the plane before you begin to see the form of the bitmap.

1. To get a better idea of what's going on with the mesh, right-click the Perspective label in the upper-left corner of the viewport and select Wireframe.

2. Select Plane from the modifier stack.

3. In the Parameters rollout, change the Length and Width Segs values to **40**. Now you can see the form more clearly.

4. Click the Render Production button to see the mesh as a rendered surface, as shown in Figure 9.89.

Now you can see that you can use a bitmap image to deform a surface. You don't have a lot of control over the details of the form, but you can create some interesting geometry using this method. For example, you can use a bitmap to create freeform terrain or a relief element for an antique jewelry piece.

FIGURE 9.89
The rendered displaced plane

THE DISPLACE MODIFIER'S MAP AND BITMAP OPTIONS

You may have noticed that the Image group of the Displace modifier parameters offered two sets of options: Bitmap and Map. Although you used the Bitmap option, you could also have used the Map option to apply a bitmap. The Map option lets you use other types of maps, such as the procedural maps offered in the Material/Map Browser. You can use both Bitmap and Map options to combine maps to displace a mesh.

Now let's go back to the Displace Modifier parameters and see what some of the other options do:

1. In the modifier stack, select Displace.

2. In the Displacement group of the parameters, click and drag the Strength spinner up to 2′6″ or 30″. The Strength value indicates the distance from the black portions of the bitmap to the white portions.

3. Click the Luminance Center check box and make sure the Center value is set to 0.5 if it's not already. The mesh drops down. The Luminance Center lets you control which shades of gray in the bitmap shift the mesh's vertices above or below the Displace gizmo. The gizmo is located on the construction grid.

4. Scroll down to the Map group and change the Length value to 11′ and the Width value to 9′. Now the surface really looks like a vacuum-formed plastic object with a flange.

5. Use the U Tile spinner to increase the U Tile value, and then do the same for the V Tile value. As you increase these values, the number of bumps across the width of the plane increases. Figure 9.90 shows the rendered plane after adjusting the Displace parameters.

Notice that in the Map group, the Planar radio button is selected. This is the default Map gizmo setting. In fact, because the Displace modifier works with maps, the Map group mimics the map settings for the UVW Map modifier.

FIGURE 9.90
The rendered displaced plane after adjusting the Displace parameters

Once you've finished working with the object, you can collapse its stack using the quad menu or the right-click menu in the modifier stack. By doing so, you will help conserve memory and help improve 3ds Max's performance. You can then start to edit the mesh by going to the sub-object level.

Using the Material Editor to Create Displaced Geometry

If you want to apply a displacement map to an object other than a NURBS surface, patch, poly, or editable mesh, you can use the displacement map in the Material Editor. This option works in conjunction with the Displacement Approximation modifier to perform the same function as the Displace modifier, but on a wider range of objects. For example, you can form a decorative feature on a building or create signage using the combination of displace, opacity, and diffuse maps in the Material Editor and then apply the resulting material to a cylinder or other geometry.

In this section, you'll create a fictitious concrete landscaping bench using an image file to create the details of the geometry (see Figure 9.91).

FIGURE 9.91
A concrete bench

The image file you will be using was created entirely in Photoshop using the Pen tool for the top and bottom bars and the Horizontal Type tool for the word *Brilliant*. This could really be anything from a scanned photograph to an imported AutoCAD line drawing. The point is that it's a bitmap image in which the dark areas represent low surfaces and the light areas represent high surfaces.

Let's get started with the bench by creating the basic geometry:

1. Choose File ➢ Reset to reset 3ds Max.

2. Make sure the Geometry button is selected in the Create tab of the Command panel; then click Cylinder.

3. Click and drag from the origin of the Perspective viewport and give the cylinder a radius of **30″**. Make the height **24″**.

4. Click the Modify tab in the Command panel and then select the UVW Map modifier from the Modifier List drop-down.

5. Scroll down the Parameters rollout, click the Cylindrical radio button, and turn off Real-World Map Size.

6. Later, if you alter the cylinder and the Map gizmo doesn't conform to the new shape, click the Fit button in the Alignment group.

With the UVW Map modifier added and set to Cylindrical, any material maps applied to the cylinder will appear around the perimeter. The next step is to create a material that uses a displacement map:

1. Open the Material Editor.

2. Select an unused material slot and change it to be an Architectural material; rename the material **BenchDisplace**.

3. Expand the Special Effects rollout and then click the Displacement button labeled None.

4. In the Material/Map Browser, go to the Maps group then expand the Standard group and double-click Bitmap.

5. In the Select Bitmap Image File browser, locate and open the file named `displace_sample .jpg`. Make sure either All Formats or JPEG File is selected in the Files of Type drop-down list.

6. Uncheck Use Real-World Scale and set both the U and V tiling to 1.

7. Click the Assign Material to Selection button, or drag and drop from the sample slot to the object, to assign the material to the cylinder.

8. Use the Orbit, ViewCube, and Pan tools to get a good perspective view of the cylinder. Change the environment background to white by choosing Rendering ➢ Environment, clicking the Background color swatch, and dragging the Whiteness slider to 0. Do a quick rendering to see the results; your scene should look similar to Figure 9.92.

FIGURE 9.92
Your first attempt
to create a concrete
bench

Your rendering doesn't really look anything like the displace_sample.jpg image. You need to add to the cylinder a modifier that gives you some control over the way the displacement map affects the cylinder:

1. In the Modifier List drop-down, select Disp Approx under the Object-Space Modifiers heading.

2. Render the scene again. This time you begin to see more clearly the effects of the displacement map.

The Displacement Approx. modifier is needed to apply the displacement map correctly to the object. There are still a few changes that need to be made, however. The amount of displacement is too great, and a single version of the map stretches around the cylinder. You want to reduce the strength of the displacement and have the map repeat four times around the perimeter so that it's readable.

The following steps will increase the number of times the displacement map displays around the cylinder:

1. Choose UVW Mapping in the modifier stack. This brings up the UVW Mapping parameters.

2. Change the U Tile setting to 4. Remember that the U setting is similar to the X-coordinate. By setting U Tile to 4, you cause the map to repeat four times around the perimeter of the cylinder.

3. Render the scene again using the Render Production tool. Figure 9.93 shows that the rendering is getting a little closer to the target.

FIGURE 9.93
The object after
changing the U Tile
parameters

By reducing the number of times the map is repeated over the surface, you have decreased the complexity of the displacement map, but in relation to the cylinder surface it is still very complex. You may recall that, in an earlier exercise for the Displace modifier, you needed to increase the number of segments in the mesh surface in order to have the displacement map take effect. You need to do the same in this situation. You need to increase the number of segments on the cylinder wall to give the displacement map enough segments to work with.

You can go back to the Cylinder object level to increase the number of segments for the side of the cylinder:

1. Right-click the Perspective label in the upper-left corner of the viewport and select Wireframe. This will allow you to see the cylinder segments more clearly.

2. In the modifier stack, choose Cylinder.

3. In the Parameters rollout, change the Height Segments value to **12** and the Sides value to **72**. The sides of the cylinder will show polygons that are close to being square.

4. Click the Render Production button again. Now you can see the map clearly.

The depth of the displacement map shows you that it isn't just a bump map. When the cylinder is rendered, 3ds Max converts the flat cylinder wall into a displaced mesh that will cast shadows and stand up to close-up views, even though the cylinder remains a plain cylinder in the viewports.

Now let's see how to reduce the depth of the displacement to something a bit more reasonable. You'll also add some noise to the Bump Map setting to give the object a sand-blasted concrete look:

1. Open the Material Editor; then go up one level to the Special Effects rollout.

2. Change the Amount setting for the displacement map to **20**.

3. Click the Bump map button labeled None.

4. In the Material/Map Browser, go to the Maps group then expand the Standard group and select Noise; then click OK.

5. Back in the Material Editor, change the Size parameter in the Noise Parameters rollout to **0.25** and change the Blur setting in the Coordinates rollout to **0.01**.

6. Click the Go to Parent button on the Material Editor toolbar; then adjust the Bump Map setting to **90**.

7. Create another rendering of the object. Figure 9.94 shows the completed bench.

FIGURE 9.94
The bench after adjusting the displacement amount and adding a Noise texture

You now have a pretty convincing model of a fairly complex form, and you created it without having to do a lot of editing. The displacement map does take a toll on rendering time, but in some situations it can save you time in building your model.

Converting a Displacement Map into an Editable Mesh

You may find yourself in a situation where you need to edit an object that you've created using a displacement map, like the one in the preceding section. Unfortunately, displacement maps take effect only when you render the image. Meanwhile, the object to which the displacement map is applied remains in its basic form in the viewports. In your exercise example, the cylinder remains a cylinder and doesn't become a displaced mesh.

You can apply two tools to gain access to the mesh that is created using a displacement map. The first is a global modifier that displays the mesh in the viewports so that you don't have to wait until the scene is rendered to see the result of the displacement map.

To see the effects of the displacement map, make sure the cylinder is selected and then select Displace Mesh (WSM) from the Modifier List drop-down. You'll have to wait a moment while 3ds Max converts the viewport display of the cylinder to show the actual mesh of the displacement map. When 3ds Max is done, you'll see the cylinder with the displacement map in mesh form (see Figure 9.95).

You can now see why the last rendering took a bit more time. With the displacement map added, the mesh is quite dense and complex. You can reduce the complexity of the mesh by reducing the number of segments in the cylinder. You can also experiment with the subdivision presets in the Displacement Approx. rollout—try the Low option first (Figure 9.96).

FIGURE 9.95
A close-up view of the cylinder with the Displace Mesh (WSM) modifier active

FIGURE 9.96
The subdivision presets in the displacement Approx. rollout

Using the Low setting will reduce the smoothness of the mesh and give it a rough appearance, so you may want to use the Low setting for meshes that will only be viewed from a distance.

THE MULTIRES MODIFIER

Try using the MultiRes modifier to reduce the complexity of objects. MultiRes reduces topology more in flat areas and leaves detail where you need it in curved surfaces.

TEXT IN 3DS MAX

In this example, a raster image of some text was used to show off the capabilities of the displacement map feature, but in most cases, you'll want to create text using the Text object found in the set of Spline Shape options of the Create tab. A text shape acts just like any other shape in that it can be extruded to form 3D objects. You can also apply modifiers to text shapes. One modifier that is especially useful with text shapes is the Bevel modifier (see the section "Bevel" in Appendix B).

You can apply any font that is available in the Windows font library to text shapes. Text can also be edited and its parameters changed, as long as it isn't collapsed into editable meshes, Editable Polys, or Editable Splines. For example, you can create a text shape that spells out *Brilliant*, extrude it, apply a material to it, and then later change the text to *absolutely brilliant*. Through the Text Shape object's parameters, you also have control over fonts, justification, size, kerning, leading, underlining, and italics.

Creating an Editable Mesh from a Displacement Map

The Displace Mesh (WSM) modifier allows you to see the displacement map so that you can use the Transform tools to adjust the size and orientation of the object within the design. It doesn't let you edit the object's surface, however. If you need to make changes on a sub-object level, you can create a special type of clone of the object that's a full mesh representation of the object with the displacement map. You can then use the clone to make further changes and hide or delete the original object.

To create this copy, use the Snapshot dialog box as demonstrated in the following exercise:

1. Choose Tools ➢ Snapshot.

THE SNAPSHOT TOOL AS A BUTTON

Snapshot can also be found on the Extras toolbar on the Array button flyout.

2. In the Snapshot dialog box, make sure the Single radio button is selected in the Snapshot group and that the Mesh radio button in the Clone Method area is selected; then click OK.

3. Use the Select and Move tool to move the Cylinder001 object to the left so that you can get a clear view of the new displacement mesh. You may experience some lag time between the time you move the cylinder and the time the cylinder actually moves on the screen.

4. Remove the Displace Mesh (WSM) modifier from the cylinder's modifier stack by selecting Displace Mesh Binding (WSM) from the modifier stack and then clicking the Remove Modifier from the Stack button below the modifier list. The Displace Mesh (WSM) modifier slows 3ds Max's reaction to your input, so deleting it will help save some time. When the Displace Mesh (WSM) modifier is removed, you see the original cylinder revert to its former shape.

5. Render the scene with the cloned cylinder. You see that it is an exact copy of the original cylinder but that the copy is an editable mesh rather than a cylinder with several modifiers attached.

USE SNAPSHOT TO CREATE COLLAPSED COPIES

You can think of the Snapshot dialog box as a tool to collapse nearly any modified object into an editable mesh.

As you've seen in these exercises, the Displace modier requires the surface to have at least enough segments to accommodate the form. This means that with complex forms, you'll have to create a mesh with lots of segments, which also means that you can quickly expand your file size using the Displace modifier. For this reason, you may want to restrict the use of this modifier to those types of geometry that can take the best advantage of its features.

CLONING WITH SNAPSHOT

The Snapshot dialog box is mainly intended to clone an animated object at a particular point in time. For example, suppose you have an animation of an object deforming over time and you want to create a clone of the object at specific points in the deformation. Snapshot is designed to perform this function. As its name indicates, Snapshot takes a snapshot of an object at a particular moment in time. The clone created by Snapshot doesn't inherit the animated motion or deformation of the source object.

In architectural applications, you may rarely, if ever, use Snapshot to clone an animated object, but you may use it more often as a tool to convert a displacement map into an editable mesh, as shown in these examples.

Additional Mapping and Material Features

3ds Max Design 2011 has a great number of material and mapping tools you can use to create interesting and highly realistic surfaces for the objects you use in your scenes. This book can't possibly go into every feature and use possible in such a robust application. In the following exercise, you will use some additional features of 3ds Max Design 2011 to create a complex material for a model that represents a stylized architectural feature similar to something you might encounter in your career.

1. Open the `ColumnSurround.max` file that you downloaded from the book's website.

 This model could represent a stylized column or some other architectural design feature, as shown in Figure 9.97. This is an Editable Poly object that was modeled from a 3ds Max Box primitive.

FIGURE 9.97
The ColumnSurround001 object

2. Select the ColumnSurround001 object.

3. Open the Slate Material Editor.

4. In the Autodesk Material Library, open the Wood group, and in the Panels rollout find the Goncalo material. Double-click it to add it to the active View1 window, as shown in Figure 9.98.

FIGURE 9.98
The Autodesk Material in the Slate Material Editor

If you look at the maps used in the Wood Goncalo material, you will see that the two Map nodes wired to the Generic_Image channel of the material are using the exact same bitmap with the exact same parameters. This is a bit inefficient, so what you can do using the Slate Material Editor is use the same bitmap node in multiple inputs on the material, thereby saving unnecessary loading of duplicate texture images and saving system RAM.

5. Right-click the Wood Goncalo node, and select Open Preview Window.

6. Click Assign Material to Selection to apply the material to the ColumnSurround001 object.

7. Select the lower of the two nodes wired to the Generic_Image channel in the active View1 window and delete it. Notice the changes in the preview window.

8. Click and drag from the output socket of the map node, and wire it to the input socket of the Appearance_Color_2_Map on the Autodesk Noise Map node, as shown in Figure 9.99. Watch the preview window return to looking as it did before.

FIGURE 9.99
Wire the Map node to the Noise node.

9. Delete the duplicate map wired to the Bump_Image channel of the Wood Goncalo material, and then wire the remaining map to the other socket in the Autodesk Noise Map node.

You have just made the material a little more efficient.

10. Now click the Render Production button.

3ds Max presents you with the Missing Map Coordinates dialog box, indicating that ColumnSurround001 requires map coordinates and may not render correctly.

11. Click Cancel to stop the render so you can UVW map the ColumnSurround001 object.

12. Close the Slate Material Editor for the moment.

13. On the Modify tab of the Command panel, add an Unwrap UVW modifier.

14. Expand the Unwrap UVW modifier, and select the Face level; then choose Edit ➤ Select All to select all the faces of the object.

15. In the Map Parameters rollout of the Unwrap UVW modifier, select Box for the mapping type.

16. In the Parameters rollout, click the Edit button to open the Edit UVWs dialog box, as shown in Figure 9.100.

Right now all the polygons of the ColumnSurround001 object are overlapping on the EditUVWs dialog box, which won't make for a particularly good UVW map.

17. In the EditUVWs dialog box, choose Mapping ➤ Flatten Mapping, and in the Flatten Mapping dialog box, accept the defaults and click OK.

This lays out all the polygons of the ColumnSurround001 object flat in the UV space, as shown in Figure 9.100. It is not the most efficient UVW map for the object, but it will work for what you are going to create.

FIGURE 9.100

The Column-Surround001 object unwrapped in the EditUVWs dialog box

18. Close the Edit UVWs dialog box.

19. On the Modify panel, right-click the Unwrap UVW modifier and select Collapse To. On the Warning: Collapse To dialog box click Yes.

20. On the Menu Bar, choose Rendering ➤ Render Surface Map. This opens the Render Surface Map dialog box, as shown in Figure 9.101.

FIGURE 9.101
The Render Surface
Map dialog box

FIGURE 9.101
The Render Surface
Map dialog box

The Render Surface Map dialog box allows you to render a number of special maps, with user selected resolutions and options, based on the UVW mapping of the selected object that you can use to enhance the materials you create for your objects.

21. Click the Cavity Map button in the Render Surface Map dialog box. After your machine processes the rendering, you will see the result in the Cavity Map dialog box, as shown in Figure 9.102.

22. In the Cavity Map dialog box, click Save Image. In the Save Image dialog box, navigate to where you are working with the files for this chapter, and name the file **ColumnSurround001_CavityMap.tif**. Click Save, and in the TIF Image Control dialog box, select 8-Bit grayscale and then click OK.

FIGURE 9.102
The rendered Cav-
ity Map dialog box

23. Close the Cavity Map dialog box and the Render Surface Map dialog box.

24. Open the Slate Material Editor, right-click the active view, and choose Materials ➤ mental ray ➤ Arch & Design. A new Arch & Design material node is created in the active view.

25. Right-click again in the active view, and choose Maps ➤ Standard ➤ Mix to create a new Mix Map node.

26. Wire the output socket of the Mix map to the Diffuse Color Map input socket of the Arch & Design Material.

27. Right-click again in the active view, and choose Maps ➤ Standard ➤ Mask to create a new Mask Map node; then create a second Mask Map node.

28. Wire the output socket of the first Mask Map node to the Bump Map input socket, and then wire the second Mask Map node to the Reflection Glossiness Map input socket.

29. Right-click in the active view, and choose Maps ➤ Standard ➤ Bitmap. In the Select Bitmap Image File dialog box, navigate to where you saved ColumnSurround001_CavityMap.tif, select it, and click Open.

30. Right-click in the active view, and create another Bitmap node. Browse to your 3ds Max Design 2011\maps\Misc folder, and load ABALONE.JPG.

31. Right-click in the active view, and create one more Bitmap node; this time load flaking paint.jpg from the same location you loaded the previous JPG.

32. Wire your map nodes so that what you have looks like Figure 9.103.

33. Double-click the Mask node wired to the Bump Map node of the Arch & Design Material node, and in the Parameter Editor click the Invert Mask option.

FIGURE 9.103
Wire your map nodes together.

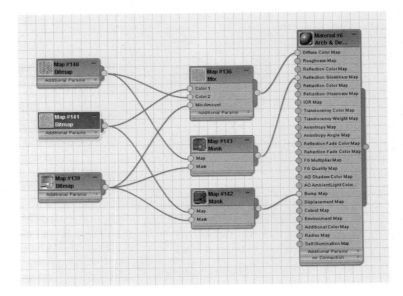

34. Double-click the Arch & Design material node to access it in the Parameters Editor.

35. In the Material Name field, rename the material to **ColumnSurround** and then apply the material to the column object in the scene.

36. Scroll to the Special Effects rollout and expand it if necessary. Click the Ambient Occlusion check box and the Round Corners check box. Change the Fillet Radius to **.25"**.

The Round Corners feature is great for creating the effect of an edge on objects that often catch glints of light, helping create a sense that the objects are real. This feature works very well on objects with straight edges such as the column you have been working with, but extremely complex objects or those with curves could cause mental ray to crash while rendering.

37. Close the Slate Material Editor.

38. On the Menu Bar, choose Tools ➤ Viewport Canvas to open the Viewport Canvas tools, as shown in Figure 9.104.

FIGURE 9.104
The Viewport
Canvas tools

The Viewport Canvas tools have been in 3ds Max since the 2010 version, but they have been greatly updated and could be considered as a new feature for 3ds Max 2011. The Viewport Canvas tools allow you to paint textures directly on your UVW mapped 3D models right in the viewport.

39. In the Viewport Paint dialog box, click the Paint brush, and select Additional Color Map from the menu.

If you select any of the bitmaps already applied to the object, you will be painting on and overwriting those images.

40. In the Create Texture: Additional Color Map dialog box that comes up use the preset size of 512, click the ellipsis box in the Save New Texture To group, and in the Save Texture To dialog box browse to where you are keeping the files for this chapter. Name the new texture `ColumnSurround001_Add_Color.tif`, and click the Save button. Make sure to set Image Type to 8-bit Color and click OK. Then click OK again in the Create Texture dialog box.

Viewport Canvas works like many layer-based painting applications, such as Photoshop, and has an incredible number of features and tools you can use to create new bitmaps for you models.

41. On the Layers floater, click the Layer menu and select New Layer, which creates Layer 1.

42. Click Layer 1 to make sure it is the current layer.

43. In the Viewport Canvas dialog box, click the color swatch and pick a color you like.

44. Now you can start painting on the column in the viewport. You can use your mouse, or pen tablet if you have one, to orbit the viewport and see how your paint strokes are applied to the model.

Take the time to really explore the Viewport Canvas tools. Try using a Brush Image to paint with another bitmap on the model. The Cavity map that you rendered earlier and used as a material mask can also be used as a mask to limit where you can paint on the model. Paint with different colors on different layers and then try seeing how the layer blending modes change the appearance of the final map. You can also switch to working on a traditional 2D view of your new texture maps if you are more comfortable painting that way. Once you are done painting, you can save you map as a layered Adobe Photoshop PSD or flatten it to save it as a TIF, PNG, or JPEG.

The Bottom Line

Create and edit materials Quality materials can add significantly to the quality of a scene. Materials are constructed by choosing a shader, setting its parameters, and then adding and adjusting maps.

> **Master It** Using the CEDFENCE.JPG file in the /maps/wood folder installed with 3ds Max as the diffuse color map, create a Standard material and assign it to an object.

Select shaders The shader that you select determines how a material appears when a scene is rendered. The most obvious difference between the different shaders is the appearance of the specular highlight.

> **Master It** Using the material from the previous Master It exercise, examine the result of assigning the different shaders to the material. Which shader results in a stretched-out specular highlight? Which shader has the most diffused highlight?

Use bump maps Image maps assigned to the Diffuse color channel of a material tend to look flat like decals or wallpaper. Adding a bump map can add apparent detail without increasing the complexity of the models.

> **Master It** Continuing from the previous Master It exercise, add a noise map to the material's Bump channel to roughen the surface. Copy and rename the material in the Material Editor and then replace the Noise bump map with the same map used as the diffuse color map. Compare the differences in the viewport.

Create a material with sub-materials Often, a model that is constructed as a single object may represent a structure composed of several objects, each with its own material. The multi/sub-object material is used to assign several distinct materials to a single object.

Master It What is one procedure for creating a multi/sub-object material?

Add entourage Adding entourage to your scenes can make them feel like they are inhabited, and help create a sense of scale, which viewers can relate to.

Master It Using the Tree01AM.tif and Tree01op.tif files you downloaded with this chapter's materials, create an entourage material with the Compact Material Editor and apply it to a plane so you can render it.

Use the Autodesk Materials The Autodesk Materials provide high-quality materials that can help you better simulate real-world materials to enhance the accuracy and realism of your renderings.

Master It Using the My_Ch09d.max file you worked on in this chapter, change the Standard Metal_Chrome_Han material into the Chrome – Polished Brushed Autodesk Material and render the scene.

Use the Displacement modifier Applying the displacement modifier or applying materials using Displacement Maps to simple objects can be a powerful way to create highly detailed or irregular forms without taking the time to build the complex geometry.

Master It Create a 50′ × 50′ plane, with 100 Length and Width segments. Apply a Displace modifier that uses the displace_sample.jpg image, which tiles six times across the surface.

Chapter 10

Using the 3ds Max Camera

If you've ever taken a presentation drawing class, you've probably been shown the importance of carefully observing the subject of your drawing. It's important to be aware of the details of a scene or landscape that might otherwise go unnoticed. By recording those details in your sketches and preliminary drawings and then addressing them in your scenes, you create a sense of depth and realism.

When you create a scene in 3ds Max Design 2011, it helps to recall those lessons in observation, even though you may not be creating a scene from real life. If you're creating a rendering of a building with lots of glass, it helps to take a look at buildings and carefully study how glass reflects the surrounding landscape. If you're doing an interior rendering, you may find it helpful to find a room that's similar in size and composition to the one you are rendering and carefully examine how the light from various sources is reflected throughout the room. By understanding the behavior of materials and light in the real world, you are better equipped to create realistic scenes in 3ds Max.

In this chapter, you'll take a look at the process of setting up your scene for a virtual photo shoot. This process includes placing a camera and setting up the relationship between the subject being shot and its surrounding environment.

In this chapter, you will learn to:

- ◆ Understand the 3ds Max camera
- ◆ Set up an interior view
- ◆ Create an environment
- ◆ Render elements for compositing
- ◆ Use the Camera Match utility

Understanding the 3ds Max Camera

So far, you have been working with the standard views, including the Top, Left, Front, Orthographic, and Perspective viewports. By constantly changing the standard views by zooming, panning, and rotating, you have learned to view objects from all angles as you modeled them. When you place a 3ds Max camera, that camera holds a particular point of view that you can use to frame a particular composition such as a helicopter (or crane) view of a large project site or an interior space for a rendering.

3ds Max cameras follow the Single Lens Reflex (SLR) film camera metaphor, where you can make adjustments such as changing the focal length of the lens from telephoto to wide angle or changing the focal depth, which is akin to changing the f-stop on the lens to capture depth-

of-field effects. Once you carefully place your camera in the scene, you can switch into this composed point of view and render the scene from within the camera.

Adding a Camera

In this exercise, you'll add a new camera in 3ds Max. You'll add a camera that shows an interior view of the courtyard on the second floor of the Villa Savoye model.

1. Open the Savoye_Camera_Start.max file from the Sybex website (www.sybex.com/go/mastering3dsmaxdesign2011).

2. Right-click the Top viewport to make it active, maximize it, and then use the Zoom Region tool to enlarge the view so that it looks similar to Figure 10.1. Make sure the Top viewport is displaying in the Wireframe rendering mode; if it needs to be changed, you can do so by clicking the Viewport Shading label and selecting Wireframe.

3. Click the Cameras icon in the Create tab of the Command panel (Figure 10.2).

FIGURE 10.1
Click and drag these points to place the camera.

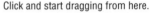
Click and start dragging from here.

Click here to set the camera target location.

FIGURE 10.2
The Cameras icon found on the Create tab

4. Click the Target button in the Object Type rollout.

5. In the Top viewport, click and drag the point shown in Figure 10.1.

6. Move the cursor toward the lower left of the viewport. As you do, you see a rubber-banding line from the point you selected in step 5. Click the point shown in Figure 10.1.

7. You've just created a camera. Click the Maximize Viewport Toggle to display the camera in all viewports, as shown in Figure 10.3. Now give your new camera a name. In the Name and Color rollout in the Command panel, change the name from Camera001 to **Mycamera**.

FIGURE 10.3
The new camera

RENAMING CAMERAS

3ds Max automatically assigns the name Camera001 to the first camera created in a scene. Subsequent cameras are named Camera002, Camera003, and so on. To help associate a camera with a view, you might consider assigning your cameras meaningful view names, just as you would name geometry in your model.

CERT OBJECTIVE

8. Right-click the Perspective viewport; then type **C**. The viewport changes to show the view from your new camera (see Figure 10.4), and the viewport label changes to match the name of the camera.

The sections of the ground plane nearest to the camera may appear to be missing. This is a phenomenon called clipping. *Clipping* is a feature in which the camera hides certain faces in the scene based on the distance from the camera. The clipping distance can be adjusted so that more or less of the scene is clipped from view.

FIGURE 10.4
The view from the new camera

THE C SHORTCUT KEY

The C shortcut key produces different results depending on the number and status of the cameras in the scene. When there is a single camera in the scene, pressing the C key switches the current viewport to the Camera viewport. When multiple cameras exist and none, or more than one, are selected, the C shortcut key opens the Select Camera dialog box, where you can select a camera from which to view the scene. When a single camera is selected, regardless of the number in the scene, the C key uses that camera as the source for the viewport. If no cameras exist in the scene, pressing the C key opens a dialog box stating there are "No cameras in scene."

Your new camera displays as a simplified camera shape, and the camera target simply displays as a small-cube helper object. The camera's field of view is also shown, when the camera is selected, as a cyan pyramid. Notice that the camera was created on the ground plane defined by the XY-coordinates. As with all newly created objects, the camera and target originate by default on the XY-plane of world space. The camera's current location won't give you a view of the courtyard, which is on the second floor. You can move the camera into position to get a courtyard view after taking a moment to study some of the camera parameters in the Command panel.

You have the option to define a variety of camera settings. At the top of the Parameters roll-out, you see the Lens setting, which adjusts the camera's focal length. A camera's focal length determines its field of view. In fact, just below the Lens setting is the FOV setting (which stands for "field of view"). If you prefer, you can enter the field of view in degrees instead of entering the focal length. When you change one setting, the other setting also changes in an inverse relationship. 3ds Max offers a default focal length of approximately 43 millimeters, or an FOV of 45 degrees, which is close to the typical focal length found in most cameras. (A setting of 43 simulates the human eye.) Below the Lens and FOV settings, you can select from a set of stock lenses—predefined focal lengths.

You might also notice the Orthographic Projection check box. This check box changes the view from a perspective to an orthographic projection. With this setting selected, your camera view will appear as a flat projection (like the top or right views) instead of a perspective view. The Orthographic Projection check box is handy for creating rendered elevations of building models or other linear models.

ADJUSTING THE CAMERA LOCATION

As with any other 3ds Max object, cameras and targets can be moved or rotated using the transform tools, although the Rotate transform is somewhat limited. The Uniform Scale option has no effect on a camera; however, the Non-Uniform Scale and Squash options change the shape of a free camera's field-of-view cone. Cameras come in two different styles that determine how the camera's orientation is managed: free and target. A target camera has both the camera and a Target helper object. The camera remains oriented toward the target regardless of which object is moved or where. The Rotate transform affects only the camera's local Z-axis, the axis that points toward the target; it can add a roll to the camera but cannot change the camera's orientation. Rotating the target has no effect on the view that the camera generates. If you look closely, you will notice a line connecting the camera and target. Selecting this line selects both the camera and the target for tandem Move or Rotate operations.

Free cameras do not have targets and can be moved by selecting the camera body only. Rotating the camera rotates the view that it generates. In most cases, the Local Reference Coordinate System should be used to rotate a free camera to better control the direction that the camera is facing.

Choosing which type of camera to create isn't difficult and, like most of 3ds Max's features, isn't permanent. A good rule of thumb is to use a target camera when the camera is stationary but must follow animation in the scene, and use a free camera when the camera's position is animated. The Type drop-down list in the Parameters rollout contains the options to switch the selected camera's type. In this exercise, you'll see how moving your camera affects its view.

1. Right-click the Left viewport. Then use the Zoom Region tool to enlarge the view of the camera and its view cone.

2. Click the Select by Name tool on the Main Toolbar. Then, in the Select from Scene dialog box, Ctrl+click the Mycamera.Target listing (Mycamera should already be selected in the list) and click OK. By doing this, you include both the Mycamera camera and Mycamera .Target in the selection.

RENAMING CAMERAS AND TARGETS

Renaming a camera automatically renames the target to match it with a .Target suffix. Renaming a target, however, does not change its associated camera's name.

3. Click the Select and Move tool; then, in the Left viewport, click and drag the Y-axis handle of the Transform gizmo. Watch the Mycamera viewport. The view looks as though you were riding an elevator up to the second floor.

4. Set the vertical camera location so that the Mycamera object is approximately 18´ above ground level. As you move the objects, watch the Y Transform type-in field at the bottom of the 3ds Max window.

While you are moving the camera location, you get immediate visual feedback by watching the Mycamera viewport. In this exercise, you moved both the camera and the target together to adjust the view. Next, you'll fine-tune the camera view by moving only the target.

If you want to match a camera to an existing Perspective viewport, you can do so by choosing Views ➢ Create Camera from View or by pressing Ctrl+C. If a camera is selected in the scene, it is modified to match the viewport. If no camera is selected, a new camera is created.

ADJUSTING THE TARGET

The Mycamera camera is at an elevation that roughly approximates the height of a person standing on the second floor. Both the camera and the target are at the same elevation. You'll want to drop the target location down a bit to center the view of the courtyard.

1. Click the Select by Name tool on the Main Toolbar again, or type **H**.

2. In the Select from Scene dialog box, locate and click Mycamera.Target. This will deselect any previously selected objects. Then click OK. You can also try to select the target using the Select Object tool. If you don't select the camera target on the first try, keep clicking without moving the mouse; this will cycle the selection through the nearby objects. Another method for selecting a target is to select the camera, right-click, and then choose Select Camera Target from the tools 1 quad menu.

3. In the Left viewport, click and drag the Y-coordinate arrow down about 3′ until the Mycamera viewport looks similar to Figure 10.5.

FIGURE 10.5
Adjust the camera target location until your view looks like this one.

3ds Max Viewport Improvements

If you are upgrading from 3ds Max 2009 or earlier, you will see that many improvements have been made to the viewports in 3ds Max:

◆ Revised viewport menus, which in 2009 and earlier required you to right-click the viewport label to launch a menu to determine shading mode, show backgrounds and safe frames, and configure the viewport layout in addition to other tools. In releases 2011 and 2010, these features are divided into three viewport menus: General, Point of View, and Shading.

◆ Viewports can show soft shadows.

◆ Viewports can show ambient occlusion.

◆ The tools for seeing viewport lighting and shadows are found on the Viewport Shading menu. Click the viewport label to access the Shading menu, then choose Viewport Lighting and Shadows to gain access to these options.

◆ A tool called XView is available from the viewport Shading menu. XView lets you diagnose problems in your geometry, such as overlapping faces, unwelded vertices, and face normal orientation.

Note that you need to be running the DirectX drivers in order to take advantage of these new features. Also, your graphics card has to support SM3 (Shading Model 3). Older graphics cards may not be able to display some of these features, such as viewport shadows. If you are an experienced 3ds Max user, take the time to explore these menus and submenus to familiarize yourself with the new location of the tools, because they have been cleverly scattered among the General, Point of View, and Shading menus.

Editing the Camera Location with the Viewport Tools

In the previous chapters, you used the viewport navigation tools in the lower-right corner of the 3ds Max window to control your Perspective and Orthographic viewports. You learned that in a Perspective viewport, the tools offered on the viewport controls changed to tools more appropriate to the perspective view. Similarly, when you have a camera assigned to a viewport, the viewport controls offer a set of tools uniquely suited to cameras. These Camera Viewport tools serve not only to alter the view in the Camera viewport but also to edit the camera's location and orientation.

USING THE DOLLY CAMERA AND FIELD-OF-VIEW TOOLS

To get a close-up view of a particular portion of your model, you typically use the Zoom Region tool or the Zoom tool in the Orthographic viewports. In a Camera viewport, there really isn't an equivalent to the Zoom Region tool. You do have two tools that have the same effect as the Zoom and Field-of-View tools for the Perspective viewport.

The Dolly Camera tool acts similar to the Zoom tool in a Perspective viewport by moving the camera toward or away from the target in a straight line. You have the added advantage of being able to see the effect of the Dolly Camera tool on the camera location. Try the following exercise to see firsthand what Dolly Camera does.

1. Select the Mycamera camera and then right-click in the Mycamera viewport to make sure it's active.

2. Click the Dolly Camera tool in the top-left corner of the viewport controls area.

3. Click and drag up in the Mycamera viewport, and notice what happens in the other three viewports. The Mycamera viewport enlarges, and you can see the camera move closer to the target in the other viewports. Notice that only the camera moves; the target remains stationary.

4. Release the mouse button, and then click the Undo button or press Ctrl+Z to return the camera to its previous location (where it was before you used the Dolly Camera tool).

UNDO VIEW CHANGE

Choosing Views ➤ Undo View Change has no effect on changes to Camera viewports. As with any other parameter modification, you can undo Camera viewport changes by pressing Ctrl+Z or clicking the Undo button on the Main Toolbar.

5. Click the Field-of-View tool; then click and drag up in the Mycamera viewport.

Notice what happens to the camera in the other three viewports; the camera's view cone decreases in size.

6. Click the Modify tab and watch the camera parameters as you adjust the Field-of-View settings. Notice that the Lens and FOV settings change with the adjustments of the Field-of-View tool.

7. Adjust the view so that the Lens parameter shows around 35mm.

The Field-of-View tool alters the camera field of view just as it does for the Perspective viewport. The only difference is that now you can see its effect by watching the camera. Field-of-View is very useful when doing interior shots; it lets you see more of an interior without the camera moving back through a wall. As you click and drag the Field-of-View tool, you see the cyan-colored field-of-view cone change in the Top, Left, and Front viewports (see Figure 10.6).

FIGURE 10.6
The field of view of a camera changes when you click and drag the Field-of-View tool.

Using the Field-of-View tool changes the size of the camera cone.

Hold down the Dolly Camera button to access two additional tools from the Dolly Camera flyout. The second tool down, Dolly Target, functions similarly to the Dolly Camera tool except that it moves the target rather than the camera. The bottom option, Dolly Camera + Target, moves both the camera and target along the vector that joins them.

A tool that performs a function similar to that of the Field-of-View tool is the camera's Perspective tool.

The Perspective tool also changes the camera's field of view, but it simultaneously moves the camera closer to or farther away from the target. This has the effect of keeping the size of the objects near the target a consistent size in the Camera viewport while the field of view changes

and the objects in the camera's periphery distort. Animating this feature creates the vertigo effect made famous in the Alfred Hitchcock movie of the same name.

CERT OBJECTIVE

If you set up a camera for a wide field of view, the perspective view may begin to exaggerate the vertical taper of tall objects. You can compensate for this exaggeration by using the Camera Correction modifier, which creates the illusion of a two-point perspective. See Appendix B, "Modifiers, Maps, and Materials," for more information.

CAMERAS DON'T COST A THING

When we teach 3ds Max classes, it seems that, inevitably, some students are hesitant to create very many cameras. As they guide people through their projects, they'll tend to move a single camera through the scene, changing its position and orientation to focus on the different features they've created. Not only is this a slow procedure, but it also eliminates the ability to efficiently re-create the exact framing of the scene from one moment to the next. Don't be frugal with your 3ds Max cameras; place them liberally throughout the scene and be sure to give them descriptive names so that you will know their intended purpose.

One question that is often asked in class is when to use a free camera rather than a targeted camera. The answer depends on whether or not the camera's position will be animated. It's almost always preferable to animate a free camera over a targeted camera. With a free camera, there is no need to accommodate the transforms of the camera's target objects. If the orientation of the camera is animated but not the camera's position, it's usually easier to animate the position of the target object, which controls the camera's orientation. When you first create a camera, start with a target camera; it's easier to orient than a free camera and you can always change it to a free camera if you prefer.

TRUCKING YOUR CAMERA VIEW

Like the Dolly Camera and Field-of-View tools, the Truck Camera tool moves the camera as it alters the camera view. You can see exactly how the Truck Camera tool works by the way that it moves the camera and target.

1. Click the Truck Camera tool in the viewport controls.

2. In the Mycamera viewport, the cursor changes to a black hand. Click and drag in the Mycamera viewport, and watch what the camera does in the Top, Left, and Front viewports.

 The camera and target move together in a path perpendicular to the direction that the camera is pointing. This is similar to using the Pan tool in noncamera viewports.

3. Click the Undo tool to return the camera and target to their previous locations.

WALKING THROUGH YOUR SCENE

Similar to the Truck Camera tool, the Walk Through tool provides tools for moving a camera through your scene. The controls for navigating the camera consist of both mouse movements

and keyboard sequences, similar to many PC-based video games. The Walk Through tool is located on the Truck Camera flyout.

1. Choose Edit ➢ Hold to save your scene's current state temporarily.

2. Click and hold the Truck Camera tool in the Viewport controls and then release the mouse over the Walk Through tool.

3. Click and drag in the Mycamera viewport. The cursor changes into a circle with a dot in the middle and the scene appears to be rotating in front of the camera. Depending on the quality and settings of your video card, the viewport may revert into a Wireframe display mode.

4. Press and hold the W key and observe the viewports. In the Top viewport, the camera appears to be moving forward in the same manner as the Dolly Camera + Target tool, but this is not the case. Look closely in the Left viewport and you will see that the camera's and target's elevations are not changing (they are not moving in a vector shared by their displacement); they are moving forward as a person would in the scene.

5. Press the Q key, and then press and hold the S key. The camera moves backward but faster than it moved forward. The Q and Z keys control the speed of the camera's movements.

6. Simultaneously hold the A key down while dragging the mouse up and to the right. The camera trucks to the left while it rotates up and to the right

7. Choose Edit ➢ Fetch to restore your scene to the state it was in prior to step 1. Click Yes in the dialog box that opens.

With a little practice, you will be able to traverse your scene easily while keeping the perspective of a person walking through it. Table 10.1 describes the keyboard controls available to the Walk Through tool.

Num Lock must be turned off when you are using the arrow keys in the numeric keypad.

TABLE 10.1: Default Walk Through Tool Keyboard Controls

SHORTCUT	DESCRIPTION
W, up arrow	Moves the camera forward
S, down arrow	Moves the camera backward
A, left arrow	Trucks the camera to the left
D, right arrow	Trucks the camera to the right

TABLE 10.1: Default Walk Through Tool Keyboard Controls (*CONTINUED*)

SHORTCUT	DESCRIPTION
C, Shift+down arrow	Moves the camera and target down
E, Shift+up arrow	Moves the camera and target up
[Decreases the space between each movement (step size) when a key is pressed
]	Increases the space between each movement (step size) when a key is pressed
Alt+[Resets the step size to the default value
Q	Increases the speed of the movements
Z	Decreases the speed of the movements
Shift+spacebar	Orients the camera horizontally and eliminates any tilt or roll
Spacebar	Prevents the camera from tilting up or down

ROTATING THE CAMERA

You've used the Orbit tool to move your point of view in the Perspective viewport. When you're working with a Camera viewport, the functionality of the Orbit tool is divided into two tools: the Orbit Camera tool and the Roll Camera tool.

The Orbit Camera tool performs the same function as clicking in the center of the green circle of the Orbit tool. Your camera location orbits about the camera target location as you drag, remaining at a fixed distance from the target. If you are using a free camera, the camera rotates around an implied target located at the center of the end plane of the field-of-view cone. This is the same location where a target is located with a target camera. You won't see the green circle that you see with the Orbit tool. If you want to limit the camera motion to horizontal or vertical, you can hold down the Shift key as you click and drag the mouse.

The Roll Camera tool performs the same function as clicking and dragging the outside of the green circle of the Orbit tool. The camera view rotates around its local Z-axis, remaining at a fixed location.

There is also a flyout option under the Orbit Camera tool. You can click and hold the Orbit Camera tool to reveal the Pan Camera tool.

The Pan Camera tool lets you change the direction in which the camera is pointing as if it were on a fixed tripod, without changing the camera's position. This is the exact opposite of the function that the Orbit Camera tool performs. Holding down the Shift key while using the Pan Camera tool constrains the motion to either a vertical or horizontal plane while moving the camera.

Setting Up an Interior View

Now let's focus our attention on the interior space. You may notice that it is difficult to see into an interior space when you are using the Perspective viewport. Placing a camera into an interior is a great way to see inside. You will switch back to a Perspective viewport to continue modeling after you have placed an interior camera. First, set up the camera to view more of the interior and less of the courtyard:

1. Right-click the Top viewport, and click the Maximize Viewport Toggle to enlarge the viewport.

2. If you need to, adjust the view so that you can get a good look at the room toward the bottom of the viewport, as shown in Figure 10.7.

3. Click the Select and Move tool; then click the Mycamera camera that you made previously.

4. Hit the spacebar or click the Selection Lock Toggle to turn on Selection Lock.

LOCKING THE SELECTION

You may find it easier to move objects with Selection Lock on because you can't inadvertently select anything else in this mode. Just be sure to unlock the selection after you're done, or you won't be able to select anything else the next time you want to.

5. Shift+click and drag the camera in the XY-plane to the location shown in Figure 10.7.

FIGURE 10.7
Copying the
Mycamera camera

Copy Mycamera from here.

Drag the copy to here.

6. In the Clone Options dialog box, make sure the Copy radio button is selected; then click OK. Note that the name of the new camera is Mycamera001.

You now have a new camera for your interior view. Next, rotate the camera so that you are looking down the length of the room instead of out the window:

1. Click the Maximize Viewport Toggle to return to a view of all four viewports.

2. Right-click the POV viewport label in the Mycamera viewport; then choose Views ➢ Mycamera001.

3. Click and hold the Orbit Camera tool in the Viewport Controls, and then select Pan Camera from the flyout.

4. Start dragging the cursor horizontally from left to right in the Mycamera001 viewport, and then hold down the Shift key to adjust the view so that it looks like Figure 10.8.

USING THE SHIFT KEY WITH A CAMERA

In 3ds Max the Shift key usually brings up the Clone Options dialog box, but in this context the Shift key is being used as a constraint. By holding it after you start dragging, as in many other software programs, the movement is restricted to a horizontal motion.

5. Click the Render Production tool to get a look at the room. Your view should look similar to Figure 10.9. Notice that there is a light source that illuminates the courtyard. This file is set up to use the scanline renderer, rather than the default mental ray renderer. Don't worry about this; it's a little faster than mental ray and will teach you about cameras just the same.

FIGURE 10.8
The new Mycamera001 viewport

FIGURE 10.9
A rendered view of the interior

Creating an Environment

In the entertainment industry, artists are employed to produce background images (called *mats* or *matte paintings*) to simulate special environments, such as mountainous terrain, a canyon, or the interior of a space station. You can employ a similar technique using 3ds Max's environment background options. The *environment* in 3ds Max is everything surrounding the objects in your scene.

The following exercise will show you how to quickly add a sky to the villa model by adding a bitmap image for a background:

1. Continue with the previous exercise, or open Savoye_Environment_Start.max from the Sybex website (www.sybex.com/go/mastering3dsmaxdesign2011).

2. Choose Rendering ➢ Environment or press 8 on the keyboard. The Environment tab of the Environment and Effects dialog box displays as shown in Figure 10.10.

FIGURE 10.10
The Environment and Effects dialog

3. Click the Environment Map button labeled None just below the Use Map check box. The Material/Map Browser appears. Locate the Maps rollout, and in the Standard folder you will see a list of map types.

4. Click the Bitmap option (Figure 10.11) in the list of map types, and then click OK.

 The Select Bitmap Image File dialog box displays. In Windows XP and earlier, the Select Bitmap Image File dialog box shows the contents of the My documents and settings\ *username*\my documents\3dsmax\sceneassets\images folder by default.

FIGURE 10.11

Select Bitmap in
the Material/Map
Browser.

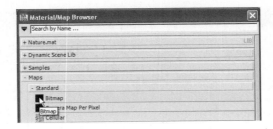

5. Locate the Maps folder under the `C:\Program Files\Autodesk\3ds Max Design 2011` program folder. Double-click the Backgrounds subfolder, and select the `SUNSET90.jpg` file. You'll see a preview of the selected file in the lower-right corner of the dialog box. At the bottom of the dialog box, you'll also see statistics about the file.

6. Click Open. Note that the filename now appears on the Environment Map button.

7. Close the Environment and Effects dialog box. Make sure that the Mycamera001 viewport is currently active, and then click the Render Production button to see the result of your background addition. This is an older file, created with a previous version of the software, so it uses the scanline renderer for this exercise. Using a background image when rendering with mental ray requires a slightly different technique. Usually mental ray renderings use an mr physical sky rather than a background image. The model is rendered with a sky in the background, as shown in Figure 10.12.

Figure 10.12 highlights a mismatch that often occurs between the lighting in the scene and the environment. Because light sources are independent of environment bitmaps, it is easy to set up lighting in your scene that doesn't necessarily go with the implied lighting in an environment image. In Figure 10.12 the environment shows a sunset while the lighting in the scene suggests midday sun. Clearly, one or the other of these two variables could be adjusted for a more realistic image. Keep this potential mismatch in mind when you design environments.

FIGURE 10.12

The sky environment
in the rendering

TURNING OFF THE VIEWPORT BACKGROUND

The environment background automatically displays in the viewport. To turn this off, choose Views ➤ Viewport Background ➤ Viewport Background and then deselect Display Background in the Viewport Background dialog box.

Making Adjustments to the Background

In many cases, the background image will need to be adjusted to fit the scene. The background image may not fit the rendering correctly, or it may be too dark or light. You might notice that the sunset background is a bit below the horizon and is a bit dark overall. In this section, you'll learn how to use the Material Editor to make adjustments to the background.

1. Click the Material Editor button in the Main Toolbar. Make sure you choose the Compact Material Editor (the original editor) rather than the new Slate Material Editor.

2. In the Material Editor dialog box, click the sample slot on the right of the bottom row. Then click the Get Material button.

3. In the Material/Map Browser dialog box, open the Dynamic Scene Lib rollout if it is not already visible.

4. Select the listing that shows SUNSET90.jpg in its title. You see a sample of the material to the left of the material label.

5. Double-click the SUNSET90.jpg listing. The sunset image appears in the selected sample in the Material Editor. Parameters for modifying the background bitmap also display in the lower half of the Material Editor. Close the Material/Map Browser.

This may be the first time you have seen a map appear by itself in the Compact Material Editor. Remember that you can't apply maps by themselves to objects—maps are usually children of materials. You can, however, apply maps directly as backgrounds

Once you've got the background image in the Material Editor, you have access to parameters that control its appearance. Next, you'll use the Coordinates rollout to offset the environment background in the viewport.

1. Go to the Coordinates rollout (Figure 10.13) and try dragging the Width and Height Offset spinners.

FIGURE 10.13
The Coordinates rollout lets you adjust the offset.

The environment background image moves in relation to the stationary geometry in the Mycamera001 viewport and in the Material Editor.

2. Right-click the label of the Mycamera001 viewport and choose Views ➤ Mycamera from the context menu.

3. Using the Pan Camera tool, drag up in the viewport to aim the camera upward.

 You now have a better view of the sky above the courtyard. If you've turned off the display of the environment map in the viewport, turn it back on now.

4. Click the Mapping drop-down list in the Coordinates rollout. Change the mapping type to Spherical Environment.

UNDERSTANDING ENVIRONMENTAL MAPPING

Cylindrical and spherical mapping wraps the environment bitmap around the inside of these two corresponding shapes. Shrink-wrap mapping conforms the map to a complex concave surface. Screen wrapping is probably the most frequently used choice because it simply pastes the bitmap flat on the background screen like a matte painting.

Notice that the image distorts as it stretches around the inside of a large sphere that surrounds the model, as shown in Figure 10.14. You can see the clouds curving slightly as they wrap around the sphere.

Fisheye camera lenses have spherical distortion appropriate to a spherical environment mapping. In order to effectively use spherical, cylindrical, or shrink-wrap environment mapping, the bitmap used must be distorted in the same way. Otherwise, a "normal" bitmap would appear stretched if used in this way.

FIGURE 10.14
Spherical environ-
ment mapping

Because you will be using the SUNSET90.jpg bitmap, you should use screen mapping to directly paste the image into the environment without distortion:

1. Change the mapping type back to Screen.

2. In the Coordinates rollout, set the Offset amounts back to 0. The bitmap will now be pasted directly into the background, as shown in Figure 10.15.

FIGURE 10.15
Screen environment mapping

Right-clicking any spinner button sets the value to its lowest nonnegative value possible. You can adjust the Offset and Size spinners as desired to move and stretch the setting sun in the background until it is in an aesthetically pleasing location in relation to the building. Now let's see how to adjust the brightness of the background image:

1. In the Material Editor, scroll down to the Output rollout and click to expand it. You'll see a graph and a set of check boxes and spinners, as shown in Figure 10.16.

2. Click the Enable Color Map check box in the Output rollout. The graph is highlighted so that you are able to adjust its settings.

FIGURE 10.16
The Material Editor's Output rollout

If you're an Adobe Photoshop user, the Color Map graph should be somewhat familiar as it is similar to Curves in Photoshop. The color map lets you adjust the tonal range of an image by manipulating the line in the graph. Right now, the line goes straight from 0,0 in the lower-left corner to 1,1 in the upper right. You can adjust the brightness, contrast, and tonal range of an image by adding control points to the line and then moving the control points. The next exercise will show you some of the Color Map functions:

1. Scroll the Output rollout up or resize the Material Editor so that you can see the entire Color Map group; then click the Add Point tool on the Curve toolbar.

2. Click the Color Map graph line at its midpoint, as shown in Figure 10.17. A square handle appears on the line.

FIGURE 10.17
Click the midpoint of the line.

Add a point here.

3. Click the Move tool on the Color Map toolbar. This button looks very similar to the Select and Move tool in the Main Toolbar.

4. Click the point you just created and drag it up and then release. Notice what happens to the sample slot image in the Material Editor. It gets brighter.

Changes to the output curves do not appear in the viewports, but they do appear in the Material Editor and in rendered views. By adjusting the line upward at its midpoint, you've increased the amount of the midtones in the image. Let's see what other options you have to edit the curve. You can get direct feedback on the effect of your changes by viewing the sample bar at the bottom of the Output rollout.

1. Scroll the Material Editor panel up so you have a good view of the sample gradient bar, as shown in Figure 10.18.

FIGURE 10.18
Scroll the Output rollout of the Material Editor panel so that you can see a view similar to this one.

Sample gradient bar

2. Right-click the point you added and moved in the previous exercise, and then select Bezier-Smooth from the pop-up list.

3. Move the point back to its midpoint position; then adjust the Bezier handles so they look like those in Figure 10.19. The sample image fades in contrast, and the gray area of the sample tonal range below the graph widens.

4. Now adjust the handles to look like Figure 10.20. The sample image increases in contrast.

5. Finally, reposition the point to the left to brighten the image so it looks like Figure 10.21.

FIGURE 10.19
The Bezier handles in a new orientation

The gray tones widen.

FIGURE 10.20
The Bezier handles set to increase contrast

FIGURE 10.21
To brighten the image, move the point to the left.

6. To apply the image changes to your model, click in the Mycamera viewport. If you have a selection set that you want to retain, right-click in the viewport and then right-click again, this time off the quad menu that appears. The background in the Mycamera viewport changes to match the sample in the Material Editor.

Besides the overall tone of the image, you can also manipulate the curves for each of the red, green, and blue color components. For example, suppose you want to increase the blue and downplay the red in the background. You can use the R, G, and B tools to isolate each color:

1. In the Output rollout, click the Copy CurvePoints check box and then click the RGB radio button at the top of the Color Map group. Copy CurvePoints forces the RGB settings to use the current curve settings.

2. Click the R and G tools (Figure 10.22) on the Output toolbar to deactivate them.

 The tool buttons should look as if they are in an up position. The curve is now blue to indicate that only the blue component of the curve is active.

3. Now move the curve point up and to the left. The sample image becomes bluer.

4. Click the R button to activate the red component. Now you see two curves, one red and one blue.

5. Click the B button to deactivate the blue component. Then click and drag the handle on the red curve (Figure 10.23) to the right just a little to reduce its strength.

6. Click in the Mycamera viewport to update the background in your model.

FIGURE 10.22
The Color Map RGB tools

FIGURE 10.23
Use Curve handles to adjust the color map.

Now the sky is bluer and a little less ominous looking, and you've seen that you have a lot of control over the background image.

You can use the Output options on any material that uses a bitmap. You can even apply an output map as a parent to those map types that do not already have a built-in Output rollout. Use the Output rollout in 3ds Max as a quick alternative to doing color correction in Adobe Photoshop or a similar image-editing program. You can also use a color-correction map to

achieve similar results. Just click the selector to the right of the material name (marked Bitmap), and choose Color Correction from the map type list. Keep the existing map as a submap, and then you can instantly adjust the hue, saturation, brightness, or contrast using the Color Correction parameters.

You can also edit the Ground-Grass Diffuse Color bitmap for the ground using the same tools you just used on the background. To gain access to the Output rollout for Maps, go to the Maps rollout, and click the button for the map you want to edit. For example, you can click the GRASS2.jpg diffuse color map for the Ground-Grass material. You'll find the Output rollout at the bottom of the map parameters that appear in the Material Editor.

Immersive Environments for Animation

One of the limitations of using a matte painting is that the illusion breaks down if the camera moves more than just a little. You can perceive the flatness of the background especially if the camera turns, because the environment bitmap does not turn with the rest of the scene.

In animations where the camera moves, you must devise immersive environments where the background remains believable. One way to accomplish this is to use an abstract background that looks the same no matter where the camera turns. Another, more complex, method is to actually model the environment with a large skydome object that envelops the rest of the scene. You will learn how to create immersive environments that can be used in animated scenes here, but you won't dive into the subject of animation until Chapter 13, "Creating Animations."

Creating a Believable Background

In animations where you are showing an outdoor flyby of a building, the background can be a simple gradient from bottom to top. Such a background will not appear to be static, because no objects in the background define a point of reference as the camera moves.

1. Continue with the previous exercise, or open Savoye_Skydome_Start.max.

2. Choose Rendering ➤ Environment. The Environment tab of the Environment and Effects dialog box appears.

3. Click the Environment Map button to open the Material/Map Browser.

4. On the Maps rollout, select Gradient from the Standard list, and notice the sample next to the Gradient label. It shows a grayscale gradient from black at the top to white at the bottom.

5. Click OK to select the gradient map.

You've switched to a gradient map for the background, but you will want to add some colors to the gradient:

1. Click the Material Editor button on the Main Toolbar to open the Compact Material Editor if it's not already open.

2. If your Material Editor displays only six sample slots, use the slide bar on the right to view the third row of sample slots just below the ones visible in the dialog box.

Alternatively, you could click the Options button on the Material Editor's vertical toolbar, and increase the number of visible material slots in the Slots area of the Material Editor Options dialog box that appears.

3. Click the undefined slot to select it; then click the Get Material button.

4. In the Material/Map Browser, grouping the Dynamic Scene Lib rollout, double-click the Map listing that shows Map #24 (Gradient) [Environment] in the name. Your actual map number may be different. The slot now shows the gradient.

Once you have the gradient in the sample slot, you can begin to adjust its parameters:

1. Close the Material/Map Browser.

2. In the Material Editor, scroll down to the Gradient Parameters rollout, and click the color swatch labeled Color #1.

3. In the Color Selector dialog box, set the Hue setting to 155, the Saturation (Sat) setting to 219, and the Value setting to 100. This defines a dark blue color for the top of the gradient.

4. In the Gradient Parameters rollout, click the color swatch for Color #2.

5. At the Color selector, set the Hue setting to 155, the Saturation to 125, and the Value to 255 to define a lighter blue shade for the middle of the gradient.

6. Click OK when you're done, and then close all of the other dialog boxes. Now you see a color gradient background in the Mycamera viewport, as shown in Figure 10.24. There may be some banding in the viewport background, but this will not appear in any rendered views.

FIGURE 10.24
Your scene with the gradient background

The new background looks like a typical clear sky with a gray horizon. It won't matter that the background remains the same throughout an animation, because the gradient colors won't give away the fact that they are not moving with the camera. Of course, you can use the gradient background for still images as well.

You can create an animated background by using an animated AVI or MOV file for a background image. Likewise, you can create an animated texture by using an AVI or MOV file for a texture map. You can also animate a still background by animating the offset value of the map over time.

Using a Texture Map and Hemisphere for the Sky

The gradient background offers the illusion of a crystal clear sky, but what if you want to add some clouds? You can simulate a cloudy sky by adding a flattened skydome over your model and then assigning to the dome a texture map that uses a bitmap of a cloudy sky. Here's how it's done.

First, you'll add the hemisphere object:

1. Click the Maximize Viewport Toggle, if necessary, to display all four viewports.

2. Right-click the Top viewport, and then click the Zoom Extents tool in the lower-right corner of the 3ds Max window.

3. In the Create tab of the Command panel, click the Geometry button and select Sphere.

4. In the Top viewport, click and drag a sphere from the center of the building, as shown in Figure 10.25. Make the sphere extend to the corner of the ground plane with a radius of about 1,060 feet. On the Parameters rollout, set Segments to 18.

5. Right-click the Front viewport, and click the Zoom Extents button.

6. In the Command panel, change the Hemisphere parameter for the sphere to 0.7. Most of the sphere will disappear, leaving the topmost portion. Change the name of the sphere from Sphere01 to **Skydome** so that you can keep track of its function.

7. Move the Hemisphere so that its base is just below the ground plane, as shown in Figure 10.26.

FIGURE 10.25
Create a sphere with a radius of 1,060 feet.

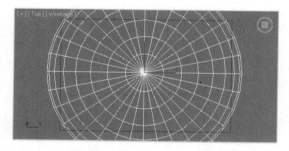

FIGURE 10.26
Move the hemisphere down in the viewport's Y-axis so that its base is just below the ground plane.

When you adjust the Hemisphere parameter, 3ds Max flattens the bottom of the sphere and places a surface on the flattened area. You need to place the bottom of the hemisphere below

the ground plane so that the hemisphere's bottom surface doesn't appear in your camera view. Another option would be to convert the object to an Editable Poly and then delete the faces that form the bottom portion.

Now you've got a dome over your model, which will become the sky. Spheres are normally intended to be viewed from the outside, so when 3ds Max creates a sphere, the normals are pointing outward. In this situation, you want your sphere to be viewable from the inside, so you need to invert the direction of the skydome's normals:

1. With the skydome hemisphere selected, click the Modify tab.

2. Right-click Sphere in the modifier stack, and then select Convert To: Editable Poly from the pop-up menu. You won't need to make changes to the skydome's parameters, so this operation will help conserve memory and simplify the object.

3. Click the Element button in the Selection rollout to enter the Element sub-object level.

4. Click the skydome to select it at the Element sub-object level. The entire dome turns red to indicate that it is composed of a single element.

5. Scroll down to the Edit Elements rollout and click the Flip button to invert the direction in which the sphere's normals are pointing. You'll notice that the Camera viewport changes so that you no longer see the background gradient. Instead you see the inside of the skydome, showing you that the normals really are flipped.

6. Back in the modifier stack, click Editable Poly to return to the object level.

The skydome is just about ready. You need to create a material to apply to the skydome to simulate the clouds. The material will also require a UVW Map modifier applied to the skydome.

1. Open the Material Editor and click an unused slot.

2. Rename the selected slot's material as **Skydome**. Make sure Material Type is set to Standard, and in the Shader Basic Parameters rollout, set Shader to Blinn. Then open the Maps rollout near the bottom of the dialog box.

3. Click the Diffuse Color Map button. Then, in the Material/Map Browser, double-click Bitmap.

4. In the Select Bitmap Image File dialog box, open the \program files\autodesk\3ds Max Design 2011\maps\Skies folder. Then locate and select CLOUD2.jpg. This is a fairly generic sky with a few clouds.

USING THE 3DS MAX SKY MAPS

The maps found in the Skies folder are very common, and their use in a production scene can often be spotted and recognized. Consider expanding your library of sky images by purchasing additional image files or by creating your own. Increase the output of these sky maps when using mental ray for your renderer.

5. Click Open. In the Material Editor you see the sky bitmap in the sample slot.

6. Deselect the Use Real-World Scale check box and set both the U and V Tiling settings to 1.0.

7. With the skydome object selected, click the Assign Material to Selection button on the Material Editor toolbar.

8. Click the Show Standard Map in Viewport button in the Material Editor.

The sky in the Camera viewport will change color but won't display the sky bitmap properly. This is because the Skydome material requires UVW mapping coordinates, which don't exist in an Editable Poly object.

You've just about finished creating the sky. The last things you need to take care of are the UVW mapping coordinates. For this situation, the best map will be the planar map. You want as much of the material map as possible to fit on the skydome. You'll get the most natural-looking sky by mapping the skydome material as a flat plane against the skydome object.

1. In the Modify tab, click the UVW Map modifier from the Modifier List drop-down list. Ensure that the Planar mapping type is selected, and then deselect the Real-World Map Size check box at the bottom of the Mapping section.

3ds Max automatically aligns the map to the skydome object and adjusts the UVW map to fit the skydome. If the gizmo doesn't fit the skydome, or you have adjusted the gizmo's size parameters and want to return to the default size, click the Fit button in the alignment area.

2. Right-click the Top viewport and click the Zoom Extents tool to get a better view of the UVW Map gizmo.

3. Right-click in the Mycamera viewport, and then switch it to the Mycamera01 viewport.

4. Click the Render Production tool to see the results. The sky appears out the window, but it is too dark (see Figure 10.27).

You can simulate clouds blowing in the wind by very slowly rotating the skydome in an animation. Read more about animation in Chapter 13.

FIGURE 10.27
The rendered Mycamera001 viewport with the sky too dark to see

If no lights are directed toward the skydome, it may appear as a dark background. You can change this by turning on Self-Illumination in the material, or you can take the following steps to add an Omni light that includes only the skydome:

1. Right-click the Top viewport.

2. Go to the Create tab in the Command panel, select the Lights button, and change from Photometric to Standard lights. Then click the Omni button under the Standard category.

3. In the Top viewport, click the center of the dome to place an Omni light there.

4. In the Command panel, change the name of the new Omni light to **skydomelight**, and deselect the On option in the Shadows group of the General Parameters rollout.

5. Open the Intensity/Color/Attenuation rollout and set the Multiplier value to 1.

Now you've got a light for the skydome. You'll want to make sure that it illuminates only the sky:

1. In the General Parameters rollout, click the Exclude button.

2. In the Exclude/Include dialog box, click the Include radio button near the top of the dialog box.

3. Select Skydome from the Scene Objects list box to the left; then click the right-pointing arrow button to move the selection to the list box on the right.

4. Click OK to close the dialog box.

 It is a good idea to also ensure that the skydome doesn't receive shadows.

5. Right-click the skydome, and choose Object Properties. In the Rendering Control group, click By Layer, and change the Properties to By Object; then turn off Receive Shadows.

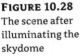

6. In the Rendered Frame Window, click the Clone Rendered Frame Window button. This makes a copy of the existing rendering so you can compare it to the next one.

7. Right-click the Mycamera01 viewport, and click the Render Production tool again. This time the sky appears brighter, as shown in Figure 10.28.

FIGURE 10.28
The scene after illuminating the skydome

EXCLUDED OBJECTS AND THE VIEWPORT DISPLAY

Objects that are excluded from illumination render correctly but still appear illuminated in the viewport. The Interactive Viewport Renderer doesn't handle this aspect of illumination as well as the other renderers, but it does display in real time.

Now you have a sky that will be correct and convincing as the animation moves through the scene. Because the sky bitmap is now assigned to an object in the model, it will remain fixed in relation to the rest of the model. The net effect will be that the sky will appropriately follow the rest of the objects in the scene as the camera moves along its path.

You can also create an interesting effect by combining the gradient background with the sky-dome sky. If you adjust the Opacity setting for the Skydome material to a value less than 70, the gradient background will begin to show through the Skydome object.

Using Render Types

Rendering in 3ds Max is often an iterative process of rendering, adjusting, and then rendering again. By rendering just a portion of your scene, you can save time by reducing the time you spend in these revision cycles. Try rerendering your scene with changes to the diffuse color, but this time render only the ground object.

1. With the MyCamera01 viewport active, type **P** to switch it to a Perspective viewport.

2. Click the Zoom Extents button to get a view of the whole model and then use the Zoom, Pan View, and Orbit tools so you are inside the skydome and can see the exterior of the building.

3. Render the scene. It should look similar to Figure 10.29.

4. Select the ground object.

5. Click the Area to Render drop-down list in the upper-left corner of the Rendered Frame Window; then choose Selected from the list.

FIGURE 10.29
The scene so far

6. Click the Render button in the upper-right corner of the Rendered Frame Window. Your Perspective viewport is rendered with just the ground object rerendered.

7. Put the Set the Area to Render option back to View.

The F9 key is the shortcut to issue the Render Last command. Render Last renders the same viewport and other rendering parameters to the same specifications as the previous rendering. This command does not bring up a dialog box and disregards which viewport is currently active. F9 does not always work, however, when input fields in certain dialog boxes, such as the Material Editor, are selected for input.

The Rendered Frame Window is overwritten with the new pixels from the selected object. In this instance, the rendering process was much faster. By rendering a selected object or set of objects, you can save some time if you're rendering just to see the results of some changes you've made to your model. There are other options in the Render Type drop-down list with which you'll want to be familiar. Here's a rundown of those options and what they do:

View Renders the current viewport in its entirety. This is the option you've used for most of the exercises so far.

Selected Renders just the objects selected.

Region Renders a selected region of the viewport. When you choose this option, you are asked to select a region in the currently active viewport, or you can select a region in the Rendered Frame Window. An adjustable marquee displays, which allows you to select a rectangular area (see Figure 10.30). Once you select an area and click the Render button in the upper-right corner of the Rendered Frame Window dialog box, 3ds Max renders only the selected portion and nothing else. If you've previously rendered the full viewport, the region you select will be overlaid onto the last rendered view in the Rendered Frame Window. This can save a lot of time if you need to rerender only a part of a view.

Crop Lets you crop an area for rendering. It works just like the Region option, but instead of leaving any previous rendering in the Rendered Frame Window, it crops the rendering to the area you selected. To rerender a cropped view, you may use the Crop Selected option.

Blowup Works like the Region and Crop options, but instead of keeping the view size the same as the overall viewport, Blowup enlarges the selected region to fill the Rendered Frame Window.

FIGURE 10.30
Selecting a region for the Region, Crop, and Blowup options

Of all the options listed, View, Selected, and Region are the ones you'll use the most. Region, in particular, can be especially useful if you want to change part of a rendering that takes a lot of time to process.

If you decide you don't want to continue with a rendering, you can press the Esc key to cancel at any time.

Render Elements for Compositing

Another way of rendering just a portion of your scene is to use render elements. These elements are quite different from render types in what they render. Rather than rendering selected objects or parts of the whole image, *render elements* split the image into its visual components that can be used later in compositing programs such as Adobe Photoshop for still images or 3ds Max Composite, Autodesk Combustion, or Adobe After Effects for animations.

Elements that can be rendered separately are the alpha, atmosphere, background, reflection, refraction, self-illumination, shadow, specular, and Z depth, or a blend of any of these image channels. To get a sense of how this works, let's try an example:

1. Click the Render Setup button on the right side of the Main Toolbar. The Render Setup dialog box appears.

2. Click the Render Elements tab at the top of this dialog box. The Render Elements dialog box appears, as shown in Figure 10.31.

3. Open the Render Elements rollout and click the Add button.

4. In the Render Elements dialog that appears, select Z Depth and click OK (see Figure 10.31).

FIGURE 10.31
The Render Elements tab of the Render Setup dialog box, and the Render Elements dialog box

> ### THE Z DEPTH RENDER ELEMENT
>
> The Z Depth element renders as a grayscale image in shades of gray representing the distance away from the picture plane (known in compositing as the camera's Z direction).

If you wanted to save this render element as an image file, you would enter the filename and folder in the Selected Element Parameters group (Figure 10.32). Rendered elements are often saved as RLA or RPF images; check your compositing software's documentation to determine the best file type to save.

If you wanted to output your render elements to Autodesk Combustion compositing software, you would enable that link and save a file as shown in Figure 10.33.

FIGURE 10.32
Name the render element in the Selected Element Parameters group.

FIGURE 10.33
Name the Combustion Workspace render element.

New to 3ds Max Design 2011 is the inclusion of 3ds Max Composite, a high-end compositing package. Choose the Open EXR (.exr) file format to save Render Elements and G Buffer channels for use in Composite. You'll learn more about 3ds Max Composite in Chapter 15, "Finishing It Off: Atmosphere, Effects, and Compositing."

Each element's parameters will appear in specialized rollouts at the bottom of the dialog box, like the Z Depth Element Parameters rollout in this example.

1. In the Z Depth Element Parameters rollout, set the Z Max value to 800′ (Figure 10.34).

FIGURE 10.34
Z Depth Element Max and Min values

2. Click the Render button at the bottom right of the dialog box. Two separate Rendered Frame Windows will appear. The first one shows the usual rendering, while the second contains the chosen render element, as shown in Figure 10.35.

3. Save your scene file as **MySavoye_Zdepth.max**.

The render element images can be brought into a compositing program where special effects can be applied based on the visual information that has been separated out as elements.

If you want to save the setup for the render elements, you can use the render preset feature. At the bottom of the Render Elements dialog box there is a Preset field. Click the drop-down arrow there to save your own preset. When you save a custom preset, you can select what categories you want in the preset. Anything found in the Common, Effects, Environment, and Render Elements dialog boxes can be saved as part of the preset. Additional categories are available that are renderer specific, so if the mental ray renderer is being used, the Processing and Indirect Illumination settings are available to be saved as part of the preset. If the scanline renderer is used, the Radiosity and Advanced Lighting settings are options.

Matching Your Scene to a Background Image

One of the most interesting uses of 3ds Max is to combine a photograph with a design model to create a view of a building as it will appear in its intended location. This is called Camera Matching, and is an excellent way to help your client understand the look and scale of the design. It can also play a crucial role in the planning phase of a project, where this type of image may be required as part of a design review submission.

There are two basic ways to do a camera match. You can strictly match the camera with a photo visually, or you can use a precise automatic method. The precise method requires that at least five points be visible in the photograph for which you have corresponding measurements in your design model. You will use this method in the following exercise.

MAKE NOTE OF THE CAMERA SETTINGS IF POSSIBLE

In this section, you'll use 3ds Max's Camera Match tools to place a model of an apartment building in a background photograph of the apartment's intended site. The apartment is located in San Francisco, California, so the model has a Sunlight system light source set up for San Francisco at 1:30 p.m. on July 4, 2011 (see Figure 10.36). It's a good idea to make note of all the camera settings that were used to take the background photograph. Information such as the focal length of the camera lens and the position and height of the camera can help you determine whether you are on the right track when aligning a model to the background. You will also want to keep track of the date, the time of day, and the direction of true north. This information will help you accurately match the sun in your design to the location of the sun in the background.

If you don't take a digital photo yourself, try checking the properties of the digital file; it frequently will tell you the lens focal length, f-stop, and time of day the photograph was taken, if the camera's date and time feature was set properly.

Setting Up the Model and the Image

Before you can align a design with a background image, you need to find at least five locations in the image that you can correlate with locations in the design. The five locations must not all be coplanar or an adequate solution will not be found. In the design, you can create an object, such as a rectangular base, that can be easily located in the photograph. The photographic image for the apartment site already has an outline of the base of the apartment drawn in for you (see Figure 10.36).

FIGURE 10.36
The background image of the site for the apartment building and a sample rendering of the apartment building

This base is 5´8˝ high and matches the building's footprint. The height of 5´8˝ was used because it is a known height in the image. The sides of the base were established by locating the building's corner in the image. Although it wasn't done for this photograph, frequently poles of known heights (*storypoles*) are placed at the future corner points of the building before the photograph is taken so that known points can be established more easily.

The vanishing points of the photograph were located so that the outline of the box could be established. AutoCAD was used to help locate the vanishing points. The photograph was brought into AutoCAD using the Image command. Then the vanishing points were established by drawing lines over the photograph.

The locations of the vanishing-point lines were carefully noted and then drawn in over the image in Photoshop. Photoshop could also have been used to find the vanishing points, but because AutoCAD offers some specialized tools for drawing vector graphics, it was much easier to find the vanishing points in AutoCAD.

A box was added to the 3ds Max design of the apartment that corresponds to the 5´8˝ tall base that was drawn over the photograph. The box will be used to align the model to the image, as you'll see in the following exercise.

Adding the Background Image

You now know that you'll need to do a little background preparation before you can match a design to a photograph. The next step is to do the actual matching in 3ds Max (see Figure 10.37).

FIGURE 10.37
The AutoCAD image with vanishing points drawn

Vanishing point to the left

Vanishing point

Layout lines

Start by assigning the background image to the 3ds Max scene file:

1. Open the file called `noriega.max`. This file contains the 3D model of the apartment building.

2. Make sure the Perspective viewport is active, and then add the background image to the viewport by first choosing Views ➢ Viewport Background ➢ Viewport Background.

3. At the top of the Viewport Background dialog box, click the Files button.

4. In the Select Background Image dialog box, locate and open the `noriegaview.tif` image file. This is the image file that contains the additional outline of the apartment base.

5. Back in the Viewport Background dialog box, select the Match Bitmap radio button in the Aspect Ratio group.

6. Be sure to deselect the Lock Zoom/Pan check box, and then click OK. After a moment, the image will appear in the viewport as shown in Figure 10.38.

FIGURE 10.38
The Perspective viewport after assigning the background image

ADDING A CONDOMINIUM TO SEVERAL IMAGES

Redeveloping downtown areas from industrial and warehouse facilities to mixed-use residential, entertainment, and commercial complexes is a common project in many metropolitan areas. Many cities are attempting to reduce the flow of citizens to the suburbs by offering safe and convenient downtown living spaces.

A friend of mine is working on a project that consists of an entire block of warehouses being demolished and replaced with one- and two-bedroom luxury condominiums. For project approval, the city's Design Review Board required renderings from several locations. Because of the downtown location, there are ample reference objects available for placing and locating the CamPoint helper objects, so this project is perfect for the Camera Match utility.

A thorough survey yielded drawings of the area and dozens of digital photographs that could be matched to the 3ds Max cameras. In many cases, the physical distances and angular relationships between objects were written and drawn directly in prints of the photographs. A total of eight camera-matched renderings were created showing the proposed structure from five different locations near the job site. If my friend hadn't used Camera Match, the renderings would have been less accurate and more difficult to produce.

You now have the image in the viewport, but you also need to tell 3ds Max that you want an image to be included as the background for renderings:

1. Choose Rendering ➤ Environment.

2. In the Environment tab of the Environment and Effects dialog box, click the Environment Map button, which is currently labeled None.

3. In the Material/Map Browser, click Bitmap; then click OK.

4. In the Select Bitmap Image File dialog box, locate and open the `noriegaview_background .tif` file. This is a duplicate of the `noriegaview.tif` file but without the outline of the base. You can also select `noriegaview.tif`, but if you do, your final rendering will contain a few stray layout lines.

5. Close the Environment and Effects dialog box.

Now you're ready to start using the Camera Match tools.

DRAG AND DROP BACKGROUND IMAGES

You can also add background images—Viewport, Rendering, or both—by dragging the file from Windows Explorer and dropping it in a viewport. When you use this technique, a dialog box appears asking to which type of background image the file is to be applied. This method is quick, but use it with extreme caution because it is not undoable.

Adding the Camera Match Points

The Camera Match tools are in two sets. The first set lets you place helper objects in the model. These helper objects, called *CamPoints*, will then be used with the second set of tools to match locations in the design with locations in the background image.

The scene contains a box named Alignobject whose sole purpose is to facilitate the alignment of the design with the background photograph. You'll use the Alignobject box to accurately place the CamPoints in the design at their appropriate locations.

Start by setting up 3ds Max to select endpoint snaps and by hiding all of the geometry except the Alignobject box.

1. Right-click the Snaps Toggle.

2. In the Grid and Snap Settings dialog box, select the Endpoint option and clear all others; then close the dialog box.

 On the Main Toolbar, click the Snaps Toggle to turn it on.

3. Use the Select by Name tool to select the green base object named alignobject.

4. Right-click to open the quad menu, and then click the Hide Unselected option in the display quad.

Now only the Alignobject box is showing. This will make it easier to place the CamPoint helpers, as shown in Figure 10.39.

FIGURE 10.39
With the endpoint snap active, place the CamPoints at the corners of the Alignobject box.

The next step is to place the CamPoint helpers in the model:

1. Click the Create tab in the Command panel; then click the Helpers button.

2. Select Camera Match from the Helpers drop-down list.

3. In the Object Type rollout, click the CamPoint button.

4. Make sure that the Snaps Toggle is active; then click the bottom-front corner of the Alignobject box, as shown in Figure 10.39. You've just added a CamPoint to the scene.

5. Back in the Command panel, change the CamPoint001 name in the Name and Color rollout to **Front Bottom**. This will make it easier to identify the CamPoint you just created.

6. Next, click the top-front corner of the Alignobject box, as shown in Figure 10.39.

7. Change the name in the Name and Color rollout to **Front Top**.

8. Place the rest of the CamPoints—Left Top, Left Bottom, and Right Top—shown in Figure 10.39, as you did for the Front Top CamPoint. Click the location in the design; then change the newly added CamPoint's name to reflect its location.

MAINTAINING A STANDARD NAMING CONVENTION

Always make sure you have a logical naming convention for the objects in your scenes. A common practice is to prefix all similar objects similarly. For example, prefix all lights with "Light" or all CamPoints with "CamPoint." Using this method will ensure that all objects of the same type will be located near each other in the Select Object dialog box.

You now have five CamPoints in place. That is the minimum number that 3ds Max needs to align a scene with a background image. The more camera match points that you can accurately place, the more precise the camera match will be. You've seen how the Alignobject box helps make quick work of placing the CamPoints in the design. You can also place the CamPoints in your design by entering their coordinates using the Camera Match Keyboard Entry rollout. But using geometry like the Alignobject box is a bit more straightforward.

HIDE THE ALIGNOBJECT BOX WHEN RENDERING

The Alignobject box was created specifically for this Camera Match operation and isn't really part of the building, so remember to hide it when you are rendering the model.

Aligning the Camera Match Points to the Background Image

The following steps will require some care. You will locate the places in the background image that correspond to the CamPoints you've just created.

1. Click the Utilities tab in the upper-right corner of the Command panel.

2. Click the Camera Match button. You'll see the CamPoint Info rollout appear with a list of the CamPoints you just created.

3. Click the Front Bottom entry in the list box at the top of the CamPoint Info rollout; then click the Assign Position button at the bottom.

4. Click the location (shown in the background image) that corresponds to the Front Bottom CamPoint in the scene (see Figure 10.40). A small cross appears at the point you click. Try to be as precise as you can in placing the cross. If you don't like the location, you can continue to click points until you have the cross placed in a location that satisfies you.

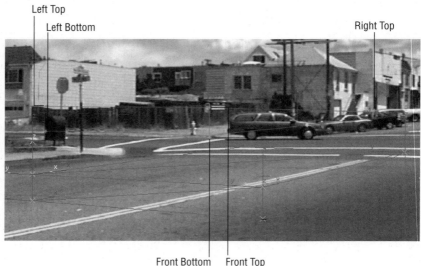

FIGURE 10.40
Click the CamPoint name in the Cam-Point Info rollout; then, with the Assign Position button active, click the points shown in the figure.

5. Because this is the first point you are aligning, you'll see a Camera Match warning message. Click Yes.

6. Select Front Top from the list in the CamPoint Info rollout; then click the Front Top corner location in the background image, as shown in Figure 10.40.

7. Repeat step 6 for each of the remaining three CamPoints.

3ds Max now has enough information to create a camera that matches the design geometry to the background image:

1. Scroll down the Command panel so that you can see the Camera Match rollout clearly.

2. Click the Create Camera button.

You will see a camera appear in the viewports and a value appear in the Current Camera Error message in the Camera Match rollout. When you click the Create Camera button, 3ds Max creates a camera that matches the view of the design with the background image.

AN ALLOWABLE CURRENT CAMERA ERROR

A good value for the Current Camera Error is any value from 0 to 1.5.

3. To see how the camera matching worked, right-click the Perspective viewport label in the upper-left corner of the viewport and choose Views ➢ Camera01. This is the camera that the Create Camera button created. The box will move into position over the image.

4. Unhide the hidden components of the building. The rest of the building appears in the viewport, as shown in Figure 10.41.

5. Hide the Alignobject box; you don't want it to appear in the rendered view.

6. Click the Render Production button on the Main Toolbar. The apartment is rendered with the background, as shown in Figure 10.42.

FIGURE 10.41
The apartment building in position

FIGURE 10.42
The rendered apartment building with the background

ADJUSTING THE CAMERA

To adjust the camera, reassign the CamPoint positions and then, with the camera selected, click the Modify Camera button in the Camera Match rollout. You can also adjust the camera manually, changing the position, rotation, FOV, and so forth to improve the camera match.

Once you have a rendering matched to a background, your work isn't completely finished. As you see in Figure 10.42, the building obscures some of the objects that are in the foreground (note the fire hydrant and the street sign). You can use an image-editing program, such as Adobe Photoshop, to bring those parts of the image back into the foreground.

Fine-Tuning a Camera-Matched View

Not all of your camera-matching projects may go as smoothly as the previous example. Due to site restrictions or other limitations, you may be able to get only three or four points to match instead of the required five points. In these situations, you have to rely more on your knowledge of the site conditions, camera locations, and camera settings. Perhaps the most important item to record is the position of the camera in relation to the site, both in plan and elevation. If you can accurately place a camera in your scene, you can usually reconstruct a camera-matched view by fine-tuning your view using the Dolly, Field-of-View, and Roll Camera tools in the Camera Controls section of the user interface. It helps to have topographical information and, if possible, aerial photographs or satellite imagery, although good site plans will work as well.

Matching the Design Image Quality to the Background

You may find that a building doesn't quite match up with the background image in ways other than orientation and size. For example, the contrast in the building may be too low compared with the contrast in the background, or there may be a grain in the background that isn't present in the rendered building. These differences can cause the design to stand out from the background, making it obvious that it is a computer rendering superimposed onto a photograph.

You can make adjustments to the lighting and materials in the scene to compensate for contrast and lighting differences, but noise in the background image has to be handled differently. You can deal with both noise and contrast by taking an alternative approach to the final rendering of the design.

Now that you've got the design aligned with the background image, you can go ahead and render the image without the background. You can then use Photoshop or another image-editing program to merge the rendered design into the background image. By doing this, you have control over the rendered image of the building apart from the background. You can add noise or adjust the contrast and color tint of the rendered design in Photoshop to match the background before the two images are merged. Figure 10.43 shows the rendering redone using this method. Compare it with the rendering in Figure 10.42, where the background and building were combined and rendered into a single image in 3ds Max.

You can also apply the Film Grain rendering effect through the Add button in the Effects tab of the Environment and Effects dialog box. Be sure to click the Ignore Background option so that only the 3ds Max objects and not the background image receive the grain, as shown in Figure 10.44.

RENDERING WITHOUT THE BACKGROUND IMAGE

To set up 3ds Max to render a view without the background, choose Rendering ➢ Environment and turn off the Use Map option in the Background group. You can always turn the background back on by reversing this procedure.

FIGURE 10.43
The rendered apartment composited with the background in Photoshop

FIGURE 10.44
Adding a Film Grain effect to the image as it is rendered

Standard Cinematic Terminology

As a design visualizer, it's a good idea to learn the standard language used to describe camera shots in the film-making world. These shot names are usually abbreviated, and the shortcut names are often used on storyboards and script treatments. The shots that describe the framing of the scene include the following:

CERT OBJECTIVE

Wide shot/extreme long shot A shot from a distance. Humans are very small. This is frequently used as an "establishing shot" that sets the location of the film.

Aerial shot Also called a *crane shot* or *overhead shot*, this is often from a plane or helicopter.

Long shot The characters/humans are seen from head to toe.

Mid shot The characters are seen from head to waist. You can identify the actions of the actors in a mid shot.

Medium close-up shot The framing of the actors is from head to chest.

Close-up shot shot (CU) This shows head and shoulders only.

Extreme close-up (ECU) Only part of the character's face is shown.

Other shot terminology describes the relationship of characters in the scene:

Two shot A shot with only two characters

Point-of-view shot (POV) A shot from the viewpoint of one character

Over-the-shoulder shot (OTS) A shot of two characters, from the point of view of over the shoulder of one, looking at the other.

There are many good sources for more information on cinematic terminology and usage. One excellent book is called *Setting Up Your Shots*, by Jeremy Vineyard (Michael Wiese Productions, 2008). This book will teach you everything you need to know to be knowledgeable about traditional camera shots and moves.

The Bottom Line

Understand the 3ds Max camera The virtual cameras in 3ds Max follow the analogy of real-world SLR cameras. You can set the focal length, set the field of view, and adjust several other parameters. Targeted cameras are oriented by moving a target object, and free cameras are oriented using the Rotate transform.

> **Master It** Create a new camera that focuses on the lower-level main entranceway, flanked by the tall, thin windows. Switch between a target and a free camera to familiarize yourself with manipulating each type.

Set up an interior view Interior cameras are more difficult than exterior cameras to properly place. The scene must be framed properly while maintaining an acceptable field of view and working within the space limitations frequently found indoors.

> **Master It** Make two clones of the camera that focuses on the outside of the entranceway. Move the new cameras and, if necessary, the targets inside the structure. Manipulate each camera so that each displays one side of the entranceway. Show as much of the windows as possible without excessive distortion.

Create an environment Most image formats can be used as the background for a rendered scene. Once an image map is selected, it can be positioned and manipulated through the parameters found in the Material Editor.

> **Master It** Select another sky image map and replace the map used in this chapter. Choose another map provided with 3ds Max Design 2011 or create your own with a digital camera. Use the controls located in the Output rollout to change a darkened sky to a brighter one, or vice versa.

Render elements for compositing 3D still images and animations must often go through a postproduction compositing process to achieve a higher level of quality or realism. Using the

Render Elements feature, you can automatically create many of the required element types at the same time the images are being rendered. Advanced image-processing software, such as Autodesk Combustion, can manipulate and composite the different images and create the final output.

Master It Open the most recent Savoye scene and create two more render elements: one for the shadows and one for the reflections.

Use the Camera Match utility When a building's model must be incorporated into a background image, you must match the 3ds Max virtual camera to the camera that took the background picture. This is accomplished by placing CamPoint helper objects in the scene and using the Camera Match utility.

Master It What is the difference between adding a CamPoint helper in the scene and assigning the position of a CamPoint helper in the scene?

A. Nothing. The terms are interchangeable.

B. *Adding* the CamPoint helper consists of locating the object accurately in the scene, while *assigning the position* of the CamPoint helper refers to selecting its proper location relative to the background image.

C. *Assigning the position* of the CamPoint helper consists of locating the object accurately in the scene, while *adding* the CamPoint helper refers to selecting its proper location relative to the background image.

D. None of the above.

Chapter 11

Organizing Objects and Scene Management

The term *scene* in 3ds Max refers to all of your models, materials, effects, and externally referenced files contained within a single .max file. In this chapter, you'll look at ways you can access and utilize your scenes while developing your renderings and animations. 3ds Max offers a variety of ways that can help you improve your workflow. You can divide a file into smaller pieces and recombine them while keeping those pieces unique. This can help you manage large scenes that require the work of several artists. Other tools let you quickly update objects in your scene or perform what-if scenarios to try different options.

In this chapter, you'll experiment with various ways of bringing in some additional furniture from the Sybex website. In the process, you'll learn how you can combine and access your scenes.

In this chapter, you will learn to:

◆ Use external references

◆ Use the Rendered Frame Window options

◆ Use the Asset Browser

◆ Create a panorama

◆ Publish a scene to the DWF format

Gaining Access to Materials and Objects from Other Files

In this section, you'll be working with groups as you did in Chapter 2, "Introducing 3ds Max Objects." You'll also use a feature called an external reference, or *XRef*, to transfer the modified fabric material from the Mybigchair.max file to the Mycouch.max file.

XRefs are a way to include other 3ds Max files in your scenes without having to combine file data into a single file. For example, you may want to create a file that contains the furniture arrangement for an office, but you may want to keep that furniture data separate from the office design file. You can XRef the furniture file into your office scene so that you can accurately locate the furniture. Because the furniture data is stored as another file, changes made to the furniture file will be updated automatically in the office file when you reload the XRef. Then, when you're done, you can remove the XRef of the office design in a single step. The furniture file then maintains its independence from the office design file. This approach avoids duplication of data

and reduces your disk storage space requirements. You can then XRef the furniture file into the office design file whenever you need to show furniture.

XRefs can be used as organizational tools to help reduce the complexity of large models by segregating similar types of objects into separate files. XRefs are also useful for dividing work between members of a design team. In an interior design project, for example, one designer can work on a floor layout while another designer works on floor patterns or lighting.

3ds Max offers two ways to use XRefs. The XRef Scenes dialog box lets you combine whole scene files into a single file. It also allows you to divide portions of a scene into separate files so that they can be edited by several individuals.

COLLABORATING ON A PROJECT

Only one individual may read and write any 3ds Max file on a local area network (LAN) at any given time. External references are a way of combining the files from several people into a master scene.

If you think you might need to edit objects brought in as XRefs, you can use the XRef Objects dialog box. You can apply transforms and modifiers to individual objects that have been imported using this dialog box, although such changes won't affect the source file.

As an introduction to XRefs, you'll use the XRef Objects dialog box in the following exercise to import a material into the MyCouch.max file. XRefs aren't necessarily the only way to import materials, but you'll use the XRef Objects dialog box in this way to see firsthand how this dialog box works.

3DS MAX AND AUTOCAD SIMILARITIES

The 3ds Max XRef tools perform the same functions as the AutoCAD XRef tools, although 3ds Max uses a different set of dialog boxes.

1. Open the MyCouch.max file from your working folder from Chapter 2 or from this book's accompanying web page, www.sybex.com/go/mastering3dsmaxdesign2011. It should look similar to Figure 11.1.

FIGURE 11.1
The MyCouch
scene

2. Press the H key.

In the Select from Scene dialog box, the icon to the left of Couch01 is surrounded by square brackets indicating that it is a group (see Figure 11.2).

3. Click Cancel to close the Select from Scene dialog box.

This will make it easy to apply a material to the entire piece of furniture because all the objects that compose the group are managed as a single object. The next job is to add the material. You used the Fabric-Blue Nap 2 material from the 3ds Max material library, but it has been modified in the Mybigchair.max file. You could reconstruct the modifications made to the material in this file, but that would be time consuming. Instead, try using the XRef Objects command to import the material and the changes that were made to it from the Mybigchair.max file.

4. Open the Application menu, and then choose References ➢ XRef Objects. The XRef Objects dialog box displays, as shown in Figure 11.3.

FIGURE 11.2
The Select from
Scene dialog box

FIGURE 11.3
The XRef Objects
dialog box

The top window in the XRef Objects dialog box lists the records or files that are referenced into the current scene. The bottom window lists the objects, materials, and manipulators within the selected record.

5. In the XRef Objects dialog box, make sure that Merge Materials is checked, and then click the Create XRef Record from File button in the upper-left corner.

6. In the Open File dialog box that appears, locate and open the Mybigchair.max file. The XRef Merge dialog box displays, as shown in Figure 11.4. Select the [Bigchair01] entry and click OK. Now the chair appears in the viewports.

7. The XRef Objects dialog box now shows the Mybigchair.max file in the upper window and, after you select the entry, a listing of objects from the file in the lower window (see Figure 11.5).

FIGURE 11.4
Select the Big-
chair01 group in
the XRef Merge
dialog box.

FIGURE 11.5
The selected object
appears in the XRef
Objects dialog box.

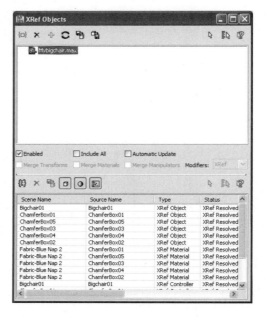

The chair is displayed in the current scene, but the chair hasn't really become a complete part of the scene. You might think of an XRef as a kind of *guest* that is visiting but doesn't maintain permanent roots in the file. Still, you can use the transform tools and modifiers on the "guest" XRef or acquire materials and objects from the XRef.

1. Click the Compact Material Editor tool in the Main Toolbar.

2. In the Material Editor dialog box, click the Get Material button.

3. In the Material/Map Browser, open the Dynamic Scene Lib rollout; then double-click the first Fabric-Blue Nap 2 listing to place the material into the current slot in the Material Editor.

4. Close the Material/Map Browser.

 You've just imported a material from the `Mybigchair.max` file into the Material Editor for your current project. You don't need the chair in your couch file, so let's remove it.

5. In the XRef Objects dialog box, select `Mybigchair.max` in the upper window.

6. Click the Remove XRef Record button at the top of the dialog box. You see a warning message asking whether you really want to remove the selected XRefs from the scene.

7. Click OK and then close the XRef Objects dialog box.

 The chair disappears, leaving your couch file as it was before you imported the chair. Now you can apply the newly acquired material to the couch.

DISABLING THE XREF LINK

To retain the XRef link to the file without actually bringing the objects into the scene, select the XRef file in the XRef Objects dialog box, and then deselect the Enabled check box below the upper window.

8. Select the Couch01 group.

9. Make sure the Fabric-Blue Nap 2 material is selected in the Material Editor window.

10. Click the Assign Material to Selection tool.

11. Close the Material Editor.

 For the final step, you'll need to make sure the couch has the same mapping coordinate scale as the other chair.

12. Click the Modify tab; then select UVW Map from the Modifier List drop-down.

13. In the Mapping group of the Parameters rollout, select the Box radio button, uncheck Real-World Map Size, and then change the U, V, and W Tile values to 0.7.

14. Save the file as **MyCouch01**.

15. Do a quick rendering of the couch. This is a legacy file that has been brought over from several releases back, so it uses the scanline renderer. Although your latest work will probably be done in mental ray, you may find yourself using the scanline renderer on older files that have standard lights and materials like this one. Your rendering should look like the couch in Figure 11.6.

FIGURE 11.6
The rendered
couch

OPTIONS FOR IMPORTING MATERIALS

You have several other options for importing materials from another file. First, you can go to the Mybigchair.max file and save the fabric to the standard material library under a new name. To do this, click the Put to Library tool in the Material Editor window. You can also set up a new material library and place the fabric there. Here are the steps for creating a new material library:

1. Click the Get Material button in the Material Editor.

2. In the Material/Map Browser, click the drop-down arrow to the left of the Search by Name field. Choose New Material from the drop-down menu.

3. Enter a name for your new material library file in the Create Material Library dialog box.

4. Drag materials you want into that library to add them.

You can then retrieve the fabric from the new library using the Material/Map Browser. This method is helpful when you are working on a team that needs to have access to a common set of materials.

A third option is to use a 3ds Max scene file as if it were a material library. Here are the steps to do this:

1. Click the Material Editor tool on the Main Toolbar.

2. In the Material Editor window, click the Get Material tool.

3. In the Material/Map Browser, click the drop-down arrow to the left of the Search by Name field. Choose Open Material.

4. In the Import Material Library dialog box, select Autodesk 3ds Max (*.max) from the File of Type drop-down list.

5. Locate and open the Mybigchair.max file.

6. In the Material/Map Browser, double-click Fabric-Blue Nap 2 in the list box. The imported material appears in the Material Editor window's sample slot.

As if you didn't have enough options already, you can also use an XRef Material Type. In the Material Editor, click the Standard button and change the type from standard to XRef Material by choosing from the list of material types. The XRef Material type will let you select a file and an object in the file, as well as the material from that object. If you have several large teams working across several locations, this is a good technique because you can have a single "master file" for all your materials and can change them for many different scenes quickly and easily. In fact, when you added the blue chair as an XRef, the material on the chair was converted to an XRef material type. When the XRef record was removed, the material reverted to Standard material type.

This is the fastest method for obtaining a material from another file.

You are able to import a material from another file using the XRef Objects dialog box. As you might guess, materials aren't the only things you can import. For example, if you want to import the seat back from Mybigchair.max, you can do so by selecting the object from the bottom list of the XRef Objects dialog box and selecting Merge. Once an object is merged, it becomes part of the current file's database (no longer an XRef). Here is a listing of the options available in the XRef Record toolbar at the top of the XRef Objects dialog box that control the files that are referenced:

Create XRef Record from File This option opens a file dialog box, allowing you to select a file containing objects to XRef.

Remove XRef Record This option removes the selected XRef'd files from the current scene.

Combine XRef Records This option combines the selected records into a single record as a housekeeping task to consolidate identical records.

Update This option compares the XRef'd file with its source file and updates the XRef if any changes have occurred.

Merge in Scene This option adds all of the objects in the selected record to the current scene and then deletes the record.

Convert Selected Object(s) to XRefs This option creates a new .max file containing the selected objects and then XRefs the new file, with the objects, into the current scene.

Select This option selects the objects in the scene that originate from the highlighted record.

Select by Name This option opens a Select from Scene dialog box. All objects in the selected XRef record appear highlighted in the dialog box.

Highlight Selected Objects' XRef Records This option highlights the XRef records in the XRef Objects dialog box that contain the XRef'd objects that are currently selected in the scene.

Here is a listing of the options available in the XRef Entities toolbar in the middle of the XRef Objects dialog box; these control the objects contained in the selected record:

Add Objects This option opens a dialog box listing objects from the selected record that are currently not XRef'd into the scene. Use this dialog box to add these files from the record into the scene as XRefs.

Delete XRef Entity This option removes highlighted XRef'd objects from the scene.

Merge in Scene Similar to the Merge in Scene button in the XRef Record toolbar, this button adds the selected entities to the scene as scene objects and removes them as XRefs.

List Objects This option controls the display of XRef'd objects contained in the selected record.

List Materials This option controls the display of XRef'd materials contained in the selected record.

List Controllers This option adds the ability to display the controllers assigned to the selected XRef objects.

Many of the toolbar functions are also located on the right-click menu available when a record or entity is selected. Additional XRef options are located below the records list, including the following:

Enabled When this option is unchecked, XRef objects do not display on the scene and are not loaded into memory with the scene.

Include All When this option is checked, all objects in an XRef record are automatically merged into the scene without user input.

Automatic Update When this option is checked, XRef objects are updated whenever the source file is saved.

Merge Transforms This option combines the Transform controllers from the source objects into the current scene. The Merge Transforms option must be selected prior to externally referencing an object into the scene.

Merge Materials This option combines the materials from the XRef'd records into the current file.

Merge Manipulators This option allows you to determine whether you have local control over manipulators. When this option is checked, any manipulator applied to the XRef'd object is merged into the scene. The manipulators coming from the XRef cannot be altered when this is unchecked.

Modifiers This option controls the handling of modifiers from XRef files. When it is set to XRef, the modifiers are contained within the XRef file and cannot be changed. *Merge* means the modifiers assigned to the XRef objects can be changed but are not reflected back into the XRef file. *Ignore* means the modifiers from the XRef file are disregarded.

Once you've imported an XRef object, you can use the transform tools to edit it. You can also modify an XRef object using the Modify tab in the Command panel. With an XRef object selected, the Modify tab gives you control over the way XRef proxy objects behave and are displayed. The options found in the Modify tab correspond to the XRef Objects entities list in the XRef Objects dialog box.

Arranging Furniture with XRefs and the Asset Browser

Using XRefs, you can begin to create a setting for the interior of the villa model. In this section, you'll use the chair—plus some other furniture from this book's accompanying web page—to create the interior setting.

During the process of arranging the furniture, you'll get a chance to explore another way of using XRefs. This time you'll use the XRef Scenes option to temporarily combine the villa model with a new furniture file to help lay out the furniture. You'll also look at how you can import geometry from one 3ds Max file to another through the Merge command and the Asset Browser. The Asset Browser is a tool that helps you manage your projects by giving you a seamless way to access data from your own computer, your network, and the Web.

Let's start by taking a look at how the Merge command can be used to import 3ds Max file data:

1. Before you save your current scene, you should strip the bitmap paths. Go to the Utility panel, click the More button, and then select Bitmap/Photometric Paths.

2. In the Path Editor rollout, select Include Material Library, then choose Edit Resources.

3. In the Bitmap/Photometric Path Editor dialog box, you'll see a list of any bitmaps that may have absolute map paths to a particular folder name. Click Strip All Paths, and click Yes in the dialog box to continue. Then close the dialog box using the Close button.

4. Save the current scene as **MyVillaCouch.max** in the same folder as the other Chapter 11 files. This will allow 3ds Max to find the associated material maps without adding the external files search path.

5. Choose Reset from the Application menu to create a new file and reset the new file to 3ds Max's default settings. The Reset Warning message displays. Click Yes.

6. From the Application menu, choose Import ➤ Merge. The Merge File dialog box displays. This is a typical Windows file dialog box.

7. Locate and open the MyVillaCouch.max file you just created. The Merge dialog box appears (see Figure 11.7).

FIGURE 11.7
The Merge
dialog box

The Merge dialog box shows a listing of objects from the file you selected. Because the Couch01.max file contains only a single group, you see the group name in the list. Had you not grouped the objects in the Couch01.max file, you would see the individual object names listed.

8. Select [Couch01] from the list; then click OK. The couch displays at the origin of the model, as shown in Figure 11.8.

FIGURE 11.8
The merged couch
at the scene origin

If the couch comes in but doesn't display the material, you may have a path issue in your file. The scene has to be able to find the bitmap file in order to display it in the viewport. This is why you stripped the paths at the beginning of this section—to ensure the bitmaps would be found.

As you saw in steps 7 and 8, Merge gives you the opportunity to select specific objects to import from other 3ds Max files—although in the case of the couch, you had only one object to choose. You can also use Merge to import cameras or geometry from other models. Unlike XRef objects, the objects you import using Merge become a part of the database of the current file and have no link to the source file.

Let's try the Merge command again by adding the chair you created earlier:

1. Move the couch 5′2″ in the X direction so that it's at the far-right side of the viewport.

RESETTING THE UNITS

You may have to change your units to US Standard Feet w/ Decimal Inches after resetting the scene earlier.

2. From the Application menu, choose Import ➤ Merge.

3. In the Merge File dialog box, locate and select Mybigchair.max and then click Open.

4. In the Merge dialog box, click [Bigchair01] and then click OK. This time you see a dialog box warning you that a duplicate material name exists in the current scene, as shown in Figure 11.9.

FIGURE 11.9
The Duplicate
Material Name
dialog box

You have four options at this point:

- You can rename the merged duplicate material by entering a new name in the input box near the top of the dialog box and then clicking the Rename Merged Material button. This will maintain both the merged material and the material in the current scene as unique materials.

- You can click Use Merged Material to replace the material in the current file with the material of the merged file.

- You can click Use Scene Material to maintain the current material and discard the duplicate in the merged file.

- You can click Auto-Rename Merged Material to have 3ds Max rename the merged material to maintain it as a unique material.

5. Click Use Scene Material. The chair displays at the origin of the file.

 Choosing this option causes 3ds Max to use the Fabric-Blue Nap 2 material currently in the file for both the chair and the couch.

6. Click the Select and Move tool from the Main Toolbar; then Shift+click and drag the chair in the negative X direction approximately 5´2˝.

7. In the Clone Options dialog box, make sure the Instance option is selected; then click OK.

Replacing Objects with Objects from an External File

You've just seen how you can use the Merge command to import parts of a scene into the current scene. Another command, called Replace, is similar to Merge but it lets you replace objects in the current scene with identically named objects from external files. This can be useful in updating scene design elements. You can also use Replace to temporarily replace complex geometry with simple *stand-in* geometry for quick-study renderings. The following exercise will demonstrate how Replace works:

1. Save your file.

2. Open the Mybigchair.max file.

3. Select the chair; then choose Group ➢ Open. This gives you access to the individual objects that make up the chair's group.

4. Click the ChamferBox02 object (the chair back) to select it; then click the Modify tab of the Command panel.

5. Select ChamferBox from the modifier stack.

6. Change the Width parameter to 2´0˝ and the Height to 2´6˝. If your chair values are already similar to those, choose something a few inches bigger or smaller. Basically, you just want to see the difference in the file.

7. Choose Group ➢ Close to close the group; then save the file incrementally.

You've made a slight modification to the chair. Now you can use Replace to see how you can update the chair in the MyVillaFurniture.max file to the new chair design.

Before you perform the Replace operation, you need to change the name of the object that forms the back of the couch. Remember that you created the Bigchair01 file from the Couch01 file, so the couch and chair share objects of the same name, even though they may not all be the same shape. The Replace command works by replacing objects in one file with objects of the same name from another file. Because you don't want to replace the back of the couch, you'll have to change the couch back object's name first.

1. Open the MyVillaFurniture.max file.

2. Select Couch01 on the right side of the Perspective viewport; then choose Group ➢ Open.

3. Click the Couch back object named ChamferBox02. Press H on the keyboard and select it by name if necessary.

4. In the Modify tab of the Command panel, change the name of the object, ChamferBox02, to **Couchback01**.

5. Choose Group ➢ Close.

Now you're ready to replace the back of the chair with the one you modified earlier:

1. From the Application menu, choose Import ➢ Replace.

2. In the Replace File dialog box, locate and select Mybigchair.max and then click Open. The Replace dialog box opens, as shown in Figure 11.10.

FIGURE 11.10
The Replace
dialog box

3. Select ChamferBox02; then click OK. You'll see a warning message asking if you want to replace the materials as well as the objects.

4. Click Yes. The chair back will be replaced with the new chair back you edited in the Mybigchair.max file, as shown in Figure 11.11.

5. Save the MyVillaFurniture.max file.

Notice that the back was replaced in both the original chair and in the instance clone of the chair. Had you made a copy instead of an instance clone, only the original chair back would have been replaced. This demonstrates that instance clones are replaced along with the original objects.

FIGURE 11.11
The new chair back
inserted using the
Replace tool

MATERIALS DISPLAYING INCORRECTLY IN THE VIEWPORTS

When you're using XRefs and the Replace option, materials do not always display correctly in the Smooth + Highlights rendered viewports. To force 3ds Max to reevaluate the materials, select them in the Material Editor, turn off Show Map in Viewport, and then turn it on again. The materials should display correctly.

Substituting Objects for Faster Viewport Performance

Maintaining and optimizing viewport performance is a constant struggle throughout the course of a project. As the number and quality of objects increases in a scene, the speed of pans and zooms and other video-intensive operations (such as playing or rendering animations) often decreases and can detrimentally affect a project's timeline. The Substitute modifier replaces the selected object in the scene with an object from another file. You can use this functionality to help sustain or improve viewport performance by swapping a high-resolution variation of a scene object with a low-resolution version from another file. Unlike the Replace command, the Substitute modifier can affect the object in the viewports, the rendered scene, or both, allowing the viewports to display a low-resolution version and the renderings to display the actual scene object. This next exercise covers the implementation of the Substitute modifier.

1. Open the VillaFurniture2.max file from this book's accompanying web page. This scene is similar to the MyVillaFurniture.max file that you recently saved, with one of the chairs converted to an Editable Poly and its components attached as a single object.

USING THE SUBSTITUTE MODIFIER WITH GROUPS

Because Substitute is a modifier, it works at the object level and you cannot substitute one group for another.

2. Select the chair on the far left.

3. In the Modify panel, expand the Modifier List drop-down and select the Substitute modifier.

4. In the Parameters rollout, uncheck the In Render check box. This causes the original geometry and not the substituted geometry to appear in any future renderings.

5. Click the Select XRef Object button.

6. In the Open File dialog box that appears, locate and select the `BigChair Optimized.max` file. This is a version of the chair in the current file that has been extremely reduced in its face count, having only about 7 percent of the faces the original has.

7. In the XRef Merge dialog box, select the ChairLight object, the only object in the scene, and click OK.

8. Both scenes contain a material with the same name, which causes a Duplicate Material Name dialog box to appear. You don't want to replace the material that exists in the current scene, so click the Use Scene Material button.

9. The Substitute Question dialog box that opens next asks if the substituted material should be applied to the selected object. Click No.

 The lower-resolution chair from the referenced scene replaces the higher-resolution chair in the current scene. Press the F4 shortcut key to turn on Edged Faces mode to see the effect more clearly. Your Perspective viewport should look like Figure 11.12.

10. Click the Render Production button in the Main Toolbar. The original, nonoptimized chair appears in the rendered scene, as shown in Figure 11.13.

FIGURE 11.12
The Perspective viewport after substituting the geometry

FIGURE 11.13
The rendered scene showing the original geometry

Importing Files with the Asset Browser

Like the Merge command, the Asset Browser lets you import a file into the current file. It doesn't let you pick which parts of a file are imported, but it does perform other functions, such as opening 3ds Max files in a second 3ds Max session or browsing the Web for materials and geometry.

As an introduction to the Asset Browser, try the following exercise. You'll use the Asset Browser to import another copy of the chair.

1. Move the middle chair to the back of the viewport.

2. In the Command panel, select the Utilities tab and then click the Asset Browser button.

 You see a dialog noting that downloaded content may require licensing.

3. Click OK. The Asset Browser opens. If the window is empty, you may need to navigate to `C:\ProgramFiles\Autodesk\3ds Max Design 2011`, as shown in Figure 11.14.

FIGURE 11.14
The 3ds Max Design 2011 Asset Browser

You can browse the contents of your computer and view thumbnail images of 3ds Max files and image files. You can then drag and drop files into 3ds Max, just as you would from Windows Explorer. One special feature of the Asset Browser is its ability to let you drag and drop 3ds Max components from websites that contain what is referred to as *i-drop content*, just as you can from any browser. In fact, the Asset Browser is an Internet browser that is built into 3ds Max.

Before you look at the Asset Browser's Internet capabilities, continue with the chair exercise to see how it works on your own computer. To display all possible files, instead of filtering geometry, images, and so forth, you can choose Filter ➢ All Files (*.*) from the Asset Browser's menu bar.

1. On the explorer bar on the left side of the Asset Browser, locate the `\3ds Max Design 2011\maps` folder and click it. The window to the right displays the image files contained in that folder, as shown in Figure 11.15.

FIGURE 11.15
Displaying the contents of a folder with the Asset Browser

2. Choose Thumbnails ➤ Small (50 × 50) from the Asset Browser menu. The images become smaller, allowing you to see more of them.

3. Click the 3ds Max Design 2011\Maps\ProMaterials folder. Again, you see a set of thumbnail views of the files. Note that the Asset Browser shows you the content of image files as well as .max files.

TURNING ON THUMBNAIL VIEWS

If all you see is a set of blank boxes, you can turn on the thumbnail views by choosing Thumbnails ➤ Create Thumbnails.

You can drag and drop image files from the Asset Browser into a 3ds Max file. If you drag and drop an image into a viewport, it becomes a background. You'll get a message asking whether you want the image to be used as the viewport background, environment background, or both. If you drag and drop an image onto an object, the image will be mapped to the Diffuse Color or Diffuse Map channel of the object's material, depending on the type of material assigned to the object.

You can also drag and drop image files into map slots or fields in the Maps, Physical Qualities, or Special Effects rollouts of the Material Editor as an alternative way of importing image maps for materials. And as mentioned earlier, you can import 3ds Max (.max) files through the Asset Browser. Try importing a chair into the current scene using the Asset Browser:

1. In the Asset Browser, use the list box to the left to locate the folder containing the Chapter 11 sample files.

2. Locate the Mybigchair.max file and select it.

3. Move the Asset Browser so that you have a clear view of the 3ds Max viewports. Then click and drag the Mybigchair.max file from the Asset Browser into the 3ds Max Perspective viewport. A context menu appears offering the Open, Merge, XRef, and Cancel options.

4. Select Merge File. Once again, you see the Duplicate Material Name dialog box.

5. Click Use Scene Material. The chair displays in the viewport. As you move the cursor, the chair follows.

6. Place the chair roughly in the center of the view and click to set the new chair location.

USING CTRL WITH THE ASSET BROWSER

If you hold the Ctrl key down when dragging geometry from the Asset Browser, the objects are placed in the new scene at the same location they reside in their original scene.

If you have the four standard viewports open in 3ds Max, the orientation of the imported object will depend on the viewport into which the object is dragged. If you drag the imported object into the Top or Perspective viewport, the object will be oriented in the normal orientation. If you drag the object into the Left or Front viewport, the object will be oriented sideways, with its Z-axis pointing toward you from the viewport.

Let's insert a few more items using the Asset Browser. This time, try inserting a lamp into the Top viewport in 3ds Max:

1. Right-click the Top viewport, click the Maximize Viewport Toggle to enlarge it, and then click the Zoom Extents button.

2. Go to the Asset Browser and locate the file called `torch1.max`.

3. Click and drag the `torch1.max` file into the 3ds Max Top viewport; then select Merge File from the context menu.

4. Adjust the location of the Torch1 lamp so that it displays on the left side of the viewport, as shown in Figure 11.16.

5. Repeat steps 1 through 4 to insert the files named `lamp01.max`, `tablelarge.max`, `tablesmall.max`, and `bruer.max`. Use Figure 11.16 as a reference to position the inserted objects.

FIGURE 11.16
Objects inserted from the Asset Browser

torch1　　　　lamp01

tablesmall　　　tablelarge　　bruer

OPENING A SECOND 3DS MAX SESSION

You can use the Asset Browser to open a 3ds Max file in a second session of 3ds Max Design 2011 by double-clicking the file's thumbnail. You may want to refrain from doing this if your system has less than optimal amount of memory.

As a rule, you can click and drag objects easily from the Asset Browser to 3ds Max using the Windows taskbar as long as you insert the objects into a non-Perspective viewport. If you must insert an object into a Perspective viewport, you can do so under two conditions. You can click and drag into the 3ds Max button of the Windows taskbar if the Perspective viewport is expanded to fill the entire 3ds Max window. If several viewports are displayed, you must click and drag directly from the Asset Browser to the Perspective viewport, bypassing the Windows taskbar. This requires that the Perspective viewport be at least partially visible, with the Asset Browser window overlapping 3ds Max. If you hold down the Ctrl key when you drag the object into the new scene, it is imported to the same location where it resides in the original file. You must follow this same procedure to click and drag bitmaps into the 3ds Max Material Editor.

Arranging Furniture with XRef Scenes

Now that you've got some furniture to work with, the next step is to lay out that furniture. Start by putting together a basic arrangement:

1. In the Top viewport, copy and arrange the furniture in a way similar to that shown in Figure 11.17.

FIGURE 11.17
The furniture arrangement

2. Next, attach the villa model as an XRef. This will give you a point of reference for the actual location of the furniture. From the Application menu, choose References ➤ XRef Scene. The XRef Scenes dialog box displays.

3. Click the Add button. The Open File dialog box displays. Locate and select the VillaSavoye_forXRefScene.max file; then click Open. You may also use VillaSavoye_forXRefScene.max from this book's accompanying web page. The filename and path displays in the XRef Scenes dialog box, as shown in Figure 11.18, and the geometry displays in the current scene.

4. Click Close. You now see the villa in the furniture layout.

5. Change to a wireframe view; then zoom out and adjust your view so that it looks similar to Figure 11.19.

FIGURE 11.18
The selected scene appears in the XRef Scenes dialog box.

FIGURE 11.19
Move the furniture into the living room in the Top viewport.

Reposition the furniture to the interior of the villa.

You see that the furniture is on the lower level of the building in the Top viewport. You want to move the furniture into the living room of the XRef villa scene:

1. Click the Select Object tool in the Main Toolbar; then place a selection region around all the furniture in the Top viewport. You may notice that 3ds Max ignores the XRef scene in the selection.

2. In the Top viewport, use the Select and Move tool to move the furniture into the living room area, as shown in Figure 11.19.

3. Switch to the Front viewport, click the Maximize Viewport Toggle, and adjust the Front viewport so that you can see the furniture and the second floor of the villa, as shown in Figure 11.20.

FIGURE 11.20
The Front viewport showing the furniture and the villa's second floor

4. Move the furniture to the second floor. Do a rough placement in the Front viewport; then zoom in and make a finer adjustment to the vertical location of the furniture.

5. Go to the Top viewport and fine-tune the furniture arrangement to fit the room, as shown in Figure 11.21.

You might notice that the XRef objects are inaccessible. They are visible and will render, complete with lighting, but you cannot manipulate any of the objects in the XRef scene.

The important thing to note here is that the coordinate system of the XRef file is aligned with the coordinate system of the current scene. Therefore, when you move the furniture to fit the XRef scene, you are placing the furniture in the appropriate location relative to the XRef scene's coordinate system.

FIGURE 11.21
Making final adjustments to the furniture placement

Next, you'll switch the relationship of the two files with which you are working. You'll close the furniture file, open the villa file, and import the furniture file as an XRef. You'll start by removing the XRef of the villa file:

1. From the Application menu, choose References ➤ XRef Scene.

2. In the XRef Scenes dialog box, select the villa file in the list box and then click Remove.

3. Click Close to exit the XRef Scenes dialog box.

4. Save the current file as **MyVillaFurniture2.max**.

Now you're ready to place the furniture in your villa file:

1. Open the `mysavoye10.max` file.

2. Open the XRef Scenes dialog box.

3. Click the Add button.

4. Locate and select the `MyVillaFurniture2.max` file; then click Open.

5. Close the XRef Scenes dialog box.

6. Right-click the Mycamera01 viewport.

 If you render the scene right now, it will be too bright. It's a good practice to use exposure control on the Render Preview window to get the right brightness and contrast.

7. On the Rendering menu, choose Exposure Control. In the Exposure Control rollout, click the drop-down arrow; then choose the Logarithmic Exposure Control and click Render Preview.

8. Make adjustments to the Logarithmic Control Parameters while watching the changes in the Render Preview Window. Try increasing the Physical Scale setting, increasing the Contrast setting, lowering the Brightness setting, and then sliding the Mid Tones setting until you like the results.

9. Finally, render using the scanline renderer. Your rendering should look similar to Figure 11.22.

10. Save your file as **mysavoyeVillawithfurniture.max**.

FIGURE 11.22
A rendered view of the villa's living room with furniture

XRefs are useful, especially when your models become complex. You can divide a model into several files and XRef them together, for example, to help keep objects organized. This can also aid in situations where you must divide design tasks between several people. You can also nest XRef files where an XRef contains other XRefs. The XRef Scenes dialog box offers other settings as well:

Add This option lets you locate and select an XRef scene.

Convert Selected This option lets you convert objects in your current scene into XRef scenes. The selected objects are saved as .max files and are removed from the current scene. They are then imported as XRef scenes back into the current scene.

Remove This option completely removes a selected XRef scene from the current scene.

XRef File This option gives you control over the way XRef scenes are linked to the current scene:

◆ Enabled lets you turn a selected XRef scene on or off. This is useful if you want to temporarily remove an XRef scene from the current scene without completely removing the link to the XRef scene. This option also removes the XRef scene from memory, making more memory available for other operations.

◆ Overlay prevents circular dependencies, which happen when a nested XRef is referenced back into itself, by loading the XRef only into the scenes that reference it. See the "XRef Scene" page in the 3ds Max Design 2009 User Reference for a complete explanation and examples of XRef overlays.

◆ Merge merges an XRef scene into the current scene, thereby ending the XRef relationship.

Update File This option controls how XRef scenes are updated:

◆ Automatic updates XRef objects whenever the source file is edited and saved.

◆ Update Now lets you manually update XRef objects from the current state of the source file.

Display Options This option controls the visibility of XRef scenes in the viewports. They have no effect on how XRef scenes are rendered:

◆ Visible turns the display of XRef scenes on or off.

◆ Box converts the display of XRefs into bounding boxes.

Ignore This option lets you control the inclusion of specific types of objects from an XRef scene. Items that are turned off won't be imported into the current scene if Merge is used.

Parent This option gives you control over the position and animation of an XRef scene by associating, or *binding,* an XRef scene to an object in the current scene:

◆ Bind is the mechanism by which you make the association. First click Bind; then select the object to which you want the selected XRef scene to be bound. The XRef scene's origin will be aligned with the selected object's pivot point. You can use a dummy object as a Bind parent object. You can then animate the bound object to animate the XRef scene.

◆ Unbind will unbind the selected XRef scene from the object to which it is bound. The Name field box at the top of the Parent group displays the name of the object to which a selected XRef scene is bound.

Using the Rendered Frame Window

While we're on the subject of file usage, you'll want to know how you can save, compare, and print rendered views using the toolbar at the top of the Rendered Frame Window (RFW). If you decide that you want to save the result from the RFW to a file, you can do so by clicking the Save Image tool on the Rendered Frame Window's toolbar.

This tool opens the Save Image dialog box, a common Windows dialog box.

In this dialog box, you can enter a filename and then select a file type for the image. You can choose from a fairly extensive list of bitmap image file types, as listed in Table 11.1.

TABLE 11.1: Bitmap Image File Types Available

FILE TYPE	EXTENSION
Audio-Video Interleaved	`.avi`
Windows Bitmap	`.bmp`
Kodak Cineon	`.cin`
Encapsulated PostScript	`.eps, .ps`
Radiance Image File (HDRI)	`.hdi, .pic`
Joint Photographic Experts Group	`.jpg, .jpe, .jpeg`
OpenEXR	`.exr`
Portable Network Graphics	`.png`
QuickTime	`.mov; requires Apple QuickTime`
SGI's Image File Format	`.rgb, .rgba`
RLA	`.rla`
Rich Pixel Format	`.rpf`
Truevision Targa	`.tga, .vda, .icb, .vst`
Tagged Image File Format	`.tif, tiff`
Silicon Graphics Image File	`.rgb, .sgi`
DirectDraw Surface Image File	`.dds`

The OpenEXR File format is similar to high dynamic range (HDR) image files. HDR image formats support a wide exposure range that stores far more information than normal images. This file format originated within Industrial Light & Magic (ILM), the visual effects company.

The OpenEXR file format has been enhanced in this release for use with 3ds Max Composite; it now holds G-Buffer and Render Element passes, all within a single file.

The Save Image for Output dialog box also lets you set some of the parameters for the chosen image file by using the Setup button. For example, if you select TIF Image File as the Save As Type file option, the Setup button will open a dialog box that lets you choose between 8-bit, 16-bit, or 32-bit color and monochrome TIFF files with or without compression.

ACCESSING ADDITIONAL IMAGE CHANNELS

The RPF file format offers support for arbitrary image channels beyond the standard RGB and alpha channels. These additional channels can be used during postproduction compositing of animations for the inclusion of special effects. When you select the RPF file format at rendering time, 3ds Max will open the RPF Image File Format dialog box, which allows you to select from a set of Optional Channels options. The RPF format is similar to the RLA format that's popular with SGI computers. This file format is particularly suited for use with Autodesk Combustion. The EXR file format provides the same functionality for use with the new 3ds Max Composite application, a compositing program that lets you make changes to your animations without rerendering, because it takes advantage of output channels such as shadow, Z-depth, pixel velocity, and so forth.

Printing Images

In addition to letting you view and save files, the Rendered Frame Window lets you print your renderings. You can print directly from the window by clicking the Print Image tool on the toolbar. This will send the print job to the default printer you have set up on your computer.

If you want to print an existing image file that you've saved, you can do so from the Save Image dialog box. Click the Save Image tool in the RFW; then, in the Save Image dialog box, locate and select an image file. If the Preview check box is selected, you'll see a thumbnail version of the file in the lower-right corner of the dialog box. You can then click the View button in the lower-left corner. 3ds Max opens another, similar RFW displaying the selected image. From this new window, you can click the Print Image tool to print the image.

VIEWING IMAGES FROM INSIDE 3DS MAX

You can open an image that you have already rendered by choosing Rendering ➢ View Image File. The image will open in its own Rendered Frame Window that you can use to print it. You can also open your rendered images in Adobe Photoshop or a similar image-editing program for greater control over cropping, print size, resolution, and so on.

Opening Multiple RFWs for Comparisons

The View button in the Save Image dialog box can be a handy tool if you want to compare a current rendering with a rendering that you have saved as a file. You can also open multiple RFWs to view several versions of your scene at once while you're rendering it. To do this, use the Clone Rendered Frame Window tool.

CERT
OBJECTIVE

This tool will open a copy of the current window contents. You can then modify your scene and render again. The cloned RFW will retain the original rendering, whereas the main RFW will display the revised scene. You can make several clones—one for each scene variation you want to try. You can minimize the windows while you are working and then maximize them later to view their contents.

Zooming, Panning, and Controlling Channels in the RFW

The Rendered Frame Window also provides a set of functions that lets you control various aspects of the window display. For example, you can enlarge an area of the window to get a closer look at a detail in your rendering. To do this, hold down the Ctrl key while you click the mouse. When you press the Ctrl key, the cursor changes to a magnifying glass. Clicking the mouse zooms in on the view. Once it is zoomed in, you can pan by holding down the Shift key and clicking and dragging the mouse. Right-clicking while holding the Ctrl key zooms the view back out. The scroll wheel on your mouse can also be used to zoom and pan in the RFW. Roll the wheel forward to zoom in and backward to zoom out. Click and hold down the scroll wheel, and then move the mouse to pan the image in the RFW.

If you want to view the red, green, blue, or alpha channel of the RFW, you can use the Enable Channel buttons on the window's toolbar, as shown in Figure 11.23. Typically, all three of the channel buttons are on. To view a single color, click the two channel buttons you do *not* want displayed. This turns them off. The Channel Display drop-down list is for RPF images. This list lets you display additional channels rendered when using the RPF file type which offers the special-effects channels.

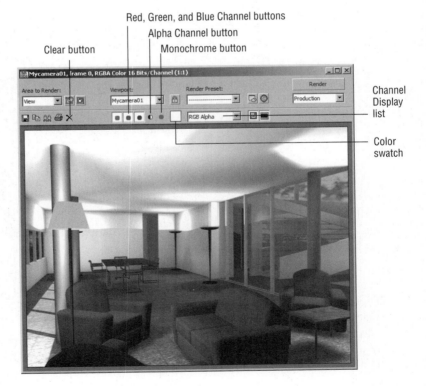

FIGURE 11.23
The Rendered
Frame Window
tools

You can also view a grayscale version of the rendering by using the Monochrome button. Finally, you can clear the contents of the RFW by clicking the Clear button.

Included at the top of the RFW are additional tools for rendering your scene without accessing the Render Setup dialog box. At the far left, the Area to Render drop-down list is where you select what portion of the current view is to be rendered. When you don't need to render the entire view, you can use the Edit Region button to define the rectangular portion of the view you need. The Auto Region Selected button automatically creates a region that encompasses all the selected objects in the view.

By default, the Viewport drop-down list displays the active viewport, which is the viewport that is rendered when the Render button is clicked. When the Lock to Viewport button is clicked, the listed viewport is rendered regardless of which viewport is active in the 3ds Max window. You can also select a render preset from a drop-down list. There are two buttons to open the Render Setup dialog box and the Environment and Effects dialogs. And of course you can render the scene in the RFW. When mental ray is the assigned renderer, many of the common mental ray tools and settings are available at the bottom of the RFW, as shown in Figure 11.24.

FIGURE 11.24
The Rendered Frame Window when mental ray is the assigned renderer

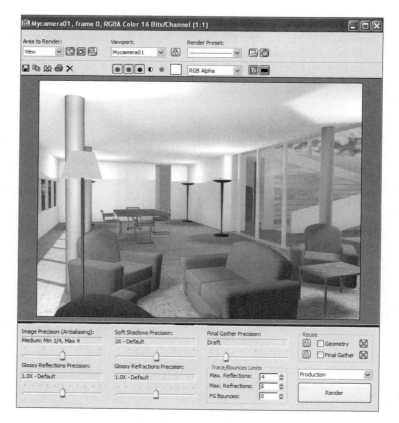

Obtaining Colors from External Bitmap Files

Perhaps one of the most interesting features of the RFW is the seemingly innocuous color swatch, located at the center of the lower toolbar (see Figure 11.23). If you right-click in the RFW, 3ds Max will record the color at the location of your cursor in the color swatch. If you right-click and drag the cursor over the contents of the RFW, you'll see a readout of the color over which the cursor passes, as shown in Figure 11.25. The readout contains additional image information you may find helpful.

FIGURE 11.25
Detecting the color and image information from the RFW

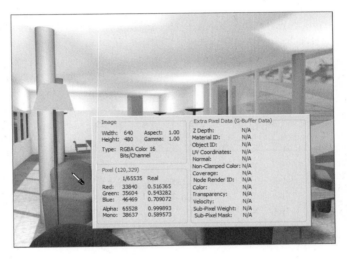

Once a color is selected and placed in the color swatch, you can click and drag this color swatch to any other color swatch in 3ds Max.

This feature of the Rendered Frame Window color swatch is significant, because with it you can import colors from a saved bitmap image file. You may, for example, be asked to match a specific color from a color chip. You can scan the color chip and save it as a bitmap file. Then, using the RFW, you can open the scanned color chip file, right-click the color, and click and drag the color from the Rendered Frame Window color swatch to the Material Editor. You can then apply the material with the imported color to an object such as an interior wall.

CALIBRATING YOUR DEVICES

If you intend to use a scanner to match colors, make sure that your scanner and printer or other output devices have been calibrated for accurate color reproduction.

Using the Asset Browser on the Internet

As you've seen, you have quite a few methods at your disposal for gaining access to files on your computer. The Asset Browser offers an additional capability of importing files from the Internet or from your company's intranet.

The methods for doing this are similar to those for importing local files. The main difference is that, instead of using the list of file folders on the left side of the Asset Browser, you use the browser functions.

You can use the Asset Browser as you would other web browsers to locate information on the Web. As mentioned earlier, you can import materials, bitmap images, model geometry, and light objects from sites that offer such items. If you prefer, you can use your favorite web browser to perform the same functions.

USING I-DROP TO ADD CONTENT

You can access a free i-drop catalog of classic designer furniture at www.ScottOnstott.com. There you will find free 3D models that you can drag and drop from the Internet directly into your own 3ds Max designs, using i-drop technology.

For this exercise, you will use the Asset Browser to locate a model and add it to your scene. Because the Asset Browser is a full-fledged web explorer, you'll need to be connected to the Internet to do the next step.

1. Open the Asset Browser or your favorite web browser and point it to www.ScottOnstott.com.

2. Using the navigation bar on the left side, choose Free Stuff ➤ 3D Models ➤ Catalog 1, as shown in Figure 11.26. If you get scripting error messages, just say no to running more scripts, and then continue.

FIGURE 11.26
Navigating to
ScottOnstott.com

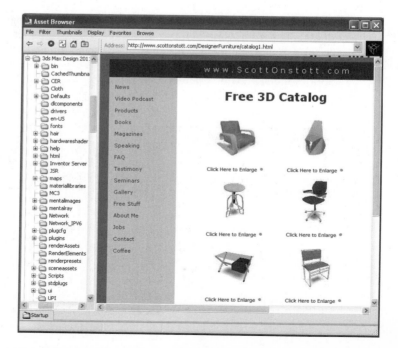

3. Select a piece of furniture that you want to download. In this example, click the thumbnail image of the red office chair (see Figure 11.27).

If you are using an Internet browser, a small pop-up window will appear. If you are using the Asset Browser within 3ds Max, the page will appear in the same window.

4. Drag the i-drop pencil from the Asset Browser to the Top viewport in 3ds Max, as shown in Figure 11.28. You'll have to carefully position the Asset Browser before you drag and drop so that you can see both the i-drop pencil and a portion of the Top viewport.

FIGURE 11.27
Select the red
office chair.

FIGURE 11.28
Drag i-drop con-
tent from the Asset
Browser into the
3ds Max viewport.

Drag the pencil symbol from here…

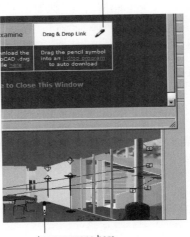

…to your scene here.

After you drag, a dialog box appears that shows the download progress.

5. A small context menu will appear in the viewport after the download is complete; it will have the Open File, Merge File, XRef File, and Cancel options. Select Merge File for this example. An Obsolete File dialog box may appear indicating that the file you are merging was created in a previous version of 3ds Max or Autodesk VIZ. If the dialog box appears, click OK. There is nothing wrong with so-called "obsolete" files; many websites offer older versions of 3ds Max files to provide backward compatibility for people still using earlier versions.

6. Move the new chair up to the second floor in the Left viewport and position it in the room. The MyCamera01 viewport will show the 3D model you downloaded (see Figure 11.29).

FIGURE 11.29
The downloaded chair added to the scene

When you are done, the i-drop content you downloaded off the Internet is automatically stored in the C:\Documents and Settings*Your Name*\My Documents\3dsMaxDesign\ downloads folder.

ADDING I-DROP CONTENT FROM THE ASSET BROWSER

You'll be able to access i-drop content with the Asset Browser in the future without having to download it again, because it is stored locally on your computer.

Tracking and Locating a Scene's Assets

Scenes in 3ds Max can contain many objects that are externally referenced from different files, as well as image maps from several local and network drives. This can create problems when files are renamed or relocated during the course of a project. For example, when you open a scene and the program is unable to locate an XRef at its assigned location, the geometry within the source scene is not available to the current scene. One solution is to keep all files in the same folder on your system. This is often not practical when assets must be shared between artists, and it creates a bloated drive when common image maps are redundantly saved in different folders.

As you learned in Chapter 9, "Enhancing Models with Materials," you have the option to assign relative paths rather than absolute paths for image maps. This allows for greater modularity of the projects and less of a chance that paths to image maps and other support files will be "broken."

It is best to maintain all of your asset files in a logical folder structure with access available to all users on the system. Regardless of how strict a procedure may be, assets get renamed or relocated, especially during software and hardware upgrades. The Asset Tracking dialog box is designed to help you locate and retarget files used in your 3ds Max scenes. This next exercise works through some of the functionality of the Asset Tracking dialog box.

1. Reset 3ds Max.

2. Locate the `MyVillaFurniture3.max` file that is currently XRef'd into `mysavoyeVillawithfurniture3.max` and move it into another folder on your system. This will cause an error when `mysavoyVillawithfurniture.max` is opened and the XRef is not located.

3. Open the `mysavoyeVillawithfurniture3.max` file. The Missing XRefs dialog box appears, indicating the name and expected location of the missing XRef file.

4. Click the OK button to close the dialog box.

5. From the Application menu, choose Manage ➢ Asset Tracking or press Shift+T. The Asset Tracking dialog box opens, displaying the name, location, and status of the files used in the current 3ds Max scene, as shown in Figure 11.30.

FIGURE 11.30
Assets can be located using the Asset Tracking dialog box.

6. If the dialog box has a tree-style view instead of a table-style view, click the Table View button in the Asset Tracking dialog box's toolbar.

 As you can see, the Unknown Status, File Missing entry in the Status column indicates that the `VillaFurniture2.max` file in the XRefs section cannot be located at its expected location. Files with their status listed as Unknown Status, Found are files that are not at their designated location but are located elsewhere in the 3ds Max search path.

 It is not necessary to remove and then add the XRef or to relocate it to its original location. You can use the Asset Tracking dialog box to retarget the XRef dependency to the new file location.

7. Highlight the offending file, and then choose Paths ➢ Set Path from the Asset Tracking menu bar to open the Specify Asset Path dialog box, as shown as Figure 11.31.

FIGURE 11.31
The Specify Asset
Path dialog box

CONFIGURING USER PATHS

If a missing file is located in any folder listed in the External Files tab of the Configure User Paths dialog box, you can use the File ➤ Reveal in Explorer option to display the location of the file in a Windows Explorer dialog box. See Chapter 9 for more information regarding the Configure User Paths dialog box.

8. Click the Browse button with the ellipses on it to open the Choose a New Asset Path dialog box, and then navigate to the new location of the VillaFurniture2.max file.

9. Select the file, and then click the Use Path button.

10. Click OK back in the Specify Asset Path dialog box to accept the new path. The status of the XRef changes from File Missing to OK and the furniture appears in the scene.

Retargeting a scene asset is only one of the functions available in the Asset Tracking dialog box. You can also strip paths from image files to force the system to access these files only from the designated user paths, view image files, or even set up custom file dependencies. 3ds Max Design 2011 is fully compatible with the Autodesk Vault asset-tracking system, and using the Asset Tracking dialog box, you can check in or out assets for editing, control revision history, and display information on a scene's editing history.

Creating Panoramas

If you've ever shopped for a car or looked at real estate online, you've probably come across a type of "virtual tour" or "wraparound panorama" that offers a 360-degree view of a space. Spawned by Apple's QuickTime VR, many software packages are available that make panoramas from a series of images. Panoramas can be made from photographs of real places or from your virtual architecture in 3ds Max.

All panorama software uses an image-distortion technique to create the seamless wraparound illusion. Because the panorama effect is image based, it is essentially a pixel phenomenon and can be efficiently transmitted on the Web. 3ds Max can export 360-degree cylindrical and spherically distorted images that you can use in a wide array of panorama-creating software. In addition, 3ds Max can export panoramas directly to Apple's popular QuickTime format. Let's use the Villa Savoye model one last time to export an interior panorama.

1. Open mysavoyeVillawithfurniture from the previous exercise or from this book's accompanying web page.

2. Select all of the cameras and Foliage objects and hide them. This isn't a necessary step, but it will unclutter the viewports and decrease the rendering time.

3. Right-click the Left viewport to activate it; then zoom into the upper floor area where you placed the furniture.

3ds Max's Panorama utility requires a camera to be placed at eye level, looking straight ahead in an interior space.

4. On the Create tab of the Command panel, click the Cameras button and click the Free button in the Object Type rollout.

5. Click a point in the middle of the second floor to place a free camera looking straight ahead, as shown in Figure 11.32.

6. Right-click the Top viewport and zoom out until you can see the new camera; then move the camera to the center of the room containing the furniture (see Figure 11.33).

FIGURE 11.32
Place the free camera for a panorama.

FIGURE 11.33
Move the camera to the center of the room.

It doesn't matter which way the camera is oriented for a panorama as long as it is facing straight ahead at eye level. The Panorama utility will automatically rotate the camera as needed to generate the panoramic image, as you will see shortly.

7. Using the Select and Move tool, move the camera to a height of 15′ in the Z direction to approximate eye level on the second floor.

8. On the Rendering menu, choose Render Setup, and then close the Common Parameters rollout. Open the Assign Renderer rollout and change the renderer from mental ray to scanline, if it isn't already.

Now, right-click in the MyCamera01 viewport; then press C to look through the currently selected free camera in this viewport.

Do not worry that the composition through this camera leaves something to be desired. The Panorama utility will utilize this camera and automatically adjust it to generate the panorama.

9. Click the Utilities tab of the Command panel, and then click the More button in the Utilities rollout to open the Utilities dialog box.

10. Click the Panorama Exporter option, and then click OK. The Panorama Exporter rollout appears at the bottom of the Utilities panel.

11. Click the Render button in the Utilities panel. In the Render Setup Dialog dialog box (see Figure 11.34), click the 2048 × 1024 button in the Interactive Panorama Exporter Common Parameters rollout. This sets a large pixel size for the entire panorama and yields higher-quality output than the default setting.

12. Make sure that Camera001 is selected in the Viewport drop-down list at the bottom of the Render Setup Dialog dialog box and click the Render button just to the right of it.

A series of six still images corresponding to the six sides of a cube are rendered and appear sequentially in the Rendered Frame Window. At the end of the automatically scripted sequence, the Panorama Exporter Viewer appears, as shown in Figure 11.35.

FIGURE 11.34
The Render Setup
Dialog dialog box

FIGURE 11.35
The Panorama
Exporter Viewer

The image that appears in the Panorama Exporter Viewer window looks blurry because of the distortion filter that was applied to create the wraparound illusion.

You can make the image look crisper by dragging the corners of the Panorama Exporter Viewer to make it smaller. On the other hand, you could have rendered more pixels in step 11 to make the panorama less blurry, but this takes additional render time. The Output Size resolution setting that you choose is for the entire panoramic image and not for each individual side. Generally, panoramas will be rather small when posted on a website, so the additional resolution may not be needed.

1. Drag the edge of the Panorama Exporter Viewer window to make the window smaller for better quality.

IMPROVING THE PANORAMA QUALITY

Try rendering the panorama at a much higher resolution to decrease the inherent blurriness. The trade-off for a sharper image is a larger file size and consequently a longer download time when the panorama is posted on a website.

2. Place your cursor directly in the center of the Panorama Exporter Viewer window, as shown in Figure 11.36. Carefully drag the cursor about ⅛″ in any direction, and watch as the image dynamically wraps around as if you are turning your head in the interior space.

FIGURE 11.36
Place your cursor in the center and drag.

You can look from side to side, up and down, and all around. Click to stop moving. For increased control or to turn small amounts, try right-clicking and dragging in the viewer window.

3. Place the cursor in the center again and hold down the middle button or wheel button on your mouse and drag down. You will zoom out of the panorama, as shown in Figure 11.37. Drag up to zoom in.

AVOID EXTREME ZOOMS

Be careful not to zoom in or zoom out too much in a panorama. Because it is a 2D image, you are actually changing the field of view of the effect, and the extremes exhibit wild distortion.

FIGURE 11.37
A zoomed-out view in the Panorama Exporter Viewer.

4. In the Panorama Exporter Viewer window, choose File ➤ Export ➤ Export QuickTimeVR.

5. Save the file and name it **MyPanorama.mov** in the QuickTime VR Output File dialog box.

OTHER QUICKTIME VR EXPORT OPTIONS

You can also export your panorama with cylindrical or spherical distortion for use in third-party panorama-generating software.

6. Close the Panorama Exporter Viewer window and the Render Setup Dialog dialog box.

7. To view your new QuickTime VR file, if you have QuickTime installed on your system, double-click the file where you saved it in the file system. QuickTime will launch (see Figure 11.38) and display the panorama in a similar fashion to 3ds Max's built-in Panorama Exporter Viewer. Drag in the center to spin the panorama.

The advantage of having your panorama in QuickTime format is that you can post it on a website and anyone who has the free QuickTime plug-in will be able to enjoy your interactive artwork; no other software is required. You must have the current version of Apple's QuickTime player installed on your system to view QuickTime VR files. You can download it for free from www.apple.com. However, QuickTime doesn't work with all Windows 64-bit operating systems at the time of this writing.

FIGURE 11.38
The panorama viewed in the QuickTime viewer

Publishing a DWF File

Still images and animations can be excellent sources of information regarding a scene. What they do not provide is the ability to interactively view a scene from user-defined views. You can't expect every client to have 3ds Max to view the scene through, and there is no viewing application available for .max files. You can, however, publish your 3ds Max scenes as Drawing Web Format (.dwf) files that can be viewed through the Autodesk Design Review software. This free viewer is available from www.autodesk.com and is installed with several Autodesk products, including 3ds Max Design 2010. You will need to make sure you have Autodesk Design Review 2011 installed to complete the following exercise.

1. Open the export_to_DWF.max file. This is a simple test scene used for expediency. If you get a message about gamma, accept the default choice.

2. Right-click in the Top viewport to make it active.

3. From the Application menu, choose Export ➢ Export to DWF.

4. In the Select DWF File dialog box that opens, name the file and select the file's location, and then click Save.

5. In the DWF Publish Options dialog box, check the Show DWF in Viewer option. This will cause the new DWF file to open in the Autodesk Design Review software after it has been created. Make sure the other options are set the same as those shown in Figure 11.39.

6. Click OK. The system pauses briefly as the DWF file is created. When it is completed, the new DWF file opens in the Autodesk Design Review software.

FIGURE 11.39
The DWF Publish Options dialog box

DWF RESTRICTIONS

There are several restrictions to the items that 3ds Max can create when publishing a DWF file. For example, environment backgrounds are represented as background colors; and environmental effects, such as fog and volumetric lights, are not included. Reflections are not shown and mental ray materials are displayed with the object's diffuse color. Take a look at the 3ds Max User Reference for a list of the objects that are supported or unsupported.

7. Click and drag in the DWF Viewer to change your viewpoint; it works similarly to using the Orbit tool in 3ds Max. Roll the mouse wheel to control the zoom factor and drag it to pan the view. You can also use the ViewCube to modify the view. Adjust the view until it looks similar to Figure 11.40.

FIGURE 11.40
The DWF file shown in the viewer

8. Many features are available in the Design Review product. If you expand the Model tab on the left side, you can see the object organization of your file. Selecting any of the objects in the model will display the Node and Object properties of the objects. On the Tools menu on the Ribbon, you can move and rotate individual objects or create a section. Let's try it.

9. Click the Tools tab on the Ribbon, and then choose Section XZ, as shown in Figure 11.41.

FIGURE 11.41
Creating a cross section

10. The front of the building and its contents are deleted in front of the Slice plane. Click and drag on the green Y-axis handle of the tripod to change the Slice plane. You can move or rotate by pressing on different areas of the tripod. Activating the end allows you to rotate, as shown in Figure 11.42.

FIGURE 11.42
Rotate the Slice plane to control the display in the viewport.

Take an opportunity to experiment with the many tools available in the Autodesk Design Review software, including the ability to slice along any plane. Autodesk has expended a lot of effort to make DWF the format of choice, and you will probably use it extensively to output your projects.

The Bottom Line

Use external references Using XRefs can increase productivity by breaking a project into smaller parts that individual artists can work on and allowing you to disassociate parts of the project as system performance decreases.

> **Master It** Extract the trees in the `mysavoye.max` or `mysavoye10.max` file as a new 3ds Max file. Change the number and arrangement of the trees in this new scene, save the configuration, and then swap this for the currently XRef'd trees.

Use the Rendered Frame Window options Using the Rendered Frame Window, you can save, print, and compare the result of your 3ds Max renderings.

> **Master It** Render the MyCamera01 viewport in the `mysavoye.max` file. Make changes to the lighting, render the viewport again, and then compare the two renderings using the RFW.

Use the Asset Browser With the Asset Browser, you can insert one 3ds Max scene into another using the dialog box to see the names of and thumbnails for the assets in any folder locally, on a network, or on the Internet.

> **Master It** Create several 3ds Max scenes consisting of a single, unique tree each. Use the Asset Browser to bring one or more of each tree into the `savoye.max` scene.

Create a panorama By creating a panorama, anybody can view the rendered result of a 3ds Max scene through the free Apple QuickTime viewer. Users can zoom and pan within the viewer to view the scene from different orientations from the original camera's location.

Master It Open the Condo AEC5.max file from Chapter 6, "Creating AEC Objects." Add a free camera centered in the main room, 6′0″ above the floor, and create a panorama and export it to a QuickTime VR file.

Publish a scene to the DWF format DWF files are gaining popularity as a means to distribute interactive access to 3ds Max scene files.

Master It Open the Condo AEC5.max file from Chapter 6. Export the condo scene as a DWF file. Open the resulting DWF in Autodesk Design Review and, using the ribbon, add a Cross Section XY Slice place to cut away a wall and see into the condo from top to bottom.

Chapter 12

Understanding Animation

Perhaps the most interesting and fun part of using 3ds Max is creating an animated presentation of your design. Animation can bring your designs to life by adding motion or change over time.

Time is the key ingredient to animation. This may sound a bit simplistic, but it will become clear as you work through the tutorials in this chapter that you need to pay close attention to the interaction of objects in your model through time. As you gain more experience animating your work, you'll start to develop an almost intuitive sense of what we call the *spacetime* of your model—the timed period of each animated segment you create. You'll become intimately familiar with this concept as you move and adjust the elements of your model. As you work through this chapter, be aware of how time is always the key component of animation.

Each camera move, light intensity change, and object movement must be carefully choreographed to create a natural flow of your vision through time. We'll show you the basic tools needed to accomplish this. You will be working primarily by keyframing within 3ds Max. This fundamental animation concept means designating critical points in the sequence (keyframes) where you want specific camera positions or lighting conditions and letting the program animate the change between those points.

In this chapter, you'll learn to:

◆ Create a quick-study animation

◆ Change the number of frames in an animation

◆ Add and edit keyframes

◆ Preview the animation

◆ Control lights over time

Understanding the World of Video Time

You may recall from childhood a special type of book called a *flipbook* that showed a hand-drawn animation of a cartoon character. Flipbooks are nothing more than a series of still pictures that, when flipped through, give the impression of motion. Today, you can purchase software that will create flipbooks for you. You could probably even create a flipbook of your 3ds Max animation.

Flipbooks demonstrate, in a physical way, how television and film work. To give the impression of motion, your television is actually flashing a series of pictures on the screen. These still images appear so fast that your mind doesn't perceive them individually, but as a smooth

stream of motion, just like the flipbooks. This process is called *flicker fusion* or *persistence of vision*, where the sequential images fuse in your perception to create the illusion of continuity through time.

Flipbooks are an example of traditional *straight ahead* animation. They are drawn one picture at a time, in order, from the beginning to the end of the sequence. After being drawn, they are shot a frame at a time with a stationary camera. In traditional cartoon animation, frames (or cels) were shot "on twos," with 12 drawings yielding 24 frames or 1 second of film animation.

This process of shooting a frame at a time can be applied not just to drawings but to actual models. When shot with a still camera, this technique is called *stop-motion animation* and is often how Claymation, such as the movie *The Adventures of Mark Twain* (1986) and other films, shorts, and commercials created at Will Vinton Studios, is filmed. The *Wallace & Gromit* episodes and movies, the *Chicken Run* (2000) movie by Aardman Animations, and movies such as *Coraline* (2009) or *The Nightmare Before Christmas* (1993) are good examples of stop-motion animation, as are the star and other creatures of the classic film *King Kong* (1933) animated by Willis O'Brien. The techniques were also used in *The Seventh Voyage of Sinbad* (1958) and *Clash of the Titans* (1981) by O'Brien's protégé Ray Harryhausen.

Traditional animators came up with a more efficient technique called *pose-to-pose* animation. In this technique, the most talented traditional animator, called the *key animator* or *key artist*, draws only the important poses, or *keyframes*, for a character to tell the story. The junior artists or interns do the tedious work to fill in all the pictures in between the poses, called *in-betweens* or simply *tweens*, to produce a smooth stream of motion. Each picture is known as a *frame*.

Technological film-making standards vary by geography. North America, most of Central and South America, and Japan use what is called the National Television System Committee (NTSC) standard for standard-definition television broadcasts and VHS and DVD recordings. This standard determines, among other factors, the number of times per second these still images appear on your TV. The rate of images per second, or frame rate as it is more commonly called, is 29.97 frames per second (fps). This means that your TV displays one whole picture or frame each 1/29.97th of a second. Therefore, for 10 seconds you will see 299.7 frames, or approximately 1,800 frames every minute. This is also called *dropframe* frame rate, because it drops about one frame an hour. NTSC-compliant television sets display an image at a resolution of 720 × 486 pixels, although each TV may crop the images around all four sides a little differently. The European standards, called Phase Alternate Line (PAL) and Séquentiel Couleur à Mémoire (SECAM), use 25 fps and 24 fps, respectively. The new HDTV standards are based on a resolution of 1920 × 1080 pixels.

As you work in 3ds Max, you can think of each of these frames as the unit of time they occupy. For the sake of our discussion, we'll round this unit of time to 1/30th of a second; therefore, 30 frames are displayed every second. This will become more apparent as you work through the tutorials.

Like traditional animators, you will be responsible for establishing the keyframes, known as *keys* in your sequence. 3ds Max will fill in all the in-between frames automatically, and you'll be able to fine-tune the way 3ds Max interpolates between your keys to control the nuances of motion.

For a comprehensive introduction to digital filmmaking, check out Dan Ablan's *Digital Cinematography and Directing* (ISBN-13: 978-0-735-71258-4). Also, Joseph V. Mascelli's *The 5 C's of Cinematography* (ISBN-13: 978-1879505414) is a classic.

Creating a Quick-Study Animation

A single image, such as a rendering, can show a lot of detail, but an animated view of a design can offer a better sense of form and space. If an animated view is properly done, you can also get a better sense of the scale of a design.

When you create an animation, you are rendering several hundred still images that are later combined to form the frames of an animated movie. Because you are generating so many renderings, animations can take quite a bit longer to produce than still images do. You can use different renderers to generate different quality results, and there is an art to finding a happy balance between render time and render quality. Each renderer has its own tricks and techniques to achieve this.

Animation in 3ds Max begins by getting into a keyframing mode. There are two keyframing modes to choose from: Auto Key and Set Key.

AUTO KEY AND SET KEY MODES

Set Key is a keyframing mode originally designed for character animators. This mode allows you to try a pose before you commit to it by saving specific keys manually. Auto Key mode, on the other hand, records the final state of all changed parameters for each keyframe, without explicit key-setting by hand.

Auto Key mode is often easier to understand and use and will be the focus of this chapter. You get into this mode by simply clicking the Auto Key button at the bottom of the user interface. You may recall that you already used this mode when you did the quick-start animation in Chapter 1, "Getting to Know 3ds Max Design 2011," when animating a car object passing in front of the building.

1. Open the SavoyeCameraAnimation_Start.max file.

2. Choose Customize ➢ Show UI ➢ Show Track Bar if it is not already selected. The track bar represents time as it flows from left to right. Keys you create will appear on the track bar when an object containing the keys is selected.

3. Click the Auto Key button at the bottom of the user interface.

 The button turns red to let you know that you are in Auto Key mode. The background behind the Time slider and the edge of the active viewport also turn red.

4. Click and drag the Time slider, which currently reads 0/100, to the far right. The Time slider sits just below the viewports and just above the track bar.

When you start to animate your model, you can think of your animation as a self-contained slice of time. That time is divided into 30 divisions per second. Each of those divisions is called a frame, and each frame when rendered will appear as a single, still image.

The Time slider shows two numbers. The first number is the current frame, and the second number is the total number of frames in your slice of time, called a *segment*. The default active time segment that 3ds Max offers is 101 frames long (frame 0 through frame 100), or a little over 3 seconds of animation at 30 fps. This time segment can be extended to longer sequences using the Time configuration tools. When you move the Time slider to the far right, you change your position in your active time segment to the last frame, or frame 100. This may seem a bit confusing right now, but the next exercise will give you a firsthand example of how time works in 3ds Max.

Longer animations may be made of multiple segments, called *shots*. Typically, video-editing software is used to composite rendered sequences from 3ds Max together into shots and provide transitions and special effects. There are many popular video-editing packages, such as Adobe Premiere, Adobe Final Cut Pro, and Avid Composer. You can also use video-compositing software such as Adobe After Effects, Autodesk Combustion, or Autodesk 3ds Max Composite (now bundled with 3ds Max Design 2011).

Adding Camera Motion

3ds Max starts out by giving you an active time segment of 101 frames numbered 0 to 100. The Time slider you just used lets you move through the frames quickly. To get a better understanding of how this works, let's add some motion to the scene:

CERT
OBJECTIVE

1. Right-click the POV viewport label, and then choose Views ➤ Camera.View.3DFRONT. You'll use this view in the animation example.

2. Right-click in the Top viewport to make it active.

3. Click the Select and Move tool; then click the Camera.View.3DFRONT camera object. When you select the camera, look in the Name field in the Command panel to verify you have the correct camera selected. This is the camera at the very bottom of the Top viewport.

4. Make sure the Time slider is at frame 100. Move the Camera.View.3DFRONT camera to the location shown in Figure 12.1.

FIGURE 12.1
Selecting and moving the 3DFRONT camera

Move the camera to this location.

Click this camera.

5. Now, right-click the Camera.View.3DFRONT viewport to activate it. Click and drag the Time slider slowly from its position at the far right to the far left and back again.

The view changes dynamically as you move the bar. Also notice that the camera moves in the other viewports, showing you its location at each frame.

You have just created a camera motion by simply selecting a frame using the Time slider and then positioning the camera in the new location for that frame. Moving objects while in Auto Key mode changes their location in time as well as within the space of the model. Had you moved the camera with Auto Key mode turned off, you would have simply moved the camera with no resulting change in the relative motion over time.

When you create a new keyframe, the parameters are *interpolated* from the previous keyframe to the new keyframe. If there is no previous keyframe for the parameters being adjusted, the parameters prior to modification are added to a new key automatically created at frame 1. Take a look at the track bar below the Time slider and you will notice two red boxes, representing the keyframes, at frames 1 and 100. By default 3ds Max Design 2011 places keyframes at Frame 1 when using Auto Key; you can change this behavior by modifying the Auto Key Default Frame setting found under Customize ➤ Preferences and going to the bottom of the Animation tab. In some earlier versions of the software, the default key was set at frame 0 rather than frame 1.

KEY COLOR CODING

Keys indicating transforms are color coded: position keys are red, rotation keys are green, and scale keys are blue. Most other keys are gray.

Adjusting the Camera Path

If you study the animation in the Camera viewport as you move the Time slider back and forth, you may notice that you alternately move closer to the building and then farther away from it. This is because the motion path of the camera is a straight line between the beginning camera location and the end location, as shown in Figure 12.2. As the camera moves through its path, or *trajectory* as it is called in 3ds Max, it also moves farther from the building.

FIGURE 12.2
The camera's trajectory

The camera's trajectory

Let's assume that you don't want that effect and that you want the camera to stay as consistent a distance from the model as possible. To achieve this, you can move the Time slider to position the camera at its closest position to the model, and then move the camera farther away at that point in time, with Auto Key on.

1. Move the Time slider to the middle of the slider position so that the slider shows 50/100. This places your camera at frame 50.

You can also enter **50** in the Current Frame text box in the animation controls area next to the viewport controls at the bottom-right corner of the user interface.

2. While Auto Key is still on, use the Select and Move tool to move the camera away from the model to a location similar to the one shown in Figure 12.3. Notice the new, red key on the track bar at frame 50.

FIGURE 12.3
The camera's position at frame 50

New camera location at frame 50

3. Right-click the Camera.View.3DFRONT viewport then click the Play Animation button in the time controls.

The viewport displays the view from the camera through the sequence of frames.

4. To stop the playback of the camera animation, click the Stop Animation button, which has replaced the Play Animation button in the time controls.

5. Right-click the Top viewport; then click Play Animation again. Notice that this time you see the camera motion in the Top viewport.

6. Click the Stop Animation button to stop the playback.

Here you see how moving the camera at a particular frame in the Time slider affects the camera motion. When you altered the camera location in this last exercise, you were actually adding a *key* or *keyframe* to the camera path. You can think of the camera path as a spline and the keyframes as control points or vertices on that spline.

The keyframes appear on the track bar only when an animated object is selected. Because the camera is selected, you can see the keyframes (see Figure 12.4). There are many ways to navigate to a precise point on the Time Slider. The Go to Time command is one technique that is convenient and fast.

1. Move the Time slider away from frame 50.

FIGURE 12.4
The bars below the Time slider indicate the location of a keyframe.

2. Right-click the keyframe at frame 50 in the middle of the track bar.

3. Select Go to Time from the shortcut menu. The Time slider moves to the keyframe location on the track bar, and the view from that location is displayed in the Camera. View.3DFRONT viewport.

The Go to Time option offers a quick way to move the current time to any keyframe location.

Viewing the Camera Trajectory

When you're working on an animation sequence, it helps to see the animation path, or trajectory, of an object. For example, if you could see the path of the camera in the last exercise, it would be easier to determine the distance between the camera and the model throughout the animation. 3ds Max offers a number of tools for displaying the camera path as well as the location of the keyframes along the path. The following exercise will show you some of those tools.

1. Make sure that the Camera.View.3DFRONT camera is still selected. Then click the Motion tab in the Command panel.

2. Click the Trajectories button near the top of the panel.

 Now you can see the path of the camera as a dotted line in the Top viewport, as shown in Figure 12.5.

3. Right-click the Top viewport, and then click the Maximize Viewport Toggle to enlarge it.

FIGURE 12.5
The Top viewport showing the camera trajectory

4. Move the Time slider to the 75/100 position to get a better view of the keyframes on the trajectory.

You can see the keyframes identified as small squares in the path. The dots in the path represent the remaining frames of the animation.

5. Use the Select and Move tool to move the camera slightly to the left to create a new keyframe.

6. Move the Time slider to the 25/100 position.

By moving the camera in step 5, you added another keyframe to the path. By using the buttons in the Create Key group in the Motion tab of the Command panel you can add a keyframe without having to move the camera:

1. Click the Parameters button, next to the Trajectories button in the Motion tab of the Command panel. The camera's trajectory disappears.

2. With the Time slider at the 25/100 position, click the Position button in the Create Key group of the Look at Parameters rollout, as shown in Figure 12.6.

FIGURE 12.6

Creating a Position key using the Motion panel

You've just added another keyframe at frame 25. Note that the Position button in the Create Key group lets you add a keyframe without changing the position of the camera. The additional keys can be used to fine-tune and manipulate the camera's trajectory:

1. Right-click the keyframe in the track bar at the 75/100 position.

2. Choose Delete Key ➢ Camera.View.3DFRONT: Position from the shortcut menu. The keyframe is removed from the camera trajectory. Repeat this step for the keyframe you created at the 25/100 position.

3. Turn off Auto Key mode. If you're not actually working on animation motion, it's a good idea to keep it turned off because any transforms or parameter changes that you apply to objects will be automatically keyed. It's a very common problem to forget to turn off Auto Key and therefore create unintended keys that mess up your camera animation.

Just as with objects in your model, you can select multiple keyframes that appear in the track bar by holding down the Ctrl key when you select or by dragging a selection window around them. You can then right-click any keyframe and select an option from the shortcut menu to edit the selected keyframes. In the preceding brief exercise, you deleted a single keyframe using the track bar right-click shortcut menu.

Controlling the Camera Trajectory Visibility

When you clicked the Parameters button in a previous exercise, the camera trajectory disappeared. This is because the path is typically visible only when the Trajectory button is selected. You can permanently turn on the trajectory visibility through the Object Properties dialog box.

1. Right-click the selected Camera.View.3DFRONT camera. Then click Object Properties in the quad menu. The Object Properties dialog box displays.

2. The By Object button in the upper-right corner of the Display Properties group should be turned on. If the button reads By Layer, click it until it reads By Object. This makes several of the options listed in the Display Properties group available.

3. Select the Trajectory check box. This turns on the trajectory display even when the Trajectories button is not clicked.

4. Click OK to accept the change and close the dialog box.

Now you can again see the camera path and keyframes for the Camera.View.3DFRONT camera object. By turning on the Trajectory display option, you can more easily edit the camera path. You'll want to turn it off, however, when you're editing other aspects of the scene, because the path trajectory can add to the visual clutter of a complex model.

ANOTHER TRAJECTORY VISIBILITY OPTION

Another way to control the trajectory visibility is to select the animated object, click the Display tab of the Command panel, and then place a check mark in the Trajectory option in the Display Properties rollout. Note that this will change the display properties of the selected object from By Layer to By Object.

Once you've established the keyframes of your animation (the beginning and end frames are also keyframes), you can edit them to further refine your camera motion. You'll see how that's done later in this chapter. For now, let's create a preview of this animation.

Creating a Preview Animation

Rendering even a short animation can be a time-consuming process, so you'll want to make sure that the motion in your animation is exactly what you want before you commit to actually producing a rendered animation. One tool that will help you determine what your animation will look like is the *preview* animation. A preview animation is a rough facsimile of how your final

animation will look. You should use it only to get a basic idea of whether your animation works in a general way. Still, it can reveal many of the flaws in your animation that might otherwise go unnoticed, such as a jerky camera motion or a camera-object collision that isn't obvious in the viewports.

PREVIEW ANIMATIONS

Preview animations are no longer made using the Interactive Viewport Renderer, which is what is used to create the display in the viewport. The preview is now handled through a viewport grab that is not affected by what you do on your computer during the rendering process. This is new behavior for 3ds Max Design 2011.

Try the following exercise to create a preview animation of your work so far:

1. Click the Maximize Viewport Toggle to get a view of all the viewports, if necessary. Then right-click the Camera.View.3DFRONT viewport to activate it. Also press F4 on the keyboard to turn off Edged Faces if the display of your file included Edged Faces.

2. Choose Tools ➤ Grab Viewport ➤ Create Animated Sequence File. The Make Preview dialog box appears, as shown in Figure 12.7.

3. Click the Create button. If this is the first time you've used this feature, you'll see the Video Compression dialog box. (You'll learn more about video compression in Chapter 13, "Creating Animations.")

4. Go ahead and click OK. If you are an experienced 3ds Max User, you'll notice that you no longer see a small version of the scene in the viewport area as the preview is created. This is new behavior with the 2011 release. After the preview is created, Windows Media Player opens and plays back the preview.

FIGURE 12.7
The Make Preview
dialog box

If you have another application designated to play back AVI files, you'll see that application rather than Windows Media Player.

The preview is rough, but it does give you a good feel for the camera motion through the model. The model itself isn't rendered, and the lighting effects aren't displayed accurately.

If you look at the Make Preview dialog box, you'll see that you have several options that control the preview animation. You can have the animation display the frame number, active grid, or light locations, for example, by selecting the check box next to each of these items. You can control the size of the animation relative to the current settings in the Render Setup dialog box using the Percent of Output input box.

If you want to limit the preview to a particular range of frames, you can specify that range in the Preview Range group. The Rendering Level drop-down list lets you determine whether the preview renders a shaded view, a wireframe view, or any other viewport rendering mode. The Output group gives you control over the Audio-Video Interleaved (AVI) settings. Finally, the Render Viewport drop-down list lets you select a viewport to render. By default, the preview animation is created using the currently active viewport.

When 3ds Max creates a preview animation, it saves the animation as a file named _scene .avi (the filename begins with an underscore character) in the C:\Documents and Settings\ *Your Login*\My Documents\3dsmax\previews folder. Every time you create a preview, 3ds Max overwrites this file without asking you whether it's OK or not. If you create a scene animation that you want to save, choose Tools ➤ Grab Viewport ➤ Rename Animated Sequence File. The Save Preview As dialog box that displays lets you save the last preview animation under a different name, thereby permanently saving the preview. After you have closed Windows Media Player, you can choose Grab Viewport ➤ View Animated Sequence File to view the last preview created.

Understanding Keyframes

The exercises you just completed demonstrate that you can add and delete keyframes on the camera trajectory. The keyframe displays as a small square on the camera trajectory. It is a point along the camera trajectory that can be manipulated in a number of ways to adjust your camera motion. A keyframe was created in the middle of the series of frames, at frame 50, when the camera was moved so that the camera path curved around the building.

The simplest adjustment to a keyframe is to transform (move, rotate, scale) the object whose keys it identifies. Notice that there are keyframes at the end and beginning of the camera path. These were created as soon as you moved the camera at frame 100. Let's try changing the view of the last frame of this camera path by moving the camera, therefore modifying the end keyframe:

1. Click the Auto Key button again to turn it on.

2. Right-click the Top viewport to make it active. Click the Select and Move tool on the Main Toolbar.

3. With the Time slider set to frame 100 (the far right), move the Camera.View.3DFRONT camera to the location shown in Figure 12.8. Notice what happens to the camera path.

FIGURE 12.8
Moving the camera
at frame 100

Move the camera here.

The tiny dots on the camera path show you the location of the camera at each frame. They also indicate the change in speed of your camera over time.

Notice that after you move the camera at the last keyframe, the dots are spread farther apart between the keyframe at frame 50 and the last frame at frame 100. This tells you that the camera motion is faster between frames 50 and 100 than it is between frames 0 and 50. You can see this because the distance between the camera's location at each frame is greater from frame 50 to 100 than it is between frames 0 to 50 while the length of time is equal. You can see another visual representation of this by creating another preview animation.

You might also notice that the camera path now crosses right through some trees. To smooth out the camera motion, and to avoid the trees, you will want to move the camera at frame 50. You can use some tools found in the Motion tab of the Command panel to help you quickly move to keyframes.

1. With the Camera.View.3DFRONT camera still selected, click the Motion tab of the Command panel. Click the Parameters button if is not already active.

2. In the Key Info (Basic) rollout, click the left arrow button so that key number 2 is displayed in the box to the right, as shown in Figure 12.9.

FIGURE 12.9
Moving the Time
slider to the time
of the camera's
second key

The camera moves to the second key associated with the selected camera, as does the Time slider. This key and the one immediately to the right of it cause the Time slider to jump to the next or previous keys that exist for the selected object.

3. Click the Select and Move tool; then move the camera to the location shown in Figure 12.10 (the trajectory is shown for clarity). There was an existing key at frame 50 that defined the location of the camera. By moving the camera with Auto Key active, the new position information replaces the old information in that key.

FIGURE 12.10

Move the camera
at frame 50.

FIGURE 12.10

Move the camera
at frame 50.

4. Right-click in the Camera.View.3DFRONT viewport, and choose Tools ➤ Grab Viewport ➤ Create Animated Sequence File. The Make Preview dialog box appears.

5. Click the Create button.

6. Replay the animation to examine the results.

The preview shows that your camera motion is too fast—your camera is moving around three sides of a building in just over three seconds. Also, the beginning and end are rather abrupt. Next, you'll learn how to increase the overall number of frames in the current animation to slow down the animation.

CONTROLLING THE ANIMATION LENGTH

Many beginning animators try to fit too much into too short a time segment. Slower motion is usually better in architectural animations, and that equates to rendering many more frames. At 1,800 frames for one minute of video, a typical animation might be several thousand frames long.

Before we move on, however, we'd like to summarize the steps involved in animating an object. You can create motion in 3ds Max by turning on the Auto Key button, selecting a point in time with the Time slider, and then transforming the object by moving, rotating, or scaling it. This creates a keyframe and possibly an animation trajectory. Once a keyframe is created, you can alter that keyframe by returning to that point in time using the Time slider and then transforming the object. If you select a frame that is not a keyframe and then move the object, you create a new keyframe. This is easy to do accidentally, so be careful when moving cameras and objects with the Auto Key button active.

Keyframes can be deleted in a number of ways, the simplest of which is to right-click the keyframe in the track bar under the Time slider and select Delete Key. An animated object must be selected before the keyframe will appear. By right-clicking the Time slider, you can also add a key at any frame without actually moving an object. Doing so opens the Create Key dialog box, shown in Figure 12.11.

You can enter the type of keyframe, as well as a source and destination time other than the default time shown in the dialog box; then click OK to accept the new keyframe settings.

FIGURE 12.11

The Create
Key dialog

Increasing the Number of Frames in an Animation Segment

At the beginning of this chapter, we mentioned that the standard frame rate for video in North America is approximately 30 fps. Therefore, in order to lengthen the time in your building animation, you need to increase the number of frames over the camera path. Right now, you have 100 frames, or about 3 ⅓ seconds of animation. Let's see what you need to do to increase your current path to 300 frames for a 10-second animation.

1. Click the Time Configuration button at the bottom of the user interface.

 The Time Configuration dialog box displays, as shown in Figure 12.12.

2. In the Animation group, click the Re-scale Time button. The Re-scale Time dialog box appears, as shown in Figure 12.13.

3. In the End Time input box, enter **300**. When you press ↵, the Length value changes to match the End Time value.

FIGURE 12.12
The Time Configuration dialog box

FIGURE 12.13
The Re-scale Time dialog box

> **SETTING THE START TIME**
>
> There is no hard and fast rule that requires that an animation must begin at frame 0. If you realize that you need to add action to the beginning of your animation, you can change the Start Time value in the Time Configuration dialog box to become a negative number. A Start Time of -90 adds three seconds to the beginning of your scene.

4. Click OK; then click OK again in the Time Configuration dialog box.

Notice that the Time slider now shows 300 for the total number of frames and that the existing keyframes have been spread out through the new animation length. You'll also see a greater number of dots in the Camera.View.3DFRONT trajectory. If you had just increased the End Time value in the Time Configuration dialog box, you would have appended 200 additional frames to the end of the animation length, but the existing keyframes would have remained at their current frames.

5. Create another preview animation, making sure that you have selected the Camera. View.3DFRONT viewport as the Render viewport. The camera now takes three times as long to circle the building, and the preview takes three times as long to create.

In the Time Configuration dialog box, you saw that you have an option to set the end time as a separate value from the length of the animation. 3ds Max lets you work with *active time segments*. An active time segment is the block of time, within your animation, on which you are currently working. Right now that block of time includes the entire time of the animation, but you can set up 3ds Max to limit your active time segment to just a few frames of the overall time length. This feature is useful if you are working on a very large animation and want to isolate your work to a specific set of frames. You'll see how to work with active time segments in the next section. Right now, let's see how to smooth out the beginning and end of the camera path so it doesn't seem so abrupt.

Accelerating and Decelerating the Camera Motion Smoothly

You don't want the camera to suddenly start or stop moving at its full rate, or your animation will seem jarring. You want the camera motion to start out slowly, and then increase speed as if you were in a car starting out from a stoplight. The same is true for the end of the camera path. You want to slow down gradually and not stop instantly. You can control the acceleration and deceleration of the camera by setting the key tangent properties. These are available in the Key Info (Basic) rollout of the Motion tab.

1. With the Camera.View.3DFRONT camera selected, set the Time slider to the first keyframe position at the far left.

2. Select the Motion tab in the Command panel, make sure the Parameters button is active, and scroll down to the Key Info (Basic) rollout. Notice that key number 1 is shown at the top of the rollout. Any changes made now will affect that key.

3. Click and hold the Out button at the bottom of the rollout. You'll see a set of buttons. These are the tangent options for the keyframe (see Figure 12.14). Tangents define the animation entering and exiting a keyframe. The tangent types are explained later in this section.

FIGURE 12.14
The available
key tangents

4. Select the Slow tangent button. This is the button that looks like the top quarter of a bell curve.

This tangent has the effect of slowing the camera motion as it approaches or leaves a keyframe. In this case, it will slow the motion as it leaves this keyframe because you used the Out tangent. Selecting the same tangent from the In flyout would cause the camera to decelerate as it approaches the key.

5. Click the Trajectories button and then zoom into the camera in the Top viewport. You'll notice that now the dots on the camera trajectory are closer together as they exit the first keyframe, as shown in Figure 12.15.

6. Create another preview animation of the camera. To see only the new beginning of the animation, choose Custom Range in the Make Preview dialog box and enter 0 and 100 in the two input boxes that become available.

You will notice that now the beginning of the animation starts out in a gradual acceleration from a stop. The bunching up of dots near the starting keyframe shows you that the frames at the beginning are closer together and there is less motion between frames. As the frames move away from the starting keyframe, they gradually spread apart, traversing a greater distance with each frame until a uniform frame-to-frame distance is reached. The net effect of all this is a smooth acceleration from the camera starting point.

FIGURE 12.15
The spacing of the
dots on the trajec-
tory indicates the
acceleration.

Now adjust the ending keyframe to decelerate the camera motion gradually:

1. Click the Parameters button in the Command panel. In the Key Info (Basic) rollout, click the right arrow button until 3 is displayed in the key number box if it is not already displayed.

2. Click and hold the In button and select the Slow button. Because you want the camera to gradually decelerate toward the keyframe, you use the In button to make the setting. Just as with the first keyframe, you see the dots in the trajectory move closer together as they approach the last keyframe.

3. Create another preview to see the results. Be sure to select Active Time Segment in the Make Preview dialog box to render the entire animation length.

In this section's second exercise, you adjusted the camera speed for the end of the camera path in a way similar to the beginning. As the frames approach the last keyframe, they gradually become closer together. The net effect is a deceleration of the camera motion.

This latest camera motion seems to move a bit faster than before. Because the frames have been moved closer to the beginning and end keyframes, they become more spread out over the rest of the trajectory, adding some speed to the camera motion. Remember that you are working with a fixed number of frames, so as you move frames closer to the beginning and end, the rest of the trajectory has fewer frames to define the camera's position, and fewer frames means faster motion.

Let's take a moment to get to know some of the other key tangent options. You already know what the Slow tangent option does. Here is a listing of all the tangent options for both in and out directions and what they are used for:

Smooth Creates a smooth transition through the keyframe. Smooth has a tendency to overshoot the smooth curvature beyond the key, sometimes resulting in undesirable behavior (see the Flat option).

Linear Straightens the trajectory near the keyframe. If Linear is used for the Out parameter of one keyframe and the In parameter of the next, the resulting trajectory between the two keyframes is a straight line, and the intervals between frames become uniform.

Step Causes the keyframe value to jump from one key to the next. If Step is selected for the In parameter of the current keyframe, the prior keyframe's Out parameter will automatically be changed to a Step tangent. Step has the effect of causing the animated values to hold steady at the current keyframe and then pop to the next keyframe's value when the Time slider reaches that frame.

Fast Causes the rate of change to increase around a keyframe. For example, using Fast in keyframe 2 of the previous exercise will cause the camera to appear to speed up around the keyframe. The trajectory also becomes straighter near the keyframe.

Slow Causes the rate of change to decrease around a keyframe. This has the opposite effect from that of the Fast tangent option.

Custom Allows you to make fine adjustments to the rate of change through a keyframe. When Custom is selected, you can edit the rate of change through a keyframe, using tangent handles, and in the Track View – Curve Editor dialog box.

Flat The Flat tangent type guarantees a smooth transition between keys and avoids the "overshoot" problems often experienced with the Smooth type. Flat is the default tangent type. When you edit any Flat tangent handle, the tangent type converts to Custom.

You'll get a chance to use some of the other tangent options later in this chapter, including the Custom tangent option. Now let's continue with a look at some of the other ways a keyframe can be edited.

Editing Keyframes

Keyframes are not set in stone, and it's a good thing they aren't. A recurring theme in this part of the book is the cycle of editing, testing, and then editing again. This process applies to keyframes as much as it does to editing materials and lights.

OTHER WAYS OF CONTROLLING SPEED

If your animation is strictly for video or film, you have no alternative for controlling speed other than increasing or decreasing the number of frames in a segment. You must adhere to the local television frame rate standards. On the other hand, if you plan to have your animation shown exclusively on a computer monitor, you have other options.

Most video playback programs for computers allow you to vary the frame rate of your animation, although you probably would not want to go below 15 fps. Any slower and you will notice the jerkiness between frames.

There are many variables that affect the quality of computer playback of animations. Color depth, image resolution, video card, system memory, file size, and file type all affect how well an animation will appear on your computer screen. In general, an MPEG 2 file will play back nicely at 30 fps. MPEG 2 offers full color at a frame size of 720×480. MPEG 2 is commonly used for satellite dish systems.

In the following exercises, you will add more keyframes and then adjust them to help you further understand how they work. You'll focus on the camera-position keyframes, but as you will learn later, these changes can be applied to keyframes for other objects in your model, such as the lights and geometry. You can also keyframe certain object parameters, such as a camera's field of view (FOV) or a door's Open parameter.

1. Move the Time slider to frame 300, and then move the camera closer to the building (see Figure 12.16).

 The camera path comes a bit too close to the trees. This in turn blocks out the view of the building. Let's add another keyframe to the camera trajectory so that we can pull the trajectory farther away from the trees without distorting it.

2. Move the Time slider to about frame 225. The camera should appear at the location shown in Figure 12.16.

3. Right-click the Top viewport; then click the Maximize Viewport Toggle to get a better look at the camera trajectory.

4. Make sure Auto Key is still turned on, and then move the camera to the location shown in Figure 12.17, creating a new keyframe number 3.

5. Click the left arrow button in the Key Info (Basic) rollout to go to keyframe 2, and move that keyframe to the location shown in Figure 12.17.

FIGURE 12.16
Move the camera at frame 300, and the camera appears at frame 225.

Move the camera here at frame 300.

The camera appears here at frame 225.

FIGURE 12.17
Move the camera to create the new keyframe 3, and move the camera at keyframe 2.

New position at keyframe 3

New position at keyframe 2

CHECKING THE AUTO KEY BEFORE EACH MODIFICATION

Verify that Auto Key mode is on before you move any keys. If you move objects when Auto Key mode is off, any changes you make apply globally to the object's entire animation. Pressing the N key will toggle Auto Key mode on and off.

Take a moment to zoom in and study the distribution of the dots along the camera trajectory. They are no longer evenly distributed over the path, except at the first and last keys. They are now crowded at the keys and spaced out as the distance from each key increases. This will create an animation that will start out slowly, and then suddenly speed up between keys.

1. To adjust keyframe 2 so that it occurs a little earlier in the trajectory, change the Time value in the Key Info (Basic) rollout to **110**.

 Notice how the trajectory changes in shape to accommodate the new setting.

2. Go to keyframe 3 and change its Time value to 200. You now have a segment of the animation where the camera motion slows down between two keyframes.

Although the new frame numbers were provided to you in this exercise, in real projects you can use the Time spinner in the Key Info (Basic) rollout to adjust the time while watching the dots in the trajectory. As you adjust the Time spinner, the dots will change their location. When the dots appear more evenly spaced, you know that the keyframe is in an appropriate location for a smoother camera motion.

Another way to even out the frames through a keyframe is to use the Normalize Time button in the Key Info (Advanced) rollout, located just below the Key Info (Basic) rollout.

When you move to a keyframe and click this button, 3ds Max adjusts the location in time of the current keyframe so that the frames are more evenly spaced. The one drawback to using the Normalize Time button is that it makes the other keyframe parameters inaccessible. The Constant Velocity option evenly spaces the frames between the current keyframe and the next.

Adding More Frames for Additional Camera Motion

Now suppose you want to add some additional camera motion to the current animation. It may seem as though you've used up all the available frames for the tour around the building. You can, however, add additional frames at the beginning or end of a segment of frames.

Adding Frames to the End of a Segment

Adding frames to the end of a segment is a fairly straightforward operation. Here's how it's done:

1. Click the Time Configuration tool at the bottom of the user interface.

2. In the Time Configuration dialog box, enter **400** in the Length input box of the Animation group; then click OK.

Notice what happens to the Time slider. Position 300 now appears at about three-quarters of the distance from the left side of the Time slider, and the overall frame count now shows 400.

Although you added more frames to the animation, the additional frames had no effect on the existing frames. The number of frames in the camera path did not change. You simply added more frames to the end of the animation. Those additional frames are not yet being utilized.

Now let's use those extra frames:

1. Move the Time slider all the way to the right so that it reads 400/400.

2. Move the camera to the position shown in Figure 12.18.

3. Click the Maximize Viewport Toggle to display all of the viewports.

FIGURE 12.18
Move the camera to a location in the courtyard.

The new camera location at frame 400

Remember that one way to create a new keyframe is to select a new frame number with the Time slider, and then, with AutoKey on, move the camera or other 3ds Max object or change a parameter. In this case, you added more time and then set the Frame slider to the new end of the segment and moved the camera while Auto Key mode was on.

Your view at frame 400 is too low in the building. You'll want to move the end location of the camera to the courtyard level. This will create an animation that will give the impression of flying over the building.

1. With the camera still selected and the Select and Move tool still active, enter **16′** in the Z input box of the transform type-ins at the bottom of the 3ds Max window.

2. You'll want to have the camera slow down as it approaches this last keyframe; so in the Key Info (Basic) rollout of the Motion tab, set the keyframe to 5 and then select the Slow option for the In tangent parameter.

If you look at the Top viewport shown in Figure 12.16, you will see that your camera trajectory moves the camera through the wall of the courtyard. You'll want to adjust the vertical location of the other keyframes so that the camera motion brings you above the building.

1. Use the Zoom and Pan tools to adjust the Left viewport view so you can see all of the keyframes in the camera path.

2. Go to keyframe 4 at frame 300 and use the Select and Move tool to adjust the vertical height of the camera so that it looks similar to Figure 12.19. You can use the coordinate readout to set the camera's Z position value to 88 feet.

FIGURE 12.19
Adjust the vertical position of the keyframes as shown here.

3. Adjust the vertical location of keyframe 3 so that it looks similar to Figure 12.19. The height of the camera at keyframe 3 is 36 feet.

4. Make sure the Camera viewport is currently active; then choose Tools ➤ Grab Viewport ➤ Create Animated Sequence File, and make a preview animation of what you have so far.

You may also drag the Frame slider from far left to right and back again. You get a sense of the motion while you watch the perspective view. This is called *scrubbing* the animation.

Adjusting the Camera Motion through a Keyframe

You'll want to refine the animation a bit more. Suppose you want to add a bit more time at keyframe 4 to pause at the bird's-eye view of the villa. You'll also want to correct the part of the animation between keyframes 4 and 5 where the camera flies through the roof.

3ds Max offers a variety of tools that let you fine-tune the animation of an object through a keyframe. Each frame can hold keys on numerous animation *tracks*. Tracks are separate containers that store independent information regarding each parameter and transform for each object in a scene. This is similar to how the audio tracks in a recording studio define a signal coming from a different microphone or instrument pickup before the mixer joins the tracks into a single audio stream.

In 3ds Max, tracks store data from *animation controllers*. An animation controller is a specialized algorithm that is responsible for recording a specific kind of animation data onto a track (position, rotation, scale, object parameters, audio, mathematical expressions, and so on). The entry point to these tools is the *Track View*, which is available in two modes: the Curve Editor and the Dope Sheet.

THE ORIGIN OF THE DOPE SHEET

The term *Dope Sheet* comes from classical animation and was a vertical chart that displayed instructions to the cameraperson.

The Curve Editor is for function curve editing and can be used to fine-tune the change in a parameter or transform value over time. The Dope Sheet is for editing time ranges and for key management. In the following exercise, you'll be introduced to both aspects of the Track View for the camera you've been working with.

1. With the Camera.View.3DFRONT camera selected, choose Graph Editors ➤ Track View – Dope Sheet to open the Track View in Dope Sheet mode, as shown in Figure 12.20. You can also right-click and select Dope Sheet from the quad menu to open the Dope Sheet.

FIGURE 12.20
The Dope Sheet showing the keys for the selected object

2. The list automatically expands to show the animation hierarchy of the selected object. You might have to scroll down in the Graph window to see the Camera.View.3DFRONT object. (See the sidebar "Auto-Expanding the Track View" if the Dope Sheet does not automatically expand the selected object's tracks.)

3. Click the Zoom Horizontal Extents tool in the View toolbar in the lower-right corner of the Track View – Dope Sheet dialog box. You can also zoom and pan within this dialog box using the built-in navigation controls.

AUTO-EXPANDING THE TRACK VIEW

Right-click in the tree-view window on the left side of the Track View – Dope Sheet dialog box to open a quad menu that is specific to the dialog box. You can choose Auto Expand and then Selected Objects Only, Transforms, XYZ Components, Base Objects, Children, and several other options. Then you won't have to click plus (+) symbols to manually expand these levels in the hierarchy. The plus symbols disappear when you choose to auto-expand their types.

CUSTOMIZING THE TRACK VIEW DIALOG BOX

Twelve modular toolbars are available for the Track View dialog box. If the Navigation: Animation Editor toolbar, with the Zoom Horizontal Extents tool, does not appear, right-click a blank section of the Dope Sheet title bar and then click the Show Toolbars option from the context menu. Choose any toolbars from the cascading menu to display them as floating toolbars. Any floating toolbars can be anchored to the Track View dialog box by dragging them to the bottom of the dialog box or below the menu bar.

The Zoom Horizontal Extents tool expands the Track View to display the entire timeline of your animation.

Take a moment to study the Track View – Dope Sheet dialog box. In the left panel, called the *Controller window,* you see a hierarchical listing of the camera's tracks. The camera name is at the top, followed by the Transform track. Under Transform are three options labeled Position, Roll Angle, and Scale. These correspond to the three types of transforms—Move, Rotate, and Scale—that you can apply to any object, as you've learned from earlier chapters. In this case, they represent the transforms applied to an object over time, such as the Move transform you applied to the camera. If you expand Object (Target Camera), you will see all of the animatable parameters for the camera, including another dozen parameters found under the MultiPass Effect entry. As you can see, it's easily possible to have thousands of animated parameters in a scene.

DISPLAYING THE ENTIRE TIMELINE

If at any time your Track View dialog boxes do not show the timeline as described in this book, click the Zoom Horizontal Extents tool shown alongside step 3 to display the entire timeline.

In the panel to the right, called the *Key window,* you see a graph representing the keys in the scene, specifically the keys that define the camera's motion. While it may appear that there are 15 keys in the Dope Sheet, there are only 5: the 5 keys on the Position track. The keys that appear on the Transform track are only indicators that keys exist on any of the tracks (Position, Roll Angle, Scale) that exist as child tracks to the Transform track. When the Transform track (the parent track) is collapsed, it is still clear that keys exist in its child tracks by their appearance on the Transform track.

The same logic applies to the keys that appear on the Camera.View.3DFRONT track; they only indicate the fact that keys exist on the camera's Object or Transform track. The frame numbers are shown on the scale at the bottom of the panel. You see the familiar keyframes that correspond to the Position track in the left panel. These keys represent the same keys that you see below the Time slider. You'll also see a light blue double-vertical line in the graph. That line indicates the current frame in the animation and can be scrubbed, like the Time slider, to examine the animation in the viewports.

Across the top of the dialog box, below the menu bar, you see a set of tools that lets you work on various aspects of the animation. You'll get a chance to work with some of these tools in the following exercises. At the bottom right, a set of navigation tools allows you to control the view of the graph. You can zoom in or out or pan using these tools. Two input boxes toward the bottom middle of the dialog box display the current position and value (if applicable) of a selected key. To the left of the input boxes is a message box that provides messages for the current operation.

In the preceding exercise, you opened a Track View dialog box that expanded and panned to show the tracks for the selected object. You can also pan through all the nodes for the entire scene. Pan the tree view on the left side of the dialog box by clicking and dragging a blank area of the Controller window when the cursor changes to look like a hand. Observe that all the scene nodes are considered children of the world and not children of a particular object. Other scene nodes include tracks for Sound, Environment, Renderer, and Objects, among others.

LOCATING THE TRACK VIEW DIALOG BOXES

The Track View dialog boxes are invaluable tools when creating animations in 3ds Max. Unfortunately, they consume a large amount of visual space and can clutter your screen and hamper productivity by requiring you to constantly open and close them. The best solution is to configure your workstation with a dual monitor setup and drag the Track View to the secondary monitor. This keeps the dialog boxes open without covering any of the viewports. The Track View dialog boxes can also be minimized when not in use or dragged partially off the screen to minimize their visibility.

You can also display a smaller version of the Curve Editor, in lieu of the track bar, at the bottom of the user interface by clicking the Open Mini Curve Editor button at the lower-left corner of the 3ds Max window. There is no corresponding mini-editor for the Dope Sheet.

Another solution is to display the Track View in one of the viewports. You do this by right-clicking the viewport label and choosing Views ➤ Track ➤ Track View – Curve Editor.

Notice that if AutoExpand is not used, some of the Object nodes have two plus signs, both a square and a round one. The plus symbols display as minus (-) signs after they have been expanded. Figure 12.21 shows the node for the WALL.13 object expanded.

The round plus symbol is used to get at the *keyable* tracks for the objects. Keyable tracks are those that can be animated. The WALL.13 object has a category inside the round plus symbol called Transform, which holds the three keyable tracks for Position, Rotation, and Scale.

FIGURE 12.21
Plus signs in the Dope Sheet's tree

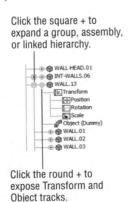

Click the square + to expand a group, assembly, or linked hierarchy.

Click the round + to expose Transform and Object tracks.

Some objects may also have an Object category that can be expanded using the round plus symbol in Track View. In 3ds Max, only the nodes appropriate to animation have keyable object tracks. For example, Camera.View.3DFRONT has an Object category that can be expanded to expose a number of keyable tracks, such as the Field of View (FOV), Target Distance, and many others, as shown in Figure 12.22.

FIGURE 12.22
Keyable tracks for the camera target object

These parameters can be animated in the object itself, like those you can manually edit on the Modify tab of the Command panel. If you do create keys on object tracks, the corresponding parameters on the Modify tab of the Command panel display red outlines around their spinners, when available, to indicate their animated status. Here the Lens and FOV parameters feature red spinner outlines, as shown in Figure 12.23, offering a visual reminder that they are animated.

FIGURE 12.23
The red spinner outlines show animated parameters.

So far you have been in Edit Keys mode in the Track View – Dope Sheet dialog box. This mode is perfect for editing individual keys and their tangents.

There is another mode of the Dope Sheet that is better suited for editing the timing of entire series of keys, called *ranges*:

1. Click the Edit Ranges button next to Edit Keys at the top left of the Track View – Dope Sheet dialog box.

2. You can drag range bars from the middle to move the entire range to another time, or you can drag the starting or ending handle to change the overall duration of the range (Figure 12.24). When the end handles are moved and the track's animation length is changed, the keys within that range are scaled proportionately. There are transforms to move, slide, or scale keys (or ranges). Scaling a parent track scales the ranges on all child tracks simultaneously. If you use the Scale Keys features on ranges, the range scales uses the current frame as the scale point. This isn't intuitive or obvious, but once you understand it, it's a powerful behavior. Experiment with these features and undo your actions after you're satisfied that you understand them.

FIGURE 12.24
The Edit Ranges mode of the Dope Sheet editor

Range bars Time slider showing current frame

The cursor changes to allow repositioning of range bars.

EDITING RANGES

Editing ranges becomes important when you want to adjust the timing of multiple animated objects and sequences relative to each other. It is much like nonlinear video editing in this respect.

Compressing and Expanding Time

Now let's see how the Curve Editor mode of the Track View can be used to adjust the camera's transition through keyframe 4:

1. From the Track View – Dope Sheet dialog box's menu bar, choose Modes ➤ Curve Editor. You can switch back and forth between the Dope Sheet and Curve Editor in this way.

 You can also click the Curve Editor (Open) button on the Main Toolbar or use the Menu Bar and choose Graph Editors ➤ Track View – Curve Editor to open both dialog boxes simultaneously.

2. Move the Track View – Curve Editor dialog box down if necessary so that you can get a clear view of the Top viewport.

3. Adjust the Top viewport so it looks similar to Figure 12.25.

FIGURE 12.25
The Top viewport

Keyframe 4

4. In the Motion tab of the Command panel, make sure that the Key Info (Basic) rollout shows key number 4. You should see the camera in the Top viewport at keyframe 4.

5. In the Track View – Curve Editor dialog box, click the Position track for the selected camera in the left panel.

 Notice that there are no child tracks below Position indicating a track for each spatial direction as would normally be the case. The default Position controller in 3ds Max is the Position XYZ controller, which provides a separate X, Y, and Z Position value for control of an object's position in each axis independently. The Bezier Position controller combines

all three directions in one track and is currently assigned as this camera's Position controller. The tracks are color coded, with red representing the X-axis, green representing the Y-axis, and blue representing the Z-axis.

These two controllers store the animation data in different ways mathematically, but they function similarly. Chapter 13 covers the different controllers and how they are assigned.

6. From the Track View – Curve Editor menu, choose Curves ➤ Apply – Ease Curve, or press Ctrl+E on the keyboard.

After you expand the Position track, you can see an Ease Curve track indented below the Position track.

7. Click the Ease Curve track in the Controller window. The Ease Curve function curve appears in the Key window as shown in Figure 12.26.

The Ease Curve graph displays a time scale in a straight line from 0 to 400. This is the current time you are using for the camera. You can adjust this curve to compress or expand time at various points along the camera trajectory. This may seem like a peculiar concept at first, but to help you understand the Ease Curve graph more clearly, consider how you used the In and Out keyframe parameters to select a tangent option. Selecting the Slow option for the first key had the effect of *compressing* or slowing time around that first keyframe. You see this graphically by the way the frame dots on the camera trajectory bunch up as they get closer to the key (see Figure 12.27).

The result is a smooth transition from a stop to the maximum velocity. Likewise, you added the Slow tangent option to the In parameter of the last key to make the camera slow to a stop instead of stopping abruptly. This is similar to compressing time before the last key.

FIGURE 12.26
The Ease Curve track for the camera's Position track

FIGURE 12.27
The frame dots bunch near the keyframe.

The Ease Curve graph lets you compress or expand time in a way similar to the Slow or Fast tangent options for the In and Out key parameters. Let's try adjusting the In and Out speed around keyframe 4 to make the transition around that key a bit smoother. First, add a key to the position on the Ease Curve graph that corresponds to keyframe 4. You'll then adjust the key to compress the time around it.

1. Click the Add Keys tool on the Track View – Curve Editor toolbar.

2. Click the line in the graph at the point that corresponds to frame 300, as shown in Figure 12.28.

 Notice that the two input boxes at the bottom of the Track View dialog box show the time coordinates of the key you just created (Figure 12.29). The numbers you see may be different from the ones shown here depending on how accurately you clicked in step 2.

FIGURE 12.28
Click in the spot shown here to add a key at frame 300.

FIGURE 12.29
Track View time coordinates

3. You can fine-tune the location of the key by entering the exact coordinate values in these boxes. The left input box sets the frame number for the selected key, and the right input box sets the key's value. Coincidentally, using the Ease Curve track, the two values will initially be identical. Click in the Frame input box to the left and enter **300**; then press the Tab key and enter **300** in the Value input box.

4. Right-click the key that you just added. You'll see the Camera.View.3DFRONT\Ease Curve dialog box, as shown in Figure 12.30.

5. In the In tangent flyout, click the Slow tangent option.

6. Do the same for the Out tangent, and then close the dialog box.

7. Close the Camera.View.3DFRONT\Ease Curve dialog box.

FIGURE 12.30
The Camera .View.3DFRONT\Ease Curve dialog box

Now notice how the ease curve looks. It levels off just before and after the new key, as shown in Figure 12.31. This leveling off indicates a compression in time around the key. A straight diagonal line as shown in the rest of the graph indicates a smooth, continuous flow of time.

FIGURE 12.31
The slope of the
ease curve

Also notice that dots in the camera trajectory seen in the Top viewport are compressed a bit more than before as they approach keyframe 4. This tells you that the camera now slows down as it transitions into keyframe 4.

To effectively use the Curve Editor, you must understand the way it displays the information about an object's animation. You already know that the graph displays the frame numbers along the bottom edge of the Key window. Vertically along the left edge of the Controller window are numbers that correspond to the value of the current key. For example, a key with a value of 35 means that an object is located 35 units from the origin along the X-axis when you are looking at the X Position track. When looking at a key on a Door object's Open track, 35 means the door is open 35 percent or, when looking at a camera's FOV track, 35 indicates the Field-of-View field is set to 35 degrees.

A sharp angle indicates a very fast change in value (vertical) over a short amount of time (horizontal). This can mean the camera is moving quickly along a particular axis or a door is flying open. Flatter curves mean less change or slower transitions. Avoid sharp turns in the curves, especially when adjusting the transforms, to reduce the amount of jerky motion in your scenes.

If you want even more control over the Ease Curve graph, you can use the Custom Tangent option:

1. With the key at frame 300 still selected, click the Set Tangents to Custom button on the Track View – Curve Editor toolbar.

 Notice that Bezier handles now appear at the key. You can adjust these handles vertically to control the shape of the curve through the key.

2. Click the Move Keys tool in the Track View – Curve Editor toolbar.

3. Click and drag one side of the Bezier handle on the key up. The curve follows the handle. Notice how the dots arrange themselves in the trajectory in the Top viewport. They start to compress and then expand again as they approach the keyframe.

BREAKING THE TANGENT HANDLES

If you hold down the Shift key while dragging tangent handles, the connection between them breaks so that they no longer move reciprocally. After they are broken apart, you can move the handles independently of one another. This creates a velocity discontinuity and can look jerky if the curve has a sharp point.

4. You don't really want this configuration for the key, so click the Undo button on the Main Toolbar to undo the change in the curve.

5. Now let's get rid of the key that's in the middle of the graph. Click that key to select it, as shown in Figure 12.32. It turns white to show that it has been selected.

6. Press the Delete key on the keyboard.

The key disappears. Notice how the curve changes. The transition into the camera position's keyframe 4 is now more gradual.

FIGURE 12.32
Selecting a key on the ease curve

Click the key in the middle of the graph.

Go ahead and make similar changes to the ease curve settings for the first and last keys:

1. Click the first key to the far left of the curve. You may need to use the scroll bars at the bottom and right side of the Controller window to access the first key. Then, click and hold the Set Tangents to Slow button and select the Slow option for the Out parameter from the flyout (Figure 12.33).

2. Click the last key to the far right of the curve and select the Slow tangent flyout option for the In parameter. The curve now looks like a gentle slope with gradual transitions between keys.

It is important to keep in mind that the Ease Curve tangent settings are independent of the Position keys. You can compress and expand time anywhere along the timeline. For example, if you wanted to have the camera slow down between keyframes 1 and 2, you could create a key in the Track View at frame 62 of the ease curve and adjust the key in a way similar to the way you adjusted the key in the previous exercises.

FIGURE 12.33
Three options for the Set Tangents to Slow button

Set both tangents to Slow.

Set the In tangent to Slow.

Set the Out tangent to Slow.

If you decide that you don't want to use the ease curve settings you've created, you can delete an ease curve by selecting the Ease Curve track in the Controller window and pressing the Delete key. You can also turn the ease curve off, choosing the Curves ➢ On/Off command from the Curve Editor menu. This way you can try different ease curves and switch between them.

CHANGING THE CAMERA'S DIRECTION

The camera will move backward along its own trajectory if the ease curve ever slopes down.

Next, let's see how to adjust the camera motion to avoid going through the roof of the villa as the camera approaches the courtyard. To do this, you'll need to use the Position track of the Track View – Curve Editor dialog box.

Adjusting the Camera Trajectory Using the Track View

Now let's take a look at another way that the Curve Editor can help you fine-tune the camera motion:

1. Move the Track View – Curve Editor dialog box up so that you can get a clear view of the Left viewport.

2. Click the Position track in the Controller window. The graph in the Key window changes to show the three position curves (see Figure 12.34).

FIGURE 12.34
The Track View – Curve Editor dialog box showing the Bezier Position track

Red X curve Green Y curve Blue Z curve

POSITION XYZ OR BEZIER POSITION CONTROLLER?

The Position XYZ controller has one function curve each on three separate tracks. The Bezier Position controller puts all three curves on one track. Each controller has its strengths and weaknesses depending on what you are doing. You have more control over each axis with Position XYZ, but you saw how the ease curve could be simultaneously applied to all three curves with the Bezier Position controller.

The Position function curves are graphic representations of the camera motions through three-dimensional space. Unlike the camera trajectory, the Position function curves display the changes in the X-, Y-, and Z-coordinates as separate lines. Each line represents a different axis

in the coordinate system. You'll see in the next exercise how you can make practical use of the function curves.

If you created a preview of the animation so far, you can see that the camera passes through the roof of the villa before landing in the courtyard. To avoid this, you can use the Position function curves to adjust the shape of the camera trajectory so that it avoids the roof. Try the following exercise to see how this works:

1. Use the Zoom and Pan tools to adjust the Left viewport to look like Figure 12.35.

2. Back in the Curve Editor, on the right end of the Position function curves, click the key at the far-right end of the blue curve. Remember that the blue curve represents the Z-axis for the position transform applied to the camera.

3. Set the In tangent of this key to Custom. You'll see a Bezier handle appear at the selected key on the curve.

4. With the Move Keys tool from the Track View – Curve Editor toolbar selected, move the Bezier handle up so it looks similar to Figure 12.36.

FIGURE 12.35
The Left viewport adjusted to show the camera trajectory approaching the courtyard

FIGURE 12.36
The Function curve with the Bezier handle pointing up and a view of the resulting camera trajectory

Moving this handle upward…

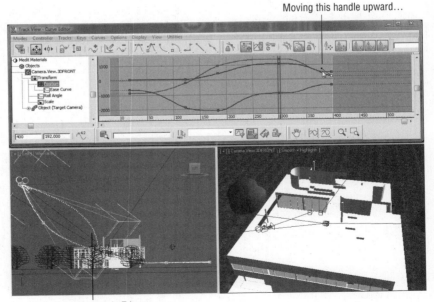

… alters the trajectory in Z here.

Notice what happens to the camera trajectory in the Left viewport in Figure 12.36: it now curves up. This helps move the trajectory away from the roof.

CONSTRAINING THE KEY MOVEMENTS

The Move Keys tool is actually a flyout containing two additional options that restrict the key movements vertically or horizontally.

By altering the Z curve of the Position function curve, you altered the trajectory of the camera in the Z-axis. If you take time to study the blue curve, you'll see that it is really a graph that represents the Z-coordinates of the camera over the 400 frames. The same is true for the X and Y red and green curves. You can manipulate the keys using a combination of the Custom In and Out tangents and by moving the keys vertically in the graph.

As you can see from this and the previous section, you have a great deal of control over the motion of an object through time and space. Next, you'll look at ways of adjusting the time so that you can add motion to the beginning of your animation.

The Custom tangent and the resulting curve in the Position track and its resulting trajectory are affected by the prior tangent setting that the Custom tangent replaces. Had the prior In tangent setting for keyframe 5 been the Smooth tangent instead of the Slow tangent, the resulting curve in the trajectory and the Z-axis curve would be different, with the frames biased toward keyframe 4.

RECEIVING IMMEDIATE FEEDBACK FROM THE CAMERA

You can adjust the camera trajectory while watching a playback of the animation in the Camera viewport. Make the Camera viewport active; then click the Play Animation button in the time controls. As you watch the playback of the animation in the Camera viewport, adjust the curve in the Track View dialog box. The Custom tangent does not change the shape of the existing curve when it is applied. That's why the previously used tangent makes a difference when you apply the Custom tangent.

USING THE TCB METHOD FOR ADJUSTING KEYFRAME TRANSITIONS

If you find that the Track view is too complex, you can also use the Tension Continuity Bias (TCB) controller for your keyframe transitions. Instead of offering a set of tangent options for the In and Out keyframe parameters, you use three settings—Tension, Continuity, and Bias—to control a keyframe transition. The TCB controller is the original (and most ancient) method used by 3ds Max for key interpolation.

You can change to a TCB controller by doing the following:

1. With an animated object selected, select a keyframe key. Then, in the Motion tab of the Command panel, open the Assign Controller rollout.

2. In the list box of the Assign Controller rollout, expand the Transform track if necessary and click the Position track to select it.

3. Next, click the Assign Controller button in the upper-left corner of the rollout.

The Assign Position Controller dialog box displays.

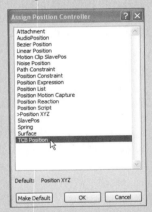

4. Select TCB Position and click OK. The Key Info rollout of the Motion tab will change to show parameters for a TCB controller.

CONTINUES

USING THE TCB METHOD FOR ADJUSTING KEYFRAME TRANSITIONS *(CONTINUED)*

You see the familiar Time and X, Y, and Z Value spinners, but you also see a graphic and five new settings named Ease To, Ease From, Tension, Continuity, and Bias. The graphic shows you an example of how the frames approach and recede from the current keyframe. The default setting shows the keys as black crosses transitioning through a bell-shaped arc. At the top of the arc is a red cross representing the actual keyframe.

You can adjust the Ease To and Ease From settings to compress the frames around the keyframe in a manner similar to the Slow tangent option you used in an earlier exercise. Using negative numbers expands the frames around the keyframe.

The Tension option alters the duration of the frames around the keyframe. A value greater than the default 25 increases the density of the frames around the keyframe, and a 0 value spreads out the frames.

The Continuity setting affects the curvature of the trajectory through the keyframe. A value greater than 25 pushes the trajectory outward, and a value of 0 causes the trajectory to form a straight line to and from the keyframe.

Finally, Bias pushes the trajectory curve to one side of the keyframe or the other, literally biasing the curve. A number less than 25 adds bias to the left side of the graphic, and a number greater than 25 biases the curve to the right side.

You can use the TCB controller to perform the same tasks as the Bezier Position controllers. For example, in place of the Slow tangent option in the In or Out key parameter, you can use the Ease To or Ease From setting to slow the camera as it approaches the keyframe. The TCB controller offers finer control from a single rollout than does the default Position XYZ controller. Also, you still have access to many of the same Track View functions you've used in previous exercises. You cannot, however, make changes to the individual X, Y, and Z Position function curves as you can with the Bezier and Position XYZ controllers.

Increasing the Number of Frames between Selected Keys

You saw earlier how you could increase the number of frames to increase the overall time and slow down the animation. You can also increase the number of frames in a specific range of frames through the combined use of the Time Configuration dialog box and the Dope Sheet. To see how this works, try increasing the number of frames between keyframe 4 and the end of the segment. Right now there are 100 frames between these two keyframes, and they are numbered from 300 to 400.

The first step is to create some additional frames to work with:

1. Click the Time Configuration button to open the Time Configuration dialog box.

2. In the Animation group, change the Length input box to read 500; then click OK to close the dialog box.

You've just added 100 frames to the animation, although you haven't actually changed the camera motion in any way. If you look at the Time slider, you can see that the keyframes are still in the same locations relative to the frame numbers. The function curves from frames 400 to 500 are straight, meaning no change to the parameters, and dashed to show that there are no keys beyond those visible in the Curve Editor. The next step is to expand the time between keyframes 4 and 5. You do this through the Track View – Dope Sheet toolbar.

1. With the Camera.View.3DFRONT object selected, choose Modes ➤ Dope Sheet to switch to Dope Sheet mode.

2. Click the Edit Keys button to switch from the Edit Ranges mode if necessary.

3. Select the Position track under the Camera.View.3DFRONT Transform track. Expand the Position track by clicking the round plus symbol and note that the Ease Curve track is also selected.

4. Hold down the Ctrl key and click the key in the Ease Curve track at frame 400, and the Position track at frame 400 as well. The keys will turn white when they are selected.

5. On the Track View – Dope Sheet toolbar, click the Scale Keys tool.

6. Now click and drag the cursor from the Position key at frame 400 to frame 500. You'll see the Position and Ease Curve keys move in the Dope Sheet graph to frame 500, as shown in Figure 12.37.

You have just scaled the keys from frame 400 to 500, without altering anything else about the animation. The camera remains hovered above the building at frame 300 (keyframe 4), and there are now 100 additional frames between keyframe 4 and the end of the animated segment. The camera's trajectory remains the same as it was before you increased the number of frames between the selected keys.

FIGURE 12.37
Scaling selected keys

ADJUSTING THE EASE CURVE SETTINGS

If you find that, after scaling a key or range of time, an object's motion does not complete its full range of motion, check the ease curve settings in the Track View. Frequently, if the ease curve data are not adjusted correctly, portions of an animated object's trajectory will appear to be missing or misplaced. It is important that any ease curves you have maintain their one-to-one correspondence with the tracks they are affecting.

Speeding Up the Preview Rendering Time

Let's take another look at a preview of the animation. Because you've increased the number of frames, you may want to adjust the preview so it doesn't take quite so long to process.

1. Choose Tools ➤ Grab Viewport ➤ Create Animated Sequence File.

2. In the Make Preview dialog box, change the Rendering Level to Flat. This is a much faster but lower visual quality algorithm suitable to checking timing and object collisions.

3. Set the Percentage of Output value to 80 to create a 640 × 480 resolution video.

4. Click the Active Time Segment radio button in the Preview Range group to make sure that the entire animation is rendered. This is important, because you added some frames to the end of the animation.

5. Make sure that the Camera viewport is selected in the Render Viewport drop-down list at the bottom of the dialog box; then click Create.

Adding Frames to the Beginning of a Segment

You've seen how to add time to the end of a time segment. Now let's look at how you add time to the beginning. You've already been exposed to some of the tools to do this. As before, you'll use the Time Configuration dialog box to add more time to the overall animation. Then you'll use the Track View dialog box to shift the animation sequence forward in the time track.

1. Click the Time Configuration tool to open the Time Configuration dialog box.

2. In the Animation group, change the Length setting to 550, and then click OK.

3. Open the Track View – Dope Sheet dialog box if it isn't already open.

4. Click the Position track of the Camera.View.3DFRONT object in the Controller window.

5. Click the Edit Ranges tool on the Track View – Dope Sheet toolbar.

 The Key window changes to show the range bars instead of the keys.

6. Click and drag the topmost Camera.View.3DFRONT bar to the right. As you do, watch the track bar at the bottom of the 3ds Max window and adjust the range bars so that the last key rests at frame 550, as shown in Figure 12.38. Notice that all of the bars move in unison.

7. Play the entire animation in the Camera.View.3DFRONT viewport.

FIGURE 12.38
Adjust the
range bars.

Notice that the last 50 frames are cut off; the camera seems to hang above the building and never reaches the courtyard. The camera motion that you had before is still stored in the scene, but some of the keys extend beyond the active time segment. You will fix this next.

1. Switch to the Curve Editor by choosing Modes ➤ Curve Editor from the Track View – Dope Sheet dialog box.

2. Select the Position track for the animated camera. Note how the function curves extend into the dark gray area past frame 550, which is now the end of the active time segment, shown in Figure 12.39.

3. Hold down the Move Keys tool and choose Move Keys Horizontal from the flyout menu.

 The Move Keys Horizontal tool allows only horizontal motion in the Curve Editor graph.

FIGURE 12.39
The function
curves extend
beyond the active
time segment.

4. Click the Move keys tool, and then drag a selection window around the three keys at the ends of the function curves.

5. Zoom into the area near the end of the active time segment in the Curve Editor. You should be able to see frame 550 listed on the track bar in the dialog box.

6. Drag the selected keys to the left and place them at frame 550.

7. Play the animation again, and observe that the camera motion is complete and the entire segment has been increased now to 550 frames.

8. It's been a long time since you've saved your work, so save the file as **MyVillaSavoye_ CameraAnimation_completed.max**.

You now have a fairly smooth animation that shows off the building from several vantage points. At this point, you may want to explore some different ways to study the results of your work.

Throughout this chapter, you've created preview animations or used the Time slider to check your camera motion. The next section will show you some additional ways to preview the motion in your model.

Other Options for Previewing Your Motion

Earlier in this chapter, you learned how to create a preview animation that gives you a pretty good sense of the speed and overall time of your animation. You can also use the Time slider to get an idea of the camera motion by manually sliding it slowly and watching the result in the Camera viewport.

A third way to study the motion in your animation is to use the time controls located at the bottom of the Command panel (see Figure 12.40).

FIGURE 12.40
The time controls

These tools work in a way similar to buttons on a VCR or DVD player, with some additions. The Go to Beginning button moves you to the first frame of the active segment. The Go to End button moves you to the last frame. The Next Frame and Previous Frame buttons move you one frame at a time either forward or backward. If you make the Key Mode toggle active by clicking it, the Next Frame and Previous Frame buttons become the Next Key and Previous Key buttons and will advance the Time slider to the next keyframe for the selected object. The Play Animation button plays the active segment in a continuous loop. The Play button turns into a Stop button when the animation is playing. The Play Animation button is also a flyout, offering you the option of playing the animation of a single selected object.

The playback is useful for getting a quick idea of how your animation is working. Try it out on what you've got so far:

1. Right-click in the Camera viewport to make it active.

2. Click the Play Animation button and watch the playback for a few seconds.

THE DIRECT3D DRIVER

Due to advances in Direct3D driver technology, you may not be able to get your viewport to adaptively degrade in this exercise. Graphics cards have made amazing progress in the last few years and can usually keep up with real-time playback except in the most complex scenes.

Partway through the animation, the playback changes to a wireframe view and displays a smoother motion, (only if your graphics card cannot keep up with the speed of the animation). Toggling Adaptive Degradation off can be helpful in large scenes that challenge the limits of your graphics card. The Adaptive Degradation toggle is to the right of the prompt area, just left of the Add Time Tag field.

3. Click the Stop Animation button to stop the playback.

When the Adaptive Degradation toggle is deselected in the Views menu, it forces the camera view to maintain a Smooth + Highlights shaded view even while playing back the camera motion. 3ds Max attempts to play back the animation at the full 30 fps. When this option is checked, 3ds Max uses adaptive degradation to achieve a full frame rate. When Adaptive Degradation is not turned on, 3ds Max may not play back the animation smoothly. You can alter the way your view is displayed to help improve the playback speed. For example, by default 3ds Max degrades the image to a wireframe for the playback. You can force 3ds Max to limit the degradation to a higher quality than wireframe by choosing Fast Shaded mode. If you choose Use Current Display mode it will maintain whatever mode you have selected.

If you want smoother playback at the expense of detail, you can use the Bounding Box setting as the degradation setting. Bounding Box is the fastest display mode, and you should need it only in complex scenes with millions of polygons, where other display modes lag behind.

1. Choose Views ≻ Viewport Configuration. The Viewport Configuration dialog box appears.

2. Click the Adaptive Degradation tab, and then click Bounding Box in the Active Object Display By Priority. To ensure that you'll actually see the Adaptive Degradation effect, you can temporarily increase the Maintain Frames per Second field to 40 or even higher if you have a superpowerful graphics card.

3. Click OK; make sure the Adaptive Degradation option is turned on at the bottom of the 3ds Max window, and then click the Play Animation button. Now the objects switch to boxes when the playback can't maintain the display of the shaded objects. The animation may be a bit rough if your video card cannot handle the playback, skipping frames to maintain the desired frame rate, but it is a bit smoother than it would be with Adaptive Degradation turned off.

As you've just seen, these options offer a variety of ways of previewing your animation. These tools will give you a sense of the motion in the animation at each change you make. They will help you refine your animation, so make liberal use of them.

Moving the Camera Target over Time

So far in this chapter, you've touched on all the major editing activities you might run into while creating a keyframed camera path. You can also make changes to the camera target. The target can be manipulated independently of the camera it is attached to. A camera target's trajectory can be completely independent of the camera itself, though you'll want to carefully choreograph the motion of both the camera and the target.

Try the following exercise to see the effects of camera target motion:

1. In the Top viewport, adjust the view so that you can see the villa courtyard, as shown in Figure 12.41.

2. Move the Time slider to the last frame so that you can see the camera in the Top viewport.

3. Make sure the Camera.View.3DFRONT camera is selected; then click the Viewport menu (the plus button), and choose Select Camera Target from the list.

4. Turn the Auto Key button on; then use the Select and Move tool to move the camera target to the location shown in Figure 12.42.

FIGURE 12.41
Adjust the Top viewport to show this view.

Last keyframe

FIGURE 12.42
Move the camera target to this location, so the camera is looking from the patio into the interior.

Move the camera target here.

Now you've created a motion for your target. The target has just two keyframes. Just as with the camera path, you can adjust the keyframe's In and Out settings, as well as the function curve settings in the track-view window:

1. In the Motion tab of the Command panel, change the In parameter flyout of the Key Info (Basic) rollout to Slow Tangent.

2. Use the keyframe selector arrows at the top of the Key Info (Basic) rollout to go to keyframe 1, and then select the Slow tangent flyout in the Out parameter.

3. Click the Play Animation button to see how the changes in the target affect the animation.

The target trajectory is often forgotten as the cause of erratic camera motion. Remember that when you start to add camera target motion, you will need to pay attention to its effect on the overall animation. If part of the animation seems too jerky and you know that you've adjusted everything for the camera path to create a smooth animation, check the target path for abrupt changes.

Controlling Lights over Time

This chapter has been devoted to showing you ways of controlling the motion of objects. In this section, you'll learn how properties of a light, such as intensity, can be changed over time.

Now let's suppose you want to fade the sunlight while simultaneously brightening the interior lights. In addition, let's suppose you want this done at the end of the animation, viewing the courtyard while the camera is no longer moving. To accomplish this in the following example, you'll use several of the tools you've already learned about in this chapter.

1. Add some time to the end of the animation. Click the Time Configuration button to open the Time Configuration dialog box.

2. Enter **600** in the Length input box, and click OK to close the Time Configuration dialog box.

3. In the Main Toolbar, click the Select by Name tool to open the Select from Scene dialog box and then click the Display All icon, if necessary, to display all the objects in the scene.

4. Select SUN from the Select Object list and click OK.

5. Choose Graph Editors ➤ Track View – Dope Sheet.

6. Click the round plus symbol in front of the Object (Target Directional Light) track to expand the list of tracks.

The SUN directional light is not currently animated. In the following exercise, you'll add keyframes to the SUN through the Track View – Dope Sheet dialog box:

1. Click the Edit Keys tool in the Track View – Dope Sheet dialog box if necessary.

2. Using the Dope Sheet's navigation tools, zoom into the area near the end of the active time segment until you can see frames 550 and 600 appear on the scale, as shown in Figure 12.43. Zoom in so the left scale is between 0 and 1.

3. Select the Add Keys tool on the Track View – Dope Sheet toolbar.

4. Click the Multiplier track in the Controller window.

5. In the Key window, click the Multiplier track at a location that is close to frame 550, as shown in Figure 12.43.

6. Click the left input box at the bottom of the Track View dialog box and enter **550.**⏎ to set the new key to frame 550.

FIGURE 12.43
Place keyframes
at frames 550
and 600.

Set frame number here.　　　Add keys here.

7. Click the Multiplier track at a location that is close to frame 600, as shown in Figure 12.43.

8. Click the Key Time box again, and this time enter **600↵** to set the new key to frame 600.

The Multiplier track of the SUN directional light now has two keys that control its value over time. These keys don't change anything yet. Remember that the Multiplier setting gives you control over a light's intensity. The final step is to adjust the Multiplier value at frame 600:

1. Right-click the key at frame 600. The SUN\Multiplier dialog box displays.

2. Change the Value input box to 0 and close the dialog box.

 You've just set up the SUN directional light to dim from full intensity to zero intensity between frames 550 and 600.

3. Switch to the Curve Editor mode and then click the Multiplier listing in the Controller window if necessary. In the Key window, you see the function curve for the Multiplier value over time, as shown in Figure 12.44.

FIGURE 12.44
Multiplier curve

In the last exercise, you added two keys to the Multiplier track. You could have added just the last key at frame 600 and set the Multiplier value to 0 at that key. This would have caused the SUN directional light to dim gradually over the entire length of the animation. The key at frame 550 ensures that the Multiplier value stays constant at 1.0 until frame 550. The Multiplier

function curve gives you a graphic representation of how this works by showing you a straight line from frame 0 to frame 550. The line then drops from frame 550 to frame 600, showing you the change in the Multiplier value from 1 to 0 between those two frames.

To see whether the modification you made really affects the model, create a preview animation of the Camera viewport from frame 500 to frame 600.

Notice that in the last frame of the sample animation, the scene still appears lit. To really darken the design, you'll need to change the ambient lighting over time in the same way that you changed the SUN directional light object.

1. Switch back to Dope Sheet mode.

ADDING KEYS IN EITHER MODE

Keys can be added in either Track View mode. The grid layout in Dope Sheet mode makes it a bit easier to select the proper frame number.

2. Scroll up the left panel to the Environment listing, under the World node.

3. Click the plus sign next to the Environment track, and then click the Ambient Light track that appears below Environment.

4. Click the Add Keys button and add two keys, at frame 550 and at frame 600, in the Ambient Light track, just as you did for the Multiplier track of the SUN directional light.

5. Right-click the key at frame 600. The Ambient Light dialog box displays.

6. Right-click the spinners for the R, G, and B input boxes to set their values to 0. You can also click the color swatch to open the Color Selector, and then adjust the Value setting to 0.

7. Close the Track View – Dope Sheet dialog box, and then rerender a preview animation. This time the design darkens to a greater extent.

8. Save the file as **MyVillaSavoye_CameraAnimation_Completed01.max**.

You still have the Omni court lights illuminating the courtyard and the Omni interior lights lighting the interior of the villa. You can perform the same steps you used with the SUN directional light to change the Omni lights' multiplier over time.

The Bottom Line

Create a quick-study animation Viewing an animation, rather than individual still images, can give you a greater sense of the size, scope, and proportion of a design project. Initial, quick-study animations usually consist of short animations with changes made to the camera's location and orientation.

> **Master It** Create a camera at the mezzanine level of any of the Condo scenes from Chapter 6, "Creating AEC Objects," oriented toward the tall windows. Animate the camera moving to the lower level and changing orientation to look into the kitchen.

Change the number of frames in an animation The 101 frames provided in the default 3ds Max scene are rarely adequate to display any significant amount of animation. It's an easy process to increase or reduce the number of frames in a scene, and this is a task that you will do often.

> **Master It** Continuing with the previous exercise, increase the number of frames to 300. Adjust the keyframes so the animation occurs over all 300 frames.

Add and edit keyframes Keyframes determine the point in time and value of nearly any parameter change in 3ds Max. Adding and editing them properly is an essential task when finalizing your animation.

> **Master It** Continuing from the previous exercise, add two keys to the camera's animation, one that raises its position before descending to the lower level and one that adjusts its rotation so that it looks at the kitchen earlier. The camera should ease into and out of its peak height.

Preview the animation Animations can take a significant amount of time to render, and unless you have a render farm setup, you may lose the ability to continue working on a scene while it renders. Creating preview animations can quickly identify animated conflicts prior to your spending the time creating a final animation.

> **Master It** Create a preview animation, at a resolution of 640 × 480, showing the modified camera path from the path from the previous exercise. Display the frame numbers in the images and save the animation as an AVI file using the Microsoft Video 1 codec.

Control lights over time Clarifying the results of the lighting in a scene is often identified as a priority early in the project cycle. Not only is a satisfactory lighting scheme required, but animated variations, such as the onset of dusk, may also need to be viewed and observed.

> **Master It** Add a quick lighting scheme to the Condo scene. Animate the lights, holding their intensity for 100 frames and then reducing the intensity to zero while turning the lights slightly red.

Chapter 13

Creating Animations

In the previous chapter, you got a fairly detailed look at how you can animate camera motion. In this chapter, you'll continue your exploration of animation by looking at methods for saving your animations as files. You'll explore how using render presets can save you time.

You'll also see how animations differ from still images in the way you put a 3ds Max scene file together. The arrangement of objects and methods you use to create a still image has different requirements from those of an animation. You'll examine some of those differences and their effect on your work.

In this chapter, you'll learn to:

- ◆ Render an animation
- ◆ Output a still image
- ◆ Render a shadow study
- ◆ Create a walkthrough
- ◆ Choose an animation file output option
- ◆ Set up a physics simulation
- ◆ Create a Particle Flow event-driven particle system

Rendering the Animation

Let's take a look at the options you have for animation output. This is a big subject, so you'll start with the basics of study animations versus finished animations.

Before you get to a point where you think you're ready for a final animation, you should generate study animations to make sure all the elements are working together. You'll want to do this because of the time it takes to generate a full, finished animation. For an elaborate design, a 20-second animation can take a long time to render, so before you commit your computer to hours or days of nonstop rendering, you'll want to be completely sure that everything is perfect.

You can create a study animation by turning off some key rendering features that may not be crucial for studying the motion of objects in your animation. You can also reduce the resolution of the study animation to help speed things up.

Creating a Study Animation

In the following exercise, you'll create an animation file to be viewed in 3ds Max. It won't be a finished product by any means. The advantage of using the Renderer output, as opposed to making a Preview animation (see Chapter 12, "Understanding Animation"), is that you will be better able to see the lighting change over time, and you'll also see how the shadows affect the animation.

The first animation you'll do will focus on the last few frames of the animation to ascertain that the spotlight is indeed dimming at the end.

1. Open Firstanimation.max. This is similar to the file that you saved in the previous chapter with a skydome object added.

2. Right-click the Camera.View.3DFRONT viewport to make it active if it is not already.

3. Click the Render Setup button on the Main Toolbar.

4. At the bottom of the Render Setup dialog box, click the Preset drop-down list, as shown in Figure 13.1.

FIGURE 13.1
Rendering presets

Rendering presets are settings from the Render Setup dialog box saved as named items in the Preset drop-down list. 3ds Max lets you maintain multiple rendering presets, as you can see from the Preset list.

5. Select Load Preset from the drop-down list. In the Render Presets Load dialog box, navigate to the renderpresets folder under the 3ds Max Design 2011 folder, select 3dsmax.scanline.no.advanced.lighting.draft.rps, and click Open.

RENDER PRESET LOCATIONS

The Render Presets Load dialog box may display the contents of the C:\Documents and Settings\ *Your Name*\My Documents\3dsmax\renderpresets folder. This is not the correct location for the render presets that install with 3ds Max Design 2011. You must navigate to the C:\Program Files\Autodesk\3ds Max Design 2011\renderpresets folder to find these.

6. The Select Preset Categories dialog box appears. Here you can select which categories of settings from the selected preset you would like to load. Leave all three categories selected and click the Load button. See Figure 13.2.

The appropriate settings are loaded from the 3dsmax.scanline.no.advanced.lighting.draft settings file.

FIGURE 13.2

Loading a preset

In this case, the Default Scanline Renderer was chosen, and settings were altered in the Advanced Lighting and Raytracer tabs of the Render Setup dialog box. Of course, these are settings that you could have changed manually in the Render Setup dialog box, but it saves time to load them all from a file.

1. In the Render Setup dialog box, make sure the Common tab is selected. In the Time Output group of the Common Parameters rollout, click the Range radio button and enter a range from **550** to **600** in the Range input boxes.

2. Click the 320 × 240 button in the Output Size group to reduce the resolution of the output if it is not already set to that output size. Fewer pixels take less time to render.

SETTING DEFAULT OUTPUT SIZES

You can right-click the resolution buttons in the Output Size area to change their default sizes.

3. Click the Renderer tab of the Render Scene dialog box and note that the Antialiasing check box in the Antialiasing group isn't selected. It was deselected when you loaded the preset earlier. This will greatly improve the speed of the rendering, but it will create a rendering that shows jagged edges on objects.

4. Switch back to the Common tab. Scroll down to the Render Output group, and then click the Files button in the Render Output group. In the Render Output File dialog box, select the AVI File (*.avi) option from the Save As Type drop-down list and enter **Myfirstanimation** as the filename. Use the Save In drop-down list to browse to the folder where you've been saving your project files.

5. Click Save. You'll see the AVI File Compression Setup dialog box.

6. Set the Compressor to MJPEG and the Quality to 90 and then click OK (see Figure 13.3).

 This dialog box allows you to select the method of compression and the amount of compression (quality) for your saved animation. You'll get a closer look at these issues in the section "The AVI Codecs" later in this chapter.

7. Click Render at the bottom of the Render Setup dialog box. The rendering process begins.

FIGURE 13.3
The AVI File Com-
pression Setup
dialog box

Notice your rendering time. Here it's blindingly fast, about one second a frame. If you have a much slower render time, go take a quick break.

Once the animation is created, you can view the rendered animation from within 3ds Max by using the View Image File command or by locating the AVI file using Windows Explorer and double-clicking it. Unlike the Preview, the player doesn't automatically launch when the rendering is complete.

1. Choose Rendering ➤ View Image File. The View File dialog box displays.

2. Locate and select `Myfirstanimation.avi`, and then click Open. Windows Media Player opens and plays back the animation. If you have another application set to play back AVI files, that application will open and play the AVI file.

As you can see, the animation is short and still pretty crude, but at least you can tell whether the lights are doing what you want them to do.

Creating a Quick Overall Study Animation

Now suppose you want to get a quick view of the overall animation to make sure everything is working as planned. In the next exercise, you'll adjust some of the frame output settings to limit the number of frames that are animated. This will help reduce the total animation time so that you'll see the results quickly. You'll use a different file format that offers a bit more control at file creation.

1. Make sure the Common tab is selected in the Render Setup dialog box, and then click the Active Time Segment radio button in the Time Output group.

2. In the Every Nth Frame input box, enter **3**. This will cause the renderer to create an animation that renders only every third frame. Consequently, the animation will take approximately one-third of the time to render all the assigned frames.

3. Click the Files button in the Render Output group; then, in the Render Output File dialog box, enter **Mysecondanimation** for the filename.

4. Select MOV QuickTime File (*.mov) in the Save As Type drop-down list and click Save. As you'll see in a moment, the QuickTime file format lets you set the playback frame rate. Quicktime output will not be available on 64-bit operating systems with 3ds Max 64 bit installed. If Quicktime is not available, use the AVI format again with MJPEG compression. The animation will play back in just over 6 seconds instead of 20.

5. In the Compression Settings dialog box, change the Frames per Second setting to **10**. Note that you can set the Quality slider and also select the color depth for the MOV file. The lower the Quality setting, the smaller the file size will be. Decreasing color depth can also reduce file size. Click OK to close the Compression Settings dialog box and return to the Render Setup dialog box.

CHANGING THE FILE SAVING PARAMETERS

After rendering a scene to a particular still image or animated file format, the dialog boxes used to set the file's parameters (compression, frame rate, and so on) no longer appear. To change the file's parameters without changing the file's type, click the Setup button in the Render File Output dialog box.

6. Click the Render button in the Render Setup dialog box. This time the rendering will take a good deal more time because you will be rendering about 200 frames overall (one-third of 600 frames). Check the Time Remaining field in the Common Parameters rollout to see an estimate of the remaining rendering time.

7. Use the View File dialog box (Rendering ➤ View Image File) to play back the animation when it finishes rendering.

LOWERING THE FRAMES PER SECOND

Rendering at 10 frames per second (fps) is near the limit of flicker fusion, where you start to perceive individual frames rather than the illusion of continuous motion. The animation will be a bit jerky but will still be a valuable sample and allow you to get a sense of timing in the segment without rendering every frame.

This animation is still crude, and you may detect that it is not quite as smooth in the playback as the previous animation, but it gives you a far better idea of how the final rendering will look than did the preview animations you used in the previous chapter, because it includes rendered light and shadow. The test animations that you render may also show you problems that need fixing. This is exactly the kind of feedback you want from tests before you commit all the time required to render the entire animation.

Adding a Moving Car

Your animation work so far has involved moving a camera around the villa. Of course, you can animate other objects in your model. Let's add a car to the villa animation to see how to control the behavior of objects other than cameras. By animating a car, you'll explore how you can rotate an object through time. You'll use a simple car model to see how you can make an object move smoothly in an animation.

First, insert a Container that has the car model inside it.

1. Right-click the Top viewport; then click the Maximize Viewport Toggle to enlarge the view.

2. Select the skydome object.

3. Right-click; then, in the quad menu, click Hide Selection.

4. Click the Application button, and choose References ➤ Inherit Container, as shown in Figure 13.4

5. In the Inherit Container dialog box, select the LowResCar_Container01.maxc file.

FIGURE 13.4
Adding the Container representing the car

3DS MAX CONTAINER FILES

3ds Max uses the extension *.maxc to identify models that have been prepared as Container files.

The car appears in the scene near the lower-right corner of the villa, just out of view of the Camera.View.3DFRONT at frame 0.

Now that you have the car in the scene, it's time to animate it. Just as with the camera, you'll need to enter Auto Key mode, select a time with the Time slider, and then move the car.

1. With the Container01 object still selected, use the Absolute Mode Transform type-in field and move the car to X = 15′ and Y = 150′.

2. Click the Auto Key button at the bottom of the interface.

3. Move the Time slider to frame 200.

4. Click the Select by Name tool. On the Select from Scene dialog box, select the Display Containers toggle to make the container appears in the list.

5. Select the Container01 object from the list, and click OK.

Click the Selection Lock Toggle so you don't have to worry about accidentally deselecting the car's Container while you are animating it.

Click the Select and Move tool, and then move the car to the position shown in Figure 13.5.

FIGURE 13.5

Move the car to the new location at frame 200.

To help you visualize the path of the car, turn on its trajectory:

1. Right-click in the viewport and select Object Properties.

2. In the Display Properties section of the Object Properties dialog box, click By Layer to change the display properties of the car to By Object.

3. Click the Trajectory check box and click OK.

Now you've got a visible trajectory. Let's adjust the beginning and ending keyframes so the car starts and stops smoothly on its path:

1. Click the Motion tab in the Command panel.

2. In the Key Info (Basic) rollout, click and drag the In flyout and select Slow.

3. Click the left-facing arrow in the upper-left corner of the Key Info (Basic) flyout to go to keyframe 1.

4. Select the Slow tangent option for the Out parameter.

5. Move the Time slider from frame 0 to frame 200 and watch what the car does.

You can see that the car moves in a straight line between the two keyframes. The orientation of the car has not changed, so the car looks like it is moving slightly sideways. Finally, the car is driving near a tree.

Next, you'll modify the trajectory of the car so that it gives the tree a wider berth. You'll also add some rotation to the car so that it looks like it's turning into the building.

1. Move the Time slider to frame 120. This is where you'll add another keyframe in order to move the trajectory away from the tree.

2. With the Select and Move tool still active, move the car to the location shown in Figure 13.6.

FIGURE 13.6
Moving the car

3. Click the Select and Rotate tool, and rotate the car so that it is aligned with the trajectory at this keyframe. By rotating the car at this point, you are adding a rotation key.

4. Now click and drag the Time slider between frames 0 and 200 to see the motion of the car.

The car moves around the tree and turns, although the turning is not well coordinated with the trajectory. The car also does not complete its turn at frame 200, where it comes to rest. You need to add a few more rotation keys to make the car's motion fit its trajectory:

1. Go to frame 200, which is now keyframe 3 of the trajectory.

2. Using the Select and Move and Select and Rotate tools, move and rotate the car so that it is nearer to the entrance of the building and oriented with the trajectory, as shown in Figure 13.7.

3. Go to frame 1 and orient the car with the trajectory.

4. Now check the animation again by moving the Time slider between frames 0 and 200.

FIGURE 13.7
Move the end loca-
tion and orient the
car with the trajec-
tory at keyframe 3.

The car now turns, but it is still somehow out of sync with the trajectory. To fine-tune the car's motion, you'll need to add some additional key locations for the rotation:

1. Set the Time slider to about frame 108; then use the Select and Rotate tool to orient the car to the trajectory. This location was chosen because it is about where the car begins to increase its turning rate, and it may be different in your scene.

2. Now test the animation again by sliding the Time slider from 0 to 200 and back.

3. Add additional keyframes if necessary to make the car rotate properly along its trajectory.

The car now follows the trajectory in a more natural, car-like fashion.

You've added several rotation keys in this exercise. Unlike the position keyframes, rotation keys do not appear on the trajectory. They do, however, appear on the track bar, below the Time slider, while the car box is selected. Notice how several keys in the track bar are both green and red, indicating that both a position and rotation track exist at that frame. The rotation keys also have parameters that can be adjusted in the Motion panel and in the Track Views.

1. With the Time slider set to 200, click the Rotation button at the bottom of the PRS Parameters rollout (not the Rotation button in the Create Key group). The Rotation key parameters appear in the Command panel.

2. Scroll down to the Key Info (Basic) rollout. You now see the settings for the rotation parameters.

If you expand the Assign Controller rollout, you will notice that it is an Euler XYZ (pronounced "oiler") controller instead of the Position XYZ controller you worked with in the camera animation. You can change the Rotation controller to Tension Continuity Bias (TCB) if you prefer (see Chapter 12 for more on the TCB controller). You can fine-tune the rotation of the car using the TCB parameters at each key, though the current settings may be just fine for this project. You've seen how you can use the Rotate transform tool over time to make the car move through its trajectory as a car normally would. You have the same types of control over the rotation of the car as you do over the position. You can also use both Track View dialog boxes to fine-tune the car's motion, just as you did with the camera in Chapter 12.

Automating Output of Multiple Still Images

Animations are great tools for presenting designs, and they can help you or your clients understand what a design will ultimately feel like to inhabit. However, animations can take a great deal of time to keyframe, preview, study, and, finally, render. The tools you use for animation can also be used to help you automate the creation of still images. In particular, they can be great timesaving tools for creating the more traditional elevation views of a building or the top, front, and side views of objects for technical illustrations. When you automate the rendering of stills, you can leave the computer unattended while each one of the stills you specify is rendered.

In this section, you'll see how you can automate the creation of elevation views of the villa by animating another camera in the scene.

Setting Up a Camera for Elevations

The first step in this automation project is to set up a camera to display an orthographic projection instead of a perspective view:

1. Click the Auto Key button to turn off Auto Key mode.

2. Adjust the Top viewport so it looks similar to Figure 13.8.

3. Click the Create tab in the Command panel; then click the Cameras button.

FIGURE 13.8
The Top viewport
and new camera

4. Click Target in the Object Type rollout; then click and drag the point indicated in Figure 13.8, directly to the left of the villa.

5. Drag the cursor to the center of the villa and release the mouse.

6. Rename this new camera `Elevation001`.

The Camera parameters need to be altered so that the camera will display a typical elevation view, which is a type of orthographic projection view:

1. Click the Maximize Viewport Toggle to view all the viewports.

2. Right-click the Camera.View.3DFRONT viewport label in the upper-left corner of the Camera viewport, and then choose Cameras ➢ Elevation001. This will allow you to see the changes you make to the Elevation001 camera settings.

3. With the Elevation001 camera selected, click the Modify tab of the Command panel; then, in the Parameters rollout, select the Orthographic Projection check box.

 Notice that the Elevation001 viewport changes to show a side view of the building.

4. Adjust the FOV spinner (FOV stands for *field of view*) so that you can see the entire building in the Elevation001 viewport.

 You'll need to make one more adjustment to the camera—lower the view in the Elevation001 viewport; it is a bit too high. You will also want to hide the background image behind the building by using the Truck Camera tool.

5. Use the Truck Camera tool in the Elevation001 viewport to drag the building to the center of the viewport, over the background image, as shown in Figure 13.9. This has the effect of moving the Elevation001 camera and its target up above the ground to the center of the building.

FIGURE 13.9
The Elevation001
viewport, showing
the orthographic pro-
jection of the villa

Setting Up the Four Elevations

With the Elevation001 camera created and its parameters set, the final step is to set up the four views using the animation features of 3ds Max. You'll turn on the Auto Key mode, and then, at three different frames, you'll set up three camera positions, one for each of the other three elevations.

1. Turn on the Auto Key button.

2. Move the Time slider to frame 2 because it is the next frame after frame 1, the Auto KeyDefault Frame.

3. In the Top viewport, move the Elevation001 camera to the location shown in Figure 13.10. Make sure that you move only the camera and *not* the camera *and* the target. You can use the Elevation001 viewport to help align the camera.

4. Move the Time slider to frame 3; then move the camera to the position shown in Figure 13.11. Again, make sure that the camera is perpendicular to the surface of the building. You can also use the Elevation001 viewport to make sure that the camera includes the entire building in its view.

5. Move the Time slider to frame 4, and then move the camera to the last elevation position, shown in Figure 13.12.

FIGURE 13.10

Move the camera to this location for the second elevation.

FIGURE 13.11

Move the camera to this location for the third elevation.

FIGURE 13.12

Move the camera to this location for the last elevation.

You now have four frames (frames 1 through 4) that show the villa's four elevations. As a final step, you'll need to create a copy of the SUN directional light that follows the camera. Typically, rendered elevation views use a light source from the upper corner of the view behind the camera, so you'll need to create a copy of the SUN to simulate that orientation.

1. Move the Time slider to frame 1.

2. Shift+click and drag the SUN directional light to the location shown in Figure 13.13.

3. In the Clone Options dialog box, give the new directional light the name **SUNelevation001**.

4. Click the Copy radio button to make the clone unique and click OK.

5. Move the Time slider to frame 2; then move the new SUNelevation001 direct light to the location shown in Figure 13.14.

FIGURE 13.13
Copying the SUN

Make a copy here.

FIGURE 13.14
Positioning the SUN for each elevation

Position at frame 4

Position at frame 2

Position at frame 3

6. Repeat step 5 for frames 3 and 4. Use Figure 13.14 to guide you in the location of the SUNelevation001 directional light.

7. Select the original SUN directional light; then, in the Modify tab of the Command panel, select the On check box in the General Parameters rollout to turn off this light. You don't want the original SUN directional light to over-illuminate the scene now that the elevations have their own animated SUN light source.

8. Turn off the Auto Key button.

BACKBURNER

Rendering animation sequences or a large number of still images can take a significant amount of time and seriously hamper your productivity. You may have even heard the term *render wander*, referring to a 3ds Max artist's habit of walking around the office while waiting for a render process to complete.

When a project's rendering time is expected to be unacceptably long, consider using Backburner to assist the rendering process. Backburner is an Autodesk utility that allows one workstation to control another, using its processor to render assigned frames from the Render Setup dialog box. This process is called *network rendering*. Larger companies often have render farms set up consisting of several workstations with no other purpose than to be used as network rendering nodes as required by the current projects. Systems in the render farm usually do not need monitors, keyboards, mice, or other peripheral devices. Another option is to use other computers that are used for day-to-day tasks in a company as a render farm in the evening.

Systems used in a network rendering setup do not need to be in a render farm; any system capable of running 3ds Max Design 2011 can be used. All machines in the setup must have 3ds Max Design 2011 installed, but this does not require purchasing additional licenses of the software. Only the controlling system, called the Manager, must have an authorized copy of 3ds Max Design 2011 installed. The systems being used by the Manager, called Servers, are not required to be authorized. Backburner can also be used in a single-system setup. This allows you to continue working in 3ds Max and the Manager while a second session of 3ds Max is opened as the Server; however, in this setup the performance degradation is often too significant to make any productivity gains. All image maps used in the rendering must be available to all the computers rendering a project.

Now that you've got the scene set up with a camera for the elevations, the rendering part is simple. 3ds Max gives you the option to render selected frames of an animation instead of the entire sequence of frames. You'll use this feature to create your elevations.

1. Stop and save your work before you begin the rendering process. 3ds Max has been known to crash when it runs out of memory, and rendering can use lots of memory. It's a good habit to always make sure you've saved before you start to render. Save your file as **MyElevationAnimation.max**.

2. Click the Render Setup button on the Main Toolbar to open the Render Setup dialog box.

3. In the Render Setup dialog box, click the Frames radio button in the Time Output group.

4. In the Frames input box, enter **1-4**. This tells 3ds Max to render only frames 1, 2, 3, and 4.

5. Click the Files button in the Render Output group; then, in the Render Output File dialog box, enter **Myelevations** for the name, and select TIF Image File (*.tif) in the Save As Type drop-down list.

6. Click Save. In the TIF Image Control dialog box, click 8-bit Color, and then click OK.

7. Click the 648 × 480 button in the Output Size section of the dialog box.

8. Make sure Elevation01 is selected in the View drop-down list at the bottom of the Render Setup dialog box, and then click Render. 3ds Max proceeds to render the four elevation views.

3ds Max will create four files, each with `Myelevations` as the first part of the name. A four-digit number is appended to the name to indicate which frame of the animation the rendering represents (for example, the first frame will be called `Myelevations0001.tif`).

Of course, you can use 3ds Max's animation tools to automate the rendering of a set of perspective or isometric views. You can now walk away and take care of other things while 3ds Max renders your views unattended. If your views take a long time to render, you may want to set things up to render overnight.

GETTING NOTIFIED ABOUT RENDERING PROGRESS

Nobody likes to stare at the slowly moving render progress bar or leave the office with a critical render in progress. Luckily, you can set up 3ds Max to notify you, by e-mail, when a render job is complete, when it fails, or when specific frames are rendered. To do this, expand the Email Notifications rollout in the Render Setup dialog box and then check the Enable Notifications option.

In the Categories section, select the frequency or cause for an e-mail notification. Finally, in the Email Options section, enter the relevant e-mail information, including the SMTP server through which the e-mail is to be sent.

The elevations you render will look a bit stark. You can add fountains, cars, peripheral objects, and people to inject some life into the images. The addition of landscaping, people, and cars to liven up a rendering is referred to as *entourage*. You can add entourage to your still images later in an image-editing program or you can include trees and people in the model to be rendered with the building. Several plug-ins are available for this purpose; the RPC plug-ins from ArchVision are widely used to this end.

Rendering a Shadow Study

Another great traditional way to use 3ds Max's animation tools is to create shadow studies. In many situations, a project may require a shadow study of a building to make sure its shadows do not adversely impact a landscape feature or another building nearby. You may also be called upon to create a shadow study to help analyze a building's heat gain and energy usage. The Daylight System tool in conjunction with the Animation tools can make quick work of such a task.

In the following section, you'll learn how to use the animation features to create both stills and animations of the building's shadows over time.

Adjusting for True North

Chapter 14, "Advanced Rendering using metal ray," shows you how to place a Daylight System into your scenes. Instead of reading the same instructions here, you'll use a file that has the Daylight System already placed for you. The Shadowstudy.max file has a Daylight System placed in the scene with the sun position set for 2 o'clock on September 21, 2010, and for the location of Paris, France. No adjustment has been made for true north yet, so you need to orient the sun correctly in relation to the building. For the villa, north is actually in the lower-left corner of the Top viewport. You can change the orientation of the compass rose and thereby change the true north direction for the project site.

CERT OBJECTIVE

1. Open the file Shadowstudy.max.

2. Click the Select by Name tool in the Main Toolbar and select Daylight01 from the list.

3. Click the Motion tab in the Command panel and turn off the Manual setting by choosing Date, Time, and Location at the top of the Control Parameters rollout, if necessary. This option locks and unlocks the Control Parameters settings.

4. Scroll down to the Location group of the Control Parameters rollout.

5. Change the North Direction setting to 225. You'll see the compass rose and Sunlight directional light change orientation and position to reflect the new north direction.

The North Direction setting interprets values as degrees in a clockwise direction, so to point north directly to the right in a positive X-axis direction, you would enter **90**. The North Direction input box does not accept negative values, so to point true north to the lower-left corner of the Top viewport, you need to enter **225**.

Now let's set up some times for the shadow study. Suppose you want to see the shadows at three-hour intervals, starting at 6 o'clock. You'll want to set the first hour a bit before the 6 o'clock time in case you want to create an animated study of the sunlight.

1. With the Daylight01 system still selected, set the Hours parameter in the Time group of the Control Parameters rollout to 3.

2. Click the Auto Key button to turn it on.

3. Move the Time slider to frame 70 and change the Hours setting to 21. Note that all of the time-related spinners turn red to show they have been keyframed.

4. Turn off Auto Key mode.

You now have a range of time that you can use to generate single images or a two-second animation showing the movement of shadows across the ground on September 21, 2010. There is one more detail you'll need to adjust before you create your study renderings.

Changing from IES Sun to a Standard Light

You may recall from Chapter 8, "Light and Shadow," that the Daylight System uses an IES Sun, which is a photometric light. Such a light produces a coarse-looking shadow when not used with the Radiosity Renderer. You'll want to change the Daylight System from IES Sun to a standard directed light to get a smooth, even shadow when you're using the Default Scanline Renderer.

1. Click the Modify tab.

2. In the Daylight Parameters rollout, change the IES Sun selection in the Sunlight drop-down list to Standard.

3. You don't need the Skylight option, so turn off the Active option for Skylight in the Daylight Parameters rollout.

Now you are ready to create the shadow study renderings:

1. In the Top viewport, adjust the view to look like Figure 13.15.

FIGURE 13.15
Adjust the Top viewport so that it looks like this figure.

2. Open the Render Setup dialog box and select 3dsmax.scanline.no advanced lighting .high.rps, from the Preset dropdown list.

3. Make sure all options are selected, and then click Load in the Select Preset Categories dialog box.

4. Click the Frames radio button in the Time Output group on the Common tab of the Render Setup dialog box.

5. Enter the frame numbers that correlate with the times of day you want to render, separated by commas. For four single views at three-hour increments, enter **20,30,40,50** without spaces.

6. Click the Files button, enter **Shadowstudy** for the filename, and select TIF as the file type. Use the Save In drop-down list to browse to the folder where you've been saving your project files; then click Save.

7. Make sure Top is selected in the Viewport drop-down list at the bottom of the dialog box and click Render. These renderings will take longer than before; you've picked the high setting, so the quality improves, but rendering progress slows accordingly.

ADD EXPOSURE CONTROL TO ADJUST FOR BRIGHTNESS

If your scene renders out too bright or too dark, you can use exposure control to compensate. Choose Rendering ➤ Environment or press the 8 key, in the top row of keys on the keyboard, to open the Environment tab of the Environment and Effects dialog box. In the Exposure Control rollout, expand the drop-down list and choose Logarithmic Exposure Control. In the Logarithmic Exposure Control rollout, select the Exterior Daylight option, and then press Render Preview to see a thumbnail of the scene. Adjust the Brightness value in the Logarithmic Exposure Control rollout to about 70 to fine-tune the brightness in the scene. You can also increase the physical scale to brighten the scene.

3ds Max will render four views of the Top viewport, each showing the shadows of the building on the ground at the times indicated for each frame.

To create a short, animated shadow study, do the following:

1. Set up the Top viewport as described in the previous set of steps.

2. Open the Render Setup dialog box, click the Range radio button, and enter a range from frame 15 to frame 75.

3. Click Files, enter **Shadowstudy** for the filename, and choose .AVI from the Save As Type drop-down list.

4. Click Render to create the shadow study animation.

The still images and the animation can be helpful tools in your work, and as these exercises demonstrate, they may not take that much time to generate.

As you've seen from the exercises in this chapter, you can have several animation sequences in a single scene. You just have to select an object to animate, depending on which animation you want to use, and then select the time range or set of frames for your final output.

You've also seen how you can create a wide variety of animations, from flybys to shadow studies. There's one more method for creating animations that you'll want to know about. You can generate a more intimate look at a design, called a *walkthrough*, by simulating the view of a building as you walk along a path. Let's see how it is done.

Creating a Walkthrough

Walkthroughs can give you a sense of what an interior space is really like. They can play a major role in selling a project to a client. They can also show you what is good or bad about a design in ways that still images cannot. This type of animation is usually created using a Path Constraint,

so you'll need a spline that indicates the walkthrough path. The camera will be created and assigned to the path using the Walkthrough Assistant.

Start by creating a path for your walkthrough using a line shape:

1. Use the Maximize Viewport Toggle to enlarge the Top viewport.

2. Click the Create tab in the Command panel, click the Shapes button, and then click Line. In the Creation Method rollout, change Drag Type to Bezier.

3. You'll want a curved path, so click and drag the start of the line at the point indicated in Figure 13.16.

4. Click and drag two more points to form the curved spline shown in Figure 13.16. Right-click to complete the path.

5. Give your new line the name **Walkthroughpath** in the Name and Color rollout on the Command panel.

FIGURE 13.16
Draw this spline for the camera path.

Click and drag these points to complete the spline.

Click and drag the start of the spline from here.

You've just created the path for the walkthrough. Remember that you can edit the curve using the Vertex option at the sub-object level in the Modify tab. You don't have to worry if your path isn't perfect. You can edit the spline to fine-tune the walkthrough animation path even after you've created the animation.

Now you're ready to create a camera for the walkthrough:

1. From the Menu Bar, choose Animation ➢ Walkthrough Assistant to open the Walkthrough Assistant dialog box shown in Figure 13.17.

2. In the Camera Creation section of the Main Controls rollout, ensure the Free option is selected, and then click the Create New Camera button. The new camera, named Walkthrough_Cam001, is created and added to the list of cameras in the Cameras section.

CHANGING A CAMERA'S SIZE IN THE VIEWPORTS

If your cameras are larger than you prefer, you can change their sizes using the Non-Scaling Object Size option in the Viewports tab of the Preference Settings dialog box. This changes all cameras' sizes along with all other nonscaling objects, such as light icons and Assembly Head gizmos.

FIGURE 13.17

The Walkthrough
Assistant dialog box

3. In the Path Control section, click the Pick Path button; then select the Walkthroughpath shape that you drew in the previous exercise. The camera moves to the first vertex on the designated path.

 The camera should be 16′ above ground so that it is at eye level on the second floor. You can't, however, move the camera, because its position is now controlled through the position of the path that it is designated to follow. You must move the path instead.

4. In the Path Control section, set the Eye Level value to 16′; then select the Move Path to Eye Level option. The elevations of the path and camera change.

Fine-Tuning the Camera's Orientation

The Walkthrough Assistant assigned the Path Constraint as the controller that determines the position of the camera, based on a percentage along the path. When the Path Constraint was applied, the camera moved to the beginning of the path and its orientation shifted to aim in the direction of the path. The Path Constraint controls the position of the object and, by default, the orientation of the camera follows the path. You have the option of keyframing its orientation to customize the view at any point in time, as you'll see next.

1. Drag the Time slider from frame 0 to frame 600. Observe that the Walkthrough_Cam001 object follows along the path it is constrained to and arrives at the end vertex of the line at frame 600.

2. Display all four viewports and then right-click in the Camera.View.3DFRONT viewport to make it active. In the Cameras section of the Walkthrough Assistant dialog box, click Set Viewport to Camera. The Walkthrough_Cam001 view now occupies that viewport. You may have to deselect the Orthographic Projection option in the Parameters section of the Camera Properties on the Modify tab.

USING MULTIPLE PATHS

Using the Path Constraint controller, you can assign more than one shape as the path for an object to follow. When more than one shape is selected, each is given a weight that determines the influence each has on the object's motion. For example, if an arc and a straight line are both assigned as the path that a camera (or any other object) must follow, with the arc having a weight of 10 assigned while the line has a weight of 2 assigned, the object will follow neither path perfectly. It will follow the arc to a degree fives times greater than it follows the line, creating a trajectory that is somewhat flattened. Were the weights to be swapped, the trajectory would be fairly straight, with a bump to indicate the smaller influence of the arc.

1. Select the Walkthrough_Cam001 camera, and then click the Motion tab of the Command panel. Make sure Position is selected at the bottom of the PRS Parameters rollout and scroll down to the Path Parameters rollout.

 There are several important options in this rollout that define the motion of an object assigned to a path constraint. The Follow option, which is checked by default, determines whether the camera changes orientation to match the tangency of the path, and the Bank option allows the object to tilt as it travels through a curved segment of the path. If your constrained object follows a vertically looping path, like a roller coaster, you need to select the Allow Upside Down option or the object will instantly flip at the apex of the loop.

2. You can set rotation keys to define the camera's orientation and override the orientation set by the Follow option. Drag the Time slider to frame 100, a point before the camera enters the curve and turns toward the end of the path.

3. With Auto Key on, click the Rotate transform and, in the Top viewport, pivot the camera about 20 degrees counterclockwise until you can see the upcoming corridor leading to the end of the path. A rotation key appears in the track bar.

THE CAMERA SHOULD MIMIC THE EYES

When you walk down a street or through a building, try to notice where you look. A few steps before a turn, you generally look in the direction of the turn for obstacles or impediments. Before you open a door, you may look down toward the knob or bar and then up into the room. Your camera movements should closely mimic the movements and focus of a person's eyes in the same situation.

4. Drag the Time slider to frame 400, just past the end of the curve, and you'll notice that the camera is rotated too far and not oriented along the path. The previous rotation key caused a 20-degree skewing of the camera's orientation, which is carried through the remainder of the camera's trajectory because of the active Follow option. You need to correct for that.

5. Rotate the camera about 20 degrees clockwise until it faces the end of the path. When you scrub the Time slider, you'll see the camera look into the turn and then straighten out as it exits.

6. You can also adjust the orientation of the camera using the Turn Head and Head Tilt Angle options in the View Controls rollout of the Walkthrough Assistant. Add more rotation keys using this method if you like.

DELETING ROTATION KEYS

To delete all the rotation keys assigned to the walkthrough camera, click the Remove All Head Animation button in the View Controls rollout of the Walkthrough Assistant.

Adjusting the Camera's Timing

Notice that the Walkthrough_Cam001 object is animated across the entire active time segment. If you'd like the walkthrough to take less time, you can keyframe the percentage the camera has progressed along its path to end at an earlier frame.

1. Drag the Time slider to frame 60.

2. With Auto Key mode on and the Walkthrough_Cam001 object still selected, change the % Along Path parameter in the Path Options group to 0 (zero).

3. Go to frame 510 and change the % Along Path parameter to 100.

4. Scrub the Time slider. Now the camera pauses for 2 seconds, takes 15 seconds (450 frames) to travel the length of the path, and pauses at the end for 3 seconds.

5. Toggle Auto Key off.

6. The time the camera takes to travel the length of the path is shortened, and now the rotation keys are not located properly. Click the rotation key at frame 100 in the track bar and drag it to frame 170. Use the feedback from the prompt line to accurately move the key.

7. Move the rotation key at frame 400 to frame 450.

The Walkthrough Assistant contains its own method for rendering previews of the current frame, eliminating the need to create them using the Render Production button.

1. Drag the Time slider to the desired frame.

2. In the Render Preview rollout of the Walkthrough Assistant dialog box, click the large Click to Render Preview button. If the results in this window are less than pleasing, go to Exposure Control (press 8 to launch the Environment and Effects dialog box), and use Render Preview there.

 Real World Scenario

THE OFFICE WALKTHROUGH

A while back, a company that was moving their corporate offices from several small floors in one building to a single, large floor in another building needed some animation assistance. Because of the nature of the company's business, there is a lot of foot traffic through their office space. The owner needed to provide a method for visitors to find the staff members they were looking for, but did not feel that there was enough workload for a full-time receptionist to direct traffic. He also wanted to reduce the amount of time that his employees were away from their desks just to usher the visitors back to their workspaces.

The decision was made to provide, for the visitors, an interactive display that would show an animation from the elevator lobby to the destination. Upon selection of a staff member's name from a list, the eye-level animation would play through and then ask the user if the animation was to be repeated. We were asked to provide animations from the elevator to each cubicle or office while another consultant put together the program, complete with a touch-screen interface.

The office was designed but not constructed; however, access was provided to the CAD files of the construction documents (see Chapter 5 for information on using CAD files with 3ds Max). Rather than design and render hundreds of separate animations, each taking time to load when requested, lines were drawn from the elevator lobby down the major corridors and then stopping at every intersection. Wherever one line stopped, one or more lines started from the same location, branching down another corridor or turning to face an office or cubicle. This allowed for the major runs, which were common to many of the destinations, to exist as independent videos while shorter animations were available for the end runs.

Based on the requested staff member's office location, the other consultant's software loaded and played the first section of animation. While it was playing, the remaining animations were loaded and then played in sequence, appearing to be a single, seamless video.

Adjusting the Path

One of the best things about using the Path Constraint is that you can easily change the camera's trajectory by editing the path:

1. Right-click in the Top viewport. Select the Walkthroughpath spline object.

2. Switch to the Vertex sub-object level by right-clicking and using the quad menu.

3. Select the last vertex and move it up.

4. Drag the vertex handle as shown in Figure 13.18.

FIGURE 13.18
Editing the walk-through path to control the camera trajectory

5. Exit the Vertex sub-object level.

6. Right-click the Walkthrough_Cam001 viewport and play the animation.

7. Save your file as **MyWalkthroughAnimation01.max**.

Observe the camera following the new trajectory from frames 60 through 500. You may keep editing the spline path as needed to complete an entire walkthrough animation.

CHANGING ELEVATIONS WITH A PATH

You can get a camera to go up or down stairs by constraining it to a path that has its vertices moved in the Z direction to accommodate the changing elevation. It is best to use Bezier or Smooth vertices in a walkthrough path to ensure gradual and continuous motion.

The Animation File Output Options

Before you render a production file, you'll want to know the animation file formats available in the Render Output File dialog box. Most of these formats are the same as those for single still images, with a few twists.

You have several format options for animation file output, each with its advantages and disadvantages:

AVI File (*.avi) AVI stands for Audio Video Interleaved, and it is perhaps the most common type of animation file on the Windows platform. You can use AVI files for both animated materials and animated backgrounds.

These AVI files can use any number of compression schemes, known as codecs (*codec* is short for compressor/decompressor). When you use this file format, a dialog box appears, allowing you to select a codec. The usual choices are Cinepak, Intel Indeo 3.2, Microsoft Video 1, MJPEG, and IYUV. You may also install other codecs onto your system, such as MJPEG or Motion JPEG codecs for specialized video output devices. (A complete discussion on codecs is beyond the scope of this section, but a brief discussion is available in the "The AVI Codecs" section of this chapter.) You may want to experiment with the codecs you have available to see which one gives you the best results.

Other AVI file settings include compression quality and the Keyframe Every Nth Frames option. The Compression Quality slider offers a trade-off between image quality and file size: the better the image quality, the larger the AVI file will be. Keyframe Every Nth Frames lets you control AVI keyframes that are not the same as the keyframes you've encountered in 3ds Max animations; AVI keyframes have more to do with the way animation files are compressed.

Targa Image File (*.tga, *.vda, *.icb, *.vst**)** This is perhaps the most universally accepted format for high-quality video animation. Rendering to the Targa format produces a single file for each frame. Because a typical Targa file is close to 1MB in size (for NTSC video), you will consume disk space in a hurry using this format. A high-definition video frame in the Targa format can be over 6MB in size. Still, it is the format of choice when you want the best-quality video output. It offers a wide variety of resolutions and color depth up to 32-bit color (24-bit plus alpha channels). Targa was developed by TrueVision, and was the first "True-Color" file format. You can use Targa files for still images, and it is a good format for transferring to Apple Macintosh systems because it usually requires little if any translation for the Mac platform.

TIF Image File (*.tif**)** This file format offers high-quality color or monochrome output. It is similar to the Targa true-color format in quality, although TIF files are used primarily for still images and prepress. This format also produces one file per frame of animation. If your images are destined for print, this file format is the best choice, but be aware that both PC and Mac versions of this file format exist. If you're sending your file to a Mac, make sure you've translated it into a Mac TIFF file. This can be done easily with Photoshop or with another high-end image-editing program.

BMP Image File (*.bmp**)** The BMP format is the native Windows image format. It is not as universally used as the Targa format for video animation; still, most Windows graphics programs can read BMP files.

JPEG Image File (*.jpg, *.jpe, *.jpeg**)** This format is a highly compressed, true color file format. JPEG is frequently used for color images on the Internet. The advantage of JPEG is that it is a true color format that offers good-quality images at a reduced file size. One drawback of JPEG is that it does introduce distortions into the image. The greater the compression used, the more distortion is introduced.

GIF Image File (*.gif**)** Although GIF files are not supported by 3ds Max as an output file format, it is an important one that should be mentioned here. This is a highly compressed image file format that is limited to 256 colors. This file format is popular because it is easily sent over the Internet and is frequently used for graphics on web pages. GIF files can also contain very small animations. You can convert a series of animated GIF frames into an animation by using a number of software tools, including Adobe Photoshop. Also, free and shareware products can turn a series of animation frames into animated GIF files.

PNG Image File (*.png**)** The PNG file format is similar to GIF and JPEG in that it is primarily used for web graphics. It has a variety of settings, mostly for controlling color depth, lossless compression, transparency, interlacing, and animation.

Encapsulated PostScript File (*.eps, *.ps**)** EPS is a file format devised by Adobe for describing page layouts in the graphic arts industry. If you intend to send your renderings to a prepress house, EPS and TIF are both popular formats.

Kodak Cineon (*.cin) The Kodak Cineon file is a 10-bit format intended for the film industry. It is a standard format for converting motion picture negative film into a digital format. Many special-effects houses use this format and other software to help create the special effects you see in movies. Frames rendered to this format are recorded as individual files.

MOV QuickTime File (*.mov) QuickTime is Apple's standard format for animation and video files. Its use is not limited to the Mac OS, however. It is somewhat equivalent to the AVI file format native to the PC, but MOV animations are of generally better quality.

Although not directly related to animations, MOV files can also be QuickTime VR files. QuickTime VR is a kind of virtual reality that uses images stitched together to simulate a sense of actually being in a location and being able to look around. QuickTime VR is frequently used on Internet real estate sites to show the interiors and exteriors of homes. It is also popular at auto sales sites that show a 360-degree view of the interiors of new cars. Photostitching applications are available to construct QuickTime VR files from a set of images.

SGI's Image File Format (*.rgb, *.sgi) and the RLA Image File (*.rla) The Silicon Graphics Image file format (SGI) has a following in the film and video industries, and Silicon Graphics has developed a format designed to work with their own animation software and hardware. The RGB (red, green, blue) format offers 16-bit color and alpha channels. The RLA format offers a greater set of options, including additional channels for special effects.

RPF Image File (*.rpf) The RPF file format is an Autodesk 3ds Max file format that supports arbitrary image channels for special effects and other types of post-processing of images. It is similar to the SGI and RLA formats. This file format is often used in conjunction when compositing scenes using Autodesk Combustion.

Radiance Image File (HDRI) (*.pic, *.hdr) Also known as high dynamic range images (HDRI), radiance image files are used for high-contrast data sets that capture a greater dynamic range than can be displayed on a monitor. HDRI files are usually composited from multiple shots taken from the same point of view at different exposure settings into one data set. Generally, you shouldn't use them in animation output due to increased memory requirements. HDRI files can be used as backgrounds and reflection maps within animated scenes. See Chapter 11, "Organizing Objects and Scene Management," for more information.

DDS Image File (*.dds) The DirectDraw Surface format, developed by Microsoft, is used to store both textures and cubic environment maps. With DirectX 9 installed on your system, you can render to the DDS format and use the files in materials, but without it you can only use DDS files in materials.

OpenEXR Image File (*.exr) Similar to HDRI files, OpenEXR image files contain additional lighting information than can be displayed on a monitor. OpenEXR was developed by and is used by Industrial Light & Magic in the production of all of their feature films. OpenEXR has been extended in this release so that all the G-Buffer and Render Element channels can be included within the single .exr file. If you use 3ds Max Composite with the EXR file format, you gain access to these individual channels for modification quickly and easily.

Several of these file formats create a single animation file, like the AVI and MOV file formats. Other file formats, such as the TGA and CIN formats, are intended as single files per frame. The

single-frame formats require an application, such as Adobe Premiere, Adobe AfterEffects, or Autodesk 3ds Max Composite, to turn them into viewable animations, although for short clips you can use the built-in RAM Player inside of 3ds Max to create viewable animations. Their chief advantage is that you can maintain a high level of quality in your animation files and then use the files as a source to produce other formats for different applications. Targa files, for example, can be rendered for the highest level of resolution and picture quality. The Targa files can then be processed through Adobe Premiere to generate AVI or MPEG-1 files for the Internet, or Motion JPEG for video output.

VIDEO POST

You can use the Video Post feature to perform nonlinear video editing of your animated sequences, including advanced transitions. This is not nearly as powerful as some of the commercially available editing programs, but it will do in a pinch when some quick editing is necessary and no other programs are readily available.

True Color vs. 256 Colors

Two of the formats we have discussed—GIF and BMP—offer 256-color output. You can get some very impressive still images from 256 colors, but when you start to use animation, the color limitation begins to create problems. One major problem is called *color banding*. This occurs when an image has a gradient color. Instead of a smooth transition of colors over a surface, you see bands, as shown in Figure 13.19. The effect is similar to that of the Posterize option in many paint programs.

This color banding may be fine for limited applications such as previewing animations, but you will want to use true color output for your finished product. True color images, such as those offered by Targa, TIF, and JPEG files, do not suffer from banding. They also offer smoother edges on models with lots of straight edges. If you don't need the absolute best quality, you might consider the JPEG output option. It provides high resolution and true color in a small file size. You can render a 10-second animation with higher-quality JPEG files and, in some cases, use less than 40MB of disk space. Most of today's desktop graphics and video-editing software can read JPEG files.

FIGURE 13.19
Two images rendered in 3ds Max. The one on the left shows what the image should look like under good conditions. The one on the right shows color banding caused by a limited color palette.

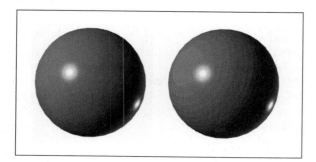

File Naming in Animations

When you choose any of the file formats other than AVI or MOV, 3ds Max generates a separate file for each frame of your animation. The name of each frame is given a number so that the frame sequence can be easily determined by video-editing programs such as Adobe Premiere or Autodesk Combustion.

3ds Max will use the name you provide in the Render Output File dialog box. For the rest of the name, 3ds Max will add a number. For example, if you enter the name **Savoye** for the animation file output using the Targa file format, 3ds Max will create a set of files with the names Savoye0000.TGA, Savoye0001.TGA, Savoye0002.TGA, and so on.

Choosing an Image Size

Still image sizes will vary depending on the medium of presentation. A minimum resolution for 8 × 10-inch prints, for example, is 1024 × 768. Larger poster-size prints will require much higher resolutions. Video animations for traditional VHS or DVD purposes usually will not exceed 720 × 480. The resolution will be determined by the type of device you are using to record to videotape or the software used to master your DVD. For example, if you were using the obsolete step-frame recording method that recorded a single frame at a time directly to videotape, you would typically render to an image size of 512 × 486. Other real-time video playback devices can use seemingly odd sizes such as 320 × 486 or 352 × 240. The horizontal resolution is stretched to fit the size of the screen, so the higher the horizontal resolution you use, the more detail appears in the final output. The aspect ratio of the animation does not change. You should check the documentation that comes with your video recording board for the specific sizes you can use for videotape.

You can use the Print Size Wizard dialog box, shown in Figure 13.20, to quickly determine the proper rendering resolution when the final destination for the image is printed media. To open the dialog box, choose Rendering ➤ Print Size Assistant.

In the Paper Width and Paper Height fields, enter the printable dimension for the artwork. This may not be the same as the paper size in situations where the printer, like most office models, does not print to the extents of the paper. In the DPI field, enter the dots-per-inch value that the image will be printed to. Click the Render button at the bottom of the Print Size Wizard dialog box to transfer the values, and then open the Render Setup dialog box. Choose a filename and type, and then click Render in the Render Setup dialog box to create your image.

FIGURE 13.20
The Print Size Assistant is used to determine the correct rendering size for image output to properly print an image.

The AVI Codecs

Earlier in this chapter, you had to choose a video-compression method for your animation files. Many methods are available, all of which degrade the video quality to some degree. Some of the methods are intended for presenting video only on a computer, while others are intended for TV monitors.

THIRD-PARTY CODECS

Several third-party codecs are available free or for purchase; one of the most popular is the DivX codec. When using a codec that does not ship with Windows, keep in mind that anyone who wants to view your animations must have that codec installed on their system as well. Be aware of this if you send an animated portfolio to a potential employer using a third-party codec that they may not have.

If your animation is destined for computer presentation, chances are you'll use the AVI file format. AVI allows you to select from a variety of compression/decompression methods, commonly known as *codecs*. You've already been introduced to a few of these codecs, but as a reminder, here's a rundown of the most common codecs and their uses:

Cinepak Designed for high-quality video playback from a computer. This codec is considered to produce the best quality.

Intel Indeo Designed for high-compression ratios, it is best suited for multimedia.

Intel Indeo RAW Applies no compression to video. Use this to maintain the highest level of image quality while transporting your file to other digital video programs such as Adobe Premiere.

Microsoft RLE Designed to keep file size down by reducing the color depth. It is primarily designed for 8-bit animations.

Microsoft Video Similar to RLE in that it reduces the color depth of the file. It is designed for 8- and 16-bit animations and videos.

None Applies no compression at all to your file. Like the Intel Indeo RAW format, this option is for storing image files at their best level of quality, sacrificing disk storage space.

BURNING ANIMATIONS TO DVDS

You can render sizable animations and burn them onto an inexpensive DVD-ROM that holds 4.7GB of data. You can buy a DVD writer for under $25; practically all new computers have them as standard equipment. Many DVD burners come with the software needed to produce DVDs that are viewable on consumer DVD players connected to television sets.

Using reactor to Animate Objects

3ds Max has an internal physics engine, called *reactor*, that is used to create animations that feature collisions between objects. Originally, reactor began as a third-party plug-in that could be purchased to add physics simulation capabilities to 3ds Max. As often happens, it was licensed by Autodesk as part of the software program; now everyone who buys 3ds Max gets reactor included. Using reactor, you can roll one object across a floor into another object and let 3ds Max figure out their movements based on the physical properties that you assign the objects. Objects used in a reactor simulation can take on a few shapes:

◆ Rigid bodies, such as a set of pool balls bouncing off the edges of a pool table

◆ Soft bodies, such as pillows flying across a room

◆ Cloth, such as comforters and tablecloths

◆ Fluid-based objects, such as inflatables floating in a pool

Objects can be fixed in place, free to move, constrained to other objects, or even attached to springs. In this exercise, you'll dump a box of toys down the stairs of the condo that you've worked on in several other chapters.

Assigning Properties to Simulation Objects

All the objects that are considered in a simulation must contain the physical information, including mass and friction, for each object. Depending on the accuracy requirements of your simulation, you don't always need precise data to input.

1. Open the Condo_startReactor.max file from this book's accompanying web page.

 This is similar to the condo files that you worked with in earlier chapters, but with much of the geometry deleted and the Default Scanline Renderer assigned as the renderer. These changes are for rendering speed only; reactor works equally well regardless of the rendering engine chosen.

 The sliding door at the bottom of the stairs is mostly open, and the railing is gone in case one of the simulation objects decides to find its way outside. A box of simple toys, blocks, and balls is positioned at the top of the stairs and animated to dump its contents.

2. Right-click a blank area on the Main Toolbar, and choose reactor from the context menu to expose the reactor toolbar. Dock the menu to the left side of the 3ds Max window.

3. In the Orthographic viewport, select the six larger spheres, as shown in Figure 13.21, or use the Select from Scene dialog box to select the objects named Ball through Ball05.

FIGURE 13.21
Select the six large spheres.

4. Click the Open Property Editor button on the reactor toolbar. Any changes made to the parameters in the Rigid Body Properties dialog box that opens are applied to the selected objects.

5. Set the Mass to 1 in the Physical Properties rollout and choose Bounding Sphere in the Simulation Geometry rollout. The Bounding Sphere option instructs reactor to calculate based on the smallest possible sphere that could hold the selected objects, rather than the surfaces of the objects themselves. This is usually quicker—and when the object is spherical in shape, as in this situation, the accuracy is not affected.

6. Select the six smaller spheres, named Ball06 through Ball11. Then in the Rigid Body Properties dialog box, change Mass to 1, Friction to 0.1, and Elasticity to 1. Choose Bounding Sphere for these as well.

7. Select all nine boxes, named Block through Block08; change Mass to 1, Friction to 0.3, and Elasticity to 0.3. Choose Bounding Box in the Simulation Geometry rollout. Like the Bounding Sphere option, Bounding Box instructs reactor to calculate based on the smallest possible six-sided box that could hold the selected objects, rather than the surfaces of the objects themselves.

8. Select the Toy Box object; then change Mass to 1, Friction to 0.1, and Elasticity to 0.3. Choose Concave Mesh in the Simulation Geometry rollout. In most nonspherical or nonbox-shaped cases, Mesh Convex Hull is the option of choice, but when the object has a recessed area, like a bowl or a cup, the Concave Mesh option is required. Concave Mesh requires a slower and more complex calculation.

9. Click the Unyielding check box so that the box's animation isn't affected by the other objects in the scene.

The box and toys are part of the simulation, and now you need to add the scene objects with which the toys may collide. To do so, follow these steps:

1. Clear your selection set, and then select the following objects: Wall_Den, Wall06, Window_Den, Floor407, Door_Patio_East, Patio_East, Planter, Planter_Dirt, Planter_Yucca, and StraightStair01.

2. Change their mass to 1, and then click the Mesh Convex Hull option.

3. In the middle of the Physical Properties rollout, check the Unyielding option to force these object to remain in a fixed location and orientation.

4. You may need to select these objects again, so type **Fixed Objects** in the Named Selection Sets field in the Main Toolbar. Press Enter after typing the name in the field.

5. Close the Rigid Body Properties dialog box.

Assigning Simulation Objects to a Collection

Not everything in a scene needs to be calculated and accounted for in a physics simulation. If a toy car wheel is to roll across a floor and then crash into a wall, the wheel, wall, and floor must be included, but not the ceiling, distant rooms, or upstairs furniture. All the included objects must be added to a collection in reactor, and only those objects included in the collection are

considered in the simulation. In this step, you will simply add the objects to the rigid body collection, in preparation for the simulation calculation.

1. Select the objects in the Fixed Objects named selection set—all the Ball objects, all the Block objects, and the Toy Box object.

2. Click the Rigid Body Collection button on the reactor toolbar. The Rigid Body Collection icon appears in the scene, and the Modify panel displays the RBCollection properties, as shown in Figure 13.22. You have just created the Rigid Body Collection.

FIGURE 13.22
The RBCollection icon and parameters

DISABLING A SIMULATION

It's not uncommon for several simulations to exist in a single scene. To turn off any simulation, select the Disabled option in the RB Collection Properties dialog box.

Setting Up and Running the Simulation

Simulations may only need to run for a few designated seconds of a much longer scene, and you can define what that length is. The simulation won't start until the designated Start Frame, and all simulations stop when the time reaches the End Frame. In this section, you will set up and run the simulation.

1. Click the Utilities tab on the Command panel, and then click the reactor button.

2. In the reactor rollout, expand the Choose Solver drop-down list, and choose Havok 3. The Havok 3 Solver is faster than Havok 1 and is better when using only rigid body objects, but Havok 3 has fewer features than Havok 1.

3. Close the Reactor Messages dialog box if it opens.

4. Expand the Preview & Animation rollout, and then set the Start Frame to **0** and the End Frame to **450** so that the simulation runs for the entire length of the scene's animation.

5. Make sure that the CamTop viewport is active, and then click the Preview Animation button on the reactor toolbar.

After a brief pause, the Reactor Preview Window opens, showing the scene from a point of view similar to the active viewport, as shown in Figure 13.23. The window appears washed out because it takes into account the lights in the scene, but not any exposure control. Your video card must be able to use an OpenGL Driver to properly display the Reactor Preview Window. This doesn't mean you need to have 3ds Max set for OpenGL, the Reactor Window will automatically use it for the preview without you doing anything special.

FIGURE 13.23
The Reactor Preview Window

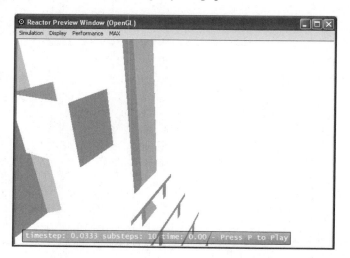

6. Press the P key to start the animation preview and then press it again to stop it. The box rises and then rotates to dump the contents down the stairs. If the box rises but nothing happens, try to scale the box so it's larger and move it down a little. This way, none of the objects will be interpenetrating at the start of the simulation.

7. Close the Reactor Preview Window and the Reactor Messages dialog box.

8. Choose Edit ➤ Hold to hold your scene in the event that the simulation doesn't run properly and must be recalculated.

9. Click the Create Animation button on the reactor toolbar, and then click OK in the reactor dialog box that opens. This indicates that the action of creating the animation cannot be undone. The scene pauses and may flash briefly as the animation is created and a key is placed at every frame for every object in the simulation that was not designated as Unyielding.

10. When the simulation is completed, right-click in the Front viewport and then drag the Time slider forward to see whether any objects were simulated inaccurately and drop through the box like in Figure 13.24.

FIGURE 13.24
Look for objects that are improperly animated in the simulation.

11. If any objects are falling through the box, correct the situation by following these steps:

 A. Select the object(s) and note their names.

 B. Choose Edit ➤ Fetch to restore the scene.

 C. Select the object(s) and move them away from the Toy Box walls. Place them above other objects if necessary.

 D. Hold the scene again.

 E. Create the animation again by repeating step number 9.

12. Play the animation again and view the animation through the Front and all three available Camera viewports (Figure 13.25).

The simulation runs well but not very accurately: the toys don't touch every step and they roll through the wall at the base of the stairs.

FIGURE 13.25
The objects are animated based on the simulation.

Refining the Settings

Four objects (Wall06, the planter, the sliding door, and the stairway) are designated as convex objects, but they are actually concave objects. Wall06 turns near the planter, forming a concave pocket, as the supports do for the stairs. On the sliding door, the glass is recessed within the frame, causing another concave pocket. The planter is essentially a large concave bowl. In this section, you'll change the designation of planter, wall, door, and stair objects.

1. Choose Edit ➤ Fetch to restore the scene.

2. Select the Wall06, Door_Patio_East, StraightStair01, and Planter objects.

> **DELETING THE ANIMATION KEYS**
>
> You may not be able to undo the animation created with a physics simulation, because this feature works intermittently, but you can select the objects animated and then delete the keys in the track bar.

3. Open the Rigid Body Properties dialog box, and then choose the Concave Mesh option.

4. While you're making changes, let's reduce the friction for the scene objects so that they slide against each other more easily. Clear the selection set; then select all the Ball and Block objects, the stairway, and the floor.

5. Set the Friction value to 0.05. The field is initially blank because more than one value is used for the different objects.

6. Select only the small balls, and set Elasticity to 1.6 to increase their bounciness. The Havok 3 Solver can't utilize Elasticity values higher than 1.9, so if you need values higher than that, you must change to the Havok 1 Solver.

7. Select the large balls, and set their elasticity to 1.

8. Hold the scene, and then create the animation once more.

9. If you're satisfied with the animation, render the scene as an animated file. You can see the animations as `reactor_CamTop.avi` and `reactor_CameraFloor.avi`, available on this book's web page.

10. Save your file as `MyCondo_ReactorComplete.max`. If you had trouble, open `Condo_ReactorComplete.max` to see a file with the correct animation in place.

Using Particle Systems

Particle systems are a means of projecting many (often more than 100,000) objects into a scene without the requirement of actually creating or inputting that much geometry. Particle systems can be used to create weather conditions such as snow or rain, fountains, hoses, a barrage of arrows, or even a lava lamp. The 3ds Max particle systems have evolved over the years, but there are basically only a few general components that need to be considered: the emitter, the particles, and any space warps involved.

The emitter As you might guess, this is the object that emits the particles into the scene. Emitters are usually nonrendering objects, but scene objects can be used to emit objects as well.

The particles When emitted, these can range from single pixel-sized dots to planes that hold images and maintain an orientation perpendicular to the viewport to instances of geometry that exists in the scene—imagine a fire hose that emits little firemen from the nozzle. Special consideration must be given as to how many particles could exist at one time and how long each particle exists in the scene before being deleted and then sent through the emitter again.

Space warps These are nonrendering objects that affect the trajectory of the particles. They can be forces, like gravity or wind, or deflectors that change the motion of a particle upon impact with the deflector.

The 3ds Max particle systems have continually evolved over the years. In their earliest form, the Spray and Snow particle systems were basically invisible planes that dropped dots on the scene objects. Third-party developers often took on the task of creating more powerful systems that could be purchased by a user and added to their seat of 3ds Max. Several of these plug-ins were purchased by Autodesk and integrated into the base product. Some of the early particle systems are shown in Figure 13.26 and are still part of 3ds Max, but they are considered legacy features that are kept around for compatibility purposes and only simple projects.

FIGURE 13.26
The legacy particle systems that are still available in 3ds Max

The addition of Particle Flow as the primary particle system in 3ds Max presented a huge increase in the capabilities of the particles but required a change in the approach as to how the systems were designed and implemented. Rather than binding a particle emitter to a series of space warps, all of which can affect the particles at one time, Particle Flow uses a flowchart style model to control the particle behavior. Within the chart, called an Event, the particles are born and then pass down the list through a series of operators and tests. Operators affect the particles in many ways, such as by defining the speed, material, or applied forces. Tests determine whether a specific condition is met, such as the particles' age or whether they've impacted a specific object. When a particle meets the conditions of a test, it's passed on to the next item in the flow or sent to another flow if directed. When a particle is passed to a test and doesn't meet the conditions, it's recycled through the same flow.

In the next section, you'll add gently falling snow outside one of the patio doors in the condo. You'll use a Particle Flow emitter to create the particles, and then use a Gravity space warp to control the direction of the particle emission.

Creating the Initial Flow

Particle Flow particle systems are dragged into a scene from the Create panel and then constructed and edited in the Particle View dialog box. The following exercise shows how to do this:

1. Open the `Particles14.max` file from this book's accompanying web page.

 This is similar to the condo files that you've worked with in this and other chapters but with much of the geometry deleted, the camera hidden, and a background image assigned. The Default Scanline Renderer is assigned as the current renderer. These changes are made to speed up the rendering process only and particle systems work equally well with the Default Scanline Renderer and the mental ray renderer.

2. From the Command panel, choose Create ➤ Geometry ➤ Particle Systems ➤ PF Source.

3. Click and drag a PF Source icon, located in the Top viewport, as shown in Figure 13.27.

FIGURE 13.27
Create a Particle
Flow particle system in the Top
viewport.

4. Zoom into the PF Source in the Front or Right viewport, and you'll see an arrow pointing in the negative Z direction. This arrow indicates the initial direction the particles will be emitted.

5. With the PF Source selected, change the object's name to Particle Snow and set the Length and Width to 15′0″.

6. Move the PF Source so that it's over the far right patio as well as a small portion of the roof, and raise it above the level of the roof, as shown in Figure 13.28.

FIGURE 13.28
Move the PF
Source over the
patio and above
the roof.

7. From the Menu Bar, choose Graph Editors ➤ Particle View or press 6 on the keyboard. The Particle View dialog box opens with the default particle system forces in place (see Figure 13.29).

8. Select and delete the two events that are not part of the Particle Snow particle system. They are labeled Event01 and Event02.

9. Click one object in the depot, and its description appears to the right of the depot. Click an operator in an event, and that operator's parameters appear to the right of the event window. The upper, smaller event is the global event and represents the parameters for the PF Source that you created in the scene. The lower event contains the operators that control the particles.

10. In the Quantity Multiplier area of the Modify panel, set the Viewport % to **10** to require that only 10 percent of the total number of particles be displayed in the viewports. This will task your video card much less than if you were to display all 20,000 particles in each viewport.

FIGURE 13.29

The Particle View dialog box

Adding and Editing the Operators

Each operator in the event has several parameters that can be edited to accomplish the desired result. Additional operators can be dragged from the depot and dropped anywhere in the event. There is no practical limit to the number of operators that a single event can hold.

1. Select the Birth operator in the lower event to expose its parameters.

2. Set the Emit Start value to **-150** and the Emit Stop value to **450**. The first parameter causes the emitter to start emitting particles at frame minus 150, exactly 150 frames before the animation begins, even though that is outside of the range of the active time segment. This results in the particles reaching the patio by the time the active time segment starts.

3. Set the Amount to **20000** to create a fairly dense snow.

DISPLAYING THE PARTICLES

If the particles stop appearing in the viewports or in renderings, make sure that the Enable Particle Emission option is checked in the Modify panel's Setup rollout when the PF Source is selected.

4. Skip the Position Icon operator. In the Speed operator's parameters, set the Speed to 10˝ and make sure Along Icon Arrow is selected as the direction. These parameter settings slow the flow of particles and force them to leave the emitter in the direction of the arrow you saw in the previous section.

5. Delete the Rotation and Shape operators by right-clicking on them and then choosing Delete from the context menu. The particles will always face the camera or viewport, so a rotation is unnecessary and the shape will be changed.

6. Drag a Shape Facing operator from the depot to the space between the Speed and the Display operators in the event, as shown in Figure 13.30. A blue line and tooltip appear to indicate the location and operator being added.

 The Shape Facing operator causes the particles to be represented, at rendering time, by planes that continuously face a selected object or camera.

7. Right-click the Shape Facing operator in the event, choose Rename from the context menu, and then rename it to **Shape Facing Snowflakes**.

8. Click the None button in the Shape Facing Snowflakes rollout's Look at Camera/Object section, and then click the CameraFloor camera in the Top viewport.

9. Drag the Time slider to frame 450 and then render the CameraFloor viewport (see Figure 13.31). The particles don't reach the bottom of the viewport, and they are much too dark. You'll address these issues in the next section.

FIGURE 13.30
Add the Shape Facing operator to the event.

FIGURE 13.31
The CameraFloor viewport showing the snowflakes so far

Adding Materials and Space Warps

The particles must be told which material is assigned to them, and this is done through an operator, rather than by dragging and dropping from the Material Editor. Space warps can affect how the particles move through the addition of gravity, wind, and several other options, as shown in this exercise.

1. Drag a Material Static operator below the Shape Facing Snowflakes operator and change its name to **Material Snowflake.**

2. To assign a material, click the None button in the operator's parameters, then open the Dynamic Scene Lib rollout and locate the Snowfall material, and click OK.

3. Render the viewport again and you'll see, as shown in Figure 13.32, that the planes have a much more snow-like appearance.

FIGURE 13.32
The Rendered Frame Window showing the particles with the Snowfall material assigned

Currently, the particles are falling perpendicular to the emitter, and they follow a straight and unrealistic trajectory. You'll add two space warps, Gravity and Wind, to alter the paths that the particles follow.

4. From the Create panel, click the Space Warps button and then click the Gravity button in the Object Type rollout.

5. Click and drag in the Top viewport to create the Gravity space warp, as shown in Figure 13.33. The size and location don't matter, but the direction it's facing does. Gravity space warps are created facing away from the viewport in which they're made.

FIGURE 13.33
Drag a Gravity space warp in the Top viewport.

6. Click the Wind button and then drag a Wind space warp in the Front viewport. Rotate the wind so that it is slightly blowing toward the building and then, for clarity, move it so that it's not located within the particle system at the top of the Front viewport (see Figure 13.34).

FIGURE 13.34
Rotate and move the Wind space warp.

7. In the Particle View dialog box, drag a Force operator below the Speed operator in the event. Force events are how you tie space warps to Particle Flow particle systems.

8. Rename the operator to **Force Gravity**. In the Force Space Warps section on the operator's parameters, click the Add button and then select the Gravity space warp in the viewports. You'll notice that the particles are moving much faster.

9. Change the Influence % value to 10 to slow down the particles.

10. Add another Force operator below the first one, rename it **Force Wind**, and then add a Wind space warp to the operator.

USING THE SAME FORCE OPERATOR FOR MULTIPLE SPACE WARPS

One Force operator can hold many space warps, but this will require that they all use the same operator parameters.

11. Change the operator's Influence % value to 8.

12. In the Top viewport, move the PF Source in the positive Y direction so that the patio is within the steam of particles; then render the CameraFloor viewport. As you can see in Figure 13.35, the snowstorm is looking better, but flakes are coming into the condo from the ceiling and walls.

FIGURE 13.35
The rendered scene after adding the space warps to the event

Adding Deflectors

While the Gravity and Wind space warps globally affect particle direction, they do not account for the particles colliding with objects in the scene. To do this, you need to add deflectors to the scene and also to the event as operators called Tests. Tests determine whether a particle has met a certain condition and what to do with it if it has. To do this, follow these steps:

1. Hide the particle system. It will be easier to maneuver in the viewports if it isn't visible.

2. Choose Create ➤ Spacewarps ➤ Deflectors and then click the POmniFlect button.

3. Drag the deflector in the Top viewport, as shown in Figure 13.36. It should overhang the front edge of the condo roof slightly.

 Unlike the other space warps you've used, the location, size, and orientation of deflectors are important. The particles must impact the deflectors for them to have any effect.

4. Use the ViewCube or Orbit tool to get an orthographic view of the outside of the condo, and switch to the Smooth + Highlights mode.

FIGURE 13.36
Drag the deflector in the Top viewport.

5. Rotate the deflector so that its arrows, indicating the deflection direction, are pointing upward, and then move the deflector to the top of the roof as shown in Figure 13.37.

6. Click the POmniFlect button again, check the AutoGrid option, and then create two more deflectors, one on each of the walls. Rotate them so that the arrows point outward as shown in Figure 13.38. It's OK if the deflectors overlap.

7. Select one of the deflectors, open the Modify panel, and then change the Time On value to **-150** and the Time Off value to **450**. This causes the deflector to deflect particles during the entire time that the PF Source is emitting particles. Repeat this for the other two deflectors.

FIGURE 13.37
Move the deflector to the roof.

FIGURE 13.38
Add two more deflectors on the condo walls.

THE DIFFERENT DEFLECTOR TYPES

Deflector names that start with P are plane shaped, S are sphere shaped, and U use a scene object as a deflector. Deflectors with Omni in the name are improvements over the legacy deflectors, and those with Dyna in the name can be used in dynamics simulations.

8. Create another POmniFlect deflector, sized and placed on the patio. Set the Time On to **-150** and Time Off to **450**. Also set the Bounce value to **0**. This deflector will hold the particles that impact it.

9. Drag a Collision test below the Material Snowflake operator and change its name to **Collision Delete**.

10. Click the Add button in the operator's parameters, and then click one of the three large deflectors. Click the Add button two more times, adding the other two large deflectors to the operator.

11. Drag a Delete operator to a blank area of the Event window (not inside the event) to create a new event. Delete the Display operator from this new event.

12. Drag from the handle on the side of the Collision Delete operator to the ring at the top of the Delete event, as shown in Figure 13.39.

 This links the Collision operator to the new event that contains only a Delete operator. Any particles that pass the test, by colliding with one of the three large deflectors, are sent to the new event and deleted. All particles that don't pass the test, by avoiding the large deflectors, continue in the scene.

13. Add another Collision operator below the Collision Delete operator and rename it Collision Hold.

14. Add the deflector over the patio to the Deflectors list. You can use the By List button to select the space warp from a list.

15. In the Test True If Particles section, make sure the Collides option is selected and then choose Stop from the Speed drop-down list to stop the particles that collide with the patio.

16. Unhide the particle system.

17. Render the CameraFloor viewport for the duration of the active time segment and save it as an AVI file. You'll see the snow fall outside of the window and collect on the patio (Figure 13.40).

FIGURE 13.39
Link the Collision test to the new event.

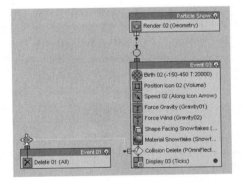

FIGURE 13.40
Snow collects on the patio.

The Bottom Line

Render an animation Animations can often give viewers a sense of size and composition unachievable using still images. Being able to produce a quality animation can mean the difference between a project being accepted or rejected.

Master It Place a new camera above and to the left of the building entrance. Render a 10-second animation of the camera descending and approaching the building.

Output a still image Still images have the benefit of allowing the viewer to spend time examining a particular viewpoint and a specific time. The images are generally produced at a much higher resolution than animations to create a better-quality printed image.

Master It Use the Print Size Assistant and the Render Setup dialog box to render four images from the camera created in the previous Master It exercise. The images are to be 300 dpi on an 8½″ × 11″ paper with a ¼″ unprintable border around the perimeter. Repeat the process creating 150-dpi images on 30″ × 42″ paper with no unprintable area.

Render a shadow study Shadow studies can help determine the need for additional, or reduced, foliage and the effects of artwork or open ceiling designs on light patterns. Producing a shadow is often a requirement when projects involve free-standing structures.

Master It Using the Shadowstudy.max file, change the location of the building to Cleveland, Ohio, and create images at 30-minute intervals from 6 a.m. to 9 p.m.

Create a walkthrough Walkthroughs are special animations that attempt to define the animation from the point of view of an individual walking through the structure.

Master It Assign a camera to a path that approaches the building from the front, passes through the entrance, and then turns to the left.

Choose an animation file output option The files that you can output from 3ds Max vary greatly in their quality and file size, and you must find an acceptable compromise between the two. A 60-second-long, 1280 × 1024 AVI using no compression may be a high-quality choice, but it can result in a file several gigabytes in size that is unplayable on most systems. The key to outputting acceptable animations is selecting appropriate file types and settings.

Master It Render 90 frames of the same animation four times, saving the output as different AVI files. With each repetition, change the codec and/or settings; then compare the output quality and file sizes. Leave the resolution the same for all the animations.

Set up a physics simulation Creating complex animations, involving many collisions between scene objects, can be very time-consuming and not very realistic. Using reactor you can assign properties to the objects involved in the animation and let 3ds Max quickly create the animation.

Master It Using the Condo15.max file, create two teapot primitives and two Oil Tank extended primitives and place them a few feet above the ground. Use reactor to animate them dropping to the floor and colliding with each other.

Create a Particle Flow event-driven particle system Particle systems can be used for a wide variety of applications in design visualization. Any time you need to have a multitude of similar objects, you can consider using a particle system. You can create things like cars in traffic, trees in forests, pedestrians in airports, etc. Particle systems also are useful for water in fountains or simulations of gas particles flowing through tubes.

Master It Create a particle system for a fountain. You don't have to actually create the fountain, just practice how the particles and forces can be used to generate it.

Chapter 14

Advanced Rendering Using mental ray

In Chapter 8, "Light and Shadow," you learned how to light the Villa Savoye model with standard lights, set up "fakiosity," and render the scene with the Scanline Renderer. That fundamental information still applies to the mental ray rendering engine in 3ds Max Design; however, mental ray gives alternative light sources that give you even more options for rendering your scenes.

3ds Max Design 2011 ships with the new 3.8 version of the robust mental ray renderer. It includes Final Gather presets for quickly assigning situation-specific parameters; the Arch & Design, Car Paint, and Autodesk Materials; global quality sliders on the Reveal toolbar for fine-tuning renderings; and mr Proxies to help make your renderings process more efficiently.

In this chapter, you will learn how to use some of the advanced features of the mental ray renderer.

Because you use them in conjunction with mental ray, high dynamic range (HDR) image files, which are another hot topic in computer graphics, will also be covered in this chapter. In this chapter you'll learn to:

- ◆ Apply final gathering
- ◆ Create a contour rendering
- ◆ Use the multi/sub-map material
- ◆ Use Skylight global illumination
- ◆ Use mr Proxy objects
- ◆ Use IES files
- ◆ Use lighting analysis

Understanding mental ray

mental ray is an optional renderer that you can use in 3ds Max, and it is the default renderer in 3ds Max Design 2011. More than just a renderer, mental ray uses special materials, photometric lights, and rendering controls. Ideally, you should decide whether to use the scanline renderer or the mental ray renderer before you begin lighting and applying materials in your scene. If you use standard materials, mental ray will be able to use them; if you use mental ray materials, the scanline renderer won't be able to render the scene correctly.

MENTAL RAY IS A COMPLETE RENDERING SYSTEM

It is up to you to educate yourself on the numerous arcane settings that can help refine the mental ray rendering process. If you plan to use it professionally, reading the technical details on mental ray in the 3ds Max Design 2011 User References is worth the effort.

RADIOSITY AND THE SCANLINE RENDERER

If you are not using mental ray, you can obtain global illumination for the scanline renderer by using Radiosity. A radiosity solution can be calculated in conjunction with the scanline renderer. The Scanline Advanced Lighting Radiosity System stores the indirect illumination data directly in the model file and then the scanline renderer processes only the direct illumination.

Not only can mental ray create a physically correct lighting simulation, but it can also render all imaginable visual phenomena (including some not possible to simulate with the Scanline Radiosity Renderer) through its fully programmable libraries of shaders.

You may remember from Chapter 9, "Enhancing Models with Materials," that shaders are the algorithms that enable the primary components of a material (the ambient, diffuse, and specular colors, for example) to be blended in different ways. With the mental ray renderer, shaders take on the expanded definition of any algorithms used in rendering.

mental ray's shaders are used in materials, lights, cameras, and in the renderer itself. The fact that shaders are programmable allows advanced animation and effects companies to push the computer graphics bar even higher. The larger firms in the film, visualization, and game markets have resources to hire programmers to write subroutines for shader libraries that feature new procedural textures, new materials, new lighting models, and much more.

Programmers can also repackage existing shaders in new ways as mental ray phenomena (scripted shader trees). Many shader libraries and phenomena (including the LumeTools Collection and Physics phenomena) ship with the version of mental ray integrated with 3ds Max Design 2011, so you'll have a lot from which to choose. Most smaller firms (including most architects and interior designers) don't have the resources to hire programmers for their projects, but they still benefit from the interest and continued shader development that mental ray enjoys in larger markets.

MANY 3D SOFTWARE PACKAGES INCLUDE MENTAL RAY

mental images' mental ray has been integrated into many of Autodesk's products including, 3ds Max, Maya, AutoCAD, the Revit family of products, and Autodesk Softimage. mental ray has also been included with Side Effects Software's Houdini, SolidWorks' PhotoWorks, Dassault Systèmes' CATIA products, and other software packages. You can find more information about mental images and see their impressive rendering galleries at www.mentalimages.com.

mental ray is a complete rendering system that can calculate almost any visual phenomenon that you want to simulate, including both direct and global illumination, caustics, ray-traced reflections and refractions, and more. In fact, mental ray is a renderer of such power and depth that entire volumes have been written on the subject. We will concentrate on the basic features of mental ray in this chapter so that you can get started on a sample project.

OTHER MENTAL RAY INFORMATION SOURCES

Please refer to *mental ray for Maya, 3ds Max, and XSI* by Boaz Livny (Sybex, 2007) and *Mastering mental ray: Rendering Techniques for 3D & CAD Professionals* by Jennifer O'Connor (Sybex, 2010) for the definitive texts on using the mental ray renderer.

mental ray takes great advantage of parallelism in information processing systems. Multiple threads of data can run in parallel (at the same time) on one or more processors in one machine or can run across several computers on a network to process your rendering.

In addition, only the incremental changes to the scene database are rendered in the sequential frames of an animation. This can save a huge amount of time, as compared to radiosity rendering, whose solution often needs to be entirely recalculated for each frame under changing lighting conditions.

NETWORK RENDERING WITH MENTAL RAY

Contact a skilled network administrator to set up mental ray for rendering in parallel across your network. Refer to Help ➤ User Reference and search for Network Rendering for additional information.

When you render an image with mental ray, you'll notice a few big differences in the Rendered Frame Window (RFW). You are probably used to the way the default renderer processes scanlines from the top of the frame down. mental ray processes frames in buckets—small rectangular blocks of pixels. As the buckets are processed, the RFW changes from black to display the rendered image. This provides visual feedback regarding the progress of each frame as it is rendering.

RENDERING WITH BUCKETS INCREASES EFFICIENCY

Processing a frame in buckets creates greater modularity that allows the massive parallelism that the mental ray renderer enjoys; each bucket can be given to a different thread for processing. Therefore, mental ray can take advantage of parallel distributed processing more efficiently than most renderers.

Figure 14.1 shows how the buckets appear in the RFW. You will see the buckets firsthand in the next section when you render with mental ray using the sample project.

FIGURE 14.1

Bucket processing in a Rendered Frame Window

Buckets that have already been rendered Buckets yet to be processed

Reveal toolbar Current buckets being rendered
 (four buckets on a quad-core system)

The order in which the buckets are rendered may seem like a mystery to you at first. By default, mental ray chooses the bucket order based on minimizing the memory cost of switching to the next one. If you're rendering buckets across a network, bucket order also is influenced by the need to minimize traffic and load-balance the processors, so the buckets may seem to appear in the RFW at random.

You may notice the addition of the Reveal toolbar underneath the RFW that contains the global quality sliders. The quality control sliders give you the ability to globally change antialiasing, material reflection/refraction, soft shadow, and Final Gather precision settings so you can easily change settings to speed up render times for tests and then increase the quality settings to fine-tune your final renderings. You will use the Reveal toolbar later in this chapter.

Setting Up mental ray

Now that you understand what mental ray can do and how it renders, there are two things you will need to do to actually start working with mental ray in 3ds Max. You'll need to verify a setting in the Preference Settings dialog box, and then you'll need to assign the renderer in the Render Scene dialog box.

VERIFYING YOUR PREFERENCE SETTINGS

In Chapter 1, "Getting to Know 3ds Max Design 2011," you saw how to change the 3ds Max Design 2011 defaults to use the scanline renderer; now you need to verify that 3ds Max is set to the appropriate settings for using mental ray.

If 3ds Max is running, save any current work you have open, and then quit and restart 3dsMax before starting these steps.

1. Once you have restarted 3ds Max, choose Customize ➤ Custom UI and Defaults Switcher.

2. Select the DesignVIZ.mentalray item in the Initial settings section in the upper left of the dialog box. Then click the Set button.

3. A dialog box will indicate that the settings will take effect the next time you start 3ds Max.

4. Quit and restart 3ds Max Design 2011.

ASSIGNING THE RENDERER

Now that you have set the mental ray defaults for 3ds Max Design 2011, you are ready to proceed with this chapter's exercises. Even though you have set up 3ds Max to use the mental ray preferences, you still have to assign mental ray as the Production Renderer for scenes that are currently set to use the scanline renderer. In the following exercise, you will assign the mental ray renderer to a scene.

1. Open the Room.max file. The sample file contains a single room interior with furnishings. The materials have already been set up for the scanline renderer and, currently, no light sources are in the model.

2. Choose Customize ➤ Preferences. Click the mental ray tab.

 Make sure Enable mental ray Extensions is selected in the General section, as shown in Figure 14.2. This option should already be selected, as it is active by default. It is important to be aware of this setting, in case you ever encounter a scene where this has explicitly been turned off (otherwise mental ray will not work).

3. Click OK to close the Preference Settings dialog box.

 Next, to finish enabling mental ray is to assign it as the Production Renderer in this scene.

FIGURE 14.2
Enable mental ray
Extensions

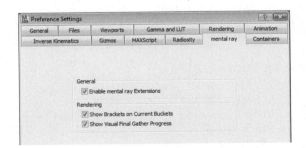

4. Press the F10 key or choose Rendering ➤ Render to open the Render Setup dialog box, and then click the Common tab. Scroll down to the bottom of the dialog box and open the Assign Renderer rollout.

5. Click the Choose Renderer (…) button next to the Production Renderer, which currently is assigned to the scanline renderer, as shown in Figure 14.3.

FIGURE 14.3
Click the Choose
Renderer button.

USING DIFFERENT RENDERERS FOR PRODUCTION AND THE MATERIAL EDITOR

Although it is possible to assign different Production and Material Editor Renderers, doing so is not recommended (they are locked together by default). It makes more sense to view materials in the same way you will render them.

6. The Choose Renderer dialog box appears. Select mental ray Renderer from the short list, as shown in Figure 14.4, and click OK.

 The scene is now enabled for rendering with mental ray, both for the Production Renderer and in the Material Editor. Notice that the tabs in the Render Setup dialog box changed after you switched renderers. Now the Indirect Illumination and Processing tabs replace the Raytracer and Advanced Lighting tabs. In addition, the controls that were on the Renderer tab have changed—they are now specific to mental ray, as shown in Figure 14.5.

7. Close the Render Setup dialog box without rendering.

FIGURE 14.4
Select mental ray
Renderer.

FIGURE 14.5
The Render Setup
dialog box

The Material Editor and mental ray

When you set up a scene to use mental ray, new materials and maps become available to you in the Material Editor—you read about some of these in Chapter 9. In addition, you can use light and camera features specific to mental ray.

Let's take a quick tour of the Material Editor to see what has changed when you're using the mental ray renderer:

1. Open the Slate Material Editor.

2. Right-click in the Active View1 window and choose Materials ➢ mental ray. This gives you a list of the mental ray–compatible materials, as shown in Figure 14.6.

FIGURE 14.6
mental ray–
compatible
materials

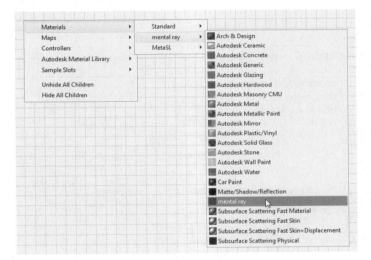

3. Select the mental ray material to add a mental ray material node to the Active View1 Window.

4. Double-click the mental ray node to display its settings in the Parameters Editor section of the Slate Material Editor.

 The mental ray material's shaders are grouped into these categories: Basic Shaders, Caustics and GI, Extended Shaders, and Optimization. Two more options appear in the Advanced Shaders rollout, as shown in Figure 14.7.

5. In the Material/Map Browser section of the Slate Material Editor, double-click the sample slot; this adds it to the Active View1 window.

 Note that you can have multiple materials in an Active View Window.

6. Double-click the Architectural material node and expand the mental ray Connection rollout at the bottom of the panel (see Figure 14.8).

FIGURE 14.7
Inside the mental
ray Material shaders

FIGURE 14.8
The mental ray
Connection rollout
from an Architec-
tural material

Shaders are organized into the same categories in which they appeared in the mental ray material. The difference is that the mental ray Connection rollout provides access to these shaders from within the Architectural material. Before mental ray was integrated into 3ds Max, the mental ray connection was a method to use mental ray shaders with standard or Architectural materials.

ACCESSING MENTAL RAY CAPABILITIES FROM A STANDARD MATERIAL

You can also find the mental ray Connection rollout in the Standard material. Using this rollout can be helpful in legacy scenes that were originally created in earlier versions of the software program.

Notice that some of the shaders are grayed out because their effects are locked to features in the host material. For example, in the Basic Shaders section, the Surface shader is locked because any map or shader applied to the diffuse map in the Physical Qualities rollout would be automatically translated to act as a Surface shader by mental ray.

These settings were not grayed out in the mental ray material because there is no host material from which to translate this information. The mental ray material itself can be used to completely describe a material's surface by choosing the appropriate shaders.

1. Double-click the mental ray material's node in the Active View1 Window.

2. In the Material Shaders rollout, click the None button next to Surface in the Basic Shaders group, as shown in Figure 14.9.

 The Material/Map Browser appears again. Expand the Maps group and then the mental ray group, which displays mental ray–compatible maps and shaders (see Figure 14.10). You can also use materials and maps from the Standard and MetaSL groups. Maps that are incompatible with mental ray will not show in any groups unless you select Show Incompatible from the Material/Map Browser Options menu.

FIGURE 14.9
Click the Surface
Map button.

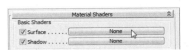

FIGURE 14.10
The Material/Map
Browser showing
the mental ray–
compatible maps

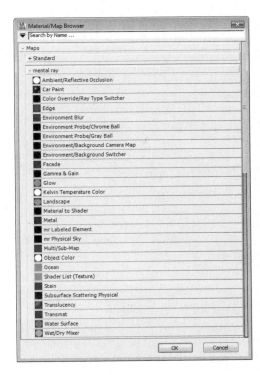

3. Alternatively, you can right-click in the Active View1 Window and choose Maps ➤ mental ray to scroll down the list of compatible maps and see how long the list is.

4. Close the Material/Map Browser and the Slate Material Editor. This completes the quick tour of the changes made to materials with mental ray.

SHADERS ARE BOTH MATERIALS AND MAPS IN MENTAL RAY

mental ray shaders can act as both materials and maps in 3ds Max. As if that isn't confusing enough, shaders can be used in lights, cameras, and the Render Scene dialog box as well.

ADDITIONAL SHADER LIBRARIES ARE AVAILABLE

Several shader libraries are included in 3ds Max's implementation of mental ray; you can mix and match these shaders as you see fit. There are shader libraries from Autodesk (3dsmax) and mental images (base, contour, and physics); and the LumeTools Collection (lume) is also included. Each shader library has its own technical help file that you can access from links in 3ds Max's User Reference.

USING 3DS MAX MATERIALS WITH MENTAL RAY

For the most part, mental ray interprets 3ds Max materials and maps the same way the scanline renderer does. However, you will get the most reliable results with mental ray by using its own purpose-built shaders, which act as both materials and maps in 3ds Max.

Because mental ray completely takes over from the scanline renderer, there are many small gaps, errors, and omissions in mental ray's ability to faithfully reproduce your intentions if you are still using the "regular" materials and maps you are accustomed to using from your experience with other renderers.

In order to use 3ds Max's materials and maps, you must translate them into mental ray's own scene description language prior to rendering—a process too complex to detail here.

USING 3DS MAX MATERIALS IN MENTAL RAY

To learn how to translate 3ds Max materials and maps for proper use with mental ray, read the extensive, detailed notes in the User Reference. Choose Help ➤ Autodesk 3ds Max Design Help. Click the Contents tab and then expand the navigation nodes for Rendering ➤ Renderers ➤ mental ray Renderer. Read "Getting Good Results with mental ray Rendering" and "3ds Max Design Materials in mental ray Renderings." You can find the complete mental ray manual by choosing Help ➤ Additional Help ➤ mental ray Reference.

If you haven't been scared off by the warnings associated with using mental ray in 3ds Max, you should be beginning to see that mental ray is an extremely complex and rich renderer—and although its marriage with 3ds Max is a happy one, it is not without its issues. The next section discusses one of the most innovative technologies used in mental ray.

Using Photon Maps

The use of the photon map in mental ray was pioneered by mental images. To understand what the photon map does, you should first review how the Radiosity Renderer stores global illumination data. The Scanline Radiosity Renderer creates a mesh overlaying the geometry in the scene that stores the data from the lighting simulation, as shown in Figure 14.11. In fact, each vertex in this mesh stores a color (called the vertex color). When these vertex colors are blended together, you see the global illumination in the viewport and rendering. A denser radiosity mesh can hold greater lighting detail but also requires more memory and longer render times and creates significantly larger files.

FIGURE 14.11
Radiosity rendering uses elements of a mesh to help determine the reflection of light within a model. Light that is reflected from one element illuminates other elements.

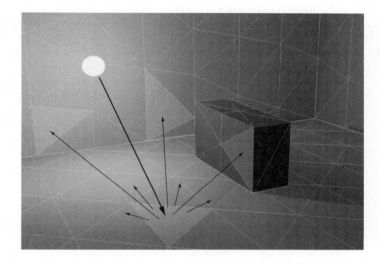

Instead of using a geometrical mesh to store lighting data, mental ray can store indirect illumination in a single map that covers all the surfaces of the model that photons (light particles) strike.

Because indirect illumination can be stored in a map rather than a geometrical mesh, it requires far less memory. On the downside, a photon map cannot be displayed in the viewport like the radiosity mesh can. You can, however, display the photon map in a rendered scene by choosing Render Setup, clicking the Processing tab, selecting the Diagnostics rollout, checking the Enable option, and clicking the Photon radio button. In mental ray, selected light sources can emit photons, which are traced through the scene. These photons are either reflected off opaque surfaces or transmitted through transparent or translucent surfaces. Depending on the Trace Depth settings, which control the number of bounces to be calculated, these photons eventually strike a diffuse surface much like a paintball would. The photons leave the intensity and color that is picked up in the interactions encountered in each photon's trajectory where they strike in the photon map. Very few of these photons actually hit the picture plane (think of it like the camera lens itself), but it doesn't matter because the photons leave their mark right where they strike—on the wall or floor, for example.

UNDERSTANDING RAY TRACING

Ray tracing works a little like a photon map but in reverse. Particles (rays) are traced backward from the picture plane, through various bounces and transmissions through surfaces in the scene, ultimately reaching the light sources that emitted them. Unlike a photon map, only the particles that hit the picture plane are considered in ray tracing. Mental ray uses a process called final gather that similarly shoots out points from the picture plane onto the surfaces visible from that particular point of view.

If you shoot only a small number of photons, the room might look like a paintball war zone. The genius of this technique is that when the photons overlap (you can also control their size), mental ray smoothes them together with a sampling algorithm. When you shoot a large number of photons (10,000 is the default), a lot of smoothing will occur in the photon map, and the indirect illumination built up by the smoothed photons begins to look good.

An important consideration to keep in mind when using a photon map is that the space in your model should be fully enclosed by geometry. Otherwise, photons would escape and, therefore, would never get recorded in the photon map. Photons must reflect or refract the number of times set by the trace depth before they are recorded in the photon map.

For example, an interior architectural space must have a ceiling to effectively use the photon map technique. For outdoor scenes, you can enclose the entire model in a skydome (see Chapter 10, "Using the 3ds Max Camera"), and the photons will be contained in the modeled environment.

SIMULATED ILLUMINATION

Direct illumination is light emitted from a source that reflects off a surface and travels directly to the picture plane, and it is easily calculated by any renderer. Computer graphics programs have been able to simulate direct light since the earliest days of Phong shading.

Indirect illumination is much more difficult to simulate and accounts for 99 percent of the light in a scene, representing all the light that is emitted from sources that does not end up hitting the picture plane. However, indirect illumination influences light that does hit the picture plane (so you see its influence in your rendering) and is critical in making realistic images.

One aspect of indirect illumination is called Global Illumination (GI), which can realistically represent the ambient light in the scene through light inter-reflection. Both mental ray and radiosity can simulate GI, although they do so in different ways. GI effects include color bleeding, which occurs everywhere but is clearly evident when a red wall is next to a white one, for example. Some red color will bleed over and give the white wall a pinkish tint. These subtle visual cues give rendered images a feeling of realism, even if you are not consciously aware of them.

With the photon map, mental ray can simulate another aspect of indirect illumination that radiosity cannot simulate—that of a phenomenon referred to as *caustics*. In the science of optics, caustics are the effects of light cast upon a diffuse surface via reflection off of or refraction through other surfaces.

You will notice caustics effects in the bright spots on the ground when you are looking through a magnifying glass, for example. Another example of caustics is the bright spots that appear on a tablecloth through a wineglass that is lit by a spot light. Caustics effects are focused, stronger light that appears on a surface.

In the real world, light can be thought of as a wave phenomenon, rather than existing as particles, rays, or photons. All the light in a physical space is experienced simultaneously. You cannot separate a portion of light in a room (thinking of it as individual rays) and say that it doesn't influence the rest of the light at the same time. All the light in a space is actually expressed as a single wave equation in quantum physics. Light is a marvelously complex phenomenon that we can only begin to simulate with computers.

Testing the Photon Map Effects

To see the effects of photon maps, as well as global illumination and caustics, let's make our first series of mental ray renderings. As a reference point, we'll begin with a single direct light source without enabling photon maps. You will first have to add a light source to the model.

1. Open the file `MentalRay.max`. This is the same sample project you saw in the previous section with its materials converted to mental ray shaders.

2. Click the Create tab of the Command panel and click the Lights category button. The drop-down has defaulted to photometric lights, which are the most appropriate lights to use to create real-world lighting simulations with 3ds Max Design 2011. Click the Target Light button in the Object Type rollout, as shown in Figure 14.12.

FIGURE 14.12
Select the Target
Light button.

Two nonphotometric light sources have been designed to work with mental ray: the mr Area Spot and mr Area Omni, which can be found in the Standard Lights drop-down. Although you can use the other standard lights with mental ray, you will get the most reliable results by using photometric lights and the mr Area lights.

3. Drag the Target light out in the Top viewport, as shown in Figure 14.13.

4. If it is not still selected, type H to open the Select Object dialog box. Select TPhotometricLight001 from the list and click Select.

5. Right-click the Left viewport to activate it. Using the Select and Move tool, drag the spotlight up just below the ceiling, as shown in Figure 14.14.

FIGURE 14.13
Creating a Photo-
metric Target light

FIGURE 14.14
Move the light
source up.

Now that you have a light in the scene, you are going to make a few changes to improve the viewport display of 3ds Max Design 2011. Taking advantage of the viewport display improvements in 3ds Max Design 2011 will help you get a better idea of how your scene will appear in the final render and can help you get to that final render faster because you will have to do fewer test renders to evaluate your lighting and materials.

1. Click in the Camera001 viewport to activate it.

2. Right-click the Shading Viewport Label and choose Lighting and Shadows ➢ Illuminate with Scene Lights, as shown in Figure 14.15.

FIGURE 14.15
Changing the
Camera001
viewport to
Illuminate with
Scene Lights

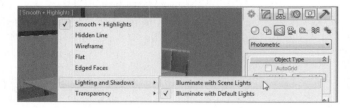

The viewport displays the Camera001 viewport as if it were lit by the light you placed previously.

3. Go back to the Viewport Lighting and Shadows menu shown in Figure 14.15 and turn on Enable Hardware Shading; then go back to the same menu and turn on Enable Shadows. Notice how the viewport changes in Figure 14.16.

Smooth + Highlights + HW appears in the Viewport Shading label to indicate that hardware shading is enabled. The shadows are projected on the objects in the scene.

FIGURE 14.16
Camera001 with scene lighting and shadows displayed

VIEWPORT HARDWARE SHADING

Viewport Hardware Shading support will be limited by your video card and its drivers. Your video hardware should support SM3.0 to take advantage of these features. You can test your hardware by choosing Help ➤ Diagnose Video Hardware. Make sure your video card is supported by 3ds Max 2011 and that your drivers are up-to-date to best take advantage of these advanced features.

CERT OBJECTIVE

The photometric light that you placed earlier supports a number of distribution methods to allow you to simulate various lighting types to increase the realism and accuracy of your renderings. The default distribution type is Uniform Spherical, as shown in Figure 14.17.

FIGURE 14.17
Photometric Light Distribution (Type)

Here are descriptions for the different types of light distributions available with the photometric lights:

Uniform Spherical This projects light evenly throughout a scene, much like a traditional household lightbulb.

Uniform Diffuse This sends light into a scene from a hemisphere and acts much like a boxed light fixture, such as the type of fluorescent light fixture you might have in your office.

Spotlight The Spotlight distribution acts like a focused light source such as your vehicle's headlights or a flashlight.

Photometric Web This distribution allows you to select an IES file that represents the way a specific real-world light fixture emits light. We will use this distribution later in the chapter.

For now, we will change the distribution type for the photometric light that you placed earlier from Uniform Diffuse to Spotlight. To do this, follow these steps:

1. If the TPhotometricLight001 object is not currently selected, click the Select by Name tool, pick the light from the Select from Scene dialog box, and click OK.

2. Go to the Modify tab and find the Light Distribution (Type) section of the General Parameters rollout.

3. Select the drop-down menu and choose the Spotlight option. Notice how the Camera001 viewport changes and the icon for the TPhotometricLight001 changes in the other viewports, as shown in Figure 14.18.

FIGURE 14.18
Viewports with the Spotlight distribution displayed

4. Right-click the Perspective viewport to activate it. Then right-click the View label to open the viewport menu. Choose Lights ➢ TPhotometricLight001 from this menu to look through the new spotlight in this viewport, as shown in Figure 14.19.

FIGURE 14.19
Looking at the table through the light

5. Using the Light Hotspot tool, located in the lower-right corner of the user interface with the other navigation tools, drag the mouse up to decrease the hotspot size in the TPhotometricLight001 viewport. You should be able to see the Hotspot gizmo decrease in size in the viewports. Temporarily change the viewport rendering mode to Edged Faces, if necessary, to see the gizmos; then change the mode back when you are done.

6. Right-click twice to stop the Hotspot tool and bring up the quad menu, and click Select Light Target (see Figure 14.20).

FIGURE 14.20
Select the target in the quad menu.

7. Press Alt+A, or click the Align button in the Main Toolbar, to invoke the Align tool and then click the dinner plate from any viewport. The Align Selection (Plate) dialog box appears.

8. Click all three check boxes for the X, Y, and Z Position options and make sure that the radio buttons for the current and target objects are set to Center, as shown in Figure 14.21. Click OK to perform the alignment.

Now the spotlight is aiming directly at the plate.

FIGURE 14.21
The Align Selection dialog box

9. Make the TPhotometricLight001 viewport active if it isn't currently. Using the Light Falloff tool (near the Light Hotspot tool), drag down in the TPhotometricLight001 viewport to increase the size of the spot's falloff. The scope of the viewport adjusts to match the diameter of the falloff circle. Your viewport should look similar to the one shown in Figure 14.22.

The Falloff gizmo should completely surround the table so that it will be fully illuminated.

FIGURE 14.22
The TPhotometric-Light001 viewport

You placed a photometric light in this scene, so you should now set mental ray to use an exposure control method that will simulate how a real camera would respond to the physically based lighting you are using in these exercises.

1. Choose Rendering ➤ Exposure Control to open the Environment tab of the Environment and Effects dialog box.

2. Navigate to the Exposure Control rollout and change the exposure control to the mr Photographic Exposure Control system, as shown in Figure 14.23.

3. Right-click the Camera001 viewport to activate it

4. Click the Render Preview button in the Exposure Control group and watch as a small thumbnail sample of your rendering appears in the gray window, as shown in Figure 14.24.

FIGURE 14.23
Set Exposure Control to mr Photographic

FIGURE 14.24
The rendered preview

RENDER PREVIEW WITH EXPOSURE CONTROL

IMPORTANT: If you are an experienced 3ds Max user, you need to retrain yourself to not just render, but instead use Exposure Control and Render Preview before rendering. Exposure Control is critical, and using Render Preview saves time and anguish.

5. The preview render is a little dark. In the mr Photographic Exposure Control group, change the Exposure Value to 4 to brighten up the image. Note how the Render Preview window changes as you adjust the Exposure Value setting.

6. Press the F10 key to open the Render Scene dialog box. Click the Render button at the bottom of the dialog box to begin your first mental ray rendering.

 The rendering will appear progressively in the Rendered Frame Window as buckets are processed. After a few seconds, you will see a rendering similar to Figure 14.25.

FIGURE 14.25
Your first mental ray rendering

The rendering in Figure 14.25 is very dark because mental ray is only rendering direct illumination and ray tracing the scene by default. There is only one photometric light source in this model, and it illuminates the surfaces it strikes directly. There is no bouncing of light with direct illumination.

Let's experiment with a photon map next. This will allow you to render indirect illumination. More specifically, let's consider GI first, because it will have the largest effect.

1. Click the Indirect Illumination tab of the Render Setup dialog box. In the Caustics and Global Illumination (GI) rollout, select Enable in the Global Illumination (GI) group.

2. In the Geometry Properties group at the bottom of this rollout, select the All Objects Generate & Receive GI and Caustics box, as shown in Figure 14.26.

FIGURE 14.26
Select the All
Objects Generate
& Receive GI and
Caustics box.

By default in 3ds Max Design 2011, no objects are set to generate caustics and GI (although they can all receive both forms of indirect illumination). By checking the box, all objects in the scene generate and receive both forms of indirect illumination. However, you must manually select which lights in the scene you want to generate caustics. You will render with caustics later in this chapter.

3. Select the green tiled floor by clicking it in the Camera001 viewport. Right-click in the viewport to open the quad menu. Select Properties from the transform quad.

4. Click the mental ray tab of the Object Properties dialog box. Select the Generate Global Illumination box to enable this feature for the floor object, as shown in Figure 14.27. Click OK to close the dialog box.

FIGURE 14.27
Select the Generate
Global Illumina-
tion box.

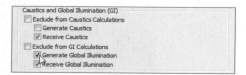

5. In the Render Setup dialog box, scroll down to the Light Properties group of the Caustics and Global Illumination (GI) rollout. Change the Average GI Photons per Light setting to 1000, as shown in Figure 14.28. This reduces the number of photons that will be emitted from all the light sources in the model from the default of 10,000.

FIGURE 14.28
Set the Average GI
Photons per Light.

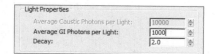

SELECTIVELY CHOOSING OBJECTS THAT GENERATE AND RECEIVE CAUSTICS

Generating photon maps is time-consuming, especially in complex scenes. You can save time by specifying exactly which objects are to generate and/or receive caustics and/or global illumination. In general, the largest surfaces in the model are the most important participants in indirect illumination. For this example, steps 3 and 4 in the previous procedure are not strictly necessary because you set all objects (including the floor) to generate GI in step 2. The sample project is so small that it doesn't take much time for all objects to generate GI. However, the amount of time needed would become more important in a complex scene. Under those conditions, you could save time by being selective about which objects generate and which objects receive both caustics and GI as set via the Object Properties dialog box.

> **CREATE TEST RENDERS WITH FEWER PHOTONS**
>
> It is a good idea to do test renders with fewer photons to get an idea of how they will appear in the space. Greater numbers of photons take ever-greater amounts of time to render, and rendering them may not be necessary at the beginning of a project's lighting phase.

1. Click the Render button at the bottom of the Render Scene dialog box. A rendering similar to Figure 14.29 will appear, showing the result of using 1,000 GI photons.

FIGURE 14.29
The rendering using 1,000 GI photons

You are able to see indirect illumination in areas that were dark in Figure 14.25. These areas are being lit exclusively by the GI photons in the photon map. Notice that some of the photons on the table and walls are greenish, indicating that they picked up that color by being reflected off the floor. You will need to make some changes to make this rendering look better.

By default, the photon size is set to one-tenth the size of the scene extents. This is usually close to the "right" size, but you can manually override the photon size by using the Radius parameter for better results.

2. Check Maximum Sampling Radius in the Global Illumination (GI) group. This enables the adjacent spinner. Change the radius size to 6″ in the spinner.

3. Do another test render by clicking the Render button at the bottom of the Render Setup dialog box. The rendering will display smaller photons, as shown in Figure 14.30.

The rendering is looking more like a paintball war zone. You can deduce that the default photon radius was approximately 1′6″ by comparing Figures 14.29 and 14.30 (based on the fact that you know the radius was 6″ in Figure 14.30).

FIGURE 14.30
The same render-
ing using a smaller
GI photon radius

The best results from a photon map occur when the photons are numerous enough and sized so that about half of their diameters overlap. It is only when the photons overlap that their colors are sampled and smoothed together.

If the photons overlap too much, there will be too much smoothing and subtle variations in lighting will be lost. If the photons do not overlap enough, they won't be smoothed, so they will still be apparent as photons in the rendering (as in Figure 14.30).

Choosing the right settings is usually a matter of doing a few test renders and observing carefully.

4. Change the Maximum Sampling Radius in the Global Illumination (GI) group to 2′. Change the Average GI Photons per Light in the Light Properties group to 100000. Click Render and watch as the rendering appears in the Rendered Frame Window (Figure 14.31). This will take a minute or so to render on most computers.

FIGURE 14.31
GI photons after
adjustment

> **USING COMMAS TO DELINEATE LARGER NUMBERS**
>
> You can't use a comma to delineate large numbers in the spinner fields.

This time, the photons are adjusted so that they are numerous enough and sized properly to blend successfully. You are now able to see much of the room that is illuminated solely by the indirect light of the photon map. Notice the color bleeding that is happening between the saturated green floor and the white walls—a characteristic and desirable effect of global illumination. Color bleeding happens in the real world and is something GI can simulate.

> **EXPOSURE CONTROL**
>
> It's imperative that Exposure Control be used when rendering using mental ray, especially when you are trying to simulate real-world physical conditions. To activate it, choose Rendering ➢ Environment, and then expand the drop-down list in the Exposure Control rollout and select either Logarithmic Exposure Control (when using the scanline renderer) or mr Photographic Exposure Control (when using the mental ray renderer). You can then adjust the settings to control the appearance of your renders.

CERT OBJECTIVE

Let's take a look at caustics next. You will be adding another light source to the scene because Figure 14.31 still looks a bit dark. The room could use more general lighting.

1. Click the Create tab of the Command panel, and click the Lights category button. Click the Free Light tool in the Object Type rollout, as shown in Figure 14.32.

FIGURE 14.32
Create a Free light
in the scene.

2. Click in the middle of the top half of the room in the Top viewport to place the light source as shown in Figure 14.33. Notice how the lighting in the Camera001 viewport changes.

FIGURE 14.33
The new light as
shown in the Top
viewport

3. Using the Select and Move tool, move the light up to the correct height in the Z direction by entering 7′6″ in the Z field of the Transform type-ins at the bottom of the interface, as shown in Figure 14.34.

PhotometricLight001 is now positioned just below the ceiling.

FIGURE 14.34
Adjust the height of the new light.

4. Click the Modify tab of the Command panel. In the General Parameters rollout, change the Light Distribution (Type) setting to Uniform Diffuse, as shown in Figure 14.35, to simulate a flush mounted ceiling light.

FIGURE 14.35
Changing the Light Distribution (Type) setting

MENTAL RAY CONVERTS INCOMPATIBLE SHADOW TYPES

In mental ray, essentially only two shadow types are available: ray-traced shadows and mental ray shadow map shadows. The other types still appear in the Shadows drop-down list; however, if selected, they are automatically converted to one of the other two types at render time. Because this is confusing, it is best to choose one of the explicitly supported types. You will get the best results with ray-traced shadows in mental ray.

5. Scroll down and open the Shape/Area Shadows rollout. You can choose from six area light types: Point, Line, Rectangle, Disc, Sphere, and Cylinder. Change the Emit Light from (Shape) setting to Rectangle and make its length and width both 2″, as shown in Figure 14.36.

A Rectangle gizmo that represents the area light shape will appear in the viewport.

FIGURE 14.36
Change the light's Emit Light from (Shape) parameters.

6. Scroll down further on the Modify tab of the Command panel and open the mental ray Indirect Illumination rollout (this rollout never appears on the Create tab). In the Global Multipliers group, change the Energy multiplier to 0.8, as shown in Figure 14.37.

FIGURE 14.37
Change the light's Energy multipliers.

This reduces the indirect illumination energy that this particular light source will emit, but it does not affect the direct illumination cast by the light.

7. Open the Intensity/Color/Attenuation rollout and select the box in the Dimming group. This will allow you to change the value to 40 percent. This reduces the amount of direct illumination that this light source will contribute to the scene.

CONTROL THE INTENSITY OF YOUR LIGHTS

If light sources have too much direct illumination intensity, they will wash out the subtle indirect illumination effects.

8. Back in the Render Setup dialog box, deselect Enable in the Global Illumination (GI) group. To test caustics, it is helpful not to get distracted by other forms of indirect illumination.

9. Select Enable in the Caustics group, as shown in Figure 14.38.

FIGURE 14.38
Enable Caustics in the Render Setup dialog box.

CERT OBJECTIVE

10. Change the viewport drop-down list at the bottom of the Render Setup dialog box to Camera001. Change the Area to Render drop-down list on the Common tab of the Render Setup dialog box to Region, as shown in Figure 14.39. By rendering a small region, you will save time by rendering fewer buckets in your test renders.

FIGURE 14.39
Set the Area to Render option to Region.

VIEWING MENTAL RAY MESSAGES

You can see what is going on with the rendering process (including any warnings) by opening the Message window. Choose Rendering ➤ Render Message Window, and leave it open when you are rendering.

11. A selection region appears in the Camera001 viewport. Drag the opposite corners of this region to enclose a smaller region around the wineglass, silverware, and plate, as shown in Figure 14.40.

FIGURE 14.40
Drag the Region
box around the
wineglass, silver-
ware, and plate.

12. Click the Render button to start the rendering.

You should hear an error sound and be presented with a mental ray dialog box that says there are no caustic photon emitters in the scene, with OK and Cancel buttons. The All Objects Generate & Receive GI and Caustics check box you selected earlier in the Geometry Properties section of the Indirection Illumination tab of the Render Setup dialog box pertains only to object geometry. This is a change from the behavior of previous releases of 3ds Max, in which this check box would affect lights as well, making lights generate caustics when this check box was enabled. This is a positive change because now you have to manually specify which lights you want to generate caustics instead of automatically having all lights generating caustics and thereby greatly slowing down your renderings. You will now set the Spotlight in the scene to generate caustics on the tabletop. Click the Cancel button on the dialog box.

13. Click the Select by Name tool on the Main Menu and select TPhotometricLight001.

14. Right-click and select Object Properties from the Transform quad menu.

15. Click the check box next to Generate Caustics and click OK.

16. Click the Render button to start the rendering. The RFW shows only the changes made within the region you selected in the previous step.

The overall rendering is much brighter now that you have added the new light source (compare with Figure 14.31). Caustic effects are usually much more subtle than GI effects, so pay close attention to your test renders to perceive them. Your Rendered Frame Window should look like Figure 14.41.

Two areas exhibit caustic indirect illumination effects: one brighter caustic area surrounds the stem and base of the wineglass, and the other caustic area makes the shadow of the wineglass on the tablecloth appear brighter.

Increasing the number of caustic photons may give the effects slightly more definition, but the results attained with 10,000 caustic photons are acceptable.

FIGURE 14.41
The rendering with caustics in the region you selected

INCREASING PHOTONS CAN BRING OUT THE CAUSTICS

If you don't see any caustic areas where you expect to see them (near glass or water usually), try increasing the number of caustic photons that your light sources emit. Be careful not to boost the number of photons too high, however, because extremely long render times may result.

17. Now that you have tested both caustics and GI, it is time to combine them in a full rendering. Enable Global Illumination in the Render Scene dialog box. Change the Render Type drop-down list on the Main Toolbar to View and click the Quick Render button. Figure 14.42 shows the results so far.

18. Save your work as **MyMentalRayGI.max**.

FIGURE 14.42
Final rendering showing caustics and GI effects

SAVING PHOTON MAPS AS FILES

You can save a lot of time in an animation by saving the photon map as a file. That way, the photon map will not be recalculated for each frame. The controls for saving and loading photon map files (* . pmap) are in the Reuse (FG and GI Disk Caching) group on the Indirect Illumination tab of the Render Setup dialog box. There are a few modes you can choose from, depending on the type of rendering you are doing. A new feature in 3ds Max Design 2010 was the ability to reduce the render flicker in animations by using the Project Points from Positions along Camera Path option in the drop-down in the Final Gather rollout. Using this setting along with the Single File or One File per frame options in the Mode group of the Reuse rollout, you can get flicker-free GI and Final Gather illumination in your animations.

In this section, you learned how to approach indirect illumination slowly by doing test renders and making the necessary adjustments to GI and caustics separately. This approach yields faster visual feedback by rendering many quick tests. Figure 14.42 shows the impressive results you have been able to achieve using a photon map in mental ray.

The next section introduces you to a technique that can improve the quality of your renderings beyond what is possible with a photon map, and you may also save rendering time.

Final Gathering

Final gathering (FG) is another technique for calculating global illumination. Originally it was used as an additional calculation used after photon map generation; now you can often skip the photon mapping and get excellent results with just final gathering alone. When you are doing exterior shots, mental ray daylighting and Final Gather will give spectacular results, without the need for any photon generation. Interior shots can also be achieved this way, especially if you use mental ray sky portals. Often interior shots are improved with photon generation combined with final gather, and if there are caustics in the scene, you'll have to rely exclusively on the photon map to simulate that aspect of indirect illumination. Therefore, FG is useful in scenes with overall diffuse lighting but is not very helpful in scenes where caustics play a major role.

Using a photon map alone for GI often leaves dark corners where photons did not reach and patchy areas of light variation where photons did not get smoothed properly. You can smooth all these rendering artifacts by using FG.

When a scene uses FG, fewer GI photons are needed, so the GI photon map can be calculated more quickly. However, FG usually increases render time overall, because additional calculations are performed after the photon map is complete.

FG works by gathering very precise GI data for a few points and then averaging the data from these points. The technique samples GI data that has already been calculated, so it should be used after you generate a photon map for the most accurate results.

Using Final Gather presets in mental ray, you can load common FG settings based on the quality of the Final Gather results required.

USING FINAL GATHER WITHOUT GENERATING A PHOTON MAP

You'll learn how to use FG without generating a GI photon map in the "Skylight Global Illumination" section. FG is conceptually very similar to the concept of regathering in Radiosity.

Let's take a look at using FG in the sample project:

1. Open `MentalRayGI.max` or continue from where you left off in the previous section.

2. Open the Render Setup dialog box if it is not already open. Click the Indirect Illumination tab.

3. Disable caustics while you are testing FG to save time by deselecting the Enable box in the Caustics group.

4. Make sure GI is set to Enable in the Global Illumination (GI) group. Also check Maximum Sampling Radius and set the value to 1´6˝.

5. Check the Optimize for Final Gather (Slower GI) option.

6. Enable FG by selecting the Enable Final Gather box in the Basic group near the top of the Final Gather rollout. Also select Draft Mode (No Precalculations) in the Advanced group, as shown in Figure 14.43.

Figure 14.43
Enable the Draft Mode setting on the Final Gather rollout.

Draft Mode Is Faster, but Leaves Artifacts

Use the Draft Mode (No Precalculations) setting only when doing test renders. It renders much faster but leaves rendering artifacts.

7. Click the Render button at the bottom of the dialog box and then wait a short time for the rendering to be processed. Look closely at the rendering, particularly around the perimeter of the glass, and you will see artifacts visible in the preview.

 If you look closely at the tablecloth, for example, you'll see rendering artifacts, which are variations in light that are apparent at the borders of the buckets. It is usually worth doing a quick preview rendering to be sure that the overall illumination looks good before doing the lengthy, finished final gathering calculations.

 One other setting can improve the quality of your final output—sampling, an antialiasing technique.

Sampling in mental ray is equivalent to 3ds Max's SuperSampling feature that is part of the materials. In mental ray, sampling is done at the scene level, so you don't have to turn on supersampling in any materials.

1. Click the Renderer tab of the Render Setup dialog box. In the Samples per Pixel group, select 4 from the Minimum drop-down. Then change the Maximum drop-down list to 16. Now many additional samples will be made for each pixel, most likely eliminating any jaggedness from the rendering.

2. Change the Filter type to Triangle by selecting the drop-down menu. Box is the default filtering mode and the fastest. The filtering algorithms provide more image sharpening as you move down the list. The sharpening filters also add more time to renderings as you move down the list in the drop-down menu.

3. Click the Indirect Illumination tab. Select Enable in the Caustics group. The final output will also render the caustic effects that you tested in the last section.

4. Deselect Draft Mode (No Precalculations) in the Final Gather rollout.

5. At the top of the Final Gather rollout, click and drag the Preset cursor to the right and choose the High option, as shown in Figure 14.44. Several parameters in the Final Gather rollout are changed to increase the quality of the FG solution.

FIGURE 14.44
Set the Final Gather preset to High.

6. Because you are rendering with Final Gather and you added the free light to the scene, you should go to the Environment tab and adjust the mr Photographic Exposure Control slightly so that the rendered image isn't too bright. A value of 5 should be about right.

7. Click the Render button at the bottom of the Render Setup dialog box to do another rendering. Be prepared to wait a few minutes for this to process. You will see three iterations of processing in the RFW. During the first two processing passes, the Final Gather points are computed and refined. In the third pass, the actual rendering is completed.

8. Save your work as **MyMentalRayFG.max**.

Figure 14.45 shows the results of all your hard work in the final output. If you don't want to wait for the render to process, you can see the results as Figure1445.tif, which you can download from the book's website.

FIGURE 14.45
The final rendering

Reviewing the Basic mental ray Workflow

Now that you have experienced the entire rendering workflow in mental ray, we'll take a moment to summarize the steps usually taken to produce final output in mental ray before moving on to more specialized topics. The first thing to do is make sure your 3ds models are as precise as possible; they should all be air-tight. Then assign mental ray materials to the objects in your scene. Next, add photometric or mental ray lighting. Neither of these last two steps is strictly necessary because most of the 3ds Max materials and lights are automatically converted to passable mental ray versions by the renderer, but you should add or convert them manually for the most reliable results.

If your scene is an exterior, you can skip photon generation. If your scene is an interior that is not illuminated by an exterior light source, you can consider generating a photon map. Then try a test rendering with a low number of GI photons. Adjust the size and number of the photons until you achieve acceptable results. If you expect caustics to play a role in your image, do more tests with a low number of caustic photons and adjust their size and number as necessary with further tests. If you feel that the photon map quality is acceptable, you are done. Use Photographic Exposure Control to "dial in" your rendering values so you have a good range of lights and darks.

You should generally add Final Gather at this point to interiors. If your scene is an exterior or is an interior illuminated by exterior sun, you can skip photon generation and just use Final Gather. Start with the lowest settings for Final Gather Precision and Image AntiAliasing. Gradually increase these values until you are pleased with the results. Adjust sampling if you notice aliasing and then process the final output.

If you can, render your job in parallel to save time. mental ray is perfect for render farming. If you plan on using it a lot professionally, it may pay to consider hiring someone to set up a network of rendering processors to ensure that you get your work done by the deadline.

 Real World Scenario

MENTAL RAY LED TO A POSITION

A few years ago there was a large project that was expected to take about three months to complete. The scope of the project included both interior and exterior animations of a small housing complex and still images suitable for both web and print media. The size of the project required temporarily taking on an additional staff member on a consulting basis. The response to the job posting was very large, with only about 10 percent of the respondents qualified for the position. Replies and portfolios came in from architects, students, artists, hobbyists, and (inexplicably) an electrician. Only a few respondents were called in for an interview.

Of those interviewed, all were good modelers with experience in architectural modeling. One applicant stood apart from the others, though, because of the quality of her renderings. She stated that she used mental ray exclusively and had displayed her extensive knowledge of the mental ray toolset. She was brought on board and ended up handling more of the project than was initially intended, freeing up employees to continue to work on the other projects in the pipeline. In the end, the client was pleased with the quality of the project, and the temporary consultant became a full-time employee. Without her expertise with mental ray and ability to generate high-quality renderings, the company might have hired a different consultant.

Contour Renderings

mental ray contour renderings are like technical line drawings of 3D geometry. Not to be confused with wireframe renderings that show all the objects' topology, contour renderings show only the outlines of objects, and often they can look very appealing, with a hand-drawn look. One of the best things about them is that they generally do not take a lot of time to set up or process. When using the scanline renderer, the Ink N Paint material will create a similar effect.

You will be using mental ray Contour shaders in the Render Setup dialog box and in a single material assigned to the Material Override setting in this nondestructive rendering technique. Once the Contour shaders are activated, you can control their settings by instancing them into the Material Editor. Let's set up the sample project for a contour rendering:

1. Open the file MentalRayContour.max. This is the original Room.max sample project with the mental ray renderer already assigned.

2. Press the F10 key to open the Render Setup dialog box if it is not already open. Click the Renderer tab and open the Camera Effects rollout.

3. Enable contours by selecting the Enable box in the Contours group, as shown in Figure 14.46.

FIGURE 14.46

Select the Enable box.

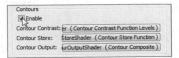

Three shaders are enabled, corresponding to the channels: Contour Contrast, Contour Store, and Contour Output.

4. Click the button marked Contour Composite in the Contour Output channel. The Material/Map Browser appears.

5. Select the Contour Only shader from the list, as shown in Figure 14.47, and click OK.

FIGURE 14.47

Select the Contour Only shader.

6. Open the Slate Material Editor. Drag the Contour Only shader from the button in the Contour Output channel to the Active View1 Window in the Slate Material Editor.

7. Select Instance from the small Instance (Copy) Map dialog box, and then click OK.

8. Click the Background Color swatch on the Contour Only node of the instanced map in the Slate Material Editor, as shown in Figure 14.48.

FIGURE 14.48

Click the Background Color swatch.

9. If necessary, change the color to white in the Color Selector: Background Color dialog box that appears. Close this dialog box after you select the color. Notice that the numerical values for the color properties go from 0.0 to 1.0 and not 0 to 255.

10. Drag the Contour Contrast Function Levels shader from the Contour Contrast channel in the Render Scene dialog box into the last available sample slot in the Material Editor.

11. Choose Instance from the small Instance (Copy) Map dialog box again.

12. Change the Angle Step Threshold to 5.0 in the Contour Contrast Function Levels (Contour) Parameters rollout. Also select Color Contrast Contours, as shown in Figure 14.49.

FIGURE 14.49

Set the Contour Contrast Function parameters.

13. Double-click the Ceiling material in the Sample Slots group of the Material/Map Browser section of the Slate Material Editor, the second slot in the top row, to add it to the Active View1 Window. You can tell this material is not currently used in the scene because it doesn't have any indicator marks in the corners of the material sample. Double-click the ceiling node to have its properties display in the Parameters Editor. Rename this material to ContourOverride.

14. Open the mental ray Connection rollout in the ContourOverride material. Click the None button in the Contour channel in the Advanced Shaders group, as shown in Figure 14.50.

FIGURE 14.50

Setting the Contour shader

15. Choose Contour Simple from the Material/Map Browser that appears. Click OK to close the dialog box.

16. Change the Width (%) to 0.1 on the Contour Simple node, as shown in Figure 14.51.

FIGURE 14.51

Set the Width (%) value of the Simple (Contour) map.

17. Keeping the Material Editor open, go to the Processing tab of the Render Setup dialog box and check the Enable box in the Material Override group, as shown in Figure 14.52.

FIGURE 14.52

Enable the Material Override option in the Render Setup dialog.

18. Now click and drag the output socket on the ContourOverride material from the Slate Material Editor to the material slot you just activated on the Render Setup dialog box, as if you were wiring them together. Choose Instance from the Instance (Copy) Map dialog box that appears and click OK.

19. Right-click in the Camera001 viewport to activate it and then click Render at the bottom of the Render Scene dialog box. Figure 14.53 shows the resulting contour rendering.

The rendering is processed very quickly without complicated materials, lights, or indirect illumination to calculate. Notice that the contours appear only after the diffuse rendering is completed in the RFW. The Contour shaders are applied after the rendering is complete based on information gathered during the rendering process.

20. Save your scene as **MyMentalRayContourDone.max**.

FIGURE 14.53
The finished contour rendering

Using the Material Override setting in the Renderer tab of the Render Setup dialog box is a powerful way to quickly create multiple renderings of scenes using single materials for testing lighting or checking your composition without worrying about changing any materials in your scene. The technique could also be used for creating renderings that look like gessoed or basswood physical models without having to assign new materials to all the objects in your scenes. You could even use this method to render out an ambient occlusion pass of your scene to use in an image-editing program to enhance the shadow detail of your renderings.

RENDERING SPECIAL EFFECTS WITH MENTAL RAY

mental ray can render several "special effects," including depth of field, motion blur, and displacement, as well as volumetric light and fog effects. Many of these effects are also available in 3ds Max with the scanline renderer, but the mental ray versions of them are often more efficient. Some of these special effects will be covered in Chapter 15, "Finishing It Off: Atmosphere, Effects, and Compositing."

CONVERTING STANDARD 8-BIT COLORS TO FLOAT COLORS

You may have noticed that the mental ray materials you are now using display color values differently than the standard materials. The values for assigning colors in mental ray materials are displayed as a range from 0.0 to 1.0 instead of the traditional 0 to 255. This allows you to select significantly more color variations. To convert a color from 0–255 to 0–1, the easiest method is to take the original value and divide it by 255, resulting in the new color value. You can also use the Color Clipboard utility, found on the Utilities tab of the Command panel, to copy 8-bit color values and paste them in Float color values, and vice versa.

Using the mr MultiMap Material

Another feature in 3ds Max Design 2011 that is very helpful in adding a sense of natural variation to your mental ray renders is the multi/sub-map material. The multi/sub-map material can be applied anywhere a map can be used in mental ray. In the following exercise, you will apply a multi/sub-map to a material in a scene:

1. Open the `MentalRayMultiMap.max` file, available from this book's website.

2. Click the Camera002_CoffeeTable viewport to make it active.

 The scene is set up with mental ray materials and GI and caustics. Final Gather is set to the High preset, and the area shadows from the light fixture near the ceiling are set to 128 samples.

3. Click the Render Production button on the Main Toolbar.

 With the render settings set to high-quality final render values, the rendering will take a while to complete. If you don't want to see the finished frame, you can cancel the render once you get an idea of what the scene will look like, but don't close the RFW.

4. On the Reveal toolbar, shown in Figure 14.54, click and drag the slider to change the Image Precision (Antialiasing) value down to Low: Min 1/16, Max 1.

FIGURE 14.54
The Reveal toolbar

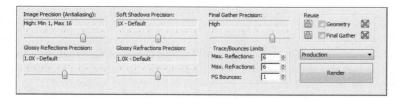

5. Set the Glossy Reflections and Glossy Refractions Precisions settings both to 0.25X – Low.

6. Set the Soft Shadows Precision to 0.25X - Low.

7. Set the Final Gather Precision to Draft.

8. Click the Render button on the Reveal toolbar.

This rendering will process significantly faster because you used the global quality sliders on the Reveal toolbar to change the values in the Render Setup dialog box. Note that dragging the slider all the way to the left is no longer the lowest setting; now this will actually turn the feature off. Watch out for this!

Now that the rendering processes quickly, you can adjust the material on the Vessel objects on the coffee table, making quick test renders as needed without taking up unnecessary time. You can see that the assortment of cylindrical objects on the coffee table all share the same material.

9. Click the Slate Material Editor button on the Main Toolbar.

10. Double-click the VesselMaterial sample to add it as a node to the Active View1 Window view, then double-click the node to its properties.

11. Click the Map button to the right of the Color (Reflectance) item to open the Material/Map Browser.

12. In the Material/Map Browser, click the multi/sub-map material and then click OK.

You will see the Multi/Sub-Map Parameters rollout in the Parameters Editor and you will see a Multi/Sub-object node appear wired to the Color (Reflectance) channel in the Active View1 window. There is a number of settings in the Multi/Sub-Map Parameters rollout, as shown in Figure 14.55. The Multi/Sub-Map parameters default to creating the maximum of 20 Color Map slots. This value can be reduced with the type-in field or by using the spinners.

FIGURE 14.55
The Multi/
Sub-Map Parameters rollout

13. Click the Switch Color/Map Based On drop-down and change the value to Random.

14. Click the Render button on the Reveal toolbar to start another test render. The cylinder objects now have different colors than the ones they had before.

15. Change the Number of Colors/Maps to Use to 12.

16. Change the values for some of the color maps (between 1 and 12, of course) to colors you like.

17. Click the Render button on the Reveal toolbar to start another test render.

18. Find the associated Color/Map value for the color on one of the cylinders that you can see in the test rendering, and click its Map button, as shown in Figure 14.56, to open the Material/Map Browser.

 You can apply any of the maps that appear in the Material/Map Browser to the sub-map color.

FIGURE 14.56
Click the Map button.

19. Select the Marble Standard Material map and click OK.

20. In the Marble Parameters rollout, change the Size value to 0.5.

21. Click the Render button on the Reveal toolbar.

 You can continue adjusting the different maps of the multi/sub-map material.

22. On the Reveal toolbar, change the values you adjusted in steps 4 through 7 to those shown in Figure 14.54.

23. Click the Render button on the Reveal toolbar to start rendering a final high-quality scene.

24. Save your scene as **MymentalrayMultiMap.max**

 Your final render should look similar to Figure 14.57.

If you don't want to complete this render, click Cancel to stop the process. In the previous exercise, you saw how using the Multi/Sub-Map parameters in the mental ray renderer allows you to create a lot of variations of materials to apply to objects in your scene. This saves you from having to create a large number of unique materials and then apply them individually to objects in your scene to add a sense of randomness.

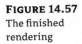

FIGURE 14.57
The finished
rendering

You also used the global quality sliders on the Reveal toolbar to reduce the render settings, allowing you to create quick test renderings without going through the various tabs and roll-outs of the Render Setup dialog box or selecting each soft shadow casting light and changing its parameters. You could also use the toolbar to select even higher settings than are available on the Render Setup dialog box if you need to address issues with antialiasing or the appearance of glossy reflections or glossy refractions.

Skylight Global Illumination

Using a Skylight to produce global illumination is a technique that has been quite popular in computer graphics. Skylight is scattered light that does not come from any particular direction, simulating the luminosity of the sky itself. Skylight emanates from a dome of infinite radius that surrounds the scene everywhere above the horizon.

ILLUMINATING A SCENE WITH NO INTERIOR LIGHTS

When you solely use a Skylight to illuminate a scene, light will not enter interior spaces that are not open to the sky. You can still render interiors using this technique by hiding the ceiling and/or roof objects, thereby allowing the scattered light from the sky to softly illuminate the scene.

If you remember the section on using photon maps, you know that global illumination is simulated with photons, and photons are emitted from light sources. However, no photons can be emitted from a Skylight because they cannot come from any particular direction, by definition.

Rendering GI with a Skylight is tricky because you must use FG to provide the GI without the benefit of a photon map. From the section on FG, you might recall that it was designed to be used after the photon map calculated at least some GI. It turns out that the FG algorithm itself

can calculate GI but for one bounce only. This means that using FG exclusively to generate GI won't yield accurate results because only the first reflection of the photons can be considered. If you are striving to make an accurate lighting simulation, do not use this method. This method is great for producing beautiful abstract renderings with little fuss.

USING FINAL GATHER ONLY

Because generating a photon map in a complex scene can be time-consuming, many of those in the film industry started using FG only and skipped the more accurate photon map process to save precious time, which is often equivalent to money.

Remember, this trick won't work for caustics because FG doesn't consider caustic phenomena. Using the Skylight for GI guarantees that soft and gentle illumination will be everywhere. It also simplifies lighting because there are no other traditional lights in this trick. Let's see how it works in our now-familiar sample project:

1. Open the file MentalRaySkylightGI.max.

2. Type H to open the Select Objects dialog box. Select the Ceiling object and click Select.

3. Right-click in the Camera001 viewport and choose Hide Selection from the display quad.

4. Click the Create tab of the Command panel and click the Lights category button. Use the drop-down to select the Standard lights option, and then select the Skylight tool in the Object Type rollout, as shown in Figure 14.58.

FIGURE 14.58
Create a Skylight in the scene.

5. Click a point under the table in the Camera001 viewport to locate the Skylight, as shown in Figure 14.59. It doesn't matter where this object is placed as long as it is oriented dome up. The Skylight will emanate light in all directions from the inside of a hemisphere corresponding to the form of its gizmo in the viewport.

FIGURE 14.59
Place the Skylight under the table.

6. Click the Modify tab of the Command panel. In the Skylight Parameters rollout, click the Sky Color swatch, as shown in Figure 14.60.

FIGURE 14.60
Change the Sky-light color.

The sky color is currently a pale blue, which is perfect for an exterior rendering. However, you are using it in an interior, so it is better to choose a pale warm color to simulate the light in the space.

7. Drag the Hue slider over into the yellow tones to warm up the scene and click Close.

USE MUTED COLORS FOR THE SKY

Do not use a highly saturated color for the Sky Color setting, because it will interact strangely with the materials in the scene.

8. Press the F10 key to open the Render Setup dialog box if it is not already open and click the Indirect Illumination tab. In the Final Gather rollout, check Enable Final Gather and check Draft Mode (No Precalculations), as shown in Figure 14.61.

FIGURE 14.61
Set the Final Gather options.

9. Click the Render button at the bottom of the Render Setup dialog box to make a test render.

10. Watch the image appear in the RFW. Click the Cancel button in the Rendering dialog box after enough buckets are processed and you have had a chance to verify that there is an acceptable level of illumination, as shown in Figure 14.62.

11. Deselect Draft Mode (No Precalculations) in the Render Setup dialog box, and then make another rendering. Prepare to wait a few minutes for this rendering to finish. Figure 14.63 shows the result.

FIGURE 14.62
Verify that there is
an acceptable level
of illumination
from the Skylight.

FIGURE 14.63
Skylight GI

INCREASING THE SAMPLES VALUES INCREASES THE RENDER TIME

This rendering could be improved by increasing the Samples per Pixel value on the Renderer tab, as you did in a previous section, to antialias the final output. You could also increase the number of Final Gather samples on the Indirect Illumination tab. However, increasing sampling requires far more rendering time, and the decision to improve the rendering quality and time depends ultimately on your computing resources and deadline.

Image-Based Lighting and Skylight

As an alternative to using a solid color in the Skylight, you can get more varied results by using an environment map to illuminate the scene. This way, there will be variations in color and intensity in the scattered light throughout the scene. This technique is called image-based lighting (IBL) in computer graphics circles. Let's try using IBL now:

1. Press the 8 key on the keyboard to open the Environment tab of the Environment and Effects dialog box. Click the None button below Environment Map, as shown in Figure 14.64.

FIGURE 14.64
Select the empty
map slot in the
Background group.

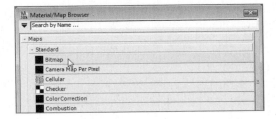

2. Select Bitmap from the Material/Map Browser and click OK, as shown in Figure 14.65.

FIGURE 14.65
Select Bitmap from
the Material/Map
Browser.

3. In the Select Bitmap Image File dialog box, browse to and select SphericalPanorama.jpg and then click Open.

4. Open the Slate Material Editor if it is not already open. Click and drag the environment bitmap from the Environment and Effects dialog box to the Active View1 Window in the Slate Material Editor.

5. Choose Instance from the Instance (Copy) Map dialog box that appears.

6. Click the View Image button in the Bitmap Parameters rollout to have a look at the image you'll be using as an environment map, as shown in Figure 14.66. Close the Specify Cropping/Placement dialog box when you are done.

FIGURE 14.66
The Spherical
Panorama.jpg
image

7. In the Material Editor, change the Mapping type in the drop-down list in the Coordinates rollout to Spherical Environment to match the distortion in the panoramic bitmap, as shown in Figure 14.67.

FIGURE 14.67
Set the Mapping
type to Spherical
Environment.

Close the Environment and Effects dialog box. To make IBL, you still need to instance the environment map into the Skylight.

8. Type H to open the Select Objects dialog box, select Sky001, and then click Select. Click the Modify tab of the Command panel.

9. Click the Use Scene Environment radio button, as shown in Figure 14.68, in the Skylight Parameters rollout.

FIGURE 14.68
Click the Use Scene
Environment radio
button.

10. On the Environment tab, in the Logarithmic Exposure Control Parameters change the Physical Scale value to 7500 to brighten up the image.

11. Click the Render Production button to do another Skylight GI rendering, but this time with image-based lighting. Figure 14.69 shows the result.

 Notice how you can see part of the environment map outside the window. This map is what is lighting the scene through the Skylight, with FG providing GI.

12. Save your work as **MyMentalRaySkylightIBL.max**. The MentalRaySkylightIBL.max file is also provided at this book's website for your convenience.

FIGURE 14.69
The rendering
with image-based
lighting

Use HDRI for Image-Based Lighting

You can get more realistic image-based lighting by using an HDR image in the Skylight and Environment Map settings. The mental ray sky is also an HDR system.

Using High Dynamic Range Images

HDR images store more information than can be displayed on a computer monitor. Monitors can display only 256 variations in light intensity for each color channel (from the blackest blacks to the whitest whites). In the real world, our eyes can perceive enormous dynamic range, from subtle candlelight to direct sunlight that is millions of times more intense.

In Photoshop, you may have experienced data loss in your image by making various adjustments to the brightness, contrast, and color balance; by sharpening; and so on. For example, when you brighten a traditional 8-bit photo, eventually you will get burnout where the pixels turn all white and there is no more tonal information. After all, how much brighter can pure white get? The answer is now many orders of magnitude brighter if you are using HDR images.

HDR images can store exposure data that varies across many orders of magnitude in brightness. You can't see all this data on the monitor at one time, but 3ds Max can use this information in a rendering. 3ds Max can also save renderings in the .hdr and other High Dynamic Range formats to preserve this more extensive visual information.

HDR Image Files Can Be Quite Large

HDR images have variable bit-depth based on how much exposure data is stored. Images that store many f-stops of exposure can grow to massive file sizes that may overwhelm the available memory in your rendering pipeline.

It is easy to use HDR images in 3ds Max. Simply select an .hdr , .pic, or .exr image, and you will see a dialog box like the one in Figure 14.70.

Figure 14.70
The HDRI Load Settings dialog box

Use the spinners to move the vertical red bars to different positions within the histogram to bracket a narrower dynamic range that can be displayed on the monitor. The preview image will get brighter or darker depending on which portion of the dynamic range you select.

Various techniques can be used to capture HDR data from the real world. One way is to take multiple photographs with different exposure levels (you want to make sure to modify only the shutter speed of the exposures, not the f-stops, which will cause a change in the depth of focus in each exposure and create artifacts in the resulting HDR image) in each shot. You can then composite all this data together using special HDR software (see the "HDR Links" sidebar). Adobe Photoshop CS3 allows you to merge a number of low dynamic range images into an HDR image. There is also a camera company that makes an HDR-friendly camera that can capture 26 f-stops of exposure in a single shot (talk about bracketing!).

USING HDR IMAGES IN 3DS MAX

You can use HDR images anywhere you use bitmaps in 3ds Max. The most common uses of HDR images are in Skylight IBL, backgrounds, and reflection maps.

HDR LINKS

Here are a few websites to explore for more information about HDR images:

HDRView This software is used to view HDR images on Windows and is free for not-for-profit use.

www.debevec.org/FiatLux/hdrview/

HDR Shop This is HDR processing and manipulation software.

www.debevec.org/HDRShop/

Photomatix This also is HDR processing and manipulation software.

www.hdrsoft.com/

Adobe Photoshop Photoshop allows you to process and manipulate HDR images.

www.adobe.com/photoshop/

RADIANCE This rendering software supports HDR images and was developed by the U.S. Department of Energy with additional support from the Swiss Federal Government.

http://radsite.lbl.gov/radiance/

RealTexture This site offers collections of HDR images on CD, plus an HDR photo-shooting service.

www.realtexture.com/hdri.htm

Spheron VR This company produces the SpheroCam HDR that captures 26 f-stops in a single shot.

www.spheron.com

Industrial Light & Magic's OpenEXR Learn about how the top-notch film effects pros use HDRI.

www.openexr.com

There are a number of ways to create HDR images for use with 3ds Max. Some use software, such as Autodesk Stitcher Unlimited, to stitch together panoramas that wrap around the greater part of a sphere. In still another technique, some photograph a chrome sphere ball to get an entire hemispherical panorama reflected in one shot (called a light probe).

In short, HDR images are popular in computer graphics today, and you can explore the cutting edge of technology if you so choose. The big film-effects production companies are using HDR workflows exclusively nowadays, so it makes sense that this technology is finding its way into 3ds Max.

The holy grail of IBL is to use real HDR environment images to illuminate virtual models using light data from the real world. At least in theory, there is no better way to realistically illuminate a virtual scene. Now you can combine all the acronyms used in this chapter by using HDR images in IBL by FG the Skylight GI (in English that is "using High Dynamic Range images in image-based lighting by final gathering the Skylight global illumination").

Using mr Proxy Objects

3ds Max scenes with a significant number of copies of the same object, or objects with extremely high polygon count, can benefit from the use of the mr Proxy object. The mr Proxy object allows you to convert a 3ds Max object to a native mental ray object. This is helpful because you don't have to have the 3ds Max object in the scene and you don't have to spend time converting to a mental ray object at rendering, which saves system resources and, more importantly, time.

In the following exercise, you will create an mr Proxy object, place a number of instances of the mr Proxy around a scene, and then render the scene.

1. Open the `MentalRayProxy.max` file that you downloaded from this book's website.

 This should be a familiar view of the Villa Savoye model that you have been working with throughout the book.

2. Click the Camera viewport to make it active and then click the Render Production button. Make a note of how long it takes to render the scene.

3. On the Create tab of the Command panel, click the Geometry button then the drop-down menu and select mental ray from the list.

4. Click the mr Proxy button, and then click and drag in the Top viewport to place the mr Proxy object.

5. With the mr Proxy object still selected, click the Modify tab of the Command panel.

6. In the Source Object group, click the None button, and then click the tree object in the lower-left corner of the Villa (as seen from the Top viewport).

 You will see the Foliage01 object listed now in the Source Object group, as shown in Figure 14.71. The options in the Parameters rollout of the mr Proxy object allow you to define how the mr Proxy object will appear in the scene. You can select to show the object as a point cloud and set the number of points used to represent the object, or you could show it as a bounding box.

7. Click the Write Object to File button to open the Write mr Proxy file dialog box, and save file as `MyTreeProxy.mib`.

FIGURE 14.71
The Parameters
rollout of the mr
Proxy object

8. In the mr Proxy Creation dialog that appears, click the radio button in front of Current Frame and the two check boxes in the Preview Generation group.

9. Click OK.

 You will see mental ray render a preview of the tree object, and a point cloud that represents the mr Proxy object in the viewports.

10. Move the mrProxy001 object so that it is in the same location as the tree you used to create it.

11. Rename the mrProxy001 object to **Tree_mrProxy001**.

12. Create instance copies of the **Tree_mrProxy001** object and place them at each of the existing trees in the scene.

13. Select the tree object you picked in step 6. From the Application menu, choose Save As ➤ Save Selected.

14. In the Save File As dialog box, save the selected tree as **Tree001.max**.

15. Click the Select by Name button on the Main Toolbar. In the Select from Scene dialog box, select all eight of the Foliage objects and click OK.

16. Press the Delete key on your keyboard to remove the selected objects from the scene.

17. Click in the Camera viewport to make it active, and then press the Render Production button.

 The scene should now render much faster than it did in step 2; however, the trees do not have any materials applied to them. You will fix that in the following steps.

18. Click the Compact Material Editor button on the Main Toolbar.

19. Click and select an unused material sample slot then click the Material Type button to open the Material/Map Browser.

20. Click and select the XRef Material from the Materials ➤ Standard group and click OK.

21. Rename the material **TreeXRefMat**.

22. In the Parameters rollout of the XRef Material, click the Browse for File button under the File Name field.

23. In the Open File dialog box, browse to and select the `Tree001.max` file you saved in step 14.

24. In the XRef Merge dialog box, select the `Foliage01` object, as shown in Figure 14.72, and click OK.

FIGURE 14.72
Select the Foliage01 object.

25. Select the mr Proxy object and then click the Assign Material to Selection button in the Material Editor.

26. Click the Camera viewport to make it active.

27. Click the Render Production button to render the scene and verify that the mr Proxy objects render with the tree texture.

28. Save your scene as **MyMentalRayProxy.max**.

You can now fill the background of the camera's field of view with a large number of instances of the mr Proxy object tree without suffering as much of a performance hit at rendering time as you would if you had used regular 3ds Max foliage objects. You have also seen how you can apply a material to mr Proxy objects that externally references its texture parameters from a separate saved file.

Using IES Files

Using the photometric lighting available in 3ds Max provides you with a great tool for visualizing how lights will affect your scenes. Earlier you changed the TPhotometricLight001 object you placed into a scene from using the default Uniform Spherical distribution model to using the Spotlight distribution type. To create an even more accurate render of what a scene would look like light with specific lights, you can change the distribution type of lights to the Photometric Web setting and specify a file that is a 3D representation of the light intensity generated by a certain fixture. These Photometric Web files are Illuminating Engineering Society (IES) files that can often be acquired from the lighting fixture manufacturers. There are some sample IES files that ship with 3ds Max in the \SceneAssets folder and with the \Luminaires sample content that you can also install.

In the following exercise, you will change the distribution type of a light in a scene:

1. Open the MentalRayIESLighting.max file from this book's website.

2. Click the Select by Name button on the Main Toolbar, and select the TPhotometricLight001 from the Select from Scene dialog box.

3. Go to the Modify tab of the Command panel, and in the Light Distribution (Type) group, click the drop-down menu and select Photometric Web, as shown in Figure 14.73.

FIGURE 14.73
Select Photo-
metric Web.

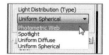

4. In the Distribution (Photometric Web) rollout, click the Choose Photometric File button, and choose the cooper.ies file that you downloaded with the Chapter 14 content from this book's website.

5. You will see a small thumbnail graphic called a goniometric diagram appear in the rollout, as shown in Figure 14.74.

FIGURE 14.74
The loaded
cooper.ies file

You can see how the icon for the TPhotometricLight001 object changed in the viewport to represent the new light distribution model you assigned.

Figure 14.75 shows the same cooper.ies file applied to a light and how it shines on two adjacent walls.

6. The Cooper light is more intense that the values the TPhotometricLight001 object had before, so you should go to the mr Photographic Exposure Control group in the Environment dialog box and adjust the exposure value to 5.

Figure 14.75
The Cooper light shining on two surfaces.

7. Click the Render Production button, and compare the results of this rendering with your previous renderings using the Spotlight distribution type.

8. Save your scene as **MyMentalRayIESLighting.max**.

 You can see that by using the appropriate Photometric Web files for the light fixtures in your scenes, you can greatly increase the accuracy and realism of your final renderings.

Using Lighting Analysis

The architecture and construction industries are becoming more environmentally conscious, or green. One aspect of green design is designing properly lit spaces that can take advantage of available daylight. This is important not only for the environment, but for human inhabitants of designed spaces. Properly designed lighting is especially important in working areas, where poor lighting design can cause eye fatigue or other unwanted physiological responses, and even create potentially dangerous working conditions.

As a visualization specialist, your responsibility is not to design correct lighting for a space; however, 3ds Max Design 2011 does provide you with the tools to help design and analyze the lighting planned by the lighting designer. The lighting analysis features in 3ds Max Design are very robust, and there isn't enough space in this book to go into them in complete detail; however, you will get an introduction to them here.

For accurate lighting analysis results, it is important to make sure that the materials and lights in a scene are as physically correct as possible. To save time, all the materials in the scene used in the following exercise have already been converted to ProMaterials (mi) and Arch & Design (mi) materials.

In this exercise, you will add a Daylight System and access the lighting analysis features of 3ds Max Design 2011 to evaluate lighting in a scene similar to the room that you have been using.

CERT OBJECTIVE

1. Open the `MentalRayLightingA.max` file from this book's website.

2. Click the Create tab of the Command panel, and then click the System button.

3. Click the Daylight button, and then click Yes to accept the Daylight System creation and set the Exposure Control value.

4. Click in the center of the scene and drag out to place the daylight system compass. Click Yes to automatically add a mr Physical Sky to the environment, and then drag again to set the Orbital Scale.

 In addition to using the mr Sun and mr Sky, you can also download weather-data files for many locations around the world from the U.S. Department of Energy's website (www.eere.energy.gov/buildings/energyplus/cfm/weather_data.cfm). You can also check and see what resources might be available from your local government websites.

5. On the Control Parameters rollout, click the Get Location button and choose Boulder, CO.

6. With the Daylight object still selected, enter 210 in the North Direction field so the direct sunlight will enter the room through the window.

7. In the time group, set the Hours value to 10 and the Minutes value to 30.

8. Click in the Camera viewport to make it active, and then click the Rendered Frame Window button on the Main Toolbar.

 The global quality sliders should all be set to Low or Draft settings. Click the Render button on the Reveal toolbar to get a relatively quick preview of what the scene looks like with the Daylight System.

 The renderer is pretty dark because you allowed 3ds Max to automatically assign the value for the mr Photographic Exposure Control. You will adjust the values now to improve the quality of the rendering.

9. Choose Rendering ➢ Exposure Control to display the Exposure Controls section on the Environment tab of the Environment and Effects dialog.

10. Select the radio button in front of Photographic Exposure.

11. Change Shutter Speed to 100 and Aperture to 4.0.

 To get the best lighting solution for an interior scene rendering with a Daylight System, you will want to create an mr Sky Portal just outside the room's window with its arrow pointing into the room.

12. Right-click in the Perspective viewport to make it active, and then orbit the view so you can see the window.

13. Click the Create tab on the Command panel, click the Lights button, and then click the mr Sky Portal button.

14. Click the AutoGrid button and drag out the mr Sky Portal on the window.

15. Switch to the Front viewport and then click the Modify tab of the Command panel. Adjust the Dimension values of the mr SkyPortal001 object to make it the size of the window, and adjust the position of the mr Sky Portal to center it in the window.

16. Click the Flip Light Flux Direction check box so the arrow emanating from the center of the mr Sky Portal is pointing into the room.

17. In the Top viewport move the mr Sky Portal so that it is just outside the window.

18. To start examining the lighting in the scene, choose Lighting Analysis ➢ Lighting Analysis Assistant. This will open the Lighting Analysis Assistant dialog box, shown in Figure 14.76.

FIGURE 14.76
The General tab

In the lower-right corner of the General tab in the dialog box, you can see that there are currently no invalid settings in the scene file.

19. Click the Lighting tab to review the settings of the Daylight and Artificial Light sources in the scene, as shown in Figure 14.77.

This tab shows you all the settings that apply to lights in the scene and allows you to select any invalid lights so that you may fix them. The Target Light and Free Light buttons on this tab are shortcuts to the Create tab so you can quickly add photometric lights to your scene.

20. Click the Materials tab to verify that there are no objects with invalid materials, as shown in Figure 14.78.

If there were invalid materials in the scene, this tab would help you find and select those objects and fix their assigned material properties.

FIGURE 14.77
The Lighting tab

FIGURE 14.78
The Materials tab

21. Click the Analysis Output tab to view the Light Meters rollout, as shown in Figure 14.79.

The Analysis Output tab provides access to the tools used for studying the light in the scene in one convenient location.

22. Click the Create a Light Meter button. This is a shortcut that prepares the Command panel to create a Light Meter object.

23. Turn on the AutoGrid feature if it isn't still active and, in the Top viewport, click and drag to create a Light Meter object on the top of the dining room table.

24. In the Parameters rollout, adjust Length Segments to 4.

25. Change Width Segments to 6.

26. You can select from four options in the Values to Display group of the LightMeter Helper object's Display rollout, as shown in Figure 14.80. Leave the radio button in front of Total Illuminance selected, as shown in Figure 14.80.

27. Using the Command panel, click the Calculate All Light Meters button.

You could also click the Calculate All Light Meters Now button on the Lighting Analysis Assistant dialog box. After 3ds Max Design processes the lighting calculations, you will see the Light Meter object in the viewports change to display the selected results, as shown in Figure 14.81. The image is displayed in Wireframe mode for clarity.

FIGURE 14.81
The calculated
Light Meter results
displayed in the
viewport

You can change the results displayed by clicking the radio buttons in front of the other options in the Values to Display group.

28. Click the Indirect Illuminance radio button of the Light Meter object to change the results displayed in the viewports.

Below the Calculate All Light Meters button in the Command panel is a button labeled Export to CSV File. This will save the results of the light meter to a comma-separated value file. This file can then be read into other software tools for further study.

29. Delete the Light Meter object.

30. On the Analysis Output tab of the Lighting Analysis Assistant, scroll down to the Image Overlay rollout.

31. Click the Create Image Overlay Render Effect button. This takes you to the Effects tab of the Environment and Effects dialog and adds the Lighting Analysis Image Overlay effect for you, as shown in Figure 14.82.

The Lighting Analysis Image Overlay rendering effect places a grid of sample points at a user-specified spacing interval over the rendered image and displays the calculated values at those projected points.

32. In the Parameters rollout for the Lighting Analysis Image Overlay effect, set the Max value in the Type and Range group to 80000.

There is a number of options you can set on the Parameters rollout, such as displaying the Camera and Daylight information in the overlay. You can also choose to fade the rendering so that the reported values are easier to see in the Rendered Frame Window. You also have the options to turn off the screen grid display and display the results of Light Meter helper objects in the camera's field of view.

FIGURE 14.82
The Lighting Analysis Image Overlay render effect options

33. Click the Render Production button on the Main Toolbar.

After the rendering has processed, the Rendered Frame Window is updated with the results from the Lighting Analysis Image Overlay, as shown in Figure 14.83. Another window, Lighting Analysis Data, also pops up; however, its content is not important.

34. Save your scene as **MyMentalRayLightingA.max**.

FIGURE 14.83
The Rendered Frame Window with the Lighting Analysis image overlay

The values provided by the Lighting Analysis Image Overlay or the Light Meter helper objects will enable the architect or lighting designer to determine if the combination of natural and artificial lighting is adequate for the type of environment being studied, or if additional fixtures or design changes are necessary.

This was a very introductory look at the lighting-analysis tools in 3ds Max Design 2011. There are a number of very informative white papers on the Autodesk website that go into much greater detail about configuring and using the 3ds Max Design lighting analysis features. If you are interested in lighting analysis, you should study those resources thoroughly.

The Bottom Line

Apply final gathering Final gathering is an optional step in calculating global illumination that can reduce the appearance of unwanted variances or rendering artifacts in the lighting.

> **Master It** Apply final gathering to an exterior view of the Savoye project from Chapter 14, "Advanced Rendering with mental ray."

Create a contour rendering Contour renderings display dark strokes along the contours of a scene's objects. This is an effect caused by using the mental ray Contour shaders and the parameters in the Camera Effects rollout.

> **Master It** Using the same techniques covered in this chapter, create a contour rendering of the interior of a condo scene from Chapter 6, "Creating AEC Objects."

Use the multi/sub-map material Creating a large number of unique maps to apply to repetitive objects in a scene to add a sense of variation or randomness can take a lot of effort. The Multi/Sub-Map rollout allows you to create one material with a number of internal variations that you can apply to objects in your scene to achieve that sense of natural randomness.

> **Master It** Create a 25 × 25 array of 1′ radius spheres, offset 3′ from each other, with a single material that will randomly change the color of the spheres through the use of the mental ray Multi/Sub-Map type of map.

Use Skylight global illumination Global illumination can enhance the appeal of a scene by simulating bounced light. This can include the color bleeding effect where color is transferred from one surface to another.

> **Master It** Add global illumination to an exterior shot of the Savoye scene from Chapter 8.

Use mr Proxy objects Using mental ray Proxy objects in scenes that require a considerable number of identical high-poly objects can save you significant file size, system resources, and render time.

> **Master It** Create and render a 25 × 50 array of mr Proxy teapots using an eight-segment teapot as the source object.

Use IES files Using Photometric Web distribution files for your photometric lights can greatly increase the realism and accuracy of your final rendered images.

> **Master It** Using the `MyMentalRayIESLighting.max` file you saved near the end of the chapter, change the light distribution type of PhotometricLight001 from Uniform Diffuse to Photometric Web, and select the `cooper.ies` file. Then render the scene.

Use lighting analysis Proper accommodation of naturally available light can greatly benefit a building's design. Using 3ds Max Design 2011's lighting-analysis tools can help architects and lighting designers successfully study how lighting affects a project.

> **Master It** Using the `MyMentalRayLightingA.max` file you saved in the last exercise, create a Light Meter helper object on top of the coffee table, calculate the light meter, and render the scene, displaying the values of the Light Meter helper on the render.

Chapter 15

Finishing It Off: Atmosphere, Effects, and Compositing

3ds Max Design 2011 has several features for adding the appearance of objects in your scene without actually adding any geometry. These features fall into one of two categories: atmospheric effects and rendering effects. *Atmospheric* effects are effects that appear to show particulate matter in the air (such as mist, smoke, or even fire). *Rendering* effects change the appearance of a rendered scene by adding objects such as glows and starbursts, but they can also be used to add hair or fur to an object in the scene. The Hair and Fur effect can be used to simulate grass in a scene.

You can also render images simulating such real-world camera effects as glare from extremely bright reflections or light sources and the depth of field created by adjusting the aperture of a camera lens.

Included with 3ds Max 2011 is Autodesk Composite, a node-based compositing application that is based on the Autodesk Toxik compositor. Compositing is the process of layering image elements on top of each other and adjusting how they are blended together to create your final image. Autodesk Composite features a comprehensive toolkit to maximize your creativity, including keying, color correction, motion tracking, paint features, full HDR support, depth-of-field effects, all at resolutions up to 4K film resolution. This chapter cannot go into all the features of Autodesk Composite, but it will give you an idea how you can work with your images, and then you can use the Composite help and learning resources.

In this chapter, you'll learn to:

- ◆ Add an atmospheric effect
- ◆ Add a grass effect using Hair and Fur
- ◆ Add the Glare effect to a rendering
- ◆ Use DOF/Bokeh
- ◆ Create stereo-pair images
- ◆ Composite the stereo pair into an anaglyph image

Adding Atmospheric Effects

When a scene is rendered in 3ds Max, the renderer calculates, among other things, the effect of the scene's lights on the surfaces of the geometry. By default, the scene is rendered as if the air surrounding the objects is clear and free of any particulates. In many cases, this is the correct assumption, and you wouldn't want to add pollution, fog, or airborne particles to the scene. Yet

sometimes, adding atmosphere effects is necessary to make the scene look more realistic, which is particularly true when dealing with lighting, fog, and fire.

3ds Max has a set of features, called *atmospheres*, that can add the appearance of airborne particles. Real-world lights cast light into their surrounding environment, and you can see the effect of the lights as both direct and indirect illumination, but you can't see the actual light rays or light cone. When the light cone appears to be visible, such as a spotlight at a movie premier or a car's headlights on a foggy road, what you're actually seeing is the light rays diffusing after hitting airborne particles such as dust, smog, or water vapor. The Volume Light atmosphere adds the light diffusion effect to selected lights in a scene.

Atmospheric effects are also helpful when adding fog to a scene, which can give the impression of desolation, eeriness, or cold, wet weather conditions. In reality, fog is comprised of an immeasurable number of minute particles that capture and diffuse light rays. This would be difficult to calculate and display accurately. You can represent fog in your scenes, including density changes and color variations, using the Fog atmosphere.

As you can guess, the Fire effect renders as a ball or tendril type of combusting materials that can change color with distance from the fire's center. Be aware that the Fire atmosphere, like Fog and Volume Light, appears only in rendered scenes and not in the viewports. Also note the Fire effect does not contribute any illumination to the scene.

These effects are designed to work with the scanline renderer, and now that the default renderer is mental ray, you may find that the scanline effects don't always work correctly. Volume Light in particular are best reserved for the scanline renderer. To create volume lights in mental ray, you can use a specialized shader called the Parti Volume Photon shader, placed on the Volume channel of the mental ray Camera Shaders group. The use of that shader is outside the scope of this book.

Creating a Volume Light

There are many times when you can use a Volume light. Any time a light beam is visible as an object in a scene, this is a chance to use a volume light. Whether it's dappled light streaming through the leaves in a forest, rays casting through a window, or even car headlights or parking lot streetlamps at night, all of these are a good use of volume lights.

In the following exercise, you'll add the Volume Light atmosphere to existing lights in a 3ds Max scene. After adding the atmosphere in the Environment and Effects dialog box, you pick the lights that will display the effect and then render the scene.

1. Open `Savoye15_A.max`. This file is similar to the Savoye files you worked with in other chapters, but with a darker environment and downward-facing spotlights added to the overhang.

FILE LOAD: GAMMA SETTINGS

If you get a File Load: Gamma and LUT warning when you open this file, choose Adopt the File's Gamma and LUT settings.

2. If it is not already the active viewport, right-click the Camera01 viewport, and then render the scene. The Rendered Frame Window should look like Figure 15.1 and show the light pools beneath each spotlight.

RENDER CAMERA OR PERSPECTIVE VIEWPORTS

The result of atmospheric effects can be seen only in rendered Camera or Perspective viewports
and not in rendered axonometric or orthographic viewports.

3. Press the 8 shortcut key, or choose Rendering ➢ Environment to open the Environment
 tab of the Environment and Effects dialog box—or you can press the Environments And
 Effects button in the Rendered Frame Window.

4. In the Atmosphere rollout, click the Add button to open the Add Atmospheric Effect dia-
 log box, as shown in Figure 15.2.

5. Click the Volume Light option and then click OK. Volume Light is added to the Effects
 field in the Atmosphere rollout.

FIGURE 15.2
The Add Atmo-
spheric Effect
dialog box

6. In the Lights section of the Volume Light Parameters rollout, click the Pick Light button. At this point, you could select each light in the scene by picking them in the viewports. Some of the lights aren't easily selected in the viewports, so you'll need to use the Pick Object dialog box.

7. Click the Select by Name button or press the H key to open the Pick Object dialog box shown in Figure 15.3. Because only lights can be assigned to the Volume Light atmosphere, only lights appear in the list.

FIGURE 15.3
The Pick Object dialog box used to select lights

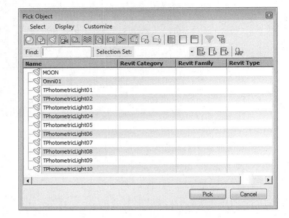

8. Highlight all the lights with names that begin with TPhotometricLight and then click Pick. The names of all the selected lights can be displayed by expanding the drop-down list in the Lights area.

9. Render the scene again (see Figure 15.4). This time the light cone can be seen from the source half the distance to the ground.

FIGURE 15.4
The rendered scene after adding the Volume Light effect

PHOTOMETRIC VOLUME LIGHTS ON 64-BIT SYSTEMS

If you are using photometric lights with the Volume Light Atmospheric effect in the scanline renderer on a 64-bit system, be aware that there are reports of render artifacts or errors and that the volumetric effects don't properly respond to the Noise parameters. We hope this will soon be remedied with a hot fix or a service pack. If you run into this error or any other errors, please submit a defect report against 3ds Max Design 2011 to Autodesk.

Adjusting the Volume Light Parameters

Like most features in 3ds Max 2011, there are many parameters that can be adjusted to tweak the appearance of the Volume Light effect. The most notable are those that modify the effect's density and color. You can change the color of the volume of light to inject emotion into a scene—for example, yellow for warmth or blue for moonlight. Use density to make the effect more visible if needed. Here you will experiment with each of those parameters:

1. In the Volume area of the Volume Light Parameters rollout, click the Fog Color swatch to open the Color Selector dialog box.

2. Select a pale yellow color (255,255,230 works well) and then click OK to close the Color Selector.

3. Render the scene again. This time the hue of the lights' cones is shifted toward yellow.

NOT ALL INSTANCES ARE AFFECTED

All the lights selected in this exercise are instances; therefore, adjusting one light's parameters adjusts that parameter for all lights. However, just because an instance is a volume light, not all the instances are volume lights, so each light must be added to the Volume Light effect.

4. Increase the Density value to 8 to increase the amount of light captured by the effect. Make sure the Exponential option is deselected and then render the scene again. With Exponential checked, the light's density falls off exponentially with distance rather than linearly, as it does when the option is off. Your Rendered Frame Window (RFW) should look similar to Figure 15.5.

FIGURE 15.5
The scene after adjusting the Density parameter

The Exponential check box is critical to use if you intend to render transparent objects within the Volume Light or Volume Fog.

You can adjust the Volume Light's parameters further as you want.

One nice tip to know is that if you put a bitmap in the Projector Map channel, you will get the bitmap throughout the volume of the light. If you need to accentuate streaks of light in a scene, this is a helpful technique.

Adding Fog

3ds Max fog comes with two different fog styles: Volume Fog and Fog. With Volume Fog, a spherical, cylindrical, or box-shaped gizmo called an *atmospheric apparatus* is added from the Helpers category on the Create tab. The fog is then created and constrained to the boundaries of that gizmo. This fog type is good for clouds or when representing a smoke or fog effect that must be limited to a specific volume.

The other type of fog atmosphere, the one that is used in this exercise, is unlimited in its extents and fills the area viewed through the camera.

ADDING THE FOG ATMOSPHERIC EFFECT

Fog is another atmospheric effect similar to the volume light but not constrained to a helper object. Let's try it:

1. If you've closed any of the windows, you can reopen the Environment tab of the Environment and Effects dialog box and then click the Add button in the Atmosphere rollout.

2. In the Add Atmospheric Effect dialog box, double-click the Fog option to select it, and close the dialog box.

 With the Fog option selected in the Effects window, the Fog Parameters rollout replaces the Volume Light Parameters rollout (see Figure 15.6). If you need to go back and adjust the Volume Light effect's parameters, simply select Volume Light in the Effects window.

FIGURE 15.6
The parameters for adjusting the fog

3. Render the Camera01 viewport. As you can see in Figure 15.7, the Fog effect starts at the camera's viewing plane and increases in density with distance.

FIGURE 15.7
The rendered scene after adding the Fog atmospheric effect

4. Although this effect frames the leaves on the tree nicely, in this case you want to just show some ground fog around the building. In the Fog area of the Fog Parameters roll-out, click the Layered radio button. The Standard area grays out, and the Layered parameters become available.

5. Layered fog has Top and Bottom parameters that set its vertical limits. Set the Top parameter to 3´0.0˝ and leave the Bottom set to 0´0.0˝ by clicking and dragging the spinners.

DON'T OBSCURE THE SCENE

Make sure the camera is above the top level. If the camera's Z position is between the Top and Bottom parameters, then it is within the fog itself, and much of the scene may be obscured.

6. Set the Falloff option to Top, so that the fog gets thinner as it reaches its upper limit. Render the scene again. Your RFW should look like Figure 15.8. The scene looks better, but you still need to work on the color and density of the fog.

7. Click the Color swatch in the Fog area, choose a dark gray/green color for the fog, and then click OK. Here we're using RGB values 60,100,60.

8. In the Layered group, change the Density values, and render. Do this repeatedly until you find a good combination of density and color.

FIGURE 15.8
The rendered scene after switching to layered fog and adjusting the falloff

ASSIGNING PATCHES OF OPACITY

Rather than controlling the density with the Density parameter, which results in an even density throughout the fog, here you'll use a map to randomly assign patches of opacity. This will add to the illusion of the fog, because it will not appear as an even computer-generated effect. Whenever you can add randomness to something, it tends to more naturally mimic reality.

1. Open the Compact Material Editor by clicking the Material Editor button or pressing M on the keyboard, select an unused sample slot, and then assign a Standard material to that slot.

2. Expand the Maps rollout and then click the None button next to the Diffuse color channel to open the Material/Map Browser.

3. Double-click the Noise Map option to select it, and close the Material/Map Browser and return to the Material Editor.

4. Click the Go to Parent button and then drag the Noise map from the Material Editor's Maps rollout to the Environment Opacity Map button, as shown in Figure 15.9.

5. Choose Instance in the Instance (Copy) Map dialog box and then click OK. Because you chose Instance, any changes made to the map in the Material Editor are reflected in the scene when it is rendered.

6. Render the scene again. It's a little better, but the changes in the fog's density are spaced too far apart.

7. Click the Diffuse Color map button in the Maps rollout to get to the material's noise map.

8. In the Noise Parameters rollout, set the Size value to 10 and the Noise type to Fractal to make the noise effect smaller and sharper. Then render the scene. Your RFW should look similar to Figure 15.10.

9. Close the Material Editor.

Drag from here...

FIGURE 15.9
Dragging a map
from the Material
Editor to the fog
parameters

...to here.

FIGURE 15.10
The scene after
adding a Noise map
to control the opac-
ity of the fog

CONTROL THE FOG'S COLOR WITH A MAP

Instead of using the Color swatch in the fog area to control the fog color, you can use a map. Similar to the way that you assigned a map to the Environment Opacity Map option, you could assign one to the Environment Color Map option as well. The fog would then get its colors from the map's colors, whether the map is a bitmap or a procedural map.

HELPING YOUR FOG INTERACT WITH THE HORIZON

The last feature that you want to address is how the fog interacts at the horizon. If you look in the Camera01 viewport, you'll see a black line in the background that sits just above the top of the land on which the building sits. This is the horizon line, and its visibility is controlled with the Show Horizon option in the camera's Parameters rollout. You can add noise at the horizon to break up the regularity of the computer-generated effect.

1. In the Layered area of the Fog Parameters rollout, select the Horizon Noise option.

2. Reduce the Size parameter to 10, and then change the Angle value to 6. The Angle value determines how many degrees below the horizon the horizon noise begins.

3. Render the scene one more time, and you should see the fog at the horizon line now broken up, as shown in Figure 15.11.

4. Save your file as **MySavoye15_A.max**

FIGURE 15.11
Horizon Noise controls the appearance of the fog at the horizon.

Adding a Fire Effect

Like the Volume Fog effect mentioned earlier, the Fire Effect atmospheric effect requires a gizmo to contain it. You can control whether the flames are reaching upward with tendrils or whether the flame is formed into a ball. Unlike real fire, the Fire effect does not cast any light into the scene and is almost always accompanied by a light. In this section, you'll create a Fire effect, which you'll add to a fire pit next to the building.

1. Open Savoye15_B.max from this book's accompanying web page.

2. Click the Helpers button under the Create panel, expand the drop-down list, and select Atmospheric Apparatus.

3. Click the SphereGizmo button. In the Top viewport, click near the center of the fire pit at the lower-left corner of the villa and drag the gizmo until it is about the size of the center of the fire pit (see Figure 15.12).

FIGURE 15.12
Creating the gizmo
in the Top viewport

4. Click the Modify tab of the Command panel and then select the Hemisphere option for the Sphere gizmo.

5. In the Front viewport, move the gizmo upward until its flat bottom is inside the fire pit.

6. Set Radius to 3′0.0″.

CHANGING THE FIRE'S SHAPE

Gizmos are subject to the same transforms that other objects are, so you can use the Scale transform to change the sphere shape to more of a capsule shape.

7. With the gizmo selected, click Select and Non-uniform Scale and then drag the Z-axis handle upward, as shown in Figure 15.13, to nonuniformly scale the gizmo along the Z-axis only.

8. In the Modify panel, on the Atmospheres & Effects rollout, click the Add button.

FIGURE 15.13
Scale the atmo-
spheric apparatus
along the Z-axis.

TURNING OFF AN ATMOSPHERIC EFFECT

You can turn off any atmospheric effect by selecting it and deselecting the Active option in the Atmosphere rollout. You can force 3ds Max to not render any atmospheric effects by opening the Render Setup dialog box, selecting the Common tab, opening the Common Parameters rollout, going to the Options section, and deselecting the Atmospherics option.

9. In the Add Atmospheric Effect dialog box, double-click the Fire Effect option to select it, and close the dialog box.

10. Open the Environment and Effects dialog box; with the Fire Effect option selected in the Atmosphere window, the Fire Effect Parameters rollout (see Figure 15.14) appears below the Effects window.

FIGURE 15.14
The Fire Effect Parameters rollout

11. Render the scene; your RFW should look like Figure 15.15.

FIGURE 15.15
The rendered scene after adding the Fire effect

12. In the Fire Effect Parameters rollout's Shape section, change Flame Type to Tendril and increase the Stretch value to 3. Stretch elongates the tendrils along the Z-axis.

13. In the Characteristics section, change Flame Size to 5 and Flame Detail to 5 to give the effect well-defined tendrils. Finally, reduce Density to 10.

14. Render the seen again to see the result of your parameter changes. Your rendering should look similar to Figure 15.16.

FIGURE 15.16
The Fire effect after adjusting the parameters

ADDING A LIGHT TO THE SCENE

As mentioned earlier, the Fire effect does not add illumination to the scene. In the real world, the light from the flames would spill onto the building and ground. You therefore need to add a light to complete the illusion. To do this, just follow these steps:

1. From the Command panel, choose Create ➤ Lights ➤ Photometric ➤ Free Light and then click near the Atmospheric Apparatus gizmo in the Top viewport.

2. Click the Align button on the Main Toolbar, and align the center of the light with the center of the gizmo.

3. Click the Modify tab. In the Intensity/Color/Attenuation rollout, click the Kelvin option, and then click the Filter Color swatch.

4. In the Color Selector that opens, choose a bright yellow or orange color to set the light color.

5. In the Intensity area, set the Candelas (cd) value to **3000** to double the light's intensity.

6. In the Colors section of the Environment and Effects dialog box, click the red Outer Color swatch and increase the redness by changing the RGB values to **227,12,12**. Click OK.

7. On the Shadow Map Params rollout, change the Bias to 0.01 and the Size to 1024.

8. In the Logarithmic Exposure Control Parameters rollout, reduce the Brightness value to 50 to darken the scene a bit and make the fire pop.

9. Render the scene; your RFW should look similar to Figure 15.17.

FIGURE 15.17
The rendered scene after adding a light

ANIMATING THE SCENE

Fires are not static; they are continuously churning and moving elements. To sell this effect in an animation, follow these steps to animate both the fire and the light:

1. Move the Time slider to frame 100 and then click the Auto Key button.

2. In the Motion area of the Fire Effect Parameters rollout, set the Phase value to 12 and the Drift value to 20.

3. Select the light in the fire pit and change the Filter color to a brighter yellow red and the intensity to **4000** cd.

4. Move the Time slider to 50, and then set the filter color to a light red and the intensity to **2700** cd.

5. Select the gizmo and then add a Noise modifier to it. In the Strength area, change the X, Y, and Z values to approximately 35′, -30′, and 4′, respectively.

6. Move the Time slider back to frame 100, and then change the X, Y, and Z values so that the Noise modifier distorts the gizmo differently over time.

7. Click the Auto Key button to turn it off.

8. Open the Render Setup dialog box and choose Active Time Segment in the Output area.

9. Save your file as **MySavoye15_B.max**.

It's always prudent to save your file before you begin a render. If the computer crashes during a render, you haven't lost any work on your Max file this way.

10. Click Files in the Render Output section, give the file a name, choose AVI or MOV as the file type, make any setup changes you prefer, and then click the Render button.

Generally, rendering directly to a movie format is not a smart way to work. When you are rendering a large number of frames, you will lose the entire movie if 3ds Max or your system crashes. Also, rendering directly to a movie file bakes the compression into the file. You should render to a sequence of uncompressed frames (then if the system crashes, you haven't lost too much time and can restart the rendering at the last completed frame) and then use the Video Post tool in 3ds Max 2011 or the Composite application to generate a movie file from the sequentially numbered frames. In this case, you'll take a chance and render directly to a movie. This could take some time, so you might want to take a short break here.

11. Play your rendered animation in Windows Media Player or Apple QuickTime—or you can choose View Image File from the Rendering menu, and this will automatically launch the correct player from within 3ds Max.

The fire churns well, and the colors change nicely. You should consider taking this exercise a little further by animating the position of the light and the radius of the gizmo. You could even use soft selection to put a noise modifier on the branches of the tree and animate the noise modifier similar to the one on the gizmo to give the appearance of the tree swaying in a gentle breeze.

Using Hair and Fur to Add Grass

3ds Max has several nonatmospheric effects that are added through the Effects tab of the Environment and Effects dialog box. Although most of these are rendering effects, such as Motion Blur, Film Grain, and Lens effects (stars, glows, lens flares, and so on), there is also the Hair and Fur effect. Although there isn't much call for hair or fur in most architectural renderings, the effect can also be used to create convincing grass and other ground cover. Like the atmospheric effects, the Hair and Fur effect can be rendered only in Perspective and Camera viewports. Rendered hair or fur is a combination of applying the Hair and Fur modifier to an object or spline in your scene and applying the Hair and Fur render effect, which is automatically added to the Environment and Effects dialog box when you apply the modifier.

1. Open Savoye15_C.max.

This file is similar to the Savoye files you worked with earlier in this chapter, but with a lighter environment, no atmospheric effects, and the Ground object was replaced with a plane that has been edited so that there are no faces beneath the building. The Hair and Fur effect is assigned to an entire object and can't have only a portion of an object passed up to it in the modifier stack. The assigned renderer is mental ray.

2. Select the ground object, the object named Plane01.

3. Apply the Hair and Fur (WSM) world space modifier to the ground. A small percentage of the actual number of hairs appears in the viewports. As you can see in Figure 15.18, the hairs are much too long.

FIGURE 15.18
The hairs as they
first appear in the
viewport

4. Open the Effects tab (not the Environment tab that you've used so far) of the Environment and Effects dialog box, and you'll see that the Hair and Fur effect was automatically added to the Effects window.

5. Select the Hair and Fur effect. The Hair and Fur rollout appears at the bottom of the Effects tab.

6. In the Hair Rendering Options section of the Hair and Fur rollout, make sure the mr Prim option is selected from the Hairs drop-down list. This option designates a procedural mental ray shader as the engine that renders the hairs.

Adjusting the Hair and Fur Parameters

The grass looks like huge, rectangular stalks sitting on the ground plane, and the color needs some work as well. In this section, you'll size the grass better and change the color.

1. With the Plane01 object selected, expand the Hair and Fur (WSM) General Parameters rollout on the Modify tab.

2. Set Scale to 1.75 to decrease the size of the hair strands, or in this case, grass blades. Set Cut Length to 75.

3. Set Rand. Scale to 30 so that each blade's length is not exactly the same and can vary 15 percent above or below the standard length.

4. Decrease the Hair Segments value to 3. The grass isn't seen up close enough to warrant the extra detail given by the larger number of segments.

 Hair and Fur gets its color from the Material Parameters rollout and not the Material Editor. You can control the color at the base of the blade (Root Color) and the tip (Tip Color) and allow a variance between the blades.

5. Expand the Material Parameters rollout.

6. Click the small gray button to the right of the Root Color swatch. This is how you assign a map, rather than a color, as the source for the grass color.

7. In the Material/Map Browser that opens, choose the Scene group to display only the maps that exist in the current scene.

8. Double-click the Surface Shader: Map # 8 (GRASS2.jpg) map.

9. Choose the Instance radio button in the Instance or Copy? dialog box and then click OK. A capital M appears on the button to indicate that a map is controlling the color.

10. Click the Tip Color swatch and then in the Color Selector assign a light green color similar to 70,105,35. The blades will now transition from the map's color at the root to the assigned tip color.

MUTANTS ARE ALLOWED

If you want to have random hairs that possess their own color, much different than the Root and Tip Color values, assign a color to the Mutant Color swatch and increase the Mutant % to more than 0.0.

11. Render the Camera01 viewport. The scene is not quite where we want it (see Figure 15.19).

FIGURE 15.19
The rendered scene after changing several Hair and Fur parameters

Refining the Ground with the Hair and Fur Parameters

Two problems exist in the scene: first, a massive number of grass blades are needed to sell the illusion of a lawn, and second, the ground object is very large. In this exercise, you'll start by deleting and reconfiguring the ground plane to make it smaller and then finish by refining the Hair and Fur parameters.

1. Make the Top viewport the only viewport, and then zoom out so that you can see the entire scene.

2. Turn off the UVW Mapping and Hair and Fur (WSM) modifiers and then click the Edit Poly modifier. If a Warning dialog box appears, click the Hold/Yes button.

3. To access the Polygon sub-object level, press 4 on the keyboard, and then select the polygons shown in Figure 15.20 and delete them.

FIGURE 15.20
Delete the selected polygons.

4. Access the Vertex sub-object level by pressing 1 on the keyboard. Move the perimeter vertices to adjust the ground plane as shown in Figure 15.21. The smaller-sized ground plane will display the same number of rendered grass blades, but they will be much denser.

FIGURE 15.21
Move the vertices to achieve this shape.

5. Exit the Vertex sub-object level and then turn the other modifiers back on. It's important to make sure you've selected the Edit Poly object level—otherwise, you will be passing an empty selection set to the Hair and Fur modifier.

6. Select the Hair and Fur (WSM) modifier and then access the General Parameters rollout.

7. Increase the Hair Count to 300,000. This may seem like a large number, but it's not uncommon for this value to be set to 5 to 10 million.

8. Reduce Scale to 0.5 and Root Thick to 0.5. These parameters shorten the blades even more and decrease the thickness at the base.

9. Render the Camera01 viewport one more time. Note that this could take a *very* long time, depending on your computer's processor and memory. This rendering calculation might take several hours using mental ray. Your completed grass should look similar to Figure 15.22.

10. Save your file as **My_Savoye15_C.max**.

FIGURE 15.22
The final rendering after adjusting the ground plane and modifier parameters

Using Glare

Earlier in this chapter you rendered a Volume Light effect and read about the Parti Volume Photon shader, which can re-create the dispersion of light against particulates in a medium. Other effects can also be simulated with the mental ray renderer in 3ds Max.

Assigning the Glare Output Shader

In a physical camera, be it film or digital, extremely bright lights or reflections that are viewed through the lens can reflect and refract on the film emulsion or on the surface of the digital sensor. This effect is called *glare*.

1. Open the Savoye15_D.max file from this book's accompanying web page.

 This is similar to the Villa Savoye files that you worked with earlier in this chapter, but with some additional detail around the villa and some spheres of various sizes and with different materials placed out in the grass.

2. Right-click the Camera.View.3DFRONT viewport to select it.

3. Click the Render Production button to have mental ray render the viewport. The Rendered Frame Window should look like Figure 15.23.

FIGURE 15.23
The rendered view

4. Right-click in the Rendered Frame Window. The mouse cursor turns into an eyedropper, and you are presented with the pixel data dialog box that tells you about the pixel that the eyedropper is sampling. Move the eyedropper over the bright portion of the large white sphere and look at the numbers in the pixel data floating dialog box. The dialog box should look like Figure 15.24.

FIGURE 15.24
The pixel data
dialog box

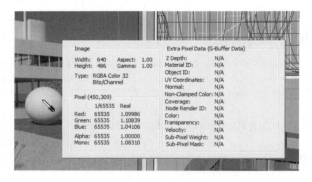

Notice that the RGB values for that pixel in the Real column are greater than 1.0. This is because the Rendered Frame Window is set to 32 Bits per Pixel and is displaying floating-point values of the High Dynamic Range rendering.

5. Right-click again in the Rendered Frame Window, and put the eyedropper over the reflection of the sun on the brass sphere (it's the middle one). You might have to use the scroll wheel on your mouse to zoom into the image to accurately pick the hot spot.

This time the RGB values are much higher; they almost reach 3.0. In a real film or digital camera, when extremely intense light hits the film or the sensor, the light can disperse through the celluloid or reflect off the surface of the sensor, creating a halo around the bright areas. You can simulate this effect in mental ray with the Glare shader.

You will re-create this effect now.

6. Click the Render Setup button on the Main Toolbar. Go to the Renderer tab and scroll down to the Camera Shaders group of the Camera Effects rollout, as shown in Figure 15.25.

FIGURE 15.25
The Camera Shaders group

7. Click the check box in front of the button labeled DefaultOutputShader (Glare) to enable that shader channel.

8. Open the Slate Material Editor.

9. Click and drag the DefaultOutputShader (Glare) button to the Active View1 Window of the Slate Material Editor, select Instance, and click OK on the Instance (Copy) Map dialog box.

10. Click the plus symbol next to Additional Params on the DefaultOutputShader (Glare) node, as shown in Figure 15.26.

FIGURE 15.26
Click to display the additional parameters.

11. Click the up arrow next to Quality and set it to 3.

12. Click the up arrow next to Spread and change it to 3 as well.

13. Click the 500 next to Resolution For, and change the value to 640, the horizontal resolution that you have been rendering the scene at.

14. Click the Render button to see the image with the glare applied. You will see the effect on the three spheres, as shown in Figure 15.27.

FIGURE 15.27
Glare on the three spheres

When you are rendering outdoor scenes using the mr Sun and Sky, be careful when using the Glare shader. The Sky itself is so intense that often it will be affected by the shader as well, and there can be an especially bright section near the horizon.

15. Save your scene as **My_Savoye15_D.max**.

Using Depth of Field

Another in camera effect that you can simulate with the mental ray renderer is depth of field. Depth of field (DoF) is created by light rays hitting the image plane from many different directions when the aperture in the lens is wide open. When the aperture is small, only parallel rays of light can hit the image plane and the depth of focus is not as pronounced.

1. Open the `DepthofField.max` file from the book's website.

2. Right-click in the Camera002_CoffeeTable viewport to make it active.

3. Click the Render Production button on the Main Toolbar to render the camera view. The Rendered Frame Window should look like Figure 15.28.

FIGURE 15.28
The rendered view

4. Click the Render Setup button on the Main Toolbar and click the Renderer tab.

5. Scroll down to the Camera Effects rollout and click the button labeled None next to the checked Lens shader.

6. On the Material/Map Browser, expand the Maps ➢ mental ray group if it isn't already, and select Depth of Field/Bokeh, as shown in Figure 15.29. Then click OK.

FIGURE 15.29
Select Depth of
Field/Bokeh.

Next, you'll adjust the depth of field:

1. Open the Slate Material Editor.

2. Drag the Depth of Field/Bokeh shader to the Active View1 Window of the Slate Material Editor.

3. Double-click the Depth of Field/Bokeh node to access the settings in the Parameter Editor.

4. Set the Focus Plane to 5′10″.

RADIUS OF CONFUSION

The radius of confusion is a physical quality of a camera system involving the lens and the focal distance and is extremely mathematical and difficult to describe. If you are interested in reading about this concept and aren't scared off by extreme math, there are a number of wiki articles about the radius or circle of confusion that you can find online.

5. Change Blade Count to 7.

6. Save the scene as `My_DepthofField.max`

7. Click the Render button on the Render Setup dialog box. When the Missing Map Files dialog box opens, click Continue. The finished rendering in the Rendered Frame Window should look like Figure 15.30.

This rendering will take significantly longer than the previous rendering because of the Depth of Field/Bokeh shader, even with only four samples and the low anti-aliasing settings. If you don't want to wait for this image to render, you can look at Figure1530.tif, which you can download from this book's website.

FIGURE 15.30
The rendering with DOF/Bokeh

When you look at the finished rendering or Figure1530.tif, you should see that the gray dual-spouted vessel and the wineglass are sharp and detailed and that everything in front of or behind those two objects is out of focus. Increasing the Samples value in the Depth of Field Parameters rollout of the shader and increasing the Minimum and Maximum Samples per Pixel values in the Render Setup dialog box can greatly increase the quality of the out-of-focus areas, but at a significant cost of greatly increased render time.

A more efficient way to create the appearance of depth of field in this rendering would be to render out the image with a Z-Depth channel and then use a compositing or image manipulation application to create the out-of-focus effect you desire.

You will now render an image that has a Z-Depth channel and other channels that you could use on your own in Autodesk Composite to create different effects.

1. Save the scene as **My_DepthofField_02.max**

2. Open the Render Setup dialog box. In the Camera Shaders group, right-click the Depth of Field/Bokeh shader and select Clear to remove it, as shown in Figure 15.31.

FIGURE 15.31
Clear the Lens shader.

3. Click the Render Elements tab and click the Add button.

4. Hold down the Control key to multi-select the Lighting, Material ID, Reflection, Refraction, Shadow, and Z Depth Render Elements options, and then click OK.

5. Click the Common tab of the Render Setup dialog box and click the Files button in the Render Output group, as shown in Figure 15.32.

FIGURE 15.32
Click the Files
button.

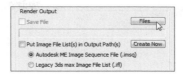

6. In the Render Output File dialog box, browse to the folder where you saved the files from the book's website, and in the File Name field enter **MyTableTop**.

7. Click the Save As Type drop-down menu and select OpenEXR Image File (*.exr, *.fxr) from the list.

8. Click the Save button, and the OpenEXR Configuration dialog box will open.

9. In the Render Elements group, click the Add button, select all the Render Elements listed, and click OK.

10. The OpenEXR Configuration dialog box should look like Figure 15.33. Click OK.

FIGURE 15.33
The OpenEXR
Configuration
dialog box

11. Click the Render button to have mental ray render and save the file. This file is also provided as `TableTop.exr` with the rest of the files from this chapter in case you do not want to render it. A high-resolution `TableTop_DOF.tif` with higher-quality sampling on the Depth of Field/Bokeh shader and the camera's anti-aliasing is also provided with this chapter's downloads.

Creating Stereoscopic Renders in 3ds Max

One of the most popular effects of the day is the resurgence of 3D, aka stereoscopic presentation. Many big movies being released are in 3D, from children's and family movies to the big action extravaganzas. Stereoscopy was first developed back in the 1830s and involves giving each of the viewer's eyes its own unique view of a scene. Each view is separated by the interocular distance—in other words, the distance between the viewer's two eyes. The intraocular distance for the average adult is about 2.5˝. This brings up some interesting possibilities and phenomena, because stereo-pair images created for viewing by children should be designed with a smaller intraocular distance. Also, certain types of images will need to be designed with a larger intraocular distance to exaggerate the perception of depth. Your brain interprets the two images and, using cues from the perspective of each image, you perceive a sense of depth from the stereo pair.

Stereographic images are also now being used in architectural and engineering graphics. Whether this too is just a fad or not, we won't know yet. This book cannot go into the rules, theory, or philosophies of stereography, and there are many, many of them, but you will get a quick tutorial of how to set up a scene with two cameras and how to render the scene in stereographic 3D. If you don't have a pair of anaglyph stereo glasses to view the finished renders, it is easy to find a store online that will sell you Red/Blue stereo glasses, which will be for the format of stereo vision that you will be using. Other methods of displaying stereographic imagery require polarized lenses, dual-synced projectors, or very high-end computer displays with synced LCD-shutter glasses.

1. Open the Savoye_15E.max file.

 This is very similar to the first file you used earlier in this chapter. You will rename the existing camera in the scene and add a new camera.

2. Click the Select by Name button from the Main Toolbar; in the Select from Scene dialog box, select the Camera.View.3DFRONT object and click OK.

3. On the Modify tab, rename the camera to **Right-Eye**.

STEREOGRAPHIC RENDERING IN 3DS MAX

There are a number of resources on the Internet for creating stereoscopic renderings from 3ds Max. Louis Marcoux has an eight-part video tutorial that goes into much greater detail on the topic, including creating camera rigs and compositing the resulting images in Video Post using MAXScript. You can find those videos and more tutorials at his website: www.louismarcoux.com.

4. With the Right-Eye camera selected, go to the Edit menu and select Clone.

5. In the Clone Options dialog box that appears, select the Instance option and in the Name field enter Left-Eye, as shown in Figure 15.34. Then click OK.

FIGURE 15.34
Clone the selected camera.

6. With the Left-Eye camera selected, click the Select and Move tool from the Main Toolbar.

7. Click the Reference Coordinate System drop-down menu and change it to Local, as shown in Figure 15.35.

8. Make sure the Transform Type-In is set to Absolute mode and enter **-2.5″** in the X Coordinate type-in field. Then press Enter on the keyboard.

FIGURE 15.35
Select the Local coordinate system.

You now have two cameras targeted at the same point in the scene and you are ready to render out the Right and Left eye views, as shown in Figure 15.36, which presents the Left-Eye and Right-Eye cameras in the lower two 3ds Max viewports. Changing the two side-by-side viewports to display the stereo-pair cameras is often a good check to see how well the stereo effect is composed. This quick technique will let you render a stereo pair once you have determined the view you want with one camera. If you want to have a camera rig where you can change the focal target or change the views, you will need a more robust setup to allow you to rotate the views and adjust the target positions without affecting the intraocular distance.

FIGURE 15.36
The stereo-pair cameras in adjacent 3ds Max viewports

When planning stereo-pair renders, it is important to know that objects between the cameras and the camera targets will appear to float out of the final composited image, and objects farther away than the camera targets will be pushed back into the image frame. Also, objects that are closer than half the distance to the camera targets may diverge so much that they appear doubled in the resulting stereo image. One last topic to be cautious of when preparing stereo-pair renders is that you want to avoid cutting off objects on the perimeter of your renders, because those objects can often break the appearance of depth in your renderings. You will need to be conscious of how objects diverge and converge in your stereo images as to avoid creating excessive eyestrain for the viewers of your stereo images or animations.

Now you will render your stereo-pair images using the Batch Render functionality of 3ds Max:

1. Choose Rendering ➤ Batch Render from the Main Menu.

2. In the Batch Render dialog box, click the Add button twice to create View01 and View02 in the task queue window, as shown in Figure 15.37.

FIGURE 15.37
The Batch Render dialog box

3. Click and select the View01 item from the task queue window.

4. Set the Camera to Right-Eye.

5. Click the Output Path button and browse to where you are saving your files for Chapter 15. Then rename the image to be saved as **MyStereo_Right-Eye.tif**.

6. Repeat the steps starting with step 3, but this time select the View02 item, select the Left-Eye camera and rename the output file to **MyStereo_Left-Eye.tif**.

7. Click the Render button in the lower-right corner of the Batch Render dialog box, and watch mental ray render the two camera views.

Now that you have the two stereo-pair images rendered, you can view them separately in the Rendering View Image File dialog box, or you can load them both into the RAM player and slide the divider over the two stacked images to see how different the perspectives are.

Keep the two images that you rendered in this exercise, because you will need them later in this chapter when you load them into Autodesk Composite 2011 to create the red/blue Anaglyph Stereo Image.

Using Autodesk Composite 2011

This portion of the chapter will go briefly into how you can use Autodesk Composite 2011 to adjust and improve your final rendered images from 3ds Max. Autodesk Composite is a full-featured node-based compositing application that is based on the acclaimed Autodesk Toxik compositor technology. Each node in the data flow is an operator that performs a function on the data (image frames in our case) in the flow. Input nodes for Composite can be rendered frames from Autodesk 3ds Max, including Render Elements files; Multi-Channel EXR; still

images from high-resolution digital cameras; footage sequences (as sequentially numbered frames) from HD or 4K digital film cameras; or even art that you create in 2D painting or drawing applications.

The data flow in Autodesk Composite progresses from left (the input sources) to right (the output nodes). The bottom of the Autodesk Composite interface is the tabbed workspace. Each tab in the workspace is set up for the different phases of the compositing workflow. The Autodesk Composite user interface is completely customizable for your workflow needs. The primary interface for working with Autodesk Composite is the Gate UI. To access the Gate UI, you can press the ~ (tilde) key on the keyboard or click the middle mouse button. The Gate UI is intended to help you maximize you speed and efficiency when using Autodesk Composite. Once you have opened the Gate UI, you sweep in a direction (usually north, east, west, or south) to access different components within the software.

Autodesk Composite features a comprehensive toolkit to maximize your creativity, including keying, color correction, motion tracking, paint features, full HDR support, and depth of field effects—all at resolutions up to 4K (or above) film resolution. This chapter cannot go into all the features of Autodesk Composite, but it will give you an idea how you can work with your images and then you can use the Composite help and learning resources.

Thoroughly learning Autodesk Composite would require a whole book as long as or longer than Mastering Autodesk 3ds Max Design 2011. However, there are a few places to find help for Autodesk Composite 2011. The first is the built in Help menu, which runs in an Internet browser. Some of the resources on the Help menu for Composite 2011 require Internet access to function. You can also find resources for Autodesk Composite in the Autodesk Toxik/Combustion discussion forums at the Area (`http//area.autodesk.com`), Digital Entertainment & Visualization Community for users of Autodesk software.

1. Close 3ds Max if it is still running. If your computer system does not have a lot of RAM, it may be a good time to reboot the computer too.

2. Start Autodesk Composite 2011.

 When you start Autodesk Composite 2011, you should be presented with the Composite Essential Skills Movies dialog box, similar to when you start Autodesk 3ds Max Design 2011, as shown in Figure 15.38. Composite has a very different interface and workflow than 3ds Max, so it is highly suggested to watch all the movies.

FIGURE 15.38
The Composite Essential Skills Movies

3. Create a new composition by clicking the File menu and selecting New, as shown in Figure 15.39.

FIGURE 15.39
Create a new composite.

4. In the Create Composition dialog box, use the Folders area on the left side of the dialog box to browse to where you are working with your Chapter 15 downloads. You can see where you are going to create the new composition in the Destination field near the bottom of the dialog box.

5. In the Name field of the Create Composition dialog box, enter **MyComposite**, as shown in Figure 15.40.

FIGURE 15.40
The Create Composition dialog box

6. Click the Create button.

7. You will see an Output node appear on the left side of the interface; the right side is the preview area, as shown in Figure 15.41.

At the bottom of the interface you will see the tabbed workspace area that was mentioned previously in the chapter.

8. On the Composition tab of the workspace, click the Format button and select HD 720p, as shown in Figure 15.42. This prepares the composition for the data that you will be importing.

FIGURE 15.41
The Output node
and Composite
interface

FIGURE 15.42
Set the format for
your composite.

9. Choose File ➢ Import to open the File Browser dialog box. Use the Folders window to browse to where you downloaded the files for this chapter from the book's website.

10. Select the `Stereo_Right-Eye.tif` image and click Import.

This image is a higher-resolution version of the first image you created with the Batch Render dialog box earlier in this chapter.

11. Click the button in the upper-right corner to close the dialog box.

Your interface should look like Figure 15.43.

FIGURE 15.43
The imported file

12. Press the ~ (tilde) key on your keyboard or the middle button on your mouse to activate the Gate UI, shown in Figure 15.44.

FIGURE 15.44
The Gate UI

13. Move your mouse through the East Gate labeled Tools. The Tools menu opens on the right edge of the screen, as shown in Figure 15.45.

14. Click the Color Correction folder, and you will see the Color Correction tools listed in the bin at the bottom of the screen.

You can scroll through the list to see the available Color Correction tools.

15. Click and drag the Photo Lab node to the MyComposite schematic view, and drop it between the Stereo_Right-Eye and Output nodes, as shown in Figure 15.46.

FIGURE 15.45

The Tools menu

FIGURE 15.46

Drag the Photo Lab node between the Input and Output nodes

As you drag the Photo Lab node over the Stereo_Right-Eye input node, if you touch the right side of the input node (called *kissing* in Composite parlance) it will connect those two nodes.

16. Once you have dropped the Photo Lab node, you can connect it to the Output node by hovering the mouse over the right edge of the node until you see it highlight. Then click and drag to connect it to the Output node, as shown in Figure 15.47.

FIGURE 15.47

Connect the Photo Lab node to the Output node.

17. Click the Photo Lab node to open its tab in the workspace area. You will see the Exposure, Contrast, Pivot, and Lift tools, as shown in Figure 15.48.

With the Photo Lab node you can adjust the exposure/contrast of all three channels simultaneously using the lock buttons or individually by disabling the locks.

FIGURE 15.48
The Photo Lab node controls

18. Bring up the exposure by a quarter stop, in other words 0.25, by clicking any one of the RGB values and dragging the mouse to the right. Or click one of the numbers and type .25 with the keyboard; then press Enter.

You should see the highlight on the spheres spread out slightly and the image get brighter.

19. Click one of the Contrast values and drag the mouse to the right. Watch as the contrast changes the appearance of the image.

20. Click the Reset button under both Contrast and Exposure to remove your edits.

21. Click the trackball under Exposure and drag the reticules to the right and slightly down, giving the image a slightly blue tint. Using the trackball, you can essentially adjust the RGB channels individually even if the channel locks are on.

22. Right-click the Photo Lab node and select Reset from the menu.

23. Click the middle button on your mouse to activate the Gate UI again, sweep through the East Gate, and choose Grain Management ➤ Add Grain. Then drag the node and place it on the connection between the Photo Lab node and the Output node, as shown in Figure 15.49.

With the Add Grain operator, you can analyze grain from one image (or sequence) such as a background plate and add that grain to a digitally rendered foreground image so that they blend together better, or you can just add grain to a completely digital rendering to make it look more like a photograph shot on film. You can also adjust the grain individually per color channel.

FIGURE 15.49
Place the Add Grain operator.

24. Click the Grain values for the R, G, and B channels and adjust them slightly. You may have to use the scroll wheel on your mouse to zoom into the preview window to see the grain, especially if you are making subtle value changes.

Autodesk Composite allows you to save grain profiles so that you can load them quickly to apply to many projects.

25. Right-click the Add Grain node and select Delete from the menu.

26. Right-click the Photo Lab node and select Delete from the menu.

Next you will add to the composite the left eye image from the stereo pair that you rendered earlier in the chapter.

1. Click the File menu and select Import.

2. The dialog box should open in the same folder you loaded the first image from earlier in these exercises. Select the `Stereo_Left-Eye.tif` image and click Import; then close the dialog box.

3. Click and drag to move the Stereo_Left-Eye.tif node above the Stereo_Right-Eye.tif node, as shown in Figure 15.50.

FIGURE 15.50
Position the
input node.

4. Hover the mouse over the connection between the Stereo_Right-Eye.tif node and the Output node and select Disconnect.

5. Press the middle mouse button or the ~ (tilde) key on the keyboard to active the Gate UI; then sweep through the East Gate and select the Pixel Expressions category.

6. Click and drag the PXL operator and place it between the Stereo_Right-Eye.tif node and the Output node, as shown in Figure 15.51.

FIGURE 15.51
Place the PXL
operator.

7. In the Preset section of the workspace, click the Load button and select the Stereo Anaglyph preset from the list, as shown in Figure 15.52.

FIGURE 15.52
Load the Stereo Anaglyph preset.

8. Click the right edge of the Stereo_Left-Eye.tif node and connect it to the In slot node of the Stereo Anaglyph node dialog box, as shown in Figure 15.53.

FIGURE 15.53
Connect the left eye image to the Stereo Anaglyph operator.

9. Click the right edge of the Stereo_Right-Eye.tif node and drag it to the RightImage slot on the Stereo Anaglyph node, as shown in Figure 15.54.

FIGURE 15.54
Connect the right eye image to the Stereo Anaglyph operator.

10. Click and drag the right edge of the Stereo Anaglyph node and connect it to the Output node, as in Figure 15.55.

FIGURE 15.55
Connect the Stereo
Anaglyph operator to
the Output node.

11. Click the Output node, and you will see a black and white image with some teal and red where the images diverge, as shown in Figure 15.56. This is because of the mode of the Stereo Anaglyph node.

FIGURE 15.56
The black and
white anaglyph
image

12. Click the Stereo Anaglyph node to open the PXL tab in the Workspace area of the Composite interface.

13. Click the Method value and change it to 2, as shown in Figure 15.57.

FIGURE 15.57
Change the
Method value to 2

14. Click the Output node again, and you should see a full-color stereo anaglyph image (see Figure 15.58).

15. The Output tab on the workspace should be open; change Pixel Format Depth to be 8 Bits, and in the Time parameters set the End frame to 2 so the duration is 1, as shown in Figure 15.59.

FIGURE 15.58
The full-color
stereo anaglyph

FIGURE 15.59
Change the Pixel
Format Depth and
Duration.

16. Click the Render tab of the Workspace area, and in the File Name field change the output name to **MyAnaglygh**. The system will add `.<FrameNo>` to suffix the rendered image name with the frame number, as shown in Figure 15.60. Change the file format to TIFF. The frame numbering is crucial if you are outputting sequences that you will convert to a movie file with Video Post in 3ds Max or another video conversion program. Make sure the path is pointing to the folder where you have been working.

FIGURE 15.60
Set the File Name
and file format
for your rendered
image.

17. Choose File ➢ Render, and then click the Start button in the lower-right corner of the Render dialog box, as shown in Figure 15.61.

18. You won't see anything happen. The Render dialog box will dismiss itself. Open the folder where you told it to save the file, and you should see `MyAnaglyph.00001.tif`.

Open it with Photoshop or the 3ds Max View Image File command, find your red/blue stereo glasses, and enjoy.

19. Save your composition in Composite, and close the program.

Adjusting your images in Composite to fine-tune to achieve the look you want is much faster and more efficient than continually tweaking settings and rerendering the images in 3ds Max trying to get a prefect render. For example, you could take the MyTableTop.exr file that you rendered earlier in this chapter and in Autodesk Composite, add highlight glare and create a depth of field look much faster with the Z-Depth channel than you could rerender the image. You can also adjust the reflections or refractions using the two channels that you added as render elements.

If you rendered out discreet image passes for each light source in your scene, you could use Autodesk Composite to blend those images together to get an almost infinite number of different lighting looks without having to adjust each light and then render out the same number of images. The power of using a compositing application with your 3ds Max Design workflow is very impressive and can save you countless hours of re-rendering when an employer or client wants to see a slightly different render.

In addition to the nodes and workflows you have seen in these exercises, Autodesk Composite can be used to key footage off blue or green screens; project camera mapping onto low poly objects to create 3D matte paintings; apply spline-based warping to create a variety of visual effects; modify sequences with raster and vector paint to clone parts of the image, or *rotoscope*; paint new information into the scene; use multiple modes of motion tracking to place new objects into an image sequence; replace computer screens, billboards, posters, or any flat elements; add motion blur to a sequence using vector channels; and add depth of field to sequences using Z-depth map channels.

Autodesk Composite can take advantage of the Backburner network rendering application that ships with Autodesk 3ds Max Design 2011. Be aware that with Autodesk 3ds Max 2011 there are two versions of Backburner that can be installed. The default is Backburner 2008; however, after you have successfully installed 3ds Max 2011, you can remove Backburner 2008 and install Backburner 2011 from the install DVD. Versions of Autodesk software prior to the 2011 release will not be compatible with Backburner 2011.

The Bottom Line

Add an atmospheric effect Atmospheric effects add the appearance of particulate matter in the air. With them, you can represent volumetric lights, fog, smoke, clouds, and even fire.

> **Master It** Add a second fog to the Savoy15_A.max file with a bottom just below the top of the building's overhang and the top 6′ above that. Give the fog a purple color, and make sure the fog is not a straight line at the horizon.

Add a grass effect using Hair and Fur Hair and Fur is a rendering effect that appears to add strands to an object at rendering. These strands can look like long, thin hair; short, thick fur; or even grass.

> **Master It** Zoom into the tree in the Savoye15_C.max file. Create a mound that rises out of the ground and covers the base of the tree. Add Hair and Fur to the mound so that it appears to be caused by a root ball under the lawn.

Add the Glare effect to a rendering Glare is an effect that is seen in real-world cameras when the intensity of the lights or reflections/refractions captured by the camera causes the light to reflect/refract within the film emulsion or on the surface of a sensor.

> **Master It** Open the TableTop_Glare.max file. Add the Glare shader and render the Camera002 viewport.

Use DOF/Bokeh Depth of field is the result of using a camera with a large aperture setting during the image exposure. The effect is seen in real-world cameras and often a rendering will appear much more realistic when there is some DOF in the image.

> **Master It** Continue with the TableTop_Glare.max file from the previous exercise. Add the Depth of Field/Bokeh shader and render the Camera002 viewport. Having Glare and DOF with good sampling settings will make the rendering take quite a while.

Create stereo-pair images Stereo 3D images are incredibly popular again, even in the architectural and engineering industries. As a visualization specialist, the odds are very high that you will encounter situations where you need to take a scene and render it for stereo viewing.

> **Master It** Using the TableTop_Stereo_01.max file, create an additional camera for the right eye with a 2.5″ intraocular distance, and then render the two cameras using the Batch Render command.

Composite the stereo pair into an anaglyph image Once you have the stereo-pair images, you need to combine them into one image you can look at with Red/Blue anaglyph glasses.

> **Master It** Use Autodesk Composite to take the two images you rendered in the previous "Master It" and render out a single anaglyph stereo image.

Appendices

In this section you will find:

Appendix A

The Bottom Line

Each of The Bottom Line sections in the chapters suggests exercises to deepen skills and understanding. Sometimes there is only one possible solution, but often you are encouraged to use your skills and creativity to create something that builds on what you know and lets you explore one of many possible solutions.

Chapter 1: Getting to Know 3ds Max Design 2011

Navigate and configure the viewports The 3ds Max viewports can be configured in several ways, including setting the quantity and configuration of the viewports.

Master It Configure the viewports so that there are three small viewports stacked on the left side and one larger viewport on the right. From top to bottom, set the three stacked viewports to be Top, Front, and Right, respectively; then set the large viewport to a perspective view.

Solution

1. Click the general viewport label menu (the plus button) at the upper-left corner of the viewport and choose Configure from the context menu.

2. Click the Layout tab.

3. In the second row of viewport configuration options, click the third option from the left.

 The viewport configuration changes to display three viewports stacked on the left and one larger viewport to the right.

4. Click in the top viewport on the left and choose Top from the context menu.

5. Click in the middle viewport on the left and choose Front from the context menu.

6. Click in the bottom viewport on the left and choose Right from the context menu.

7. Click in the large viewport on the right and choose Perspective from the context menu.

8. Click OK to close the dialog box and reconfigure the viewports.

Dock and float toolbars The 3ds Max user interface has several customizable features, including the ability to hide or expose and dock or float the program's toolbars.

Master It Detach the Command panel from the right side of the 3ds Max window and release it so that it floats in the middle of the 3ds Max window. Select the Command panel again and attach it to the left side. Expose a hidden toolbar and dock it to the left of the Command panel.

Solution

1. Place the cursor to the right of the Utilities tab. The tooltip will read "Command Panel."

2. Click and drag the Command panel and release it over the viewports. The Command panel is now floating.

3. Right-click the floating Command panel title bar, and choose Dock ➤ Left.

4. Release the mouse. The Command panel is now docked to the left side of the viewports.

5. Right-click the blank area of any toolbar.

6. From the context menu that appears, select any of the unchecked toolbars. That toolbar appears in the UI.

7. Click the new toolbar's title bar and drag it to the far left boundary of the viewports and release the mouse. The toolbar docks to the left of the Command panel.

Copy objects and use the transform tools The transform tools (Move, Rotate, and Scale) are the most commonly used tools in 3ds Max. With them, you can position, orient, and scale your objects as required in the scene. You can quickly create a copy in 3ds Max, a process called *cloning*, by holding down the Shift key while using any of the transform tools.

Master It Make a box that is 3′ long, 10″ wide, and 8″ high. Make five instance clones of the box and rotate each clone 20 degrees more than the previous clone. Stack the boxes like a spiral staircase, with an increasing amount of swing with each stair and leaving no vertical or horizontal gaps in the stairs.

Solution

1. Create a box and, in the Parameters rollout, set Length to 3′, Width to 10″, and Height to 8″.

2. Click the Select and Move tool in the Main Toolbar.

3. Hold the Shift key down and drag the Z-axis handle up until the Z readout in the transform type-ins reads approximately 8″, then release the mouse.

4. In the Clone Options dialog box that appears, set Object to Instance, and Number Of Copies to 5, and then click OK. The five clones appear in the viewports.

5. With the Move transform still active, select the first clone, the second box from the bottom, then enter 8. If the box moves out of sight, undo the command, then, in the Units Setup dialog box, set Default Units to Inches and move the box again.

6. Repeat the process with the remaining steps, setting each one's height exactly 8″ higher than the previous.

7. Click the Select and Rotate tool in the Main Toolbar.

8. Starting with the second box up, select each box, then enter a Z rotation value, 20 degrees higher than the previous step, in the transform type-ins.

9. Switch to a four-viewport layout and set the Top viewport to the Wireframe rendering mode.

10. Using the Move transform, select each box in the Perspective viewport, and move it into position in the Top viewport.

Create a named selection set Whenever any objects are selected in 3ds Max, the selected objects are referred to as a selection set. Often, you may need to repeatedly select the same objects for different operations. By creating named selection sets, you can quickly select objects by selecting the selections set name from a drop-down list.

Master It Continuing from the previous Master It exercise, rename the boxes to Step1, Step2, Step3, and so on, starting with the top step. Make and test two named selection sets, one containing the lower three steps and another containing the even-numbered steps.

Solution

1. Select the boxes named Step1, Step2, and Step3.

2. In the Named Selection Sets input box in the Main toolbar, enter a name for the selection set containing the lower three steps, then press enter key.

3. Click a blank area of the viewports to clear the selection set.

4. Expand the Named Selection Set drop-down list, then click the name that you just entered. The three lower stairs are selected.

5. Select the boxes named Step1, Step3, and Step5.

6. In the Named Selection Sets input box in the Main toolbar, enter a name for the selection set containing the three odd numbered steps, then press enter key.

7. Click a blank area of the viewports to clear the selection set.

8. Expand the Named Selection Set drop-down list, then click the name that you just entered. Every other step is selected.

Chapter 2: Introducing 3ds Max Objects

Apply a modifier Modifiers provide many ways to manipulate an object that may not be possible by manually transforming the object's sub-objects. The order in which the modifiers appear in the modifiers stack determines the final result.

Master It Create a Teapot primitive and apply the Slice modifier to it. Raise the Slice plane sub-object until it passes through the middle of the object. Choose the Remove Top option from the Slice Parameters rollout to delete everything above the Slice Plane. Add a Cap Holes modifier to the top of the stack.

Solution

1. To access the Slice Plane sub-object, click the plus (+) symbol next to the Slice entry in the modifier stack.

2. Select the Slice Plane sub-object level in the modifier stack, and then click the Select and Move transform in the Main Toolbar.

3. Drag up the Z-axis handle of the Move Transform gizmo to raise the level of the Slice Plane.

4. In the Slice Parameters rollout of the Modify panel, select the Remove Top option. Everything above the Slice Plane disappears.

5. To exit the Slice Plane sub-object level, click Slice in the modifier stack or press the 1 key, in the top row of keys and not the numeric keypad.

6. Expand the modifier list and apply the Cap Holes modifier. The holes at the top of the teapot are covered with faces. Your scene should look similar to the following image.

Make a clone of a 3ds Max object The type of clones you make determines whether modifiers and parameter changes affect the clones as well as the original. Copies are distinct objects, instances maintain the changes between all clones, and references maintain all changes below the reference bar.

Master It Select the teapot from the previous exercise and make two clones: one instance and one reference. Turn off the Slice modifier for the instance, and then apply a Twist modifier and increase the amount of twist reflected in the objects. Select the reference clone, and apply a Spherify modifier to the top of the stack.

Solution

1. Use the Move transform to make a clone of the teapot by dragging it with the Shift key pressed.

2. In the Clone Options dialog box, choose the Instance option.

3. Clone the original teapot again, but this time choose Reference in the Clone Options dialog box.

4. Select the instance clone and turn off the Slice modifier by clicking the lightbulb next to the Slice entry in the modifier stack. The Slice modifier is disabled for all three clones.

5. Expand the modifier stack and choose Twist from the list of available modifiers. You can press the T key several times to locate the modifier in the list.

6. In the Parameters rollout, increase the Angle value until the teapots show a significant twist.

7. Select the reference clone, expand the modifier list, and apply a Spherify modifier. The following image shows the result when a 115-degree twist is applied to all the teapots and the Spherify modifier, set to 50 percent, is applied to the reference clone only.

Manipulate a group Groups provide a method for associating separate objects so they act as if they are a single object. Groups can be opened, allowing individual member objects to be selected or exploded, or the members associated with it to be changed.

Master It Make one clone each of the teapots from the previous exercise. Select the three original objects and make them into a group. Remove the spherified teapot from the group, and then add the remaining two non-spherified teapots to the group.

Solution

1. Select all three teapots, hold down the Shift key, and use the Move transform to create the clones. The type of clone selected does not matter for this exercise.

2. Use the Select Object tool or the Select Objects dialog box to select the original three teapots.

3. On the Group menu, choose Group. Name the group **teapot group**.

4. To remove the teapot from the group, choose Group ➢ Open, select the spherified teapot, and then choose Group ➢ Detach.

5. Select one of the remaining teapots in the group, and choose Group ➢ Close.

6. To add the other teapot objects to the group, select the two non-spherified teapots, choose Group ➢ Attach, and click the group to add it to the group.

Chapter 3: Creating Shapes with Splines

Draw shapes with splines Two-dimensional splines can be used as the building blocks for more complex, three-dimensional objects. You can draw splines from scratch using the Line tool or start with a parametric shape and then collapse it to an editable spline.

Master It Create a rainbow-shaped set of splines—in other words, a series of concentric arcs.

Solution Using the Line tool, do the following:

1. Create a line with three vertices: one at each end of the arc and one at the middle.

2. At the Vertex sub-object level, change all the vertices to Bezier.

3. Adjust the handles to create the initial arc shape.

4. Select the Scale transform from the Main Toolbar.

5. Hold down the Shift key, click the spline, and drag toward its center point.

6. In the Clone Options dialog box, enter the number of arcs that you want, and then click OK.

 The arc's clones are created. You could have also started the exercise using the Arc parametric shape. The Arc method has the advantage that the arc endpoints remain in-line with each other when they are scaled.

Outline and extrude splines Outlining splines provides a way to create a new spline sub-object that parallels the original. This is faster and more accurate than creating the second spline manually and then attaching it to the original. Extruding splines is the most common method for creating 3D objects from 2D splines.

Master It A column surround is a shell that covers a structural column to give it a more appealing appearance. Create a 16′-tall, 2″-thick, semicircular column surround with a 16′ outside radius.

Solution

1. Use the Arc tool (Create ➤ Shapes ➤ Arc) to create an arc in the Top or Perspective viewport by clicking to set the start point, dragging and releasing to set the endpoint, and then clicking to place the middle of the arc.

2. In the Parameters rollout, set the Radius to 16″ and the From and To values to 0 (zero) and 180 respectively. This creates a 16″ outer radius over a 180-degree span.

3. Convert the arc to an editable spline.

4. Access the Spline sub-object level, and then select the single spline that makes up the arc.

5. In the Geometry rollout, type **2″** in the Outline field, and then press ↵.

6. Exit the Spline sub-object level.

7. From the Modifier List drop-down list, apply the Extrude modifier to the spline; then set the Amount parameter to 16′.

Modify closed splines with Boolean tools Nearly any shape can be formed using the standard Editable Spline tools. Rather than adding, deleting, and adjusting vertices, it is often faster and easier to create two or more simple shapes and combine them for a more complex shape.

Master It Using the spline Boolean tools, create the cross-sectional shape of a fluted column, similar to the shape shown here.

Solution

1. In the Top viewport, use the Circle tool to draw a circle that will represent the outermost radius of the column. Move the circle to the origin

2. Create a smaller circle that encroaches into the larger circle. The smaller circle will be used to form the flutes themselves.

3. In the Main Toolbar, make sure the Reference Coordinate System is set to World; if it is set to View change it to World. Then click the Rotate tool, and then choose Use Transform Coordinate Center from the Coordinate Center flyout in the Main Toolbar. This will cause the smaller circle to rotate about the origin, which is currently also at the center of the larger circle.

4. Turn on the Angle Snap Toggle on the Main Toolbar.

5. Hold down the Shift key and drag the blue Z ring of the Rotate Transform gizmo until the smaller circle is copied and rotated 30 degrees.

6. In the Clone Options dialog box, set Number of Copies to 11 and then click OK. Twelve smaller circles now surround the larger circle, and are evenly spaced 30 degrees apart.

7. Select the larger circle and convert it to an editable spline.

8. In the Geometry rollout, click the Attach Mult. button; then, in the Attach Multiple dialog box that appears, select all the smaller circles. Click Attach to attach all the smaller circles, as spline sub-objects, to the larger circle and close the dialog box.

9. Access the Spline sub-object level and select the larger circle.

10. In the Geometry rollout, click the Subtraction button to the right of the Boolean button.

11. Click the Boolean button, and then click each of the smaller circles anywhere outside of the larger circle. The smaller circles and any areas shared with the larger circle are deleted, leaving the fluted shape.

12. Exit the Spline sub-object level.

Chapter 4: Editing Meshes and Creating Complex Objects

Create openings with ProBoolean operations Using the ProBoolean operations, you can join meshes (union), delete one object and any volume it shares with another object (subtraction), or delete two objects while retaining the volume of the share (intersection).

Master It Using the ProBoolean tools, cut an archway into a box primitive representing a wall. The archway is to be 3′ wide and 8′ high at the top of the arch.

Solution

1. Set your units to US Standard Feet w/Decimal Inches.

2. Create a long box in the Perspective viewport that is 6″ wide and at least 8′6″ tall.

3. Create another box that is 3′ long, 2′ thick, and 6′6″ tall. This will be the straight section of the archway.

4. Make a cylinder with a radius of 18″ and a height of 2′; change Height Segments to 1.

5. Turn on Slice and slice the cylinder from 90 degrees to 270 degrees. You are left with half of a cylinder.

6. Click the Rotate tool in the Main Toolbar and then enter **-90** in the Y field of the transform type-ins at the bottom of the UI. The cylinder rotates so that the flat surface is facing down.

7. Click the Move transform tool and then right-click the 3D Snap tool and turn on the Vertex snap.

8. Select the cylinder object and press the spacebar on the keyboard to turn on the Selection Lock toggle.

9. Place the mouse near one of the corners of the cylinder and watch for the Vertex Snap icon.

10. When the Vertex Snap recognizes the corner, click and move the cylinder to the top of the archway box.

11. Select one of the objects, and then click Create ➢ Geometry ➢ Compound Objects ➢ ProBoolean.

12. Select Union in the Operation section, click the Start Picking button, and then pick the other archway object. The two objects are combined as a single object. Click the Start Picking button again to turn it off.

13. Move the archway object so that it protrudes from either side of the wall.

14. Select the wall, and then click Create ➢ Geometry ➢ Compound Objects ➢ ProBoolean.

15. Select Subtraction in the Operation section, click the Start Picking button, and then pick the archway object. The archway object disappears, leaving an archway-shaped void in the wall.

16. Save your file.

Designate a modeling template image Using a template image applied to geometry, such as a plane or a box, can be very helpful in the modeling process. These image planes can be used to display reference information, such as plans, sections, or elevations, needed to aid the modeling process.

Master It So you can use it to model the building's elevation, add an image plane that uses the House.jpg file provided with 3ds Max to your Front viewport.

Solution

1. Right-click in the Front viewport.

2. Click the Create tab, the Geometry button, and then make sure Standard Primitives is selected from the drop-down.

3. Click the Plane button, and then in the Front viewport draw out a plane object. Set the Length and Width segments to 1.

4. In the Material Editor, create a new material and name it **ElevationTemplate**.

5. Click the Diffuse Map slot, and select Bitmap from the Material/Map Browser.

6. In the Select Bitmap Image File dialog box, browse to your 3ds Max program directory, open the Maps folder, and then open the Backgrounds folder.

7. Select the HOUSE.JPG file and click OK.

8. In the Coordinates rollout of the material, deselect Use Real-World scale, set the U and V tiling to 1, and deselect the Tile box for both.

9. Click the Go to Parent button to get to the top of the ElevationTemplate material.

10. Select the Plane object, click the Assign Material to Selection button in the Material Editor, and then click the Show Standard Map in Viewport button.

11. With the Plane01 object selected, rename it to **ElevationTemplate** and deselect the Real-World Map Size box in the Parameters rollout. The House.jpg file will now display in the Smooth, Hidden Line, and Flat shaded viewports.

12. Reviewing the image, you can see the two front doors. If you estimate that the doors are standard 6′8″ in height and are about 70 pixels tall, the entire image is 512 pixels by 480 pixels. This would make the image plane 45.6′ tall and 48.64′ wide.

13. Make the ElevationTemplate plane 45′7″ in length and 48′7″ in width.

14. With the ElevationTemplate object selected, right-click the Select and Move tool to bring up the Move Transform Type-In dialog box and set the X value to 0 and the Z value to 22′9.5″ to set the image plane on the zero Z elevation.

15. To keep from accidentally moving, scaling, or rotating the ElevationTemplate object, with it selected go to the Hierarchy tab of the Command panel, click the Link Info button and check all nine boxes in the Locks rollout.

Create and modify objects with box modeling Virtually any real-world object can be created using box modeling methodology. Instead of combining primitive objects, you can take a plane or a box and extrude/bevel, inset, and otherwise build up new polys to model anything you wish.

Master It Create any object you want using box modeling techniques.

Solution

1. Choose any object you want to model.

2. Collect Reference materials, either photos or drawings.

3. If possible, find an actual object that you can hold in your hand as a 3D reference.

4. Once you have the reference materials, mentally dissect the object to determine how you might model it.

5. If you have 2D reference photos or drawings, map them to planes in the viewport.

6. Create a box or plane and add an Edit Poly or Edit Mesh modifier, or convert to an Editable Poly or Editable Mesh object.

7. Use various box modeling methods such as extrude, bevel, and inset to build up polygons.

8. Use transforms to select and move, select and rotate, or select and scale these polys.

9. Switch to edge or vertex mode, and use these tools to refine your model. Chamfer edges to round corners.

10. Use Smoothing groups to define hard edges and smooth curved surfaces on the model.

Attach objects to a mesh The Attach option of an Editable Poly object causes objects to become Element sub-objects of an existing Editable Poly. This creates a single object from multiple objects and reduces the memory requirements of the object.

> **Master It** Create a short tube primitive to act as a simple, round picture frame. Taper the tube. Create a short cylinder to represent the picture backing. Use the Attach option to attach the backing to the frame.

> **Solution**

> 1. Choose Create ➢ Geometry ➢ Standard Primitives ➢ Tube.

> 2. Create a tube in the Top viewport.

> 3. Increase the number of sides to smooth the tube a bit, and note the smaller of the two Radius values.

> 4. Click the Move tool and then enter **0** in each of the transform type-in fields. This moves the tube to the origin.

> 5. Click the Modify tab, expand the Modifier List drop-down, and choose Taper.

> 6. Lower the Amount value until you achieve a slight inward taper.

> 7. Choose Create ➢ Geometry ➢ Standard Primitives ➢ Cylinder.

> 8. Create the cylinder in the Top viewport. Enter Radius and Sides values equal to the smaller radius and Sides values for the tube. Height Segments can be set to 1, and the cylinder's height should be miniscule.

> 9. Click the Move tool and then enter **0** in each of the transform type-in fields. This moves the cylinder to the origin and centers it on the tube.

> 10. Select the frame, right-click, and choose Convert ➢ Convert to Editable Poly.

> 11. Click Attach in the Edit Geometry rollout, and then click the cylinder. The cylinder is attached to the tube.

> 12. Click Attach to turn off the tool.

Create clones with Array and Snapshot The Array and Snapshot tools both provide a method of creating many clones of scene objects. The Array tool creates them in patterns of rows and columns, and the Snapshot tool creates clones by capturing their appearance at any point in time.

> **Master It** Create a window that's 4′ wide by 6′ tall. In the Front viewport, create an array of windows that are spread out 8′ on-center horizontally and 12′ on-center vertically.

> **Solution**

> 1. Using box primitives (or skip ahead to Chapter 6, "Creating AEC Objects," to see how to use the AEC objects), create a 4′ × 6′–tall window. Group it if necessary.

> 2. With the window selected, click the Array tool from the Extras toolbar.

> 3. In the Incremental X field at the top-left corner of the dialog box, enter **8′**.

4. Enter 10 for the number of windows to be created horizontally in the 1D Count field.

5. Click the 2D radio button.

6. Enter 3 for the number of rows of windows to be created vertically in the 2D Count field.

7. Enter **12´** in the Z field in the Incremental Row Offsets area.

8. Preview the array, and then click OK.

Chapter 5: Working with External Design Data

Create topography with splines Using the Terrain compound object, you can create flowing or layered surfaces defined by the height, shape, and location of the included splines.

Master It Create a Terrain object in a shape that represents a valley that extends between two peaks. The summit of the peaks should be approximately 1,000´ above the ground plane and the valley should extend approximately 200´ below it. Contour lines should be present for every 100´ of elevation change.

Solution

1. Using the Line tool, draw two long, thin contour lines to represent the valley. One contour line should completely encompass the other. Be sure to drag the cursor whenever you place a vertex so the vertices are smooth rather than sharp. Use several vertices to define an area. In this exercise, whenever a dialog box appears asking if 3ds Max should close the spline, click Yes.

2. Draw one more line around the valley line to represent the land at ground level. The area of this shape should be large enough to encompass the valley and both mountains.

3. On one side of the valley, draw a large closed spline representing the base of the mountain.

4. Draw nine more somewhat concentric shapes that will become the incremental contour lines.

5. Repeat steps 3 and 4 on the other side of the valley.

6. Using the Move tool and the transform type-ins, move the outer and inner valley contours to -100´ and -200´, respectively.

7. Move the outer contour lines for the mountains up 100´, and then move each subsequent line 100´ higher than the previous.

8. Select the lowest valley line, and then choose Create ➢ Geometry ➢ Compound Objects ➢ Terrain.

9. Click the Pick Operand button.

10. Click each contour line in sequence from lowest to highest. When picking the mountain contours, alternate peaks when selecting contours at the same altitude.

11. Select the type of surface to display in the Form section of the Parameters rollout.

Import AutoCAD plans into 3ds Max The File Link Manager is a utility that incorporates an AutoCAD drawing into a 3ds Max scene while maintaining a link between the two files. Changes made to the DWG file are reflected in the 3ds Max scene whenever the drawing is reloaded.

Master It Create a File-Link Preset so you can repetitively use the same settings when you file-link a drawing file into the 3ds max scene.

Solution You must create a file linking preset that contains the file linking parameters that you want to retain. Here is the procedure:

1. Click the Application menu and choose References ➢ File Link Manager.
2. On the Attach tab, click the File button, and then locate and select the DWG file to link.
3. Click the Presets tab and then click the New button.
4. Give the new preset a unique name, and then click OK.
5. Select the preset, and then click Modify.
6. Set the desired parameters in the three tabs of the File Link Settings dialog box, and then click Save.
7. Click the Attach tab.
8. Expand the Preset drop-down list and select the new preset.
9. Click Attach This File.

Use the Substitute modifier It is best to use your CAD application and 3ds Max Design to each of their strengths: drafting 2D plans with blocks for laying out space arrangements and then linking that plan into 3ds Max, extruding walls, and then using the Substitute modifier to replace 2D CAD blocks with the appropriate 3D models for rendering your views and presenting to the designers or clients.

Master It Using the File Link Manager, attach `Classroom01.dwg` into a new 3ds Max scene. Using the Substitute modifier, replace the circles of the StudentDesk blocks with the `Chair.max` file and the rectangles with the `Worktop.max` file.

Solution

1. Reset 3ds Max.
2. In the empty scene, click the Application menu and choose References ➢ File Link Manager.
3. Click the File button and select the `Classroom01.dwg` file. Select the Entity Blocks Preset that you created earlier in this chapter and click Attach this file. Close the File Link Manager.
4. Select one of the rectangles and go to the Modify tab.
5. Apply a Substitute modifier to the rectangle.
6. From the Parameters rollout of the Substitute modifier, click the Select Xref Object button.

7. Using the Open File dialog, browse to and select the `Worktop.max` file.

8. In the Xref Merge dialog box, select Worktop01, click OK, and click Yes on the Substitution Question dialog box asking if you want to assign the Substitute Object's material.

9. Select one of the circles and repeat steps 6 through 9. Use the `Chair.max` file to replace the circles in the AutoCAD blocks.

Import Revit files into 3ds Max Revit is Autodesk's premier building information modeling (BIM) software. Using Revit, every element of a building's construction is modeled as a 3D component. Revit's lights, materials, and views can all be incorporated into a 3ds Max scene.

Master It What is one method of bringing the components of a Revit file into 3ds Max?

A. Use the File Link Manager to link the Revit file to the 3ds Max scene.

B. Save the Revit file in Revit 2009 or earlier, and then use the File Link Manager to link the Revit file to the 3ds Max scene.

C. Save the Revit file in Revit 2009 or earlier, and then click the Application menu and choose References ➤ Import to import the Revit file to the 3ds Max scene.

D. Export the Revit file as an FBX file, and then use the File Link Manager to link the exported Revit file to the 3ds Max scene.

E. Use the Layer Manager to define the Revit layers to import, and then drag the file from Windows Explorer to a 3ds Max viewport.

Solution The correct answer is D. You must use an existing FBX preset or create a new file linking preset that contains the file linking parameters that you want to retain. Here are the steps:

1. In Revit, choose File ➤ Export ➤ FBX and then click Save.

2. In 3ds Max, click the Application menu and select References ➤ File Link Manager.

3. On the Attach tab, click the File button, and then locate and select the FBX file to link.

4. Click the Presets tab.

5. Select the most appropriate Autodesk Revit FBX preset.

6. Click the Modify button.

7. Verify the desired parameters in the File Link Settings: FBX Files dialog box, and then click Save or Cancel, and verify the other FBX presets or copy an existing FBX Preset and modify it for your needs.

8. Click the Attach tab.

9. Expand the Preset drop-down list and select the most appropriate FBX preset.

10. Click Attach This File.

Chapter 6: Creating AEC Objects

Create a wall with a linked door or window Many walls in actual structures contain doors and windows, and the tools for creating them in your 3ds Max scenes can significantly reduce the amount of time required to complete a project.

Master It Draw a spline to represent the floor area of a rectangular room 20′ × 40′ in size. Create walls around the perimeter that are 15′ tall and do not encroach inside the perimeter line that you drew. Fill one of the tall walls with floor-to-ceiling fixed windows and place a door in the opposite wall.

Solution

1. Draw a spline using the Keyboard Entry method or the Rectangle primitive.

2. Choose Create ➢ Geometry ➢ AEC Extended ➢ Wall.

3. Set the Height parameter to 15′.

4. Set the Justification to Left.

5. Turn on the Vertex Snap option; then activate the 3D Snap toggle.

6. Select one vertex of the spline, and then select the next three vertices in counterclockwise order.

7. Click the initial vertex; then choose Yes in the Weld Point dialog box that appears. Right-click to terminate the command.

8. Activate the Edge/Segment snap option.

9. Choose Create ➢ Geometry ➢ Windows ➢ Fixed.

10. Click the top edge of the wall, and then set the width, depth, and height of the window. The depth is defined by the width thickness of the wall; the width and height can be arbitrary.

11. Set the Height parameter to 15′ and Width to 4′.

12. Use the Move transform type-ins to move the window to 0 (zero) in the Z-axis so that it sits on the floor.

13. Move the window until it is approximately 2′ from one corner of the room.

14. Hold the Shift key down and copy the window to the side where the majority of the wall remains. Use the Vertex Snap option and select vertices at the outside, lower corners as the initial and subsequent points for the move operation.

15. In the Clone Options dialog box, select the Instance clone type and set Number of Copies to 8; then click OK. A total of nine windows occupy one of the long walls.

16. Choose Create ➢ Geometry ➢ Doors ➢ Pivot.

17. Using the procedure from steps 10 through 13, create a pivot door that is 3′6″ wide and 7′6″ tall. Your scene should look similar to the following image.

Build a staircase Staircases can be complex assemblies that must meet a fixed set of parameters, including transitional height and stair count. 3ds Max comes with a library of parametric stairs that can meet most of your needs.

Master It Delete the stair that you made for the condo scenes in this chapter. Replace it with a spiral staircase that transitions from the lower floor to the mezzanine.

Using a procedure similar to the one described in the "Changing Elevations with Stairs" section, replace the straight staircase with a spiral staircase using Create ➢ Geometry ➢ Stairs ➢ Spiral Stair. Use the same count, riser height, and other parameters from the straight stair object. Your scene should look similar to the following image.

Create a railing Railings partition spaces and guide or restrict foot traffic through a facility or room. The Railing parametric object included in the 3ds Max toolset provides many parameters, such as ones for setting the number and style for the railings and posts.

Master It Select the railing on the mezzanine level of the condo scene in this chapter. Modify it so that the lower railing, which currently passes through the middle of the railing system, is moved to the bottom. Replace the pickets with solid fill.

Solution

1. Open the last condo scene that you worked on, or Condo AEC5.max from this book's web page.

2. Adjust the Perspective viewport so that you can see the railing.

3. Select the railing, and then click the Modify tab of the Command panel.

4. In the Lower Rail(s) section of the Railing rollout, click the Lower Rail Spacing button.

5. In the Lower Rail Spacing dialog box that appears, expand the drop-down list in the Parameters section and choose Space from End, Unbounded. The lower rail moves to the bottom of the railing system.

6. Close the Lower Rail Spacing dialog box.

7. Scroll down to the Fencing rollout.

8. Expand the Type rollout and choose Solid Fill. The posts and pickets are replaced with a solid panel.

Add parametric plants The AEC foliage objects included in 3ds Max can quickly populate a scene with any number of trees found in the library. Each tree can be unique or an instance of others.

Master It Replace the yucca tree in the condo scene with a small weeping willow from the plant library. Make sure it doesn't encroach into the nearby walls. Adjust the tree to your liking, and then copy it and the planter to two more locations. Change the Seed value to make the two new trees different from the original and from each other.

Solution

1. After the first tree is created and adjusted, use the Move transform with the Shift key held down to make the two clones. It's important to make the two clones as copies, rather than instances, so the change to the Seed value is not reflected in all of them.

2. Change the Seed value for each of the two clones.

3. Move and rotate the trees as required to maintain a gap between the walls and the foliage. When the trees are selected, your scene should look similar to the following image.

Chapter 7: Organizing and Editing Objects

Loft a shape Lofting is the practice of extruding a two-dimensional shape along the length of another two-dimensional shape. There are few restrictions on the shape component of the loft object, but the path component must consist of a single spline.

Master It Use the Loft tool to create a table leg that is 32″ tall. The table leg is to start as a 1″-diameter circle and end as a square that is 1½″ on a side.

Solution

1. In the Perspective viewport, draw a circle with a Radius value of 0.5″.

2. Draw a rectangle and set the Length and Width values to 1.5″.

3. Click the Line tool and expand the Keyboard Entry rollout.

4. Click the Add Point button.

5. Enter **32″** in the Z field, and then click Add Point again.

6. With the line still selected, choose Create ➢ Geometry ➢ Compound Objects ➢ Loft.

7. Click Get Shape, and then pick the circle in the viewport. The circle is lofted along the line.

8. Expand the Path Parameters rollout.

9. Make sure the Percentage radio button is selected, and then enter **100** in the Path field.

10. Click the Get Shape button again, and then select the rectangle. The circle transitions to the square.

Organize objects with layers By assigning the objects in your scenes to layers, you can define which layers are hidden, frozen, rendered, and subject to a radiosity calculation. New objects are always created in the current layer using the current layer's color.

Master It Make three instance clones of the table leg from the previous Master It exercise. Also make two teapot primitives and a 32″-long, 32″-wide, and 2″-tall box. Place the two-dimensional shapes in one layer and hide the layer. Place the legs in one layer, the square in one layer, and the two teapots in one layer. Assign each layer a unique name and layer color.

Solution

1. Select the table leg and click the Move tool in the Main Toolbar.

2. Hold the Shift key down, and then drag the X or Y transform handle.

3. In the Clone Options dialog box, choose the Instance options, set the number of copies to 3, and then click OK.

4. Choose Create ➢ Geometry ➢ Standard Primitives ➢ Teapot, and then create two teapots in the Perspective viewport.

5. Choose Create ➢ Geometry ➢ Standard Primitives ➢ Box, and then drag a box out in the Perspective viewport.

6. Without deselecting the box, in the Parameters rollout enter **32** in the Length and Width fields and **2** in the Height field.

7. Click the Layer Manager button in the Main Toolbar.

8. Select the two 2D shapes and the line; then, in the Layer dialog box, click the Create New Layer (Containing Selected Objects) button.

9. Click the New Layer Name input box in the Layer dialog box and enter a descriptive name.

10. Repeat steps 8 and 9 for the table legs, box, and teapots. If any colors in the Color column on the Layer dialog box are identical or similar, select the color swatch, and then pick a new color in the Layer Color dialog box.

11. Click the dash icon in the Hide column for the layer containing the 2D shapes. The shapes disappear in the viewport.

Deform an object with the Noise modifier Applying the Noise modifier to any object adds apparent randomness to the object's surfaces. This can often add a sense of realism to a scene by eliminating the perfect roundness and flatness of many objects created in 3ds Max.

Master It Select the potted tree in the last condo scene you saved, add the Noise modifier to it, and then adjust the Noise parameters so that the trunk of the tree is slightly more jagged than it currently is.

Solution

1. Select the Yucca object you renamed previously.

2. In the Modify tab, expand the Modifier List drop-down list and assign the Edit Mesh modifier.

3. Activate the Vertex sub-object mode and select the lower one-third of the tree.

4. In the Soft Selection rollout, check the Use Soft Selection option.

5. Increase the Falloff until the tree is affected just below where the fronds start.

6. Go back up to the Modifier List drop-down and add a Noise modifier to the stack.

7. Adjust the Strength setting in the X and Y values and then reduce the Scale setting until you get the results you desire.

Model with the Symmetry modifier In many cases, objects are symmetrical across one or more axes. Rather than attempting to model both sides of an object, you can model one side and then, using the Symmetry modifier, adjust the other side automatically to appear as its reciprocal.

> **Master It** Being able to quickly modify objects you have already built to create new objects is an important skill. Open the last condo scene in which you modified the pedestal. Create a clone of the first pedestal you built, modify one side of the pedestal, and then make the new pedestal model symmetrical.
>
> **Solution**
>
> 1. Open the last condo scene you were in when you were working on the pedestal loft object.
>
> 2. Click the Select and Move tool on the Main Toolbar and then select the pedestal loft object.
>
> 3. Hold down the Shift key and then click and drag a clone of the pedestal to the right. Set Clone Options to Copy and name the clone **NewPedestal**.
>
> 4. Add an Edit Mesh modifier to the NewPedestal object.
>
> 5. Select and expand the Edit Mesh modifier from the stack.
>
> 6. Activate the Vertex sub-object mode.
>
> 7. Select the front view.
>
> 8. Select some vertices along the right side of the pedestal and move them in the positive X direction.
>
> 9. Deselect the points you selected and moved.
>
> 10. Close the Edit Mesh modifier.
>
> 11. Add a Symmetry modifier to the top of the stack.
>
> 12. Select the Flip option in the Parameters rollout. Your new pedestal should be symmetrical now.

Extrude with the Sweep modifier Similar to the Loft compound object, the Sweep modifier extrudes one 2D object along the length of another. While the Loft tool is more powerful, with more controls and features, the Sweep modifier is faster, can be applied to multiple objects, and comes with a library of 2D shapes.

> **Master It** The goal of this exercise is to make a round bumper to fit around the box that you made in the previous exercise. The large, flat surfaces of the box should transition seamlessly into the bumper. Use the Sweep modifier to extrude a half-round shape that fits precisely around the box.
>
> **Solution**
>
> 1. Continuing from the second "Master It" exercise, create a 32″ × 32″ rectangle in the Top viewport.
>
> 2. In the Modify tab, expand the Modifier List drop-down list and assign the Sweep modifier to the rectangle.

3. In the Section Type rollout, select the Half Round shape from the Built-In Section drop-down list.

4. In the Parameters rollout, set the Radius value to 1″.

5. In the Sweep Parameters rollout, set the angle to -90, and then set the Pivot Alignment area by clicking the button in the middle of the left column.

Align objects Visualization specialists frequently must move one object so that it sits directly on, or butts precisely against, another object with no gaps or overlaps. The Align tool is often the best choice when you need to align the minimum or maximum axis values of different objects.

Master It Continuing from the previous exercise, you need to align the table legs with the box so that the top of each leg is aligned to the bottom of the table and two of the rectangular edges at the top of each leg are aligned with the outside edges of the box. Move the teapots so they lie within the perimeter of the box, and then align the bottom of the teapots with the top of the box. Align the bumper so that it is centered around the box.

Solution

1. If necessary, click the Maximize Viewport Toggle to display four viewports and switch the Top viewport to Wireframe mode.

2. In the Perspective viewport, select a table leg, click the Align tool in the Main Toolbar, and then pick the box to which you will align the table leg.

3. In the Align Selection dialog box, select the X Position and Y Position options, and then select the Maximum options in both the Current and Target Object columns. The top-right corner of the leg, as shown in the Top viewport, is aligned to the top-right corner of the box.

4. Click OK.

5. Select another table leg, click the Align tool in the Main Toolbar, and then pick the box to which you will align the table leg.

6. In the Align Selection dialog box, select the X Position and Y Position options, and then select the Minimum options in both the Current and Target Object columns. The bottom-left corner of the leg, as shown in the Top viewport, is aligned to the bottom-left corner of the box.

7. Click OK.

8. Select another table leg, click the Align tool in the Main Toolbar, and then pick the box to which you will align the table leg.

9. In the Align Selection dialog box, select only the X Position option and then select the Minimum options in both the Current and Target Object columns. The left edge of the leg is aligned with the left edge of the box.

10. Click Apply. Select only the Y Position option, and then select the Maximum options in both the Current and Target Object columns. The top-left corner of the leg, as shown in the Top viewport, is aligned to the top-left corner of the box.

11. Click OK.

12. Select the last table leg, click the Align tool in the Main Toolbar, and then pick the box to which you will align the table leg.

13. In the Align Selection dialog box, select only the X Position option, and then select the Maximum options in both the Current and Target Object columns. The right edge of the leg is aligned with the right edge of the box.

14. Click Apply. Select only the Y Position option, and then select the Minimum options in both the Current and Target Object columns. The bottom-right corner of the leg, as shown in the Top viewport, is aligned to the bottom-right corner of the box.

15. Click OK.

16. To align the bottom of the box to the top of the legs, select the box, click the Align tool, and then pick one of the legs. Select the Z Position option only. Select Minimum for the current object and Maximum for the target object. The box moves to the top of the legs.

17. Click OK.

18. In the Top viewport, move the teapots so they are within the perimeter of the box.

19. In the Perspective viewport, select both teapots, click the Align button, and then pick the table. The settings from the previous alignment option (Z Position, Current Object: Minimum, Target Object: Maximum) are retained and appropriate for this operation. Click OK.

20. Select the bumper object, click the Align tool, and then pick the table. To align the bumper to the box, select the X, Y, and Z position options and then select Center for both the current and target objects. The bumper is centered on the box.

Rename objects A good naming convention is invaluable when a scene becomes complicated, with many objects to control and select. The Rename Objects tool is invaluable for quickly renaming several objects to a standard naming convention.

Master It Again continuing from the previous exercise, use the Rename Objects tool to rename the four table leg clones to objects named Table_Leg_01, Table_Leg_02, Table_Leg_03, and Table_Leg_04.

Solution

1. Click the Manage Layers icon in the Main Toolbar to open the Layer dialog box.

2. In the Layer dialog box, highlight the TableLegs layer and click the Select Highlighted Objects and Layers button. The four table legs should highlight. If the Table Bumper highlights, deselect everything. Select the Table Bumper and then highlight the TableTop layer and click Add Selected Objects to Highlighted Layer. Reselect the objects on the TableLegs layer if necessary.

3. Choose Tool ➢ Rename Objects to start the Rename Objects tool.

4. In the Rename Objects dialog box, make sure the radio button next to Selected is selected.

5. Select the box in front of the Base Name field.

6. Select the box in front of the Numbered field and set Base Number to 1.

7. In the Base Name field, enter **Table_Leg**.

8. Click the Rename button.

9. Click the Select by Name button from the Main Toolbar. You should see your properly named table legs highlighted in the Select from Scene dialog box.

Chapter 8: Light and Shadow

Create and adjust the different light types Lighting is an important component of any 3ds Max scene, and proper lighting schemes add to its quality. The various types project light into the scene in different ways.

Master It What is the difference between a spotlight's falloff and its far attenuation?

Solution *Falloff* is the angular limit within which a spotlight will cast illumination. The amount of illumination falls off from 100 percent at the limits of the hotspot to 0 percent at the perimeter of the falloff.

Attenuation defines the distance the light travels from its point of origin. Attenuation is defined by a Start distance and an End distance. The light has full intensity from its point of origin to the Start distance, declining intensity from the Start distance to the End distance, and 0 illumination is projected beyond the End distance.

Render a scene 3ds Max scenes are generally output to image files or animated files for viewing. Choosing the proper output file type is important to manage the file size and quality.

Master It Render a camera view, and save the file as a JPEG file with a Quality value of 100. Render it three more times with Quality values of 90, 50, and 30. Compare the four files for both quality and file size.

Solution

1. Open a 3ds Max scene.

2. Open the Render Scene dialog box.

3. Click Files in the Render Output section.

4. In the Render Output File dialog box, specify the file location and name, and then click the Setup button.

5. In the JPEG Image Control dialog box, set the Quality to 100 and then click OK.

6. Click Save, and then click Render in the Render Scene dialog box.

7. Repeat steps 3–6 three times, changing the Quality value and filename each time.

8. Open the files in your favorite image editor or viewer, as well as Windows Explorer. You'll see image quality degrading as the Quality value lowers, while the file size reduction is even more severe.

Define shadow effects Shadows are an important feature of any 3ds Max scene. They convey information regarding the intensity and type of illumination. Shadows also define where in the scene an object resides by tying it to the surrounding objects.

Master It What is the procedure for causing an object to not cast shadows from a specific light?

Solution

1. Select the light.

2. In the General Parameters rollout, click Exclude.

3. In the Exclude/Include dialog box that appears, select the object in the left window.

4. Click the right-facing double arrow button to move the object to the right window.

5. Make sure both the Exclude and Shadow Casting radio buttons are selected.

6. Click OK.

Save and restore scene states Scene states let you save and restore the parameters of the lights in a scene. They can save a great amount of time by eliminating the need to note each light's parameters and on/off status, and other parameters, to accommodate different lighting conditions.

Master It Open the file you saved in the "Using Scene States" section in this chapter. Save the light parameters as a lighting scheme, change the parameters, and then restore the new scheme.

Solution

1. Open the file.

2. Choose Tools ➤ Manage Scene States.

3. In the Manage Scene States dialog box, click Save.

4. In the Save Scene State dialog box, enter a name for the scene state.

5. Select the Light options in the window, and then click Save.

6. Modify the parameters of the lights in the scene.

7. In the Manage Scene States dialog box, select the scene state that you just created.

8. Click Restore.

Chapter 9: Enhancing Models with Materials

Create and edit materials Quality materials can add significantly to the quality of a scene. Materials are constructed by choosing a shader, setting its parameters, and then adding and adjusting maps.

Master It Using the CEDFENCE.JPG file in the /maps/wood folder installed with 3ds Max as the diffuse color map, create a Standard material and assign it to an object.

Solution

1. Open the Material Editor.

2. Click an unused material; then click the Arch & Design button and select the Standard material from the Material/Map Browser.

3. Expand the Maps rollout and click the None button next to the Diffuse Color option.

4. Double-click the Bitmap map item in the Material/Map Browser.

5. In the Select Bitmap Image File dialog box, navigate to the /maps/wood folder from the 3ds Max install, select CEDEFENCE.JPG, and then click Open.

6. Create an object in the scene and select it.

7. In the Material Editor, click the Assign Material to Selection button.

8. Click the Render Production button in the Main Toolbar to review the material on the object.

Select shaders The shader that you select determines how a material appears when a scene is rendered. The most obvious difference between the different shaders is the appearance of the specular highlight.

Master It Using the material from the previous Master It exercise, examine the result of assigning the different shaders to the material. Which shader results in a stretched-out specular highlight? Which shader has the most diffused highlight?

Solution

1. Create a sphere in the scene and apply the wood material to it.

2. In the Material Editor, increase the Specular Level and Glossiness values to better define the specular highlight.

3. Render the scene and observe the result of the parameter changes on the object.

4. In the Shader Basic Parameters rollout, expand the drop-down list and choose a different shader.

5. Click Quick Render to see the result of changing the shader.

6. Repeat steps 4 and 5 for the remaining shaders.

7. The shader that stretches out the specular highlight is the Anisotropic shader. The shader that diffuses the specular highlight the most is the Oren-Nayar-Blinn shader.

Use bump maps Image maps assigned to the Diffuse color channel of a material tend to look flat like decals or wallpaper. Adding a bump map can add apparent detail without increasing the complexity of the models.

Master It Continuing from the previous Master It exercise, add a noise map to the material's Bump channel to roughen the surface. Copy and rename the material in the Material Editor and then replace the Noise bump map with the same map used as the diffuse color map. Compare the differences in the viewport.

Solution

1. Expand the Maps rollout in the Material Editor.

2. Click the None button next to the Bump label.

3. In the Material/Map Browser, select Noise and then click OK.

4. Adjust the values in the Noise Parameters rollout to your liking. Then click Go to Parent.

5. Render the scene.

6. Copy the sphere in the scene, making sure not to create an instance.

7. Copy the material in the Material Editor by dragging it to another unused slot.

8. Rename the new material.

9. In the new material, drag any of the None buttons in the Maps rollout over the Bump Map button to clear it.

10. Drag the Diffuse Color Map button and drop it over the Bump Map button.

11. Choose Instance in the Copy (Instance) Map dialog box.

12. Assign the new material to the new sphere.

13. Render the scene and compare the two materials.

Create a material with sub-materials Often, a model that is constructed as a single object may represent a structure composed of several objects, each with its own material. The multi/sub-object material is used to assign several distinct materials to a single object.

Master It What is one procedure for creating a multi/sub-object material?

Solution

1. Select a material slot.

2. Click the Material button and choose Multi/Sub-Object from the Material/Map Browser.

3. Choose whether to discard or keep the existing material.

4. Set the number of sub-materials.

5. Click a sub-material button, and then set that sub-material's parameters.

6. Click the Go to Sibling button, and then adjust the parameters of the next sub-material.

7. Repeat step 6 for the remaining sub-materials.

Add entourage Adding entourage to your scenes can make them feel like they are inhabited, and help create a sense of scale, which viewers can relate to.

Master It Using the Tree01AM.tif and Tree01op.tif files you downloaded with this chapter's materials, create an entourage material with the Compact Material Editor and apply it to a plane so you can render it.

Solution

1. Reset 3ds Max Design.

2. Open the Compact Material Editor.

3. Click the Material Type button and select Standard from the Material/Map Browser.

4. Rename the Material to **TreeEntourage**.

5. Expand the Maps rollout and click the None button next to the Diffuse Color option.

6. Double-click the Bitmap map type in the Material/Map Browser and navigate to the folder where you downloaded the Chapter 9 files and select Tree01AM.tif, and then click Open.

7. Uncheck the Use Real-World Scale option, set the Tiling values to 1, and deselect the Tile options for both U and V mapping directions.

8. Click the Go to Parent button.

9. Scroll down in the Maps rollout and select the None button in the Opacity slot of the material.

10. Double-click the Bitmap map type in the Material/Map Browser and navigate to the folder where you downloaded the Chapter 9 files and select Tree01OP.tif, and then click Open.

11. Uncheck the Use Real-World Scale option, set the Tiling values to 1, and deselect the Tile options for both U and V mapping directions.

12. Click the Go to Parent button.

13. In the Front viewport, create a plane object, deselect the Real-World Mapping Size option, and keep the plane selected.

14. In the Material Editor, select Assign Material to Selection.

15. Click the Render Production button in the Main Toolbar to review the entourage tree material.

Use the Autodesk Common Materials The Autodesk Materials provide high-quality materials that can help you better simulate real-world materials to enhance the accuracy and realism of your renderings.

Master It Using the My_Ch09d.max file you worked on in this chapter, change the Standard Metal_Chrome_Han material into the Chrome – Polished Brushed Autodesk Material and render the scene.

Solution

1. Open your My_Ch09d.max file.

2. Select one of the Cab Handle objects in the background of the perspective view.

3. Click the Material Editor button on the Main Toolbar.

4. Select one of the unused material sample slots and then click the Get Material button.

5. In the Material/Map Browser, scroll down to the Scene Materials group and expand it.

6. Right-click the Scene Materials group and select Filter Selected Objects to only see the material(s) applied to the currently selected object.

7. Double-click the Metal_Chrome_Han material to select it, and then right click the Scene Materials Group and unselect Filter Selected Objects, then close the Material/Map Browser.

8. In the Material Editor, select the next unused Material Sample Slot.

9. Click the Get Material button to open the Material/Map Browser and go to the Autodesk Material Library group then expand the Metal group; Scroll down and double-click Chrome – Polished Brushed to place it in the selected Compact Material Editor sample slot.

10. Select the Metal_Chrome_Han material sample and click the Select by Material button.

11. The Select Objects dialog box opens, showing the DoorHandlex objects selected; click Select.

12. Select the Metal Chrome – Polished Brushed material sample and click the Assign Material to Selection button.

13. Deselect all objects.

14. Render the scene.

Use the Displacement modifier Applying the displacement modifier or applying materials using Displacement Maps to simple objects can be a powerful way to create highly detailed or irregular forms without taking the time to build the complex geometry.

Master It Create a 50′ × 50′ plane, with 100 Length and Width segments. Apply a Displace modifier that uses the `displace_sample.jpg` image, which tiles six times across the surface.

Solution

1. Reset 3ds Max Design 2011.

2. Create a 50′ × 50′ plane.

3. Set the Length and Width Segments to 100.

4. Apply a Displace modifier to the plane.

5. In the Image group, select the None button in the Bitmap area and browse to the `displace_sample.jpg` image.

6. Set U Tile to 2.0.

7. Set V Tile to 3.0.

8. Adjust Displacement Strength to 6″.

9. Render the scene.

Chapter 10: Using the 3ds Max Camera

Understand the 3ds Max camera The virtual cameras in 3ds Max follow the analogy of real-world SLR cameras. You can set the focal length, set the field of view, and adjust several other parameters. Targeted cameras are oriented by moving a target object, and free cameras are oriented using the Rotate transform.

Master It Create a new camera that focuses on the lower-level main entranceway, flanked by the tall, thin windows. Switch between a target and a free camera to familiarize yourself with manipulating each type.

Solution

1. Open the file.

2. In the Top viewport, zoom into the main entrance, leaving room to place the camera.

3. Choose Create ➢ Cameras in the Command panel, and then click Target.

4. Click to place the camera outside of the building, and then drag and release near the entrance to place the target.

5. Move the camera up so that it does not rest on the ground plane.

6. Change the camera and target locations to adjust the orientation of the camera.

7. Click the Modify tab.

8. In the Parameters rollout, expand the Type drop-down list and choose Free Camera. The target disappears.

9. Change the orientation of the camera using the Rotate transform.

Set up an interior view Interior cameras are more difficult than exterior cameras to properly place. The scene must be framed properly while maintaining an acceptable field of view and working within the space limitations frequently found indoors.

Master It Make two clones of the camera that focuses on the outside of the entranceway. Move the new cameras and, if necessary, the targets inside the structure. Manipulate each camera so that each displays one side of the entranceway. Show as much of the windows as possible without excessive distortion.

Solution

1. In the Top viewport, select the camera that focuses on the outside of the entranceway as well as its target.

2. Click the Select and Move tool in the Main Toolbar.

3. Hold down the Shift key and move the camera and target so that the camera is inside and to the left side of the entranceway.

4. Choose Copy in the Clone Options dialog box.

5. Right-click the label for the current camera viewport, and choose Views and then the name of the new camera.

6. In the Top and Right viewports, move the camera and target to frame the scene properly—focusing on the right side on the entranceway's interior. You can also adjust the camera's properties as required.

7. Repeat steps 1 through 6, cloning the last camera made, to create the camera that focuses on the left side of the entranceway's interior.

Create an environment Most image formats can be used as the background for a rendered scene. Once an image map is selected, it can be positioned and manipulated through the parameters found in the Material Editor.

Master It Select another sky image map and replace the map used in this chapter. Choose another map provided with 3ds Max Design 2011 or create your own with a digital camera. Use the controls located in the Output rollout to change a darkened sky to a brighter one, or vice versa.

Solution

1. Open the file.

2. Open the Material Editor.

3. Select the sample slot containing the Skydome material.

4. Expand the Maps rollout.

5. Click the Diffuse Color Map button containing the `CLOUD2.jpg` map.

6. In the Bitmap Parameters rollout, click the Bitmap button.

7. In the Select Image File dialog box, navigate to and select a different sky image. The images can be found in the `3ds Max Design 2011/maps/Skies` folder. You must have installed the omitted maps from the Autodesk website, as covered in Chapter 9, "Enhancing Models with Materials," to have these files.

8. Expand the Output rollout.

9. Make any adjustments that you prefer.

10. Render the scene to display the changes.

Render elements for compositing 3D still images and animations must often go through a postproduction compositing process to achieve a higher level of quality or realism. Using the Render Elements feature, you can automatically create many of the required element types at the same time the images are being rendered. Advanced image-processing software, such as Autodesk Combustion, can manipulate and composite the different images and create the final output.

Master It Open the most recent Savoye scene and create two more render elements: one for the shadows and one for the reflections.

Solution

1. Open the file.

2. Open the Render Scene dialog box.

3. Click the Render Elements tab.

4. In the Render Elements rollout, click the Add button.

5. In the Render Elements dialog box, click the Shadow and Reflection options, and then click OK.

6. In the Render Scene dialog box, click Render. Three Rendered Frame Windows open, with two of them appearing blank.

7. In each of the blank Rendered Frame Windows, click the Display Alpha Channel button in the toolbar. You'll see the areas in shadow or the faces that reflect the environment in white while the other areas remain in black.

Use the Camera Match utility When a building's model must be incorporated into a background image, you must match the 3ds Max virtual camera to the camera that took the background picture. This is accomplished by placing CamPoint helper objects in the scene and using the Camera Match utility.

Master It What is the difference between adding a CamPoint helper in the scene and assigning the position of a CamPoint helper in the scene?

A. Nothing. The terms are interchangeable.

B. *Adding* the CamPoint helper consists of locating the object accurately in the scene, while *assigning the position* of the CamPoint helper refers to selecting its proper location relative to the background image.

C. *Assigning the position* of the CamPoint helper consists of locating the object accurately in the scene, while *adding* the CamPoint helper refers to selecting its proper location relative to the background image.

D. None of the above.

Solution The correct answer is B.

Chapter 11: Organizing Objects and Scene Management

Use external references Using XRefs can increase productivity by breaking a project into smaller parts that individual artists can work on and allowing you to disassociate parts of the project as system performance decreases.

Master It Extract the trees in the `mysavoye.max` or `mysavoye10.max` file as a new 3ds Max file. Change the number and arrangement of the trees in this new scene, save the configuration, and then swap this for the currently XRef'd trees.

Solution

1. Open either of the specified files.

2. Delete everything in the scene except the trees. You can do this quickly by selecting all the objects with names that begin with "Foliage" in the Select Objects dialog box and then clicking the Invert button.

3. Open the XRef Scenes dialog box.

4. Select the XRef, and then click Remove.

5. Close the XRef Scenes dialog box.

6. Rearrange, copy, or modify the trees.

7. Choose File ➢ Save As and save the file under a new name.

8. Open the same file that you opened in step 1.

9. Select and delete the trees.

10. Choose File ➢ XRef Scene.

11. Click the Add button, navigate to the new tree file, and then click Open. The trees, in their new configuration, surround the building.

12. Save the file.

Use the Rendered Frame Window options Using the Rendered Frame Window, you can save, print, and compare the result of your 3ds Max renderings.

Master It Render the MyCamera01 viewport in the `mysavoye.max` file. Make changes to the lighting, render the viewport again, and then compare the two renderings using the RFW.

Solution

1. Open the `mysavoye.max` file and right-click in the MyCamera01 viewport.

2. Choose Rendering ➢ Render, or click the Render Scene button, to open the Render Scene dialog box.

3. Make sure Single is selected in the Time Output section.

4. Click the Render button. The render is displayed in the RFW.

5. In the RFW toolbar, click Clone Rendered Frame Window. A copy of the RFW opens.

6. Make changes to the lighting by selecting the lights and changing their parameters, or make the changes in the Light Lister.

7. Render the viewport again. The RFW is overwritten with the new rendering, but the clone remains. Compare the two renderings.

Use the Asset Browser With the Asset Browser, you can insert one 3ds Max scene into another using the dialog box to see the names of and thumbnails for the assets in any folder locally, on a network, or on the Internet.

Master It Create several 3ds Max scenes consisting of a single, unique tree each. Use the Asset Browser to bring one or more of each tree into the savoye.max scene.

Solution

1. Open the tree file that you created in the first Master It section of this chapter.

2. Delete all but one tree, and then save this tree as a new file.

3. Change the parameters of the tree, and then save it as another new file.

4. Repeat step 3 several times until you have a significant library of unique but similar trees.

5. Open the file that you saved in step 12 of the first Master It exercise.

6. Remove the external reference containing the tree file.

7. Choose Utilities ➢ Asset Browser in the Command panel.

8. Navigate to the folder containing your new trees.

9. Drag each of the new trees into the scene.

Create a panorama By creating a panorama, anybody can view the rendered result of a 3ds Max scene through the free Apple QuickTime viewer. Users can zoom and pan within the viewer to view the scene from different orientations from the original camera's location.

Master It Open the Condo AEC5.max file from Chapter 6, "Creating AEC Objects." Add a free camera centered in the main room, 6′0″ above the floor, and create a panorama and export it to a QuickTime VR file.

Solution

1. Open the Condo AEC5.max file.

2. Choose Create ➢ Cameras ➢ Free, and then place a free camera in the Front viewport.

3. Adjust the camera's location so that it is centered in the room and 6′0″ above the main floor.

4. Choose Utilities ➢ More ➢ Panorama Exporter.

5. In the Panorama Exporter rollout, click the Render button.

6. In the Render Setup dialog box, set the Output Size to a value large enough to show detail in the panorama.

7. Click the Render button.

8. In the Panorama Exporter Viewer dialog box, choose File ➤ Export ➤ Export QuickTime VR.

9. In the QuickTime VR Output File dialog box, assign the file a name and destination; then click the Save button.

Publish a scene to the DWF format DWF files are gaining popularity as a means to distribute interactive access to 3ds Max scene files.

Master It Open the Condo AEC5.max file from Chapter 6. Export the condo scene as a DWF file. Open the resulting DWF in Autodesk Design Review and, using the ribbon, add a Cross Section XY Slice plane to cut away a wall and see into the condo from top to bottom.

Solution

1. Open the Condo AEC6.max file.

2. Choose File ➤ Publish to DWF, give the file a name, and then click Save.

3. Accept the default options in the DWF Publish Options dialog box. Click OK.

4. Open the DWF file in the Autodesk Design Review.

5. In the Autodesk Design Review Ribbon, expand the Tools tab, and then choose the Section XY tool.

6. Drag or rotate the Cross Section tripod until one of the exterior walls is removed.

Chapter 12: Understanding Animation

Create a quick-study animation Viewing an animation, rather than individual still images, can give you a greater sense of the size, scope, and proportion of a design project. Initial, quick-study animations usually consist of short animations with changes made to the camera's location and orientation.

Master It Create a camera at the mezzanine level of any of the condo scenes from Chapter 6, "Creating AEC Objects," oriented toward the tall windows. Animate the camera moving to the lower level and changing orientation to look into the kitchen.

Solution

1. Open any of the condo scene files from Chapter 6. (These files are available on the website as well; see www.sybex.com/go/mastering3dsmaxdesign2011.)

2. In the Top viewport, place a target camera in the mezzanine and the target near the windows. The cameras, as a category, have been hidden and this will expose cameras that already exist in the scene.

3. Change the Perspective viewport to view the scene through the new camera.

4. In the Front or Left viewport, adjust the height of the camera to match a person's eye level at the mezzanine for the camera, and the lower level for the target.

5. Move the Time slider to frame 100, and then click the Auto Key button.

6. Change the locations of the camera and target so that the camera is at eye level of the lower level, near the windows, and the target is in the kitchen.

7. Turn off the Auto Key button, and then play the animation.

8. If necessary, place the Time slider at frame 100, turn on Auto Key mode, and make any adjustments to the camera and target locations.

9. Save your file.

Change the number of frames in an animation The 101 frames provided in the default 3ds Max scene are rarely adequate to display any significant amount of animation. It's an easy process to increase or reduce the number of frames in a scene, and this is a task that you will do often.

Master It Continuing with the previous exercise, increase the number of frames to 300. Adjust the keyframes so the animation occurs over all 300 frames.

Solution There are two ways to complete this task: increase the number of frames and move the keys, or scale the animation and keys at the same time. To adjust the scene using the first method, follow these steps:

1. Click the Time Configuration button in the time controls area.

2. In the Animation section of the Animation Controls dialog box that opens, set the Frame count to 300, and then click OK.

3. Select both the camera and target.

4. In the track bar at the bottom of the 3ds Max window, select the keys at frame 100 and drag them to frame 299. Watch the status bar for visual feedback as you move the keys. This method should be used when the animation of only certain objects should be altered.

5. Play the animation.

To scale the animation and keys at one time, follow these steps:

1. Click the Time Configuration button in the time controls area.

2. In the Animation section of the Animation Controls dialog box that opens, click the Re-scale Time button.

3. In the Re-scale Time dialog box, set the Length value to 299, and then click OK. Use this method when the animation of all objects in the scene must conform to the new animation length.

4. Play the animation.

5. Save your file.

Add and edit keyframes Keyframes determine the point in time and value of nearly any parameter change in 3ds Max. Adding and editing them properly is an essential task when finalizing your animation.

Master It Continuing from the previous exercise, add two keys to the camera's animation, one that raises its position before descending to the lower level and one that adjusts its rotation so that it looks at the kitchen earlier. The camera should ease into and out of its peak height.

Solution

1. Continuing from the previous exercise, drag the Time slider to approximately frame 70.

2. Click the Auto Key button, and then raise the height of the camera above its initial height.

3. Right-click the new key at frame 70 on the track bar, and then choose Camera01: Z Position from the context menu that appears.

4. In the Camera01: Z Position dialog box, click the In tangent button and choose the Slow tangent option. Choose the Slow tangent for the Out option as well.

5. Move the Time slider to approximately frame 200.

6. The animated camera is a target type, so its orientation is determined by the location of its target object. Select the camera's target and raise it in the Z-axis until the kitchen starts to come into the view.

7. Turn off Auto Key mode and play the animation. The camera raises, easing into and out of the peak position, and lowers to its final position, showing the kitchen earlier than in the previous exercise.

Preview the animation Animations can take a significant amount of time to render, and unless you have a render farm setup, you may lose the ability to continue working on a scene while it renders. Creating preview animations can quickly identify animated conflicts prior to your spending the time creating a final animation.

Master It Create a preview animation, at a resolution of 640 × 480, showing the modified camera path from the path from the previous exercise. Display the frame numbers in the images and save the animation as an AVI file using the Microsoft Video 1 codec.

Solution

1. Right-click in the Camera01 viewport.

2. Choose Animation ➢ Make Preview from the Menu Bar.

3. In the Make Preview dialog box, check the Frame Numbers option in the Display in Preview section.

4. In the Image Size section, increase the Percent of Output value to 100.

5. In the Output section, choose AVI, and then click the Choose Codec button.

6. In the Video Compression dialog that appears, select Microsoft Video 1 as the compressor, and then click OK.

7. In the Make Preview dialog box, make sure that Active Time Segment is selected in the Preview Range section.

8. Click the Create button. 3ds Max creates the preview animation.

9. Click Animation ➤ View Preview to examine the preview animation that you made.

10. Save your file.

Control lights over time Clarifying the results of the lighting in a scene is often identified as a priority early in the project cycle. Not only is a satisfactory lighting scheme required, but animated variations, such as the onset of dusk, may also need to be viewed and observed.

Master It Add a quick lighting scheme to the condo scene. Animate the lights, holding their intensity for 100 frames and then reducing the intensity to zero while turning the lights slightly red.

Solution

1. Place four or more instance clones of an Omni light near the ceiling.

2. Create four Omni lights below the floor. The second set of lights should be instanced to each other, but not to the lights near the ceiling.

3. The lights below the floor should be weak and not cast shadows. Their purpose is to illuminate the horizontal faces below the ceiling lights, which would appear dark with only the upper lights in the scene.

4. Adjust the upper lights so they don't wash out the scene, but don't spend too much time adjusting them (that isn't the focus of this exercise).

5. Move the Time slider to frame 99, turn on Auto Key mode, and then select one of the upper lights.

6. Change the light's Multiplier value, and then reset it to its original value. This doesn't result in an animated change in the value, but it does place a key for the multiplier at frame 99 and cause the value to hold steady for the first 100 frames.

7. Click the color swatch in the Intensity/Color/Attenuation rollout, note the Hue value in the Color Selector dialog box, change the Hue value, and then click Close. Reopen the Color Selector dialog box, and then change the value back. Similar to the previous step, this sets a key that will hold the color value steady for the first 100 frames.

8. Repeat steps 6 and 7 for one of the instances of the lights below the floor.

9. Move the Time slider to frame 299, and then open the Light Lister.

10. Change the Multiplier for both of the lights listed to 0 (zero).

11. Select each of the color swatches in the Light Lister and drag the Hue slider to the left, into the red range.

12. Close any open dialog boxes, turn off Auto Key mode, and then render the animation as a preview. The lights hold their values for the first 100 frames and then slowly turn off and turn slightly red.

Chapter 13: Creating Animations

Render an animation Animations can often give viewers a sense of size and composition unachievable using still images. Being able to produce a quality animation can mean the difference between a project being accepted or rejected.

Master It Place a new camera above and to the left of the building entrance. Render a 10-second animation of the camera descending and approaching the building.

Solution

1. Open one of the Villa Savoye scenes from this chapter.

2. Right-click in the Top viewport and zoom out so that you can see the front of the building and a good amount of area outside the building.

3. Choose Create ➢ Cameras ➢ Target.

4. Click in the lower-left corner of the Top viewport to place the camera, and then drag toward the building and release to place the target.

5. In the Left viewport, move the camera up until it is above the building.

6. Right-click the viewport label for an existing Camera viewport and switch that viewport to the view from the new camera.

7. Move the Time slider to frame 300.

8. Click the Auto Key button.

9. Move the camera toward the building and lower. Move the target to achieve the final animation view that you prefer.

10. Turn off Auto Key mode.

11. Click the Render Scene button in the Main Toolbar.

12. In the Common tab of the Render Scene dialog box, click the Range radio button and set the Range values to 0 and 300, respectively.

13. In the Render Output section, click the Files button.

14. Enter a filename and type, and then click Save and Render to close the two open dialog boxes. Additionally, you may need to address the parameters available in a settings dialog box.

15. The animation renders to the specified file.

Output a still image Still images have the benefit of allowing the viewer to spend time examining a particular viewpoint and a specific time. The images are generally produced at a much higher resolution than animations to create a better-quality printed image.

Master It Use the Print Size Assistant and the Render Setup dialog box to render four images from the camera created in the previous Master It exercise. The images are to be 300 dpi on an 8½″ × 11″ paper with a ¼″ unprintable border around the perimeter. Repeat the process creating 150-dpi images on 30″ × 42″ paper with no unprintable area.

Solution

1. Make sure the Camera viewport is active.

2. Choose Rendering ➤ Print Size Assistant.

3. In the Print Size Wizard, make sure Custom is selected at the top of the Paper Size section, and then click the Inches option in the Choose Unit section.

4. Enter **10.5** for the Paper Width, **8** for the Paper Height, and **300** for the dpi.

5. In the Rendering section, make sure the Save File option is checked, and then click the Files button.

6. Enter a filename and file type in the dialog box that opens, and then click Save.

7. Your Print Size Wizard should look similar to the following screen shot. Click the Render Setup button in the Rendering section.

8. In the Time Output section of the Common Parameters rollout, choose the Frames option, and then enter four frame numbers to render, each delineated with a comma.

9. Click the Render button at the bottom of the Render Setup dialog box.

10. The four selected frames are rendered to 10.5″ × 8″ images at 300 dpi.

11. Repeat steps 2 through 9 using **42** for Paper Width, **30** for Paper Height, and **150** for the dpi in step 4.

12. The selected frames are rendered to a 40″ × 32″ image at 150 dpi.

Render a shadow study Shadow studies can help determine the need for additional, or reduced, foliage and the effects of artwork or open ceiling designs on light patterns. Producing a shadow is often a requirement when projects involve free-standing structures.

 Master It Using the Shadowstudy.max file, change the location of the building to Cleveland, Ohio, and create images at 30-minute intervals from 6 a.m. to 9 p.m.

Solution

1. Open the Shadowstudy.max file.

2. Use the Select Objects dialog box to select the [Daylight01] group, and then click the Motion tab in the Command panel.

3. In the Location section of the Control Parameters rollout, click the Get Location button.

4. In the Geographic Location dialog box that opens, expand the Map drop-down list and choose North America.

5. Select Cleveland OH in the City list, and then click OK.

6. In the Time section, set the Hours value to **6**.

7. Turn on Auto Key mode and drag the Time slider to frame 600.

8. In the Time section, change the Hours value to **21** (9:00 p.m.). Turn off Auto Key mode.

9. Right-click in the Top viewport.

10. Open the Render Scene dialog box.

11. The time frame for the shadow study is 15 hours, or 30 half-hour increments. With a 600-frame available animation length, the increment between renderings is 20 (600/30).

12. In the Time Output section, select the Active Time Segment option, and then set Every Nth Frame to 20.

13. Enter the resolution in the Output Size section.

14. Click the Files button in the Render Output section, and give the renderings a filename and type.

15. Click Render.

16. The shadow study files are rendered and saved.

Create a walkthrough Walkthroughs are special animations that attempt to define the animation from the point of view of an individual walking through the structure.

Master It Assign a camera to a path that approaches the building from the front, passes through the entrance, and then turns to the left.

Solution

1. Open one of the Villa Savoye scenes from this chapter.

2. Right-click in the Top viewport and zoom out so that you can see the front of the building and a good amount of area outside the building.

3. In the Top viewport, draw a line that begins well outside the building, passes through the entrance, and then turns to the left.

4. Choose Animation ➢ Walkthrough Assistant.

5. In the Camera Creation section of the Walkthrough Assistant dialog box's Main Controls rollout, select the Free option, and then click Create New Camera.

6. Make sure the new camera is selected; then, in the Path Control section, click Pick Path and select the line that you drew in step 3.

7. Set the Eye Level parameter to 5´5˝, or whichever height you prefer, and then check the Move Path to Eye Level check box.

8. Right-click in an existing Camera viewport, and then click Set Viewport to Camera.

9. Render the scene, and then make any required adjustments.

Choose an animation file output option The files that you can output from 3ds Max vary greatly in their quality and file size, and you must find an acceptable compromise between the two. A 60-second-long, 1280 × 1024 AVI using no compression may be a high-quality choice, but it can result in a file several gigabytes in size that is unplayable on most systems. The key to outputting acceptable animations is selecting appropriate file types and settings.

Master It Render 90 frames of the same animation four times, saving the output as different AVI files. With each repetition, change the codec and/or settings; then compare the output quality and file sizes. Leave the resolution the same for all the animations.

Solution

1. From this chapter's files, open one of the Savoye scenes that has an animated camera.

2. Make the camera's viewport active; then open the Render Scene dialog box.

3. Set Time Output Range to span 90 frames.

4. In the Render Output File dialog box, click the Files button, name the file, and assign AVI as the file type.

5. Click the Setup button. In the AVI File Compression Setup dialog box, choose a compressor and quality. Leave Keyframe Rate at its default.

6. Click OK, and then Save to close two of the open dialog boxes.

7. Click Render to render the scene to the specified AVI file.

8. Repeat steps 4 through 7 three times, changing the filename in step 4 and the Compressor and Quality parameters in step 5.

9. Open each of the files in Windows Media Player and compare their qualities. Look at the file sizes in Windows Explorer and see if there is a correlation between file size and file quality.

Set up a physics simulation Creating complex animations, involving many collisions between scene objects, can be very time-consuming and not very realistic. Using reactor you can assign properties to the objects involved in the animation and let 3ds Max quickly create the animation.

Master It Using the Condo15.max file, create two Teapot primitives and two Oil Tank extended primitives and place them a few feet above the ground. Use reactor to animate them dropping to the floor and colliding with each other.

Solution

1. Open the Condo15.max file.

2. In the Top viewport, create two Teapot primitives and two Oil Tank extended primitives.

3. Move them all above the floor.

4. Select the two teapots and then open the Rigid Body Properties dialog box.

5. Set Mass to 1.0 and choose the Concave Mesh option in the Simulation Geometry rollout.

6. Deselect the teapots and then select the two Oil Tank objects, set Mass to 1.0, and choose the Mesh Convex Hull option.

7. Deselect the Oil Tank objects, select the Floor407 object, set its Mass to 1.0, choose the Bounding Box option, and then check the Unyielding option.

8. Select all five objects and then click the Create Rigid Body Collection button in the reactor toolbar.

9. Click the Create Animation button.

10. Render the scene.

Create a Particle Flow event-driven particle system Particle systems can be used for a wide variety of applications in design visualization. Any time you need to have a multitude of similar objects, you can consider using a particle system. You can create things like cars in traffic, trees in forests, pedestrians in airports, etc. Particle systems also are useful for water in fountains or simulations of gas particles flowing through tubes.

Master It Create a particle system for a fountain. You don't have to actually create the fountain, just practice how the particles and forces can be used to generate it.

Solution

1. Reset 3ds Max Design 2011.

2. On the Create panel, choose Particle Systems from the drop-down list.

3. Create a PF Source in the Perspective viewport.

4. Turn on Angle Snap, and rotate the PF Source.

5. Play the animation. The particles fly up into the air.

6. Create a Gravity space warp in the viewport, centered beneath the Pflow emitter.

7. Open Particle View by pressing 6 on the keyboard.

8. Adjust the emit Start and Stop values, and increase the amount. Set the emit Start and Stop so the particles appear throughout the default 100 frames.

9. Adjust the Size and Divergence settings to create a tapered effect.

11. Add an Age Test below the Shape operator. Set the age to 12 frames.

12. Create a new event and add a Force operator to it.

13. Select the Force operator, and add the Gravity space warp to the Force operator.

14. Adjust Strength of the gravity to a low value like .5.

15. Drag a Collision test after the Force operator.

16. Add a POmniFlect into the viewport to catch the falling particles. Rotate it and position it below the PF Source emitter.

17. Add the POmniFlect to the collision.

18. Set Bounce to 0 and Friction to 100, so the particles will collect on the deflector.

19. Create a camera view and add a Shape Facing operator. Assign the camera to the Lookat controller.

20. Add a Material Static operator to adjust the material.

21. Create a material with an opacity-mapped gradient, and assign the material via the Material Static operator.

Chapter 14: Advanced Rendering Using mental ray

Apply final gathering Final gathering is an optional step in calculating global illumination that can reduce the appearance of unwanted variances or rendering artifacts in the lighting.

> **Master It** Apply final gathering to an exterior view of the Savoye project from Chapter 14, "Advanced Rendering with mental ray."

> **Solution**

> 1. Open SavoyeExterior_MasterIt.max.

> 2. Assign mental ray as the renderer.

> 3. Click the Indirect Illumination tab of the Render Scene dialog box.

> 4. Disable Caustics if necessary and enable both Global Illumination and Maximum Sampling Radius.

> 5. Increase the Maximum Sampling Radius value to about 1′ and turn on Optimize for Final Gather (Slower GI).

> 6. In the Final Gather rollout, check the Enable Final Gather option and, in the Advanced group, check Draft Mode (No Precalculations).

> 7. Create a Daylight System and Photometric Free Lights equivalent to the Omni-Interior lights to replace them, and then delete all the standard lights in the scene.

> 8. Do a test render.

> 9. Make any adjustments to the lights, deselect Draft Mode (No Precalculations), and then render the scene again.

Create a contour rendering Contour renderings display dark strokes along the contours of a scene's objects. This is an effect caused by using the mental ray Contour shaders and the parameters in the Camera Effects rollout.

> **Master It** Using the same techniques covered in this chapter, create a contour rendering of the interior of a condo scene from Chapter 6, "Creating AEC Objects."

> **Solution**

> 1. Open one of the Chapter 6 condo scenes.

> 2. Hide any EASYnat or RPC objects.

> 3. Assign the mental ray renderer to the scene.

> 4. In the Render Scene dialog box's Renderer tab, enable the Contours option in the Camera Effects rollout.

5. Click the Contour Output button.

6. In the Material/Map Browser that appears, click the Contour Only (Contour) shader. Click OK to close the Material/Map Browser.

7. Open the Compact Material Editor, and then drag the shader from the Contour Output button to a sample slot. Choose Instance in the Instance (Copy) Map dialog box that appears.

8. Click the Background Color swatch in the Contour Only (Contour) Parameters rollout in the Compact Material Editor, and then set the color to white.

9. Drag the shader from the Contour Contrast button from the Render Scene dialog box to a sample slot in the Material Editor. Make this an instance as well.

10. Lower the Angle Step Threshold parameter in the Material Editor.

11. Select another unused sample slot. Rename the material to **ContourOverride**. Change the Diffuse Color to white.

12. In the white material's mental ray Connection rollout, click the Contour button in the Advanced Shaders area, and then select the Simple (Contour) shader from the Material Map Browser.

13. Reduce the Width (%) value in the Material Editor.

14. Create and position a camera or click Ctrl+C in the Perspective viewport to create a camera from that view.

15. Go to the Processing tab on the Render Setup dialog box and enable the Material Override setting. Then drag the ContourOverride material from the Material Editor into the material slot of the Material Override.

16. Render the Camera viewport.

 The viewport renders and then displays the contours. Your rendering should look similar to the following image.

Use the multi/sub-map material Creating a large number of unique maps to apply to repetitive objects in a scene to add a sense of variation or randomness can take a lot of effort. The Multi/Sub-Map rollout allows you to create one material with a number of internal variations that you can apply to objects in your scene to achieve that sense of natural randomness.

Master It Create a 25 × 25 array of 1′ radius spheres, offset 3′ from each other, with a single material that will randomly change the color of the spheres through the use of the mental ray Multi/Sub-Map type of map.

Solution

1. Reset 3ds Max Design 2011.

2. Create a 1′ radius sphere primitive near the World Origin.

3. Open the Material Editor and select an unused material sample.

4. Click the Map button for the material's Diffuse color channel.

5. Select the multi/sub-map material and set the Switch Color/Map Based on Value option to Random.

6. Apply the material to the sphere.

7. Click the Array button on the Extras toolbar.

8. Use the Array dialog box to create a 25 × 25 array, offsetting the spheres so they don't overlap.

9. Adjust the Perspective viewport so you can see the entire array.

10. Render the Perspective viewport.

 The Perspective viewport renders, showing you the array of spheres with the colors from the multi/sub-map feature randomly applied to the different spheres.

Use Skylight global illumination Global illumination can enhance the appeal of a scene by simulating bounced light. This can include the color bleeding effect where color is transferred from one surface to another.

Master It Add global illumination to an exterior shot of the Savoye scene from Chapter 8.

Solution

1. Open SavoyeExterior_MasterIt.

2. Move one of the existing cameras or create a new camera that views the exterior of the building.

3. On the Environment tab, change the Ambient Light value to 0.

4. Assign the mental ray renderer to the scene.

5. Under the Lights category of the Create command panel, click the Skylight button and then place a Skylight on the ground outside the building.

6. Change the sky color by clicking the Sky Color swatch in the Skylight Parameters rollout. Choose a pale blue color.

7. Render the scene.

Use mr Proxy objects Using mental ray Proxy objects in scenes that require a considerable number of identical high-poly objects can save you significant file size, system resources, and render time.

Master It Create and render a 25 × 50 array of mr Proxy teapots using an eight-segment teapot as the source object.

Solution

1. Reset 3ds Max Design.

2. In the Top viewport, create a teapot primitive and set Segments to 8.

3. From the Create tab of the Command panel, select the mental ray list of objects.

4. Click the mr Proxy button.

5. Click and drag in the Top viewport to create the proxy object.

6. With the mrProxy001 object selected, click the Modify tab of the Command panel.

7. In the Source Object group, click the None button and then click the Teapot01 object.

8. In the Proxy File group, click the Write Object to File button.

9. In the Write mr Proxy file dialog, name the Proxy object and click Save.

10. Click OK to accept the mr Proxy Creation dialog box settings.

11. Select and delete the Teapot001 object.

12. Using the Array tool from the Extras toolbar, create an array of teapots 25 across and 50 deep.

13. Click in the Perspective viewport to set up a view you like.

14. Render the scene.

15. Save your scene as **MyTeapotParade.max**.

Use IES files Using Photometric Web distribution files for your photometric lights can greatly increase the realism and accuracy of your final rendered images.

Master It Using the MyMentalRayIESLighting.max file you saved near the end of the chapter, change the light distribution type of PhotometricLight001 from Uniform Diffuse to Photometric Web, and select the cooper.ies file. Then render the scene.

Solution

1. Open the MyMentalRayIESLighting.max file.

2. Select PhotometricLight001.

3. Click the Modify tab and choose the Helpers button.

4. Click the Emit Light from (Shape) button, and change it to Point.

5. Click the Light Distribution (Type) drop-down menu and select Photometric Web.

6. In the Distribution (Photometric Web) rollout, click the < Choose Photometric File > button.

7. Browse to and select the `cooper.ies` file.

8. Click the Render Production button and compare this rendering to the previous rendering you did with this file.

9. Save your scene as **`MyMentalRayIESLighting2.max`**.

Use lighting analysis Proper accommodation of naturally available light can greatly benefit a building's design. Using 3ds Max Design 2011's lighting-analysis tools can help architects and lighting designers successfully study how lighting affects a project.

Master It Using the `MyMentalRayLightingA.max` file you saved in the last exercise, create a Light Meter helper object on top of the coffee table, calculate the light meter, and render the scene, displaying the values of the Light Meter helper on the render.

Solution

1. Open the `MyMentalRayLightingA.max` file.

2. Select the Camera viewport and change the view to Camera02_CoffeeTable.

3. Click the Create tab and choose the Helpers button.

4. Click the LightMeter button, and then activate the AutoGrid function.

5. In the Camera viewport, create a LightMeter helper object on top of the coffee table.

6. Once the LightMeter helper object is placed, click the Calculate All Light Meters button.

7. When the processing is complete, open the Effects tab of the Environment and Effects dialog.

8. Uncheck the Show Numbers on Entire Image (Screen Grid) option.

9. Check the Show Numbers from Light Metering helper objects.

10. Click the Render Production button on the Main Toolbar and see the results in the Rendered Frame Window.

11. Save your scene as **`MyMentalRayLightingA2.max`**.

Chapter 15: Finishing It Off: Atmosphere, Effects, and Compositing

Add an atmospheric effect Atmospheric effects add the appearance of particulate matter in the air. With them, you can represent volumetric lights, fog, smoke, clouds, and even fire.

Master It Add a second fog to the `Savoy15_A.max` file with a bottom just below the top of the building's overhang and the top 6′ above that. Give the fog a purple color, and make sure the fog is not a straight line at the horizon.

Solution

1. Open the `Savoy15_A.max` file.

2. Open the Environment tab of the Environment and Effects dialog box.

3. Click the Add button and then add a second Fog atmospheric effect to the scene.

4. In the Fog section of the Fog Parameters rollout, click the Fog Color swatch and then select a purple color from the Color Selector that opens.

5. Click the Layered radio button.

6. Set the Bottom value to 16´ and the Top value to 22´.

7. Click the Horizon Noise check box.

8. Render the scene.

Add a grass effect using Hair and Fur Hair and Fur is a rendering effect that appears to add strands to an object at rendering. These strands can look like long, thin hair; short, thick fur; or even grass.

Master It Zoom into the tree in the Savoye15_C.max file. Create a mound that rises out of the ground and covers the base of the tree. Add Hair and Fur to the mound so that it appears to be caused by a root ball under the lawn.

Solution

1. Open the Savoye15_C.max file.

2. Zoom into the base of the tree in the Camera01 viewport.

3. Create a large sphere at the base of the tree. Use the Hemisphere parameter and the Move tool to reduce the amount of the sphere by chopping off most of the portion that remains underground and move it into place.

4. Convert the sphere to an Editable Poly and then delete the polygons at the flat bottom of the sphere.

5. Add a UVW Map modifier to the sphere, deselect Real-World Map size, and choose Spherical as the Mapping type.

6. In the Material Editor, get the material from the ground and assign it to the sphere.

7. From the Modify panel, add the Hair and Fur (WSM) modifier to the sphere.

8. Set Scale to approximately 20.

9. In the Material Parameters rollout, click the gray button next to the Root Color parameter and then choose Mtl Editor in the Browse From section of the Material/Map Browser.

10. Double-click the Grass2.jpg map listed, and then choose Instance in the Instance or Copy? dialog box.

11. Render the scene.

Add the Glare effect to a rendering Glare is an effect that is seen in real-world cameras when the intensity of the lights or reflections/refractions captured by the camera causes the light to reflect/refract within the film emulsion or on the surface of a sensor.

Master It Open the TableTop_Glare.max file. Add the Glare shader and render the Camera002 viewport.

Solution

1. Open the `TableTop_Glare.max` file.

2. Click the Render Setup button.

3. On the Renderer tab, scroll down to the Camera Effects rollout and the Camera Shaders group.

4. Click the Output shader button.

5. From the Material/Map Browser, open the Maps ➢ mental ray rollout.

6. Select the Glare shader and click OK.

7. Open the Slate Material Editor.

8. Drag the Glare shader to the Active View in the Slate Material Editor, select Instance, and click OK.

9. Expand Additional Params.

10. Adjust the Quality, Spread, and Resolution For options, and then close the Slate Material Editor.

11. Render the scene.

Use DOF/Bokeh Depth of field is the result of using a camera with a large aperture setting during the image exposure. The effect is seen in real-world cameras and often a rendering will appear much more realistic when there is some DOF in the image.

Master It Continue with the `TableTop_Glare.max` file from the previous exercise. Add the Depth of Field/Bokeh shader and render the Camera002 viewport. Having Glare and DOF with good sampling settings will make the rendering take quite a while.

Solution

1. Continue with the `TableTop_Glare.max` file.

2. Click the Render Setup button.

3. On the Renderer tab, scroll down to the Camera Effects rollout and the Camera Shaders group.

4. Click the Lens shader button.

5. From the Material/Map Browser, open the Maps ➢ mental ray rollout.

6. Select the Depth of Field/Bokeh shader and click OK.

7. Open the Slate Material Editor.

8. Drag the Depth of Field/Bokeh shader to the Active View in the Slate Material Editor, select Instance, and click OK. You can leave the Glare shader in the Active View1 window.

9. Double-click the Depth of Field/Bokeh shader to access its properties in the Parameters Editor.

10. Adjust the Focus Plane setting so that its distance will make an object in the image the focal point.

11. Change Blade Count to 7.

12. Increase Samples to 8.

13. Render the scene.

Create stereo-pair images Stereo 3D images are incredibly popular again, even in the architectural and engineering industries. As a visualization specialist, the odds are very high that you will encounter situations where you need to take a scene and render it for stereo viewing.

Master It Using the TableTop_Stereo_01.max file, create an additional camera for the right eye with a 2.5″ intraocular distance, and then render the two cameras using the Batch Render command.

Solution

1. Open the Tabletop_Stereo_01.max file.

2. In the Top viewport, zoom in and select the Camera002_CoffeeTable camera.

3. Clone the camera as an instance and name the new camera **Camera002_CoffeeTable_R**.

4. With the new camera still selected, select the Select and Move tool.

5. Change the Reference Coordinate System to Local.

6. In the Absolute Transform Type-In, move the new camera 2.5 inches along the X-axis.

7. On the Rendering menu, select Batch Render.

8. Add two views to the task queue.

9. Select the View01 item and the change Camera to Camera002_CoffeeTable.

10. Set Output Path to the folder where you have been working on the Chapter 15 files and set the filename to **Camera002_CoffeeTable_L.tif**.

11. Select View02 from the task queue, and set Camera to Camera002_CoffeeTable_R , Output Path to the correct folder, and the filename to **Camera002_CoffeeTable_R.tif**.

12. Click the Render button to render both images.

Composite the stereo pair into an anaglyph image Once you have the stereo-pair images, you need to combine them into one image you can look at with red-blue anaglyph glasses.

Master It Use Autodesk Composite to take the two images you rendered in the previous Master It and render out a single anaglyph stereo image.

Solution

1. Save your work in 3ds Max and close the program, and then start Autodesk Composite.

2. Create a new composition called **TableTop** and save it in your working directory.

3. Import the stereo-pair images.

4. From Pixel Expressions, add a PXL operator to the composition panel.

5. Select the PXL operator and load the Stereo Anaglyph preset.

6. Connect the _L image to the In, and connect the _R image to the RightImage slots of the Stereo Anaglyph operator.

7. Select the Stereo Anaglyph operator and change Method to 2.

8. Connect the output of the Stereo Anaglyph operator to the Output node.

9. On the Output tab, change the Image Format to custom, the width to 640, and the height to 480.

10. On the Output tab, change the pixel format to 8 Bits.

11. On the Output tab, change the End value to 2.

12. On the Render tab, change the file format to TIFF and the folder to your working folder.

13. Choose File ➢ Render.

14. Verify the destination folder and filename.

15. Click the Start button.

16. View your rendered anaglyph stereo image with red/blue glasses and enjoy.

Appendix B

Modifiers, Maps, and Materials

3ds Max Design 2011 offers a multitude of modifier and material options—so many, in fact, that to do a tutorial on all of them would require a multivolume book. After reading the first few chapters of this book, however, you'll have a good understanding of how 3ds Max works, and you'll be able to use most, if not all, of the modifiers and materials with a little experimentation and some help from this appendix.

This appendix is intended to give you general information about the modifiers and materials and to show you what types of features are available. If you need more detailed information about the modifiers and materials, consult the 3ds Max Design Help System, which offers full descriptions of the options and parameters for all the items discussed in this appendix. Choose Help ➤ Autodesk 3ds Max Design Help. Click the Search tab in the panel to the left, enter the name of the item in the Type In the Word(s) to Search For input box, and then click List Topics. If you see only a single panel in the User Reference, click the Show button in the User Reference toolbar.

Modifiers

The tutorials in this book cover the most commonly used modifiers in 3ds Max. Every now and then, you'll need to use one of the modifiers that is not discussed at any length in this book. For those situations, you can find a description of the modifier in this section. This description should be enough to get you started. Even if you don't need all these modifiers now you may want to review their functions so that you'll know what's available.

The modifiers are all on a single drop-down list. The modifier list is broken down into three categories: Selection modifiers, World-Space modifiers, and Object-Space modifiers. This appendix presents the modifiers in the same order as they appear in the drop-down list, starting with the Selection modifiers. Not all of the modifiers appear in the modifier list simultaneously, because the list changes depending on the type of object currently being edited. Only the modifiers that work with the selected object are displayed in the list, so modifiers will appear and disappear in the list, depending on what you have selected in the viewport.

Selection Modifiers

The Selection modifiers allow you to gain access to the sub-object levels of objects. Once sub-objects are selected with a Selection modifier, other modifiers can be placed above them in the stack to affect only the sub-object selection. This process is also referred to as *passing a sub-object selection up the stack.* To add a modifier to the top of the stack that affects the entire object, rather

than just a sub-object selection, first apply another Selection modifier; then, without making a sub-object selection, apply the next modifier. The entire object is again affected by any modifiers applied to the top of the stack.

MESH SELECT

The Mesh Select modifier allows you to gain access to the sub-object level of an object to select part of the object. You can then apply another modifier to affect only what you selected with Mesh Select. For example, you could use Mesh Select to select part of an object, and then you could apply the Taper modifier to only the selected part. You can use Mesh Select to pass selections up the stack to other modifiers or to gain access to mesh sub-object selection for Patch and NURBS surfaces. You can also use Edit Poly and Edit Mesh modifiers to select sub-object levels like you do when using Mesh Select.

PATCH SELECT

The Patch Select modifier allows you to gain access to the sub-object level of an object to select part of the object. It works in a similar manner to the Mesh Select modifier, but Patch Select treats objects as if they were editable patches rather than meshes.

SPLINESELECT

The SplineSelect modifier lets you affect sub-object selections of splines. Much of the functionality of the SplineSelect modifier is also found in the Edit Spline modifier.

POLY SELECT

The Poly Select modifier is similar to the Mesh Select modifier as it lets you select sub-objects of Editable Poly objects to be passed up the stack.

VOL. SELECT

The Vol. Select modifier lets you make sub-object selections based on a volume. You have the choice of four volume types: Box, Sphere, Cylinder, and Mesh Object. A Selection gizmo in the shape of the volume type you select appears in the design. You can then select the sub-object level of the Vol. Select modifier to move the Volume gizmo into place to make the selection. This is very powerful because you can base the selection on an object. For example, you can animate an object moving across a terrain and have the vertices in the terrain selected based on the position of the object.

NSURF SEL

NSurf Sel allows you to place sub-object selections anywhere in the stack of NURBS objects. This is similar to the Mesh Select modifier but is available only for NURBS objects.

World-Space Modifiers

World-Space modifiers (WSMs) are modifiers that use the World Space as their point of reference, as opposed to the Object Space of the object to which they are bound. The MapScalar

modifier is a good example of a WSM, because it associates the map of an object with the World Space and isn't affected by the Object Space of the object to which it's attached. An object using the MapScalar modifier can be scaled to any size or shape, and any maps attached to the object won't be scaled.

IDENTIFYING THE MODIFIER TYPES

The World-Space modifiers can be recognized by their (WSM) postfix.

CAMERA MAP (WSM)

At times, you may want an object to be invisible while it maintains a presence in a scene. For example, suppose you have a fairly detailed background image that shows a garage, and you want to create the illusion of a car entering the garage. You can create a simple box with an opening similar in shape to the background garage opening, and then use the Camera Map modifier to blend the box into the background. Once you do that, you can animate the car to drive into the box. The net effect is that the car appears to drive into the garage in the background image in your final animation. This allows you to keep the geometry simple yet still have an animation that shows a fair amount of detail.

The Camera Map modifier applies a planar UVW map to an object, and it aligns that map so that it's perpendicular to a specified camera. The map is typically the same as the background, giving the illusion of an invisible object. Because the object can cast and receive shadows, you can create different effects. For example, if you're using the Camera Match tool to match a building design to a photo of a building site, you can use the Camera Map modifier to include shadows on buildings in the background.

This modifier can be used when a camera is in motion, as it updates the map at each frame. There is also an Object-Space modifier (OSM) version.

DISPLACE MESH (WSM)

Displace Mesh lets you deform a surface using a bitmap image. It's similar to including a displacement map in a material to an object, but instead of simply creating the illusion of a bumpy surface by changing the surface normals, Displace Mesh actually changes the geometry to a bumpy surface. See Chapter 9, "Enhancing Models with Materials," for a detailed description of the Displace Mesh modifier.

If you assign a displacement map to an object, you usually won't be able to see the effects of the map until the object is rendered. The Displace Mesh modifier allows you to see the effects of a displacement map while you're editing. Displace Mesh can also let you convert a displacement map into an Editable Mesh, as described in Chapter 9.

DISPLACE NURBS (WSM)

The Displace NURBS modifier performs the same function as the Displace Mesh modifier, but it is applied to NURBS objects.

Hair and Fur (WSM)

The Hair and Fur (WSM) modifier can be applied to objects to create a number of effects, including grass, in your rendered scenes. See Chapter 15, "Finishing It Off: Atmosphere, Effects, and Compositing," for an explanation on the use of the Hair and Fur (WSM) modifier.

LS Colors (WSM)

Lightscape was a stand-alone Autodesk product for calculating radiosity solutions. Lightscape is no longer available or supported by Autodesk, but legacy scenes can be imported into 3ds Max. The LS Colors modifier converts Lightscape radiosity mesh colors to Autodesk 3ds Max vertex colors. This is useful when you import a lighting solution (*.ls file) from Lightscape into 3ds Max.

UTILIZING LIGHTSCAPE MATERIALS

You can also use the Lightscape Materials utility to aid in the conversion of lighting solution data into 3ds Max.

MapScaler (WSM)

CERT OBJECTIVE

Apply this version of the modifier when you want the material map to maintain its original scale, regardless of the scale of the object to which it is applied. This modifier allows you to "lock" a map's scale so that changes to the object don't affect the associated map. Use the Object-Space modifier (OSM) version to lock the associated map's scale to Object Space instead.

PatchDeform (WSM)

This modifier allows you to deform an object based on the form of a Patch object. A Patch object is an object that can be formed into a smooth, curved surface by editing its vertices. You can, for example, create a plane and then convert the plane into an editable patch. The vertices of the editable patch can then be edited to shape the plane into a smooth, curved surface of any shape you want. Such a surface can be used to deform other objects, using the PatchDeform modifier. The object moves to the location of the patch with the WSM version. See also the OSM version of this modifier.

PathDeform (WSM)

The PathDeform modifier works in a way similar to the PatchDeform modifier but uses a spline or NURBS curve instead of a Patch object. For example, you can use this modifier to deform an object along the path of the spline. An example of this would be the curving of text to conform to the shape of a round column or sphere. The object moves to the path used for the deformation in this version of the modifier. See the OSM version also.

SUBDIVIDE (WSM)

The Subdivide modifier allows you to manually apply a radiosity mesh to an object. Subdivide works in a similar way to the Radiosity Meshing parameters, but instead of applying a mesh globally, Subdivide lets you apply a mesh to single objects or even sub-object levels. Because it's a modifier, it can be edited directly from the modifier stack. The size of the subdivided mesh is locked to World Space with this modifier; if you scale the object, the mesh stays the same size.

SURFACE MAPPER (WSM)

The UVW Map modifier has a fixed set of seven mapping options that allow you to apply a map to most forms. But what happens when none of those options will work for your design? If you have an organic form that requires custom mapping, you can use the Surface Mapper modifier.

The Surface Mapper requires that you create a NURBS surface that you edit to the form of the required map. You form the NURBS surface around the object to which you are applying the map and assign the same material to both the NURBS surface and the object. Once this is done, you apply the Surface Mapper modifier to the object or objects. The map is projected onto the modified object(s), based on the direction of the normals on the NURBS surface. In this version of the modifier, the scale of UVW space is tied to World Space; if you scale the object, the UVW coordinates remain in their original size.

SURFDEFORM (WSM)

The SurfDeform modifier works in a way similar to the PathDeform modifier but uses a NURBS surface instead of a curve. You can use this modifier to deform an object, based on the shape of a NURBS surface. This version stays locked to World Space.

Object-Space Modifiers

Object-Space modifiers directly affect the object that they are applied to in the local coordinate system of the object itself. Object Space is generally described in UVW coordinates when dealing with texture maps.

AFFECT REGION

The Affect Region modifier lets you apply a bulge to a surface. Two points control the bulge. One point sets the base of the bulge, while the other locates the tip of the bulge. Each point can be adjusted independently of the other. You can control the bulge's shape through Falloff, Pinch, and Bubble parameters.

AUTOMATIC FLATTEN UVS

This is the same as the Unwrap UVW modifier. This modifier is automatically applied by the Render to Texture operation.

BEND

You can bend an object on any axis by using the Bend modifier. You can control the degree of the bend, the place where it occurs, and the axis about which it occurs. This modifier is demonstrated in Chapter 2, "Introducing 3ds Max Objects."

BEVEL

Bevel allows you to extrude a 2D shape and add beveled edges. The Bevel Values rollout for this modifier allows you to set the height of the extrusion. You can use three levels of beveling. Each level has its own height and outline settings, so you can control beveling by adjusting the height and changing the outline value, and then expanding or contracting the shape of the outline at the selected level. The Surface parameters let you control the segments of the extrusion and whether the sides are curved or straight. Typically, Bevel is used to bevel text, but it can be used for other 2D shapes (see Figure B.1).

FIGURE B.1
A sample of the Bevel modifier used on text

Bevel level 1
Bevel level 2
Bevel level 3

BEVEL PROFILE

Bevel Profile is like a simplified Loft tool. You can use it to extrude a shape along a path. This modifier is an excellent tool for creating extruded forms such as elaborate picture frames or curved stairs. To use it, you draw an outline of the object, using a spline. Draw another spline indicating the profile of the object. Select the outline and then apply the Bevel Profile modifier. In the Parameters rollout of the Bevel Profile modifier, click the Pick Profile button and select the spline you want to use as the profile. The outline is extruded to the shape of the profile (see Figure B.2).

FIGURE B.2
An example of the Bevel Profile modifier

Resulting surface Bevel profile

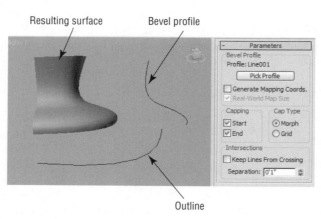

Outline

Once you've extruded a shape using the Bevel Profile modifier, you can modify the shape by adjusting either the profile spline or the original extruded shape. Bevel Profile is similar to the more powerful Sweep modifier discussed later in this appendix.

CAMERA CORRECTION MODIFIER

Wide-angle camera views tend to exaggerate the three-point perspective view of tall objects. The tops of buildings, for example, appear to taper to a sharp point too quickly. The Camera Correction modifier enables you to reduce this distortion.

The Camera Correction modifier is unusual in that it isn't found in the Modifier List drop-down. To use it, you must first select the camera you want to work on, right-click the camera, and then select Apply Camera Correction Modifier from the tools 1 quad menu, as shown in Figure B.3.

FIGURE B.3
Accessing the Camera Correction modifier

APPLYING THE CAMERA CORRECTION MODIFIER

You can also apply the Camera Correction modifier by first selecting the camera and then choosing Modifiers ➤ Cameras ➤ Camera Correction.

Once you've done that, you can adjust the camera view using the options in the 2-Point Perspective Correction rollout that appears on the Modify tab of the Command panel.

CAMERA MAP (OSM)

Similar to the Camera Map (WSM) modifier example earlier in this appendix, at times you may want an object to be invisible while it maintains a presence in a design. For example, suppose you have a fairly detailed background image that shows a garage, and you want to create the illusion of a car entering the garage. You can create a simple box with an opening similar in shape to the background garage opening, and then use the Camera Map modifier to blend the box into the background. Once you do that, you can animate the car to drive into the box. The net effect is that the car appears to drive into the garage in the background image in your final animation. This allows you to keep the geometry simple, yet still have an animation that shows a fair amount of detail.

The Camera Map modifier applies a planar UVW map to an object, and it aligns that map so that it's perpendicular to a specified camera. The map is typically the same as the background,

giving the illusion of an invisible object. Because the object can cast and receive shadows, you can create different effects. For example, if you're using the Camera Match tool to match a building design to a photo of a building site, you can use the Camera Map modifier to include shadows on buildings in the background.

The Object-Space version of this modifier is a better choice when there is no camera motion. (See also the "Matte/Shadow" section later in this appendix.)

CAP HOLES

Some editing procedures will leave openings in a mesh. You may, for example, use the Slice modifier to slice an object into two halves. Each half will have an opening at the Slice plane. The Cap Holes modifier can be used to close the openings.

In 3ds Max, a hole is a closed loop of edges with a single face. Cap Holes works best on planar holes, but it also works on nonplanar holes. Cap Holes is a very useful tool when used in conjunction with the STL Check modifier; if you find problems in a mesh with the STL (stereolithography) check, using Cap Holes may fix those problems.

CLOTH

The Cloth modifier is used for simulating cloth objects that must interact dynamically with other objects in your scenes. The Cloth modifier can be used to simulate flags, or tensile structures in your projects. The Cloth modifier can also be used with the Garment Maker modifier.

CROSSSECTION

The CrossSection modifier is a powerful tool that lets you connect splines to form surfaces. (If you're an AutoCAD user, you can think of CrossSection as a super Rulesurf or Edgesurf command.) This modifier is called CrossSection because with it you can draw cross sections of an object and then join the cross sections together to form a surface.

When used in conjunction with the Surface modifier, CrossSection lets you form elaborate patch surfaces by defining the surface edge with two or more 3D splines. First you draw the splines; then you attach them to form a single object, using the Attach option in the Modify tab. You then apply the CrossSection modifier, which connects the vertices of the separate splines. Finally, you can "skin" over the splines with the Surface modifier (see Figure B.4).

FIGURE B.4
Creating a surface using the Cross-Section modifier and the Surface modifier

Spline shapes CrossSection modifier applied to shapes

Surface modifier applied to cross-sectioned shapes

The order in which the splines are created is as important as the location of the starting vertex of the splines. You want to be sure that the splines *point* in the same direction, with the beginning vertex of each spline placed in the same orientation relative to the rest of the spline. Figure B.5 shows how all the splines are oriented with their starting points (the yellow vertices) to the left of the figure.

FIGURE B.5
Aligning the spine vertices

The splines are oriented in the same general direction.

If you collapse the stack of a surface created using the CrossSection and Surface modifiers, you have a patch surface that can be edited in the same way as any other patch surface.

DELETEMESH

You can think of the DeleteMesh modifier as a tool that lets you try out deletions in a mesh before committing to the change. Because it's a modifier, it can be placed anywhere in the modifier stack. Here's how it works: go to the sub-object level of an object and make a selection of the item you want to remove. If it's a surface patch or NURBS surface, you can isolate mesh surfaces for deletion by using the Mesh Select modifier. Once you've made your selection, apply the DeleteMesh modifier. The selection will be deleted. Because DeleteMesh is a modifier, you can restore the deleted items by removing DeleteMesh from the modifier stack.

DELETEPATCH

You can think of the DeletePatch modifier as a tool that lets you try out deletions in a Patch object. Because it's a modifier, it can be placed anywhere in the modifier stack. It works in a similar way to the DeleteMesh modifier (described in the previous section). Because DeletePatch is a modifier, you can restore the deleted items by removing DeletePatch from the modifier stack.

DELETESPLINE

DeleteSpline is similar to DeleteMesh except that it works on splines rather than on meshes. Sub-object selections are limited to vertices, segments, and splines.

DISP APPROX

The Disp Approx modifier allows you to apply a displacement map to an object through a material channel. A tutorial for this modifier can be found in Chapter 9.

Displace

The Displace modifier allows you to apply a displacement map directly to an object without having to do it through a material. This is similar to the DispApprox modifier, but no materials are required.

Edit Mesh

Like the Edit Spline modifier, Edit Mesh seems a bit redundant, as it duplicates the parameters for Editable Meshes. However, Edit Mesh offers great flexibility in editing meshes by allowing you to position edits in the modifier stack. You can experiment with changes in a mesh, maintain other modifiers and parameters that would otherwise be altered by mesh edits, or edit multiple mesh objects.

The Edit Mesh modifier uses much more memory than does a simple Editable Mesh object. For this reason, try to avoid using this modifier unless you really need the flexibility it offers.

Edit Patch

The Edit Patch modifier lets you edit an object as if it were an Editable Patch object. The Edit Patch modifier uses a good deal of RAM, as it must make a copy of the selected geometry in RAM in order to perform its functions. Nevertheless, Edit Patch is offered for those occasions when you want to try out options, or when prior modifiers or parametric options must be left in place.

Edit Poly

The Edit Poly is yet another modifier that lets you edit an object as if it were a simple geometric object, an Editable Poly object in this case. Using the Edit Poly modifier gives you control of all of the Editable Poly tools without actually converting the mesh to an Editable Poly. Use this modifier only to experiment with the tools and then convert the object or collapse the modifier stack to save the edits and reduce the file size and RAM usage. Edit Poly is generally preferred over Edit Mesh because of its richer toolset.

Edit Spline

The Edit Spline modifier may seem redundant because it duplicates the parameters for Spline objects, with a few limitations. Edit Spline offers flexibility in editing splines by allowing you to position edits anywhere in the modifier stack. For example, you can use Edit Spline to test spline edits. Because it's a modifier, you can easily discard changes made using Edit Spline by deleting it from the modifier stack—something you cannot do using the basic parameters for a spline. Edit Spline is also useful for applying changes to several shapes at once by applying a single Edit Spline modifier to a set of objects. You may also want to maintain other modifiers that would otherwise be affected by changes to the basic parameters of the shape.

> **Consider Memory Usage with the Edit Spline Modifier**
>
> The Edit Spline modifier uses much more memory than does a simple editable spline object. For this reason, try to avoid using this modifier unless you really need the flexibility it offers.

EXTRUDE

Extrude is used to extend 2D shapes into the third dimension in a linear fashion. 3ds Max shapes, NURBS curves, and shapes imported from CAD programs can all be extruded. The Extrude modifier offers the option to cap ends, which closes the openings formed by the top and bottom of an extruded, closed shape. You can also select the type of mesh that is created with Extrude.

FACE EXTRUDE

The Face Extrude modifier allows you to extrude only selected faces of a mesh. You must first make a selection of faces on the sub-object level of an object. You can then apply the Face Extrude modifier to affect the selected faces. Although you can use the Extrude option at the sub-object level of an Editable Mesh or Editable Poly, the Face Extrude modifier uses fewer resources and offers a few additional options, such as Scale and Extrude from Center. You can achieve a beveled effect with these options. A selection modifier must be placed below Face Extrude and a sub-object selection must be passed up to it.

FFD ($2 \times 2 \times 2$, $3 \times 3 \times 3$, $4 \times 4 \times 4$)

The Free Form Deformation (FFD) modifiers let you deform objects in a general way by offering lattice control points to pull and stretch objects. When you apply an FFD modifier, a lattice box appears around the selected object. You can use the control points on the box to push or pull the object's form (see Figure B.6). The lattice box is a type of gizmo and doesn't represent actual geometry.

FIGURE B.6
A chair with the
FFD $4 \times 4 \times 4$
modifier

The FFD modifiers are offered in three types: $2 \times 2 \times 2$, $3 \times 3 \times 3$, and $4 \times 4 \times 4$. Each type places a different box around the object. The FFD $2 \times 2 \times 2$ modifier, for example, places a box with control points at each corner.

FFD (Box)

The FFD (Box) modifier is similar in function to the previous FFD modifiers but adds the capability to control the number of control points. With FFD (Box), you aren't limited to the $2 \times 2 \times 2$ through $4 \times 4 \times 4$ lattice of the FFD modifier, as shown in Figure B.7.

FIGURE B.7
An FFD (Box)
modifier applied
to a chair using a
$5 \times 6 \times 7$ lattice

FFD (CYL)

Like the FFD (Box) modifier, FFD (Cyl) allows you to set the number of control points in the control lattice, but instead of a box, FFD (Cyl) places a cylindrical lattice around the object.

FILLET/CHAMFER

The Fillet/Chamfer modifier lets you convert a spline vertex into a filleted (rounded) corner or a chamfered corner. It works only on vertices that connect straight segments, and it won't join two disconnected segments. To use it, select a shape and then apply the Fillet/Chamfer modifier. The Vertex sub-object level is automatically opened, allowing you to select a vertex for editing. You can either select a vertex and enter a fillet or chamfer value in the Edit Vertex rollout, or set a fillet or chamfer value first and then select a vertex and click the Apply button.

GARMENT MAKER

The Garment Maker modifier allows you to create 2D patterns for objects to be used with the Cloth simulation system.

HSDS

HSDS stands for Hierarchical Subdivision Surfaces. The HSDS modifier subdivides the surface of an object. You can use it to help smooth out a curved surface of an object without reducing the object to a mesh.

LATHE

Lathe is used to revolve 2D shapes into the third dimension in a circular fashion. 3ds Max shapes, NURBS curves, and shapes imported from CAD programs can be lathed. The Lathe modifier offers the option to cap the ends, which closes the openings formed by the beginning and end of a lathed shape. You can also select the type of mesh that is created with Lathe.

LATTICE

The Lattice modifier lets you convert the segments of a shape or the edges of an object into struts and the vertices into joints. The effect is similar to that of converting a mesh object into a wireframe, but expressing the wireframe as renderable geometry (see Figure B.8). A geodesic dome is a good architectural example of using a latticed geosphere.

You can change the selected object so that only its joints appear, as shown in Figure B.9.

FIGURE B.8
A tapered cylinder
converted into a
lattice

FIGURE B.9
A tapered cylinder
with its joints con-
verted into octahe-
drons

In addition, Lattice allows you to display both joints and struts to form some unusual objects. You have control over the number of sides of the struts or the type of geometry used at the vertices. You can also change the scale of the joints and struts.

LS Mesh

This modifier refines a Lightscape mesh object (imported from Lightscape). This modifier is designed to be used in conjunction with the Lightscape material and the LS Colors modifier.

MapScaler

Apply this OSM version of the modifier when you want the material map to maintain its scale relative to the scale of the object. Changes to the object's scale will affect the associated map's scale also. Use the WSM version to lock the associated map's scale to World Space instead.

Material

When you apply a multi/sub-object material to an object, you need to assign a material ID to selected faces of the object in order to correlate the sub-material with the selected faces (see Chapter 9 for a look at multi/sub-object materials). The Material modifier lets you do just that.

The Material modifier isn't needed for Editable Meshes or Editable Polys. It's intended for other types of objects that don't offer access to mesh-level editing. For those objects, you need to apply the Mesh Select modifier first in order to select mesh faces. You can then apply the Material modifier to assign a material ID.

MATERIALBYELEMENT

The MaterialByElement modifier applies the different materials of a multi/sub-object material to the different elements of an object. This is done randomly.

MELT

The Melt modifier allows you to make an object appear as if it were melting. The modifier is applied parametrically with settings for the amount of Melt, Spreading based on a percentage, and a Solidity value.

MESHSMOOTH

MeshSmooth does just what the name implies: it smoothes a mesh so that sharp corners are rounded. It does this by increasing the complexity of the mesh. The smoothed form can be edited by using control vertices (CVs) in a way similar to NURBS CVs. MeshSmooth is similar to the TurboSmooth modifier described later in this appendix.

MIRROR

Mirror performs a similar function to the Mirror tool on the 3ds Max Main Toolbar. Instead of creating a second object when the Clone Option indicates to do so with the Mirror tool, the Mirror modifier creates a second set of geometry, using the Copy option, but both instances of the geometry are elements of the same object. Because it's a modifier, you can control the mirror effect as part of the object's modifier stack.

MULTIRES

The MultiRes modifier is similar to the Optimize modifier, with the added option to specify the level of simplification as a percentage or number of vertices. The more powerful MultiRes has generally replaced Optimize for mesh simplification operations.

NOISE

The Noise modifier randomly repositions the vertices of an object to simulate an uneven surface. You can adjust the strength of the noise to create a relatively smooth surface or a mountainous terrain. The effectiveness of Noise is dependent on the amount of segmentation of the object.

NORMAL

When you create geometry in 3ds Max, the normals of the geometry are pointing outward and you don't have control over their orientation. You can gain control of the normals of 3ds Max geometry by collapsing the stack and reducing the geometry to an Editable Mesh. Unfortunately, once you do that, the geometry loses its parametric functions. The Normal modifier lets you control the normals of 3ds Max geometry without forcing you to give up parametric functions.

NORMALIZE SPLINE

The Normalize Spline modifier places additional control points along a spline. The control points are spaced at regular intervals. This can be useful when using splines for motion paths where a constant speed is required.

OPTIMIZE

The Optimize modifier simplifies the geometry of an object while maintaining an acceptable level of detail. This offers the benefits of faster rendering time and less RAM usage. This modifier has effectively been replaced by the MultiRes modifier.

PATCHDEFORM

This modifier allows you to deform an object based on the form of a Patch object. A Patch object is an object that can be formed into a smooth, curved surface by editing its vertices. You can, for example, create a plane and then convert the plane into an editable patch. The vertices of the editable patch can then be edited to shape the plane into a smooth, curved surface of any shape you want. Such a surface can be used to deform other objects, using the PatchDeform modifier.

The object remains in its current location while being deformed. See also the WSM version of this modifier.

PATHDEFORM

The PathDeform modifier works in a way similar to the PatchDeform modifier but uses a spline or NURBS curve instead of a Patch object. For example, you can use this modifier to deform an object along the path of the spline. An example of this would be the curving of text to conform to the shape of a round column or sphere. The object does not move to the path with this modifier. See also the WSM version.

PRESERVE

The Preserve modifier lets you "clean up" a mesh that has been edited on a vertex sub-object level. Often when a mesh is edited by moving vertices, the resulting form takes on a rough appearance. The Preserve modifier will help smooth out that rough appearance.

To use the Preserve modifier, you must first make a copy of the object you want to modify. Make your changes to the copy's vertices, and then, with the vertex sub-object level still active, apply the Preserve modifier. Use the Pick Original button of the Preserve modifier to select the original object from which you made the copy. You can then use the other Preserve modifier controls to adjust the mesh.

PROOPTIMIZER

The ProOptimizer modifier allows you to interactively optimize the polygon/vertex count of selected objects with a number of parameters while maintaining the appearance of the object. There is also a Batch ProOptimizer utility that allows you to optimize multiple files simultaneously.

PUSH

If you need to create a bulging or shrunken appearance, you can use Push. The Push modifier has a single parameter that pushes or pulls the vertices of an object from its center.

QUADRIFY MESH

The Quadrify Mesh modifier can be used to increase the geometry of your model and covert the triangular geometry to quadrilateral polygons. This modifier can be very helpful on Boolean objects and objects to which you want to apply the MeshSmooth or TurboSmooth modifiers.

RELAX

Relax is similar to Push, but instead of pushing vertices out from the object's center, Relax softens the corner edges of an object or generally relaxes an object's shape to something smoother, with less-pronounced surface changes, by evening out the distribution of vertices in an object based on the parameters you select.

RENDERABLE SPLINE

This modifier lets you set the renderable parameters of spline objects, including those that are brought into 3ds Max through importing or file linking (see Chapter 5, "Working with External Design Data") from an AutoCAD-based application, without collapsing the splines to editable splines.

> **3DS MAX VERSUS NON-3DS MAX SPLINES**
>
> Splines made in 3ds Max do not require the use of the Renderable Spline modifier because they already have the same controls available in their Rendering rollout.

RIPPLE

Ripple modifies an object's surface to produce a concentric rippled effect. You can control the amplitude, wavelength, phase, and decay of the ripple.

SHELL

This modifier extrudes a flat or curved two-dimensional or three-dimensional surface, giving it volume and solidity.

SKEW

The Skew modifier skews an object, as shown in Figure B.10. You can control the direction and strength of the skew. You can also limit the skew to a portion of the object.

FIGURE B.10
A cylinder skewed using the Skew modifier

SLICE

Slice allows you to define a plane through which objects can be cut. There are two ways in which Slice can affect an object. The most obvious is splitting a single object into two distinct objects. Slice gives you the option to keep both parts of the split object, or you may hide one part. Slice also lets you refine an object along the intersection of the slice plane with the object.

SMOOTH

The Smooth modifier applies autosmoothing to the surface of an object. Although you can usually apply smoothing to an Editable Mesh at the sub-object level, Smooth allows you to control the smoothing as an item in the mesh's modifier stack.

SPHERIFY

The Spherify modifier lets you distort an object into a spherical shape. It offers a single parameter that lets you control the amount of distortion you can apply to the object.

SQUEEZE

Squeeze lets you move the vertices of an object along the Z-axis. The vertices closest to the object's pivot point are moved the farthest. If you apply Squeeze to a box, for example, the vertices at the center of the top surface are pushed or pulled farther than the ones toward the edge, creating a bulging effect or a cupping effect, as shown in Figure B.11.

Squeeze can also be made to affect the vertices along the Y- and Z-axes to create a flare or a crimping effect, as shown in Figure B.12.

FIGURE B.11
Cupping and bulging a box with the Sqeeze modifier

FIGURE B.12
Crimping and flaring a box with the Squeeze modifier

STL CHECK

If you plan to export your 3ds Max model for use with stereolithography (STL) equipment, you can use the STL Check modifier to check your design for correct export. STL Check is also used after performing Boolean operations. Use STL Check to see if the Boolean introduced any discontinuities or errors in the mesh. If so, add a Cap Holes modifier and then collapse the mesh.

STRETCH

If you just want to squash or stretch an object along a single axis, you can do so using the Stretch modifier. If you apply a positive Stretch value to this modifier, the object elongates along the selected axis while contracting along the other two axes, as shown on the left in Figure B.12. Applying a negative Stretch value causes the object to shrink along the selected axis while bulging out in the plane of the other two axes, as shown on the right in Figure B.13.

FIGURE B.13
Sample boxes that are stretched and squashed using the Stretch modifier

SUBDIVIDE

The Subdivide modifier, an OSM version of the Subdivide WSM modifier, allows you to manually apply a radiosity mesh to an object. Subdivide works in a similar way to the Radiosity Meshing parameters; however, instead of applying a mesh globally, Subdivide lets you apply a mesh to single objects or even sub-object levels. Because it's a modifier, it can be edited directly from the modifier stack.

SUBSTITUTE

The Substitute modifier lets you substitute one object for another. This feature is useful if you have a complex design and want to simplify part of it to help speed up editing or rendering. You can substitute a simple object for a complex one while editing. Then, at render time, you can have 3ds Max restore the original complex object. You may also do the reverse for quicker rendering of sample views. The Substitute object can come from the current design or from an external file. Substitute objects are removed by deleting the Substitute modifier from the stack.

SURFACE

The Surface modifier applies a patch surface over a set of interconnected spline segments. The segments must all be of one object and must be joined at their vertices. The Surface modifier applies patch surfaces to three- and four-sided polygon formations of the interconnected segments. See the CrossSection modifier earlier in this section.

SurfDeform

The SurfDeform modifier works in a way similar to the PatchDeform modifier but uses a NURBS surface instead of a Patch object. You can use this modifier to deform an object, based on the shape of a NURBS surface, similar to the way you would use a patch surface.

Sweep

The Sweep modifier is similar to the Bevel Profile modifier in that it extrudes a shape along a spline path. Sweep is much more powerful in that it can use multispline, noncontiguous shapes as paths, eliminating the need to break complex splines into individual objects. Sweep is very fast, can use any shape as the cross section, and has a library of cross-sectional shapes, mostly relevant to structural steel components, from which to choose. Sweep also lets you use custom-defined shapes. See the tutorial in Chapter 7, "Organizing and Editing Objects," that uses this modifier.

Symmetry

Like the Mirror modifier, the Symmetry modifier mirrors the selected object about a plane to replicate the geometry. The Mirror plane can be oriented in the X-, Y-, or Z-axis, and the Flip option swaps the side used as the reference side. The offset between the two halves is determined by moving the Mirror sub-object perpendicular to the orientation of the plane. See the tutorial in Chapter 7 that uses this modifier.

Taper

The Taper modifier allows you to taper an object along a specified axis. See Chapters 2 and 4 for a more detailed look at the Taper modifier.

Tessellate

The Tessellate modifier divides the faces of a surface into multiple, smaller faces. It can have the effect of smoothing a surface. You can also use it to increase the number of faces in a region of a surface for further editing. If Tessellate is applied to an object, all the faces of the object are tessellated. You may also enter the Face sub-object level to select a specific set of faces for tessellation (see Figure B.14).

Tessellate is also an option in the Face, Polygon, and Element sub-object levels of Editable Meshes and at all levels of Editable Polys.

FIGURE B.14
A surface
before and after
tessellation

TRIM/EXTEND

The Trim/Extend modifier works just like the Trim/Extend options in the sub-object level of Editable Spline objects. You can trim open spline segments to other existing, overlapping segments within a single object, or you can extend open segments to other segments within the same object that lie in the direction of the segment end. The Trim/Extend modifier is offered for those situations where it's preferable to include Trim/Extend operations within the modifier stack.

TURBOSMOOTH

The TurboSmooth modifier smoothes geometry by subdividing the mesh and is comparable to the MeshSmooth modifier. TurboSmooth, however, calculates and implements the smoothing much faster and has a streamlined user interface. The MeshSmooth modifier has a larger toolset and should be used only when access to these tools is required.

TURN TO MODIFIERS

Turn To modifiers let you convert objects from one type to another with the modifier stack. You can then apply other modifiers to control the converted object.

Turn to Poly Converts objects to polygonal objects

Turn to Patch Converts objects to patches

Turn to Mesh Converts objects to meshes

TWIST

The Twist modifier deforms an object by twisting it along a selected axis. Figure B.15 shows a box that has a Twist modifier.

FIGURE B.15
A twisted box

UNWRAP UVW

CERT
OBJECTIVE

This modifier is used to assign planar texture maps to sub-object selections. Unwrap UVW can also assign UVW coordinates to a model. The Automatic Flatten UVs (Unwrap UVW) modifier is applied during the Render to Texture process where each object is UV mapped so that the resulting textures can be applied to the object surfaces.

UVW Map

This modifier lets you control the orientation of maps on the surface of an object. It also lets you control the size and aspect ratio of a map in relation to the object to which it is mapped. UVW Map offers a set of mapping types that allow you to tailor the map to the shape of an object. For example, if you are applying a material to a cylindrical shape, you can use the Cylindrical Mapping parameter that projects the map in a cylindrical form. A UVW Map gizmo gives you a visual reference for the location and orientation of the mapping parameters. You can use the transform tools to adjust the Map gizmo. When paired with selection modifiers, different parts of a single object can have different mapping coordinates.

UVW XForm

You can use the UVW XForm modifier to control the way a material map is applied to an object. Many 3ds Max objects offer built-in mapping coordinates, such as the general coordinates for standard primitives and lofted objects. Unfortunately, those built-in mapping coordinates don't offer the tiling and offset options found in the UVW Map modifier. The UVW XForm modifier is offered to allow tiling and offset control over mapping in objects that have built-in mapping.

Wave

The Wave modifier produces a linear wave effect on the selected geometry. You can control the amplitude, wave length, phase, and decay of the waves; the amount of segmentation in the object determines the smoothness of the wave. More segments produce smoother waves.

XForm

The transforms (Move, Rotate, Scale) are not transferred to other objects or instances; all objects must be selected for any transform to have an effect. The XForm modifier is intended to allow transforms to exist within the modifier stack. XForm modifiers cause transforms to be applied to all objects with the instanced modifier in their stack. This makes it useful for trial purposes, since you can easily delete the XForm modifier from the stack—something you cannot do with the standard transform tools on the Main Toolbar. This is most important when applying a Scale transform to an object that is in a hierarchy. If you scale the XForm gizmo, you avoid problems. If you simply scale at the object level, that Scale transform will be passed down to the children and will usually introduce skewing and other distortions during animation.

Materials and Maps

Mastering Autodesk 3ds Max Design 2011 focuses on a few of the materials available in 3ds Max, and for 80 percent of your projects, your needs won't go beyond the material types shown in the tutorials of this book. For the remaining 20 percent, you'll find the range of materials offered by 3ds Max indispensable.

This section provides a description of all the materials available in the 3ds Max Material/Map Browser for use with the Default Scanline Renderer. Just as with the preceding "Modifiers" section, you may want to read about these material options for future reference.

The mental ray Materials

The latest release of 3ds max uses mental ray 3.8. The specialized mental ray material and map shaders are covered in Chapter 9. You can refer to the User Reference for detailed notes on the many mental ray shaders that are available. In the Material/Map Browser, there is a mental ray materials rollout with a complete list of the types now available. Materials that import from Revit via FBX are assigned the new Autodesk Material type to ensure complete compatibility between 3ds Max Design and Revit. This is a mental ray material new to 2011. It features an ease-of-use interface, with fewer controls and less confusion for the novice. As with Standard materials, there are material libraries, with preset materials available for you to use. This material was preceded by the ProMaterial type, a similar mental ray material. Before there were ProMaterials, the Arch & Design (A&D) material was the primary mental ray material in use.

For complete information about individual material types, see the Types of Materials topic in the 3ds Max Design Help. The mental ray materials included in this release are listed here.

ARCH & DESIGN

This is the most widely used material by mental ray visualizer. It has the most complete accessibility to all the functions you can control and consequently the most complex interface. It uses templates like the Architectural Material. When in doubt, use A&D materials.

AUTODESK CERAMIC

This limits your choices to Porcelain or Ceramic (unglazed earthenware) and lets you enable bump (crazing) and relief mapping (patterns stamped in the clay). Matte/Satin or HighGloss are the shininess options.

AUTODESK CONCRETE

Choose the type of sealant and type of finish. This also includes a weathering option.

AUTODESK GENERIC

This is probably the material you want to start using first as you explore the new Autodesk Materials. It has all the features available in one place. Features include color, image, image fade, glossiness, highlights, direct and oblique reflectivity, transparency/translucency/refraction, cut-out, self-illumination, and bump channels. Cut-out is a separate opacity masking channel, independent of the transparency channel.

AUTODESK GLAZING

This is a window glass shader. You select how many sheets of glass, reflectance, and color. More sheets creates more reflection/refraction. Don't use this for solid glass objects; use this for windows and curtainwalls.

AUTODESK HARDWOOD

This lets you choose between furniture and flooring; also there is a stain color as well as finish types.

Autodesk Masonry CMU

This limits your choices to masonry or concrete masonry unit (CMU), relief stamping, and finishes.

Autodesk Metal

This includes eight types of metal, finishes, patina, and relief stamping options.

Autodesk Metallic Paint

This is a preset layered material with four layers: one for color, one for flecks, a pearl (polish) layer, and a top coat. This functionality is also available using the Car Paint material.

Autodesk Mirror

This has no choices at all, except a tint color. Mirrors reflect 100 percent of the objects and environment. Use this on both planar and curved surfaces alike; it is not limited to flat surfaces.

Autodesk Plastic/Vinyl

This limits choices to solid or transparent plastic, or vinyl, finish, bump, and relief maps.

Autodesk Solid Glass

Use this for nonwindow glass objects, such as goblets, cut glass bowls, chandeliers, and so on.

Autodesk Stone

This use for polished or unfinished stone based on a diffuse channel map, with bump and relief channels.

Autodesk WallPaint

This is just color, application (brush or roller or spray), and finish (flat, satin, eggshell, high-gloss).

Autodesk Water

This has ocean, pond, stream, reflecting, or swimming pool options, plus color for the sea option only. Sea color options include Tropical, Algae Green, and Murky Brown. You can make some pretty rank-looking swimming pools with this—someone make a "too much chlorine" shader quick! Don't expect too much from the Wave Height option; tsunamis are not included.

Car Paint

This is a layered material type, with four layers preset. A color layer, a flake layer, a polish layer, and a dirt layer make up the components of this material.

Matte/Shadow/Reflection

Use this just as you would use the Matte/Shadow material for the scanline renderer.

MENTAL RAY

If you're going to use the stand-alone mental ray renderer, use this material. It's designed for rendering outside of 3ds Max Design 2011.

SUBSURFACE SCATTERING FAST MATERIAL, SUBSURFACE SCATTERING FAST SKIN, SUBSURFACE SCATTERING FAST SKIN+DISPLACEMENT, AND SUBSURFACE SCATTERING PHYSICAL

All the Subsurface Scattering materials mimic the appearance of light passing through a top layer and scattering within a second layer.

mental ray Shader Map Types

The mental ray shader map types included in this release are listed here. See the 3ds Max Design Help (the Material Shaders Rollout topic) for details about each of these.

AMBIENT/REFLECTIVE OCCLUSION

Ambient occlusion is often called a dirt shader, crevice shader, or detail shader. It adds gradation into fine detail areas, adding realism.

CAR PAINT

This is the same four-layer material functionality described earlier, available as a map.

COLOR OVERRIDE/RAY TYPE SWITCHER

Put this in any channel where you want to replace the color or image that's currently applied with a different one of your own choosing. You can use this to override many different channels, including environment, photon, and final gather illumination.

EDGE

This blurs edges on bump-mapped objects in profile.

ENVIRONMENT BLUR

All the environment shaders work on different aspects of the background; this one adds blur to the environment map rendering.

ENVIRONMENT PROBE/CHROME BALL

This is used to map the correct ray direction based on a light probe (chrome ball). By shooting a gray or chrome ball in a scene, you can match CG lighting to the actual lighting in a photo or film sequence.

ENVIRONMENT PROBE/GRAY BALL

See above, Environment Probe/Chrome Ball.

ENVIRONMENT/BACKGROUND CAMERA MAP

This projects the background map based on a camera position.

ENVIRONMENT/BACKGROUND SWITCHER

This lets you have one map to use as a background and a second for environment map reflections.

FACADE

This speeds rendering by placing "cardboard cutouts" in the scene, replacing complex geometry.

GAMMA & GAIN

Also called Utility Gamma & Gain, this adds a simple multiplier to a color or map. Use this to intensify maps, similar in usage to the Output rollout on the standard bitmap.

GLOW

This adds an aura around a light or object, simulating light coming from an object or source.

KELVIN TEMPERATURE COLOR

Color temperature, a numeric measure of light energy, can be defined using this shader. Generally, changing this is similar to changing white balance on a video camera; it tints everything to blue or orange.

LANDSCAPE

This maps textures to terrains based on slope and height and includes noise and image adjustments too.

MATERIAL TO SHADER

This lets you assign Max Standard materials as a shader map for mental ray.

METAL

Metal creates realistic metallic surface treatments in mental ray.

mr LABELED ELEMENT

This is used to output any branch of a shader tree to a render element.

mr PHYSICAL SKY

This is used in conjunction with mr Sun and Sky; it provides an environment map with a sun disk. horizon, and ground plane. Adding a bitmap in the haze channel lets you create clouds in the mr physical sky.

Multi/Sub-Map

This is a special shader that assigns multiple maps or colors to a single parameter of a material. It's useful for randomizing coloration of arrays of objects that would otherwise appear too regular and artificial.

Object Color

Applies the wireframe color as a map in any material. There are additional white and black channels used to blend these into the color.

Ocean

This is a water shader that creates realistic wave patterns over an ocean as seen from a great distance.

RPC_texture

Use this so mental ray understands RPC Textures on RPC cars, people, vegetation, and so on.

Shader List (Texture)

This lets you build up multiple shaders in a list, so the output of one becomes the input for the next.

Stain

This is combined with other shaders to provide "discoloration" in the main shader.

Subsurface Scattering Physical

This gives the illusion of two layers in which light passes through the top and is dispersed in the underlayer.

Translucency

This simulates how surfaces look as light passes through a surface from back to front.

Transmat

Short for transparent material, this is used with parti-volume shaders to make transparent the enclosing surface of a volume.

Water Surface

This simulates how water looks based on angle of viewing, changing reflection, and changing transparency accordingly.

Wet/Dry Mixer

This creates two surfaces (one wet, one dry) with separate bitmap textures for each (one shinier and more saturated than the other).

Materials (Blue Spheres)

When you select both the Materials and Maps options in the Show group of the Material/Map Browser, you'll see a list of options that show either a blue sphere or a green parallelogram. The items at the top of the list with the blue spheres are the material types; the green parallelograms indicate the map types. The main difference between the two is that the materials in the list represent types of materials available, whereas the maps are components of materials and cannot be applied directly to objects.

NONE

This option allows you to remove a material specification from the Material Editor.

ADVANCED LIGHTING OVERRIDE

This material is used to fine-tune legacy radiosity materials. This material gives you direct control over the radiosity properties of a material. This material is an adjunct to the base material and has no effect in nonradiosity renderings. You can control properties such as reflectance, color bleed, and transmittance. It used to be called Radiosity Override in early releases.

ADVANCED LIGHTING OVERRIDE AND THE ARCHITECTURAL MATERIAL

The Architectural material has an Advanced Lighting Override rollout with the same controls available in this material.

ARCHITECTURAL

This is a version of Standard materials that has a unique interface created for architects. It is physically accurate and designed to be used with the Radiosity Renderer. See the 3ds Max Help System for more information on Architectural Materials; they are legacy materials. If you have switched your default settings and custom UI using the non–mental ray settings, it will make these materials the default in the Material Editor. DWG files may import with these materials if they come from older versions of Autodesk CAD programs.

BLEND

You can mix two materials into a single material by using the Blend material. Blend offers the ability to control the strength of each material.

COMPOSITE

Composite materials allow you to superimpose up to 10 materials. You can apply additive or subtractive opacity to each material or control the strength of the individual materials.

DIRECTX SHADER

The DirectX Shader allows you to apply DirectX (Direct3D) shaders to objects in your viewports. Using DirectX shading will give you a better idea how your objects and materials will look in applications such as game engines or other real-time applications.

DOUBLE SIDED

You can assign a different material to the front and back or the normal and non-normal sides of an object with a single surface by using the Double Sided material. When you select this material type, you can use the Double Sided basic parameters to select a material for the Facing material and another material for the Back material. This is different from the 2-Sided option available in several materials, which applies the same material to both sides of all surfaces.

INK 'N PAINT

The Ink 'n Paint material is used for creating nonphotorealistic renderings and can be used to create the appearance of 2D cartoons, technical illustrations, and stylized architectural renderings.

MATTE/SHADOW

A Matte/Shadow object has the effect of making itself and anything behind it invisible so that you can see through the scene all the way to the background. It's most frequently used in conjunction with environment maps where a design is to be blended into the background image. For example, suppose you have a fairly detailed background image of a city's downtown area, complete with skyscrapers. To create the illusion that your new building exists in the midst of the existing structures, first place your building in 3ds Max accurately in relation to the other buildings in the background image. Next, create simple boxes in the foreground and modify them to match the perimeters of the buildings in the background image. Apply the Matte/Shadow material to the boxes, and it will appear that the buildings in the background are actually in front of your 3ds Max building.

You can also use Matte/Shadow objects to add shadows to objects in a background image. For example, suppose you are using the Camera Match tools to match a car design to a background image of the building's site. In the real world your design would cast shadows on the ground, but in your 3ds Max scene you would leave out the ground so that the ground in the background image could come through in the rendering. Unfortunately, when you do this the design doesn't cast a shadow on the ground because the ground does not actually exist as geometry in the scene. This unnatural absence of a shadow creates an odd, floating appearance. You can add a ground plane to your design and assign the Matte/Shadow material to this ground plane. The ground plane will be invisible when it's rendered; yet it will receive a shadow, creating the illusion that the car is casting a shadow on the ground of the background image.

Figure B.16 shows a rendering of a car using the background from the Camera Match exercise of Chapter 10, "Using the 3ds Max Camera." Notice the shadow of the car in the image. To obtain that shadow, a surface was placed under the car, and a Matte/Shadow material was applied to the surface. The Receive Shadow option was also turned on for the Matte/Shadow material.

Matte/Shadow materials behave in a way similar to the effect of the Camera Map modifier. The main difference here is that the Camera Map modifier is view dependent, while the Matte/Shadow material affects all views.

FIGURE B.16
A 3D car model is
rendered onto a
background image.

MULTI/SUB-OBJECT

The Multi/Sub-Object material is like a collection of separate materials under a single material name. Multi/Sub-Object materials are useful in situations where you want to assign multiple materials to a single object. See Chapter 9 for more on the use of Multi/Sub-Object materials.

RAYTRACE

Raytraced materials reflect and refract light in a way that simulates one of the ways light actually works. The term *ray tracing* comes from the way the program traces the path of light from a pixel in the rendered image back to the light source. Raytraced materials are best used for transparent or shiny materials, such as glass or water that reflect or refract light. Figure B.17 shows a rendering of a sample file from 3ds Max. The goblet in the figure uses a raytraced material.

FIGURE B.17
A goblet rendered
using the Raytrace
material

SHELL MATERIAL

The Shell material is used for storing and rendering baked textures created by the Render to Texture feature when the Baked Materials setting is Save Source (Create Shell), which is the default setting. The Save Source (Create Shell) option allows for the creation of a Shell material while saving the original one with options for displaying in the viewport and/or rendering.

Shellac

A Shellac material lets you create a shellac effect by combining two materials. One, called the Base material, is used for the underlying base. The second, the Shellac material, is applied over the base with some transparency. You can control the transparency and blending of the Shellac material.

Standard

The Standard material was formerly the default material in the Material Editor. It's covered in some depth through the tutorials in this book. It offers a wide variety of shaders, and you can include several different types of maps (described in the next section). With the available combination of shaders and maps, you can create nearly any effect you need for materials.

Top/Bottom

The Top/Bottom material lets you assign a different material to the top and bottom of an object based on the object's local Z-axis. An example of this might be a two-tone car body. You can control the position and blending of the two materials.

XRef Material

When you externally reference (XRef) an object or scene into the current scene, that object or scene's materials come with it. The XRef material allows you to XRef any material from another scene into the current scene's Material Editor without bringing any geometry with it.

Maps (Green Parallelogram)

The materials discussed in this book allow you to apply maps in several different ways. Maps can be used to control reflection, opacity, bumpiness, transparency, and so on. This book focuses on the use of bitmaps for most of the material map applications, but there are several other map types that you'll want to know. This section describes the different map types and how they might be used.

None

This option is used to remove a map assignment from a material.

Bionatics Normal Map

If you have installed the EASYnat plug-in from Bionatics, you will see the Bionatics Normal Map option in the Material/Map Browser. This map, when applied to EASYnat plants, affects the intensity of the maps in relation to an object's surface angle.

Bitmap

The Bitmap option is described thoroughly in this book. It allows you to use any bitmap image as a material map. It's perhaps the most flexible option, because thousands of bitmaps can be acquired from a wide variety of sources. You can create fairly credible materials through the use of bitmaps.

BnxNormalMapTex

If you have installed the EASYnat plug-in from Bionatics, you will also see the BnxNormalMapTex option in the Material/Map Browser. This map is automatically applied when using EASYnat's materials and should not require any changes by you.

Camera Map per Pixel

The Camera Map per Pixel map projects a bitmap image from the direction of a specified camera onto objects in the scene and is beneficial in the use of matte paintings in renderings.

Cellular

The Cellular map is a procedural map that creates a variety of cellular, or granular, material effects. With this map, you can create materials ranging from terrazzo to polystyrene foam. The Cellular map is fairly complex, so you may want to experiment with it on your own to see what types of results it produces.

Checker

The Checker map is a procedural map that creates a checkerboard pattern. You can assign a color or another map to the squares of the checkerboard. You can also add noise to create a more natural appearance and specify the amount of tiling in each direction. The Checker map can be useful when trying to visualize UVW Mapping on an object; you can apply the Checker temporarily, and then, when the UVW Mapping is accurate, replace it with your final texture.

Color Correction

The Color Correction map allows you to adjust the appearance of a child map, using a number of tools similar to what you would find in an image editing application.

Combustion

The Combustion map works in conjunction with Autodesk's Combustion compositing software.

Composite

A Composite map is a map formed from the combination of other maps. Mask maps are used to control blending of the composite maps.

Dent

Dent is a procedural 3D map that produces a random, dented surface. You can control the depth and size of dents through the map's parameters. You can also apply other maps to the Dent map to create a multicolored surface.

Falloff

The Falloff map is primarily used as an opacity map. When applied to an object as an opacity map in its default mode, the object appears most transparent at its center and least transparent around its edges, like a clear balloon or glass ball. This is the same effect as the Falloff setting in the Extended Parameters rollout of the Standard material, with some added control.

FLAT MIRROR

The Flat Mirror map is used primarily as a reflection map. It produces a mirror-like finish on a flat surface, reflecting the environment and objects nearby. To use this material, you must apply it directly to coplanar faces of an object on a sub-object level. This can be done by including Flat Mirror in the reflection channel in a sub-material of a Multi/Sub-Object material. It is a good practice to reduce the Amount value for the reflection channel when using a Flat Mirror (unless an actual mirror is being modeled) to reduce the reflection amount to a more realistic value.

GRADIENT

The Gradient map lets you create a color gradient using two or three colors. You can perturb the gradient by applying a noise parameter.

GRADIENT RAMP

The Gradient Ramp map is similar to the Gradient map, but it allows for a greater range of colors.

MARBLE

The Marble map simulates the appearance of marble. You can control the color of the marble veins and the background, and you can also adjust the size of the veins.

MASK

The Mask map uses two maps. One map is used as a base map, while the second map is a mask. The mask controls the visibility of the base map.

MIX

The Mix map allows you to combine two colors, two maps, or a color and a map and adjust the influence of each on the material.

NOISE

The Noise map creates randomness in the form of a grayscale pattern. Noise can be used to create a bump pattern or a granite surface. Parameters let you adjust the scale and intensity of the noise.

NORMAL BUMP

The Normal Bump map allows you to apply specially created Normal Maps to objects to add detail to the object and are usually used in the Bump or Displacement components of a material.

OUTPUT

Bitmaps offer control over the bitmap image through the Output rollout. Such controls aren't available for many of the procedural maps. The Output map is like a modifier for procedural maps that gives you the same Output rollout options as bitmaps.

Particle Age

The Particle Age map affects the appearance of a particle according to its age. There are three phases you can assign to a particle by percentage of its age.

Particle MBlur

The Particle MBur map can be applied to a particle system to change the opacity of the particles leading and training edges according to how fast the particles are moving.

Perlin Marble

Perlin Marble creates a marble pattern using what is called the Perlin Turbulence algorithm. The Perlin pattern has a more swirled appearance.

Raytrace

Like the Raytrace material, the Raytrace map provides raytraced reflection and refraction for objects to which it is assigned. It's most suitable for highly reflective surfaces or transparent materials. Using the Raytrace map in a material slot, rather than as a material, allows you to limit the portions of the object that are raytraced and reduce the amount of processing time required to render a frame. See "Raytrace" in the earlier "Materials" section for more information.

Reflect/Refract

The Reflect/Refract map simulates reflection and refraction of backgrounds in the environment of the design. It does this by mapping the environment onto a cube surrounding the mapped object and then using that cube as a reflection map.

RGB Multiply

The RGB Multiply map combines the effects of two maps. This map is commonly used for bump maps.

RGB Tint

The RGB Tint map lets you apply a color tint to another map. You first insert the RGB Tint map; then, through its parameters, you attach a second map. You can then use the R, G, or B color swatch in the RGB Tint parameters to tint the second map.

Smoke

The Smoke map creates noise in a smoke-like pattern. It's more commonly used as an opacity map for simulating smoke than as a diffuse color map.

Speckle

The Speckle map creates a speckled appearance using two colors, two maps, or a color and a map. You can use it for diffuse or bump maps to create a speckled-egg look.

SPLAT

Splat produces a splattered-paint look. Its controls are similar to those for Speckle. You can use two colors, two maps, or a color and a map to produce the splat effect.

STUCCO

The Stucco map is designed to create a stucco surface and is commonly used as a bump map.

SWIRL

Swirl creates a swirl pattern from two colors or maps.

THIN WALL REFRACTION

The Thin Wall Refraction map creates the illusion of refracting glass. When applied to a thin box representing a glass panel, it offsets the view behind the glass panel, simulating a refracted appearance. This map requires less time to render than the Reflect/Refract map or the Raytrace map. Therefore, in well-lit, close-up views, it offers a good alternative to those maps.

TILES

The Tiles map is a procedural map that allows you to parametrically control the appearance of courses of brick or block. You can control the type of tile joint as well as the color and texture of the tile pattern through this map. Several common brick and block patterns are available to select from and then customize.

VERTEX COLOR

You can apply regions of color to an Editable Mesh by assigning color to vertices in the mesh. These vertex color assignments become visible when you apply the Vertex Color map to the mesh. To apply a color to a vertex, select the mesh and then click the Modify tab. Click the Vertex option in the Modify tab's Selection rollout, select a vertex or set of vertices, scroll down to the Vertex Color group, and edit the colors. After assigning a color to a vertex, create a material that uses the Vertex Color map as a diffuse map; then apply the material to the object. The Terrain object automatically applies a Vertex Color map when you create Color by Elevation.

WAVES

The Waves map simulates the surface of water. It can be used as a diffuse color map and bump map at the same time to create a rippling, water-like surface. You can control the amplitude and size of ripples.

WOOD

The Wood map simulates the qualities of wood grain. It is a 3D procedural map, which means that the wood-grain effect is carried through the volume of the object to which it is applied. If you cut a notch out of the object, for example, you'll see the grain accurately reproduced in the notch, as in a real piece of wood. You have the option of controlling two colors for the wood grain, the grain thickness, and the amount of noise or straightness in the grain.

Appendix C

Inverse Kinematics and MAXScript

3ds Max Design 2011 offers a comprehensive system that allows for the animation of complex assemblies through the use of hierarchies, parent-child relationships that let groups of objects be animated as a single object. The hierarchies can be animated through both *forward* and *inverse* kinematics. In this appendix, you'll create hierarchies and add inverse kinematic controllers to a model of a light fixture.

3ds Max Design 2011 also offers a full-featured scripting language called MAXScript. This scripting capability enhances the functionality of the software beyond what can be accomplished with the predefined user interface. Although it is beyond the scope of this appendix to teach MAXScript in depth, you will get a high-level overview of the software's terminology as well as a hands-on taste of using a script.

Assembling an Articulated Luminaire

In this section, you will learn how to make an *assembly* that wires important parameters from a light source together with a light fixture shown with a streamlined user interface. The assembled structure is called a *luminaire* in 3ds Max Design 2011.

You will also learn the basics of *kinematics* in this section in order to link the joints of an articulated desk lamp in a realistic fashion. Kinematics is the study of articulated motion, and you will be learning the differences between forward and inverse kinematics with the desk lamp model. When you are done, you will have a luminaire that you can quickly drop into a working scene and adjust in a user-friendly way.

Transforming Pivot Points

You begin by adjusting the pivot points of the sample model in preparation for linking its joints together in a hierarchy. Each one of these objects (except the base) has a joint where two parts meet. The pivot point of each part must coincide with that object's axis of rotation.

1. Open the file Luminaire01.max from the book website. The scene appears as shown in Figure C.1.

FIGURE C.1

Desk lamp geometry

2. Examine the parts of this simple desk lamp model. Press H on the keyboard to open the Select Objects dialog box. There are five parts to this lamp: Arm01, Arm02, Base, Hood, and Swivel. Select each object in turn and identify it on the screen.

3. Switch to the Front viewport, and select the Hood object. Zoom into the area where Hood meets Arm02.

4. Click the Hierarchy tab of the command panel. Click the Pivot button, and turn on Affect Pivot Only in the Move/Rotate/Scale group.

5. Click the Select and Move tool. Move Hood's pivot to the center of the round joint on the right by dragging the Transform gizmo. Turn off the Affect Pivot Only button when you're done.

6. Repeat steps 3–5 for Arm01 and Arm02 by moving their respective pivots to the center of each of their round joints. If you need precision, you can use the Align tool to align to another pivot or the center of another object.

Aligning the Light Source with the Fixture

You may notice that a lightbulb geometry has been modeled to fit inside the desk lamp's hood. Next you'll add the light source:

1. Click the Create tab of the command panel, and select the Lights category button. Select Photometric from the drop-down list if it isn't visible currently, and click Target Light in the Object Type rollout.

2. Drag out a target point light in the Top viewport without regard to its position or the position of its target.

3. Move the point source itself inside the lightbulb in both the Top and Front viewports.

4. Right-click the Top viewport to activate it; then select Light001.Target and press Alt+A to invoke the Align command.

5. Instead of trying to click the alignment object, press H to use the Pick Object dialog box, which is nearly identical to the Select Objects dialog box, and select Light001 from the list.

6. In the Align Selection dialog box, check the X Position and Y Position options and clear Z Position. Choose Center for both Current and Target radio buttons to align the target directly below its source. Click OK to accept the changes, and close the dialog box when you're finished.

7. Select TPhotometricLight001 and switch to the Modify tab of the command panel.

8. In the General Parameters rollout on the Light Distribution (Type) group, choose Spotlight from the drop-down list. In the Color section, change the bulb color to Halogen.

9. Change the intensity to 3,000 candelas and click the Resulting Intensity check box to activate the Dimming feature; 100 percent is now 100 percent 3,000 candelas.

10. Rename TPhotometricLight001 to **Light001**.

Using Schematic View

Schematic View is an application that helps you visualize the relationships between *nodes* in a scene. Nodes are containers for objects' geometry, transforms, modifiers, materials, relationships, and so on. Visualizing nodes can be especially helpful when establishing parent-child hierarchical links, as you are about to do with the desk lamp.

The Connect and Unlink Selected tools are available in Schematic View, allowing you to set up hierarchies causing one object's (the parent) transforms to affect other objects (the children) based on the parent's pivot point. You can arrange nodes in a structure resembling the model you are linking, which gives you a visual reference to the kinematic chain you want to animate.

1. Click the Schematic View (Open) button on the Main Toolbar.

2. Click the Connect button on the Schematic View toolbar.

3. Click the Light001 node, and then drag a link to the Hood node in Schematic View. Your cursor will change to the Connect icon while you are dragging, and a rubber band will connect your cursor and the Light001 node.

DRAGGING NODES IN SCHEMATIC VIEW

Always drag nodes from the child to the parent in Schematic View. In the case of the lamp, you want the Hood's transforms to be passed on to the Light001 object.

4. Connect Light001.Target with Hood also by dragging a link between these two nodes. The Hood is now said to be the parent of the light and its target. Light001 and Light001 .Target are siblings in this family hierarchy metaphor.

5. Continue making relationships in Schematic View by linking Hood to Arm02 next. Then connect Arm02 to Arm01. Arm01 should be linked to Swivel and, finally, Swivel should be the child of Base. When you are all done, your hierarchy should look like Figure C.2. Notice that the whole family is made up of children of Base. This is as intended so that you will be able to move the entire model with the base.

CORRECTING NODE LINKS

If you make any mistakes connecting nodes, you can use the Unlink Selected button to make corrections, or you can open the Luminaire02.max file from the Sybex website.

FIGURE C.2
The Lamp's node
hierarchy

FORWARD KINEMATICS

So far, you have established links between various nodes in your model. These links establish what is called a *kinematic chain*. Kinematics is the study of moving objects or systems.

In forward kinematics (FK), you transform the top node in the hierarchy to affect the entire chain. For example, rotating your upper arm at the shoulder (the top node in your arm) affects your forearm, hand, and fingers, but you can rotate your hand without affecting your upper arm. Let's see what this means with your lamp:

1. Close the Schematic View dialog box. Choose Edit ➤ Hold to experiment without worrying about altering the scene.

2. Press F4 to turn on Edged Faces mode. Select the Base object and move it in the Perspective viewport. Observe that all the objects move together because they are linked to this top ancestor.

3. Select Arm02 and move it. Notice that Arm02, Hood, the light, and its target move as one. However, Arm01, Swivel, and Base remain behind. Only the object and its children are affected. The object's parents stay at home, as shown in Figure C.3.

FIGURE C.3
Children and
descendants
move together.

INVERSE KINEMATICS

3ds Max has a range of inverse kinematics (IK) systems available for your use. The oldest is the IK system found on the Hierarchy tab. This system lets you animate a hierarchical chain by moving the child rather than the parent. In Inverse Kinematics, the chain is resolved in reverse fashion. You transform the bottom node in the hierarchy and thereby affect all of its ancestors. Instead of all moving with the child, the nodes in IK try to stay connected while the top node stays behind. This is similar to lifting somebody's hand over their head, causing the forearm and upper arm to raise as well. Again, an example is the best way to understand this concept:

1. Switch to the Hierarchy tab of the command panel.

2. Click the IK button and then click the Interactive IK button to turn on this feature. Any transforms you now perform are in IK mode until you turn this button off.

3. Select Light001.Target and move it in the XY plane. Observe how all the nodes move as they need to in order to stay connected with all the other nodes in the chain (see Figure C.4). All nodes move except the Base node, which is called the *terminator* of the IK chain.

4. Turn off Interactive IK mode and choose Edit ➤ Fetch to end your experiment. A dialog box will appear asking if it's OK to restore. Click Yes.

FIGURE C.4
Moving the target
animates the chain.

USE HOLD TO TEMPORARILY SAVE YOUR SCENE

Choosing Edit ➤ Hold saves into the /autobak folder a file called maxhold.mx, which contains a complete copy of your scene. There is only one maxhold.mx file available, and every time a Hold is performed, the file is overwritten. Choosing Edit ➤ Fetch replaces your current scene with the contents and settings from the last maxhold.mx file created. The Fetch command is not undoable.

IK SOLVERS

The more advanced and recent IK systems use a type of controller called an *IK Solver*. IK Solvers are applied via the Animation menu. There are four different IK Solvers available. The HI (History-Independent) solver is the one that works best for character animation, and the HD (History-Dependent) solver is most frequently used for animation of machine parts that require sliding joints or use joint constraints. The IK Limb Solver is designed for fast animation of two jointed parts (an arm and a leg, for example). The Spline solver lets you animate an IK chain by moving vertices in a line.

JOINT CONSTRAINTS

You may have noticed that when you were experimenting with moving the light's target in IK mode, even though the lamp parts stayed connected, they got all twisted out of shape. We all know that in the real world, these kinds of simple mechanical joints have a limited range of motion. When you specify *joint constraints*, you set up each joint with information about how it is allowed to rotate, how far, and how easily. Joint constraints help make the desk lamp's motion more realistic.

1. Click the Select and Rotate tool; then switch to the Parent Reference Coordinate System in the drop-down list on the Main Toolbar when working with joints. This is especially important if any of your objects have rotated pivots that do not align to the World Coordinate System.

2. Select the Hood object and, if necessary, switch to the Hierarchy tab of the command panel. Make sure the IK button is still selected and Interactive IK mode is off. Scroll down to the bottom rollout called Rotational Joints. Right-click in the Perspective viewport, and perform a Zoom Extents Selected on Hood.

ADDING THE VIEWPORT DEFAULT LIGHTING

Your lamp may appear very dark in the viewports. This is because the only light in the scene is pointed away from the lamp, and there is no other illumination available. The images in the book are shown using additional lighting for clarity. You can force the scene's default lighting to display in a viewport, even when you have already added light sources. Choose the Viewport general label (the plus button) and then Configure. On the Lighting and Shadows tab in the Viewport Lighting Options (Viewport shading) group, select Illuminate Scene With: Default Lights. The accompanying radio buttons allow you to select default lighting with either one or two lights. This setting does not affect the output of a scene that is rendered using the Render Scene or Quick Render method.

3. Notice that the green Y axis ring of the Transform gizmo indicates the direction this joint should rotate. Deselect the Active check boxes in the X Axis and Z Axis groups in the Rotational Joints rollout. Now this joint will be allowed to rotate in only one direction, as designed.

4. In the Y Axis group, select Limited. Then drag the From spinner down to about -45 degrees. The Hood will rotate in the viewport as you set this joint limit and then return to its original orientation when you release the spinner.

5. Drag the To spinner to about 45 degrees to set the upper rotation limit.

6. Set Damping to 0.5 to give this joint 50 percent resistance to being rotated.

7. Select Arm02 and deselect Active for both the X- and Z-axes since this joint also should rotate only in the Y direction. Check Limited and set the limits from -45 to 45 degrees. Give this joint 50 percent damping also.

8. Press the Page Up key to move to the next ancestor up in the hierarchy (Page Down moves down the hierarchy). You should now have Arm01 selected.

9. Deselect Active for both the X- and Z-axes for this joint. Limit this joint to a range of motion between -30 and 30 degrees without damping.

10. Press the Page Up key again to advance to the Swivel object. This time, deselect its X and Y Active axes. You don't need to set limits for the swivel joint, because it can spin all the way around.

11. Page up to the Base object. Uncheck Active for all three rotational joint axes since the base shouldn't rotate at all.

12. Switch the Reference Coordinate System back from Parent to View now that you are done setting joint constraints (see step 1).

13. Finally, you must select the base as terminator of the kinematic chain. Select the base in the viewport. The terminator will not move relative to the rest of the chain. Open the Object Parameters rollout near the top of the IK Hierarchy panel. Check Terminator, and you are done.

You have now set up the joint constraints for the articulated desk lamp model. The lamp moves in a realistic fashion, based on what each one of the mechanical joints' range of motion allows.

Testing IK Joint Constraints

Now that you have gone to all the trouble of specifying how each joint is allowed to rotate, how far, and how easily, it is time to test the model and see whether it meets your expectations.

1. Choose Edit ➢ Hold whenever you are testing. There are some things in IK that cannot be undone, so holding is always a good idea.

2. Click the Hierarchy tab, then the IK category button, and turn on Interactive IK mode.

3. Select the Light001.Target object, click the Selection Lock Toggle at the bottom of the UI or press the spacebar to lock your selection, and move the target around in all directions. Observe the motion of all of the parts of the desk lamp model. If you want to tweak anything in its settings, now is the time to do it.

4. When you are satisfied with the behavior of the desk lamp, turn off Interactive IK mode and choose Edit ➢ Fetch.

The lamp should move in an accurate and realistic fashion. You can easily transform all the parts of the fixture by dragging the light's target wherever you want illumination.

Using the HD Solver

One problem with investing so much time into building an articulated model is that it requires your colleagues to share the same high level of knowledge to take advantage of your work. If they don't understand IK, then they won't be able to articulate the model as you intend.

One thing you can do to make your model more user-friendly is to apply the HD Solver to the IK chain. No longer will users of your model need to understand the difference between forward and inverse kinematics in order to use your functioning model.

The HD Solver makes it unnecessary to switch in and out of Interactive IK mode to transform the articulated model. All the IK calculations are applied to your model permanently, and people can articulate it right away without understanding the technicalities of IK.

1. Select the Light001.Target object. You must select the child end of the chain in this step.

2. Choose Animation ➢ IK Solvers ➢ HD Solver. A rubber band will attach to your cursor. Instead of trying to click an object, you can be more specific by selecting it by name. Be careful not to make a mistake; this step is not undoable.

3. Press H to open the Pick Object dialog box. Select Swivel and click Pick. (See Figure C.5.)

FIGURE C.5
Picking the Swivel
object

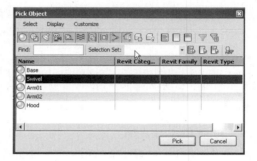

You selected the Swivel object in step 3, and not the Base object, because the HD Solver should not be bound to the terminator (that's just how it works). Remember to bind it to the second object from the top of the hierarchy. The HD Solver will now display in the viewport. A small green cross appears by the Light001.Target; additional orange crosses indicate joint positions, as seen in Figure C.6. Moving the green cross will show you the IK system in action.

INDENTING THE HIERARCHY

Check Display Children or Display Subtree in any Select Objects (or similar) dialog box to display the hierarchy as indents in the list.

FIGURE C.6
Animating with
the HD Solver

BINDING THE END EFFECTOR TO ITS PARENT

The *end effector* is the object that you move to transform the chain when you're using the HD Solver. In this case, the end effector is the light's target.

You will find that you cannot move Light001.Target away from where it was when you applied the HD Solver. Fortunately, the lamp is not "stuck" in this position forever. The simple solution is to link the end effector to its parent:

1. Select the Light001.Target object.

2. Switch to the Motion tab of the command panel. Click the Parameters button if it's not already selected and then scroll down near the bottom of the IK Controller Parameters rollout. Click the Link button under the End Effectors Group.

3. Select the Base object from the Perspective viewport. The base is now linked as the parent to the end effector. In other words, you have linked the bottom and top of the chain together, making a complete mathematical unit.

Testing the Articulated Chain

Now that you have applied the HD Solver to the kinematic chain and bound the end effector to its parent, it is important to test the behavior of the system to make sure it works the way you designed it. If you discover any problems in the testing, you will know you have to go back and fix them before you assemble the luminaire in the next section. If the desk lamp moves in a realistic fashion without using Interactive IK mode, it passes the test. Let's test the articulated chain now:

1. Choose Edit ➤ Hold for this test.

2. Move the Base object. The entire desk lamp hierarchy should move freely. If the light's target seems stuck in position, go back and bind the end effector to the top parent as described in the previous section, "Binding the End Effector to Its Parent."

3. Move the light target with Interactive IK mode turned off. The parts of the desk lamp should articulate to keep up with the target object. The joints should move in a realistic way, where each joint moves within prescribed limits, with damping where appropriate.

4. Press H on the keyboard to have a look at the object hierarchy. The base is the terminator and the top-level parent. Light001.Target is the end effector and is a sibling with light01 at the bottom of the hierarchy. If the indentation of the list isn't visible, go to the Select

from Scene dialog box's Customize menu and choose Display Children; then close and expand the Base object to display the hierarchy.

5. Choose Edit ➤ Fetch after you are satisfied that your scene is working properly. If you made any mistakes, go back and correct them, or open the Luminaire05.max file to continue.

ASSEMBLING THE LUMINAIRE

An *assembly* is a containing data structure that organizes a light fixture and its light source into a simplified interface called a *luminaire*. You can think of an assembly much like a group but with an added feature called a *head*. The head is classified as a helper object that contains the simplified user interface. Let's assemble the luminaire now:

1. Select all the objects except for Light001.Target. Remember to leave the light's target out of the assembly so that you'll be able to transform it independently later on. Everything going into the assembly will be treated as one object (much like a group).

2. Choose Group ➤ Assembly ➤ Assemble. The Create Assembly dialog box appears.

3. Type **DeskLamp001** in the Name box. Notice that Luminaire is the only head object listed because there is only one head helper that ships with 3ds Max Design 2011. Click OK.

CREATING HELPERS WITH MAXSCRIPT

It is possible to create custom assembly head helpers with the MAXScript programming language.

4. Click the Modify tab of the Command panel. Observe the simplified interface of the assembly object.

5. Press H on the keyboard and notice that the assembly shows up as a group in the list.

WIRING PARAMETERS

The assembly's interface is very simple and contains only the Dimmer spinner and Filter color swatch. The only problem with the interface of the assembly is that it doesn't actually work yet.

Right now there is no behind-the-scenes connection between the user interface components of the assembly head and the actual parameters of the light source they represent. To make this connection, you will *wire* the parameters now:

1. Select the DeskLamp001 assembly.

2. Choose Group ➤ Assembly ➤ Open. Red selection brackets appear around the opened assembly.

IDENTIFYING OPEN ASSEMBLIES

An open assembly displays red selection brackets while an open group displays pink selection brackets. Remember these colors; they'll help you identify and differentiate among the various ways of organizing objects.

Notice that there is a green 2D symbol of a lamp that appears on the grid near the base. This symbol represents the assembly head itself and appears only in an opened assembly object. Here we've isolated the symbol so it's easier to see, as shown in Figure C.7.

FIGURE C.7
Assembly symbol

3. Select the head helper symbol. Press H to examine the hierarchy. The assembly head is the DeskLamp001 object itself when the assembly is opened. Close the Select Objects dialog box.

4. Right-click in the Perspective viewport on the assembly head and select Wire Parameters from the transform quad.

5. A small context menu will appear. The parameters are organized into two categories: Transform and Object (see Figure C.8). From this small menu, choose Object (Luminaire) ➤ Dimmer.

6. A rubber band will be attached to your cursor. Click the Light001 light source object, as shown in Figure C.9.

FIGURE C.8
Select the parameter in the context menu.

FIGURE C.9
Pick the Light001 object.

ARC ROTATE USING THE KEYBOARD

You may have to Arc Rotate so that you can see under the lamp if you can't see the spotlight symbol. You can Arc Rotate in the middle of any function by holding down the Alt and Shift keys and then dragging with the middle mouse button/scroll wheel pressed. The Arc Rotate gizmo does not appear in the viewport, but the functionality is available.

7. Again, from a small context menu, choose Object (Target Point) ➢ Multiplier, as shown in Figure C.10.

8. The Parameter Wiring dialog box appears with the Dimmer in the head selected in the left window, and the Multiplier for the light selected in the right column. Click the Two-Way Connection arrow and then click the Connect button to wire these parameters together. Close the dialog box.

9. Right-click the head object again and select Wire Parameters from the quad.

10. Choose Object (Luminaire) ➢ Filter Color from the context menu.

11. Click the Light001 object with the rubber band. Choose Object (Target Point) ➢ Filter Color.

12. Establish a two-way connection between the Filter Color parameters as you did in step 8 (see Figure C.11). Click Connect and close the Parameter Wiring dialog box.

FIGURE C.10
Select the parameter in the context menu.

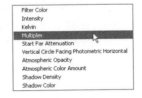

FIGURE C.11
Wiring parameters

Click here to establish two-way control.

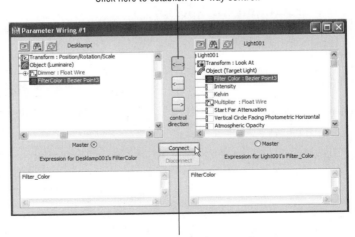

Then click Connect to wire the parameters.

13. The last step is to close the assembly. With the DeskLamp001 head still selected, choose Group ➤ Assembly ➤ Close.

 The parameters from the assembly head are now wired together with the light source parameters they represent.

14. Save your work as **myLuminaire07.max**. (Also provided on the Sybex website for reference is Luminaire07.max, which includes additional lighting to illuminate the lamp, and a floor object to catch the light and shadows.)

ALTERING THE LIGHT SOURCE PARAMETERS

Try changing the Filter Color and Dimmer in the assembly and render the scene to see how the light source responds. Or you can see it interactively in the viewport if you go to the viewport POV menu and choose Lighting and Shadows ➤ Illuminate with Scene Lights and Enable Hardware Shading.

The desk lamp model is completed. The complexities of the articulated IK hierarchy and the photometric luminaire are hidden within the user-friendly assembly, where you can easily adjust the intensity and filter color of the light source. You can articulate the desk lamp by moving the light target in a very intuitive fashion.

3ds Max Scripting with MAXScript

MAXScript is a powerful programming language designed for nonprogrammers that gives you the ability to create, manipulate, animate, and control objects in your scene. Nearly everything you can do in 3ds Max Design can be performed or controlled from a script, and most menu and toolbar buttons you use in 3ds Max Design run scripts to perform their functions.

In this section, you will learn the basics of MAXScript and create and modify a simple script for creating an array of objects.

Understanding MAXScript

One of the easiest ways to understand how a script command is formatted is to open the MAXScript listener by choosing MAXScript ➤ MAXScript Listener, and choose MacroRecorder ➤ Enable (Figure C.12).

FIGURE C.12
Enable the
MacroRecorder

With the listener enabled, all scripts triggered or commands you would use to create objects will show in the upper view of the listener. For instance, when you create an object such as a box in a viewport, the MAXScript command may look like this:

```
Box lengthsegs:1 widthsegs:1 heightsegs:1 length:4 width:10 \
    height:25 pos:[0,0,0]
```

Copying that command into the lower window of the MAXScript Listener will run that script and create the box. Any command entered in the lower window will run instantly; however, a script program is typically created and edited from the MAXScript editor (MAXScript ➢ MAXScript Editor) and can be as simple as the command to create a box or as complicated as a full application with a user interface (UI) to read and write custom geometry, access databases, or perform other unique and complex functions within 3ds Max Design. Simple scripts for performing repetitive commands can be created by performing the actions in 3ds Max Design and then copying and pasting the scripts into the MAXScript editor. Figure C.13 shows a sample script.

FIGURE C.13

MAXScript Editor sample script

In the MAXScript Editor, you press Ctrl+E to evaluate (run) the script program. Scripts can be saved to a file and assigned to menu buttons to be quickly run at any time. Scripts can be automatically evaluated when 3ds Max Design is first run by placing the script into the `C:\Program Files\Autodesk\3ds Max Design 2011\Scripts\Startup` folder. Scripts can be encrypted to protect intellectual property and prevent reverse-engineering with the MAXScript command `encryptScript`.

When working with scripts, you are often creating and accessing *objects*; these objects may be renderable geometry, arrays of numbers, variables, renderers, and so on. Accessing and controlling the object typically requires knowing the name of the object and adding a dot after the name, and then a command or parameter name and optionally new values to pass to the object. To change the height of the box created earlier, you could perform the command `$Box001.height = 5` to explicitly set the height of an object named Box001. To add 5 units to the existing height, you would use a command like `$Box001.height = 5 + $Box001.height`. The MAXScript listener will echo the new height in the view and the object will reflect the new value.

MAXScript is a complete programming language that includes the ability to loop operations, subdivide sections of programs into functions, and react to user interface events such as pressing a button or changing a value or option. A UI is created by manually defining objects or by using the MAXScript Editor and the Tools ➢ New Rollout menu option to graphically create and edit the UI elements and the events that are triggered.

USING MAXSCRIPT

The easiest way to learn a new subject like programming is to take something that works and modify it to see how the parts function. If the program stops working correctly, you more easily know where to look to troubleshoot the problem, and troubleshooting is an essential skill in programming. The following simple script will create a one-dimensional array of teapots in your scene:

```
myX = 0      -- Initial Teapot Position
myY = 0
myZ = 0
myXOffset = 10       -- X Offset for each teapot
myQuantity = 5     -- How many teapots
myRadius = 3     -- Radius of the teapots

delete $myObj* -- Delete all scripted objects

for i = 1 to myQuantity do
(
    obj = Teapot radius:myRadius smooth:on segs:4 handle:on \
        spout: on lid:on \
        mapcoords:on realWorldMapSize:on \
        pos:[myX, myY, myZ] isSelected:on

    obj.name = uniquename "myObj"      -- Add unique numbers to name
    myX += myXOffset      -- Increment the X location
)
```

Type the code into the MAXScript Editor and press Ctrl+E to run the script.

As shown in the first line of code, placing two minus signs (--) in a line causes MAXScript to ignore the remainder of the line, allowing you to add descriptive comments in the code. The first three lines of this script create the variables myX, myY, and myZ that set the initial position of the first teapot. As teapots are created, the number in myXOffset is added to myX to create the next teapot in a new X location. The total number of teapots is defined by myQuantity, and the teapot radius is in the variable myRadius.

In this example, after variables are declared, the next line deletes any objects in the scene with a name that starts with myObj;. The * is a wildcard that means "any additional characters," and any object starting with that name will be deleted. This has an effect only after the code is run once and teapots exist in your scene.

The next section is a for loop that creates the array of teapots; the code between the parentheses will be run repeatedly until the desired number of loops is reached as defined by the myQuantity variable. The i = 1 code creates an incrementing variable i with an initial value

of 1, and i will be used to keep track of the loops. Within the loop parentheses are three commands: the command to make a teapot, a command to change the name of the new teapot, and code to increment the myX variable for the next loop.

A teapot is created in the first four lines of code within the loop; at the end of the first three lines is a \ that means the current line is continued on the next line and the next line is seen as part of the first line. These four lines could be on a single line and are split for clarity. The code that starts `obj = Teapot` creates a new variable called `obj` that is a reference to the new teapot object and allows you to later perform additional operations on the teapot. Each teapot parameter is then listed with a colon and then a value or variable, for example `radius:myRadius` and `handle:on`. For the position of the new teapot, the code `pos:[myX, myY, myZ]` controls the location. The three values for X, Y, and Z must be placed between the braces and separated by commas.

The next line, `obj.name = uniquename "myObj"`, accesses the `name` parameter of the new object and replaces it with a new name myObj concatenated with the next in a series of numbers determined by the `uniquename` command. Commands and parameters for objects are accessed by placing a dot after the object name and then the parameter you want to control. For instance, you can change the number of segments of the teapot object by using the command `obj.segs = 12`.

The final line of code takes the current teapot position myX and increments it by the number in the variable myXOffset. The code `+=` is a shortcut for incrementing the variable on the left with the variable or value on the right. With each loop the myX position is changed so the teapots are offset from one another.

Appendix D

The Autodesk 3ds Max Design 2011 Certification Exams

Mastering Autodesk 3ds Max Design 2011 has been selected by Autodesk to be an Official Training Guide for its 3ds Max Design 2011 professional certification exams. There are two levels of certification: the Certified Associate level and the Certified Professional level. The exam for the Certified Associate level consists of 30 computer-administered questions that include multiple choice, matching, and point-and-click. The exam for the Certified Professional level is a performance-based test that requires you to perform tasks in 3ds Max Design in addition to answering questions.

3ds Max Design 2011 Exam Preparation Road Map

Autodesk certifications are industry-recognized credentials that can help you succeed in your design career, providing benefits to both you and your employer. Autodesk certifications are a reliable validation of skills and knowledge and can lead to accelerated professional development, improved productivity, and enhanced credibility.

Autodesk highly recommends that you structure your examination preparation for success. This means scheduling regular time to prepare, reviewing this exam preparation road map, using Autodesk Official Training Guides, taking an assessment test, and using a variety of resources to prepare for your certification. Equally important, actual hands-on experience is recommended.

The 3ds Max Design 2011 Certified Associate exam consists of 30 questions that assess your knowledge of the tools, features, and common tasks of 3ds Max. Question types include multiple choice, matching, and point-and-click (hotspot). The exam has a one-hour time limit (in some countries the time limit may be extended).

The 3ds Max Design 2011 Certified Professional exam is a performance-based test. The exam is composed of 20 questions. Each question requires you to use 3ds Max Design 2011 to create or modify a data file, and then type your answer into an input box. The answer you enter will be either a text entry or a numeric value. The exam has a 90-minute time limit (in some countries the time limit may be extended).

To earn the credential of 3ds Max Design 2011 Certified Professional, you must also pass the 3ds Max Design 2011 Certified Associate exam. You can pass the exams in any order.

To recertify from 3ds Max Design 2010 Professional to 3ds Max Design 2011 Professional, you need only pass the 3ds Max Design 2011 Certified Associate exam.

Assessment Tests

Autodesk assessment tests will help identify areas of knowledge that you should develop in order to prepare for the certification exam. At the completion, you will be able to review the items you missed and their correct answers. Contact an Autodesk Certification Center for more information at http://autodesk.starttest.com.

ATC® Instructor-Led Courses

The Autodesk Authorized Training Center (ATC®) program is a global network of professional training providers offering a broad range of learning resources. Visit the online ATC locator at www.autodesk.com/atc.

Recommended Experience Levels for 3ds Max Design 2011 Certification Exams

Actual hands-on experience is a critical component in preparing for the exam. You must spend time using the product and applying the skills you have learned.

2011 Certified Associate Exam Mastering 3ds Max Design 2011 course (or equivalent) plus 100 hours of hands-on application

2011 Certified Professional Exam Mastering 3ds Max Design 2011 course (or equivalent) plus 400 hours of hands-on application

Certification Study Icon

As you work your way through this book, you'll see an icon in the margin when a topic that should be studied is being covered. Pay careful attention to the techniques and tools discussed there, and you should be well prepared for the examination.

You may also want to study the topic in the 3ds Max Design 2011 Help to gain complete knowledge about the UI elements, parameters, and functions of the tools. Use the Index or Search tab in the Help to navigate to the pertinent pages.

Exam Objectives

To help you focus your studies on the skills you'll need for these exams, we've included two tables: Table D.1 lists the sections and objectives for the Certified Associate exam, and Table D.2 lists them for the Certified Professional exam. The objectives in the tables are from the Autodesk Certification Exam Guide. These tables direct you to the chapters in this book that will help you master the objectives for each exam.

TABLE D.1: Certified Associate Exam Sections and Objectives

TOPIC	OBJECTIVE	CHAPTER OR APPENDIX
UI/Scene Management	Identify object selection options	1
	Describe differences between coordinate systems	4
	Describe viewport configuration and navigation	1
Modeling	Identify the category of an object or group of objects	1
	Demonstrate knowledge of scene setup	1
	Classify cloned object types and features	1
	Identify ProBoolean options	4
	Explain snap functions and settings	3
Camera	Recognize camera workflow	12
	Identify camera controls	8
Animation	Describe options for displaying the location and direction of animated objects	12
	Identify animation editors and their functions	12
	Explain graph editor features	12
Materials	Identify material types and features	9, B
	Recognize functions of the Material Editor	9, B
	Explain settings for Arch&Design and Autodesk Materials	9
	Identify workflow for using Image File Formats	9
	Identify mapping and material options	9
Lights	Identify industry standard lighting terminology	8
	Describe light processing concepts and terminology	8
	Recognize light setting options	8
	Identify lighting preset options and their purpose and benefits	8

CONTINUES

TABLE D.1: Certified Associate Exam Sections and Objectives *(CONTINUED)*

TOPIC	OBJECTIVE	CHAPTER OR APPENDIX
Rendering	Identify options to control the area of a rendering	14
	Describe rendering process workflow	13
	Recognize functions of the Rendered Frame Window	13
Global Illumination	Identify Final Gather setting procedures	14
	Explain Global Illumination usage and terminology	14
Effects	Identify particle system features and setup	13
IK	Explain the different IK systems usage and features	C
Dynamics	Explain Rigid Body usage and features	13

TABLE D.2: Certified Professional Exam Sections and Objectives

TOPIC	OBJECTIVE	CHAPTER OR APPENDIX
Modeling	Use modifiers in cross product workflow	5, B
	Demonstrate modeling workflow processes	4
	Create and utilize modeling references	4
Camera	Demonstrate camera setup	10
Animation	Edit animations using graph editors	12
	Set up and use Tracks to control an object	12
Materials	Set up object mapping	9
	Demonstrate mapping modifier features	9
	Describe the results obtained by using specific Arch&Design Material Settings	B
	Use material editor features	9
Lights	Demonstrate how to set up and evaluate the use of physically-based lighting tools	8, 14
	Set up and evaluate the results of using common lighting systems	8, 14

TABLE D.2: Certified Professional Exam Sections and Objectives *(CONTINUED)*

TOPIC	OBJECTIVE	CHAPTER OR APPENDIX
Scripting	Edit a MAXScript to perform the desired result	C
Rendering	Configure a scene for rendering using efficient rendering workflow	14
	Describe the effects obtained by using specific render effects and settings	15
Global Illumination	Demonstrate knowledge of GI and Caustics	8
Effects	Demonstrate knowledge of particle flow	13
IK	Create and edit a basic IK system and evaluate the results	C
Dynamics	Set up and run a rigid body simulation in reactor	13
Scene Assembly/ Pipeline Integration	Demonstrate cross product workflow knowledge	5

Index

Note to the Reader: Throughout this index **boldfaced** page numbers indicate primary discussions of a topic. *Italicized* page numbers indicate illustrations.